# Present Tense: An American Editor's Odyssey

## Books by Norman Cousins

PRESENT TENSE: AN AMERICAN EDITOR'S ODYSSEY 1967

IN PLACE OF FOLLY 1961

DR. SCHWEITZER OF LAMBARÉNÉ 1960

IN GOD WE TRUST 1958

WHO SPEAKS FOR MAN? 1953

THE GOOD INHERITANCE 1952

TALKS WITH NEHRU 1951

MODERN MAN IS OBSOLETE 1945

A TREASURY OF DEMOCRACY 1942
(edited by N.C.)

THE POETRY OF FREEDOM 1945
(coedited with the late William Rose Benét)

# Present Tense

An American Editor's Odyssey

by Norman Cousins

McGraw-Hill Book Company

New York    Toronto    London    Sydney

To the Staff of the *Saturday Review*

# Preface

An editorial page is an exercise in present tense. The editorial may scrutinize history; it may try to anticipate the future; but most of all it is an encounter with the present. Over the past quarter-century—the period of the current editorship—the *Saturday Review* has been examining the contemporary arena. Its gaze has been fixed on man's relationship to his political and natural environment. During this period, a geographic community for the first time was extended to the entire world. Man was still subject to all the demands and decisions that had always been part of his national life, but it now mattered severely whether there might be too many people on the earth, whether one individual with access to a nuclear trigger could start the human species on an irreversible downward spiral, and whether a conventional territorial clash between two nations might become the tragedy of the race. The world had become one before it became whole.

These were the dominant themes, then, of the editorial page of the *Saturday Review*, but they did not block out a wide range of other interests and concerns. This book attempts to reflect that range, from the apocalyptic to the roseate, from the plural abstract to the singularly real, from the creative and sprawling achievements of twentieth-century art and science to the mock heroics and the sideshows of the contemporary tent.

The writings in this book, then, reflect the issues and diversions that preoccupied the editorial page and the editor's articles. My work on the magazine began in March, 1940; the period of my editorship began in October, 1942. This book, therefore, is something in the nature of a personal journal kept during a time of vast acceleration of causes, forces, and effects. The story begins with World War II, runs through to Hiroshima and the early postwar years during which man first tried to cope with the implications of an atomic age; through the revolution of national independence for most of the nations of Asia and Africa symbolized by Bandung; through the upheavals in Korea, Suez, Laos, and the Congo; through the development of missiles and sputniks and spaceships; through the nuclear test-ban treaty; and up to Vietnam.

This book is divided into two sections. The first is about the *Saturday*

*Review* itself, the people who founded it, its progress, its adventures in the world of communications. The second is about the past twenty-five years, as reflected in the editorials and articles in the magazine.

Caution: Part I is not to be regarded as a detailed or documented history of the *Saturday Review* or even as a fully objective account. These pages are supremely personal in purpose and manner, being in the nature of background notes. If I give substantially less attention to current members of the staff than to the early editors, it is not because my esteem for my contemporaries is any the less profound but because they speak for themselves in the pages of the magazine.

In general, the material in Part II is grouped chronologically rather than thematically. The attempt here is to reflect a reaction or response to events or issues as they happened. The selection is arbitrary. The yardstick is nothing more complicated than those things I felt most intensely at the time.

The one exception to the chronological approach is the section on two special projects: the Hiroshima Maidens and the Ravensbrueck Lapins. The Maidens were a group of scarred atomic-bomb victims who were brought to the United States for plastic surgery and psychotherapy. The Lapins were a group of Polish women who had been victimized by Nazi medical experimentation in World War II and who were also brought to the U.S. for medical care. The various pieces that appeared in SR over a period of several years dealing with both the Maidens and the Lapins have been reworked into a single narrative, and form a subsection within Part II.

With a few exceptions, the materials appearing here have not previously been published in book form. These exceptions include several editorials on nuclear testing (*In Place of Folly*) and some passages on Albert Schweitzer (*Dr. Schweitzer of Lambaréné*). The only changes or deletions in the editorials or articles from the form in which they originally appeared were made for the purpose of avoiding repetition of ideas already discussed or for correcting errors in the original editing or typesetting.

A note about an aspect of the SR editorial page: From the start, SR's editorials have been signed. Henry Seidel Canby, who originated the custom, believed that responsibility for the magazine's viewpoints should be clearly fixed. True, an editorial by its very nature is chargeable to the magazine as a whole; but Canby felt that such plurality conferred too much immunity. The reader had a right to know—not approximately but precisely. There was also the effect on the writer. Something happened, Canby believed, when a man knew he must show his face. This was the custom we inherited; this is the custom we proudly maintain.

Some acknowledgments. Dana Little was of prodigious assistance, reducing to a finite number an endless array of details involved in putting together this volume. Dori Lewis made many valuable editorial suggestions and helped shape the form of the book. Mary K. Harvey prepared a comprehensive background memorandum on the campaign for the treaty to outlaw nuclear testing. Jack Cominsky, my closest associate and SR's publisher since 1942, gave me the benefit of his notes and memories.

More generally, I acknowledge my debt to the staff of the *Saturday Review,* beginning with its two founding editors, Amy Loveman and Henry Canby, who turned over to me their tenderest possession, the magazine itself.

*N.C.*

*New York City*

# Contents

# Credo for the *Saturday Review*

Fundamentally, to publish a magazine that people will read and respect;

To believe, not as rote or strained slogan, but as rigid fact, that a magazine is by natural right the property of its readers;

That, because of this, editors are but temporary custodians, their tenure related to and dependent upon their confidence in the judgment and intelligence of the reader;

That such confidence is best established by avoiding both the condescension of talking down and the presumption of talking up;

That a magazine, like a person, requires, in order to be effective, certain qualities—readily identifiable and beyond obliteration;

That high among these qualities is a response to values, the capacity to create values, and the passion to defend values;

That other essential qualities include clarity, curiosity, insight, incisiveness, integrity, good taste, good will, conviction, responsibility;

That what is written is believed by the writer and written to be believed by the reader;

That the magazine should reflect a sense of adventure and excitement about life in general and about books and ideas in particular;

That honest sentiments, honest passions, and honest indignations are among the highest expressions of conscience, that there is no need to feel shy or awkward or embarrassed in their presence, and that they are not to be waved aside;

That cynicism at best is a waste of time; at worst, a dangerous and potentially fatal disease for individuals and civilizations both;

That ideals are the main business of writers, and that people will respond to ideals far beyond the anticipations of their nominal leaders;

That believing all this need neither limit nor inhibit a sense of fun and the enjoyment of laughter;

That editing, finally, is not paring but creating.

—Norman Cousins

From the *Saturday Review*'s 25th Anniversary Issue, August 6, 1949

Part One

# The Life and Times
# of the
# *Saturday Review*

# I

The magazine of ideas stands midway between the newspaper and the book as a reflection of its time. It is freed of the need to capture history in headlines, but it stays as close as it can to the surge of events. It lives in the arena it seeks to comprehend and chronicle, trying to stick its head up high enough to see the interaction between pressure and resistance and, in Toynbee's celebrated phrase, between challenge and response. It is interested both in the movement of ideas and in the faces in the crowd. It has a sense of history even though its style and purpose are not consciously historical.

Thus measured, the *Saturday Review of Literature* was a magazine even when, as a weekly book-review supplement, it was part of a newspaper. The fact that it appeared on newsprint didn't obscure its predominant periodical qualities and purpose. This purpose was to penetrate the contemporary complex and to try to connect it to its origins. Such a design —like the character of SRL itself—was not the result of front-office directives but of the convictions and compatible personal chemistries of four individuals—Henry Seidel Canby, Amy Loveman, Christopher Morley, and William Rose Benét. They were the founding editors; from the start, they seemed almost destined to be joined in a common creative purpose. They were exhilarated by the opportunity to apply their individual and combined critical talents to the literary output of their time. They took full advantage of the possibilities afforded by an independent journal for wide-ranging, searching appraisal. Their literary station enabled them to move naturally and surely in the broad field of ideas.

What was most characteristic and important about Dr. Canby and his associates was their sense of connection and responsibility to the period in which they lived. Their purpose was to perceive the vital balances of their age. They tried to look beyond the events, the manners, and the aberrations that lent themselves all too easily to striking labels and catch phrases—catch phrases that were to become fixed totalities in the minds of later generations. The world of the 1920s that emerged from the pages of SRL was not just a world of rum-runners, spangled flappers, jazz, high-flying stocks, Teapot Domes, Gatsbys, Kennicotts, and Babbitts. It was a world which produced scholars and scientists who successfully challenged theories that had held for centuries; a world that was tooling up for the great changes of the 1930s and 1940s; a world that was at least as interested in examining values as it was in playing with them; a world in which teachers such as Dewey, Kilpatrick, and Rugg were laying down new educational foundations: a world in which poets, old and young, all the way from A. E. Housman and W. B. Yeats to Robert Frost, Robinson Jeffers, and Stephen Vincent Benét, were finding responsive audiences; a world which relished the intellectual splendor and contrast afforded by George Bernard Shaw and H. G. Wells; a world which, for all its vaunted twitching, could sit still long enough to enjoy recognized story-tellers like Ellen Glasgow, Edith Wharton, Thomas Hardy, Joseph Conrad, and E. M. Forster, and still notice new writers like Ernest Hemingway, Sinclair Lewis, and William Faulkner; a world which knew the enjoyment of laughter that men like Robert Benchley and Ring Lardner could provide.

The high value placed by SRL on balance and perspective was nowhere more evident than in the attention given both to the creative flow outside America and to the cultural prospect inside America herself. The magazine did not underplay or shun the kind of artistic environment that was attracting some of America's best-known writers to Paris, or Vienna, or Bayreuth, but the emphasis was on assessing vital elements in the American past. The editors saw no conflict between their response to the stimulus of new moods or ideas and their desire to recapture an important part of the national heritage. Canby believed that Whitman, Thoreau, Emerson, and James deserved to be brought to full size before the contemporary generation. If SRL's editors stood aloof from anything, it was the debunking that was then in such high fashion. They were too busy forging connecting links between past and present to be tempted into the irrelevance of cynicism.

This insistence on a rounded and reflective view of life made a profound impression on me when I came to SRL early in 1940. And one of the first things I did was to find out as much as I could about the history of this magazine and the people who gave it life.

## II

It all started one day late in 1919 when Donald Scott, then the vice-president of a New York daily newspaper edited primarily for businessmen, put through a telephone call to Professor Henry Seidel Canby, of the Yale University English Department. Mr. Scott said he wanted to see Professor Canby at the earliest possible moment on a matter of literary importance. A meeting took place several days later at the Yale Club in New York.

Henry Canby, then forty-two, had won a reputation in academic circles for his work in literary criticism, much of it on the *Yale Quarterly*. He

had been called upon frequently by book publishers for advice on manuscripts dealing with the early period of American literature. Rarely did
the advice prove faulty; Canby was a shrewd, precise assayer of literary
worth. There was nothing gaudy or self-serving about his criticism. The
critic's job, as he saw it, was to bring good taste and a trained intelligence
to bear on the evaluation of a book.

Mr. Scott said he was acting in behalf of Mr. Edwin F. Gay, general
manager of the *New York Evening Post,* a newspaper then edited
primarily for members of the financial and business community. Mr. Gay
wanted Canby to recommend someone who might start a literary supplement for the *Post.* The editor for the new section would have complete
freedom and would receive a considerable measure of front-office support.

Henry Canby mentioned several names, carefully traced the background of each man, drew up a balance sheet of personal and professional assets, and gave his estimate of possible availability.

Then Mr. Scott asked his key question: How would Canby himself
like the job? Would he be willing to give up an academic career for the
newspaper business?

Henry Canby said he would give Mr. Scott his answer in a few days.
When the answer came it was yes.

Three members of the *Evening Post* staff were assigned to the new
supplement: Christopher Morley, who only recently had started a column
on the paper; William Rose Benét, former *Post* copy boy and poet; and
Amy Loveman, researcher and assistant librarian. The human combination was just right. The group quickly developed a mutual affection and
a team relationship. There was no fumbling or meandering in their selection and presentation of material. The literary values were readily apparent. The judgments were unambiguous and carefully buttressed. The
supplement may have been new but there was nothing immature or
groping about it.

Henry Canby set the judicious, authoritative tone in his own writings
and presided over the staff with calm certainty of purpose and unquestioned good will. Indeed, the most characteristic thing about Canby was
absence of rancor. As a critic, he never denounced; he merely registered
a dispassionate and documented disapproval. The editor's chair for him
was not a saddle for hobbyhorses or galloping ghosts. Canby didn't regard a book as an outlet for personal frustrations, or as a chance to
display superior knowledge. His allegiance was to clearly defined principles of literary criticism.

"Henry can do the impossible," Amy Loveman used to say. "He's a
born persuader."

And so he was. He would win his point not because he overwhelmed
people but because people had no difficulty in trusting him. Indeed, it
was impossible not to be impressed with his sweeping beacon-light ap-

proach to issues and ideas. No other man I knew was more at home with a qualifying clause. When he had something to propose you could be sure it had been thoroughly worked over and calibrated.

Dr. Canby was actively engaged in helping émigré writers. As president of the American Center of the P.E.N. Club (poets, playwrights, essayists, editors, and novelists), and as secretary of the National Institute of Arts and Letters, Canby gave strong direction to the Center's and Institute's efforts to defend writers abroad who were under political pressure and attack. He was a champion of creative freedom and the conditions that made it possible. He helped make it possible for these writers, wherever they were, to express their concerns—without fear or apology. Together with his wife, Lady, he helped arrange for the translations of their books, bringing them to the attention of responsive publishers. Many émigré writers and critics made their debut in this country in the pages of SRL.

Physically, he appeared unreasonably unprepossessing and underproportioned. But, like John Adams, he benefited from high compression and maximum energy utilization. He had extraordinary persistence and staying power.

Canby and his group won recognition for their supplement out of all proportion to the modest circulation of the newspaper. In fact, the *New York Evening Post* had difficulty in competing against a large evening field, including the *New York Evening World* and the *Sun*. In 1924 Thomas W. Lamont, president of J. P. Morgan & Co. and publisher of the *New York Evening Post*, sold the newspaper to the Curtis interests in Philadelphia. According to one version, probably apocryphal, Cyrus K. Curtis arrived in New York one Saturday, shortly after acquiring the *Post*. Emerging from the Wall Street subway at noon, he observed the Wall Street brokers as they picked up the *New York Evening Post* and ejected the literary supplement with a single flip of the wrist, thus giving Wall Street what was known as its "Saturday book look." He proceeded to the offices of the *Post* nearby and made known his decision to discontinue the special section.

Mr. Lamont, profoundly disturbed by this development, offered Dr. Canby the necessary backing to start an independent weekly literary review. A young man by the name of Henry R. Luce, who had studied under Canby at Yale and who, with several classmates, was starting a newsweekly magazine, offered hospitality and publishing facilities. Canby readily accepted. The offices of both magazines were established at 236 East 39th Street. The first issue of the *Saturday Review of Literature* appeared on August 2, 1924, and carried the imprint of Time, Inc., as publisher. Luce was listed as president and Canby as vice-president. Canby's name also appeared as editor; Amy Loveman and William Rose Benét were associate editors, and Christopher Morley was contributing editor.

The symbol for the new magazine was a line drawing of a phoenix rising from the ashes. It had been William Rose Benét's idea and he used it as an integral part of the heading for the department "Phoenix Nest" he conducted in *SRL* until his death in 1950. It was a decorative but jaunty bird, looking less like an enactment of the classical legend than an indignant creature whose tail had been accidentally singed.

The format of the new magazine was newspaper supplement size, printed three columns wide in distinctive type. The leading editorial, written by Dr. Canby, was in the nature of a credo:

> A literary review without a program is like modern man without his clothes—healthy, agile, functioning in all his senses, but regarded as less than respectable, even by his friends. Yet what is a program but a reflection of temperament! A sanguine, full-blooded man thinks well of his universe, a melancholy man thinks ill of his, and each makes his program. There is more honest philosophizing in many a casual newspaper column, or blunt plain man's opinion, than in elaborate sets of principles chosen to fit a prevailing mood.
>
> We cannot escape from our moods but we need not capitalize them for the supposed benefit of bored contemporaries. The *Saturday Review* is to have a guiding purpose, that must be drawn not from the temperament of the editorial staff but from things as they are in literature. . . .
>
> A critic of literature must be aware of his good fortune and unblushingly embrace his subject, leaving reticence and prejudice behind. The half-hearted intellectual afraid of his enthusiasm is as much of a charge upon criticism as the entranced sentimentalist. One suffers from too little love to give and the other from too little sense in loving.
>
> But in pursuing literature, a literary review (which is a kind of literary personality with motives and character) must have two purposes, especially in America. There are two functions of literature that, so far as I am aware, have not been clearly distinguished in their modern aspects, although the general difference has been the cause of many a lively row. Literature can be timeless and literature can be timely. . . .
>
> I shall drop then in conclusion those somewhat formal terms . . . and say that criticism, which is part of the living fabric of contemporary literature, must be keenly aware of both past and present, and a partisan of both. It must be like a modern university where one seeks Principles, but also works in laboratories of immediate experience amidst the vivid confusion of experiment. In one guise a gray-beard philosopher searching for the Best, but also in the mood of youth, watching the three-ringed show under the great tent of Today—yet discriminating in both—that is the double function of criticism and this *Review*.

In that first issue of *SRL* Amy Loveman wrote a review of a novel, *Woodsmoke*, by Francis Brett Young. All the qualities which were to win her distinction as a critic can be observed in that review: the attempt to see a book not only in the reviewer's terms but in terms of what the author was trying to do; the sense of balance and fairness that prevented her from seizing upon a single startling aspect of a book and raising it to a monopoly status; the existence at all times of basic critical values carefully developed out of a remarkable working knowledge of the best in literature; and a final neat loop of appraisal that could be grasped readily by the inquiring reader.

There was something else in that first review that was characteristic of the reviewer. Miss Loveman praised Mr. Young for a story that drew its strength from the author's "sympathetic vision of a world in which human nature, cast back upon elemental conditions, retains even at its most pitiful a certain essential dignity."

In that one sentence is to be found the essence of her own optimism. She could contemplate all the violence and meanness and mobilized evil of the age, yet never forget the ultimate strength that was to be found in human decency. She was not appalled by the dualism in man; all that mattered to her was that moral catharsis and the chance to do better came with the gift of life.

In those early days Henry Canby may have set the policy for SRL but Amy Loveman set the tone and spirit. From the start she had been optimistic about the magazine. Her writings were an argument for idealism without self-deception, for awareness of living issues without meaningless immersion, and for recognition of the power of hope. She had no patience with the cynicism that went in and out of fashion; she thought nothing was more wasteful than defeatism—whether in literature or life. This large view never left her.

Both on the newspaper literary supplement and on SRL, Amy Loveman assigned most of the books for review, wrote reviews of her own, handled a regular department in the magazine called "The Clearing House," in which she answered requests from readers for out-of-the-way information, edited copy, pasted up the dummy, read page proofs, and put the magazine to bed at the printer's. She answered most of the office mail, made sure that Henry Canby, Bill Benét, and Christopher Morley ate their lunches on time, kept the publishers and authors happy by going to their parties, and supplied that most valuable of all functions in a magazine office—finding the lost manuscripts of anguished authors who somehow forgot to make a carbon copy.

Early one evening Christopher Morley cried out in horror that a valuable photograph had suddenly disappeared from his desk. He had borrowed it from an English publisher and had promised to return it within two weeks. The problem was promptly turned over to Miss Loveman, who made the usual search, then expressed her hunch that the photograph had slid off the desk into the wastepaper basket, which had been emptied an hour earlier by the cleaning women.

Miss Loveman rushed downstairs and discovered that the dump truck had been gone thirty minutes. She obtained the address of the dump, taxied there, and picked her way through a mountain of crumpled paper, cigarette butts, apple cores, remains of box lunches. After two hours she emerged triumphant from the city dump with the missing photograph.

Miss Loveman had ready rapport with people, regardless of their age or rung on the social or cultural ladder. Once she got into conversation with a taxicab driver who, after inquiring about her occupation, revealed that his main interest in life was poetry, and that he wrote verse whenever he wasn't actually driving. There was a spirited conversation about techniques in poetical expression. When Miss Loveman arrived at her home the driver said goodbye, adding it was nice to be able to meet someone in the same line of business. The incident delighted Miss Loveman and she told it often. Nothing was more remarkable about Amy Loveman than her gift for friendship or the ease with which she did things for other people. People would say she was the only person they knew who could be thoughtful without having to think about it.

Almost everywhere she went she met people who wrote poetry. Invariably they would follow up the meeting by submitting verse for publication in the *Saturday Review*. Amy had the incredibly difficult job of returning 98 per cent of these submissions, and it is a tribute to her genius in human relationships that her rejection letters never lost her a friend.

She never got tired of reading poetry—good, bad, and in between—all during her years on SRL and the Book-of-the-Month Club. With it all, she never wrote a poem in her life. "I wouldn't dare to," she said, "knowing how well supplied the world already is with bad verse."

How many books she had to assess or process over the years for SR and BOMC she herself never dared to guess. The bad books, and there were many of them, failed to exhaust or depress her. Now and then she would come across something of quality and her delight could not have been more complete if she had discovered an unpublished novel by Jane Austen.

On the bookshelf behind her desk, conveniently within reach, were her favorite reference books, the most conspicuous of them being the *Dictionary of American Biography*. She could relive the moments in history when the big men had to make their big decisions and she could retain a sense of freshness and excitement in her appreciation. For her, Winston Churchill was like a summing-up of everything that was right with the human race. She liked the epic forward thrust and the mammoth optimism of the man; she was enchanted with the Churchillian contempt for the difficult and his sense of outrage toward the impossible.

"No one can say I'm not an optimist," she once said about herself. "I have always been an optimist. And I've never been disappointed."

It is doubtful, however, whether anything gave her greater satisfaction than to be able to work with new writers, helping to remove the roadblocks in the way of publication. Her advice was precise, crisp, practical, built on a solid foundation of reasonable explanation. And underlying everything else was an almost epic kindness. This combination of incisiveness and kindness characterized her entire life.

If Henry Canby supplied the philosophy and the generalship, and Amy Loveman the basic energy for the forward thrust, Chris Morley was the literary crown prince and Bill Benét the conscience of the staff.

Christopher Morley brought a quality of sagacious merriment and controlled omniscience to *SRL*. He moved about the world of letters with the greatest of ease and delight, a master of literary forays and excursions. There was an aspect of magic to the man; whatever he touched turned to a species of literary gold, minted with scholarship and a robust appreciation of life.

Few American essayists of his time had greater energy or inventiveness. Almost none knew better the beautiful distinction between humor and wit, between routine jokes and creative whimsy. He had a radar-like faculty for picking up the incongruous and converting it on his scope into a wry observation or felicitous thought, fortified by an enriching and apt allusion. What a treasure trove of out-of-the-way information he was able to draw upon. But he never reached into it for the purpose of random ornamentation; what lured him was the chance to make visible the interconnections between art and life. It was most natural that he should have been the editor of Bartlett's *Familiar Quotations*.

He was a bookman's bookman. He very early appointed himself an ambassador for books to the public at large, speaking for all those who shared in the creative act of the book—author, publisher, printer, librarian, bookseller. If the bookseller had a finer friend, I didn't know of him. "What is on my mind," Christopher Morley once wrote, "is the fact that the bookstore is one of humanity's great engines . . . one of the greatest instruments of civilization."

The literary missionary in him never knew fatigue. Once he persuaded a stenographer at *SRL* to read Francis Thompson's essay on Shelley. He was entranced the next day when, wide-eyed and obviously converted, she asked for more. It was clear to him that she had experienced the magic of transport; he concluded that he had helped make a better world. "When one is weary of writing about books," he said, "one thinks of the moment when some young person finds his way for the first time into some book of genuine truth and beauty, seeing the world momentarily anew and feeling the glow of that immortal heat when we know ourselves collaborators with Destiny in the endless fashioning of life."

There must be at least fifty books and published essays which carry his name. Each of them is in the nature of a tribute to the joyous art of knowledgeable living. He made you think he would go to the end of the world for a moment of creative splendor. His colleagues had that feeling about him every time he took off for Hoboken across the Hudson River (he called it the "Seacoast of Bohemia") where he helped to stage off-beat plays to suit the civilized taste. "I suppose," he remarked, "that people born and reared in the theater would take the glamor of an antique playhouse more for granted and would be too tony to find beauty flourish in so mean a habit. Please be that some of us shall never take things for granted nor lose the jocund faculty of amazement."

Chris Morley was not the easiest man in the world to get along with. He could make his personal fancy seem like a towering test of principle. He could be caustic, prickly, petulant. But all this became inconsequential alongside his charm, his laughter, and his readiness to do handsprings for a good book or a good idea. Among his favorite quotations was a line in a letter from Keats to Reynolds: "Now it appears to me that almost any man may, like the spider, spin from his own inwards his own airy Citadel." Christopher Morley was such a man; his Citadel had the kind of crisp airiness that freshened other minds and kept forever new a wonderful respect for the creative imagination.

Bill Benét stayed close to his poetry and Phoenix Nest assignments on *SRL*, but in his restrained, patient way he would argue for greater involvement by the magazine in issues concerning creative freedom. He was also, Amy Loveman said, something of a soft touch and would evoke her strongest protective instincts. Her favorite story about him illustrated his need for constant surveillance. She said that Bill was trustful to the point of innocence and defenselessness, and that his friends had a special obligation to keep him from being hurt.

"Any person with a sob story can get anything he wants out of Bill," she said. "During the pit of the depression, a violinist came to the office and asked to see one of the editors about a personal matter. The receptionist immediately sent him in to see Bill, who listened sympathetically as the visitor, after identifying himself as first violinist with the Pittsburgh Symphony Orchestra, spoke of his predicament. He said the orchestra had been temporarily suspended because of lack of funds. He had come to New York but had been here for two weeks without finding a job. And he had just received a message from Pittsburgh asking him to return at once because his wife was fatally ill. The doctors thought she had a chance if surgery could be obtained. He needed money for the trip home and for the operation. He said he was a great admirer of *SRL* and of Bill Benét's column.

"Bill was having a difficult time himself but he immediately gave the violinist thirty dollars. He did even more. He said he would arrange a benefit party. He telephoned Mrs. Thomas Lamont, told her of the violinist's needs, and asked if she would invite friends to her home for an evening musicale at which the violinist would play. A collection would be taken up. Mrs. Lamont readily agreed. Bill also spoke to me about it and asked if I could bring at least a dozen people to the benefit. I invited at least thirty, of whom twenty accepted.

"Bill really threw himself into the effort. His hope was that he might be able to raise at least $1,000 to help the violinist meet some of the costs of his wife's illness and his living expenses. Some seventy persons assembled in the Lamont home on the appointed night. Everyone came, that is, except the violinist.

"The people all sat around waiting for the performance to begin. Bill, with great dignity, finally announced that the guest of honor would probably not appear. In response to popular demand, he recited his own poetry for an hour or more, and saved the evening from being a total disaster. But nothing I or anyone could say to Bill later could convince him that there was not some extenuating circumstance that would show the man with the violin case to have acted in good faith."

I violate chronological tidiness here to relate a small sequel. Several years after the incident involving the benefit concert that never came off, and about a month after I started to work for *SRL*, the telephone receptionist asked me to come out to the waiting room to see a gentleman. I did so. He said he was an admirer of the magazine, identifying himself as first violinist for the Pittsburgh Symphony Orchestra who had come to New York to find work because the orchestra was temporarily suspended. He said he had just received word that his wife was desperately ill and he needed money to return to Pittsburgh.

Amy's account of the incident came immediately to mind. I could hardly believe that this man had forgotten he had already worked this particular mine. I asked him to wait for a moment, then went directly to Bill and told him about the visitor outside with the violin.

"Wonderful," Bill exclaimed and followed me out to the reception room.

The "violinist" saw Bill a split second before Bill saw him and had the full shock of recognition. He bolted for the exit door and disappeared down the stairs. Bill called after him to slow down; he feared the man might slip on the stairs in his headlong flight and break his neck. But the man from Pittsburgh had no intention of applying the brakes. He must have negotiated the eight flights in thirty seconds.

"Poor chap," Bill said. "He probably thought I would turn him over to the police; I just wanted to talk to him."

Bill made a religion out of believing in people and helping them. No one in the United States did more to encourage poets of all ages. He would suffer visibly whenever he had to write a note of rejection, especially when a poetry submission was accompanied by a letter showing the writer to be a person of good feelings and high hopes. Sometimes Bill's desire to help people was reflected in his choice of material for his Phoenix Nest department. Members of the literary community had a sense of this;

some of them said, privately or in print, that *SRL's* poetry section was flabby, lacking in standards, and incompetent. Moreover, Bill was accused of being far behind new trends in poetry.

The accusations were unfair and untrue. Bill made a strong distinction between material selected for the Phoenix Nest and material he approved for the body of the magazine. While he might give hospitality to border-line poems (generally rather short) for his own column, he was completely discriminating in the selection of *SRL* material.

His attitude toward new trends in poetry was far from rigid. What he objected to was not experimental poetry per se but the tendency of some abstractionists to disregard or disparage the classical tradition. He saw no conflict between new forms and the established values. He felt the *Saturday Review of Literature* should provide space for experimentation, but he didn't want the magazine to separate itself from the great literary tradition, or to become a house organ for any private club or clique. In his own work Bill was no slave to convention; he employed free verse and unobstructed expression. "The Dust Which Is God" was no excursion into conventional versification. It was venturesome and challenging, but was not alien to anyone who had grown up on Tennyson or Yeats.

Perhaps the most succinct account of Bill's family background is contained in a letter he wrote in 1945 to the Reverend Earle C. Reynolds, now of Meade, Kansas. The Reverend Reynolds was doing research on Stephen Vincent Benét and had asked Bill for some family background. The following is from Bill's reply:

> Stephen Vincent Benét was born on July 22, 1898, the year of the Spanish-American War, on Fountain Hill, South Bethlehem, Pa. On his father's side he was of Spanish descent, the family having originated in Catalonia, migrated to Minorca, and his forebears came from Minorca to St. Augustine, Fla. My grandfather was born in St. Augustine, went to the University of Georgia, and then to West Point. On our mother's side, our great-grandfather, William Rose, was also a graduate of the Military Academy.
>
> My grandmother's (Mother's mother's) name was Rose. They were English and Scotch-Irish stock. My father was born in Kentucky, his mother being a Kentuckian. We are therefore about half Southern and half Northern. In the Civil War my grandfather was, of course, in the United States Army, a Federal (later Chief of Ordnance). Stephen brought to the writing of *John Brown's Body* a knowledge of the feelings of both the North and the South. Also he spent some boyhood years in Augusta, Georgia, went to school there and entered Yale from there. He also went to a military school in California earlier. My father being in the Ordnance Department of the Army was ordered from place to place as all Army officers are and we lived, after Stephen was born, in Buffalo, N.Y., near Albany, N.Y., where I went to school, in California, in Augusta, etc. I was

out of college in California, and went to New York and married there.

I am twelve years older than my brother. Stephen began writing at an early age as everyone in our family was fond of poetry. My father was something like Field Marshal Wavell, the present Viceroy of India, in his love of English poetry. He used to read many fine things aloud to us. He was a great reader and loved his library. My mother read a great deal also. We were a bookish family. . . .

After Bill Benét's death in 1950 Amy Loveman served as interim poetry editor in addition to her regular duties. She screened the poetry submissions for the one poem out of perhaps five hundred that would be acceptable. She corresponded with those writers whom she felt deserved a personal critique or encouragement. As mentioned earlier, Bill Benét loathed printed rejection forms as much as the aspiring contributors did. To the fullest possible extent he handled submissions with personal letters. Amy Loveman went as far as she could in maintaining this tradition. She also screened the new volumes of poetry for review and selected the reviewers.

The search for a successor to Bill Benét lasted six years, and ended with the selection of a brilliant young professor of English literature at Rutgers University, John Ciardi, about whom I write later in these pages.

### III

*SRL*'s founding quartet lived with Time, Inc., about a year and a half. Apparently the theory that two new struggling weeklies were easier to publish than one didn't hold. In any case, *SRL* moved to 25 West 45th Street in 1925 and took a view of the publishing horizon from the eighth floor.

In those early days *SRL* found some 20,000 readers who quickly became devoted to it and formed a cheering section. And it performed the kind of service for the world of books that had never existed in America on a national scale. The editorial franchise was discernment—both in literature and life. But it was a limited market place despite the intensity of response, and only Mr. Lamont's generosity enabled the magazine to continue. Indeed, the *Saturday Review*'s own experience for a long time seemed to bear out what the magazine world had accepted as a truism— no "literary" publication, no magazine of "ideas," could live without a subsidy, especially if issued as a weekly, with multiplied costs. Part of the same theory held that the only way for a weekly to succeed was as a mass magazine, offered to the public at a price lower than the actual per unit cost, the difference as well as the profit to be provided by advertising revenue.

For a long time—too long—the theory held water. One by one magazines concerned with the arts or with opinion were hopefully and even auspiciously started, only to be snuffed out. *The Dial, The Freeman, The Bookman,* and any number of others, all of them excellent products and deserving of a robust existence, made strong but eventually fruitless attempts to disprove the notion that, in a nation of well over a hundred million people, there was no room for intellectual periodicals.

By 1936, *SRL's* financial condition had sharply deteriorated. Mr. Lamont was forced to reduce his subsidy. Henry Canby, then fifty-nine, had expressed the hope he might have more time for his literary studies and for his duties as chairman of the Board of Judges for the Book-of-the-Month Club. George Stevens, the talented young managing editor, and Amy Loveman surveyed the field and fixed their gaze on Bernard De Voto, then thirty-nine, essayist, historian, and lecturer in literature at Harvard College.

George went to Cambridge and received a prompt turn-down from De Voto. Several weeks later, however, De Voto indicated he wanted to pursue the matter. Stevens returned to Cambridge with Noble Cathcart, then publisher and business manager of *SRL.* At the end of a long evening session, they could rejoice in their acquisition of a new editor. De Voto's first issue as editor was dated September 26, 1936. He contributed a fairly short statement of his editorial philosophy following Dr. Canby's editorial of introduction, declaring himself a defender of the literary tradition established in *SRL* by his predecessor:

> It is enough that, under Dr. Canby, the *Saturday Review* has had an individuality and an excitement beyond any other literary journal of its time. I believe that it has had an integrity of its own also: at least I have felt freer in its pages than I have sometimes felt elsewhere.
>
> I can only say that I hope to maintain that individuality, excitement, and integrity. I believe that the values of literature are genuine values. I believe that clear thinking is one of the most difficult and most desirable things in the world, and that all absolutes are dangerous. I believe that the free meeting of diverse intelligences is as necessary to literature as to society itself. I believe that literature is so interstitial with the life of its times that all attempts to separate them are folly. Beyond that, I also believe that the present age in American literature is the richest we have ever had—and that America is a nation sufficiently great to abide all the confusion, folly, and despair of these times, and to triumph over them in its own terms and in harmony with its own traditions and institutions.

De Voto's tenure lasted one year and five months. Apparently there had been some misunderstanding about the requirements of the editorship. It is likely that De Voto regarded his role as editor largely in terms of intellectual leadership. To be sure, Stevens and his colleagues respected that kind of leadership, but they tended to define it in less abstract terms than did De Voto. It wasn't so much that they expected him to assume full administrative responsibility. Apart from the editorials, there was the matter of the magazine's total thrust, the kind of writers who became identified with *SRL,* and the issues that infused its pages.

*SRL* could provide no such luxury; the staff was at rock bottom; no one took so much as a two-week vacation. George Stevens had the delicate task of clarifying the situation. De Voto was a man of generous and buoyant spirits, but he could also be blustery and intransigent. He returned to Cambridge in March 1938.

Amy Loveman, Henry Canby, and Noble Cathcart then made the decision that should have been made a year and a half earlier: they told George Stevens he was to be the new editor.

Stevens, thirty-four at the time, was well acquainted with the book industry. Before coming to *SRL* in 1933 he had been vice-president and staff editor of W. W. Norton & Co. He certainly knew every aspect of *SRL,* having worked in both the business and editorial departments. He was a superb judge of writing—especially fiction. Some of his book reviews could serve as a model for journalism classes. He was also a good administrator. The magazine began to reflect his craftsmanship. But the depression difficulties persisted.

Mr. Lamont's subsidy was discontinued altogether in 1938. After that the magazine was on its own. It was kept going because its creditors were a hardy band of optimistic gamblers.

It was about this time—at the end of 1938—that Harrison Smith threw out a lifeline. Mr. Smith was then partner in the book-publishing firm Harrison-Hilton Books, soon to become Smith and Durrell. Earlier firms in which Mr. Smith had been a founder or co-founder were Jonathan Cape and Harrison Smith, Inc., and Harrison Smith and Robert Haas, Inc. He had also been an editor with Harcourt, Brace & Company.

Not even Henry Canby or Amy Loveman, as they themselves acknowledged, had Hal Smith's touch for recognizing a good story. Hal was William Faulkner's first publisher, although much of the credit for discovering Faulkner belongs to Lenore Marshall, the poet, who worked as first reader for Hal Smith at the time. Hal was also Sinclair Lewis's personal editor and confidant. Hal knew how to help an author flesh out his characters and lead them from one scene to the next in the development of a story. Even when Sinclair Lewis was no longer published by Smith, Lewis would come to him for advice.

It is diversionary and disproportionate here, but I cannot resist a story bearing on the close relationship between Lewis and Smith. One day, shortly after he received the Nobel Prize for Literature, Sinclair Lewis showed the scroll to Hal Smith over drinks at the Yale Club. What transpired was told me in these approximate words by Hal himself:

"We were talking about the Nobel Prize and Red said he didn't know what to do with it. I thought awhile and said, 'Red, it's about time you did something for Yale. Why don't you give the Nobel scroll to Yale?'

"Red surprised me by saying it was a corking good idea and got up from the table and said he wanted to do it right away, now. He obtained a large brown paper bag from the waiter, inserted the scroll and told me to follow him.

"We went across the street to Grand Central and got a train to New Haven. Red had fortified himself for the voyage with some bottled goodies that had been supplied by the bartender at the club. By the time we reached New Haven, Red was convinced that his benefaction would make up for all his failures as an alumnus over the years. He was singing 'Boola Boola' softly as the cab turned up Chapel Street.

" 'One minute,' Red said to me, 'How are we going to give it? To whom?'

" 'I really think we ought to donate it to the library,' I said.

" 'Right you are,' he said. 'Driver, take us to the library.'

"It was a Saturday football afternoon and the library was practically empty. We went over to the main desk. I called over one of the clerks and told him that the gentleman with me was Sinclair Lewis who wanted to give Yale University his Nobel Prize for Literature which he was carrying in the large brown paper bag.

"The young man looked at Red and the paper bag and I could tell from the expression on his face that he wasn't impressed. He said he wasn't authorized to receive any Nobel prizes for the university and that we would have to come back on Monday to see the chief librarian. Red wasn't too pleased and said he would take his bag up to Cambridge and give it to Harvard. The young man was completely unruffled by the threat. I knew Red was steamed up and would go through with his notion about Harvard. I wanted to save the prize for Yale. So I told the young man to telephone the president of the University and tell him that Mr. Sinclair Lewis was waiting in the library to give the University the Nobel Prize for Literature. The young man grunted, picked up the telephone, spoke to someone, then turned to me and said he was sorry, the president of Yale University happened to be at the football game.

" 'We're wasting time,' Red said. 'Now look here, young man, you take this bag and give it to the president with my compliments.'

" 'I am sorry, sir,' the young man said, 'but I am not authorized to accept any prizes.'

"That was when Red really blew his top. He said he didn't propose to spend the entire day trying to unload a Nobel Prize on anyone. He tossed the paper bag to the young man, then grabbed my arm and stormed out. We took the next train back to New York. Long before we arrived at Grand Central, Red had forgiven me for the entire excursion. Anyway, that's how Yale happens to have a Nobel Prize for Literature."

The story, or parts of it, may be apocryphal, but that is the way Hal told it.

Hal provided sustenance for *SRL* at a time when its prospects were morose. He literally took *SRL* into his own already cramped book-publishing office on the eighth floor of 420 Madison Avenue. Amy Loveman, Henry Canby, Bill Benét, and Chris Morley were all squeezed into a single office barely large enough to hold their desks.

George Stevens had the adjoining office; it was about seven feet by eight feet. Two secretaries completed the staff; they sat in the combination passageway and file area. It was a tight squeeze.

Even with a sharp reduction in overhead, *SRL* continued to operate in the red. Harry Scherman, president of the Book-of-the-Month Club, who had always been close to *SRL*, helped to meet the deficit. At one time or another, Henry Canby, Christopher Morley, and Amy Loveman were as prominently identified with the Book-of-the-Month Club as they were with *SRL*. Mr. Scherman, generally regarded as one of the nation's most talented writers of direct-mail promotion, not only wrote new subscription mailing pieces for the magazine, but gave *SRL* the use of the Book-of-the-Month Club membership list—without charge. This resulted in a gain of at least 10,000 new readers—more than a 50 per cent increase.

There can be no question that this one act saved the life of the magazine at a critical time.

The infusion of subscriptions made possible by Mr. Scherman's generosity reduced the annual deficit but it did not eliminate it. A magazine is perhaps the only product in the United States that is sold to its customers for less than the cost of manufacture. *SRL* was certainly no exception. In 1939 the yearly subscription rate was three dollars; the newsstand rate was ten cents per copy. But the cost of producing a single subscription for the year was close to eight dollars; a single copy cost about fifteen cents. The difference had to come from advertisers. Here, however, *SRL's* situation was more difficult than that of most magazines because it was dependent on book publishers for its primary advertising support. Traditionally, book publishers received substantial advertising discounts—generally 40 per cent below the regular advertising rates. Moreover, book-publisher advertising was expensive to run, for much of it was received in the form of raw copy rather than plates. *SRL* had to absorb the expense of typesetting and revisions.

# IV

This was the general situation at the time I was hired by *SRL*. My coming to the magazine was accidental. In 1939 I was on the staff of *Current History,* a monthly journal of world affairs founded by *The New York Times* shortly after the end of World War I. *Current History* had been published in 1936 from *The New York Times* by M. E. Tracy, former columnist for the Scripps-Howard newspapers, and John Casman. Mr. Tracy was one of the most remarkable men I have ever known. He was educated at the Perkins Institute for the Blind in Boston. Despite his handicap, he kept up with world events on a daily basis. Few men I have known have had as wide a range of knowledge.

This is not the place to write at length about M. E. Tracy, to whom I owe so much. Suffice it to say he edited *Current History* for four years, then sold it to E. Trevor Hill, who moved it from its comfortable old quarters in the famous old World Building at 63 Park Row, at the foot of the Manhattan entrance to the Brooklyn Bridge, to 420 Madison Avenue, to which *SRL* had also just moved.

I had met both Miss Loveman and Dr. Canby earlier in connection with *Current History's* annual non-fiction book awards. Now that *Current History* and *SRL* were both in the same building, it was inevitable that the staffs of both magazines would come into frequent contact. Miss Loveman introduced me to Mr. Smith.

One day, sharing the same elevator, Mr. Smith asked me if it was true that I had decided to give up editing in order to become a professional ballplayer.

I laughed and said I had no idea where he had picked up such a notion.

"Somebody told me he saw you playing baseball at the Yankee Stadium a few weeks ago on a tryout for the Yankees," he said. "I also learned that you're now considering an offer."

The elevator arrived at the eighth floor before I finished explaining to Mr. Smith what had happened. It was true that I had played at the Yankee Stadium, but it had nothing to do with a tryout for the Yankees. The occasion was a Metropolitan Newspaper League game. The *New York Post* was playing the *New York World-Telegram*. Even though I had not been on the *Post* for more than three years, I was still the regular shortstop. This made me what was known as a "ringer." The baseball competition among the New York newspapers escalated from year to year. It began innocently enough with only editorial staff workers, but some of the papers began to reach into their composing rooms for tough, hard-hitting baseball talent. Then the *Post* broadened its interpretation of the eligibility requirements to include the alumni.

Unfortunately, Hal never got the story straight. He persisted in spreading the word that he personally saved me from a career as a professional baseball player by offering me the editorship of the *Saturday Review*.

The factual account of how I became editor was just as implausible. I got the job because no one else would take it. Being in the same building, I came to know Hal Smith, George Stevens, Amy Loveman, and Henry Canby. And on those evenings when Amy Loveman was working late, I would drop by to lend a hand, especially in editorial production. Then, when George Stevens received an offer in December 1939 to head the New York Office of J. B. Lippincott Company, Hal Smith and Amy Loveman asked me if I would join SRL as executive editor. Elmer Davis, essayist and critic, would be invited to serve on the editorial board and would contribute editorials from time to time.

My acceptance was immediate. The most satisfying part of my job on *Current History* had been the reviewing of books on world affairs. The prospect of working on a magazine devoted to books was irresistible. George Stevens and Amy Loveman were most generous and painstaking in instructing me about the job. It involved assigning books for review, developing articles, editing copy, writing editorials, dummying the magazine, and seeing it through the press. Amy Loveman, of course, would help in all these respects.

I was twenty-five at the time. It seemed clear to me that, in addition to the post of executive editor, the magazine needed someone of the stature of Henry Seidel Canby at the top of the masthead. I brought the matter up repeatedly during those early months. Henry Canby took the view that the presence of Elmer Davis on the staff, plus his own availability as consultant, gave SRL the kind of representation at the top I had suggested. I persisted, however, and we drew up a list of ideal names, among them Carl Van Doren, Edmund Wilson, Clifton Fadiman, and Van Wyck Brooks. Hal Smith, Henry Canby, and I then dutifully made the rounds. The men we approached were highly qualified but also highly rational. I suppose we must have seemed a little foolish in our effort to persuade them to accept what must have seemed a certain invitation to a bankruptcy party. The answer in every case was no. They were of no mind to engage in a tilting contest with creditors, however genial. In the end, then, I got the editor's job by default.

Appropriately, even symmetrically, perhaps, my first job had been on the *New York Evening Post*—as education writer—which gave me a certain kinship with SRL's founders. With them, I shared confidence in the existence of a strong and growing audience in America for a magazine that made good taste its franchise—good taste in the things that make for an exciting life of the mind. I believed in books as molders of ideas and shapers of events.

The editor's job, as I saw it early in 1940, was not to raze a magnificent structure in order to get rid of the mortgage, but to retire the debt by broadening the base. The bookkeeping liabilities were large, but the human assets were even larger. We had everything we needed, in fact, except cash in the bank and a business staff.

For the next two and a half years it was rough going. There were times when only the disposition of a printer to be influenced by honeyed words without any real honey in back of them kept the magazine alive.

For a long stretch we paid our contributors nothing. In this epithelial fashion we hung on from week to week.

During this long period, however, when we were forced to execute maneuvers that would make the circus Wallendas seem like tired porch sitters, we became increasingly convinced that the magazine could ultimately be made to support itself. We were certain there was a growing market for a literary magazine that would be concerned with ideas as well as with books, that would see books not as ends in themselves but as part of a surging and changing world. Such a magazine would try to deal with serious issues without taking itself too seriously; it would try to war against stuffed-shirtism (we hoped to be able to avoid the possible danger of self-injury involved in such a crusade); it would recognize that good books, like plants, demanded certain conditions in order to exist.

We had long-range projects we wanted to initiate, several different series of special issues we wanted to undertake, and we needed the wherewithal not only for editorial expansion but for staffing the business department. We lost the services in those days of good and gifted people because we couldn't meet our payroll—people like Frank Taylor, our advertising director, who had a family to support and was forced to leave and who was to become one of New York's leading book editor–publishers.

In 1942, my title was changed from executive editor to editor. What was most memorable about *SRL* that year, however, was that two men became associated with the magazine who were to have central roles in its growth. One was E. De Golyer, a scientist and booklover who also happened to have, among his many talents, a knack for knowing where to look for oil, and who was to become chairman of *SRL*'s Board of Editors. The other was J. R. Cominsky, who left *The New York Times* to become our business manager and publisher.

First, E. De Golyer. Almost everyone called him De or Mr. De. *Who's Who* and the formal records spelled it out—Everett Lee De Golyer, petroleum geologist and leading citizen of Dallas.

I met Mr. De Golyer through John Williams Rogers, the author and playwright, who got permission from Mrs. De Golyer to show me Mr. De's famous book collection. Mr. De happened to be there and took me on a personal tour. He handed me original manuscripts of articles that had been published in *SRL*, then opened the door to a small storage closet and showed me a complete file of the magazine.

Mr. De asked me to stay to dinner. The next day I asked him if he would like to own the magazine.

"I don't know why it took you so long to ask," he said. He held out his hand: I took it, and that was that.

"Just one condition," he said. "If you spend one goddam cent for lawyer's fees in drawing up any papers to formalize the deal, it's off. We've already shaken hands; that's enough."

As I came to know Mr. De, I sensed he had more sides to him than a group of mobiles. Put him in one setting and he could be as coldly analytical as a brain surgeon describing the difference between a synapse and a ganglion. Put him in another setting and he could be as compassionate and tender as an Irish setter in a nursery.

No man had more respect for the scientific method; yet few have gotten more mileage out of their hunches—even when all the evidence seemed to go the other way. His mind was like a spark jumping across gaps. Once, when a subordinate reported to him that he had dug five dry holes in a field, having gone down to 12,000 feet, De told him to stay put and go down another 2,000 feet. The rest was almost inevitable. They hit oil at 14,000.

When I asked De what caused him to give the order to drill the additional footage, he bit hard on the end of his twisted Mexican cigar, grinned, and said: "Damned if I know, I'm just lucky."

Then he turned pensive.

"Look," he said, "luck isn't just a matter of having a pot in your hand when it rains Kentucky bourbon. Maybe it's a matter of knowing what to do when you get dead-ended by the printed guides and instructions. Organized and systematized knowledge can carry you only so far in a field where the answers thin out very fast. You've got to be able to generate a sort of momentum of the senses to carry you into zones where the book doesn't operate. If you say this is a pretty highfalutin way of describing a hunch, I'll agree with you."

I once asked Mr. De to tell me about his Potrero del Llano No. 4 strike for Mexican Eagle Oil—the most productive single well in a half century of petroleum exploration. He had been a college kid at the time. Would he say that his fantastic discovery of Big ME was the result of a hunch?

He laughed.

"I was pretty raw then," he said. "Even so, I had spent a fair number of hours thinking about this crazy business. I had been out in the field one summer with Willard Hayes, of the U.S. Geological Survey. I'd read the books carefully and listened to some fellows who seemed to know a thing or two that wasn't in the books. I began to think of ways of finding oil that weren't confined to the conventional methods. One of them worked. I was lucky."

"In that case," I said, "you were lucky in the sense that your original theories worked. But you had to have the theories even before you could test your luck. You just didn't happen to point a finger at a spot in the earth and say, 'Let's poke a hole here.'"

"I'm not going to argue with you," Mr. De said. "I'll just rest my case on a single observation. You can take it as a law of success that when a fellow happens to hit it big, the more honest he is about saying how lucky he was, the more disposed people are to credit him with being a wizard. Anyone worth a damn doesn't have time to think of himself as successful; he's too busy mulling over all his mistakes and muffed opportunities."

Mr. De was a founder of Amerada, one of the world's great petroleum development companies. He is credited with spectacular discoveries for Amerada in the Seminole Plateau in 1930. He pioneered in torsion balances and the refraction method. He had a leadership role in the Geophysical Research Corporation, with its history-making record in Texas and Louisiana. He was Assistant Deputy Petroleum Coordinator for war in World War II. He astounded the petroleum world with his then-revolutionary estimates about the oil reserves of the Persian Gulf area. He was president of the American Institute of Mining and Metallurgical Engineers.

Not so well known was the nature of the man himself. Indeed, he was something of a legend in the petroleum industry. Some oilmen frankly said they could never figure him out, regarding him as a combination of maverick and refugee professor. They were baffled by the amount of time and attention he gave to things that had nothing to do with petroleum. They couldn't quite understand why he should go running off for days at a time just to track down a book by some Spanish fellow named Cabeza de Vaca. They were startled by tales that he would postpone or cancel important business appointments just to spend time with all those "writing people" who were always coming out to the house.

But there was nothing feigned about this side of Mr. De. He had an abiding delight in book collecting and the creative life. In his own writings he would spend hours on a sentence just to make sure it turned right. He filled out thousands of catalogue cards by hand in preparing his notes for what was to be the major literary effort in his life—a history of the petroleum industry—a project his illness prevented him from completing.

His private library, like the man himself, was wide ranging, well organized, primed for instant and constant action. It is doubtful if anyone owned finer private collections in the fields of Southwest Americana and folklore, the early exploration of America, the history of science, Charles Darwin, or Morleyana (he owned practically everything Christopher Morley ever wrote, some of it in original manuscript). He presented his collection on the history of science, running into thousands of volumes, to the University of Oklahoma without condition or stipulation. "No point in giving them money or a building," he said, "They've got plenty. But did you ever know of a university that didn't need good books?"

He knew people all over the world—government officials, industrial leaders, fellow oilmen, scientists, writers, editors, newsmen, printers, booksellers, college presidents and professors, cabdrivers, headwaiters. But he picked his intimate friends carefully. Put him down with fellows such as Frank Dobie, Buck Herzog, Tom Lea, Cleveland Amory, Savoie Lottinville, Paul Horgan, Lon Tinkle, or John William Rogers—and he would have the time of his life. Or turn him loose in a good bookstore, such as the one he helped Elizabeth Ann McMurray build in Dallas, or Lew Lengfeld's emporium in San Francisco, and he would be difficult to dislodge.

For fifteen years De was the owner of the *Saturday Review* and my boss. Not once in all that time did he suggest or intimate that the editorial page or the magazine take any turn to coincide with his own views. He gave me, quite literally, all the freedom in the world. My main problem was not to fight for editorial independence, but to justify the independence I had. He never took a cent out of *SR*, and when there was no longer any question about its ability to go it alone, he transferred his ownership to the people who had the responsibility for publishing it.

He went by the political name of conservative; but he taught me a great deal about genuine liberalism and the largeness of the human spirit. He taught me, too, not to place stock in stereotypes—whether they went by the name of industrialists or intellectuals. The *Saturday Review* would not be alive without him. Some weeks before he died in 1956 he told me he got a bigger kick out of the success of the magazine, after so many years at the bottom of the barrel, than out of his biggest oil strike.

The other part of our twin blessing in 1942 was represented by J. R. (Jack) Cominsky. I had met Jack in 1938 when I worked on *Current History*. He had called on us to talk about advertising in the Sunday magazine section of *The New York Times,* of which he was then advertising director. As mentioned earlier, *Current History's* offices were in the famous old New York World Building at 63 Park Row, at the foot of the Manhattan entrance to the Brooklyn Bridge. At one time the building was high on the list of New York's sight-seeing attractions. It was almost twenty stories tall with its graceful dome and spire. It had easily the most commanding presence of any structure on what at one time was known as "newspaper row" in New York.

Jack was a Rochesterian. Though he lived and worked in New York City, his center of gravity was Rochester, where he grew up, went to college, and became city editor (at the age of twenty-five) of the *Rochester Democrat and Chronicle.* It was easily apparent that he had a prodigious emotional investment in Rochester. He took pride in the university, in the Eastman School of Music, in the varied activities of the Eastman Kodak Company, in the symphony orchestra, in the art museum, and in the city's legendary figures. His wife, also a Rochesterian, was a concert pianist and augmented Jack's interest in music.

It is possible that Jack came to our offices at *Current History* only once. But I recall no other visitor who made a deeper impression on me. I remember thinking at the time that his advertising position at *The New York Times* must have been important indeed to have lured him away from his editorial bent. One thing in particular stuck in my mind. I had two baskets on my desk, one for unedited copy, the other for outgoing edited copy. In the former basket was an article on the first page of which was the following sentence: "President Roosevelt has no intention of seeking additional farm legislation, providing he can get enough cooperation for his existing program."

Jack happened to glance at the article in the basket and politely called my attention to the grammatical error. The correct word, of course, was "provided," not "providing."

Three years later, when we knew we would need a new advertising and business manager for the *Saturday Review,* I thought immediately of Jack Cominsky. He had the business experience we needed. Of equal importance was the fact that he had the deep-rooted cultural background and interests that would enable him to know what the *Saturday Review* was all about. How could we pry him loose from *The New York Times?* Certainly not with cash. I knew we couldn't afford to pay him more than a fraction of what he was receiving at *The Times.* I decided it would be worth talking to him just the same.

We met for lunch at the Seymour Hotel restaurant, just across the street from the magazine's offices at 25 West 45th Street, to which *SRL* had returned after three years on Madison Avenue.

Everything Jack said that day made sense. Once or twice I tried to interrupt in order to resume my story, but there was no breaking into his exuberance. And the more he talked the more convinced I became that he was our man. Anyone with this combination of energy and singleness of purpose would also have the fortitude to see it through at *SRL.*

"Jack," I finally succeeded in saying, "I was hoping I might be able to persuade you to be our business and advertising manager. We're almost broke and can't pay you as much as I'm sure you're getting. Until a few months ago we weren't even paying our contributors, but we've got the help now of a man by the name of E. De Golyer, and I have a hunch we might make a good team. We're just starting a regional cultural inventory of America. The first issue is on the American Southwest. John H. McGinnis, Frank Nash Smith, Lon Tinkle, and John William Rogers are helping to put it together. The next special issue will be on the South. Virginius Dabney, Roark Bradford, David Cohn, and Ralph McGill will help us with that one."

No man ever had a more encouraging response than I did from Jack as I soared in my description of the future for a journal of ideas and the arts that would address itself to the market place of good taste. I spoke of the magnificent legacy we had in SRL and the fact that Henry Canby and Amy Loveman were completely in accord with my plans for the magazine.

Jack almost exploded with excitement. The two of us must have made an interesting duo that day in the Seymour Hotel café as each added fuel to the other's optimism. Our hopes grew ever larger and brighter. Finally, after almost three hours, I realized we were the only ones left in the restaurant. But I still hadn't received a direct answer from Jack to my original proposal.

"Think about it," I said, "and let me know."

Jack looked at me as though I were being completely irrelevant. "Of course I'll come," he said. "I'm going to have to give *The Times* two weeks' notice. In the meantime, I'll be putting some ideas on paper."

That was how it began. Within two days after Jack joined the staff I had the unmistakable sensation of a new throb somewhere deep in the hull of SRL. Jack threw himself into the work of the magazine with a totality that made it apparent this was to be the great passion of his life. No one arrived earlier or left later. He even came into the office on weekends, sorted the mail, wrote memos, and prepared the work of the business department for a fast start on Monday mornings. He was something of a walking filing system. I can't think of a vital statistic about the magazine that he didn't carry with him. Once, on a dare from me, he emptied his inside pockets; I counted sixty-nine important papers or letters. Even this, however, was insignificant alongside his fast-accumulating mental storehouse of information about the magazine. Once, while working on an editorial late at night, I wanted to make a reference to an article we had published some months earlier. I telephoned Jack at his home; he gave me the correct title, author's name, date of publication, and main points of the article.

We may not have been able to pay all our bills but Jack gave us the sense that we were merely passing through a brief discomfort. If he had the slightest bit of good news he would deliver it in a way that made us feel we were on the verge of an Olympian triumph. If he had bad news, he kept it to himself. His optimism was harnessed to the kind of energy that made good things happen.

We had good times together. Shortly after the end of the war New York City was crippled by a transportation strike. Jack and I were scheduled to speak on a radio program over the city station, WNYC, located in the Municipal Building downtown, next to the old World Building. We were lucky enough to get a cab going down. Getting back was a different story; it was rush hour. I spied a horse and wagon waiting for a traffic light to change. I sprinted for the wagon and offered the driver three dollars to take us uptown.

"Mister, I ain't never taken passengers before. This wagon's for old furniture. Where ya gonna sit?"

"We'll sit in the back, on the floor," I said.

"It's pretty hard back there. There ain't no cushions."

"In the business we're in," I said, "we grow our own cushions."

I called out to Jack and told him the transportation crisis was solved. We climbed up the back of the wagon, our inexperience clearly reflected in our groping assault on the tailgate.

The ride uptown must have taken at least an hour. Every now and then our host would shout to us to ask how our "cushions" were holding out. Truth to tell, they were wearing pretty thin, but we were having too good a time to admit any second thoughts. Besides, it gave Jack an unobstructed chance to talk to me about his adventures on the *Rochester Democrat and Chronicle*.

The most important thing Jack did for the *Saturday Review*—in a long inventory of important things—was to force us to look ahead. Within two days after he arrived he asked for a prospectus of our plans, describing all the special issues and projects scheduled for the year ahead. Thus armed, he could approach the book publishers and try to stir them up.

The main value of Jack's suggestion, of course, was that it compelled us to get moving on specific ideas that otherwise might have remained in the dream stage. Also, it produced a number of new ideas for translation into actuality. Jack's expectations proved to be correct. An improvement in the total picture became apparent within a matter of months. While we were not yet in the black, we were at least able to pay our contributors. Our prospects were better than they had been for some years.

Jack's aim was to make the magazine financially independent of book-publishing advertising. He believed that diversification of advertising was one of the strongest assurances we could have of editorial freedom. It took ten years or more for Jack's program to reach the point where it became clearly visible and the results fully felt, but he had the confidence and persistence to see it through.

When I reported to Mr. De on our progress early in 1943, I began with Jack Cominsky.

# V

The editorial broadening of the magazine was not the result of any single decision. Long before I came to *SRL*, Henry Canby, George Stevens, and Amy Loveman had often discussed the appropriateness of a more inclusive cultural journal. Henry Canby's original intention was to call the magazine *The Saturday Review*. This title, however, had been preempted by the English weekly of the same name, and Dr. Canby added *of Literature.*

In my early discussions with Henry Canby and Amy Loveman concerning the general direction in which the magazine ought to go, I found the strongest concurrence and support for a wider treatment of ideas and the arts. We all agreed that new features should not take space away from the book-review section but should be added to it. The underlying principle of expansion was that book reviews would continue to be the editorial center of the magazine.

As the magazine grew, in fact, we were able to institute something we had never had before—a full-fledged book-review staff. Assigning books for review had never been anyone's full-time job. In the early days Amy Loveman would go through the shelf of new books twice a week, doing most of the assigning herself and consulting with the other editors in areas where they had special competence. When SR became solvent, one of the first things we did was to create a separate department concerned solely with assigning and processing books for review. For head of the department we selected Raymond Walters, Jr., whom I had known and admired when he was an editor of *Current History.* As book-review editor, Ray broadened our range of reviewers. He was especially proficient in bringing books together for group reviews. Ray was a skilled, quiet editorial craftsman. He also compiled and edited *Writing for Love or Money,* a selection of articles drawn from SR on writing as an art and as a profession. My name appeared as editor of the volume. I should never have consented to it. The work was done by Ray and he deserved all the credit. *The New York Times* lured Ray away from us in early 1958. We regretted losing a man of his stature and capacity. His assistant, Rochelle Girson, was promoted to book-review editor in 1958. Miss Girson had a wide background and experience at SR, having worked with Miss Loveman as well as Ray Walters. Eventually, the Book Review Department was to consist of of several full-time staff members, among them Rollene Waterman (later Saal), who became Miss Girson's assistant in 1958, and Ruth Brown, her successor as of 1961.

Under Miss Girson's talented editorship new regular features were introduced to the section. In 1958 Granville Hicks began to contribute a weekly short literary essay or review. Hicks's own books on American literature and his literary viewpoint in general seemed to us to be compatible with the traditions of literary criticism established by Henry Canby. Other features added include a column by Robert J. Clements on the European literary scene; a regular report on the trade publishing front by David Dempsey; a wide-ranging column on books, authors, and literary issues by John K. Hutchens; a monthly column, "On the Fringe," by Haskell Frankel, dealing with people who make book news; a section on paperback books by Rollene Saal. Mary Gould Davis superintended

*SRL*'s reviews of children's books until 1954, when she was succeeded by Frances Landers Spain. In 1959, the juvenile book editors consisted of a team from the Bank Street College of Education in New York headed by Irma S. Black. In 1961 Miss Alice Dalgliesh, who had been editor of Books for Young Readers at Charles Scribner's Sons for over twenty-five years, became *SR*'s authority in the field. Miss Dalgliesh retired in 1966 and was succeeded by Mrs. Zena Sutherland, former editor of the Bulletin of the Center for Children's Books at the University of Chicago and television consultant and author. The most recent contributor to *SR*'s book section is J. H. Plumb, eminent British historian and fellow of Christ's College, Cambridge, whose new monthly feature "Perspective" was added in the fall of 1966.

The Book Review Department provided much of the internal excitement in the affairs of the magazine. I have never ceased being astounded by the ease with which we could get into trouble with book reviews. Henry Canby and Amy Loveman often spoke to me about their difficulties over the years in keeping books from being sent out for review to friends or enemies of the authors. Here were the questions they always tried to ask themselves in assigning a non-fiction book:

1. Is the prospective reviewer an established authority in the field covered by the book? If not, don't send the book.
2. Has the prospective reviewer written a book, or does he plan to write a book, on precisely the same subject as the book under review? If so, don't send the book.
3. Is the prospective reviewer a personal friend or antagonist of the author? If so, don't send the book.
4. Have the prospective reviewer's own books been reviewed by the author of the book under consideration? If so, don't send the book.
5. Is the prospective reviewer known to be a strong opponent of the central idea or ideas in the book under consideration? If so, don't send the book.

In fields where many of the experts were identified with one point of view or the other—as in the case of the Soviet Union or Communist China —the application of the five-point yardstick described above often left us with a shelf of unassigned books. In some cases we felt reasonably sure all the points had been checked off only to discover, after the review appeared, that we had slipped.

Amy Loveman wrote a "credo of reviewing" for the magazine in the issue of July 25, 1931. In it she said:

> We believe the cardinal sin of a reviewer to be the exploitation of himself instead of interpretation of his subject. While we hold that the public is better served in regard to certain types of books by the review that presents or discusses their subject matter in relation to their field as a whole rather

than analyzes the volumes in detail, we are certain that there is no place in a just literary journal for the critic who uses it for the mere display of his own erudition, for the advancement of personal peccadilloes or the waging of personal controversies.

*SRL*'s reviews were written not primarily for specialists and academicians but for the intelligent reader who thought it important to be well informed about the wide range of new books. This didn't mean that the editors would bypass all books of a specialized nature. Some of them warranted extended treatment. For the most part, however, the reviews would be directed to the broad spectrum of books, fiction and non-fiction, intended for the general reader.

Much has been said in recent years about the lack of toughness in reviewing media, including the *Saturday Review*. The implication was that a deliberate effort was made to avoid offending publishers because of advertising. Several points were generally overlooked in this casual indictment. First, out of the many thousands of new books received each year, only a fraction can be sent out for review. The weeding-out process involves some degree of quality control. Second, it is not necessary to lacerate a book and its author in order to be critical. Nothing is easier than to find a few flaws in a book and proceed to tear it apart on those grounds. An author may spend two years in writing a book—and a reviewer two days or perhaps as little as two hours in reading it or writing about it. It is no more than fair to expect the reviewer to be sure of his ground before proceeding with the demolition, if such is his intent.

The reviewer must be concerned primarily with the merits of the book, of course, but he should state the author's thesis even before he passes judgment on it. He must give some idea of what the book is all about; he must relate it to other books in the same field and to the previous output of the author; he must make clear his own yardsticks of criticism. It is obviously impossible to write an essay on every book. Conversely, it is not always easy or fair to deal with a book in a single paragraph.

Perhaps the most striking example of a slashing review that should never have been published by *SRL* was Sinclair Lewis's review of Bernard De Voto's *The Literary Fallacy* in 1944.

De Voto, as indicated earlier, was not weighted down by reservations in style or approach. Language to him was no feeble instrument. Occasionally he engaged in personal forays. Somewhere along the line he had managed to insult Sinclair Lewis.

Lewis was infuriated by De Voto's frequent references in *The Literary Fallacy* to the ignorance of American writers in general. De Voto had charged that our novelists and writers paid too little attention to American history or science. Lewis persuaded Hal Smith to let him review De Voto's book for *SRL*. It was easily the most vitriolic review that ever appeared in this magazine—not excluding John Ciardi's attack on Anne Morrow Lindbergh's *The Unicorn and Other Poems*. Lewis ridiculed De

Voto's physical appearance. He excoriated him for his errors. Nothing that Lewis had ever written in his own satirical works was as stinging as his commentary on De Voto.

I had serious reservations about publishing Lewis's review without severe editing. The standing rule at *SRL*—that a reviewer enjoyed complete freedom of criticism and opinion—did not seem to me to constitute a hunting license for personal quarry. I expressed my doubts but in the end was overawed by Lewis's reputation; we ran the review as written. The episode had the effect of making me think through the existing principles that applied to book reviewing. I felt that complete freedom of reviewing was unworkable and an abdication of the editor's responsibility. At the very least, we had to be reasonably careful about keeping the book-review section from becoming a personal battleground. We were not going to plunge pell-mell into showy, shiny, brutal literary criticism just to get us talked about.

Two of *SRL*'s features that appeared at the very end of the magazine and that indeed sometimes faced each other often produced more comment than anything up front. I refer, of course, to Double Crostics, an invention of Mrs. Elizabeth S. Kingsley, introduced in 1934, and the Personals Department, instituted in the first issue.

The credit for discovering Double-Crostics belongs to George Stevens. It was he who discovered Mrs. Kingsley and gave the puzzle its name.

Double Crostics was to crossword puzzles what chess is to checkers. It utilized the basic form but contained an extra dimension in that the filled-in squares became a striking quotation. Mrs. Kingsley quickly became an institution. When she pronounced judgment on the meaning or derivation of a word, that was the end of the argument. Her interests and predilections, reflected in her choice of quotations and definitions, ranged from Greek mythology to music and contemporary baseball heroes. Sometimes she would spend three or four days in concocting a single out-of-the-way definition to bedevil her valiant but often helpless readers. She encouraged her followers to use reference books. She said she used reference books to make the puzzle and saw no reason why the reader shouldn't use them, too.

Eighteen years and 973 puzzles later, Elizabeth Kingsley retired in 1952. As befitted a queen, she passed along her reign to Mrs. Doris Nash Wortman, who had her own style and created her own inimical controversies. Mrs. Wortman had apparently learned one lesson from her predecessor. When making word games, be sure of your ground in the first place and, if attacked, never yield an inch of it in the second place. Mrs. Wortman, however, had an asset that Mrs. Kingsley never enjoyed. We had arranged with one of the nation's most skilled word puzzlers, Laura Hobson, the novelist, to work out Double Crostics in advance of publication each week—as an ambassador-at-large for the readers, making certain that we weren't putting them at too great a disadvantage with some of the definitions, and acting as a sentry against mechanical or other errors.

Mrs. Wortman died in June 1967. Her Double-Crostics reign had lasted fifteen years. She had given the puzzle an accent of intellectual challenge that was the delight (and sometimes the despair) of many thousands of Crostickers.

The Personals column began in 1932 when Louis Untermeyer advertised to find out whether anyone wanted to acquire a pair of Sardinian donkeys. I have always suspected Chris Morley and Bill Benét of skillful seeding in those early Personals columns, but they never owned up to it. At any rate, within a few months after its start, seeded or unseeded, the Personals feature in *SRL* was being talked about. Little wonder. Consider some of the early notices:

> 'TIS SPRING! What Rose-in-hand will toss a petal into cup of old Khayyam?

> WOULD LIKE CORRESPONDENCE with wealthy old widdy woman in the twenties who can steer a boat and arrange for petrol while I type the American Novel in the turgid waters of Puget Sound.

> GENTLEMAN, about to be stumped by arrival of out-of-town nephew, aged 17, is looking for young, pretty, and intelligent girl to date said nephew. Box 183.

> WHITE HAT. Would the beautiful girl who tried on the white hat in Saks Fifth Avenue care to meet the man who sat at the adjoining table? S. S. Box 73.

> S. S. Box 73. Missed your notice. Eager to meet. Be at same place Tuesday noon. WHITE HAT.

Some of the Personals notices produced thousands of responses. So far as we know, however, the item that broke all records consisted of only nine words:

> OIL WIDOW would like to hear from interested party.

An estimate of the replies was that there were about 3,600 "interested parties." I had no doubt that the widow, whoever she was, was able to solve her problem.

Wherever I went, I met people whose lives had been changed by the Personals. In Seattle, following a lecture, a woman came forward and embraced me. "I just want to thank you," she said, "for my family."

I drew back, straightened my tie, and looked at her closely.

"What I mean," she said, "is that I met my husband through the Personals column. Not until after five months of correspondence did I discover he lived around the corner."

In Atlanta, the head of a bank telephoned me during my visit to that city to express thanks for his job. He had made the original contact years earlier through the Personals column.

Ultimately, it became necessary to exercise careful surveillance of the Personals department, especially the part of it that led to blind meetings. Inevitably, perhaps, charlatans had begun to prey on the users of the column, exploiting trust in the magazine for their own purposes. With heavy hearts, Jack and I were forced to discontinue correspondence notices or other items that might expose people to harm. For the first few weeks after the new policy was in effect we thought, judging from the volume of protest, that we might have made the biggest mistake of our lives. We decided to stick it out nonetheless, and were pleased that the storm blew itself out by the end of the year. The Personals department suffered in volume for a few weeks and then began to expand along less romantic and more practical lines.

## VI

One of the most important moves we made toward broadening the magazine editorially was to engage John Mason Brown as critic-at-large in 1944. The suggestion had originated with Amy Loveman. Like most of us on *SRL*, John Brown had been a veteran of the old *New York Evening Post*. During World War II he had served in the U.S. Navy. Few plays John Brown wrote about carried as much dramatic impact and suspense as his own part in the amphibious landing at Normandy.

John had been aide to Admiral Alan G. Kirk on the USS *Augusta*, flagship of the American invasion fleet. Admiral Kirk assigned John the job of monitoring the loudspeaker during the invasion landing. John did a running commentary for the men on board, connecting them to the historical enterprise in which each had a major role. His words enabled the men to penetrate the constricted field of vision imposed by war on the individual warrior. John Brown could lift the men below decks out of their interior limbo and make them integral to the battle.

Some years later Admiral Kirk told me that, for sheer brilliance of observation and ability to convey the essence of an incredibly complex and fast-changing situation, he had never seen the equal of John Mason Brown's dramatic performance on June 6, 1944.

Such an evaluation would come as no surprise to anyone who has heard John Mason Brown on the public platform. Within a short time after he began his lecturing career, John Brown became the most popular speaker in the country, a distinction he retained for more than thirty years. I knew of no contemporary critic who had a greater gift for the felicitous use of the English language. He had complete command over the quintessentials, whether in describing a play, a person, or an event.

He was proof of the proposition that words are the ultimate art. The pictures he painted in the listener's mind had far greater substance and color than that which the eye alone could perceive. John Brown demonstrated that the most potent theater could be staged within the human imagination—without curtains, props, or special lighting effects. And so he went around the country, a composite performance by himself, providing not only dramatic criticism of a very high order, but a versatile sampling of the plays themselves.

What appealed to me especially about John Brown was that his approach to the theater paralleled *SRL*'s approach to books. His interest in the theater was exceeded only by his interest in the human drama. He paid his readers the compliment of believing that their interests were as wide-ranging as his own, their sensitivities no less keen, their concerns no less deep. What he once wrote of Edith Hamilton, for whom he had total admiration, was no less true of himself: He said that Miss Hamilton was "a popularizer but not a vulgarizer, a liaison officer between the finest that has been and the finest that is." She "wrote from the heart as well as the head." Her "learning and living are linked. Large as is her erudition, her vision is larger."

John Mason Brown's writings in the magazine progressively widened until they embraced the world of the creative arts as a whole and, indeed, the arena of events and ideas. He brought his critical intelligence and remarkable command of the language to bear on a wide range of subjects. In fact, few writers I know have made more imaginative use of the unique advantages offered by a magazine for combining the public interest in the topical with the critic's interest in the generic and the historical. He would write about Clifford Odets one week, locating him in time, space, and the human condition. The next week he would contribute an essay on a new book about Horace Walpole by Wilmarth Lewis. Then he would drop out of the magazine for several weeks in order to gather material for a series of articles on the Nuremberg Trials—a series, incidentally, which still stands as one of the best-rounded accounts and appraisals of that event—whether from the standpoint of political or juridical history. I was especially struck with his description of some of the men on trial:

> A sorrier group of men than those who had found their Valhalla in the Nuremberg dock could scarcely be imagined. The prison pallor—that pallor which can reduce the most florid complexion to a whiteness not unlike a fish's belly—was upon them. . . . Their bodies, like their authority, had shriveled. Only the cruelty in their faces remained undwindled. Inescapable as this was, it was insufficient to encompass their mass crimes. They had lean, though not hungry, looks. It was not so much that they had become thin as that they had ceased to be gross. The change in their diet did not end with a different menu. They were nourished by what they had

eaten but starved for that which they had once fed on. Adversity had whittled away their persons no less than their powers.

No assignment we gave John Mason Brown used him more fully perhaps than his coverage of the Presidential election campaigns. All the bizarre sounds of the nominating conventions were duly noted—John Brown had not been a student of the theater for nothing—but he was also able to discern the deep currents underneath the corn. His sense of drama was in balance with his sense of history.

In 1955 John Mason Brown took leave of absence in order to begin work on his study of Robert E. Sherwood, playwright, author, historian, adviser to presidents. Sherwood's qualities called irresistibly to a mind like John Mason Brown's. For Sherwood represented a combination of poetic sensitivity and craggy practicality. His mind and life were interwoven in the texture of living history but he never lost vital contact with tradition. His unabashed love of America didn't make him insensitive to its imperfections.

More than a year before embarking on his book about Sherwood, John Brown had suggested that Henry Hewes, a staff writer with *The New York Times* and lecturer on the theater at Sarah Lawrence College and at Columbia University, be assigned the openings which John himself, for various reasons, wasn't able to cover. When John's return seemed to be indefinitely deferred by the multi-volume study of Sherwood, it was natural that Henry Hewes should become *SR*'s drama critic.

Hewes, tall and attenuated like a sketch from the old *Vanity Fair*, was totally devoted to the theater. He wrote about new plays and the history of the theater with knowledgeability and zest. He became editor of *Famous American Plays of the 1940's*, *The Best Plays of 1961–62*, and *The Best Plays of 1963–64*. At *SR*'s editorial meetings Henry expresses strong ideas on all subjects under discussion. He has an earnest, enthusiastic quality and places high value on his commitment to the magazine. And, like his predecessor, he is a popular platform personality.

One of the advantages to the magazine provided by the lecture platform was that it give us access to a broad range of listeners, all of whom, in effect, were sampling one section or another of the magazine. Incidentally, this was part of my own justification for taking time away from the magazine in order to speak publicly.

I am sure we all enjoyed our lecturing experiences, but I doubt that any one of us relished them more than Bennett Cerf, who contributed "Trade Winds" from 1942 to 1957. Bennett loved everything about public speaking—the receptions and dinners and after-lecture chitchats that often ran late into the night. Most speakers try to shun the social activities that go with lecturing. Receptions, especially, call for considerable fortitude. The shower of random noises has a disorienting effect. Oliver Wendell

Holmes (and dozens of others, no doubt) has been credited with the remark that he had two fees for his lectures: $500, if his hosts did not offer hospitality or entertainment; $1,000, if they did. The reverse could probably be said of Bennett. He thrived on public contact.

"Let's face it," he once remarked. "I'm pure ham. I like the platform, the billing, the lights, and everything that goes with it. I like 'show' people. I've got stars in my eyes—and always will. The other day a cab-driver turned around and said: 'Aren't you Bennett Cerf? Sure you are. I seen you on TV *What's My Line?*' I like that."

This unself-conscious exuberance was reflected in his Trade Winds column. Christopher Morley had originated the column; in his hands it had been a bookman's log, with entries covering visits to bookstores or items about publishers' row. Chris loved to decorate the column with typographical doodads, such as fingers pointing into paragraphs in the style of old-fashioned grocery ads. Bennett also carried material about the trade, generally drawn from his own publishing experiences and contacts. But the distinguishing and characteristic ingredient in his handling of the column was humor. Next to people he loved funny stories. Each column contained a generous supply of anecdotes. Trade Winds started Bennett Cerf on his career as a professional raconteur and laugh man. It was on the basis of his column that Simon & Schuster persuaded Bennett to publish his *Try and Stop Me*, a comic compendium that was followed eventually by a dozen or more humorous books or anthologies.

Some of *SRL*'s subscribers objected to what they thought was an unnecessarily frivolous and somewhat undignified department, but most of the readers cheered him on. I not only acquiesced in the turn he gave to Trade Winds, but gave him full support. I sometimes cribbed stories from his advance columns and used them at the beginning of my lectures. But Bennett got even. Once he came to hear me speak at the New York Town Hall. My talk was directed to world affairs, with the Berlin airlift crisis and the spread of nuclear weapons accounting for a large part of a rather somber report.

"That's pretty potent stuff you're dishing out," Bennett said to me after the talk. "If you could just lighten it up with a funny story here and there, you'd be surprised how much easier it would be for your listeners to stay with you. It's especially important to begin with the kind of story that puts your audience in a good mood and gives them a chance to hobnob with people in the news. You've got to bring in the big names."

"But I don't know any funny stories that involve people with big names," I protested.

"Norman," he said, "You meet them all the time. You just have to have an ear out for good copy. Who was the last celebrity you met?"

"Not counting you?"

"Come on, now."

"Well, last Tuesday in Albany, at the Board of Regents meeting, I sat next to General Eisenhower."

"Good. What happened?"

I told Bennett that while I was being introduced the General leaned over and whispered in my ear that I looked a little nervous. The General was right; I *was* nervous, and I admitted it.

Then, in a low voice, the General gave me his secret for overcoming his nervousness. "Whenever I get up to speak," he said, "I transfer my embarrassment to the audience."

I asked the General how he did that.

"Simple," he said. "Just look straight at them and imagine everyone out there is sitting in his tattered old underwear."

The effect on Bennett as I told the story was electric.

"Great, great," he said. "That's an ideal opening. It's funny, it's true, it happened to you, and it involves the biggest name in the country right now. Now the next time you speak, just tell the story as an opener and see the difference it makes."

Three weeks later, at a civic forum in St. Louis, I told the Eisenhower story. It was a complete dud. No laughs. In fact, the anecdote fell so flat that my lecture was uphill all the rest of the way.

After the talk a gentleman came up to me. "About that story of Eisenhower and the underwear," he said, "Was that really true?"

"Yes," I said. "It happened just as I told it. Why do you ask?"

"Well, Bennett Cerf spoke here last week and said it happened to him."

I forgave Bennett. Anyone who hears a story automatically becomes its owner. The important thing is to tell it first. A few of Bennett's best stories I reluctantly had to cut from his column because they were fairly raw. Bennett let out anguished cries every time it happened, but he was back on the telephone the next day with his customary bounce and heartiness.

In all the years he contributed Trade Winds, Bennett's copy was never carelessly prepared or late. He was one of the most disciplined writers I have ever known. It was a mystery to me how he managed time for his Random House affairs, which included business and editorial operations; for his lectures, which sometimes took him from the office for weeks at a time; for his own books and periodical writings which, in addition to the *Saturday Review*, included a regular newspaper column and a regular Sunday-supplement newspaper feature; and for his television programs.

Bennett finally recognized that even he had finite dimensions to his capacity. After fifteen years at the *Saturday Review* he told us he couldn't carry the column any longer. We had a farewell party in his honor. When he got up to acknowledge our toasts, he started to tell some stories but it was easy to see his heart wasn't in it.

"I guess I'm not in a funny mood today," he said finally. "What I want to say is that Trade Winds started me off on a totally new career and I've never been happier with any connection than with the *Saturday Review*. And that reminds me of a story . . ."

And that was the way it ended, not with a whimper but a gag. We replaced Bennett with two writers—John Fuller and Jerome Beatty. Both were good roving reporters with a strong interest in the world of books. Each had his own flair and special areas of enthusiasm. Fuller was the most avid games man I had ever known. He collected them by the thousands, a substantial percentage of which found their way into his column. He also had an eye for the bizarre.

Jerry Beatty, editorial consultant to *Esquire,* and formerly a staff writer on *Collier's, Pageant,* and *Coronet,* was not so unpredictable as Fuller but he came closer to the original bent of the column under Morley. He was especially interested in literary curiosa and in unusual publishing events.

In July 1966, Herbert R. Mayes, former editor of *McCall's* magazine, became a regular contributor to Trade Winds. For years I had tried to persuade Herb to contribute to the column. I couldn't think of any American editor who had a wider or richer store of experiences in the world of publishing and communications in general. After years of resistance Herb finally agreed to write one column. Reader response was both strong and favorable and Herb agreed to take a regular turn on the page.

Long before these changes in Trade Winds, of course, other departments and columns had been integrated into the magazine. It was Horace Sutton who convinced us in 1947 that it was possible to embark on a type of travel coverage substantially different from anything that had appeared in general magazines up to that time. Sutton, young, red-haired, energetic, positive in convictions and outlook, spoke of his belief that one of the great revolutions in human history was about to get under way. He forecast a world in which countless thousands of Americans would be visiting far-off places—not just for the purpose of seeing famous sites but because they would be even more interested in history-in-the-making. Long-range travel, he predicted, would become a normal way of life. He saw a new dimension in travel-writing which not only provided the expected information on what to do and what not to do, but connected Americans with life as it was actually lived in the places they would be visiting. His department would be called "Booked for Travel" and would use books, quite literally, for its point of departure.

When Horace started his department in 1947, 200,000 Americans possessed valid passports. In 1966, 1,500,000 Americans had passports. Horace's editorial initiative, with the help of William D. Patterson, SR's associate publisher, enabled the magazine to translate the new American interest in travel into a major part of the magazine's growth.

For a man who makes a living out of visiting far-off places, Horace is a remarkable homebody. He is never happier than when he is with his family, with at least two weeks stretching in front of him before his next trip. He loves to come into the office to discuss editorial and publishing problems. One day in 1961 he announced he had just accepted a job as editor of *Paradise of the Pacific*, a monthly journal published in Honolulu. He said he thought he could continue to edit his department in *SR*, for he expected he would still do considerable traveling. We agreed, and Horace moved his family to Hawaii, and became a first-class editor-publisher.

For a long time, I had secret thoughts of turning Horace Sutton to general reporting and article-writing—at least occasionally. He is a talented observer, he knows how to use words, and he has a gift for penetrating complex and murky situations. My hopes for Horace in this direction were fully realized early in 1967 when he went to Indonesia to do a comprehensive story on the political purges. His article on that subject was one of the most incisive and informative pieces of foreign correspondence ever to appear in the *Saturday Review*.

We were indebted to John Mason Brown for introducing us to James Thrall Soby, our first "Fine Arts" department head. Soby, as chairman of both the Department of Painting and Sculpture Exhibitions and the Trustees' Committee on the Museum Collections of the Museum of Modern Art, began his regular column on art in *SRL* in 1946. He ranged with style and distinction over the entire world of art.

In 1959, following James Soby's retirement, Arnold H. Maremont, of Chicago, a good friend of the magazine, suggested the possible availability of Katharine Kuh, former director of the Chicago Museum of Art who, he believed, might be willing to come to New York and join the staff. We invited Mrs. Kuh to contribute several articles and were delighted with the result. She was alive to the eternal need for experimentalism in the arts but didn't make the mistake, as some art critics do, of repudiating everything that had been done before. It is one thing to be receptive to new approaches; it is another thing to allow oneself to become intimidated by them to the point where one becomes part of an uncritical cult. Within a year after Mrs. Kuh began her column we began to see evidence of the leadership position she was winning for *SR* in the field of art.

Cleveland Amory, author of *The Proper Bostonians, Who Killed Society?* and *The Last Resort*, satirist and social historian, introduced the column, "First of the Month," in 1957. The column is an effort to sort out the main events. Its main value, however, is not so much as a highlight news summary but as an outlet for Amory's talent as a spotter of incongruities and paradoxes, especially when they involve public celebrities. His column also reflects an astounding range of personal interests, running from a passionate concern for humane treatment of animals to golf and new strategies in chess. As a golfer, he can outdrive many professionals.

Hollis Alpert and Arthur Knight began in 1950 to provide SR with highly mature, competent reviews of films, and won virtually every award for distinguished criticism of motion pictures. Robert Lewis Shayon and Gilbert Seldes alternated for several years in writing about radio and television. After Seldes became dean of the Annenberg School of Communications at the University of Pennsylvania, Shayon conducted the column himself. He is as aware of TV's failings as any critic, but few items of genuine merit escape his attention. Ivan Dmitri introduced us to the concept of photography as a fine art. Dmitri, an artist himself, conceived and carried out a series of "Photography in the Fine Arts" issues in conjunction with special exhibitions he arranged in museums around the country. Margaret Weiss joined the staff as photography editor in 1961. Peggy's artistry in living is clearly reflected in her approach to photography as an art.

Martin Levin, the anthologist, revived Bill Benét's old Phoenix Nest department in 1958 by bringing into the magazine an extraordinary variety of talent—all the way from Richard Armour, George S. Kaufman, John Updike, H. Allen Smith, and Ogden Nash to James Thurber, Ben Hecht, P. G. Wodehouse, Frank Sullivan, and Henry Morgan. There is an impression that the anthologist's job is the easiest one in literature. Not so in the case of Levin, who worries and fusses over his department with an intensity few writers give to their own work.

Goodman Ace, generally credited with being the most sought-after comedy writer in television, agreed to write a short weekly piece called "Top of My Head," early in 1964. It soon became one of the most-quoted sections of the magazine.

From the start, I relished the job of selecting cartoons for the magazine and have never relinquished it, no matter what else had to be delegated. After a particular tense morning in the office, with work piling up because of the heavy traffic of visitors and telephone calls, I found this task something akin to therapy. Especially did I enjoy the series, "Through History with J. Wesley Smith," by Burr Shafer. A piano merchant in Santa Ana, California, Shafer gained fame as a cartoonist. His cartoon character, J. Wesley Smith, was a bumbling, bulbous, middle-aged man who had a propensity for turning up with maladroit comments in famous historical situations. J. Wesley, in short, was a creature of the absurd.

One cartoon showed him in the boat with George Washington crossing the Delaware. "Please sit down, General," J. Wesley called out, "you're rocking the boat."

Another cartoon showed J. Wesley with shield, spear, and helmet stepping on a fellow-soldier's heel. Said J. W. S.: "Pardon me, Achilles."

One more: Mr. and Mrs. J. Wesley Smith, accompanied by their three youngsters, are shown entering a glade. J. Wesley, dour-faced, is carrying a large picnic basket. Mrs. J. Wesley is speaking. "Don't be silly. Mr. Thoreau will be *delighted* to see us."

The J. Wesley Smith series was anthologized in two books and became the most popular cartoon feature in the magazine. Burr Shafer died in 1965; the magazine reprints old J. W. S. favorites from time to time.

These departments were distinct from the development of our special supplements, or magazines-within-a-magazine. The first of these supplements, instituted in 1947, was concerned with music, live and recorded, and was edited by Irving Kolodin, who had worked on the *New York Sun* in the field of music criticism since 1932. Kolodin's main characteristics as a critic are his solidity, the strength of his reasoning, and the clear visibility of his critical yardsticks. His competence as a critic extends to all fields of music, but he has a special interest in the opera. Kolodin does more than select records for review; he evaluates recordings and live performances. Important recordings never escape his notice. Manufacturers and artists might not like his verdict at times, but no one ever questions his ability or integrity.

The Recordings Supplement is a series of special sections on newly recorded music, live performances, music developments throughout the world, jazz and the dance. Irving's concern and expertise in each of these fields are readily apparent. Nothing goes into his section that doesn't meet his own rigid standards.

Kolodin correctly forecast the rebirth of the phonograph industry through the medium of long-playing records. For almost two decades the phonograph had been eclipsed by radio. Few believed that a slow turntable and technological advances in sound quality could not only bring about the return of the phonograph but could give rise to a major new American industry. Kolodin designed *SRL*'s music supplement to reflect his certainty that the 33 r.p.m. record would have major acceptance.

Kolodin also proved to be right about the 45 r.p.m disc. He contended in the magazine that 45 r.p.m. was against the public interest, being a poor and unworkable straddle between the 33 r.p.m. and the old 78 r.p.m. RCA, which had invested large sums to support its conviction that the 45 r.p.m. had a large place in the future of the phonograph industry, withdrew its advertising from *SRL*. Eventually, it became clear that the public verdict was against 45 r.p.m.; RCA discontinued 45 r.p.m. production, and resumed its advertising in the Recordings Supplement.

Kolodin's acuteness and his phenomenal knowledge of opera history and performance were never more in evidence than when his ear detected a fraudulent recording of Verdi's *Ballo in Maschera*, released in 1950. After listening to the recording, presented as a "classic" edition with a list of prominent Italian singers, Kolodin's suspicions were aroused. In collaboration with opera experts at the Met, he pinpointed the recording as a Metropolitan broadcast of years earlier, featuring Jan Peerce and Leonard Warren, among others. As music detective, Kolodin also revealed in 1953 that a recording of Wagner's "Ring" cycle, presented as a product of an East German company, was actually a transcription of a Bayreuth broadcast.

Five years before the concept for a Lincoln Center of the Performing Arts took shape, Kolodin wrote a lead article for *SR*, projecting a ten-year plan for making a major music center out of the Metropolitan.

He has a lean social life; he scrupulously avoids developing close friendships with performers or people whose work he may have to evaluate. He rarely makes appointments for lunch. I have seldom seen visitors in his office. Except for those occasions when his wife Irma accompanies him, he generally makes the rounds of concerts and operas alone. He is at the top of his profession not just because of his innate talents but because he has been willing, quite literally, to invest the whole of his life in his art and work. There is no member of the staff for whose professional competence I have higher regard.

Eventually, Irving Kolodin also became the editor of a substantial venture by *SR*—the special programs produced for the Metropolitan Opera and Lincoln Center. This was a major undertaking; sometimes as many as a dozen different editions had to be published each week to accommodate last-minute program changes. Irving absorbed the added responsibilities with characteristic strength and grace. Jack Cominsky and Marion Urmy assumed the responsibilities for business management and over-all publication.

The Science Supplement, under John Lear, was started in 1956. Lear, a conscientious, hard-working editorial craftsman with a granite-like integrity and a blazing sense of justice, had been an editor on *Collier's* magazine, then recently defunct. All these qualities went into the making of a new section which dealt with science and technology, especially in terms of its implications on public policy. My conception of the new supplement, as I discusssed it with John Lear, put the emphais on research—what was being done in fields ranging all the way from medicine to astronomy; what the principal problems were; fields in which greater research was needed, etc. John wanted the emphasis to be on important issues confronting the scientist—issues that had social and political implications. He wanted to treat research as a special department in the section. He asked me to suspend judgment until after several issues had been published. I was glad I did so; he was right. Later in this section, I have more to say about John Lear.

The third monthly supplement, dealing with education, was unique in at least one respect. It had been proposed to us in 1960 by the Fund for the Advancement of Education, under the auspices of the Ford Foundation. In effect, the proposal was that the Foundation and SR would form an editorial partnership for the publication of a monthly educational supplement. The arrangement would last for at least three years.

It seemed to us a most attractive opportunity, for it would enable SR to provide a genuine measure of leadership in the effort to upgrade the nation's educational policies and programs. The editor would be Paul Woodring, Distinguished Service Professor of Education, Western Washington College of Education, and author of *A Fourth of a Nation, New Directions in Teacher Education,* and *Let's Talk Sense About Our Schools.* Staff members included James Cass, former consultant to the Governor's Committee on Higher Education in New York state, former director of the Research and Development Division of the National Citizens Council for Better Schools and co-author with Max Birnbaum of *Comparative Guide to American Colleges;* Frank Jennings, long-time contributor to the *Saturday Review* and author of *This Is Reading,* as well as several English textbooks; John Scanlon, former editor of the *Amherst* (Mass.) *Journal* and government official.

The Education Supplement more than lived up to our expectations. It was able to achieve that rare combination of good writing and authority that editors strive for so valiantly but don't always achieve. In 1965 the arrangement with the Ford Foundation was transferred to the Charles Kettering Foundation, then expanding its interest and concern in the field of education. Charles F. Kettering, Jr., vice-president of the Foundation, assured us that the main desire of his group was the continued independence, improvement, and growth of the section.

With the education section well established and operating monthly, Paul Woodring expressed a wish to spend more time teaching and writing. He suggested that James Cass, whose editorial talents were a vital factor in the wide acceptance of the section, be given the operational responsibility and share with him the policy-making functions. This change took place formally in June 1966. In September of 1966, Peter Schrag, former Associate Secretary of Amherst College and author of *Voices in the Classroom,* joined the Education Supplement as Associate Editor.

The Communications Supplement rounded out the monthly cycle of special supplements. Richard L. Tobin, long-time newspaperman and journalist, war correspondent and city editor, news editor for TV and radio, and director of public affairs at the *New York Herald Tribune,* initiated and founded a new section in SR that provided major coverage and appraisal of the world of news-gathering and reporting. The greatest single lack in news coverage, he believed, was news about the press itself. He felt there were also important opportunities for evaluating the fields of advertising and public relations.

Dick Tobin became SR's managing editor in 1961. He injected the right amount of atmospheric calm into our collective editorial metabolism. Most of the departmental editors—and the editor himself—tend to show the effects at times of working under pressure. Dick lowers the temperature; the rest of us are the beneficiaries. He superintends a long checklist: What is in our articles bank? What is our schedule of leading articles for seven or eight weeks ahead? What editorial material, whether in articles, features, book reviews, or the special supplements, lend themselves to cover treatment? What are the personnel problems that require special handling? Dick puts all these sundry matters or problems into tidy bundles and then reviews them with me. He makes it possible for me to stay close to those aspects of the magazine I feel belong on my desk: the final selection of the articles; final cover choices and cover lines; special treatment of themes or "takeouts." On Fridays and Mondays I go over the page proofs of the entire issue with Dick or Pearl Sullivan, the editorial production chief, or Al Balk, Features Editor.

Al Balk came to SR in 1966 from Chicago, making the transition from free-lance writer to editor. His predecessors as SR Features Editor were Peter V. Ritner, who became editor of the Trade Book Department in The Macmillan Company, and James F. Fixx, who became Executive Editor of *McCall's* Magazine in 1966. The feature editor's job involves handling all the columns for the magazine, and sometimes a great deal besides; doing a large part of whatever rewriting is necessary in the articles; and acting as an assistant managing editor.

For the first twelve years of my editorship I had put the magazine to bed each week. I went to the printer, working at the compositor's stone. In 1952 I relinquished this part of the job to Eloise Perry Hazard, a young lady who, despite physical frailty, had extraordinary patience and a prodigious capacity for the tough, grinding work that the physical production of a magazine entails.

Pearl Steinhaus Sullivan, who had been working in advertising production, succeeded Eloise in 1959. Pearl had wide experience and an incredible store of energy. As the magazine grew, it became necessary for her to bring in assistants—Ardeane Tratzki being her first lieutenant—but Pearl insists on maintaining her place at the make-up desk herself, where she personally pastes in the last inch of galley proof.

For our cover designs and special layouts, we turned to Irving Spellens, consulting artist. Under his direction, SR's appearance was substantially improved.

Perhaps the greatest contribution of all to my emancipation from editorial chores came in 1959 when Cleveland Amory recommended Hallowell Bowser to by my personal editorial associate. For a long time, I had been inundated by the flow of magazine materials and correspondence. Hal Bowser helped to stem this tide and freed me for the part of the job I relished most—planning for the magazine and working directly with the staff. Hal's interests range all the way from microscopy to abstract philosophy. He comes by his encyclopedic knowledge honestly, having been on the staff of *Funk & Wagnalls Encyclopedia* before coming to SR. Most of all, Hal has the kind of overview and wit that makes him something akin to office sage. I found myself turning more and more to Hal Bowser for answers to all sorts of questions and problems. In my mail each day I receive perhaps a dozen or more fairly complicated requests. I pencil the notation AP ("Advise please") in the upper right-hand corner of each letter. The next day the letter is returned by Hal with a memorandum containing a reasonable analysis of the proposal or request, often with an astonishingly complete historical account of the project, and an incisive statement of the alternatives. "The lively editor," Harold Ross once said, "is a man who learns how to delegate his ulcers." Hal has the resilience and philosophical calm to make the both of us ulcer-free.

Hal constantly astounds me with odd bits of information on events and personalities. When, for example, the editors met with Lancelot Law Whyte, the British philosopher, Hal mentioned Mr. Whyte's role in helping to finance private research in jet aircraft in 1936. On another occasion, when we met with Sir Isaiah Berlin, the British historian-philosopher, Hal referred to the time when Sir Winston Churchill dined with Irving Berlin, the songwriter, in the mistaken idea he had invited Sir Isaiah.

Most of the discussion so far about the growth of the magazine has centered on the new departments and their staffs. We had the good fortune to become associated with a number of people who, even if they do not write regularly, make important contributions to the magazine. These include Harrison Brown, of the California Institute of Technology, whose specialized knowledge range across many areas of science and who takes a strong interest in world planning and population control; Joseph Wood Krutch, critic-essayist, humanist, and author of numerous books, among them *The Measure of Man, The Desert Year,* and *More Lives Than One;* Elmo Roper, public opinion analyst and expert in American communications; Walter Millis, journalist and historian, and author of *The Road to War;* John Steinbeck, who contributed short essays until his own writing compelled him to end our informal association; and Frank C. Jennings, educator and author, who was extremely helpful, as we mentioned earlier, in the basic planning of the Education Supplement.

Early in 1964 SR added regular coverage and commentary from Washington by Henry Brandon, U.S. correspondent for fourteen years for the *Sunday Times* of London. Brandon has the kind of insistent knowledgeability and toughness that is the mark of a first-rate Washington correspondent. He has something more: historical perspective and the ability to comprehend the context in which major government decisions are made.

The most recent addition to the staff is Theodore C. Sorensen, former special assistant to President John F. Kennedy and author of *Decision Making in the White House* and *Kennedy*. Sorensen remained as a White House aide with President Lyndon B. Johnson until February 1964. I had several talks with Sorensen, both in Washington and New York, in the hope of persuading him to join *SR*. I couldn't think of anyone with whom I would feel more comfortable or proud in sharing the editorial page. I knew that Sorensen's special qualities of acuity, soundness, and vision would have a strong appeal for *SR* readers.

Sorensen wanted to finish his book on President Kennedy before making any long-term commitments. A multitude of offers were pressing in on him. Universities tried to lure him with special chairs; at least two national industries wanted him as head of their trade associations; some of the nation's leading law firms wanted him on their staffs. In the end, Sorensen decided to divide his time largely between the practice of law and editorial work for the McCall Corporation in general and the *Saturday Review* in particular.

The growth in the departments and special monthly supplements was matched by the circulation and business growth of the magazine. It is important here to say something about Nathan Cohn, who came to *SRL* as controller and treasurer in 1948; W. D. (Pat) Patterson, who became associate publisher in 1950; and Marion Urmy, who became assistant to the publisher in 1953, and as *SR*'s office manager always manages to retain her calm in the middle of a seemingly constant maelstrom.

Earlier I spoke of Jack Cominsky's remarkable combination of fixed purpose and enthusiasm. I think I also referred to my own optimistic interaction with Jack on magazine matters. Many of the important decisions we made for *SR*, however, were not the sole product of this joint exuberance, but of the balanced team formed with the addition of Nathan Cohn and Pat Patterson.

I had known Nat ever since he was fifteen. He had broken virtually every scholarship record in every subject. He was quiet, good-humored, unfailingly relevant in everything he said or did. Appropriately, perhaps, his formal training was as a stock market analyst. I hesitated to ask him to give up a sturdy and no doubt lucrative career on Wall Street, but he had precisely the qualities we needed. Jack and I tended to the kind of optimism that frequently caused us to see our problems as smaller than they actually were. Nat never minimized a problem in his life. When he agreed to join the staff, Jack and I knew what it meant to have a man on the premises who was preoccupied with the need to balance a budget. Nat not only kept our accounts in order; each week, at the editorial conference, when the size of the magazine was being fixed, Nat was there to remind us of our promise not to stray too far from the space allocations he specified. What astounded us about Nat was that he could project *SR*'s income and expenses six months away and come within 1 per cent of the forecast. Like Jack and Pat, Nat had strong editorial interests. No one on the staff read the magazine with a sharper eye; at least, no one sent in as many issues marked up with more typographical or grammatical errors.

Pat Patterson, too, had had an early editorial background. He had been foreign correspondent for the Associated Press; most of his service had been in Mexico City. During the war he had been with the Office of War Information, assigned to London. Pat's editorial skills and his understanding of our editorial objectives were a prodigious asset. He worked alongside Jack Cominsky and helped to build and administer a business and advertising staff that at one time consisted of two men and that eventually numbered more than thirty.

Pat—big, burly, congenial—loved to sit back and dream aloud about the magazine. All we had to do to cause his ruddy face to dissolve into a sunset-like grin was to suggest a long talk about future plans for SR. Communication to him, like wine, was to be savored, not gulped.

Perhaps more than any other man on the staff, Pat understood and shared my compulsion for vigorous sports. After graduating from Yale, he had had a tryout by the New York Baseball Giants. Pat and I had good times together when we played in baseball and basketball benefit games for the March of Dimes. The teams had been recruited from among people in the publishing industry and the arts in general who had had college sports backgrounds. Inevitably, the games tended to deteriorate into a comic routine. Pat enjoyed the burlesque but this didn't keep him from making the kind of all-out effort expected in traditional football rivalries between Yale and Harvard.

I never had difficulty in engaging Pat in foot races through the streets while we were on our way to lunch or appointments outside the office. It wasn't that we were in a hurry necessarily; it was just that the cramped routine of desk life produced an irresistible desire to break out and run. Once, during a race across Madison Avenue, Pat suddenly cried out behind me, "Stop, thief!" That slowed me up.

No other man I have ever known, not even Horace Sutton, had more wanderlust in his blood than Pat Patterson. His passion for travel was surpassed only by his knowledge of the travel industry. This expertise made him one of the most respected and sought-after figures in the field. In 1954 he was given the assignment by the travel industry of drawing up an analysis and forecast for the coming year. The thoroughness and scope of the report were such that he was asked to write an annual report and forecast, "The Big Picture," which became an annual event in the industry. Pat was an excellent business counterpart to Horace Sutton in the field of travel. The substantial development of the magazine in that field is the direct product of that association.

Pat helped build an effective advertising sales team for the magazine, men and women who had to convince the agencies that *SR* deserved consideration even though it couldn't furnish the circulation numbers of the big journals. In the forties and early fifties this was one of the most exhausting jobs in the magazine world. Helene Slaght, Lyn White, Robert Burghardt, Joe Luyber, and Fletcher Udall took the discouragement and the battering that came from trying to get *SR's* story across to people who had never heard of the magazine. In a sense, they were the real heroes, for they kept going under circumstances that would have been crushing to people less committed to the magazine. Eventually the magazine was to command the services of Harry Morris, who worked alongside Jack and Pat in putting the advertising staff on a national footing.

A special word about Helene and Lyn. Advertising saleswomen are not unusual; these two, however, would be remarkable in any company. They possess an excellent combination of devotion to the magazine, sympathy with its basic purposes, and tenaciousness in dealing with prospects.

In 1945 Jack brought in Bert Garmise as circulation-promotion manager. Apparently the word got around very quickly that *SRL* had found a man of extraordinary abilities, for six or seven magazines tried to steal Bert away from us. Eventually, Bert went into business for himself as circulation-promotion consultant. We were pleased to become his first client. Taking his place in 1950 as regular circulation manager of *SR* was the highly experienced Raymond F. Goodman. In a sense, therefore, we had the best of both possible worlds—Bert as adviser and Ray as full-time operating head of the Circulation Department.

# VIII

The freedom with which we have always been able to discuss important issues in *SR* was far different from the conception I had had of what happened in the making of magazines.

Journalistically speaking, I had been weaned on Lincoln Steffens. If you knew the score you knew that the honest editor didn't have a chance. He was a pressure point on an assembly belt operated by remote control. The pressure came from owners, stockholders, advertisers, politicos—anyone, in fact, who had a claim on the front office. As for advertising, well, everyone knew that you couldn't live without it but if you got it you couldn't live decently with it, either. Or so the muckrakers and the hard-boiled ex-newsmen contended. It was a grim, dim view underscored in many of the books and plays about journalism during the twenties and thirties.

It didn't take me long after joining the *Saturday Review of Literature* to realize I had been weaned from the wrong bottle. My apprehensions belonged back on the shelf with the old copies of the muckraking journals. The only pressure on me was to do a good job. The man who hired me, Harrison Smith, kept pushing me to accept one basic fact: to recognize that I had his complete support. Amy Loveman, Henry Seidel Canby, and E. De Golyer not only did not resist change but helped to bring it about. I became aware very early that I had one of the most exciting and challenging assignments in American journalism. That feeling never changed. To work with books and ideas; to see the interplay between a nation's culture and its needs; to have unfettered access to an editorial page which offered, quite literally, as much freedom as I was capable of absorbing— this is a generous portion for any man.

Not infrequently, I would be urged by friends to devise controversies for the magazine. I resisted the advice—not because I was opposed to controversy but because I believed our first need was to develop a corps of writers and editors who had conviction, courage, and integrity. To the extent that controversy was useful, it would flow naturally out of the unbridled views of these men. In short, the problem was not in inventing controversy, but in defining reasonable and responsible methods for conducting it.

The stormiest controversies in the magazine's history were largely unplanned. One of the earliest of these was between a banker and a poet. The subject matter had nothing to do with poetry, but Bill Benét was one of the principals. Another controversy concerned Ezra Pound and T. S. Eliot. The third grew out of John Ciardi's review of a book of poems by Anne Morrow Lindbergh. Still another controversy concerned fluoridation. All these issues, of course, were in addition to the dominant and continuing debate over the implications of nuclear energy.

We begin with the banker vs. poet. In the spring of 1943 *SRL* published an unusual dialogue between William Rose Benét and Thomas W. Lamont. In his *SRL* Phoenix Nest for May 22, 1943, Bill Benét made a passing reference to a book on economics, *The Coming Showdown,* by Carl Dreher. This was part of the comment by Benét that touched off the debate:

> The self-righteousness of capital toward the recent high-handed conduct of John L. Lewis (and of most of the press, which can always be counted upon to side with the big money) brings to mind the fact that, as Carl Dreher says in *The Coming Showdown,* there was also a "sit-down strike of capital in the face of a national crisis." But that was some time back, of course, and events move fast, and people forget. Yet also "the people do get the general drift of events. . . . They know that the profits of big business have gone up. They know that the yield of the excess-profits tax for the first year of rearmament was no more than a drop in

the bucket of military expenditures, and that Congress is still squeamish about dipping deep into war profits." They have a strong suspicion that capital is cashing in on the war. So . . . beneath the appearance there will be that "class suspicion and hatred" which the Big Boys are always muttering about when they are not too busy promoting it with all the means at their command.

Benét never pretended to be writing for *The Economist,* but his casual remarks about business and morality provoked what Mr. Lamont called a "long but respectful and amiable letter":

> Having started originally in newspaper work and for years followed the course of the public press, I have always felt that its independence, just as in England, has been recognized and accepted as one of the glories attained up to the present time only by Anglo-Saxon peoples. Have I been wrong about this all this time? And are you able, moving as you do more closely in journalistic circles than I can hope to do, to assure me that you are right as to this lack of "independence" in the press?
> . . . I do not believe you need to be concerned about the Big Boys in industry. On the contrary, I assure you from personal knowledge that what we have to be concerned about is this: namely, that many of our industrial concerns under present tax legislation, far from cashing in on the war, are more likely to be dangerously depleting the corporate reserves they will surely need to meet the task of reconversion of their plants from war uses and machines to peacetime production when the war ends. Of course, we may squeeze the corporations until the pips squeak, but let us leave them enough to prepare for this vital task of reconversion. . . .

My memory is vague about Bill Benét's reaction to the letter; but I can almost hear him saying: "Oh, well . . . I really don't want the last word; I don't think I'd know what to do with it if I had it."

It was characteristic of Lamont, too, that he ended his written discourse with an invitation to Benét to join him at the Coffee House or Century for a "cool drink," when he hoped Benét would fix [him] up with a simple little international plan that would prevent wars."

I'm certain the two men met to talk it over. And I'm equally certain that after rather vigorous initial amenities no reference was made to the subject that brought them together.

We come now to the controversy over Ezra Pound in 1949 in which most of the critics for whom we had deep respect were opposed to us. The controversy grew out of a series of articles by Robert Hillyer opposing the 1952 award of the United States Library of Congress Bollingen Prize in Poetry to Ezra Pound. Mr. Hillyer also criticized the influence of T. S. Eliot on contemporary poetry. He contended that the award was largely the result of Eliot's lobbying for Pound. Pound had renounced American citizenship and had gone to Italy to embrace fascism before World War

II, becoming Mussolini's leading propagandist against the United States. Hillyer was outraged that an acknowledged traitor should be the beneficiary of Eliot's intervention. Hillyer's articles also tried to establish a direct connection between the award to Pound and the rising influence of what he described as the "obscurantist" school in American poetry, of which he accused Eliot of being the high priest.

It was generally assumed that Bill Benét, as poetry editor, had initiated the articles by Hillyer. This is incorrect. In 1949 I had gone to Japan for several weeks. Harrison Smith, as associate editor, was in charge editorially. Hillyer, a poet and critic, had discussed the implications of the Bollingen Award with Hal Smith. Our policy at SR was to open our pages to various viewpoints, even if they sharply clashed with our own. Hal felt that Hillyer was entitled to his say and encouraged him to develop his ideas into a series of articles.

When I returned from Japan the pieces had not yet appeared but were in type. I realized they would create a storm and would expose the magazine to considerable criticism and counterattack. But I agreed with Hal that a writer of Hillyer's stature should have access to the magazine. And, while I disagreed with Hillyer's blanket charges against the "obscurantists," I thought the award to Pound by an agency of the U.S. government was certainly open to question. During World War II, as editor of *U.S.A.*, published by the U.S. government for distribution abroad in at least a dozen languages, I had to review the texts of enemy propaganda activities. Month after month I would read Pound's incredibly obscene fulminations against the United States and the American people. He reserved his most severe invective for Franklin D. Roosevelt. His repertoire included such phrases as "Roosevelt, that cheap Jew kike," or the "moron Americans," or "the Jew-infested United States." He said he anticipated with relish the crushing defeat of the United States and the triumph of fascism.

I didn't believe that a man's poetry should be judged according to his political opinions or activities. But neither did I believe that a violent crusade against this nation and its culture was completely irrelevant in the specifications for a cultural award carrying the name of the U.S. government. It would have been an entirely different matter if the award to Pound were being given by a private group. But it wasn't. The auspices were official; the American people, therefore, had the right to consider whether an official or quasi-official award should be given to a man who had hired himself out to an enemy, whose extreme pronouncements had been directed at this nation, its history, its culture, and traditions. The Library of Congress Bollingen Award was one of the highest cultural prizes in the nation. Was there no requirement for cultural responsibility or integrity in the conditions, explicit or implicit?

I thought that Hal was right in deciding the issue deserved at least to be aired. So did Bill Benét and Amy Loveman. We believed it was unfair to assume, as Hillyer did, that the purpose of the judges in giving the award to Pound was to restore his respectability as part of an effort to save him from the consequences of the treason charges. (Pound was then in a U.S. hospital as a mental patient.) We also took exception to the vehemence of Hillyer's statements about "obscurantists" in American poetry who "conspired" to bring about the award. But we all felt Hillyer was entitled to his say.

The storm that broke following the publication of the Hillyer articles was the most severe up to that time in the history of the magazine. We were the subject of a scathing editorial attack by *The Nation*. We received a protesting letter signed by twenty-five esteemed poets. If controversy confers benefits upon a magazine, we became aware it also had its risks. It resulted in too much abuse and charges of bad faith—on both sides.

In any event, I learned a great deal from that particular episode. If I had it to do all over again, I think I would have argued against the notion that we were obligated to publish *both* Hillyer articles. I would have accepted the piece that raised the question about giving an award to Ezra Pound carrying the name of the U.S. Library of Congress. But I doubt I would have felt that the second article, which carried Hillyer's objections to what he termed the "obscurantist" school, was essential to his objections to the award. In any case, I learned we should try to strike a balance between the obligation to provide an outlet for authoritative spokesman and the responsibility to avoid wild shooting parties. I am not suggesting the existence of personal animus behind the Hillyer pieces. I feel strongly there was none. But enough questions were raised by the Hillyer pieces to have made me somewhat less permissive in the future.

We come now to the John Ciardi–Anne Morrow Lindbergh controversy. In order to present the full flavor of this controversy, it may be useful to provide some background. John Ciardi, it will be recalled, succeeded William Rose Benét as poetry editor of *SRL* in May 1956. I had been following with admiration John Ciardi's contributions to *The Nation* during the early 1950s. His writing was crisp, articulate, provocative. I knew that Bill Benét had thought highly of him, even though in many ways Ciardi was his quintessential opposite in style and approach to poetry.

Though generously proportioned, Bill Benét had a suggestion of frailty about him. Perhaps it was the rounded nature of his features, the sensitivity of facial expression, and the softness in his voice that contributed to the general impression of gentleness. John Ciardi looked like a combination of a Hemingway big-game hunter and a charging fullback who had carried half the opposing football team on his back in a successful plunge for the touchdown.

Bill, as I have noted earlier, was kind to all comers to the point of personal exhaustion. John is extremely affable but highly discriminating in the people on whom he would lavish attention. Bill suffered visibly whenever he had to reject the work of someone he knew or who had a profound emotional investment in having his work published. John Ciardi is the least temporizing man I ever met. If he doesn't like a poem or an article he feels it is disservice to the writer to lead him on. He has no talent for ambiguity, either in his opinions or his relationships. His column in the magazine is a genuine reflection of his full personality.

Mostly, he writes about poetry and his experiences as editor, critic, and lecturer. But he also writes about other things that excite or infuriate him —all the way from the mysteries of fine bourbon to pilots who ditch their planes over population centers.

Few of the octaves of experience and feeling that give color and fire to the English language are beyond his reach, a fact that was very much in evidence in his pieces on Anne Morrow Lindbergh. In SR January 12, 1957, Ciardi reviewed Mrs. Lindbergh's *The Unicorn and Other Poems*. Here are some representative excerpts:

> . . . as a reviewer not of Mrs. Lindbergh but of her poems I have, in duty, nothing but contempt to offer. I am compelled to believe that Mrs. Lindbergh has written an offensively bad book—inept, jingling, slovenly, illiterate even, and puffed up with the foolish afflatus of a stereotyped high-seriousness, that species of esthetic and human failure that will accept any shriek as a true high-C. If there is judgment it must go by standards. I cannot apologize for this judgment. I believe that I can and must specify the particular badness of this sort of stuff. . . .

> . . . she is constantly in trouble with the simplest of rhymes (here "heart-apart") and that, lacking first a sound grammatical sense and second anything like a poet's sense of words and their shades of meaning, she is defenseless against her rhyme-schemes and will commit any absurdity while entangled in her own harness.

> Nor is "absurdity" too strong a word. I can certainly sense the human emotion that sends Mrs. Lindbergh to the writing, but I can only report that what emerges in the writing is low-grade poetry and low-grade humanity. As a person Mrs. Lindbergh must certainly have richer resources than these, but whatever those personal resources the fact remains that they simply do not make their way through bad writing. I must believe that the art of poetry is more important than Mrs. Lindbergh or than you or than me, and that bad observance of that art is an assault on one of the most enduring sanctions of the total human experience. . . . For a person of poetic pretensions to misuse language itself in so slovenly a way is certainly akin to Original Sin, and in the absence of the proper angel, I must believe that it is the duty of anyone who cares for the garden to slam the gate in the face of the sinful and abusive . . .

> . . . finally, and as a sort of ultimate absurdity, what must certainly be the neatest trick of the literary season:

> Down at my feet
> A weed has pressed
> Its scarlet knife
> Against my breast.

Compare the now classical examination answer that reads: "Dante was a great transitional figure: with one foot he stood in the Middle Ages, while with the other he saluted the rising sun of the Renaissance." The student could perhaps be forgiven—he was racing the clock. But what will forgive Mrs. Lindbergh this sort of miserable stuff?

Within the time it took for the nearest subscriber to post a letter and have it delivered, we knew we had run into a storm. Nothing in the previous history of the magazine got under the skin of more readers. We could have filled at least three full issues with nothing but the reactions of shocked subscribers. As it was, we broke all records for our letters-to-the-editor department by devoting at least seven full pages to reader reaction, the first massive wave of which was against John Ciardi.

Hal Smith wasn't sure we were wise in making public disclosures to the extent of opposition to Ciardi's review, especially when we published letters requesting subscription cancellation. I was concerned about the cancellations, of course, but I couldn't imagine anything healthier for the magazine or the state of American literature in general than the fact that a controversy over poetry had become something of a national conversation piece. All the news-wire services covered the story.

Hal Smith was pleased by these developments but feared that the initial huge preponderance of anti-Ciardi mail would array the bulk of the readership against the magazine. Again, I felt the effect would actually strengthen the readers' tie to *SR*. The fact that we were willing to take such a generous licking on our letters pages indicated we were genuinely interested in a dialogue with our readers. A magazine by its very nature tends to tell people what to do. It was good for the readers, I thought, to get back at the editors.

As it turned out, our decision to provide a full reflection of reader displeasure in the first available issue touched off an even greater pro-Ciardi demonstration in succeeding issues. In no time our pages became a pitched battlefield. Judging by the thousands of letters we received, there weren't many readers left who didn't get into the act. At one point the erroneous impression apparently took hold that letters would be tabulated only if they were accompanied by a cancellation of subscription. Thus, it was not at all unusual to receive a letter that began: "One of your subscribers writes that he wishes to disassociate himself from a magazine that will tolerate John Ciardi. I wish to disassociate myself from a magazine that tolerates attacks on John Ciardi." I was somewhat more reassured by a letter that said: "I have been reading your letters-to-the-editor debate about John Ciardi and I see that fourteen readers have canceled because of their distaste for John Ciardi. Lest this cause you to panic and fire him, I personally promise to deliver two dozen new subscribers within two weeks." And he did.

One cable read: "Bolivia casts two votes for John Ciardi."

What finally convinced me that we had better terminate the controversy, if we could, was a person-to-person telephone call from Oregon to my home that got me out of bed at 2 a.m. A woman operating on Pacific Coast time identified herself as the president of a local literary society and said she had been delegated to report that the members of her group, then in session, had voted three to one in favor of Mrs. Lindbergh. I thanked her and went back to bed.

Finally, the debate turned on the editor. A fairly substantial number of readers seemed to feel I was unfair in not pronouncing final judgment for the magazine. "What makes you think you are entitled to the luxury of sitting it out?" one subscriber asked. Truth to tell, I had been drawn into the affair emotionally, as had everyone else, and didn't need much urging to do a piece. It was, I suppose, something of a straddle, but at least it gave me opportunity to try to lower the temperature of the controversy.

Eventually, the debate subsided. One aspect of the aftermath was highly gratifying. Most of the readers who had canceled during the height of the debate sent in requests to be restored to our lists. Some of them, in fact, were indignant that we had cut them off. "Just because I got into the swing of the thing and asked you to cancel shouldn't have caused you to take me literally," one of them said. "Good God, haven't you ever lost your temper?"

Did the magazine come out of the Ciardi–Lindbergh controversy with a net gain or loss? I have no way of knowing. That is not what is important. What is important is that poetry and values in literary criticism had come into national focus. Moreover, the debate was instructive for SR's editors in that it highlighted problems in the responsible conduct of magazine debate.

Next to John Ciardi, the editor on our staff who has been most involved in controversy has been John Lear, our Science editor. His first major bout was with some of the drug companies. He was disturbed by the apparent race among the manufacturers to be the first to reach the market with spectacular items for maladies or infections that had been difficult to treat or cure—without the rigorous testing that could establish the high order of safety required for human use. In the case of one new drug, John's suspicions were aroused by the nature of the manufacturer's advertising brochure. It displayed some dozen calling cards of physicians in various parts of the country, making it appear that these doctors had tried the product and were testifying to its efficacy. John sent telegrams to the addresses listed, asking for verification. He then followed up the telegrams with personal telephone calls. As he suspected, the cards were completely fictitious, although the form of presentation in the advertisement was obviously intended to be authoritative. John's disclosure in the magazine focused widespread attention on and concern over schemes for promoting new drugs.

Another of John's prime targets was pricing policy. He revealed that some antibiotics, for example, cost pennies to produce but were sold for dollars. He was not opposed to a generous markup; what troubled him was the level of pricing on some drugs that bordered on the extortionate.

Still another recurrent theme in the Science Section had to do with the indiscriminate use of the miracle drugs. John had access to research showing that antibiotics and cortisone were being used far more generally than the maladies of the patients required or the delicate balances of their bodies permitted. Not all people were able to tolerate the drugs. The result was that the harmful effects of the drug in some cases were even worse than the illnesses they were supposed to cure. This was especially true of penicillin and cortisone.

Senator Estes Kefauver, then the head of a special Senate subcommittee examining practices and policies of drug manufacturers, frequently consulted John Lear. At one point, in fact, Senator Kefauver gave John substantial credit for the many reforms brought about as the result of the investigation.

A good many private physicians supported John Lear in these battles, judging by the mail, but the opposition to him was sharp and unrelenting. I received a substantial number of letters questioning his integrity. Some said he was in the secret employ of those drug firms that were eager to see their competition disadvantaged.

I suppose the letter writers had no way of knowing that they had used the least convincing argument against John Lear it would have been possible to concoct. What is most characteristic about John Lear, as I said earlier, is his total integrity. He can be stubborn and tenacious when under attack. But to question his honesty is like doubting Pablo Casals' ability to draw a bow. No other writer or editor I have ever known is less likely to be pushed or pressured in a direction in which he doesn't want to go. The one thing I never doubt is the unimpeachable character of the man and his work. I was outraged by letters that tried to insinuate that he was personally motivated.

The biggest battle that grew out of John Lear's editing of the Science Section was over fluoridation. The editorial problem presented by his position was that the preponderance of doctors, dentists, and scientists among our readers disagreed with him strongly. On the other hand, among his supporters were some groups with extremist coloration. Typically, John Lear was neither intimidated by the massed authority arrayed against him nor put off by the undesirable nature of some of the support. He had made a careful investigation into fluoridation, discovered that many questions had yet to be answered, and that there were enough authentic cases of harmful side effects from fluoridation to warrant the fullest possible public scrutiny and debate. He was also mindful of the civil rights issue represented by forced medication.

After John had assembled all the material for his first takeout on fluoridation he came to my office and told me about his plans. He said he knew he was embarking on a course that would put the magazine on the unpopular side of an important public issue, with many of my own friends among the opposition. But he believed that the evidence on fluoridation raised substantial questions that were not now being answered. He left the material with me.

For the next two days I studied the material and did some independent research. It seemed to me that fluoridation's opponents were in error in saying it did no good, and its advocates were in error in saying it did no harm. Fluoridation did both. It helped prevent cavities, but it also affected some people adversely. Sensitivity to certain chemicals varies widely in people. The big question, therefore, was not only whether fluoridation did more good than harm but whether the government had the right to jeopardize the health of some people even when there was an advantage to many.

It was foolish to fight fluoridation on the grounds that it was not an effective agent in the prevention of tooth decay. The findings were conclusive on that point. But a wider scrutiny also indicated that some people were allergic to fluorides, even in minute amounts. I came across documented cases of people who suffered illnesses of varying severity from fluoridation, all the way from acute headaches to a disintegration of the connective tissue, producing symptoms that were similar to those associated with rheumatoid arthritis.

I returned the material to John, congratulated him, said I realized we were in for a hot time, and that most of our constituents would probably be against us, but I agreed he had the obligation to proceed.

We were prepared for a storm but we had no idea that it would assume the proportions it did. The American Dental Association and hundreds of individual dentists berated the *Saturday Review* for being indifferent to the health problems caused by cavities and poor teeth in general. They said fluoridation was an inexpensive way of preventing these problems. As for the allegations of harm produced by fluoridation, they accused us of having been taken in by quacks and right-wingers. Among those who attempted to refute John Lear were distinguished heads of medical schools and research clinics, some of them my warm personal friends.

It was powerful stuff and it gave me some sleepless nights. But there was no definitive refutation of the evidence that some people were incapable of tolerating fluoridation. How many? No one knew, but the number was not so important as the fact they existed. In any event, it seemed reasonable to suggest that an attempt be made to find out more about the nature and extent of this sensitivity before a decision was reached.

The attempt to dismiss, without adequate documentation, the issue of possible harm seemed to me to be a key point in the controversy. When I brought up this point in discussion with some dentists, they said that authoritative evidence of danger was lacking. How did one define the word "authoritative"? In our possession were the letters of a distinguished Swedish medical Nobel Prize winner, a medical official of the government of India, several research papers in medical journals—all of them saying substantially the same thing; namely, that cases had been observed of many patients with fluoride poisoning in varying degress.

There was also substantial evidence of entire communities where fluoridation had succeeded without reported cases of illness or difficulty. And there were about one hundred communities that had abandoned fluoridation after negative experiences of one kind or another.

The mixed evidence made one thing clear. Fluoridation was not an open-and-shut case. Some facts were still missing. Was it irresponsible to suggest further research before the commitment was made? Another element in the case called for additional investigation: If only a small amount of fluoride could affect the bone structure of the teeth, why would that same amount be too small to affect other organs of the body? The fluoride was not applied directly to the teeth. It went into the blood stream. How could we be sure that such a chemical in the blood stream was neutral except in one place? Admittedly, there were comparatively few cases in which specific harm had been documented. But further research might indicate that the percentage was higher than supposed. Why waste time arguing the matter? Why not find out?

The controversy on our letters pages grew week by week. We were accused of know-nothingism, of consorting with extremists and political rowdies. The accusations hurt but no one came forward with the definitive evidence that all people were equally able to tolerate fluorides. Some of our correspondents kept peppering us with evidence that tooth decay was arrested by fluoridation. This was never the main point at issue. The case against fluoridation was not that it didn't succeed in preventing cavities, but that it might also succeed in doing other things, not all of them desirable. In any event, what puzzled me profoundly about the issue from the medical point of view was that I had supposed that most doctors and dentists would have insisted on the principle of individual prescription where there was evidence of varying effects. For those people who wanted fluorides in water for their children, and where tests demonstrated an ability to tolerate the chemicals, the medication could have been inexpensively obtained. And if the argument was that there was a social good in making the medication available to all without cost, the answer was that the community could have provided free toleration tests and free fluorides—at only a fraction of the cost of fluoridation.

What was the outcome of the debate? I don't think we won it, but I don't think we lost it either. We lost some readers we especially regretted losing, although I suppose these were more than offset by the number of readers who subscribed. As in the Ciardi controversy, it was meaningless to attempt an appraisal on the level of net loss or gain of readers. My hope was that we had made a contribution, however small, to the national debate on the subject. And I hoped, too, that we had been able to indicate our respect for the people who disagreed with us. If the debate were decided on the basis of which side mobilized the greater number of lustrous experts, I am afraid we would have lost. But the history of medicine is replete with instances in which the positions taken by leading authorities are later reversed. This is no criticism of the experts; it would be irresponsible of them to shift their ground every time they felt a tremor. But progress is made not only by the experts; it is made by researchers, many of them obscure, who develop new facts and correlations that become the basis for new theories and practices of the authorities and the administrators.

Finally, then, our argument was for more research. If this research should someday indicate that our position was based on error, we will crusade in *SR* for water-supply medication with no less zeal than we crusaded against it.

The most sustained debate in the magazine's history grew out of nuclear fission and its implications on war and peace. To the extent that any single theme or program has dominated the editorial policy of the magazine during the past two decades, it has to do with the impact of atomic energy. The editorial "Modern Man Is Obsolete," appearing shortly after the bombing of Hiroshima, attempted to define some of the challenges represented by the new age—challenges not just to the nation's foreign policy but to its economy, politics, education, and culture in general.

The most controversial aspect of nuclear energy, of course, arose over the testing of nuclear weapons. The magazine took the full plunge into that debate and, indeed, had a role in helping to start it. Some of the earliest information on radioactive fallout appeared in the pages of *SR*. In June 1956, Professor Barry Commoner, biologist at Washington University, St. Louis, called to *SR*'s attention reports in the files of the U.S. Atomic Energy Commission revealing that detectable traces of radioactivity had turned up in vegetation over wide areas. Cows grazing on grasses dusted by radioactivity had produced contaminated milk.

By 1956, the full dimensions of the actual and potential danger began to be apparent. The issue, as SR's editors saw it, was basically a moral one. No country engaged in the testing of nuclear explosives had been able to confine fallout to its own territory. Winds carrying radioactive poisons were indiscriminate. If the United States or the Soviet Union took the position that other peoples should be expected to sustain the radioactive hazard because it contributed to security, the other nations could not be blamed if they asked that they not be taken for granted.

By 1957, radioactive strontium began to turn up in the teeth of children in various parts of the world. This meant that the substance was also finding its way into their bones. Even without respect to the radioactive health dangers, continued nuclear testing severely reduced the chances for bringing the world nuclear arms race under control.

All these arguments against testing, of course, produced powerful counter-arguments. It was contended, first of all, that continued testing was vital to the national security. Our defenses demanded a wide range of nuclear devices, it was said; it was impossible to develop these devices without testing. As for radioactivity, it was argued that the dangers were fictitious. And even when it was established beyond question that some of the poisons had turned up in human bone, it was said that no danger was involved. Indeed, one of the proponents of testing asserted that radioactivity extended life. This contention, of course, was promptly refuted by medical researchers.

SR played a part in the "Declaration of Conscience," an impassioned appeal against testing by Albert Schweitzer, issued in 1957 under the auspices of the Nobel Peace Committee in Oslo. SR also brought groups of Americans together to consider the question and to take appropriate action. Naturally, the magazine's position and its activities in all these respects produced substantial opposition.

It is doubtful if anything in the history of the magazine made the editors prouder than a letter from President Kennedy, following passage by the United States Senate of the limited test-ban treaty, commending them for their efforts over the years for bringing nuclear testing under control.

Related to the control of the nuclear arms race, of course, is the need to develop the United Nations fully and to give it the effective instruments of world law. This theme has been consistently emphasized on the editorial page and in the articles. The magazine has attempted to deal with the specifics of strengthening the UN, especially with reference to financial support, peace-keeping operations, and the wide range of activities carried on by UNESCO and the technical development and relief agencies of the UN.

Other recurrent themes in the magazine have been on the need to protect the conditions of creative freedom and expression; the need to educate on every level in the cultures and problems of other peoples, especially in Asia and Africa; the need for enlarged educational facilities and programs beyond the university; the need to combat environmental contamination, especially in air and water; and the problem represented by the growing casualness toward violence in entertainment and literature and, indeed, in everyday life.

Basic to all these issues, as the editors see it, is the need to assure the individual that he is far from helpless and that his role is central for bringing about essential change and in protecting important values.


## IX


*Perhaps the best way of continuing the* SR *narrative at this point is to turn to some of the anniversary pieces that appeared on the editorial page. The purpose of these pieces was to give a full accounting to our readers, talking frankly about some of the problems and decisions we had to make. The following editorials provide something of an interior history of the magazine. The first of these editorials, which appeared March 17, 1959, also deals with some of the personal problems of an itinerant editor:*

Some personal notes as the editor completes his nineteenth year at the *Saturday Review*:

The two questions that most frequently come this way are less editorial distance: "How is it possible to operate a magazine from Madras or Hiroshima or Lambaréné? How can you get anything done when you spend so much of your time, quite literally, up in the air?"
and philosophical than mechanical. The first question has to do with
The second question is personal and functional: "Isn't it pretty risky to subject yourself to the hazards of so many different climates and foods?"

As for the first question, the largest part of the answer is the obvious one. SR has a staff and a very good one. The publisher, in addition to being a first-rate businessman, has a wide editorial background. The associate publisher, the articles editor, the production editor, the book-review editors, and the department heads make up an effective editorial team. True, a considerable portion of the editor's job cannot be delegated. Even here, however, the telephone, the airplane, and the post office are effective aids on a magazine that has the world and the human situation as its main editorial franchise.

Like everything else, the editor's job has been revolutionized by the air age. There is hardly a place in the world that cannot be reached by mail in forty-eight hours. I have had airmail bundles of work only two and a half days old from New York delivered to me at a jungle hospital in French Equatorial Africa. On another occasion, a postman on a bicycle met me coming out of a Japanese inn in Nagasaki and handed me page proofs of a forthcoming issue of SR. On the contrary, it took three days for an office folder to reach me on the Upper Michigan peninsula.

The airplane has made it not only possible but essential for an editor to move his desk from place to place. It is no longer necessary to form secondary judgments. The big events are now a community matter. On the purely operational level, the airplane is an ideal office. Nowhere outside of a plane have I found such productive working conditions. Conversely, when at my desk in New York, I find that my main business each day is to preside over interruptions. I have little time for reading in New York, less time for writing. Sequence in thought is annihilated. One takes things as they come, and they come in short, uneven bursts. I became sufficiently objective about my job once to keep track of everything that happened in the course of an average day. The telephone rang on the average of once every six minutes. There were at least seven callers each day. As a result, the important business with the staff had to be squeezed into ninety minutes or less. This doesn't even begin to take into account the mail folder, which uses up all the intervals.

On a plane, however, especially when we are high above the clouds, the fragmentation disappears. Sequence comes to life again and the mind has a chance to regroup itself for consecutive thought. The meal tray serves as an excellent stand for the typewriter and the seat beside you, if empty, is an adequate side table for working papers. One hour in the sky office is the equivalent of about four hours on land in terms of actual output.

There are distractions, of course. But they are nourishing distractions. Nowhere in the world is there grandeur of such dimensions and such proximity. Sometimes, when you fly above a storm, you can see vast cloud masses catching the light of the sun. The result is a Grand Canyon of color multiplied by infinity. Once, flying from Seattle to San Francisco, there were three distinct cloud levels, with absolute clearing between each one. Each level had its own character, its own display. The first was a massive purple floor, swelling and bulging when we were close to it. The second layer was full of tunnels and caverns, exploiting every gradation of gray and black. The third level abandoned itself to the full play of color from a submerged sun, with gentle formations suggesting lakes of gleaming silver, or long, lemon-colored slopes meeting a pale green-blue sky.

Another time, flying from Beirut to Karachi, we darted in and out of sky-filling thunderheads, each of which looked as though it were made up of all the combined mountain masses in the world. The thunderheads ran up to 40,000 feet or more, growing fatter and more menacing on their way up, and then, suddenly, they flattened out on the top, connecting with each other to make a giant white roadbed. Underneath were the long caverns, deep gray on one side, streaked blue on the other. For more than an hour we rode through the caverns until we finally hit a long open clearing.

One need not even mention the sunsets when seen from high in the air. The combination of the brilliant but fast-waning light and the swift movement of the plane away from the sun changes the skyscape so rapidly that no two minutes are the same. It is a developing wonder and makes a moving picture that stays in the mind. And, if you catch the late sun just right as you fly east, you can see thin golden threads spinning off the propellers.

As I say, these are nourishing distractions and I welcome as many of them as I can find. Indeed, I accumulated some dozen skyscapes to think back upon. It is the kind of hobby that goes naturally with the kind of job that has the world for its locale.

We come now to the second question, having to do with constant changes of diet and climate and the effect on one's health.

In general, if you want to get close to the life of other peoples, especially in Asia and Africa, you would do well to leave your apprehensions behind and take the plunge. If you are in good health, you will have little to fear. Now and then, of course, you are apt to find yourself in a delicate situation when a few qualms will cross your mind. At the Schweitzer Hospital in Lambaréné, for example, one visits the leper village not without some personal uneasiness. Modern medical theory supports the view that leprosy is somewhat akin to tuberculosis and that there are varying stages and degrees of contagion. If the leprosy involves the muscles or nerves, it is not believed to be infectious. If it involves the skin, however, especially in the case of open sores, there is the possibility of contagion. Inflammation of the nasal membranes with consequent discharge is believed to be a source of infection. Children contract the disease through constant intimacy with leprous members of their families.

Dr. Schweitzer is careful to the point of seeming overcautious in admonishing outsiders not to have physical contact with leper patients at his hospital. The chance of infection is extremely small; even so, the doctor is stern with outsiders. For himself, he is exposed constantly regardless of the virulent condition of some lepers.

It isn't always easy, however, to follow Dr. Schweitzer's admonitions. While walking through the leper village one day, I met a leper who introduced me to his wife. She was carrying a baby of perhaps twenty months. The father said the child was leprous. His nose was running and he had sores all over his face. As I chatted with the parents, the baby twisted in his mother's arms and reached out for me to take him, which I did almost by conditioned reflex. To do otherwise under the circumstances would have been awkward. For the next few weeks I was conscious of my slightest inclination to sniffle or sneeze. Most men in good health think they are indestructible and immortal—until they get a cold, when they are certain they will die within the hour. I confess that my experience with the leper baby made me feel mortal in the extreme.

This is not to say that I have been totally immune to infection or illness while abroad. I suppose I have sampled every species of dysentery recorded. I have had to make numberless unscheduled, speedy departures from receptions or social functions all the way from Djakarta to Mexico City. At such times, philosophical calm seems only vaguely attainable and, in fact, quite academic.

Generally speaking, however, the risk while traveling is extremely small. Such deviations as occur are more the result of sudden changes in one's routine than of basically unhealthy situations. Much of the danger is the result of an excessive idea of one's capacity with respect to food and is not peculiar to geographical variations. The pursuit of new foods can be a delightful adventure, but it is often carried to unreasonable lengths and can produce deceptively intense but fortunately temporary discomforts.

Experiences such as these, of course, are not the exclusive possession of Americans abroad. They apply equally to visitors to our own shores. Friends of mine from Asia have complained about food upsets that may have been less the result of quality than quantity. In addition, the foreign visitor has to cope with exhaust gases from buses, trucks, and cabs on a scale unknown abroad. The heavy monoxide fumes from vehicles are added to the industrial smoke in American cities and produce headaches and severe nausea in persons unaccustomed to them.

Foreign visitors are also disturbed by our crowds. When Americans think of dense population masses they are apt to think of cities in India or Japan. Yet nowhere in the world are there more humans crowded into smaller space than in New York City. I have seen the teeming millions of Asian cities, but nowhere have I seen greater human congestion than in the Grand Central area of New York City during the lunch hour. The business of navigating even a short distance through the crowded sidewalk calls for special knowledge and top physical conditioning. Little wonder that many foreign visitors who see New York for the first time have the feeling of being overwhelmed and exhausted—almost to the point of illness.

The editors have had the good fortune to be hosts to visitors from India, Pakistan, or Japan. We could tell that the noonday crowds charging through New York streets produced an effect akin to panic on some of our guests. They had never seen so many people under such compressed conditions before. All this, combined with a rich diet and the accelerated American pace, causes more than a few Asian visitors to long for the comparative calm and openness of Calcutta or Karachi.

In any event, Americans need not fear that they are in mortal jeopardy every time they set foot outside the continental limits of the United States. Nor need they believe that such minor discomforts as they may encounter have an exclusively American label. Discomfort and upsets, like politics, are the products of people rather than places.

Speaking personally, the principal hazard I have encountered throughout the world is not food or climate but being mistaken for the editor of *The Saturday Evening Post*. For years I have wanted to express my regrets to Mr. Ben Hibbs of that worthy journal. I do so now.


*The following editorial, published on February 18, 1961, addressed itself to an important change in the affairs of the* Saturday Review:

No solemn discussion of world problems this week. Just a personal report to friends of the family. An important change takes place this issue in the affairs of the magazine; the *Saturday Review* joins a major American publishing family. The terms provide for autonomy and continuity of management, staff, and editorial policy. The prospects are robust. First, however, some background.

When E. De Golyer acquired ownership of the *Saturday Review* in 1941 it had a small but noble readership (23,000) and a whopping deficit. Within a few years SR developed a pattern of consistent growth; it doubled and redoubled its readership. The magazine's backing was strengthened further still when Marshall Field, Sr., became a minority stockholder in 1946. Shortly before his death in 1956, Mr. De Golyer transferred majority ownership to me. It has become a rather substantial enterprise. We are somewhat startled, in fact, to see SR's name listed by publishing trade journals among the nation's leading magazines in advertising revenue. True, it hasn't happened overnight; even so, it's a little difficult to develop a fresh-linen approach to life after so much early practice with napkin rings.

Speaking personally, nothing in my life, next to my family, has meant more to me than the *Saturday Review*. Being able to work on one of the very few magazines in America wholly owned by its staff; the privilege of writing an editorial on Sunday night and sending it directly to the press on Monday morning without going through the meat-grinder of policy clearance; the feeling of mutual respect and independence between the editorial and business departments—blessings such as these, for a man up to his ears in causes, are no small portion. William Benton was right when he described my work on SR as not a job but a precious way of life.

I had occasion to reflect on all this only a few weeks ago when I attended a meeting of editors of national magazines. Most of the discussion concerned internal shop problems. It was said, with no demurrers, that the editor's importance and independence of operation were being consistently narrowed, even minimized. At one time in the history of American journalism, it was pointed out, the editor occupied the central and commanding position on a magazine; today, the locus of power and responsibility is elsewhere. I didn't argue against the proposition; it would have been too subjective and I didn't want to clap hands over my good luck in public.

At the same time, I have not been unmindful of some basic problems affecting my relationship to the *Saturday Review*. One of them involves the supremely relevant fact that I am not going to live forever. A doctor may give you delicate intimations of your mortality, but a lawyer feels he has to rub your nose in it. In particular, SR's lawyer made me aware of certain complications in the ownership structure of the magazine that would occur in the event of my death. There is no point in detailing these complications except to say that my wife would have to sell my share of the ownership just to meet the government tax on it. Another factor Jack Cominsky and I had to take into account was our increasing dependence on printing and paper facilities and services over which we had no control.

One day at lunch I discussed some of these problems with an old friend, Herbert Mayes, editor of *McCall's*. Herb Mayes has a surer and more creative grasp of magazine publishing than any other man I know. He told me about the structure and operating methods of the McCall Corporation. It had its own facilities, including printing, engraving, and subscription fulfillment. It had something even more important—men at the top who believed that the editorial product came first. He referred specifically to Norton Simon, who represented effective ownership control, and Governor Arthur B. Langlie, president of the McCall Corporation. Herb Mayes was not being theoretical; he had worked on magazines for thirty-five years and he felt that only since coming to *McCall's* had he been able to function on a fully creative basis.

Herb Mayes said Norton Simon had a philosophy of life that could readily comprehend what the *Saturday Review* was all about. Mr. Simon had a strong interest in education and the fine arts; he was a member of the Board of Regents of the University of California. One thing was certain: If our problem was how to continue to put out a magazine we believed in, while avoiding the risk of a forced sale in the event of my death, Norton Simon might have the answer.

A few days later Herb Mayes arranged a meeting. I found Norton Simon soft spoken, reflective. We talked less about publishing problems than about ideas. He followed world affairs closely and had a deep concern about the response of the individual to the stresses of his society.

He said he liked the *Saturday Review* and asked if Mr. Cominsky and I wanted to pursue the possibility of SR's affiliation with the McCall Corporation under terms that would maintain SR as an autonomous and editorially independent publishing entity. In fact, he said, the McCall Corporation would have no interest in such an affiliation unless we could give assurances of continuity of management.

Then came two meetings with the operating head and president of *McCall's*, Arthur Langlie, who had served as Governor of Washington for sixteen years before coming to his present post in 1957. Governor Langlie spoke about the company, its philosophy and methods of dealing with the public and its employees, its facilities, its prospects and problems. He had a knack for throwing a good descriptive loop around a complex idea. I especially liked his emphasis on constructive change. His views on SR were most gratifying.

We also had a meeting at the offices of SR, where other members of our staff had a chance to meet Mr. Simon. I have no way of knowing what kind of impression we made on him; I do know he made a fine impression on us. The general outlines of an agreement began to take shape.

Herb Mayes and I then went to Los Angeles to meet Mr. Simon and his associates on their home grounds. Mr. Simon was the head of Hunt Foods and Industries, which owned a controlling interest in the McCall enterprises. Working with him in close proximity were a half-dozen alert, creative young people. It quickly became apparent to me that they were all pulling together in favor of the new association with SR.

That evening, we had dinner with Mr. and Mrs. Simon in their home. I had heard about the Simon art collection, but I was hardly prepared for the scope of the art treasures on their walls. Mrs. Simon has multiple artistic interests, clearly reflected in the home and the pattern of family living. She reads selectively and intensively, with strong interests in art, education, and *belles lettres*. I was pleased to learn that Mrs. Simon had read SR for years, knew its history and its special interests, and had, in fact, read aloud from the magazine to her husband. I was heartened by her intimate knowledge of the *Saturday Review*'s editorial department and her own identification with some of the projects SR had undertaken.

The next morning Herb Mayes and I flew back to New York and reflected on the rapid progress made toward the solution of our problem since our talk only a few weeks earlier. At the office I gave a running report to the staff on the Los Angeles expedition. A few days later I left for the Far East on a trip that had been scheduled many weeks earlier. Mr. Cominsky and our lawyers took over the negotiations.

I rather welcomed the idea of being out of the country. It would give me a chance for uncrowded, sequential thought outside the pressure-cooking atmosphere of the office. Before the arrangements for affiliation with the McCall Corporation were consummated, I wanted to be able to anticipate all my later second thoughts and come to terms with them. It was a grim experience. By the end of my trip I could qualify as an expert on the deep silences at night in far-flung places such as London, Karachi, Bombay, New Delhi, Calcutta, Bangkok, Vientiane. I came by that knowledge honestly—staying awake and thinking about *Saturday Review*, its past and its future, its staff and its readers. I tried to guess what Amy Loveman's advice would have been. I wondered whether Mr. De Golyer, who was a born maverick and prized independence above all things, would tell us to take the plunge. Finally, I wasn't sure how I would function in the new structure. All but four years of my professional life had been spent on *Saturday Review*. In a sense, we grew up together. Any change, however essential and favorable, was bound to tear me in half.

When I returned to New York last week, a proposed contract was ready. It called for what in legal terminology was known as a "pooling-of-interests" transaction rather than a purchase. The main provisions:

1. *SR* would exchange all its stock for approximately 10 per cent of McCall stock.

2. The *SR* group would maintain a participative stock interest in the McCall Corporation.

3. *Saturday Review* would not become a division of the McCall Corporation, but would be continued as an autonomous corporation, with a Board of Directors of its own.

4. *Saturday Review* would have a seat on the McCall Corporation Board of Directors.

5. The McCall Corporation would make available to *SR* such additional facilities and resources as would apply constructively to *SR*'s growth potential.

6. Present *SR* management was to be retained under a long-term contract.

7. The editor was to continue to fix and carry out editorial policy, also under a long-term contract.

It was a good contract; I would have been myopic to have expected anything better. In fact, I felt fortunate to have been abroad during the home stretch of the negotiations; I might have gotten in the way.

Even so, the last three days before the actual signing were the toughest of my life. I had just been around the world but I could think of no longer or more impassable distance than was represented by the dotted-line space at the bottom of a stock-transfer statement. Three things helped. One was the fact that John Wharton, whose friendship and advice have meant much to me over the years, was on hand to help resolve my last-minute doubts. The second was that Jack Cominsky, without whose energetic enthusiasm even our presses would refuse to roll, vigorously supported the change. The third was the positive atmosphere in the office once the full nature of the new arrangement was made known. Harrison Smith, Pat Patterson, Nat Cohn, Irving Kolodin, John Lear, Horace Sutton, John Ciardi, Dick Tobin, Henry Hewes, Rochelle Girson, Hal Bowser, Jim Fixx, Pearl Sullivan, among others, asked all the relevant questions. Once they got the answers, they looked and acted like people who understood the process of change and the real factors that make for forward thrust. Confidence such as this has within it potent fuel for the psyche; it will carry us a long way. In fact, we have a sense of surge and dramatic opportunity at an important time in the history of ideas.

*In* SR *for February 29, 1964, this account of life under the new owner-ship appeared on the editorial page:*

Three years ago this month the *Saturday Review* became part of the McCall Corporation. Our reasons for making the change were discussed on this page at that time. Since then readers have written asking whether we felt this change has worked out for the best. This piece, then, is in the nature of an interim report.

From the beginning, the stance of the McCall Corporation was that the resources and facilities of the company were available to us for such use as we might wish to make of them, but that McCall's would take no initiative in that direction. Editorial and business policy would continue to be made by the *Saturday Review*.

One obvious and substantial facility, of course, was McCall's printing division, which possessed some of the finest magazine press equipment in the world. For many years the *Saturday Review* had been printed by the Blanchard Press, with its Rumford Press division in Concord, New Hampshire. From the first day of our relationship, Mr. Francis Ehrenberg, head of the Blanchard Press, found ways of being of service to the *Saturday Review* far beyond the high quality of printing he provided. During the depression years, the difference to a magazine between being on the presses and being in the morgue was often represented by the kind of printer you had for a friend or, more precisely, the kind of friend you had for a printer.

Francis Ehrenberg was such a friend. At the time McCall's acquired *SR*, therefore, we made known our desire to stay with Blanchard as long as possible. The McCall Corporation concurred in this decision. It was natural and inevitable, of course, that ultimately our printing would be done inside the family. This change will take place later this year. In making it, we wish to express our high opinion of and gratitude to Mr. Ehrenberg and all the workers of the Blanchard Press and its Rumford division.

Another use of the McCall resources has to do with the special full-color art sections that have appeared in the magazine from time to time. It would not have been possible, for example, for us to have published the recent special section in color on private art collections without the kind of facilities that McCall's arranged to put at our disposal. The section was produced in record time and the insert was shipped to Rumford in Concord, New Hampshire, to be bound into the finished copies.

Another prime benefit to SR has come about through the Editorial Committee, consisting of the editors of *McCall's, Redbook,* and the *Saturday Review,* the three units of the magazine division of the company. Instead of confining itself to publishing problems, the Editorial Committee has unabashedly sought to broaden its knowledge about the principal issues of our time. Among the men who have met with the committee in sustained discussion—and sometimes debate—have been U Thant, Secretary-General of the U.N.; Adlai Stevenson, U.S. Ambassador to the U.N.; McGeorge Bundy, Presidential assistant; Franklin D. Murphy, Chancellor of the University of California; Robert M. Hutchins, president of the Center for the Study of Democratic Institutions; Richard M. Nixon; Senator William Benton; Gabriel Hauge, economist; Alvin C. Eurich, president of the Aspen Institute for Humanistic Studies; Francis Keppel, U.S. Commissioner of Education; Henry R. Luce, editor of *Time* and *Life;* Ambassador Llewellyn E. Thompson; John B. Oakes, chief of the editorial page of *The New York Times;* Paul G. Hoffman of the United Nations Special Fund; General Lucius D. Clay.

On one occasion the entire Editorial Committee journeyed to Dublin, New Hampshire, to spend a full day with Grenville Clark, the distinguished private citizen and co-author of *World Peace through World Law,* who for more than half a century has had a constructive influence on the long-term relationship of the United States to the rest of the world.

The course and outcome of these meetings, as might be expected, have been somewhat varied; but they have been unfailingly productive in stimulating dialogues on the key questions before America and the world. In some instances, material developed at the meetings has gone into the making of editorial content for the magazines.

The new relationship has not been without challenges or problems. About a year ago there was reason to believe that some of the editorial positions taken by the *Saturday Review* might be detrimental to *McCall's.* When the question came to a head, Norton Simon and Herbert Mayes, representing leadership of the company, said that whether or not this was true, the editors of the *Saturday Review* could not and should not change their positions or policies on this account. It was natural, Mr. Simon said, that freedom, whether applied to a magazine or a society, should create problems and even penalties. But it was even more important to be aware of the benefits of freedom and put them to work. He suggested that we look past the penalties to the opportunities. The net result of the episode was a substantial boost to our morale.

Another problem concerned cigarette smoking. When the U.S. Surgeon General's report on the health hazards of smoking was published, *SR* decided to suspend cigarette advertising until the Federal Trade Commission clarified the relevant questions of public policy. Even though this decision was likely to raise difficulties for the other magazines in the company, Mr. Mayes, as president of the company, upheld the right of each magazine to make its own decision.

During the past three years, *Saturday Review* has enjoyed the greatest growth of readership in its history, rising from 250,000 to almost 400,000.* We have no particular long-term circulation goals, any more than we did when the magazine numbered 20,000 readers not so many years ago. Whether we reach a million readers or more than a million is of less consequence than producing a magazine that is read rather than viewed, and genuinely respected rather than merely received.

In advertising, the *Saturday Review* last year was first among all weekly magazines in revenue increase over the previous year. Here, too, we hope to do even better, but this is in proportion to all our other plans and hopes for the magazine.

During the deliberations preceding the sale to McCall's three years ago, one of the negative arguments advanced by friends we consulted was that we would be under so much pressure to produce a favorable operating statement that the entire tone of the magazine would be adversely affected. In actual fact, the reverse has proved to be true. Mr. Mayes and Mr. Simon have emphasized that they are less interested in having us make a good showing financially than in seeing us put out the finest magazine of its kind in the world.

This is a tall order but it makes for a creative and dynamic atmosphere. No editor could ask for more.

*Another personal report to the readers was published little more than a year later (April 24, 1965) on the editorial page:*

This is an informal report about a surprise party that took place a few days ago at the *Saturday Review*. With few exceptions, the entire staff was assembled in the editorial bullpen in the magazine's new home at 380 Madison Avenue, New York, N.Y. Guests included U Thant, Secretary-General of the United Nations, his deputy, C. V. Narasimhan, and all the members of the board of directors of the McCall Corporation, of which *SR* is a division.

The occasion was the editor's twenty-fifth anniversary on *SR*. Did the

* Circulation as of June 1, 1967: 510,000.

party come as a genuine surprise? It did. I thanked the speakers—U Thant, Jack Cominsky, my long-time associate and publisher of *SR*, and Herbert Mayes, president of the McCall Corporation. But I never got around to saying even a portion of the things that should have been said. I was much too flustered.

The size of the staff—some one hundred strong—was difficult to take in when I saw them all in one place. In 1940 the total number of full-time employees was perhaps half a dozen, all departments included. The resources of the magazine were then so slender that all the original founding editors voluntarily went on part time—Henry Seidel Canby, Amy Loveman, William Rose Benét, and Christopher Morley. Dr. Canby came to the office several times each week, gave advice on articles and essays, and wrote occasional editorials.

On those rare occasions when all four founders were in the office at the same time, the result was a happy shower of intellectual and reminiscent sparks, with Chris Morley and Bill Benét doing most of the igniting. They were their own best gallery and played to it within an inch of their soaring capacities. There could be no higher reward for the men than to evoke Amy Loveman's sense of delight. Amy seemed to them, and to all who knew her, to represent the optimum in human graciousness, generosity of spirit, and personal splendor.

These were the faces I missed most when I looked out on the assembled staff during the surprise anniversary party. Bill Benét had died in 1950, Amy Loveman in 1955, Chris Morley in 1957, and Henry Canby in 1961. Not once in all the years I have worked on the *Saturday Review* have I forgotten that it is first of all their magazine. I couldn't help thinking how pleased they would have been with the spacious, efficient new offices and, even more, with the way their early struggles for a self-supporting cultural journal had finally been justified.

I missed seeing George Stevens, my predecessor on the magazine and, since 1940, editor of J. B. Lippincott Co., in Philadelphia. Thinking back now on those early days, I try to see myself as George Stevens must have seen me—not yet twenty-five years old, still freighted with the appearance of a teen-ager (John Mason Brown quipped that I looked almost pre-natal). How could they have taken me seriously? But they did, and I am forever in their debt.

Two other faces were missing from the party, Harrison Smith and E. De Golyer, both vital in the history of the magazine, both my warm personal friends. Hal Smith continued to serve as active Associate Editor until two years ago, when age and illness combined to keep him away from his desk. Mr. De asked no favors of *SR*'s editors and he issued no directives. He knew the meaning and requirements of editorial independence; he asked only that he be allowed to help create the conditions that favored it. Mr. De died in 1956 after a prolonged illness. His biography is now being written by Professor Lon Tinkle of Southern Methodist University. It should be a major contribution to contemporary Americana.

There were new faces at the anniversary party—the people at McCall's who acquired ownership of the *Saturday Review* little more than four years ago. Many questions were asked by our readers at the time: Would the basic character of SR be changed? Would the *Saturday Review* lose its accent and independent editorial viewpoint?

Far from feeling swallowed up or overwhelmed in a large organization, the editors have a sense of occupying a major position within the McCall Corporation. SR has direct representation on the McCall Board of Directors and its editor is chairman of the Editorial Committee for the entire company.

Norton Simon has been much in the news in recent months. What impresses you most about the man is that the only thing greater than the range of his activities and the call on his energies is his total focus on and insight into any matter before him. I have never seen him in a situation where he has been caught without having done his homework. Indeed, on several occasions I have been embarrassed because he was able to come up with more precise information than I had on SR affairs.

Now for some purely personal notes. What is to me perhaps the most awesome fact about my twenty-fifth anniversary at SR is that it happened. Starting in mid-August last year, and for most of the next five months, I was sidelined by a disabling illness that began on the last day of a trip abroad. There was a rather rapid deterioration of connective tissue in the spine and joints of arms, hands, and legs, plus loss of weight. The case eluded precise diagnosis. Assuming that the basic illness would be arrested and that I would be able to resume my work at SR but that I might be left with limitations of mobility and function, I naturally pondered what physical activity I would miss the most. I was somewhat surprised to find that what pained me most was not the prospect of being separated from my usual globe-trotting or lecturing or an active life in sports, especially tennis and golf. What was most difficult to take was the possibility that I might not again be able to play the organ.

Something else became clear to me during that time. I was able to resolve doubts about my future on SR. After almost a quarter century and with the magazine on solid ground, I had early last year begun to think that perhaps at last the time had come for a change. There was a chance to go into government service; also, an invitation to become head of the East-West Center in Hawaii, in which I had a deep interest. Both invitations exercised profound gravitational pulls. But illness is a great clarifier. I knew very quickly I would not accept either offer. I also knew that the most important thing in my life was to resume my work at SR. Being able to get back on the job in time for the twenty-fifth anniversary became an unrelenting obsession.

The episode taught me something about modern medicine. I am certain my recovery was accelerated far more by the confidence that Dr. William Hitzig gave me in myself than by all the vaunted medication, most of which I didn't take anyway. I learned that one of the most important things a doctor can do for a patient is to spend time with him and give him some understanding of the ability of the human body to meet its needs, given reasonable peace, nourishment, and will to live. There has been regeneration of the damaged tissue in spine and joints. Muscle atrophy has stopped and new muscle has formed. Weight has been regained, with something to spare. It may have been Stendhal who wrote that it is one of life's great tragedies that infants are unable to sense and comprehend the wonder of life unfolding inside them. The privilege has now been mine.

I think back on a long series of exciting events in the process of recovery, all of which produced feelings of indescribable delight—the first time since the illness began that I could flex the fingers of my left hand (for hours I observed this phenomenon, staring at the hand in stark wonder); repeating the process a few weeks later with the right hand; the first time I was able to turn a doorknob by myself; the first time I was able to tie my own shoelaces; the first time I could reach up to take down a book from a high shelf; the first time I sat upright without supporting devices in a regular chair; the first time I could move pieces on a chessboard by lifting them rather than pushing them; the first time I was able to hold a golf club, even if I couldn't swing it properly; the first time I was able to stand up unsupported in a charging surf; the first time I could stand on tiptoe; the first time I could hold a camera with steady hand; the first time I could use a typewriter; the first time I went out on a tennis court and felt complete freedom of movement in shoulder, elbow, and wrist; the first time I was able to use all fingers with full mobility on the organ; the first time I was able to shake a man's hand instead of holding out my forearm, as I had done for months. All these experiences were akin to starting life all over again. And the recovery has continued, day by day and week by week.

Wondrous though all these "firsts" were, nothing gave me deeper pleasure than the *SR* anniversary party.

For when I looked around the room at the party for my 25th anniversary at *SR*, I saw more than faces, present and past. I saw a long series of projects and causes with which the magazine identified itself. I am proud that *SR* was the first magazine to report and write in depth about the implications of the atomic age, and to maintain its concern. I am proud of the part *SR* played in the campaign for a ban on nuclear testing. I am proud of *SR*'s role in bringing about reform in the manufacture and dispensing of unsafe drugs, and in giving its readers such an early and authentic awareness of the problems and possibilities of space travel. I am proud of the way *SR* anticipated the far-reaching changes in music records and recording equipment. I am proud of its service to and standing in the educational community. I am proud of its leadership position in the field of travel. I am proud of its stand on cigarette advertising. I am proud of what it has done in relating the world of books to the world of ideas, and the battle it has waged for freedom of intellectual inquiry.

Most of all, though, I am proud of the people who read the magazine and of their partnership with the editors on special projects. *SR*'s readers successfully carried out a program in Hiroshima for the "moral adoption" of hundreds of children whose parents had died in the atomic explosion. *SR*'s readers helped make it possible to bring the Hiroshima Maidens to the United States for plastic surgery. *SR*'s readers helped provide medical and psychological treatment for Polish ladies who had been injured in forced medical experimentation by Nazi doctors during World War II. I am proud of the support *SR*'s readers gave only recently—and are still giving—to Paul Brand's work in fighting leprosy in India.

The most exciting part of each day at *SR* is going through mail from readers from all over the world. Do the opinions of our readers make a difference? Yes. It is hard for me even to estimate the number of times I have thanked readers for a well-deserved rap over the knuckles. Whether with respect to participation in our causes or criticism or encouragement, the readership is the most rewarding aspect of the editor's experience on the magazine. There is a sense that the magazine is being read, thought about, worked over. There can be no sweeter feeling for an editor than this.

For all these reasons and more I am glad to be back. I do not take the privilege of this editorship lightly. Freedom is the highest prize on this earth. It is also the most precarious and fragile. To work on *SR* is to take part in a widening adventure in intellectual freedom. It is not easy; the responsibilities that go with freedom are not without fatigue. But at least there is more of a sense of being alive than in almost any other work I can think of. For this, and for many other things, I thank *SR*—the people who own it, the people who produce it; and the people who read it and enable it to grow.

Part Two

# The Editorial Page

## 1940–1967

# The Forties

*Adolf Hitler and Benito Mussolini, as Axis partners, had something to do with the development of the* Saturday Review *into a weekly journal of ideas and the arts. The world was being hammered into an iron form alien to freedom and creative growth—and therefore to human life. There was a mobilization against the free flow of ideas and the phenomenon of a rational society. A counter-mobilization was required. The* Saturday Review *wanted to be part of that counter-mobilization.*

*This didn't mean that we were turning away from books. What it meant was that we were turning with books to the conditions that made possible the creative life of the mind. Our job as we saw it was not just to appraise literature but to try to serve it, nurture it, safeguard it.*

*We gave increased attention to books as vehicles for ideas. We made a special effort to relate books to what was happening in the world. It was in this sense that the* Saturday Review *became a journal of ideas.*

*This section begins with some editorials and articles written during 1940–1945, the war years.*

## Can We Stay Out?

It seems obvious that the biggest issue in American life today, even bigger than our most important domestic problems, is whether we can stay out of the European war. It is an issue which is likely to dominate the presidential campaigns. Up to now most of the candidates have stepped lightly around the question of our foreign policy, but they will begin to be pressed for answers by an anxious electorate which has suddenly discovered that the war in Europe is real and that many millions of people are facing mass murder. It is certain that the candidates will vie with each other in attempting to furnish satisfactory answers; soon the air may be filled with supposedly flawless proposals for an American foreign policy which will keep us out of the war. It is almost equally certain that the next few months will find a steady stream of books—indeed, the trickle has already begun—telling us how to preserve our neutrality.

But candidates and authors, if they are pressed hard, will be forced to admit or should admit that there is no single foreign policy which can stand up under the pressure of changing events. There are too many variables involved in the equation of neutrality to justify the belief that any single personality or any single plan can guarantee us immunity. We want to keep clear of the war *physically* but we are already in the war *emotionally*. But the bridge from emotions to actions may be shorter than we think. And yet we cannot and should not stop forming attitudes toward the war; thank God we still have the right and ability to feel outraged, to moralize, to become excited. At the same time we must be prepared to recognize that our sympathies can exert tremendous pull upon our course of action. This may be true to a larger extent today than ever before; the radio has given the war a proximity and an extra dimension it never had for us in 1914.

Another and perhaps even more important variable is the unpredictability of events themselves. It would be easy for us to embark upon a fixed policy of isolation or "Continentalism," as Charles A. Beard prefers to call it in *A Foreign Policy for America*, if we knew in advance the identity of the victor plus his intentions following victory. While it is simple enough to say we will have no part of Hitler, we do not know that Hitler will have no part of us. The possibility of a challenge to America from a victorious Germany may seem incredible or even laughable. But we must bear in mind that Germany has been attempting and has been accomplishing the supposedly impossible for seven years; this is Adolf Hitler's strongest argument with his people. Hermann Rauschning, in *The Voice of Destruction*, quotes Adolf Hitler as saying that "National Socialism alone is destined to liberate the American people from their ruling clique and give them back the means of becoming a great nation," and that there were "strains" in America which were "an assurance that the sound elements of the United States will one day awaken as they have awakened in Germany."

This, we repeat, is merely a report of a conversation, but in deciding for ourselves whether it is fact or fancy we may be helped by another quotation from the Rauschning book. Adolf Hitler, says the author, told him that the Nazis could and would capture foreign countries from within as well as from without:

> When I wage war . . . in the midst of peace, troops will suddenly appear, let us say, in Paris. They will wear French uniforms. They will march through the streets in broad daylight. . . . The confusion will be beyond belief. But I shall long have had relations with the men who will form a new government—a government to suit me. We shall find such men, we shall find them in every country. We shall not need to bribe them. They will come of their own accord. Ambition and delusion, party squabbles and self-seeking arrogance will drive them. Peace will be

negotiated before the war has begun. I promise you, gentlemen, that the impossible is always successful. The most unlikely thing is the surest. We shall have enough volunteers, men like our S.A., trustworthy and ready for any sacrifice. We shall send them across the border in peacetime. Today you don't believe me. . . . But I will accomplish it, move by move. . . . Our strategy is to destroy the enemy from within, to conquer him through himself.

This book was published before the German Trojan Horse invasion of Norway. Even those who prefer to believe Rauschning is using his imagination for British propagandist purposes will have to admit the amazing and frightening parallel between what he reported and what is actually happening today.

Even if a victorious Germany is too exhausted to turn her dynamism in the direction of the Western Hemisphere there is still no assurance that other factors might not bring us into direct conflict. Should the defeat of Great Britain and France be the signal for a re-distribution of empire, what position would we take, especially toward the Far East? Raymond Leslie Buell, in his *Isolated America,* believes one result of a German victory might mean an American war with Japan.

These are but a few of the factors which make it difficult to say with certainty what we shall have to do in order to stay out of the war. While we know what developments may serve to bring us in, we do not know whether the absence of those developments will keep us out. If we could at least be certain that we are the sole masters of our destiny the picture might not be so dark. But outside events over which we have no control unfortunately have some control over us.

*—May 18, 1940*

# Not Recrimination but Resolve

It is almost inevitable, in times such as these, to find scholars and writers turning back to history for a re-assembling and revaluation of the events leading up to the large-scale disasters which today are blasting away a substantial, perhaps fundamental, part of the structure of civilization. But even these investigations leave many questions unanswered—questions relating to the moral as well as physical unpreparedness of great nations and peoples, America included, in the face of grave dangers.

Archibald MacLeish places a large share of the blame upon the post-World War pacifist or semi-pacifist writers, of which he was one, whose works served to condition people against positive attitudes. Seeds of cynicism have been planted, he says, which have resulted in indifference among many people, especially the younger generation, toward moral values involved in the present war. Similar beliefs have been expressed by Walter Millis, who looks back and finds that the anti-war literature of the twenties and thirties, among which his own *Road to War* occupies a conspicuous place, has made the mistake of speaking of war in terms of absolutes, thus helping to seal the minds of people against changing conditions and changing events which make it clear that the evils of war are relative, and the ultimate in evil may not necessarily be represented by mass murder on the battlefield but by mass slavery of men and ideas.

Along with these statements is the warning—implied in the case of MacLeish, explicit in the case of Millis—that America must accept and fulfill her obligations toward the preservations of moral values in the world, by force of arms, if necessary. This change of heart or attitude—call it what you will—not only by MacLeish and Millis, but by a large number of other writers—may seem a paradox: the contradiction in fundamental philosophy between the MacLeish and Millis of, let us say, 1930, who were pro-pacifist, and the MacLeish and Millis of 1940, who are anti-pacifist.

And yet, there is no paradox, no contradiction, no inconsistency. The same motives which turned MacLeish and Millis and the others to the writing of pacifist literature until very recently are also behind their support of the fight against Hitlerism today. The least common denominator of their philosophies continues to be humanitarianism. The form may change—it was against war then and it is against barbarism now—but the substance remains the same. A Hemingway who cried out against the evils of war in *Farewell to Arms* picked up a gun and went off to war to fight the evils of something he felt was worse than war in Spain. In the World War liberals led the interventionist movement; in the years that followed they led the anti-war movement; today the trend seems to be returning to intervention again. Have the liberals changed sides? No; only targets.

But there are consequences of even a change in targets, as Mr. MacLeish has demonstrated. Many of those who are not old enough to remember the importance of moral factors contributing to our participation in the last war and who were nourished during their most formative years on books such as Hanighen's and Engelbrecht's *Merchants of Death,* or Millis's *Road to War,* or Remarque's *All Quiet on the Western Front* —each of them an excellent work but each telling only part of the story— may have learned their lessons, as Mr. MacLeish fears, only too well.

Whatever the effect of our post-war literature, nothing can be gained now by continuous raking over of old coals. One of the disturbing developments in recent weeks has been an increasing tendency among writers to concern themselves unduly with blame-fixing; in many quarters the pointing of fingers has become a constant preoccupation. It would be unfortunate but perhaps characteristic of the American intellectual if he should allow the issue to become an end in itself, sublimating all thought and energy into polemics over the past, instead of bending himself to the problem at hand.

This is no time for recrimination. There is a big job to be done that needs doing quickly. The lightning, catastrophic successes of Nazism have shaken in many people their faith in the ability of America to maintain either the instruments or institutions of democracy. They have become confused, uncertain, intimidated. They must be told—even if the telling runs counter to the American worship of success—that success does not necessarily make right, any more than might makes right. They must be rallied around a re-definition of the meaning of human dignity, of the need to preserve a free interchange of ideas. A common ground must be cleared on which Americans can stand in unison and resolution.

Much of this job can be done by our writers, if only they will do it.

*—June 29, 1940*


# The One Indispensable

It requires no range-finder to detect that the air in liberal circles is quivering with disillusion and confusion, or to confirm our fears that almost all our favorite dogmas or ideas of only a few years back have been obscured or obliterated under the pressure of changing events. To refresh your memory concerning those ideas, take down a representative armful of books published half a decade or so ago. Turn to—among others—Dos Passos or Farrell or Dreiser or Hemingway in fiction; to Chase or Sheean or MacLeish or Mumford or Frank in non-fiction. It is difficult to draw a least common denominator from the analyses and conclusions of their books, but a little addition shows that the sum total approximates a number of attitudes and convictions having wide acceptance at the time. War was to be condemned under all conceivable circumstances; there was a general distrust of economic and social America as constituted to cope with the needs of the people, or to survive a crisis; centralization or concentration of power was regarded as not only desirable but inevitable; socialism or some form of a rigidly planned economy were put forward as responsible solutions.

We have been right in expecting that these beliefs might shortly be put to the test, but we have been frequently wrong in anticipating the conditions under which the tests would be made, and more often wrong in pre-judging the results. We scorned war and therefore the instruments of war because we ourselves had no quarrel with other peoples within the visible future, and because we seemed to think that *all* civilization had at last outgrown war. The beautiful glow of this vision obscured the reality that forces far more destructive than war might be loosed which would issue a challenge and determine the rules and conditions under which that challenge might be contested or inflicted. Obscured, too, were other factors: the pulling power of our own ideals and emotions under fire; the possibility that lack of instruments of warfare, far from being an automatic guarantee of lasting peace, might be regarded by better-armed powers as an invitation to war; the likelihood that civilization would not outgrow war until it could produce a dominant species of beings as far above man as man is above animal, overcoming the problems of race suicide with as great success as man himself in overcoming the problems of fire, water, and weather.

Similarly, the prescriptions we wrote for the ills of society have been filled in a manner as disappointing as it is confounding. We called for greater centralization of power, but we were thinking only in terms of power for greater good, forgetting that it could also be used for greater evil. Those of us who said that socialism alone could eliminate our poverty and suffering were surprised and frightened when under that name emerged full-blown personal dictatorships which extended the realm of suffering far beyond the ordinary imagination, and which bent their primary efforts not toward justifying their power but toward maintaining and extending that power. Even less, perhaps, was it suspected that countries flying the banner of socialism—national or international—would threaten directly our own fundamental concepts of living and thinking, or that we might have to fight those countries for our very lives.

Little wonder that contemporary literature is strewn with disillusion. Little wonder that there is so much propping-up of convictions with straws, so much groping on the fringes of reality, so much dread of the future. To paraphrase the title of Freda Utley's new book (the most recent and perhaps the best of the disillusion confessionals), the dreams we have lost are many.

What, then, remains? If we are in a fight now—and we are—what is left that we are fighting for? The feeling continues to grow that we are fighting for time to think. We are fighting for time to keep decisions in our own hands, even though we may not be sure now what those decisions may be. We are fighting for time to probe deeper the lessons of the past to learn why it is that history has played strange tricks with our convictions, twisting them into such unrecognizable and antagonistic realities. We are fighting for time to build or resurrect ideals that will brave the years.

Time to think. It is a strange fight but no fight ever had a nobler goal.

*—October 12, 1940*

# Still Required Reading

The twenty-seven-year war between Sparta and Athens was so thick with history, so crowded with various combinations of circumstances, that it is more than likely that a parallel can be found for every war that was ever fought. Even so, the reader of Thucydides will find it difficult to escape the feeling that the Peloponnesian War and World War II stand apart from all other wars in their peculiar attraction for each other. This is not just because Sparta was the supreme land power, and Athens the supreme naval power; nor just because the former sought to win by invasion and the latter by blockade; nor just because the war started as a matter of local sovereignty involving a small state and spread until it engulfed the entire Greek world; nor just because the war was really but the second phase of a war that had been fought many years earlier without any conclusive resolution of the issues.

The war between the Greek giants—like the war between the European giants—came about and was fought because two worlds were in conflict. It was the "we-or-they" struggle between democracy and oligarchy—the equivalent in the pre-Christian era for the totalitarian state. This was not a war in the conventional sense, limited to one nation at war with another nation, as Thucydides points out with characteristic understatement and objectivity. It was a war of conflicting opinions, where people disagreed with their neighbors and were willing to fight those neighbors in order that their own ideas might prevail. It so happened that certain groups of Athenians, for example, sympathized with Sparta, secretly or otherwise, not only because they may have felt the war was unjust but because Sparta happened to have a form of political organization better suited to their pocketbooks or their prejudices or whatever it was that principles were called in those days. These Athenians probably did not consider themselves disloyal to Athens—or at least to what they thought the Athenian ideal should be—but they could not reconcile such a conception with democracy, then at its height in Athens, just as the oligarchy was at its ebb.

Thus the problem was not only one of war but of civil war as well, which made for an infinitely more bloody and disastrous conflict. This revolutionary aspect of the larger struggle became increasingly important as the war unfolded. Those states which were not already involved found themselves drawn in through the medium of internal conflict; the oligarchic faction in each state would call on Sparta for help, and the democratic faction on Athens. "In times of peace," says Thucydides, "there would have been neither the pretext nor the desire to ask a foreign power to help decide a domestic struggle. But in times of war, with alliances at the command of either faction, opportunities for bringing in the outsider were never wanting."

Thucydides adds that the "sufferings which the internal conflicts entailed upon the countries were many and terrible, but no worse than will occur time and time again, as long as man remains the same."

But you will read Thucydides not only because here is a voice that carries across from a distance of two thousand years, but because you will want to know why it was that Athens lost and democracy died. It will be small consolation to know that the oligarchy didn't last either, or that the enemies of democracy at home met their just deserts. The important thing is that democracy—and civilization with it—died once and you will want to know whether there is anything tangible connected with it that you can identify and say to yourself that it can be prevented from happening again.

Democracy died then; but it is doubtful whether it died on the battlefield. Athens virtually won the war in 425 B.C. when Sparta, her legend of invincibility on land shattered, sued for peace. From that point on, the complexion of the war changed. Athens allowed her old side interest, imperialism—already responsible for many difficulties, particularly among states she needed as allies—to dominate more than ever her war tactics and objectives. Forgotten was the advice of Pericles to attempt no new conquests. The expansionists were now in the saddle; apparently the war to preserve democratic institutions was fine as far as it went but it didn't go far enough.

This is, of course, not the whole story; there are so many factors entering into the picture, particularly at the time that Sparta requested the armistice, that it should be fairly simple for anyone with a point to prove to find one to his liking. An isolationist today may argue that the history of Athens proves that we will be committing suicide by entering the war; while his opponents may argue that Athens went into the war because her vital interests were threatened and considered those interests, one of which happened to be no less an item than the preservation of democratic institutions, worth fighting and dying for if that was the only way they could be secured. Whichever the point of view best tailored to your own convictions or hunches, the fact is inescapable that at the end of more than a half-dozen years of fighting, a truce was called while Athens considered terms—but Athens, as Thucydides says, decided "to grasp for something further."

What would have happened if Athens had stopped in 425 B.C. will remain one of the great riddles of history. It is possible that she might have succumbed anyway—and Greece along with her; that she might have fallen before Rome. In any event, we know what happened when she decided to go after bigger things.

—*June 7, 1941*

# Warrior against Troglodytes

There were no parades in Prague last Saturday, no celebrations to mark an important day in the history of the Czechoslovakian people. It was the anniversary of an event associated with the story of civilized progress, but this is Occupied Europe in 1942, and the philosophy of the nihilist has no room for anything related to civilized progress. And so the people of Czechoslovakia last Saturday carried quietly in their hearts the memory of John Amos Comenius, who taught them that in order to be good citizens of Czechoslovakia they had to be good citizens of the world.

He was born in Moravia three hundred and fifty years ago, on March 28, 1592. He was born at a time when progress was still something of a phenomenon, for it was only the dawn after the Dark Ages and everywhere big clubs were wielded by small minds trying to hold back the day. He was born John Amos Komensky but history knows him by his Latinized name—appropriately so, for he was a Latin scholar and writer of stature. History also knows him as the outstanding Czechoslovakian of the seventeenth century, a man of vision and ideas, a teacher whose influence, whether in regard to educational concepts or democratic philosophy, was to leap across the oceans and become stronger through the centuries. And whether as educator or democrat, Comenius is still new, still strong and challenging, still filled with the vibrant and timely quality that we like to think belongs to the word "modern." More than three centuries ago he charted the techniques and goals of the present-day progressive educator. He stressed the importance of stimulating the intellect; he steered clear of dogma; he favored learning by doing, understanding between parent and teacher, and, in fact, almost every tenet now associated with "new" trends in contemporary educational theory. He was the first to champion so effectively free, compulsory general education for both sexes, the first to come out so boldly for academic freedom. To him is owed a debt of gratitude not only by the modern illustrated textbooks but by our illustrated magazines as well, for Comenius was the first Westerner to conceive and project a picture book, which he called the *Orbis Pictis*.

But it is in the field of political philosophy that Comenius's importance for our own times is emphasized. His approach was strictly that of an educator, but his eyes were able to see the reality of mutuality among peoples. He saw great hidden collective strengths in the similarities among men everywhere, and deplored the ignorance which made them stress their differences. But he saw books as speaking a universal language and looked forward to the day when books which could be read by all would tell them that the human race is really the human family, that nations must come together if they are to survive.

The civilized minds of his day recognized the value of the man and his work, but the small minds, the troglodytes, did not understand him, and because they did not understand were disturbed and tried to destroy him and his work. He was the target of bigotry. Spanish troops swept away his property. Comenius died in 1670 but his many writings, notably *The Gate of Tongues* and *The Great Didactic*, continued to live and grow in importance.

Such is his stature and meaning for our times that Comenius is as much a part of the fight today as any of our living writers who devote themselves and their writings to the preservation of a world where books are not suspected, feared, and destroyed, but examined, analyzed, and integrated, if worthy, into the general body of knowledge. But if Comenius is fighting our fight, no less are we fighting his. For the small minds and troglodytes are still with us; they are at grips with us on the battlefield and some of them are even to be found at home, tugging at our sleeves while we are trying to take aim, obstructing, impeding, belittling, believing the worst and doubting the best—scornful of the issues at stake and blind to the consequences if we should fail. Or perhaps they are not afraid of failure because they cannot bring themselves to believe that what we have is worth preserving. It is almost too bad that shortsightedness such as theirs cannot be put where it belongs—back in the eleventh century.

*—April 4, 1942*

## Remember Lidice

*Statesmen, historians, writers, readers:*
    You have been looking for a single statement to unite all peoples everywhere who are making common cause with us in the fight for survival. You want it to be simply stated, yet carry the eloquence of demonstrable truth. You want it to ring with clarity, yet be rich and deep in its universal appeal. Some of you have already made efforts at creating such a rallying cry. Many are noble, inspiring. But we ourselves have not produced *the* one brief affirmation that could answer all questions and remove all doubts in a way that could have equal meaning and importance for every human being everywhere.

    Yet the search can now be ended. There is now such an affirmation. We have not produced it, but the enemy has. By one of those queer twists of irony, it has remained for Nazi Germany to provide for the cause of the

United Nations a single brief statement so towering, so powerful, that nothing we have said or can possibly say can surpass it. It tells us—all of us—what we are fighting for and what we are fighting against. It is an answer to cynics, scoffers, disbelievers, belittlers. It is dated June 10, 1942. Listen carefully. This is what it says:

> The investigation of the murder committed on Deputy Reich Protector for Bohemia and Moravia, S.S. Upper Group Leader Reinhard Heydrich, revealed beyond doubt that the population of the township of Lidice near Kladno gave shelter and assisted the murderers.
>
> In addition, evidence was found of hostile actions committed against the Reich, and subversive printed matter as well as arms and ammunition dumps, illegal radio transmitting station, and huge supplies of rationed commodities were discovered.
>
> In addition, the fact was ascertained that inhabitants of this township were in active service of the enemy abroad.
>
> After ascertaining these facts, all male adults of the town were shot, while the women were placed in a concentration camp, and children were entrusted to appropriate educational institutions.
>
> The township was leveled to the ground and the name of the community extinguished. The inhabitants of Lidice near Kladno numbered 483.

This statement was in the form of an official communiqué, and was no doubt intended as a bold display of strength to frighten off new attacks on Nazi hangmen. Actually, it is one of the most important documents in the history of World War II. For it not only sums up compactly and tersely the issues at stake in this war, but serves as an authorized confession of one of the most sickening and horrible mass crimes since Attila —Hitler's blood partner and trail blazer. It has thus remained for the Nazi to provide the sharpest and most damning description ever drawn of the nature of Nazism.

Here is something to sink down deep, something to store away against the day when weariness or cynicism may set in, causing us to wonder whether the game is worth the candle and perhaps wonder what the whole mess is about anyway. For it is all too easy at such times to lose our grip on our basic convictions, perhaps because our goal seems so far away as to be misty and unattainable; perhaps because the present is measured so heavily in terms of blood and tears and sweat that the scales of the future seem meaningless.

At such times, remember Lidice. Remember that Lidice is only symbolic of all the towns and cities and nations that have been set on fire, one by one, as part of a war of extermination, in which the enemy agrees with us that he can never break a living free people, and so, thus agreeing, kills them.

It is well that the story of Lidice was told in the form of an official Nazi communiqué. Otherwise, it is possible that the "cautious" and "conservative" among us would have warned against being deceived by atrocity propaganda. It is strange, when you think of it, how we have allowed ourselves to become so saturated with a fixed pattern of thinking that we have a rigid and almost stereotyped reaction when confronted by a word such as "atrocity" or a term such as "barbarous crimes." For twenty years we have waged a relentless war not against the things that bring on atrocities or against atrocities themselves but against the word "atrocity" itself.

Even the British government, terrified lest it be accused of spreading vicious atrocity propaganda, sat on the news of the Hong Kong atrocities for weeks before it finally let the world know what actually happened, and then almost timidly and half-afraid, as though it were offending not civilized morality but civilized credulity.

What we have seen these last two generations comes close to being the treason of reason. We didn't think that barbarism was ever again possible, therefore, Q.E.D., barbarism couldn't exist.

And where did all this sweet reason lead us? It led us to refuse to believe the bare truth when Japan first bombed Shanghai six years ago; no, we told ourselves, such wanton slaughter was unthinkable, so we preferred the comfort of saying that the Japanese airmen were merely poor marksmen: they were trying to blast Chinese warships in the harbor and not kill civilians. It led us to "reserve judgment" when the reports came out that the Polish people were being systematically exterminated. And, most humiliating of all, it led us to say no, no, it can't be so, when the news of the attack on Pearl Harbor burst upon us while we were enjoying a good Christian Sunday, so we nodded in agreement when the radio commentators helped fill in the missing parts by declaring that this could never be the *real* Japanese navy—only a few officers running amok who would commit hari-kari before they could be repudiated and summarily dealt with by the emperor.

What balderdash. What an utter abdication of realistic thinking. What we meant in all this flow of sweet reason was that *we, ourselves,* wouldn't have been capable of such abominations, therefore no one else could. So now we discover that atrocities are atrocities, that towns are being burned and thousands upon thousands of civilian males are systematically exterminated and the women carried off and the children spared, the better to mold them into the new order. This is what this war is about.

Remember Lidice.

*—July 11, 1942*

# The American Folly

There is something curiously paradoxical today in the changed relation-ship between the book and film world and the everyday world in which Americans live. Once—and not many years ago at that—many of us picked up a book or went to the movies for an hour or two of escape. But the war has reversed that. Today we live in what is actually a world of escape and take a brief dip into reality every now and then in our diversions.

When you read on-the-spot reports such as *Guadacanal Diary*, by Richard Tregaskis, or *Men of Bataan*, by John Hersey, or *Queens Die Proudly* by W. L. White, or *One World*, by Wendell Willkie; or even books of fiction such as *The Dead Look On*, by Gerald Kersh, or *The Voice of the Trumpet*, by Robert Henriques—when you read these books you are strangely lifted out of the fantastic and unreal world that is America today and plumped into a world of substance and reality, a world where basic values are at stake, where blood is flowing in mounting torrents to keep the meaning of America alive.

The contrast is even more striking with motion pictures—perhaps because the film is a much more compact and dramatically effective vehicle than books. You go to see a film such as *In Which We Serve*, or *Desert Victory*, or *Prelude to War* and come away dazed and blinking—dazed because your brief excursion into the real world of 1943 has been full of raw stuff; blinking because it is difficult to get adjusted again to the world you actually have to live in and work in. This world is much different from the one you have seen when it took shape on the screen. This world—that is, the American world today—is an incredible world which no word describes so aptly and tragically as the word "escape"—in the sense that we are detached from the needs of the present.

Does "escape" seem too harsh when applied to America? How else would you describe a nation that is in a fight to the death yet thinks it can afford the luxury of interminable wrangling, pulling, tugging? How else would you describe a nation where there are men in the Congress who regard as their main enemy not Hitler but the President of the United States, and who count as a supreme triumph anything that will embarrass, hamstring, or obstruct him? How else would you describe a nation where the abolition of government agencies, regardless of the nature of their work or their urgency on the war front or home front or both, is eagerly sought by congressional blocs not to expedite the war against Germany and Japan but to expedite the war against a competing political party? How else would you describe a nation where efforts to stabilize wages and prices and taxes are constantly thwarted because each group wants the other group to make whatever sacrifices have to be made; where organized pressure groups are relentlessly grubbing whatever they can while the getting is good? And finally, how else would you describe a nation where there are race riots and devastating and irresponsible strikes?

Don't take comfort in the notion that this is the democratic way. This is not the democratic way, unless we are to say that the democratic way is disintegration and insanity. There is always a wide margin in democracy for cleavages and divergences; indeed, in normal times democracy thrives on them. But there comes a time when the margin must shrink, when differences must be subordinated to common resolution in the face of a common danger. To stray far out beyond the margin, to allow what are really minor differences to become magnified and intensified to the point where more important issues are sidetracked or obscured; to obstruct or impede the national welfare because of petty politics or prejudice—all this is inexplicable treason.

Yet the profoundly disturbing reality is that this is the picture of America today—a nation which has yet to grasp the imperatives of the hour. There is no "home front" in the sense that there is a solid wall of resistance. There is no such wall and we may as well face it. Selfishness, shortsightedness, stubbornness have eaten into the wall and have left big, gaping openings. Armies can win battles and nothing more. It is the nation as a whole which alone can prove its ability to survive.

Can it be that when it comes to a showdown we haven't got what it takes? Can it be that a nation born in the blood of freedom's battle has so far wandered from its heritage as to be ignorant of the bold requirements of continued freedom and self-preservation? Can it be that all these internal explosions will serve only to pave the way for the destruction, demolition, or overthrow of American democracy at home without a single enemy shell, bullet, or bomb touching our shores? If so, we had better call the boys home now, for there is nothing left for them to save.

*—June 26, 1943*

# What I Learned About Congress

*A Willing Pupil Takes A One-Day Course*

This is a report of a visit to Washington for the purpose of learning about the Congress at first hand from Senator Robert A. Taft of Ohio. The trip grew out of a poem, "Recess for the Boys," by William Rose Benét, appearing in the Phoenix Nest of the *Saturday Review*. Senator Taft read the poem, which satirized absenteeism in the Congress, then wrote to Mr. Benét, terming the criticism unreasonable and inviting the Pulitzer Prize poet to visit him for the purpose of learning just how the Congress actually works.

This was the second time within a year that Mr. Benét had been tendered a distinguished invitation to learning. The first invitation came last summer from Thomas W. Lamont, head of the house of J. P. Morgan & Company, following a column by Mr. Benét on war profits. Mr. Lamont disagreed and offered to augment Mr. Benét's education in economics. The present invitation came from one of the most prominent and active senators in Congress, son of a former President of the United States, and himself a "dark horse" possibility for the Republican Presidential nomination, according to some political commentators.

The staff urged Mr. Benét to accept; clearly, solicitude for Mr. Benét's education was becoming a matter of considerable national importance.

But Mr. Benét found it impossible to accept. Other plans precluded even a one-day trip to Washington, and the keeper of the Phoenix Nest called upon me to pinch hit. Needless to say, I jumped at the chance, conscious of serious educational deficiencies of my own on the Congress requiring expert attention. First, however, it was necessary to find out whether Senator Taft approved the change in the batting order. The Senator affably agreed, suggested a date, and supplied an advance outline of the following course of study:

*Morning Classes*

  9 to 10 A.M. Senator's office, general routine, mail, organizing notes for committee meetings.
  10 to Noon. Observation in the theory and practice of a Senate committee.
  Noon to 1 P.M. Observation in the theory and practice of the Senate itself. Vantage point: gallery.

*Afternoon Classes*

  1 to 1:45 P.M. Refueling in the Senator's lunchroom. Instruction optional.
  1:45 to 3 P.M. Resumption of Senate theory and practice from the gallery.
  3 to 4 P.M. Parallel instruction at the House of Representatives. Gallery observation with the Senator.
  4 P.M. to as long as necessary. Summary lecture, at the Senator's office, the pupil to remain during visitors' calls.

As it actually turned out, the course was well planned, though somewhat intensive, and there was little deviation from the original outline. I arrived in Washington the evening of June 14, and set out early the next morning in high anticipation inevitably tinged with nostalgia at the prospect of going back to school. The scarcity of cabs, the heavy traffic, and my remarkable facility in getting lost within five seconds after entering any government building, all combined to make me about twenty minutes late, something I had vowed to myself I would not let happen. I did not want to give the idea that senators get to their offices any earlier or work any harder than editors of literary magazines. With profound chagrin, I learned that my mentor had arrived at 8:50 A.M., had asked for me, had worked for about fifteen minutes, then had stepped out of the office. While waiting for him to return, I became acquainted with Mr. I. Jack Martin, the Senator's secretary, a congenial, somewhat slight man of about thirty-five, who was most cooperative in providing valuable basic orientation in office routine.

I learned from Mr. Martin that the Senator receives an average of 250 letters a day, though on peak days the number is so high they don't even bother to count it; I learned, too, that many of the letters or telegrams come from organizations and pressure groups; that it is impossible for the Senator himself to read all the letters, let alone answer them; that Mr. Martin screens through the most important ones for the Senator's personal attention; that the others are assorted, collated, tabulated, and filed after they are acknowledged—usually in the form of mimeographed letters. I learned that the Senator is interested in the we-want-you-to-do-thus-and-so mail but not dependent on it and generally uninfluenced by it. Even the pressure telegram, talking at the top of its capital letters, must go through the same processing as the less formidable regular correspondence.

I learned that the Senator is assisted by a staff of seven: a "secretary" who is actually the office manager and special assistant; a research or correspondence chief; and five secretarial stenographers or typists. The research chief and a secretarial clerk work in an additional office provided for Senator Taft in the Capitol itself, within easy distance of the Senate Chamber and the Committee rooms. Not all senators enjoy these dual facilities, but Mr. Taft's membership on seven important committees, as well as the fact that his regular quarters in the Senate Office Building are somewhat small, were responsible for the extra corner office in the Capitol.

My orientation was interrupted at this point by a young lady who told Mr. Martin that the Senator had entered his office and was waiting to see me. Senator Taft rose from his desk to greet me as I walked in. He was as I had imagined him—a tall, rather lean, fair-complexioned man of about fifty or fifty-five, with pleasant gray eyes, small nose, large, full mouth, and a small chin that does not recede quite so much as it appears in the newspaper photographs. He is semi-bald and the effect is to give him an elongated and severe appearance from a distance, almost in the manner of a Grant Wood portrait. But close up, his face becomes much softer, extremely youthful. His voice is well modulated, his diction excellent, his choice of words simple yet effective. He has a direct, pleasant manner and looks more like the head of a chemistry department or economics department of a Midwest university than the popular conception of a senator—broad beamed fore and aft. He maintains an even composure, although he occasionally seems preoccupied.

Senator Taft began by discussing the general program for the day, spoke about the morning's correspondence, ruffling through the papers on his desk and coming up with a letter concerning something that was said by the president of an Eastern university at a board of directors' meeting of a large insurance company. The university president had been quoted as saying that he had just discussed the coming Republican National Convention with Senator Taft, who had confided to him that in all probability Governor Dewey would not be nominated on the first ballot, that there would be a deadlock between Dewey and Bricker, and that the plan was to break the deadlock by nominating Taft.

All this flabbergasted the Senator. He rang for a secretary and began dictating a letter. Politely but briefly, he told the university president that he was as surprised as he was bewildered, especially since the two hadn't seen each other for at least two years. But more important to him, he wrote, than the surprise or the bewilderment was the embarrassment. He had pledged his support to Governor Bricker and was prominent in organizing his campaign. References to his own candidacy, particularly when attributed to himself, might make it appear that he was only giving lip service to Governor Bricker and had plans and ambitions of his own.

Senator Taft finished the letter, sighed wearily, then smiled and said: "The old boy must be ga-ga."

I told the Senator that I myself had seen and heard numerous reports saying approximately the same thing. Surely there must have been some basis somewhere for it.

"If there is, this office has had nothing to do with it," he said. "I am not a candidate. The only thing I am getting ready to campaign about is for reelection as Senator from Ohio."

The phone rang. That gave me a chance to look around the office. It was furnished adequately, though somewhat mustily, with the heavy black leather fittings and glass-door bookcases that are as inseparable apparently from a senator's office as franked envelopes. There was a generous assortment of family pictures. There was one of Mrs. Taft and several photographs of the four Taft boys, three of whom are now in military service. The largest picture in the room, standing on the floor and leaning against the fireplace, was a colorful sepia photograph of the Senator's father, President William H. Taft, snapped informally in his carriage as he lifted his hat to enthusiastic onlookers. Directly above it, on the mantel, was a brass statuette of President Taft. (Later I learned that Robert Taft idolized his father from early childhood and still does; that he goes out of his way to be nice to anybody who knew or has a kind word for his father.)

Next to the statuette on the mantel was a row of brightly jacketed books. I got up to examine the titles. Among them were Pierre Van Paassen's *Forgotten Ally*, Louis Fischer's *Empire*, Philip C. Nash's *World Order*, Ely Culbertson's *Total Peace*, Edward Stettinus's *Lend Lease*, Carlos P. Romulo's *Mother America*, Philip Kinsley's *The Chicago Tribune: Its First Hundred Years, Horace Walpole, Gardenist*, and David Dallin's *Soviet Russia's Foreign Policy*.

Not a bad selection, I thought.

As I had looked over the books, the Senator had been observing me—somewhat apprehensively, I thought. When his phone call was completed, he spoke about the books with some anxiety. They had been sent to him with the compliments of the author or the publisher, he explained. The books he read were in his library at home. I made whatever mental adjustments were necessary.

By this time, it was past 10 A.M. and we were overdue at the special committee meeting scheduled for that morning. Senator Taft said that it was to be a closed meeting of the newly created Senate Committee on Post-War Economic Policy and Planning, and that he had arranged with Senator Walter F. George, the chairman, that I be permitted to sit in. On the way down to the committee room, he explained that the committee was currently working on Senate Bill 1730, designed to cushion the shock of unemployment in the reconversion period immediately after the war. The bill provided for what the sponsors believed was a comprehensive program of unemployment insurance.

We entered the committee room, there were brief introductions, and I was seated on one side of the rim of a mammoth raised horseshoe desk. The nameplate in front of me read "Claude E. Pepper." The Senator from Florida, apparently, was unable to attend. The senators present, viewed left to right around the horseshoe from where I sat, were Scott W. Lucas, of Illinois; Alben W. Barkley, of Kentucky, the Democratic majority leader; Senator Taft; Carl Hayden, of Arizona; Walter F. George, of South Carolina, the chairman; Arthur H. Vandenburg, of Michigan; and Warren R. Austin, of Vermont.

Under consideration was Senate Bill 1730. It sought to insure unemployment insurance, as it were, by standing in back of the unemployment insurance programs of the individual states. Each state has already enacted an unemployment insurance program, ranging from benefits of $10 a week in some states to $22 a week in Connecticut, over a period ranging from fourteen weeks in Arizona to twenty-four weeks in California. The states have established funds with an aggregate total of some

6 billion dollars. Should any state fail to meet its obligations under its own plan, the Federal government would underwrite the deficit, according to the bill.

Most of the discussion concerned the relative advantages of the plan for one state as against another, for the small state as against the large, for the agricultural state as against the industrial, etc. It was apparent that two or three members of the committee were somewhat disturbed lest their own states suffer in relation to some hidden advantage held by another. After that, an inevitable brief dispute arose over states' rights vs. Federal powers, with Senator Taft championing the former and Senator Barkley the latter. Senator Taft then suggested that the Federal government make it possible for the states to extend the period of unemployment payments, when, as, and if necessary. Both sides seemed to think this suggestion reasonable.

After some further discussion on methods of collection and administration, Senator Taft signaled me to follow him.

Once outside, he explained that nothing new was likely to come up at his own meeting and asked whether I might care to attend a hearing of the Military Affairs Committee. The prospect intrigued me and the Senator phoned his secretary to serve as my escort. While waiting for Mr. Martin, I asked the Senator some questions. Unemployment insurance was fine as far as it went, but wasn't the basic problem one of creating a sound economy which in itself would provide against unemployment? Unemployment insurance was the least that the Congress could do, but was it also the most that it intended to do?

The Senator replied that the committee was proceeding on the basis of one thing at a time. The first problem to face the country at war's end, he said, would be the dislocations inherent in the demobilization, and the unemployment insurance was only an attempt to tide over the country until such time as reconversion and retooling could be accomplished. Moreover, he said, the Senate had already undertaken reconversion legislation.

And what about the longer range? What about the continuing problem of achieving a healthy economy? Consider the paradox: during war, we operate under a peak load with the bulk of the manpower drained off; during peace, we operate under a limited load with the bulk of the manpower available but largely unused.

The Senator acknowledged the problem, said he had certain ideas concerning a sound economy based on free enterprise. He said that free enterprise could never get going again under a continued policy of high government spending, and that this policy could create a tremendous momentum for inflation. "We've got to put on the brakes," he said.

I asked him whether under certain circumstances it might not be impossible or inadvisable to put on such brakes. If free economy didn't start up by itself, wouldn't government be compelled to help? Did not the committee's own unemployment insurance act prove that the government had to accept responsibility for economic dislocations? And what if the unemployed were still unemployed after twenty weeks or whatever the period of benefits might be?

In that case, said the Senator, he supposed there would have to be a period given over to work relief.

And if that wasn't enough?

"Then I guess we would have to keep men from starving by giving them checks outright," he said.

At that moment, the Senator's secretary arrived. Senator Taft arranged to meet me in the Senate gallery when Congress convened at noon, and he returned to his postwar committee.

When we arrived at the meeting of the Military Affairs Committee, I discovered that the same bill under discussion at the Post-War Committee session was also being considered here. After a half hour of approximately the same question-and-answer routine as the one I had just heard, with almost the identical considerations of states' rights, equality of benefits, administration costs, etc., I whispered to Mr. Martin, asking whether it was customary for Senate committees to duplicate each other's work. His answer was that the Military Affairs Committee was at present studying demobilization and that this particular bill came within its purview. He added that subcommittees of both groups were to meet the following morning for the purpose of integrating their work and findings.

In any event, by this time I had become reasonably aware of Senate Bill 1730 and I was eager to get over to the Capitol for the next step in my education. We got up and left. It was almost noon, time for the Senate to convene.

One of the most fascinating things about Washington is the underground passage between the Senate Office Building and the Capitol. The distance is perhaps no more than a quarter of a mile, but senators are the most pathetic pedestrians in the world, so there is an electric car system operating by means of an overhead rail with only a single ground track on which the car is balanced. The vehicle looks like a cross between a mountain cable car and a tunnel-of-love contrivance at Coney Island. It seats twelve people, strung out in pairs, with the operator in the center, and you go zipping along at a merry pace expecting the whole contraption to take off in flight at the first curve. Enchanted, I stayed on for an extra ride, and I hope my official guide wasn't too embarrassed. All that was missing from the general getup was a brass ring as you looped around the last turn.

If you are ever in Washington on one of those deadly summer days when the whole place feels like the black hole of Calcutta under a sun lamp, take my advice and stick it out in that cool cellar passage, every now and then shuttling back and forth on that breeze-blessed tram. If you rate temperature reduction above fragrance, then that ride is something out of this world. You don't have to be a senator to get on, although you will be expected to give up your seat if the place suddenly becomes chock full of senators and there isn't enough room. Another advantage possessed by senators is that they can keep a car waiting for them even before they arrive simply by pressing a buzzer in the elevator on the way down. Sometimes a senator may be fairly bursting to get over to the Capitol or back to his office, so he presses the buzzer three times. This is almost the equivalent of a four-alarm fire; and even if the tram has started on its way to the other side, it has to go into abrupt reverse to pick up its dashing cargo.

My cellar adventure resulted in my being five minutes late for the next class. The Senate had already convened when I entered the gallery with Mr. Martin, but it was difficult to know that by observing the men on the floor. Perhaps a half-dozen men were seated on the Democratic side of the chamber, a dozen on the Republican side, and men were walking up and down as well as in and out, and the chatter sent up a constant drone. The presiding officer, in the absence of Mr. Wallace, was Senator Guy M. Gillette, of Iowa, who was earnestly engaged in a side conversation with Senator Barkley.

Through it all came the overtones of some solid oratory. Someone was making a speech that I never would have believed had I not actually heard it. It seemed too typical to be true. It was about the virtues of the *great* American middle class, about how everyone was taking advantage of that *great* bulwark of American democracy, and how it was high time the Congress recognized its tremendous responsibility to the *great* white class. Senator Barkley, quickly realizing that the speaker had intended to say "white-collar class," politely tried to correct the blunder, but that only served to stiffen the speaker, and he became more and more emphatic about less and less as he went along. What he had been leading up to so eloquently amounted to a demand for higher ceiling prices.

Another senator chimed in to support the claim. He told about the ominous situation as it pertained to hogs and cattle and predicted a meat shortage in the near future. Two sentences later he was complaining about freight cars loaded with beef at sidings waiting futilely for buyers.

"Mr. Chairman," someone was saying, "this is the most outrageous situation I have ever heard of in my life."

Then someone said he wanted to pass along to the Senate a statement that had been told him in confidence about the cattle situation, but he was not at liberty to state the source of the information although he would be glad to divulge the source should anyone want to know it ( *sic* ). This confidential information, he said, was that the cattle situation was the most confused it has been in years.

Period.

The matter of unfair hog prices was being aired with considerable gravity when an usher tapped my shoulder and told me that visitors were not permitted to take notes. Spying the press gallery at the other side, I thought it would simplify matters if I continued my notes from the section, only to discover that only representatives of daily newspapers are entitled to work there. Not even weekly newspapers or news periodicals such as *Time* or *Newsweek* or *United States News* can use the Senate press gallery. This was an interesting curiosity and I asked the guard whether those magazines had tried to get the rule changed.

"Now don't start that war all over again," he said. "If you're from a magazine you'll have to rely on your memory."

When I returned to the gallery, Senator Taft came up to take me to lunch. He was accompanied by Senator John A. Danaher, of Connecticut, my own state.

On the way to the Senate restaurant, Senator Taft said he couldn't understand what all the noise was about that morning on the imminent shortage of beef, remarking that the present beef inventory was extremely high, yet only a few months ago the same scares were raised. I asked whether it was purely coincidental that the beef-shortage scares were almost automatically followed with a proposal of higher prices. The Senator smiled.

The Senate lunchroom is as free of decorative ostentation as a cane chair. There is a large table in the center which can accommodate perhaps fourteen or sixteen persons; the remaining tables are average sized and are spread alongside the walls. On the far side of the room I observed Senator Robert La Follette sitting with his young son, aged eight or nine. There was a generous sprinkling of women around the room, most of them wives or daughters of senators.

Whatever the situation may be around the rest of the country with regard to runaway restaurant prices, the Senate menu certainly indicates and justifies the existence of an OPA. For seventy-five cents or a dollar you can order a meal unobtainable under a dollar and a half in New York or under two dollars in any commercial restaurant in Washington itself.

Most of the discussion at lunch was shop talk about mail, answered and unanswered, about long-distance telephone calls from irate constituents, about lobbyists, about legislation, about other senators. I learned that the average congressman lives in constant dread of form letters sent over his signature to people who ought to receive personal attention; that he never has enough time to take care of his job properly; that what with committee meetings, Senate sessions, and the plaguing daily mail, he keeps falling behind even though he may keep his office open three or four nights a week.

Toward the end of the meal, someone rushed up and asked my hosts to hurry back onto the floor. It seemed that Senator Bridges was crying for help on some appropriations measure.

So far as I could see, the plea didn't make much of an impression.

"That type of thing gives me a pain in the neck," Senator Danaher said. "What makes him think I'd be of any help? What say, Bob"—turning to Senator Taft—"let's get out there and vote the other way—but only when we're good and ready."

Meanwhile, Senator Wherry, the party whip, was going from table to table, in the Senate lunchroom, relaying Senator Bridges's call for succor. If anyone got up promptly, I failed to notice it.

After lunch, we returned to the Senate gallery, with Senator Taft sitting alongside me and identifying the various members of the Congress. A debate on a supplementary appropriation bill was on the floor at the time and we leaned forward to hear Senator Kenneth McKellar, of Tennessee, as he orated on states' rights. At that moment, someone who had just come down the aisle whispered to Senator Taft, who turned to me and said, simply:

"American bombers are over Japan."

Down below, on the floor of the Senate, young men rushed up and down relaying the news.

Once the messengers left, there was nothing to indicate that anything exceptional had happened. Confusion and small talk. Senators strolling in and out. A handful of men in their seats. I had the strange feeling that I was in a never-never land utterly removed from the war. I thought of American planes over Japan, wondering where they came from, wondering how many might never return. And out of the mist of the strange world in which I found myself words would come drifting up to me from the floor, words about hogs and prices that ought to be higher, about items on appropriation bills that ought to be put in or left out, about states' rights. . . .

Finally, a dark man stood up in the far corner of the floor and asked to be recognized. It was Senator Claude Pepper, of Florida.

"Mr. Chairman," he began, "word has just been received that American B-29 planes have bombed Japan proper. I believe it is only fitting that the Senate should pause at this time both to pay tribute to our aviators and to reflect upon the historic importance of this news. It means that the theories of long-range, land-based aviation have proven themselves. It means that the war will be brought home to the enemy as never before. It means that America has come a long way from the brink of chaos on which it found itself on the evening of December 7, 1941. It means that . . ."

He was interrupted. Senator Clyde M. Reed, of Kansas, was asking a question.

"Did I understand the Senator from Florida to say that B-29 planes were the ones that did the bombing?"

Senator Pepper nodded.

"Well, then," sang out Senator Reed, "does everyone here know where those marvelous machines come from? They come from good old Kansas."

Thus saying, the Senator chuckled loudly and went back to his seat, obviously very happy with himself for having given his all for dear old Kansas.

After a momentary exposure to the face of reality, the Senate had snapped back into place.

I stepped outside for a breath of air.

Next stop was the House of Representatives. Senator Taft escorted me over. We didn't say much. Our minds were 9,000 miles away.

I confess that I was in no mood for the general pandemonium that burst upon me when I walked into the House gallery. I had expected confusion and disorder far beyond what I had witnessed in the Senate, since the House has more than four times as many members and physically is at least two or three times as large, but I was prepared for nothing like this. Let me try to give the picture as I saw it:

Perhaps one-fifth of the representatives were in their seats and were listening to the business at hand. The others were either clustered together in talkative little groups or were walking around chattering, or both. One of the congressmen was bouncing a young child on his knee. Twice each minute the speaker had to rap for order; a comparative hush would follow the last rap of the gavel but would last perhaps five or ten seconds and the general commotion would start up all over again.

Since it is next to impossible to hear any congressman from his seat, a microphone is set up at the rostrum in front of the speaker's platform. A tall, young-looking congressman was speaking into the microphone at this time. The amplification system blared out his words but the combination of the over-all din and the poor acoustics made it difficult to snatch more than a phrase here and there. It was a curious and disturbing experience. People talking, talking. Hardly anyone listening. Now and then someone would ask to be heard, interrupting the speaker at the microphone. He would be recognized from the chair despite the general blur, and he would shout from his seat, but you couldn't hear anything. His lips would move, but that would be all. Or perhaps he would hurry down to say something in front of the microphone, but it only served to magnify the meaningless confusion.

With the feeling that I had aged at least ten years, I returned to Senator Taft's office for the concluding portion of the course. I sat alongside the Senator's desk while he carried on his regular business, the most conspicuous feature of which was its enforced lack of continuity. Unending interruptions by telephone calls, unexpected visitors, and office details reminded me somewhat of the editor's office of a magazine with which I have some familiarity.

There were telephone calls from Clarence Streit, the author of *Union Now*, who wanted the Senator to join him at dinner; from John D. M. Hamilton, who inquired on the progress of the Bricker campaign; from John T. Flynn, who wanted to show the Senator a statement he was preparing; from Alice Roosevelt Longworth, who extended a social invitation; and from several others from within the building.

So that my instruction would be as complete as possible, the Senator invited me to remain in his office while he received visitors. This may or may not have been disconcerting to the callers. It is possible that some of them left earlier than they had originally planned. I took some comfort in the knowledge that I could reciprocate in some measure at least for the Senator's many favors.

It was now close to six o'clock, and I wanted to take up some general questions with the Senator that had occurred to me during the course of the day. First of all, I confessed my disappointment and apprehension at what I had seen on the floors of the Congress. Even the Senate, for all its traditional dignity, seemed to be less a deliberative than an *adlib*erative body. So far that day I had heard nothing except jockeying around to favor one group or another at the expense of another. Was the Senate becoming nothing more than a sounding board for petty gripes?

"There's no place quite like this in the world," Senator Taft answered. "Anyone can get up at almost any time and talk about anything under the face of the sun. It makes for a good deal of confusion and a good deal of noise. There is a saying that the Senate gets its business done by unanimous consent or physical exhaustion. Sometimes you wonder whether anything at all is accomplished. But the surprise, actually, is how much really does get done despite all the appearance of disorder.

"When I first came here as a freshman senator, it took me a year to get over my disillusion. Back in the State Legislature in Ohio everything was done with a sense of order and purpose. Here, I spent the first few months doing almost nothing except finding out where I was supposed to be and at what time, and trying to pick my way through the confusion. But after a while I got the hang of things and came around to the realization that, even if we do blunder through somewhat, the important thing is that free government is maintained—whatever its faults."

This seemed like the logical finale to my education on the Congress, and I got up to leave. I expressed my gratitude to the Senator, whom I found to be an effective and engaging teacher, and he, in turn, extended an open invitation to me to return at any time for postgraduate work.

On the train that night, I went over the day's lessons. Uppermost in my mind, of course, was the Congress as I had actually seen it in action. I could still hear the bedlam, reminding me of an indefinite extension of the seventh-inning stretch at a ball game. I wish I could say I exaggerate. I wish I could say that so long as they blunder through, as Senator Taft put it, there is no point in bothering about it or even wondering about it.

True, I had been there at a bad time. Appropriation bills always make for chaotic and uninteresting sessions. Even so, I honestly can't help being bothered about it. I honestly can't help wondering about it. Yes; I know it is a thousand times better than a hall full of men whose minds click and keep pace just as do their heels. It is a thousand times better than hundreds of mouths chanting "Ja!" in unison. And if disorder and commotion are the price we have to pay for democratic institutions, then the price is utterly cheap and let the confusion reign supreme. But surely there must be a happy medium somewhere.

It hasn't always been this way. The Congress hasn't always been a sounding board making big noises over small things. When De Tocqueville wrote his now-classic study of the American government more than a hundred years ago, he was impressed with the tremendous sense of responsibility and prestige of the Congress. When Bryce wrote his *American Commonwealth* only fifty years ago, he, too, came away with a feeling of the towering dignity of the legislative branches of our government. But both writers also seemed to recognize that this magnificent framework had to be periodically strengthened; they seemed to recognize that the flexibility of the Congress could under certain circumstances become as great a disadvantage as it was an advantage.

It would be presumptuous of me to say what these "certain circumstances" are, but I should like to report my feeling that the blame cannot be placed upon the individual members of the Congress or the Congress itself as an institution. I agree with Jerry Voorhis, who asked people in a recent magazine article to "stop kicking Congress around." If the Congress goes, we can kiss our democracy good-by. The problem before us is to find out why and how it is that the Congress has gotten this way, and then see if we can't help to restore something of an equilibrium.

What, then, is wrong with the Congress? It isn't only the noise and the confusion, for those, after all, may be only external exercises which can be blotted out by a pair of sturdy earmuffs. But what troubles me is that the noise and confusion may be indicative of inner weaknesses.

In the first place, a congressman's job is markedly different from what it was a generation or more ago. It is absolutely impossible for a congressman today to meet all the demands upon him which are now inherent in the job. At one time legislation was his chief concern. Today, legislation must take turns with dozens of other jobs, and this applies to representatives and senators both. The mail alone, if it is to be handled right, is a full-time job. There are at least twice as many letters today flooding in upon the Congress as there were ten years ago. Personal calls from constituents are heavier than ever before, and a congressman who wants to keep his job can't afford to turn away too many of them.

Then, too, the congressman has inevitably become more of a lobbyist than he is a legislator. He is expected not only to vote but to use his influence in getting others to vote. He is expected to intercede for a business firm in his state or district which feels it is being discriminated against by a government agency.

Most important, of course, is the matter of The Party. There are meetings and conferences and phone calls and letters, and sometimes hurried trips home to straighten out political snarls. There is no point in being falsely altruistic about this; a man who is interested enough to run for office in the first place is also interested in being reelected.

What this all amounts to is that the largest part of a congressman's time is almost inevitably taken up with activities which bear on his reelection. If this seems to be putting it too strongly, then we can at least say that the largest part of his time is taken up with activities that have little or nothing to do with a national legislative program. Certainly this is bound to reflect itself in the work of the Congress as a whole. Men who are preoccupied with comparative trivia off the floor of the Congress do not experience a revelation in high statesmanship the moment they step on the floor.

There is a disposition to excuse all this by saying that the real work of the Congress is done in committee, and that most congressmen keep up with current business by following *The Congressional Record*. While I do not doubt that congressmen have come to lean on the committees and *The Record*, I fail to see this as an adequate substitute. Otherwise, we shall have to admit that the floors of the Congress are the greatest gymnasium for shadow-boxing in the world.

Still on the subject of time requirements, what about keeping well informed? That takes time, and plenty of it. I see no evidence to indicate that this particular demand has not frequently become expendable. If wisdom depends upon knowledge, and knowledge upon information, and information upon time, one can readily understand how there is hardly time to be wise.

Faced with this drastic assortment of demands, the average senator or representative finds it impossible to attend the full daily session of his branch of the Congress. Yet his name must appear on the roll calls; he must vote; occasionally he must make himself heard. Thus we have the peripatetic, or perhaps we should say perapathetic, congressman who drops in and out, but who can never stay long enough to sink his teeth into any real legislative meat. Thus we have the noise and the confusion, which, as I said earlier, are actually and ominously indicative of deep-seated causes and strains.

Some members of the Congress have protested that there has been afoot for the last few years an attempt to undermine not only the power but the prestige of the Congress. If the institution of the Congress has been weakened, then only the Congress can answer for that. Only the

Congress can fix its own level. It can be as great or as inept as it chooses to be. It can play a vital part in the shaping of the peace or can trail meekly behind. It can be progressive or retrogressive, constructive or obstructive. There is no ceiling over its possibilities. But before these possibilities can be fulfilled, they must be recognized for what they are. A man who does not know where he wants to go is hardly likely to get there.

*—June 24, 1944*

## Will Educators Lose the Peace?

In 1922 an American writer was anxious to learn what European and American children were being taught about the Great War, as it was then popularly known. The answer, he was convinced, would determine in large part both the nature and the duration of the peace. History's lessons, if mistaught, misunderstood, or ignored, might have to be learned again the hard way.

The writer was William G. Shepherd. At home, of course, it didn't take much probing to reveal that American elementary and high-school instruction in the causes and conduct of the war was almost nonexistent or so perfunctory and inadequate as to be worthless. This occasioned no public outrage; nor was there any reason for one. The prevailing public mood had turned against the war and the feeling was that the less said about it the better. A corrosive cynicism had eaten into the early ideals of the war; and if the teachers had any inclination to assume dynamic leadership in moving toward positive goals, they kept it carefully concealed; nor did the textbooks as a whole reveal any incisive attitude toward the war.

What about Europe? Obviously, the best way to find out would be to undertake a survey firsthand. Mr. Shepherd went to Europe, interviewed educational supervisors and teachers throughout Europe, and came back with his worst fears realized. Even more than in America, Europe had sloughed off the responsibility for teaching its children about the war. Educators had another war on their hands—a tug of war between countless factions in each country over what should be taught and by whom, with the result that children were lucky to have anything taught them about the war at all. This was much more serious than mere decentralization; in many places it came close to educational anarchy. Consider, for example, the situation as Mr. Shepherd found it in Germany. There were as many educational policies as there were districts. The only thing all courses and textbooks seemed to have in common was that all mention of the war itself was scrupulously avoided.

Mr. Shepherd went to see Dr. Carl Heinrich Becker, secretary of the Prussian Ministry of Education, who readily admitted that "not a single word was being taught about the greatest war that history has known up to that time." Teachers were not allowed even to mention it, he added, while history books were rigidly inspected to make sure no reference to the war, however slight, might slip by.

"Is this done purposely?" asked Mr. Shepherd.

Dr. Becker replied that it was, and then explained that "politics" was to blame. "You see," he said, "there are six different parties in Prussia. Each party has a different idea about the causes of the war, the events, and the mistakes. As soon as the ministries of education start to prepare a story of the war for the school children some leader of a party arises to say that the story is wrong in some detail. Then we have to drop the whole thing and start all over again. We must find some story that will suit all the parties, including the Socialists and the extremists on both sides. It is impossible and we have quit trying."

Even in the matter of a straightforward chronology of the war, the factions disagreed. Four experts were assigned to the project, and while no one quarreled over the dates, there was bitter argument concerning what happened on those dates. The chronology was abandoned.

Mr. Shepherd asked about the German revolution of 1918. That, too, was a difficult question for the schools to handle. Asked to explain it, the teacher was instructed to talk mainly about the revolution of 1848, and, when pressed about 1918, to say that 1918 was a sequence of 1848.

"And that," concluded Dr. Becker, "is as far as we can go in telling the children about the recent affairs in Germany."

What Mr. Shepherd saw in France was disturbingly part of the same pattern, even though the colors seemed a little more subdued. The Minister of Public Instruction in Paris was apparently too cautious to make a statement, and delegated a subordinate to answer Mr. Shepherd's questions.

According to this official, schoolteachers in France welcomed the end of the war, with its military regulations in the classroom, and immediately began to give their own versions concerning what happened. Since no textbooks were available, each instructor took it upon himself to explain the war.

As was to be expected, the reaction set in, largely through parents who complained that their children were being lied to about the war. The parents had their own calcified versions and it didn't take them long to find out which teachers were dispensing conflicting ones. Socialist workmen said their children were being indoctrinated with imperialist ideas; upper-class parents were horrified to discover that their heirs were being exposed to Marxist dogma. And so forth.

Pressed by all sides, the French Education Ministry, like its counterpart in Germany, took the easy way out. The only way of satisfying everybody, apparently, was to drop the war as if it had never existed. Textbooks? Yes; attempts had been made to have impartial, authoritative textbooks written, but the textbook writers were no better than the teachers and the parents; they had stories of their own and they were stuck with them. And so was France.

The whole difficulty, the official explained to Mr. Shepherd, was that there were seven influential parties in France. It was almost mathematically impossible to write a textbook dealing with the war that would be certain to please all seven of them, to say nothing of pleasing the teachers and the parents.

"When," asked Mr. Shepherd, "do you think you will be able to begin studying the history of the war in your schools?"

It is doubtful whether the official realized at the time that there was any cause-and-effect implication in his reply. "We will begin," he said, "when the next generation dies."

What he meant, he added, was that it would take that long before the white-hot prejudices of the time would cool off, enabling scholars to undertake an authoritative study. The irony, of course, is that he predicted the literal truth.

Mr. Shepherd went to London, hoping to find at least some crumbs of reassurance, but came away without even that. He spoke to Mr. Richards, in charge of the English school inspectors, and asked the same questions.

He learned that the Government had no policy on the war, and that the local school boards prescribed the courses and the textbooks. Any schoolmaster or member of a school board could go to any publisher and purchase any book he wished. The function of the Government was limited to regular inspection and, if the local boards wished it, occasional advice. Some textbooks had been written on the war and were already in use in some schools.

"All our textbooks," Mr. Richards explained, "are written anonymously. No reliable and well-known textbook writers have attempted to write any schoolbook of the war. All the school histories that have appeared, with a few exceptions, have been thrown together for greedy publishers by hack writers. The paper is poor; the illustrations are unspeakably bad; and the statements of facts are absolutely unreliable.

"Every one of these unsigned textbooks found by our inspectors in use in the schoolrooms is immediately thrown out. Since there are no other textbooks, the schoolchildren of England are not learning the history of the war."

Back in the United States, Mr. Shepherd became the architect of a magnificent understatement when he observed that "although in Germany, France, and England every child must learn to read, the printing press is paralyzed, and the historian is palsied when it comes to the task of telling the new generation about the war."

Does anyone doubt that the failure of education and educators—or, more precisely, the failure of nations—to teach the new generation after World War I helped to bring about World War II? Does anyone doubt that the success of *Mein Kampf* was due in some part, at least, to the fact that it was able to exploit an ignorance created just as surely as disease is created by poverty? Does anyone doubt that the educational vacuum existing in Germany after the last war was an open invitation for Adolf Hitler? Does anyone doubt that the lack of courage, cohesion, and intelligence in dealing with the problem of education in Germany was only symptomatic of large fissures and indecisions, to which the school system made its full negative contribution?

Does anyone doubt that the failure of the democracies to meet their educational responsibilities in the 1920s was directly connected with the cynicism and defeatism that not only helped Nazism in its rise to power, but enabled Germany to go as far as she did; namely, within one ace of making the entire globe into the shape of a swastika?

Finally, does anyone doubt that the same conditions which formed the background of the educational failures of Europe and America after the last war are present today? The end of the war in Europe will be marked by a struggle for power in each nation. Again there will be six, seven, eight, or more parties. Again the conflict of prejudices and politics. Again the pressure on the schools to teach this doctrine or that. Again the temptation to solve the problem of what to say about the war by saying nothing. And again, we suppose, the feeling that nothing can be done until the next generation dies.

Here is a problem as tangible as a brush fire. It has nothing to do with abstract educational theory or philosophical meditations over the purposes and functions of education. The question it poses is much more direct and compelling, even, than what to do with the Nazi teacher after this war—now the favorite bone of contention in academic circles. The question, stripped of everything else, comes down to this: *Can we prevent world-wide anarchy in education after this war?*

Some educators may argue that the question is properly one for society as a whole to answer; that they are actually only the servants of that society. And society may answer back that educators are being paid not only to teach but to formulate educational policy. Either way, arguments such as these, if they come up, are undiluted escapism and belong to the same atmosphere of recrimination, finger-pointing, pressure, and counter-pressure that had such ominous consequences once before.

There is a movement under way in this country and abroad for an international office of education. What an opportunity for such an office to guard against the recurrence of an educational breakdown by assuming real leadership after this war. What an opportunity to act with courage, imagination, and intelligence. Why would it not be possible, for example, for such an office to appoint a committee of leading historians, men whose allegiance to scholarship is greater than their individual partisan views, and charge them with the responsibility for writing the story of the last five or ten years? No one expects that differences will not exist within such a group; but at least there would be a realization by every member that the very purpose of the group is to *reconcile* these differences in order to avoid an ugly or disastrous anarchy or near-anarchy. The chances, too, are that people within each country would be more apt to respect the work of a nonpartisan group of internationally famed scholars than the work of someone within their own country who is certain to be tarred with a brush of special interest.

This is not suggested as a cure-all. There are no cure-alls in this world. But the important thing is to get public thinking started on this question before the jealousies and cleavages and sharp contests for power that are almost certain to follow this war take their toll of the schools, which can least afford it.

*—September 16, 1944*

## Mr. Willkie

We write not so much about a former candidate for the Presidency of the United States as about a man who both understood and belonged to his age, who was able to communicate that understanding with perceptiveness, sincerity, and courage.

We write, then, about the author of *One World*, perhaps the most important book to come out of this war. This although *One World* lacks the fiery persuasiveness of *Common Sense* or the striking power of the *Liberator* papers. Of what, then, does its greatness consist? Its unprecedented audience for a book of this type? Only partially—though it is estimated that close to 20 million Americans have read it in one form or another. What makes *One World* of lasting importance is that it held up a mirror to the future. The central question of our time—and this holds true for peoples everywhere—is whether the world can see itself for what it is. It is a crisis in self-recognition. The face of the world underwent an abrupt change in a single generation, a change which, measured in terms of previous history, would be spread out over a century or two or more. And yet the mind behind the face remained unchanged, hardly able to adjust itself to the shattering experience of the past, let alone attune itself to the present or anticipate the bold dimensions of the future.

"When I say that peace must be planned on a world basis," he wrote, "I mean quite literally that it must embrace the earth. . . . Men and women are on the march, physically, intellectually, spiritually. . . . Men need more than arms with which to fight and win this kind of war. They need enthusiasms and a conviction that the flags they fight under are in bright, clean colors. The truth is that we as a nation have not made up our minds what kind of world we want to speak for when victory comes.

"America must choose one of three courses after this war: narrow nationalism, which inevitably means the ultimate loss of our own liberty; international imperialism, which means the sacrifice of some other nation's liberty; or the creation of a world in which there shall be an equality of opportunity for every race and every nation. . . ."

Generalizations, these, but generalizations that have the look and feel of honesty and urgency. They pointed to, and indeed called for, a structure of world peace far more coherent and cohesive than anything yet made public at the official conferences of the leading powers. How eloquent the difference between the precise and unabashed convictions on the organization of one world into a genuine governmental unit, and the feeble, vague gestures toward an undefined form of "international cooperation" made in such apparent heroism in the present political campaign. For the great danger today is that we may not realize that the issue facing us is not isolation vs. international cooperation so much as it is strong international commitments vs. lip-service international "organization." And the danger of the latter is indistinguishable from the danger of no organization at all. Even a new League can perform no miracles if it is designed only to correct the mistakes of 1919 and not to take care of the vastly advanced problems of 1944.

He died in 1944. "I live in constant dread," he once wrote, "that the war may end before the people of this world have come to a common understanding of what they fight for and what they hope for after the war is over." He dedicated his life to that cause, though by so doing he alienated the dominant section of his own party, which persisted in confusing America's relationship to the world with the rough-and-tumble of domestic politics. Had he wished to genuflect, had he wished to string along with the politics-as-usual crowd at a time when the earth itself quivered with the weight of what was at stake as millions of men fought for a future which their leaders had not sufficiently defined—had he wished to do this, he might have been rewarded with another nomination for the Presidency. But he didn't want it under those terms; just as he was convinced that the American people wouldn't want him under those terms either.

He lost the nomination but he gained the respect and good will of millions of Americans in both political parties who saw in him a powerful and independent force for world good, realizing that world good was inseparable from American good. They were comforted and reassured by his very presence; he was a rugged and ominous menace to those who were tempted to play political football with world problems; no one knows how many political speeches were rewritten or revised because of that unseen influence. Whatever measure of true internationalism exists in his party he brought about largely by himself. And for the years to come, there was always the feeling that he was something of an insurance policy against anything happening without the American people being able to know about it in advance.

He was a bulwark for the making of tomorrow. There is no reason why we should deprive ourselves of the full measure of his greatness. In his ideas are to be found the bold definitions of the opportunity before us, the virile and towering promise of the future. Wendell Willkie continues to be a great asset to America, and an even greater one to the world.

*—October 14, 1944*

# Quiet, Please!

We learn from our 46th Street neighbor, *Variety*, the much-respected Bible and fever chart of the entertainment industry, that war pictures are "poison at the box office" right now; and, indeed, that in Philadelphia the owner of one theater prominently displayed the ingenious line, "This Is Not a War Picture," in its advertising for a film called *Two Yanks Abroad*. It was felt that war-weary Philadelphians might take one look at the title and stay away in droves on the rash and unjust assumption that it had something to do with a war currently being fought overseas.

There are, of course, two parts to the problem. One is that—as with *Two Yanks Abroad*—people may be scared away by what seems to be a war title even though it is not a war film. The other is that people may be lured into a theater by a non-war title such as *The Seventh Cross*, only to discover too late that they have been made the victims of an organized swindle and are forced, *nolens volens*, to sit through an hour or more of moving picture entertainment in the form of a war story. Hence the need for proper labeling which, after all, is the consumer's only real protection in matters such as these.

What has happened in Philadelphia may not be typical of the nation, but, even if it is, it is understandable and natural. Consider, if you will, the privation and suffering to which the average American civilian has been subjected in this war. Only enough gasoline to take care of essential needs in getting around, with only taxicabs and other forms of transportation as alternatives; hardly enough of the best cuts of meat unless one goes to the trouble of eating occasionally at restaurants; not enough butter for bread or other dishes, compelling the nation to turn to indistinguishable substitutes or even to jam or cheese; long—too long—lines in front of liquor stores with the probability that one's favorite scotch may be out of stock with nothing but rum or bourbon and fifty-seven other varieties to take its place; the insolence of headwaiters at night clubs who, refusing to set up a new table for you in the front row, will give you only a third-row table for your five-dollar tip; the smaller-type face being used as a war necessity by newspapers in their stock-market quotation listings, causing severe eyestrain in following your rising stocks—rising ever higher now that there is no longer any danger that the war will end suddenly and without proper warning. We have been saving for last the most drastic privation of all, now rapidly becoming the nation's number-one problem: shortage of standard-brand cigarettes, an unmitigated calamity, comparable only to a planetary collision or the absence of a fourth hand at bridge.

This, it goes without saying, is only a partial list; but we are reluctant—pardonably, we hope—to provide a fuller and more drastic tabulation lest some irresponsible readers enclose it in a letter to a serviceman whose supreme enjoyment of life in general may lose some of its edge if he is given a clue to the egregious suffering on the home front. It would be only slightly less unfortunate if this catalogue of catastrophe were to fall into the hands of civilians in the occupied or liberated areas of Europe, diverting them from their own troubles which, though of lesser conse-quence, nevertheless loom large when they directly affect the individual.

There is no choice for us but to suffer in silence. For more than two thousand years the Spartan spirit has slept; but we can bring it back to life and give it new meaning by exercising forbearance in the trials con-fronting us such as even our Puritan fathers were not called upon to face. And we have a right to ask the cooperation of all groups in our society to the end that this organized silence may be as effective and widespread as possible. Radio news announcers should be compelled by law to whisper the latest reports from the front; newspapers must abandon the screaming headlines about the war, taking the news off the front page and giving it the benefit of the reduced decibels of the second section; books and magazines should follow the lead of the movies by doing their utmost to sidestep anything touching on the war, and adapting the Philadelphia labeling device—i.e., "This Is Not a War Book," or "This Is Not a War Article," etc. Which reminds us:

This is not a war editorial.

—December 20, 1944

# Waiting—for What?

There is a grotesque lack of urgency in too much of the writing and think-ing today on the subject of planning for a peace that will stick. We are referring to the fairly prevalent notion that the most we can hope to do after this war is to postpone the next one for thirty years or so. Fre-quently related to this is the idea that there may have to be a few more wars before man can finally outgrow international murder or get it out of his system. Presumably, if only we wait long enough, war will solve itself.

This unhurried and semi-scholarly approach to war has all the dangers of its charms. It makes it too easy for us to slide into an attitude of philo-sophic resignation about the future. Why get excited or expend any en-ergy over the problems of lasting peace if a few more wars are inevitable anyway? An easy chair becomes a private Mt. Olympus as we contem-plate the future of mankind; there spreads before us a Homeric pano-rama with vast ups and downs which, for all their volcanic changes, are nevertheless part of an inexorable pattern. Naturally, the inexorable is beyond the power of any individual. Why try to affect the pattern? Why, indeed?

But an even greater fallacy is the assumption that we can afford the luxury of several more wars. It should be no secret that the next war, if it comes, will be global suicide. In that sense, it *will* be the last war. The prospect, after such a war, of being able to muster up enough men, maté-riel, and morale, in anticipation of another war, is scientifically nonexist-ent. This is no Sunday-supplement scare; the cold, mechanical truth is that the destruction of humanity is now close to a mathematical formula. Many parts of the equation have already been worked out in this war; the others are even now taking shape in the experimental laboratories of the world. Why should we suppose that the techniques of destruction have now reached their peak and that warfare cannot possibly be any worse? After the war between Rome and Carthage, people were convinced that organ-ized warfare had reached the ultimate in horror and sheer destructive-ness. After the Napoleonic wars, and even after World War I, people were still toying with the same illusion. But war is like a geometric pro-gression where the successive numbers soon get completely beyond human control or comprehension.

Consider the progression as it concerns a coming war—war that is sup-posed to be just another in a series of kinks that man must work out of his muscles before he can enjoy the unrestricted use of his limbs. It will not be a war with armies in the field as it is today, any more than the trench warfare of World War I has been carried over to the present. It will be a war of national populations ranged against each other. It will be

a war operated by means of push buttons and levers, releasing and directing armadas of high detonation through the sky. It will be a canopy of
death making the present V1 and V2 robombs and rocket bombs seem like
flimsy kites alongside B-29 Superfortresses. There will be switchboards of
annihilation, with one button for a large city such as Detroit, and another
for New York, and so forth. It will not be a long war, because when all
the buttons are pushed and all the levers are pulled—and the moment it
starts each nation will run to its own switchboard—that will be the end of
everything, literally, figuratively, definitively.

We are not speculating. If this sounds like a nightmare, try to visualize just one thing: the mass production of the robomb or the rocket
bomb. Forget everything else. Forget the buttons and the levers and the
switchboard. Consider only mass production applied to robombs. Why
should it be any more difficult to turn out hundreds of thousands of robombs than it is to turn out hundreds of thousands of planes?

We say this not by way of scaremongering, but because we are appalled
to find people still reflecting leisurely about means by which the next war
might be put off, or feigning a philosophy of acceptance of the inevitable,
by which they mean a few more wars as part of a more-or-less normal
evolution of civilization. But at this particular time in history it is no
longer possible to make peace on the installment plan. We must play for
keeps this time—or else. If we bring anything less than this to bear at the
peace table, we bring futility.

What we should like to see after this war, as part of a collaborative international program of education, is a traveling exhibit that will acquaint
the peoples of the world with some factual information concerning what
a new war would be like. The exhibit would attempt to report, simply
and factually, what science is like during the twentieth century—its potential for omnipotent demolition and extinction, and alongside that, its
potential for better living.

The people would draw their own conclusions. The biggest of these, we
believe, is that unless the new international controls are as correspondingly great as the switchboards of war, then that new war becomes inevitable. But such controls would also require an organization of nations far
beyond anything that has been suggested or even hinted at in any of the
official conferences. This is not by way of disparaging the world's political
leaders. World citizenship cannot be handed down from the top. It will
radiate from humanity itself or not at all.

—*March 3, 1945*

# F.D.R.

This is no passing sorrow. Its dimensions are bottomless; its meaning takes on added fullness with each succeeding day. The sense of shock and disbelief gives way to a deep and permeating sense of loss. It is as though a piece of the future had slipped away and part of ourselves with it.

The vastness of the tragedy, coinciding with the end of the struggle in Europe, has produced a tremendous orchestration of human emotion. For the writer or historian, the story has the stuff of epics. And just as the tragedy of Lincoln inspired a teeming and ever-growing literature on his life and times, so in the months and years ahead will there be a continuing and expanding fascination in the Roosevelt story.

The first time we saw him was in October, 1937, at a press conference in the White House. The room was tightly packed with newsmen, and we prowled around the edge of the crowd, trying to get a full view of the man behind the desk. The President had just come back from Chicago, fresh from his now-historic "quarantine-of-aggressors" speech.

The air was tense; not since the last war had a president been so outspoken in criticizing nations with which we maintained diplomatic relations. What gave the speech its bristling, challenging quality was that it came at a time when pacifist, anti-World War II sentiment was at its height. Correspondents pressed close to the desk and kept up a rapid fire of questions.

Finally, at the left side of the room, we were able to find a vantage point which gave us a full, clear view of the President. We shall never forget F.D.R. as we saw him then. He was tanned, robust, electric with life. We remember thinking that we had never seen a healthier-looking human being. We remember thinking, too, that we had never seen a more magnificent head. His face was alert, strong, compassionate. He had an eager, expectant look that every now and then would dissolve into a smile or laugh that would win back a smile or laugh from every person in the room.

The White House press conference was the greatest show in Washington and everyone knew it, including the President. Many newshawks would come heavily armed with concealed bear traps which were carefully baited with seemingly innocent questions. But they were up against the most agile bear you ever saw. It was wonderful to see the way he would jump in, snatch the bait, and jump out again, swinging the trap around so neatly that the man who baited it would frequently find himself inside. It was a game that everyone enjoyed playing, most of all the President. You could tell, too, that these seasoned old war horses of the

Washington press corps loved and respected Mr. Big, even though many of them were constantly prodded by the front office to find some way of putting him on the spot. They loved and respected him because he looked, acted, and spoke the part. They would say that you could see him for the first time, and without knowing anything about him, say to yourself, "That man looks as the President of the United States must look."

There was also the look of greatness. It was inevitable. Anyone who could come back out of retirement, after having been afflicted with a dreadful disease that shrank his limbs and made it impossible for him to walk unaided, would be great for that reason alone. You could see his braces where they entered his shoes, huge pieces of steel that seemed to reach inside you as well. It did things to you because 130 million people were leaning on this man and the weight, if anything, was making him stronger and bigger.

But within a few years history itself was to lean heavily on him. We didn't see him again until early in 1944, and it was only a passing glimpse. It was still the same magnificent head. You could read the hopes of millions of people all over the world in his eyes and in the lift of his chin. But you could see other things as well. The rugged youthfulness was gone. He had lived lifetimes. His face was lined with a thousand lines and each line told a story. You could see American boys dying in far-off places, you could see the homeless and the wretched and the damned everywhere, you could see the unutterable tragedy of a bleeding world.

All this you could see and more. You could see the certainty of victory, you could see the grand designs for a family of nations, you could see the flickers of world citizenship. There were anguish and faith in that face, compassion and affirmation, suffering and courage. It was this mixture of profound pain and promise, this supreme symphony of emotion, that seemed to symbolize the man as well as the age.

When he died, something deep died in each of us. No one can ever define it, but it was there and we knew it when it was gone. But when he died, something strong was born in each of us as well. No one can define it either, but we know it has something to do with the obligation— even more than the inspiration—to make good.

*—April 21, 1945*

# To the Class of '45

This is a warning against an illusion—the illusion of completion. It is a natural illusion and easy to understand. This very occasion almost bristles with the physical evidence helping to support it. Your caps and gowns, the very word valedictory, your diplomas, the congratulations of your family and friends, the textbooks and notebooks and papers you will put away in your attic perhaps—all this helps to intensify the illusion that you have completed your education, that you have done all that is to be done by way of equipping yourself with whatever knowledge or learning you will need in life. We assure you that it is with the greatest respect to your college and to the faculty that we tell you, sincerely and with the utmost good will, that your education is incomplete.

For the past four years—no, it would be more accurate to say for the past sixteen years—you have taken part in, or have been exposed to, various mental and intellectual exercises designed, for better or worse, to develop your thinking apparatus. We are not saying, mind you, that you have not been equipped for specialized work or professions in the adult world. What we are saying is that the word education is a misnomer if it means learning and nothing more. In terms of your experiences since you were five or six years old, it has meant an attempt by the community at large and your family to pry open your mind and give it a chance to grow. Mr. George Bernard Shaw has said that education is only a buck-passing device by parents who couldn't retain their sanity if you stayed around the house. But Mr. Shaw, as usual, may be overstating the case.

The mind is a curious instrument. It is like a muscle that grows soft and flabby without exercise. And the longer it is allowed to remain idle, the more difficult it is to get it back in thinking trim. Dr. Oliver Wendell Holmes, in his charmingly irreverent book of light essays, *The Professor at the Breakfast Table,* says that the human mind is like a checking account. As long as you keep putting enough money in the bank, your checkbook is the most magic book in the world. All you have to do is dip your pen in the ink, make a few flourishes, and your check becomes the open sesame to your heart's desires. But just stop making ample deposits, and the magic evaporates with a curt and imperious message from the bank, "No funds." Many persons, Dr. Holmes said, have a corresponding mental experience. They keep drawing on their intellectual reserves long past the time they have put anything in to draw against. Unfortunately, however, there is no bank to serve notice that they are out of mental funds. So they continue, in their conversation, in their letters, in their everyday activities, to do their mental business even though they are intellectually bankrupt.

Beware of this intellectual bankruptcy. It can happen with the greatest of ease despite four years of what is technically known as higher education. All you have to do is coast for a year or two, allowing your mental assets to dwindle, and you can cancel out a large part of the formal educational transaction you are now concluding. What you put into your mind between the age of twenty-one and thirty-five will determine to a large extent how much meaning you can put into your life and how much meaning you can get out of it. These are the vital years of cerebral growth and retention, assuming, of course, that there has been some activity and development during the previous years.

How is this CRP—Cerebral Refurbishing Program—to be done? The answer is fairly simple. By doing it. By retaining your curiosity about the world; by being interested in and concerned with the phenomena of life and living; by learning how to listen; by being able to integrate new knowledge and new interests with old; by what might be called the intellectual "follow-through" which can pursue ideas beyond their surface state.

That word "ideas" is important. It is to the mind what air, water, sun, and food are to the body. "Ideas," says W. Macneile Dixon, the English philosopher, in his *The Human Situation*, "are the most mysterious things in a mysterious world. . . . They are beyond prediction. They appear to have a life of their own, independent of space and time, and to come and go at their own good pleasure. . . . They are living, powerful entities of some kind, and as infective as fevers. Some, like flowers, are the creatures of an hour; others are of a prodigious vitality and root themselves, like oaks, in the soil of human nature for a thousand years. Ideas, like individuals, live and die. They flourish, according to their nature, in one soil or climate, and droop in another. They are the vegetation of the mental world."

James Russell Lowell went even further than that. He viewed ideas not only as mental offspring, but as the ovarian eggs of the next generation's or century's civilization. "These eggs are not ready to be laid in the form of books as yet," he wrote; "some of them are hardly ready to be put into the form of talk. But as rudimentary ideas or tendencies, there they are and they will go into the making of the future."

And where are such germinal or seminal minds? Lowell answered by suggesting that you follow "the course of opinion on the great subjects of human interest for a few generations or centuries, get its parallel, map out a small arc of its movement, see where it tends, and then see who is in advance of it or even with it; the world calls him hard names, probably; but if you would find the ova of the future, you must look into the folds of his cerebral convolutions."

The value of your education cannot be measured in terms of the facts and information you have been able to retain. If your education has provided you with nothing except facts, that education has been a failure. More important than your ability to remember facts is your ability to appraise them, to know a fact when you see one, to be able to go to the right places for facts when you need them.

Education—the good education, that is—can help you to move out beyond the narrow and calcifying confines of the ego so that you can identify yourself sympathetically—no, that word is not strong enough—identify yourself *compassionately* with the main stream of humanity.

*—June 9, 1945*

*In 1945 the specific danger represented by Adolf Hitler and his allies was turned back, but the war ended in a way that defined a different and larger challenge. The first atomic bomb over Hiroshima changed contours of human history. It liberated man from one danger but confronted him with the ultimate problem of safeguarding the planet for human life. The main question now was whether man was intelligent enough to survive—and then make that survival meaningful.*

*As of August 6, 1945, when an atomic bomb was first used against human beings, the* Saturday Review *had defined for itself a purpose that was to shape and perhaps dominate its pages for the years ahead. The reasoning behind that purpose and challenge was first expressed in an editorial titled "Modern Man Is Obsolete," published in the August 18, 1945, issue. The little book that followed under the same title attempted to develop the central theme and anticipate the requirements of a world under law. In any event, the use of nuclear energy for military purposes and the inadequacy of absolute sovereignty to deal with the implications of nuclear energy became, and still are, the dominant editorial theme and preoccupation of the magazine.*

## Modern Man Is Obsolete

Whatever elation there is in the world today because of final victory in the war is severely tempered by fear. It is a primitive fear, the fear of the unknown, the fear of forces man can neither channel nor comprehend. This fear is not new; in its classical form it is the fear of irrational death. But overnight it has become intensified, magnified. It has burst out of the subconscious and into the conscious, filling the mind with primordial apprehensions. It is thus that man stumbles fitfully into a new age of atomic energy for which he is as ill-equipped to accept its potential blessings as he is to counteract or control its present dangers.

Where man can find no answer, he will find fear. While the dust was still settling over Hiroshima, he was asking himself questions and finding no answers. The biggest question of these concerns the nature of man. Is war in the nature of man? If so, how much time has he left before he employs the means he has already devised for the ultimate in self-destruction—extinction? And now that the science of warfare has reached the point where it threatens the planet itself, is it possible that man is destined to return the earth to its aboriginal incandescent mass blazing at fifty million degrees? If not—that is, if war is not in the nature of man—then how is he to interpret his own experience, which tells him that in all of recorded history there have been only three hundred years in the aggregate during which he has been free of war?

Closely following upon these are other questions, flowing out endlessly from his fears and without prospect of definitive answer. Even assuming that he could hold destructive science in check, what changes would the new age bring or demand in his everyday life? What changes would it bring or demand in his culture, his education, his philosophy, his religion, his relationships with other human beings?

In speculating upon these questions, it should not be necessary to prove that on August 6, 1945, a new age was born. Nor should it be necessary to prove the saturating effect of the new age, permeating every aspect of man's activities, from machines to morals, from physics to philosophy, from politics to poetry; in sum, it is an effect creating a blanket of obsolescence not only over the methods and the products of man but over man himself.

It is a curious phenomenon of nature that only two species practice the art of war—men and ants, both of which, ironically, maintain complex social organizations. This does not mean that only men and ants engage in the murder of their own kind. Many animals of the same species kill each other, but only men and ants have practiced the science of organized destruction, employing their massed numbers in violent combat and relying on strategy and tactics to meet developing situations or to capitalize on the weaknesses in the strategy and tactics of the other side. The longest continuous war ever fought between men lasted thirty years. The longest ant war ever recorded lasted six and a half weeks, or whatever the corresponding units would be in ant reckoning.

It is encouraging to note that while all entomologists are agreed that war is instinctive with ants, not all anthropologists and biologists are agreed that war is instinctive with men. The strict empiricists, of course, find everything in man's history to indicate that war is locked up with his nature. But a broader and more generous, certainly more philosophical, view is held by those scientists who claim that the evidence to date is incomplete and misleading, and that man *does* have within him the power of abolishing war. Prominent among these is Julian Huxley, who draws a sharp distinction between human nature and the *expression* of human nature. Thus war is not a reflection but an expression of his nature. Moreover, the expression may change, as the factors which lead to war may change. "In man, as in ants, war in any serious sense is bound up with the existence of accumulations of property to fight about. . . . As for human nature, it contains no specific war instinct, as does the nature of harvester ants. There is in man's make-up a general aggressive tendency, but this, like all other human urges, is not a specific and unvarying instinct; it can be molded into the most varied forms."

But even if this gives us a reassuring answer to the question—is war inevitable because of man's nature?—it still leaves unanswered the question concerning the causes leading up to war. The expression of man's nature will continue to be warlike if the same conditions are continued that have provoked warlike expressions in him in the past. And since man's survival on earth is now absolutely dependent on his ability to avoid a new war, he is faced with the so-far insoluble problem of eliminating those causes.

In the most primitive sense, war in man is an expression of his competitive impulses. Like everything else in nature, he has had to fight for existence; but the battle against other animals, once won, gave way in his evolution to battle against his own kind. Darwin called it the survival of the fittest, and its most overstretched interpretation is to be found in *Mein Kampf,* with its naked glorification of brute force and the complete worship of might-makes-right. In the political and national sense, it has been the attempt of the "have-nots" to take from the "haves," or the attempt of the "haves" to add further to their lot at the expense of the "have-nots." Not always was property at stake; competitive advantages were measured in terms of power, and in terms of tribal or national superiority. The good luck of one nation became the hard luck of another. The good fortune of the Western powers in obtaining "concessions" in China at the turn of the century was the ill fortune of the Chinese. The power that Germany stripped from Austria, Czechoslovakia, Poland, and France at the beginning of World War II she added to her own.

What does it matter, then, if war is not in the nature of man as long as man continues through the expression of his nature to be a viciously competitive animal? The effect is the same, and therefore the result must be as conclusive—war being the effect, and complete obliteration of the human species being the result.

If this reasoning is correct, then modern man is obsolete, a self-made anachronism becoming more incongruous by the minute. He has exalted change in everything but himself. He has leaped centuries ahead in inventing a new world to live in, but he knows little or nothing about his own part in that world. He has surrounded and confounded himself with gaps—gaps between revolutionary science and evolutionary anthropology, between cosmic gadgets and human wisdom, between intellect and conscience. The struggle between science and morals that Henry Thomas Buckle foresaw a century ago has been all but won by science. Given time, man might be expected to bridge those gaps normally; but by his own hand he is destroying even time. Communication, transportation, war no longer wait on time. Decision and execution in the modern world are becoming virtually synchronous. Thus, whatever bridges man has to build and cross he shall have to build and cross immediately.

This involves both biology and will. If he lacks the actual and potential biological equipment to build those bridges, then the birth certificate of the atomic age is in reality a *memento mori*. But even if he possesses the necessary biological equipment, he must still make the decision which says that he is to apply himself to the challenge. Capability without decision is inaction and inconsequence.

Man is left, then, with a crisis in decision. The main test before him involves his will to change rather than his ability to change. That he is capable of change is certain. For there is no more mutable or adaptable animal in the world. We have seen him migrate from one extreme clime to another. We have seen him step out of backward societies and join advanced groups. We have seen, within the space of a single generation, tribes of headhunters spurn their acephalous pastimes and rituals and become purveyors of the Western arts. This is not to imply that the change was necessarily for the better; only that change was possible. Changeability with the headhunters proceeded from external pressure and fear of punishment, true, and was only secondarily a matter of voluntary decision. But the stimulus was there; and mankind today need look no further for stimulus than its own desire to stay alive. The critical power of change, says Spengler, is directly linked to the survival drive. Once the instinct for survival is stimulated, the basic condition for change can be met.

That is why the quintessence of destruction as potentially represented by modern science must be dramatized and kept in the forefront of public opinion. The full dimensions of the peril must be seen and recognized. Then and only then will man realize that the first order of business is the question of continued existence. Then and only then will he be pre-pared to make the decisions necessary to assure that survival.

In making these decisions, there are two principal courses that are open to him. Both will keep him alive for an indefinite or at least a reasonably long period. These courses, however, are directly contradictory and represent polar extremes of approach.

The first course is the positive approach. It begins with a careful survey and appraisal of the obsolescences which constitute the afterbirth of the new age. The survey must begin with man himself. "The proper study of Mankind is Man," said Pope. No amount of tinkering with his institutions will be sufficient to ensure his survival unless he can make the necessary adjustments in his own relationship to the world and to society.

The first adjustment or mutation needed in the expression of his nature, to use Huxley's words, is his savagely competitive impulses. In the pre-

Atomic Age those impulses were natural and occasionally justifiable, although they often led to war. But the rise of materialistic man had reasons behind it and must be viewed against its natural setting. Lyell, Spencer, Darwin, Lamarck, Malthus, and others have concerned themselves with various aspects of this natural setting, but its dominant feature was an insufficiency of the goods and the needs of life. From Biblical history right up through the present there was never a time when starvation and economic suffering were not acute somewhere in the world.

This is only part of the story, of course, for it is dangerous to apply an economic interpretation indiscriminately to all history. Politics, religion, force for force's sake, jealousy, ambition, love of conquest, love of reform —all these and others have figured in the equations of history and war. But the economic factor was seldom if ever absent, even when it was not the prime mover. Populations frequently increased more rapidly than available land, goods, or wealth. Malthus believed that they increased so rapidly at times that war or plague became Nature's safety valve. This interpretation has undergone some revision; however, it is not the interpretation but the circumstances that raise the problem.

Yet all this has been—or can be—changed by the new age. Man now has it within his grasp to emancipate himself economically. If he wills it, he is in a position to refine his competitive impulse; he can take the step from competitive man to cooperative man. He has at last unlocked enough of the earth's secrets to provide for his needs on a world scale. The same atomic and electrical energy that can destroy a city can also usher in an age of economic sufficiency. It need no longer be a question as to which peoples shall prosper and which shall be deprived. There is power enough and resources enough for all.

It is here that man's survey of himself needs the severest scrutiny, for he is his own greatest obstacle to the achievement of those attainable and necessary goals. While he is willing to mobolize all his scientific and intellectual energies for purposes of death, he is unwilling to undertake any comparable mobilization for purposes of life. He has shattered the atom and harnessed its fabulous power to a bomb, but he balks—or allows himself to be balked—when it comes to harnessing that power for human progress. Already many representatives of industry have counseled words of synthetic caution, informing a puzzled public that we shall not see the practical application of atomic energy for general use in our lifetime. If it works out this way, it will not be because of any lack of knowledge or skill, but only because of the fear in certain quarters that atomic energy will mean a complete revamping of the economic structure, with the probability that it would be operated as a government utility or public service.

The cry is certain to go up against further government experimentation with atomic energy for peacetime purposes, and industry will demand that government withdraw and give it the right to carry on its own experiments. These experiments, however, would most likely be no more consequential than if the atomic bomb had been left to decentralized chance. Moreover, it takes enthusiasm to fertilize invention, and there is as yet little discernible enthusiasm for atomic energy in those quarters which are asking for the right to sponsor its peacetime uses. However understandable this lack of enthusiasm may be, it should not blind public opinion to the critical importance of having research for practical use carried on with the same urgency, the same fullness, the same scope and intensity as it has been for war ends thus far.

The size of the opportunity is exceeded only by the size of the promise. But even as man stands on the threshold of a new age, he is being pulled back by his coattails and told to look the other way, told that he must not allow his imagination to get out of hand—all this at a time when he should know almost instinctively that if he can put the same courage, daring, imagination, ingenuity, and skill that he demonstrated in winning the war into meeting the problems of the new age, he can win the peace as well.

He must believe, too, that mobilization of science and knowledge in peace should not be confined to cosmic forces, but must be extended to his other needs, principally health. What a fantastic irony that organized science knows the secret of the atom but as yet knows not a fig about the common cold! Who can tell what advances in medical knowledge might accrue to the welfare of mankind if as much mobilized effort were put into the study of man as there has been of matter! Cancer, heart disease, nephritis, leukemia, encephalitis, poliomyelitis, arteriosclerosis, aplastic anemia—all these are anomalies in the modern world; there is no reason why mobilized research should not be directed at their causes and cure. Nor is there any reason why even old age should not be regarded as a disease to be attacked by science in the same intensive fashion.

Surveying other adjustments he will have to make if he chooses the positive course, man must consider himself in relation to his individual development. He can have the limitless opportunities that can come with time to think. The trend during the last fifty years toward shorter work weeks and shorter hours will not only be continued but sharply accelerated. Not more than half of each week will be spent earning a living. But a revolution is needed in his leisure-time activities—which so far have come to be associated almost entirely with the commodities of vended amusement. Once before the world knew a Golden Age where the development of the individual—his mind and his body—was considered the first law of life. In Greece, it took the form of the revolution of awareness, the emancipation of the intellect from the limitations of corroding ignorance and prejudice.

Once again, if man wills it, he can be in a position to restore that first law of life. But he shall have to effect a radical transformation in his approach to and philosophy of education, which must prepare him for the opportunities and responsibilities not only of his chosen work but for the business of living itself. The primary aim should be the development of a critical intelligence. The futile war now going on between specialization and general study must be stopped. There need no longer be any conflict between the two. The individual will need both—specialization for the requirements of research, general knowledge for the requirements of living. As for the problem of time in which to accomplish these dual objectives, formalized education until the twenty-fifth or thirtieth year is doubtless indicated; but it should not abruptly end there. Education, like the capacity of the mind itself, has no rigid boundaries. Unlimited exploration should be the first imperative of any educational program.

We have saved for last the most crucial aspect of this general survey relating to the first course: the transformation or adjustment from national man to world man. Already he has become a world warrior; it is but one additional step—though a long one—for him to become a world citizen. This is not vaporous idealism, but sheer driving necessity. It bears directly on the prospects of his own survival. He shall have to recognize the flat truth that the greatest obsolescence of all in the Atomic Age is national sovereignty. Even back in the old-fashioned Rocket Age before August 6, 1945, strict national sovereignty was an anomalous and preposterous holdover from the tribal instinct in nations. If it was anomalous then, it is the quintessence of anomaly now. The world is a geographic entity. This is not only the basic requisite for world government but the basic reason behind the need. A common ground of destiny is not too large a site for the founding of any community.

Reject all other arguments for real world government—reject the economic, the ideological, the sociological, the humanitarian arguments, valid though they may be. Consider only the towering problem of policing the atom—the problem of keeping the smallest particle of matter from destroying all matter. We are building on soap bubbles if we expect this problem to be automatically solved by having America, Britain, and Canada keep the secret to themselves. That is not only highly improbable, but would in itself stimulate the other nations to undertake whatever additional research might be necessary over their present experimentation to yield the desired results. In all history there is not a single instance of a new weapon being kept exclusively by any power or powers; sooner or later either the basic principles become generally known or parallel devices are invented. Before long the atomic bomb will follow the jet plane, the rocket bomb, radar, and the flame thrower into general circulation. We must not forget that we were not the only horse in the atomic derby; we just happened to finish first. The others will be along in due time.

Nor can we rely on destructive atomic energy to take care of itself. Already there is the tempting but dangerous notion to the effect that the atomic bomb is so horrible and the terror of retaliation so great that we may have seen the last of war. This is quasi-logical, but war is no respecter of logic, relative or absolute. And if history teaches us anything, it is that the possibility of war increases in direct proportion to the effectiveness of the instruments of war.

Far from banishing war, the atomic bomb will in itself constitute a cause of war. In the absence of world control as part of world government, it will create universal fear and suspicion. Each nation will live nervously from one moment to the next, not knowing whether the designs or ambitions of other nations might prompt them to attempt a lightning blow of obliteration. The ordinary, the inevitable differences among nations which might in themselves be susceptible of solution might now become the signals for direct action, lest the other nation get in the first and decisive blow. Since the science of warfare will no longer be dependent upon armies but will be waged by push buttons, releasing radio-controlled rocket planes, carrying cargoes of atomic explosives, the slightest suspicion may start all the push buttons going.

There is the argument, of course, that each nation will realize this; that is, that the first button might lead to universal catastrophe as all the other nations rush to their switchboards of annihilation. Here, too, there is the unwarranted presupposition of reason. In an atmosphere of high tension and suspicion, reason is an easy victim. Moreover, there will always be the feeling that one nation can escape though all the others may go down. What a temptation for the blitzkriegers!

No; there is no comfort to be derived from the war-is-now-too-horrible theory. There is one way and only one to achieve effective control of destructive atomic energy and that is through centralized world government. Not loose, informal organization. Not even through an international pool, or through an international policing agreement. A police force is no better than its laws, and there can be no laws without government. Finally, the potency of the weapon must dictate the potency of its control.

There is no need to discuss the historical reasons pointing to and arguing for world government. There is no need to talk of the difficulties in the way of world government. There is need only to ask whether we can afford to do without it. All other considerations become either secondary or inconsequential.

It would be comforting to know that the world has several generations in which it might be able to evolve naturally and progressively into a single governmental unit. In fact, it might seem that the Charter of the United Nations has made an adequate beginning in that direction, providing the machinery for revision which might lead within fifteen or twenty years to a real world structure. But the time factor has been shattered. We no longer have a leeway of fifteen or twenty years; whatever must be done must be done with an immediacy which is in keeping with the urgency. Once the basic peace settlements are arranged, the United Nations must convene again for an Atomic Age inventory, undertaking an over-all examination of the revolutionary changes in the world since its conference in San Francisco in the long-ago spring of 1945.

If all this sounds like headlong argument, posing methods or solutions which seem above the reach of mortal man, the answer must be that mortal man's reach was long enough apparently to push science and invention ahead by at least five hundred years during five years of experimentation on atomic energy. His ability to do this not only indicates that he can extend or over-extend himself when pressed, but emphasizes the need to do the same with government.

In meeting this need, man need not be frightened by the vastness of the differences which shall have to be accommodated within the world structure. We can agree with Macneile Dixon in *The Human Situation* that "Many are the races and many the temperaments. There are vehement and hotheaded men, selfless and conciliatory men. They display, varying as they do in appearance, talents, behavior, every type of unpredictable reaction to their surroundings. There are sybarites and ascetics, dreamers and bustling active men of affairs, clever and stupid, worldly and religious, mockers and mystics, pugnacious, loyal, cunning, treacherous, cheerful, and melancholy men. There are eagles among them, tigers, doves, and serpents. 'He was a comedian on the stage,' said the wife of a celebrated funny man, 'but a tragedian in the home.'" All these differences are in addition to those of ideology, politics, and geography.

And yet it is not in spite of these variations but because of them that man is now in need of a general amalgam. If those variations did not exist, if man's actions were uniform and uniformly predictable, then man would be as free of war as the vegetable kingdom. The differences point up the problem, not the problem the differences. The important question is not how great an obstacle the differences might be to the setting up of a closely knit world structure, but whether man will be in a better position to reconcile those differences within world government than without it.

Man must decide, moreover, what is more important—his differences or his similarities. If he chooses the former, he embarks on a path that will, paradoxically, destroy the differences and himself as well. If he chooses the latter, he shows a willingness to meet the responsibilities that go with maturity and conscience. Though heterogeneity is the basic manifestation of nature, as Spencer observed, a still greater manifestation is the ability of nature to create larger areas of homogeneity which act as a sort of rim to the spokes of the human wheel.

True, in making the jump to world government, man is taking a big chance. Not only does he have to create the first world authority, but he will have to make sure that this authority is wisely used. The world institution must be compatible with—indeed, must promote—free institutions. This challenge is not less important than the challenge to establish world government itself, for all through history there has been too great a contradiction between ideals and institutions and the forces which have taken over those ideals and institutions. Another way of saying this is that we have too often allowed the best ideas to fall into the hands of the worst men. There has not been a great ideal or idea which has not been perverted or exploited at one time or another by those who were looking for means to an end—the end being seldom compatible with the idea itself. The greatest idea ever to be taken up by the mind of man—Christianity—was for centuries violated and corrupted by its very administrators. Alexander's vision of a brotherhood of man fell victim to its own force—force based on might-makes-right. Mohammed dreamed of a universal religion based on the noblest of ethics, and taught that conversion by the sword was no conversion at all; yet his followers built an empire largely at the point of the sword. Passing from religion to politics, we have only to consider the immediate past. It was in the name of socialism and social progress that fascism came to Italy and Nazism to Germany.

That is the double nature of the challenge: to bring about world government and to keep it pure. It is a large order, perhaps the largest order man has had to meet in his 50,000-odd years on earth, but he himself has set up the conditions which have made the order necessary.

All these are the various mutations and adjustments needed in the expression of man's nature, in his way of life, his thinking, his economics, his education, his conditioning and orientation, and his concept of government in an Atomic Age. But if he rejects this, the first course, there is yet another way, an alternative to world government. This is the second course. Preposterous as this second course may seem, we describe it in all seriousness, for it is possible that through it man may find a way to stay alive—which is the central problem under consideration in this paper.

The second course is relatively simple. It requires that man destroy, carefully and completely, everything relating to science and civilization. Let him destroy all machines and the knowledge which can build or operate those machines. Let him raze his cities, smash his laboratories, dismantle his factories, tear down his universities and schools, burn his libraries, rip apart his art. Let him murder his scientists, his doctors, his teachers, his lawmakers, his mechanics, his merchants, and anyone who has anything to do with the machinery of knowledge or progress. Let him punish literacy by death. Let him abolish nations and set up the tribe as sovereign. In short, let him revert to his condition in society in 10,000 B.C. Thus emancipated from science, from progress, from government, from knowledge, from thought, he can be reasonably certain of safeguarding his existence on this planet.

This is the alternative to world government—if modern man wishes an alternative.

*—August 18, 1945*

# The Paralysis of Conscience

America has renounced isolation. We have done it officially. We have signed state papers committing us to world cooperation. We have at last become internationalist.

At least that is what we keep telling ourselves. But it is doubtful whether America has ever been more truly isolationist than at this moment. We are willing to dip our pens in the international inkwells, signing whatever documents have to be signed, but we have only a blank stare when the time comes to do the job described in the type above the signatures. We are internationalist, all right, on paper and in the form of the thing, but something strange happens when we have to match form with substance.

Pick up your newspapers. If you look often enough and hard enough, you may find reports about what is happening in the rest of the world. You may find reports on the real condition of man in A.D. 1945. You may find reports about the millions of homeless and sick and damned everywhere. You may find reports about European church groups which are bewildered and bitter over the failure of the United Nations Relief and Rehabilitation Administration to perform as so grandiosely advertised.

But all this accounts for only a small portion of the items in the newspapers. You will find interesting first-page reports about one of the biggest booms in America's history. You will find reports about traffic jams and crowded highways as gasoline rationing is lifted. You will find reports about other traffic jams—in front of vacation resorts, department stores, restaurants, and places of amusement. You will find reports about the glorious possibility that nylon stockings will be available before Christmas. You will find full-page advertisements competing for your attention and your dollar, inviting you to deplete new stocks on hand or on order of private airplanes, frozen-food freezers, imported linen, electric irons, platinum jewelry, refrigerators, washing machines, electric stoves, brass fireplace fixtures, electric heating pads, pressure cookers, feather-and-down pillows, steel-base sink cabinets, calf handbags, carpet sweepers, vitamins, chromium-plated bars, health lamps—and almost anything else that was withheld from a long-suffering public during the war years.

What does it mean to be internationalist? Does it mean that what happens elsewhere is none of our concern as long as we can sign a document now and then and send over a few bags of old clothing? Does it mean that millions of people must struggle to stay alive on a bare-subsistence level while we install our deep-freeze units and stock up on vitamin pills?

All over the world today people are wondering about America. The reservoir of good will that Wendell Willkie, in his *One World*, feared was running low has now almost run dry. How can it be otherwise when a nation that proclaims its devotion to world cooperation isolates itself morally and acts as though the main purpose of the war was to see how fast it could reconvert to new kitchen equipment? How can it be otherwise when we are so conscienceless about our own largesse, assuming that our good fortune and our advantages are as natural as the earth itself?

This moral isolation goes far beyond the disparity and the disproportion of wealth and welfare between us and the rest of the world. It involves our shocking failure thus far to accept the responsibility for moral leadership that was laid at our door at the end of the war. Our use of the atomic bomb turned that responsibility into an obligation. We possess the most hideously successful and most indiscriminate killer in history, but we have used it in a vacuum. We have not so far met the opportunity to equate the atomic bomb with an atomic solvent, to equate force with reason, stating to the peoples of the world the full implications of destructive atomic energy, as we understand them, and calling for the building of a real world structure for the greater welfare and security of all.

What is this atomic solvent? It is not a chemical compound or a gadget. It is world public opinion at work, a powerful solvent for the difficulties and differences that are keeping peoples apart. This could be the propitious moment, the grand moment, with the tremendous psychological advantages it offers at the end of a great war to take the moral leadership in bringing the atomic solvent into play. But that propitious moment is slipping. And the world is slipping, too, back into old systems of isolation and power politics and spheres of influence—the ovaries of war.

—*October 6, 1945*

## Sovereignty in an Atomic Age

The word "sovereignty" is a fortress in the mind. It creates powerful protective images. It crystallizes the idea of security.

We cling to these images, but the tragedy is that the fortress has paper walls. A tragedy, because we assume that national sovereignty still offers us security and freedom of national decision. A tragedy, because we assume it still means a guarantee of national independence, the right to get into war or stay out of it. We even debate the question of "surrendering" some of our sovereignty—as though we still have something to surrender. There is nothing left to surrender. There is only something to gain—the security provided by a common world sovereignty.

At the heart of sovereignty throughout history there has been security based on the advantage of geography or military might. For sovereignty has been inseparable from power. But by the end of World War I the validity of national sovereignty had sharply changed. The development of air power alone, apart from all other aspects of the world's inexorable trend toward close interrelationship, outdated traditional concepts of independence among nations. Yet we preferred to believe that there was no connection between a world being locked into a single piece and its over-all organization. Unfortunately, our unreadiness or unwillingness to see this connection did not cause the connection to disappear.

So much did this connection exist that it led to World War II. Despite six years of that new war, despite jet planes, rocket planes, despite the abrupt telescoping of a thousand years of human history in the release of atomic energy, despite the loss of millions of lives, we still act as though sovereignty can function as it did two thousand years ago.

Can it be that we do not realize that in an age of atomic energy and rocket planes the foundations of the old sovereignties have been shattered? That no longer, as Mr. Gerald Johnson has pointed out in these pages, is security to be found in armies and navies, however large and mighty? That no longer is there security based on size and size alone? That any nation, however small, with atomic energy, is potentially as powerful as any other nation, however large? That in an Atomic Age all nations are now directly accessible to each other—for better or worse? That in the erasure of man-made barriers and boundaries all the peoples of the world stand virtually unarmed in the presence of one another? That they are at the mercy of one another, and shall have to devise a common security or suffer a common cataclysm? That the only really effective influence between peoples is such influence as they are able to exert morally, politically, ideologically upon each other? That the use of disproportionate wealth and abundance of resources by any nation, when applied for bargaining purposes, does not constitute influence but the type of coercion against which severe reaction is inevitable?

All these questions have been in the making for centuries, but the triumph over the invisible and mighty atom has given them an exactness and an immediacy about which there can be no mistake. The need for world government was clear long before August 6, 1945, but Hiroshima and Nagasaki raised that need to such dimensions that it can no longer be ignored. And in the glare brighter than sunlight produced by the assault of the atom, we have all the light we need with which to examine this new world that has come into being with such clicking abruptness. Thus examined, the old sovereignties are seen for what they are— vestigial obstructions in the circulatory system of the world.

Much of the attachment to old concepts of sovereignty, as well as the reluctance to face squarely its limitations in the modern world, grows out of apprehension over the control a world authority might have over the internal affairs of the individual state. There is the fear, for example, that the individual constitutions would be subject to central control. There is the fear that institutions built up over centuries would exist only at the pleasure and discretion of a superstate.

Natural and understandable though these concerns may be, they have their source in confusion over a distinction that should be made between world *sovereignty* and state *jurisdiction.* A common world sovereignty would mean that no state could act unilaterally in its foreign affairs. It would mean that no state could have the instruments of power to aggress against other states. It would mean that no state could withdraw from the central authority as a method of achieving its aims. But it would *not* mean that the individual state would lose its *jurisdiction* over its internal affairs. It would *not* mean the arbitrary establishment of a uniform ideology all over the world. It would *not* mean the forcible imposition of nondemocratic systems on democratic states, any more than it would mean the forcible imposition of democratic systems on nondemocratic states.

Although the idea of bestowing democracy on all other peoples throughout the world seems both magnanimous and attractive, the fact remains that democracy is not to be had just for the giving or the taking. It cannot be donated or imposed from without. It is an intricate and highly advanced mechanism capable of existing, like man himself, only under certain conditions. It depends not only on the love of freedom, but on the ability to carry the responsibilities of freedom. It requires enduring respect for numberless principles, not all of them incorporated into formal law. It requires adherence to the principle of majority rule with preservation of minority rights. It is as much a way of living and a philosophy of life as it is a form of political organization.

This does not mean, however, that peoples not now democratic must be restrained from moving toward democracy. Nor does it mean that the conditions under which democracy can come into being cannot be nurtured and developed. So far as a central authority is concerned, one way to help in that development can be by providing a greater external harmony that will permit a greater internal harmony.

In creating this higher sovereignty, we naturally wonder whether history has any advice to offer. History tells of two experiences worth our examination. The first happened in Greece more than two thousand years ago; the second happened in America a century and a half ago. Neither experience can properly be termed a parallel or a precise guide to the present. Strictly speaking, no precise guide to the present is to be found anywhere. Never before has the world known such a profound and sudden shock; never before has there been so little in the way of previous experience to build upon. But while we should not overstretch historical analogy, neither should we fail to take into account the operation of certain historical principles whose validity might seem to apply to our own time.

Early Greece—that is, the Greece of the pre-Christian era—was not a state but a bundle of states. Although geographically united, it was politically disunited, with trade rivalries and frequent wars. The need for one nation to rise out of all the small city-states was apparent to many Greek leaders, but no one city-state was willing to take the initiative in building a genuine, common sovereignty. Several leagues or confederations were attempted, but broke down because the strongest states arrogated supreme power to themselves. Moreover, leagues of nations were arrayed against each other within Greece itself, with small states in the south clustered around Sparta, and the small states in the north clustered around Athens. This struggle between Athens and Sparta, growing out of their inability to come together within a single governmental organization, cost Greek civilization its very life.

Greece's failure is worth noting because it illustrates the consequences of disunion for states within a related group. It is worth noting, too, because it served as one of the strongest arguments for a union of the states during the making of the American Constitution. Throughout the minutes of the Constitutional Convention, and throughout *The Federalist*, which interpreted and analyzed the work of the convention, we find frequent reference to the Greek experience.

The causes and the effects of the Greek failure, said *The Federalist*, "cannot be too highly colored, or too often exhibited. Every man who loves peace, every man who loves his country, every man who loves liberty, ought to have it ever before his eyes. . . ." Readers were told that if the Greeks had been "as wise as they were courageous," they would have transformed their loose and competing leagues into a real union. *The Federalist* believed that had such a union been formed after the war against Persia, when both Athens and Sparta were for once united in defense of Greece, there might never have been a Peloponnesian War culminating in the ruin of both states and in the decay of Greece itself. America, said *The Federalist*, should be the "broad and solid foundation of other edifices, not less magnificent, which will be equally permanent monuments of their errors."

There is a disposition to deny the value of America's success at international organization one hundred and sixty years ago because the states were supposedly so compact, so homogeneous, so closely knit in their cultural and political and economic patterns.

Yet a fact frequently overlooked is that the American Revolution did not create the United States. The United States were created largely through their differences, differences so intense that only a common sovereignty could prevent international anarchy within the American group.

Listen to Thomas Paine on the "homogeneous" quality of the colonial peoples at the time the international organization that is the United States was founded:

"If there is a country in the world where concord, according to common calculation, would be least expected, it is America. Made up, as it is, of people from different nations, accustomed to different forms and habits of government, speaking different languages, and more different in their modes of worship, it would appear that the union of such a people was impracticable. But by the simple operation of constructing government on the principles of society and the rights of man, every difficulty retires, and the parts are brought into cordial unison."

Paine's footnote to this paragraph indicates that the melting pot was not peculiar to a later period in American history. "That part of America," he said, "which is generally called New England, including New Hampshire, Massachusetts, Rhode Island, and Connecticut, is peopled chiefly by English descendants. In the state of New York about half are Dutch, the rest English, Scotch, and Irish. In New Jersey, a mixture of English and Dutch, with some Scotch and Irish. In Pennsylvania, about one-third are English, another third German, and the remainder Scotch and Irish, with some Swedes. The states to the southward have a greater proportion of English than the middle states, but in all of them there is a mixture and beside those enumerated, there are a considerable number of French, and some few of all the European nations, lying on the Coast."

Paine went on to point out that the American experience proved that diverse peoples did not have to be subjugated to be brought together, but that they could achieve common government through common consent. Government, he said, was not a "thing made up of mysteries," but a "national association acting on the principles of society."

In examining, therefore, the Greek and American experiences, we find one central point worth considering in relation to the problem before us today: states within a related group must live as one or suffer as many. A corollary is that the differences among peoples are not a deterrent in meeting the need for over-all government, but actually both a precondition and a basic reason behind the need.

What validity does this have for the world today? First, do the nations of the world belong to a related group? If so, how and to what extent?

The world has at last become a geographic unit, if we measure geographic units not according to absolute size but according to access and proximity. All peoples are members of this related group, just as the thirteen American colonies belonged to a related group, and just as the city-states of Greece belonged to a related group. The extent of this relationship need only be measured by the direct access nations have to each other for purposes of war. And the consequences of disunion are as applicable to the world group today as they were to individual groupings of states in the past. The unorganized geographic units of the past have given way to the unorganized unit of the present. It is a unit without unity, an order without any order.

In a world where it takes less time to get from New York to Chungking than it took to get from New York to Philadelphia in 1787, the nature and extent of this geographic entity become apparent. All natural distances and barriers vanish. Never before in history has the phrase, the human family, had such a precise meaning. This much all of us—American, European, African, Asiatic, Australian—have in common: Whether we like it or not, we have been brought together or thrust together as members of a world unit, albeit an unorganized world unit. Within that unit, to be sure, are divisions and subdivisions, but they are all heavily interdependent. There is little point in musing or speculating whether this unit is desirable or whether it deserves our support. The fact is that it exists.

Here we must meet the argument that, even though the world may be a geographic unit, it is too large, too unwieldy, for the creation and operation of a governmental unit. But size alone does not limit the area in which government can function. Unwieldiness is entirely relative to the instruments of control. For harmony among states depends upon relationships; and relationships among states depend upon law and respect for law.

No less an authority on international organization than *The Federalist* tells us that "the larger the society, provided it be within a practical sphere, the more duly capable will it be of self-government." By "practical," *The Federalist* meant both necessity and workability. Thus a state could be as large as the need behind it, as long as it possessed effective machinery for its administration. And two thousand years before *The Federalist* Aristotle considered the limitations upon the size of a state and decided that it could be determined by the range of a man's voice. Accessibility seemed to Aristotle to be the prime requisite of a governmental unit. According to this definition, radio has converted the entire world into a small enclosure capable of central government. But radio is only one of the instruments available for drawing the peoples of the world together under a common sovereignty. The revolution in communication and transportation can give them a practicable mutuality such as even the people of any one nation a hundred or more years ago never knew among themselves.

This mutuality—a mutuality built on present and future needs—is more important than physical dimensions. It is more important than differences and difficulties. It is important to whatever extent the survival of the human race is important.

—*October 13, 1945*

# We're on Dizzy's Side

Right off the bat, we've got our money on Dizzy Dean to win his fight with the English teachers who are trying to throw him off the air as a play-by-play baseball announcer.

In case this blistering struggle may have escaped you in the general profusion of minor matters such as atomic energy, the O.P.A., and the Big Four disagreement over Germany, we are glad to sketch in the general background.

Of course you remember Dizzy Dean. He was an Arkansas cotton picker who came up to the Big Leagues some fifteen years ago to pitch for the St. Louis Cardinals, and a sweet pitcher he was, too. He had the strongest arm since Iron Man McGinnity and kept proving it by taking his turn on the mound almost every other day. He was supposed to be as fast as Walter Johnson and though he couldn't curve them or mix them up as did the great Matty, his assortment was better than most. The Cardinals waltzed into several National League pennants on the strength of his hurling.

Now the Ol' Diz had much more than just a fancy arm. He had the best-lubricated and most frequently used voice apparatus the national pastime has ever known. It was said that he developed his decibels down in Arkansas as a hog caller; and the loudspeaker system didn't exist that couldn't be out-thundered by the mighty Diz—with or without cupped hands. His disputes with umpires were not monologues—no umpire's dispute ever is—but from where they sat in the bleachers the customers could quite easily hear Diz's side of it.

But all studies of Diz as a human sound track would quickly reveal that his windpipe was less important than his glottis. The range, pitch, and volume were overshadowed by the actual formations of the sounds. It was what Diz said that really attracted attention. And no one ever accused him of burdening his auditors by changing his script. Diz was strictly a broken-record orator, and the consistent message he kept delivering to the world reflected his profound conviction that he was the best baseball player who ever lived.

And when there suddenly appeared on the scene another pitching Dean—brother Paul, just as audible, invariable, and insistent—the national pastime knew that lightning could strike twice. But Diz enjoyed seniority whenever they were together and made all public announcements. "Me and Paul," he would allow as how at the beginning of every season, "me and Paul will win fifty games for the Cards this year."

And they usually did, even though Diz sometimes had to win twice as many games as Paul in order to do it. Paul's throat muscles may have been as well developed as Dizzy's but right there the family baseball resemblance ceased. After a few years—as was inevitable—Paul was shipped to the minors, corrugated vocal cords and glass arm and all. But Brother Diz kept on going in the big time, piling up the victories week after week and sometimes day after day—a popular figure with the fans, not in spite of his pneumatic-drill proclamations but because of them.

When you watched Diz, you could forgive him for anything. You were attracted by the graceful rhythm of his pitching motion: the long, majestic sweep of his arm as he prepared to let the ball fly; the poised, calm alertness after the pitch. That was what really counted, and you knew it when batter after batter swung ineptly at pitches they couldn't even see. And even when Diz's laryngorrhea became particularly bad, you charitably thought of the thirteen strike-outs the day before and felt very warm in your heart toward him indeed.

But—to paraphrase Mr. G. B. Shaw—some statistically certain accidents caught up with Dizzy Dean. He always did like to bat and run the bases, and once, in a world series game against Detroit, he got on base as a pinch hitter. Racing down to second base, he was felled by a swiftly re-layed throw that caught him squarely in the back of his neck. He shook that long head of his, laughed or seemed as though he were trying to laugh it off, and went right on playing. Later, they discovered that Diz had been out cold on his feet but didn't know it. A year or two later, in an all-star game, as we remember it, he seriously injured his right foot trying to slide in an attempted steal. Diz needed that foot to step into that long, pitching motion of his. No longer could he have the vital follow-through.

But Diz didn't want to say good-by to baseball. His voice was unimpaired, which meant to him that practically half his baseball assets were intact. After a few short years out of the limelight, he put these assets to work by becoming the announcer for radio broadcasts of the St. Louis Cardinals' and Browns' ball games.

Never before in history have man and machine been so perfectly wedded to each other as Diz and his microphone. The fact that he could be heard even beyond the impressive range of his own voice seemed like a custom-made miracle. He became possessed of such power as he had never known when he had been laboring out there on the hill under a St.

Louis tropical sun. Now he could cuss out umpires, call the turn on strategy, relieve himself of choice descriptions, and, in general, have the time of his life. Radio listeners, too, became inordinately fond of Diz; he sounded like a combination of Bob Burns, Red Barber, and the kid next door. They liked his language—some of it authentic American baseballese, but most of it just plain Dizzy Dean. "I wished the umps adden't done that," he said ruefully when he didn't agree with a called third strike. "That batta shooda walked on accounta he was right in waitin' it out." Or: "The runner just slud inter third safely, but he was awmost throwed out, the lucky stiff." Or: "Just look how calmly and confidentally the batter is standing up down there next to the plate." Or: "The side is out and the runners are left at their respectable bases."

And the listening customers loved it. They knew just what Dizzy meant when he said that the batter was a-sendin' a tall can o' corn out into center, or when the runner couldn't get his tail out of the way of a hit-and-run play. The customers loved it, that is, except for the English teachers. Last week it was learned that some of them had carried the case against Dizzy to the Federal Communications Commission. They protested that Mr. Dean was an unquenchable and bottomless source of some of the most egregious errors in grammar and syntax that had ever been given wavelength frequency. They argued that their students were suffering because of the broadcasts, and demanded that Mr. Dean's franchise or whatever it was that enabled him to be heard be discontinued.

So far, no word has come from the Federal Communications Commission. Dizzy knows about the episode but seems to be taking it in his stride. "Maybe I am butcherin' up the English language a little," he is quoted by the Associated Press as saying. "Well, all I gotta say is that when me and Paul and Pa was pickin' cotton in Arkansas, we didn't have no chance to go to school much. But I'm glad that kids are gettin' that chance today."

The editors of the *Saturday Review* take their stand with Dizzy. Anyone—young or old—who is interested enough in baseball to tune in on Dizzy's broadcasts has already heard just as bad or worse treatment of the American language from his general contact with the sport, either on the sand lot fields or on the side lines. Abuse of English is the standard occupational disease of the national pastime—a disease which, if cured, would do irreparable damage to the patient. Not a small part of the vigor of the American language comes from our sports; and we are sure we can count on Henry Mencken to join with us in a holy crusade to put Dizzy back on the air should the Missouri teachers succeed in their efforts at grammatical decontamination of the baseball broadcasts. But we have a hunch that the teachers won't get to first base.

—*August 3, 1946*

# Hating War Is Not Enough

There is an unconnected and unfinished quality about much of the recent literature on the war. Too many books and poems are apparently written out of the conviction that all that is needed to end war is to describe it, to make people uncomfortable when they read about it. As after World War I there is under way a tremendous artistic outpouring against the horrors of war. You pick up *War Is No Damn Good*, by R. Osborn, and see page after page of bitter, searing drawings—raw satire and commentary on the futility of authorized mass murder. You pick up *Casualty*, by Robert Lowry, and read of convulsive misery and death in battle and behind the lines. You read a new poem by Alfred Kreymborg— eloquent, powerful, piercing—showing war as a naked and festering corpse.

You read all this, and you are moved. But there is nothing new about it, nothing that you haven't read before, nothing that hasn't already been said with as much or more energy and passion. From Homer to Hemingway there is a solid carpet of books describing war, in Tolstoy's phrase, as "a terrible, an atrocious thing." If there is any field of human error that has been adequately mirrored and condemned in the world's literature, it is war.

But it is not for want of originality that we are concerned over the direction being taken by the current anti-war novels and poems. Restatement and reiteration of valid themes are a legitimate and essential function of literature. Our complaint is rather that it is not enough to generate and intensify a hate of war in order to end war. It is not enough to shudder over word or line pictures of bloated bodies floating up on a beach, or of maggoted corpses piled up like cordwood. All the poetic fervor in the world against war will not abolish war if men do not understand how wars begin and how peace must be made. Indeed, it has happened that a sense of horror alone may actually be part of a drift toward war. Never before in history was there such a grandiose campaign to make people literate about the horrors of war as existed in this country during the period from 1919 to 1939. Hemingway, Dos Passos, and Remarque were only a few of the novelists who contributed to what amounted to a national conviction that if only we could squirm enough, we would never again have to fight. Almost every magazine carried, as a public service, advertisements of World Peaceways with its driving messages on the insanity of war.

But the war came anyway, not only in spite of our anti-war literature, but perhaps to some extent because of it. Apparently Mr. Hemingway and World Peaceways failed to convince Adolf Hitler. Or, if they convinced him of anything, it was that we were too busy hating war, too frightened of war itself, to give any thought or effort to stopping it.

Again, today, too many writers are viewing war as a thing apart, as an isolated phenomenon of horror—completely detached from causes and implications. There seems to be a slipping away in our memories of why and how Hitlerism happened and how it was that we were brought into the war. There is a revulsion against the symbols and the trappings of war, and once again the feeling is gaining ground that we have only to bury our weapons to preserve and ensure the peace.

But just getting the tools of war out of sight is not enough. Disarmament is not the answer. Neither is armament. The first offers no protection against aggression and may in fact incite it; the second tends to make war inevitable as the frictions generated by mounting competitive stockpiles of explosives become incendiary. The answer, if there is an answer, must lie in the direction of establishing an authority which takes away from nations, summarily and completely, not only the machinery of battle that can wage war, but the machinery of decision that can start a war.

Until such time as the United Nations is strengthened into an organization from which no state can withdraw or secede under any circumstances; until its decisions are made compulsory and binding; until it has authority over the individual in limited and well-defined areas relating to mutual security, such as atomic weapons and all weapons adapted to mass destruction—until then, we shall be without even the minimal equipment necessary to prevent war. Such equipment will not automatically destroy all of the roots of conflict, but it may at least dispose of the shoots until such time as we can build not merely a structure of precaution and prevention, but a structure of justice.

*—January 4, 1947*

# Wanted: Men to Make Catastrophes

For a demonstration of supercharged tempers set off by hair-trigger action, observe two New York City taxicab drivers whose cars are locked together with dented fenders as the result of a mutually lost race for an opening in heavy traffic. Observe how the insistent, violent honking of the other cars piled up in the snarl is all but blotted out as the human sound machine takes over. Observe not only the depth and carrying power of the decibels but the range and virtuosity of the language itself. Then observe how the chin-to-chin communication system is replaced by the more direct toe-to-toe method in which the participants soon become virtually indistinguishable not only from each other but from their rumpled fenders.

To observe this is to observe an event repeated so many times each day in New York as to become almost as symbolic of the town itself as Radio City, Grover Whalen's waxed mustache, or a news photo of the mayor arriving at the scene of a four-alarm fire at five in the morning to take personal charge.

But there was a brief moratorium on taxi tempers in New York last week. Peace drifted down from the heavens as though by divine dispensation. It was the day of the heavy snow—a snow so persistent that even the few surviving veterans of the "I-Remember-the-Blizzard-of-'88" Club were forced to disband in despair after almost sixty years of ceaseless and superior snickering at intervening snowstorms.

It was shortly before noon, and the town had not yet begun to close down. The streets were clogging rapidly and visibility was so poor you couldn't see a zebra at ten paces. Some of the cabs were still operating and I had been lucky enough to flag one down. As we branched off from Times Square, another cab turning into the same street but coming from an opposite direction hit us squarely port and aft. Both cars spun around like overwound toys and came to a stop with their rear wheels embedded in snow piles.

I got out cautiously and braced myself for the inevitable clash of sovereign egos. But none came. Instead, there was only the most touching mutual solicitude.

"Sorry, Mac," said the driver of the other cab with genuine concern. "My fault. Couldn't see nothin'."

"Couldn't see nothin' neither," my driver said self-consciously, as he inspected first a badly dented rear mudguard and then the position of the wheels in the snow pile. "Ain't this the damnedest snow? Oughta have my head examined for being out today. Shoulda stood in the garage but the boss said try it for a coupla hours but don't take any calls to Brooklyn."

"Yeah. Gonna pull in myself soon's I get ridda this call. Hope I didn't bang you up too much."

"Nah. I'd just like to see the boss try'n dock me for this one. I warned him this morning I wasn't gonna be responsible for no damage."

As the passenger of the other cab and I stared in disbelief and wonder the driver of my cab went to his trunk, took out a shovel and a couple of old burlap bags, and went over to help the other driver get his car free of the drift. He grunted and wheezed as he shoveled and shoved while the other driver, behind the wheel, synchronized his acceleration with the rhythm of rocking motion from behind. The chains finally found the friction they needed and set up a mighty whirring sound as the car shook itself free and moved forward.

After both cabs were in the clear, the drivers stood together in the cold chatting amiably, one having provided cigarettes, the other a light from his cupped hands. Their faces were wet and red, and the snow, by this time, had laid down a thick, hard crusting over their caps and coats. The men were talking shop—whether to turn up for work the next day, how deeply the storm would cut into their earnings, how many people offered a $5 bonus to be taken over the bridge to Brooklyn. As they turned around and walked to their cabs, the other driver called out: "S'long, Mac. See you again sometime. Look me up at Parmelee if you ever wanna switch. Name's Callahan. Just ask for Stump Callahan." My driver said, "Sure, Stumpy, sure. May take you up on it. I'm Irv Moscowitz. Metro Cab. G'bye."

That evening, people who lived in apartments next to each other for years but who hadn't exchanged a word during all that time were swapping not only butter and eggs and sandwiches but accounts of their terrifying and soul-shattering experiences during the day. In hotel lobbies throughout Manhattan, marooned commuters from Flatbush, Brooklyn, and Greenwich, Connecticut, who usually see one another only in newspaper caricatures, slept snugly if not cozily next to each other in hotel chairs and sofas. In the suburbs, all the ingredients that go towards making up the most rigid caste-system-within-a-caste-system on earth— one car vs. two cars vs. three cars; public school vs. private school; Cornell vs. Dartmouth vs. Princeton vs. Yale vs. Harvard, etc; one house servant vs. two house servants vs. three house servants, etc.; one guest room vs. two guest rooms vs. three guest rooms, etc.; first-generation wealth vs. second-generation wealth vs. third-generation wealth, etc.—all these ingredients were set aside as neighbors stopped sizing up each other with slide-rule eyes for the moment and got down to the business of forming snow-shoveling and rescue crews. Farther out toward the country, neighbors who lived in constant terror of being invited out to dinner by each other were pooling their jeeps and station wagons and heavy cars in order to open up their private roads and the public arteries—while their wives dug down into the deep-freeze units to build up a common food bank.

The only trouble with the storm was that it wasn't severe enough, didn't last long enough, didn't cover enough territory. For the world neighborhood is badly in need of a natural catastrophe that can pull it together. Little more than two years after the organized wreckage of one war came grinding to a halt, the momentum for another war has been gathering with such speed and force that the main question is no longer will it come, but when.

There was an idea two years ago that only a real world organization could keep the Great Neighborhood from being ripped apart and its peoples blasted from the skies by the ingenious discoveries of talented scientists. And the preamble to that organization was magnificent and inspiring, for it said that its purpose was to prevent the scourge of war. But when the nations of the Neighborhood came to the part of the document where they had to prove that they meant what they said in the preamble, they said nothing. No real rules of the game. No machinery. Nothing that could stick. Would Soviet Russia agree to set up real laws and then abide by them? Well, it would go along with the others for the ride but would have to retain for itself the right to approve any decision—no matter how many of the others were in the majority. How about the United States? Well, now, the United States was in a somewhat more favorable position, because it could count on the support of more nations than Russia, but no, thanks, the United States would like to insist, too, on going its own way when it wished. So both giant nations got together at least that once and agreed on a convenient way of disagreeing. The veto.

It didn't take very long for the two nations, knowing that each one suspected the other; knowing, too, that the other most certainly believed that war was inevitable in the long run and that therefore each had to prepare for anything that could happen in the short run; knowing, too, that any unfriendly nation anywhere in the world was a potential base of political and military action and that it therefore had to be protected or utilized or both—it didn't take very long for the two nations, under the circumstances, to find themselves in the identical position other nations have been in throughout history. Hamilton sized it up pretty well one hundred sixty years ago when he said that neighboring nations of equal power were natural enemies and that in the absence of either a common authority or a common danger they would compete unilaterally for security; but this required additional power, and since additional power threatened the security of the other, the thunder and the lightning were already in the making.

It is late, but not too late, to shine up the ideal of the common authority so that it will have real substance and meaning. But if that common authority is not to be, perhaps what is needed is a common danger. It brought us together once before and might do it again. And since there is no national power threatening the two giants, we may have to call upon nature to help do the job. Here is a real field for the scientists. They have been able to bend the skies to their will, first through flight and now by manufacturing weather. They have successfully prodded innocent and unsuspecting clouds into releasing rain and have now been able to manufacture snow by carefully seeding the sky with pellets of dry ice.

Let the scientists now turn all their inventiveness and resourcefulness into the making of a world-wide downpour or blizzard of such duration and dimensions as would enable the presiding occupants of the planet to develop some perspective on their common problems. If the common danger of another war seems too remote to the human species to cause it to take appropriate measures soon for the common safety, then let it be confronted with a type of danger here and now that gives it no choice except to work together.

Let the skies open up and speak for peace in a way that man can understand as plainly as he does the feel of cold or heat. Let the great deluge or the great blizzard come. Let the oceans swell and the rivers overflow their banks. Let the cities and the towns of the world be shut down, their power cut off, their roads blocked, their cars and their trains stalled, their food supply threatened. Let the rains and the snows continue until such time as man can comprehend that the common action and intelligence which he knows are required to meet the assault of water and ice are no less crucially required to prevent political catastrophes. And let the disaster continue until man decides finally what his future role on this planet is to be—a fawning, misshapen, hunted creature scratching away feebly at the parched skin of the earth for food and fuel after the last of the great wars, or a human being sharply aware that the common destiny and individual destiny are one and that the privilege of human existence carries with it the obligation of nobility. What is nobility? It is difficult to say. But whatever else it may be or not be, it is never without reason, courage, and conscience.

*—January 10, 1948*

# Bangling the Language

For some years the popular impression has prevailed that the English-American language has been steadily expanding in range, variety, and color. Every so often we see impressive lists of new words which, with the blessings of the lexicographers, have passed into the blood stream of the general vocabulary. But very little is said about the fact that many useful words are dying out each year—not because they lack value or vitality but because of increasingly lazy habits of writing and speaking.

For the fact remains that our language may actually be shrinking—despite the highly publicized stream of new recruits drawn regularly from slang, sports, entertainment, new trades, and current events. This shrinkage is represented by the loss of thousands of pithy, precise, essential words—words which, in a sort of Gresham's law applied to vocabulary, have been driven out over the years by flat, juiceless expressions. A recent edition of Shakespeare, for example, provided explanations for 2,400 words * which had long since passed out of general usage. True, a large

* The working vocabulary of the average high-school student has been estimated at 6,000 words.

# The Editorial Page, 1940–1966

number of these words deserved to die, either because they were replaced by sharper, more satisfying words, or because they were strictly a product of their times. But this still leaves a fair number of words which are as indispensable to the language today as they were when Shakespeare used them.

Could anyone think of a better word for defining someone who steals house servants out from under the unsuspecting noses of his best friends than the word *slockster?* This is not slang but a lost word from standard Anglo-Saxon English. Is there a better verb to describe the act of pushing and poking about in a crowd than the verb *to prog?* Is there any excuse for using the expression "petty liar" when the correct but forgotten word for it is *fibster?* Is there any single word in use today that can express more readily the ability of the fingers to enable the brain to recognize objects through touch alone than the lost word *felth?* And what shorter way of referring to an unweaned infant than the old word *suckerel?* Or *taverner* for tavern keeper? Or *nappy* for midday sleepiness?

If economy of expression is a virtue, then we have injured the language through the loss through disuse of such words as *flinders* (combining fragments and splinters); *janglesome* (combining nerve-racking and quarrelsome); *lanken* (combining leanness and lankiness); *keek* (combining peeping with slyness); *maffle* (combining stammering and blundering); *sloomy* (combining dullness, laziness, and sleepiness all at once).

Only sloominess in our thinking could be responsible for the fact that although we use the word "smattering" we have neglected the much more useful noun from which it is derived, *smatters,* to describe small matters or trifles. Similarly, we use the trite expression "smash it to smithereens," but overlook the word *smither,* an excellent way of describing a tiny fragment. The word "ungainly" is in common usage today but not so its affirmative opposite, *gainly,* a handy way of describing someone who is shapely, elegant, provocative. The word "same" has an equally useful variant, *samely,* which can be used instead of the phrase "always the same." We use "bereave," but what about *reave?* ("To *reave* the orphan of his patrimony"—Shakespeare's *Henry VI.*)

In the matter of precision, is there any one word that describes an attitude not so strong as the word dislike but stronger than the word indifferent? Yes; the word is *mislike.* Incidentally, there is a long list of other words which, combined with the prefix *mis,* make for an effective and lucid use of English. *Misproud*—proud for the wrong reason; *misgo*—arrive at the wrong place; *misexpense*—using money for the wrong purposes; *misbelieve*—to acquire mistaken convictions; *mislive*—to lead a wasted life; *misfare*—to have things turn out poorly, etc.

If one of the proofs of a virile language is its ability to generate verbs with striking power and pithiness, then we have been enfeebling English by neglecting such trenchant verbs as *to tolter*—move with slowness and heaviness; *to strome*—walk up and down while pondering some decision; *to rax*—reach and stretch at the same time; *to bangle*—fritter away an inheritance by carelessness and stupidity; *to gowl*—weep in anger rather than sorrow; *to spuddle*—assume pompous airs in the execution of a minor mission; *to stodge*—overstuff grotesquely; *to thrump*—bump into people in a crowd; *to slorp*—eat gluttonously and with monstrous sound effects.

Picturesque, time-saving expressions we have bangled over the years would include *barrel-fever* or *jug-bitten* to describe the disease of alcoholism, or, even more directly, the noun *bouse*, which combines souse and booze. *Knee-crooking* is probably the etymological ancestor of the expression "brown-nosing," so commonly used in the recent war to describe self-debasement in honeying up to a superior. *Forswat and forswunk* is a good phrase to describe someone who is grimy and sweaty after he emerges from a long day's toil in the coal pits. The word *fluttersome* could hardly be improved upon for a picture of someone gadding about at a party talking with much emotion and little sense. The victims of such flutterers would aptly be termed *tirelings*. Those who can converse only by arguing and snapping and by exhibiting their tempers would be described as *toitish*.

In no branch of language is there greater need for endless reinforcements than the uncomplimentary reference. Consider these lost gems: *gowk*—an open-mouthed fool; *jabbernowle*—a slow thinker and a bore; *chuff*—a Shakespearian favorite to describe someone who converts his extra wealth into extra chins; *mome*—someone not quite arrived at, but well on his way to, the status of a blockhead; *sumph*—the same man upon becoming a blockhead; *scroil*—a slick, mean fellow; *bummel*—a small-time tramp; *dumble*—short for dumbbell.

Is it too much to hope that words such as these may be restored to the language? Far from it; we have only to consider that a large number of words which had virtually disappeared toward the end of the nineteenth century have been since rediscovered and are in common use today: *deft, blurt, gab, kindle, glower, glamor, hotfoot, grub, malodorous, forbear, foreword, afterword, lush, reek, pixie, quash, runt, sheen, sag, sleuth, slick, snack, uncanny, tinsel, snarl, bolt, imp, tryste, sliver, slogan, kink, dump, croon, cleave, mole, monger.*

The value of new or rediscovered words is not that they enlarge one's choice in speaking or writing with greater precision, suppleness, color. Certainly no one wants to be *wordridden*, a lost but handy word describing a slave to words for words' sake. They used to tell the story, incidentally, about the English fishwife who looked on blandly when Daniel O'Connor accused her in court of being a perjurer, thief, strumpet, and procurer, but who put her foot down when he called her a parallelogram.

*—July 10, 1948*

# The Fifties

*Five years after the end of World War II, the American people were still in a crisis mood. This was not so much a matter of continuing scarcities, at home or abroad, as it was of uncertainty. An atomic armaments race had now formally begun; the feelings of solidarity or mutuality of purpose between the United States and the Soviet Union had long since been dissipated. The sense of insecurity that had dominated much of the thirties and forties had carried over to the fifties. And the central question in the minds of many people was whether ever again in their lifetimes they would live without fear of war. Prosperity was high and becoming higher, but there were tremors underneath.*

## Where Hell Begins

Gian-Carlo Menotti came up with an intriguing personal definition of hell a few weeks ago at New York's Town Hall. Mr. Menotti said that "hell begins on the day when God grants us a clear vision of all that we might have achieved, of all the gifts which we have wasted, of all that we might have done which we did not do. . . . For me, the conception of hell lies in two words: 'too late.'"

Another definition of hell is furnished by T. S. Eliot in that highly polished and meticulously written but frosty and detached play, *The Cocktail Party.* "What," asks the leading character, "is hell?" Then he proceeds to supply his own answer: "Hell is oneself. Hell is alone, the other figures in it merely projections. There is nothing to escape from and nothing to escape to. One is always alone." Later another character in Mr. Eliot's play supplements this conception of hell by picturing it as "the final desolation of solitude in the phantasmal world of imagination, shuffling memories, and desires."

It is a fascinating game, these personal definitions of hell. The other day I found myself playing this game in a somewhat inappropriate place —a strato-cruiser plane high up above the earth, high above a flooring of light-colored clouds. Here in a gleaming fairyland of skyscape and heaven I dwelled on hell.

I began by agreeing with Mr. Menotti. But even on his own terms I felt there was a hell more fiendish than the one he described. The torture that comes with a sudden vision or realization of squandered talent and unfulfilled creativeness is bad enough, but not nearly so bad as the torture of knowing what needs to be done, and not being able to dislodge the deep internal block that prevents it from being done. There is a locked door somewhere shutting the talent off from the will. It is not true that genius will always out: genius can decay and destroy itself in the rust of its own corrosive juices. The retrospective hell over the unachieved is a small oven compared to the living hell of coping with a mysterious inner vault which volition alone cannot unlock.

Mr. Eliot's hell has this much in common with Mr. Menotti's: both are intensely personal. At the core center of Mr. Eliot's Gehenna man is aware that he will never be able to shatter his loneliness. He discovers the "final desolation of solitude." Here, too, it seemed to me that there must be hotter and sharper thorns at hell's center than those that stab at the naked loneliness of man. My intensified hell begins where man actually worships his solitude—because he fears his fellow man. He shrinks from the sight of men because he detects cunning in their eyes, designs in their minds, violence in their hands. He contemplates his brothers and knows only primitive uncertainty. To be alone is his only refuge from the transience of their affections, the terror of their suspicions, the explosiveness of their antagonisms.

Even this section of hell has an inner circle where the anguish is further compounded. Here man attains the ultimate in fear: he fears himself. He believes he is imprisoned in his own body. He feels he is chained to qualities and impulses he can neither comprehend nor control. He is first baffled, then terrified, by his responses to situations which, in anticipation, he can measure against high principle but which, in reality, leave him bereft of any moral standard. He finds himself shackled to a tyranny more absolute than any he has known outside himself—an inner tyranny which enfeebles the conscience and dictates over it. In such a fear and in such a hell, self-hate is inevitable and indeed becomes a crusade.

There is yet another hell beyond the hell in which "one is always alone," in Mr. Eliot's phrase. It is a hell in which man succeeds in piercing his loneliness, succeeds in establishing his bond with the generality of men—only to discover a collective loneliness in the universe. The iron walls of the self may be torn down in a magnificent triumph of common purpose and common conscience as men discover they are but single cells in a larger and common body. But it is not enough. For hell begins where larger identification stops. No loneliness is as great as that which severs the society of man from identification with the totality of all life and all things.

We now come to hell's own hell. The torment experienced by those at this innermost station may not be easily described but at least the sufferers may be recognized. This is the hell of those who possess a natural idealism yet turn their backs on it; who know the meaning of nobility yet resist it; who can comprehend dignity yet shun it. Finally, it is the hell of those who have an awareness of what is meant by the gift of life, yet fail to justify it.

*—May 27, 1950*

# In Defense of a Writing Career

A few weeks ago a journalism senior visited the offices of the *Saturday Review* in New York. He was looking for an editorial job. He was hardly seated when he began to express serious doubts about the career he had selected and for which he had invested so many years of study.

"I like to write," he said. "My idea of heaven is a big back porch in the country overlooking a green valley, where I can squat in front of a typewriter and poke away till the end of time. Next to that I'd like a job on a magazine or in a book-publishing house. But it's no use. Either as a writer or editor the chance of breaking in is so slight that there's hardly any point trying. And I haven't got enough of that folding green paper to endow myself with my own back porch and let the rest of the world go hang."

This was a new twist. Generally, the journalism seniors stride into the *SRL* offices in the spring with more bounce and spirit than the second act of *La Bohême*. They may be detoured; they may be diverted; but they won't be discouraged and they won't be dismayed. They know exactly what they want to do and where they want to go. Yet here was a young man regretting that he had ever persuaded himself to make writing a career. He meant it, too. His face couldn't have been more emancipated from enthusiasm than if he had been dreaming of flying to Paris in a Constellation only to wake up and discover that all the time he was in a subway car stalled under the Hudson River in the tubes to Hoboken.

I was anxious to find out more about both the dream and the awakening. Why did he decide to take up journalism in the first place and what suddenly soured him? Why so great a gap between the original vision and the present disillusion?

He answered those questions fully and frankly. For almost two months he had devoted almost every hour of his spare time to visiting magazine and publishing offices, canvassing the possibilities of employment. He had also spoken to a number of prominent authors, soliciting their advice about the glories and perils of free-lance writing.

None of the national magazines wanted him, he said, although he was quite sure that at least a few of them really needed him. And, judging from what he observed, even if he could crack open a spot for himself at *Life* or *Time* or *Newsweek* or *Collier's* or the *Atlantic* or *Harper's*, he wasn't sure that it would be a wise thing to do. No possibility for advancement. The good jobs were all sewed up and would be for years to come. Most of the magazines were edited by a few men, who, despite the ulcers and anxiety neuroses of their calling, would probably live forever. Men such as Mr. Luce, Mr. Hibbs, Mr. Weeks, and Mr. Allen quite obviously weren't going to step down—at least not during the second half of the twentieth century, and those on the next echelon were all braced to resist any replacements or reinforcements for perhaps even longer.

On the news magazines the most you could hope for was perhaps breaking out of the open arena of the researchers, where men engage facts like toreadors do bulls, into the well-populated pen of the assistant editors. Here the facts are digested—sometimes passing into the blood stream of the magazine without leaving a trace. Salaries of the assistant editors are adequate though not spectacular. Above everyone, however, is the iron ceiling of anonymity. One's writing is as shorn of individuality and personality as toothpicks being processed out of a plank of wood. When the mountain labored it at least brought forth a live mouse; here you labor over your typewriter for a week and produce half of a dead overset galley—unsigned, of course.

Newspapers were out of the question, my young friend continued. All right, perhaps, as an opening gambit, just to get it out of your system so you could say you were a newspaperman once. A nice thing to have in your past but not in your future. True, you meet such interesting people, or so they say, but there's not much creative inspiration in the written material or the weekly pay check. Of course, my friend said, it is a different proposition if you are lucky enough to become a syndicated columnist, conjuring up your own assignments in various corners of the world. But it's obvious, he said, that heavy-pay jobs such as this are all filled.

What my friend wanted most of all to do, of course, was to write a novel. He had spoken to a number of prominent writers and had made something of a survey of the creative-writing field—all of which had convinced him that the way was practically barred to all but a few fortunate newcomers. He then proceeded to give me the results of his investigation, which showed that Norman Mailer's *The Naked and the Dead*, for example, had been rejected by a large number of publishers. And Betty Smith's *A Tree Grows in Brooklyn*. And Gertrude Diament's *Day of*

*Ophelia*. And Mildred Jordan's *One Red Rose Forever*, spurned by twenty-two. And Mika Waltari's *The Egyptian*, ignored by eleven.

Let us suppose, he said, that a young author sending in his first manuscript relied on a single publisher's judgment. Suppose he received a rejection slip the first time out. Wouldn't he be justified in thinking that the publisher knew more about writing than he did; and gave up his writing career right then and there? But even if he preserved his confidence in his own work, submitting his book to publisher after publisher, what was he to do if he received rejection slips from them all? Does anyone know how many Norman Mailers or Betty Smiths there might be whose manuscripts were turned down by all the publishers?

Putting all this together, the journalism senior concluded that he had made a serious error six years earlier when he had decided, on the basis of his editorship of the high-school paper, that he had a natural talent for a professional career as writer.

It was a bleak picture, I admitted, but an incomplete one. There were some facts worth considering which justified the choice of writing or editing as a career for anyone with a reasonable amount of talent. I agreed it's a difficult field to break into, but then, again, what profession isn't?

In talking to him about the magazine and publishing offices he had canvassed, for example, it became apparent that he had failed to apply any imagination to the problem before him. All he had done was to write for an appointment with a key person and then go in to present his credentials.

"What else was there to do?" he asked.

One thing he might have done, I replied, was to recognize that he had arranged a dead-end tour for himself. There was no reason to believe that his own cold application for employment would stand out in bold relief above the hundreds upon hundreds of other applications— all of them qualified young people. A job applicant ought to know the history of that publication, a great deal about its format and editorial content, something about the particular audience it is trying to reach, and what the problems seem to be in reaching it.

All this is pay-dirt knowledge. It's not easy to come by, but it's worth trying to get, for it can give an applicant a toe hold on an interview. Most good jobs don't open up; they are created. You create a job by presenting not only yourself but an idea that reveals your own knowledge of the publication and your understanding of its audience and its needs.

Next, for the newspaper business. First of all, let's modify the Hollywood stereotype somewhat. It isn't true that every newspaperman is comprehensively slouched—slouched hat, slouched shoulders, slouched smile, and slouched psyche. I've met some hard-bitten cynics among newspapermen, to be sure, but I've also met them in politics or teaching, for that matter. And I've met many newspapermen who take their profession seriously, give it the best they've got, are affirmative, idealistic, progressive. The pay doesn't begin to compare with that, say, of the corporation lawyer, but I've known a number of newspapermen who did fairly well by their families by using their spare time to good advantage in free-lance writing. Offhand, I know of at least six newspapermen now writing novels and perhaps three more writing nonfiction books, and, despite the high mortality of unsolicited manuscripts, I'd be willing to bet that the majority of them will have their works accepted and published.

This brings us to the final problem surveyed by my journalism-senior friend—in particular, writing a new book and getting it published. I can agree with him readily that the orphan of the publishing industry is the unsolicited-manuscript department. I believe it to be a fact that no other branch of a publisher's organization is as understaffed—qualitatively as well as quantitatively—as the unsolicited-manuscript department. The pay for first readers in many houses isn't much higher than for bookkeeper assistants or even for shipping clerks. Some publishers spend thousands of dollars in sending their editors on a tour around America, beating the brush for concealed literary talent, but are reluctant to spend more than a few dollars to appraise fully and competently such talent as may be found in their own mailbags. It has occasionally happened that an editor on tour will make the discovery of an exciting new manuscript which only the week before had been routinely shipped back with a form letter by his own firm. One publisher, on the occasion of the firm's anniversary, blandly announced in an advertisement that with only a single exception he had never accepted an unsolicited manuscript. It would have been interesting to get a box score on some of the important books that he happened to miss.

I am not completely unaware of the publisher's problem. When hundreds of book-length manuscripts are received each week—many of them looking more like tied-up bundles of left-over leaves from last fall—it would put a publisher out of business if he had to maintain a highly qualified staff of readers who gave thorough consideration to every single manuscript. What has happened is that a sort of literary Gresham's Law has been in operation for many years, the bad manuscripts driving out the good.

At one time the biggest joy in a publisher's life was represented by the thrill of discovery in chancing across an unsolicited manuscript that heralded a new talent. But that was back in the days when a publisher's mail could fit on top of his own desk instead of requiring something in the order of a coalbin, as happens today. And that was before so much of the publisher's time was taken up with arrangements for reprint rights, motion-picture negotiations, correspondence with bookstores, and other business matters—to say nothing of the care and spoon-feeding of authors.

Some publishers have long since recognized this problem and their own responsibility in meeting it. In most cases they have worked out something of a triple-platoon system whereby the first shock wave of manuscripts is absorbed by a corps of readers who have authority to reject only the blatantly inadequate. All the others are passed along to somewhat more specialized readers, who make no final decisions themselves but who winnow out the worth-while books for the editors, who constitute the third platoon. It is an expensive system, if done by competent and well-paid people all along the line, but it does succeeed in filtering out, in many cases, the really deserving books, which, so far as the general public is concerned, would seem to be the main function of book publishing.

Meanwhile, the first novelist would do well to stay out of the bottomless pit that is the unsolicited-manuscript department. That is, to stay out if he can. At the very least, no manuscript ought to be submitted without the benefit of an advance letter to the publisher attempting to establish some contact on a responsible level and seeking some genuine expression of interest. The reply to such a letter is not, of course, conclusive, but its tone and responsiveness may serve as a guide. It is sound policy, moreover, to write to firms whose lists over the years reveal no prejudice against beginners.

It would be even better, of course, if the young novelist were able to obtain the backing of a recognized third party—perhaps a book reviewer or a teacher or another author who might be sufficiently interested to recommend a particular manuscript to a publisher. Strategically, this puts the young author in the happy position—if the plan works—of being courted. Of all the consummations in a writer's heaven most devoutly to be wished, none can quite compare with the postal ecstasy of opening a letter from an established publisher which begins: "Dear Mr. Smith: It has come to my attention that you have just written a book . . . ," etc., etc.

Perhaps the most meaningful and fruitful way of all to fashion a key to the literary kingdom is through such writing and study units as exist at such universities as Iowa, Michigan, Cornell, Alabama, and Stanford—although I doubt that there are more than a dozen really first-rate writing courses at the university level in the country. The men and women who head these workshops are known and respected in the publishing offices and are constantly pursued by publishers for promising names. These magistrates of writing talent have built up over the years a position of respect and importance.

Finally, there are the various literary awards, of which the Avery Hopwood Awards in creative writing occupy such an important place. There are fifty-three local, regional, and national writing prizes and distinctions of one sort or another—many of which lead to publication. The value of these contests, however, is represented not only by the prizes themselves, but by the fact that a manuscript generally receives a much more careful and competent reading than in the ordinary course of submission through the unsolicited-manuscript channels. Leading national publishers, such as Harper or Dodd, Mead or Houghton Mifflin or Farrar, Straus, accept many manuscripts for publication out of their prize-contest hoppers in addition to the winners.

All in all, I told my young friend that anyone with ability who selects writing as a career today need not fear that all the doors are shut or that once inside there is no place to go. The difficulties are real but they are not insuperable so long as there is a reasonable degree of familiarity with what not to do and a fair amount of ingenuity in pursuing alternatives.

Writing as a career is a good life and a rewarding one. It represents a continuing challenge. Each writing project is like a difficult battle, requiring a skilled combination of strategy and tactics to accomplish a specific objective. It demands a mobilization of concentration—and concentration is or should be one of the higher gifts of human mental activity. It is the most agonizingly difficult work at times but, as John Mason Brown recently said about creative writing, it is the sweetest agony known to man. This is the one fatigue that produces inspiration, an exhaustion that exhilarates. Double-teaming the faculties of imagination and reasoning and keeping them coordinated and balanced are a tiring process, but you've got something to show for your efforts if you succeed. I suppose that was why Socrates liked to refer to himself as a literary midwife—someone who helped to bring ideas to birth out of laboring minds. As a master of cerebral obstetrics, Socrates also knew and respected the conditions necessary for the conception of ideas and recognizing the need for a proper period of germinating reflection.

With all these delights of the creative process it may seem extraneous and crass to mention the tangible inducements, but it may be said for the record that some people in the writing profession eat very well. Some authors even make as much money as their publishers, and a few of them a great deal more. True, there is a sort of Law of the Dominant Fraction these days by which the government can obtain the larger part, but retention of capital has always been the prime problem of authors anyway, with or without respect to taxes. A not-inconsiderable advantage is also afforded by the fact that this is one profession in which one can take a trip to Paris or Switzerland or the Riviera or the Antarctic, for that matter, for the purpose of obtaining material and vital repose for one's next book and be able to charge all the costs of this soul-stretching safari up to deductible business expenses.

Apart from all these reasons—biological, philosophical, materialistic—

in favor of a writing career, there is yet another reason as significant as it is compelling. That prime reason is that there is great need in America today for new writers. I am not thinking here of a technical shortage of supply, for production is still several light-years ahead of consumption. The need I am thinking of for new writers has to do with the type of book and voice America is hungering for today. That type of book will not be afraid to deal with great themes and great ideas. It will not be afraid to concern itself with the larger visions of which man in general and America in particular are capable, for America today is living far under its moral capacity as a nation. It will not be afraid to break away from the so-called hard-boiled school of writing which has made a counterfeit of realism precisely because it ignores the more meaningful aspects of life.

This need of which I speak has come about because too many writers have been writing out of their egos instead of their consciences; because too many of them have been preoccupied with human neuroses to the virtual exclusion of human nobility; because too many of them, in their desire to avoid sentimentality, have divorced themselves from honest sentiment and honest emotion. Indeed, we have been passing through what later historians may regard as the Dry-Eyed Period of American Literature. Beneath the hard and shiny surface of the school of the supersophisticated there is no blood or bones, merely a slice of life too thin to have meaning. Instead of reaching for the grand themes that can give literature the epic quality it deserves, too many writers have been trying to cut the novel down to the size of psychiatric case histories.

Beyond this is the need for writers who can restore to writing its powerful tradition of leadership in crisis. Most of the great tests in human history have produced great writers who acknowledged a special responsibility to their times. They defined the issues, recognized the values at stake, and dramatized the nature of the challenge. Today, in the absence of vital moral leadership on the official world level, it is more important than ever that writers see themselves as representatives of the human community. For the central issue facing the world today is not the state of this nation or that nation, but the condition of man. That higher level today needs its champions as it never did before. There is no more essential and nobler task for writers—established writers, new writers, aspiring writers—than to regard themselves as spokesmen for human destiny.

*—June 17, 1950*

# Save the Libraries

One of the world's richest storehouses of cultural treasures before it was destroyed by the bombs in World War II was The Zwinger, of Dresden. The Zwinger was a Versailles-like palace dedicated to the preservation of the glories of the creative spirit in man.

One thing about The Zwinger has always intrigued me. Its name. The Zwinger, literally, is a general name for a prison or place of confinement. I have never been able to make up my mind whether The Zwinger was named in anger or irony. Perhaps the latter; to invest such a place with the image of a prison may reflect a somewhat grim awareness of the fate of too many cultural repositories. Mere preservation of works of art is lifeless imprisonment; they become victims of solitary confinement under indefinite sentence.

This is not to say that the American general public fails to honor works of art or books. Indeed, what the American library suffers from today is excessive public veneration and insufficient public support. People bow from the bottom of their cerebral lobes as they pass a library's august columns; they speak in memorial-chapel whispers when they venture inside the far-from-pearly library gates; they observe an almost statuesque solemnity in front of the catalogue cards. There is plenty of hushed awe but very little of the welcome tinkle of silver.

As a result, the average American community today is not far from finding itself in a critical position with respect to its library facilities and services. When Andrew Carnegie established his nationwide community library endowment the population of the United States was about half what it is today. Meanwhile, in the last half century the educational level of America has had the most prodigious rise in human history, with respect to numbers and time. Assuming that there is some connection, however frighteningly slight at times, between education and books, it should be apparent that the American people have all but outgrown their present library facilities. Hundreds of new communities in the United States are without any public libraries at all. Meanwhile, many hundreds of established libraries are operating in structures badly in need of extensive repairs. Even without reference to the drastic need for expansion, existing equipment in many cases is fast approaching obsolescence. Budgets for new books, the librarians tell us, are only a fraction of what is required just to keep the library's shelves up to date. As for the new developments that properly fall within the sphere of the public library which likes to regard itself as a community center—such developments as documentary-film departments, music-recording departments, microfilming, etc.—only a small handful of public libraries in the country have been fortunate enough to be able to keep up with the times.

All these difficulties of the public library—particularly in the field of research—have added enormously to the burden of the college and university library. Increasingly, the university library has been called upon by the community and the region to meet a wide variety of needs which formerly could be handled locally. The time is not far off, it seems to me, when the university may be asked to take a direct and leading part in meeting the fast-approaching crisis in community library service. Whether this is done as an extension division of the university, supported by public funds, or on a cooperative basis by colleges and universities over a statewide or regional area, or in cooperation with existing public library facilities, are questions which may have different answers in different parts of the country.

One thing seems certain: public library service in the United States cannot carry on much longer without major reinforcements. Basically, however, the matter comes down to public support. Whether through direct taxation or as part of the community education budget or through voluntary contributions, the library in a democratic society must sooner or later be maintained on a democratic basis. It would be nice to suppose that there is another Andrew Carnegie somewhere getting ready to give $53 million for local libraries. It would be nice to suppose that there are dozens of John Jacob Astors and Samuel Tildens and James Lenoxes and Enoch Pratts sprinkled all over the United States waiting to establish the seven- and eight-figure endowments in every city and community to meet the new and enlarged needs. Yes, I suppose it would be nice to believe that all this might happen, but don't count on it. True, millions of dollars are still being made these days but I understand that not all of them are being retained.

It would be nice to assume, too, that every community may be as fortunate as Louisville, Kentucky, which boasts a mayor who spends almost as much time in the local library as he does in the city hall, who isn't afraid to run on a ticket of solid accomplishment in behalf of the public library, and who is lucky enough to have one of the nation's top librarians as his partner. But here again one must not count too soon on a literary revolution in politics sweeping the nation. It is more likely that most of the nation's mayors will continue to operate as of yore, largely unmarred and uncontaminated by contact with the local library institutions.

Such being the case, the issue rests squarely with the American people themselves. It is doubtful, however, that public support will be forthcoming unless the libraries—public and university both—do a better job of presenting their case to the public than has been done until now. A large Southern city recently polled its citizens to find out whether the city ought permanently to dispense with its public library. Happily, about 95 per cent of those polled promptly answered "no"—do not abolish the library. The next question concerned the use the person answering the poll had made or expected to make of the library. Unhappily, almost 90 per cent of those polled had never been in the library and never expected to be. There seemed to be something of a feeling that libraries were resting-places for the unemployed or shelters for the aged or homework stations for schoolchildren or high-ceilinged havens for highbrows who weren't out grappling with realities and meeting payrolls.

Even in such library-conscious cities, comparatively speaking, as Baltimore, Providence, and Cleveland, where the public libraries are municipal showplaces, seven out of ten people have never taken out a library card. The national average is considerably lower. There are countless millions of underprivileged Americans who have never stepped inside a public library. The big job is to get them to come in. No doubt the prospect of success in such a venture would give some of our librarians the shivers. But, as Milton was good enough to remind us, one of the most salutary gifts of human intelligence is that it can transform a threatened hell into a potential heaven. It may very well be that the nation's public libraries will have to pass through the purgatory of a public invasion before librarians can enjoy the paradise of reading rooms with sufficient candlepower, sufficient manpower, and sufficient stack space. The very act of bringing people in large numbers into the libraries will serve to acquaint the general public not only with the benefits of personal library affiliation but with the need for an up-to-date plant that can do full justice to the community. Moreover, if the future of the library in America depends mainly on general-citizen backing rather than individual endowments, it is doubtful whether such large-scale support is obtainable without large-scale participation.

Such a magnificent invasion opens up all sorts of opportunities for revamping some of the public attitudes toward libraries in particular and books in general. I am afraid that too many people regard the library as a place which furnishes all the answers and not enough people see it as a battleground of ideas. The dynamic library is more than a book repository or an exchange station or a fact-dispensing unit; it is a place where one can exercise one's own ideas, where he puts those ideas to the test. In short, I have in mind a headquarters for the cross-fertilization of ideas.

Now for the books themselves. I should like at this point to preach a dangerous and subversive gospel. The world of books has become far too static. Too many people accept uncritically what is said in books just because it is in print and between hard covers. There is too much acclaim for the great books and not enough of the continuing and searching examination and reappraisal of what books say, regardless of their reputation.

The easiest way to stifle progress is to go in for a sort of literary ancestor worship. One of the most intensive periods of stagnation in recorded history was in early medieval Europe, when even children could and would quote freely from Aristotle. That was when Aristotle was the sun in the scholar's heaven around which all knowledge revolved. Since Aristotle was the last word in scholarship, hardly anyone dared to utter any words of his own. The end result was that there were long generations of intellectual Aristotelian parrots who lived in Aristotelian cages and hatched Aristotelian eggs. No one would have been more shocked or disturbed at the spectacle than Aristotle himself, whose own method of teaching was to stimulate the spirit of free inquiry, concerned as he was with the development of a critical intelligence. And I suspect that Aristotle would have applauded Bacon for demonstrating that there were vast uncharted areas beyond Aristotle—large, fertile fields for creative thought and scholarship. We are indebted to Bacon, too, for showing us that the greatness of a book lies not only in its mastery of a subject but in its power to inspire better books on the same subject.

The library is not a shrine for the worship of books. It is not a temple where literary incense must be burned or where one's devotion to the bound book is expressed in ritual. A library, to modify the famous metaphor of Socrates, is the delivery room for the birth of ideas—a place where history comes to life.

Directly related to this need for the development of the critical faculty in reading is the need for continuing education in America on a high level. By continuing education I am thinking here not of a glorified naturalization course or delightful instructions in how to convert your hobby into a business—most hobbies have too much business in them anyway. What I have in mind is the fact that one of the biggest problems facing America today is not the education of children but the re-education of adults. Almost daily, man has heaped on his head and shoulders problems of such complexity and intensity that only a generation ago were denied even to his speculations. History is no longer waiting to be read; it saturates the air itself. Man has been projected as from the mouth of a cannon onto a world stage with no rehearsal in the part of the world citizen he is called upon to play. Moreover, he is bewildered by the multiplicity of players with their strange accents and even stranger actions. There is much he doesn't like about it and a great deal that he fears, and he hasn't been able to read far enough ahead in his lines to know how it is all going to turn out. All he knows is that he is involved beyond exemption or recall and that he must somehow keep the curtain from coming down.

To live at a time when the term "human destiny" is no longer a philosophical abstraction is to be confronted by the need to justify the uniqueness of man. Being alive today imposes an awesome responsibility—a responsibility to be measured in terms of transcendent values. As it concerns the American people, this responsibility means vital moral leadership on a world scale—if we are not to cancel out the meaning of our own history.

I do not mean to suggest that the university can by itself bring about the needed public awareness of the throbbing new changes that Americans—individually and collectively—are called upon to meet. What is required is a far-reaching mobilization of the moral and intellectual—no less than physical—resources of a democratic society. In such a mobilization, however, the American university has an important part to play. A new conception of adult education is needed, one which takes it out of the category of marginal importance in our national life and regards it as central in the over-all pattern of American education. First of all, I suppose we will have to shatter the myth that formal education, up through college, necessarily represents an adequate education. The need today is for continuity—continuity that will enable the individual to maintain some basic comprehension at least of a fast-changing world, that will enable him to avoid the feeling of helplessness that has swept over so many people who have thrown up their hands when confronted with the recurring crises of an atomic age and who no longer feel that as individuals they can exercise any influence or control over their own collective destiny.

I know this all sounds pretty cosmic but we live at a time when the cosmic has become the casual. Most importantly, we live at a time when the scholar has a greater responsibility for the protection and preservation of his works than ever before. It is not always true that a democracy in times of emergency has been able to provide leadership equal to crisis. The disintegration in Athens after the death of Pericles, when a tanner named Cleon attempted to cut the nation's problems down to his own size, is not the only example in history of a democracy which discovered that the responsibilities of leadership shifted from the nominal leaders to the people. I very much doubt that the type of moral leadership required in the world today is dramatically in evidence on an official level. This would seem to place a special responsibility and opportunity before those elements of our society which deal with the life of the mind and which recognize those transcendent values which give meaning and purpose to human existence.

I am not arguing here for the abolition of the ivory tower. My argument is that all towers are in jeopardy today—particularly the towers of the mind. The scholar or the poet or the artist or the scientist who is most concerned about creative work must recognize, surely, that he cannot turn his back on those conditions which alone make such creative work possible. The charred wrecks of the libraries or laboratories or studies of a hundred cities in Europe and Asia should offer additional stimulus, if stimulus is needed, in the direction of a grand mobilization of thought in behalf of the human situation.                    —*July 1, 1950*

# Woodrow Wilson and His Clients

Monday, September 25, is the thirty-first anniversary of one of the saddest and most costly days in American history. It was on that day that Woodrow Wilson made his last public speech. He was fighting to win over the American people to the cause of the League of Nations, for he was convinced that the war just ended would become merely the opening episode of a continuing tragedy if the nations failed to establish world law. And the biggest test was right here in America. Public opinion was slow in seeing the connection between world peace and world law. Traditionally, too, the American people had been accustomed to waiting for a problem to come to a boil before doing anything about it. Wilson's case rested on the need to anticipate crisis as the best means of crushing it.

Imagine the unutterable anguish of the man who had managed to convince millions of people all over the world of this, only to return home to find that leaders of the opposing political party had been capitalizing on the desire of Americans to forget about the war, forget about Europe, forget about involvements. And the campaign against the League was succeeding. Hence Wilson's decision to carry the fight for peace to the people. It was to be a tour that would attempt to crack open the isolationist heartland. The compressed schedule called for about one hundred speeches before audiences in almost every state stretching from Ohio to the West Coast—all in a few short weeks.

The best account of that trip—Wilson's last public trip—is to be found in a compelling and evocative book, *Woodrow Wilson as I Know Him*, by Joseph P. Tumulty, his confidant and friend who served as private secretary for eleven years. The book appeared in 1921 and is now out of print, but it is hoped that the publishers can be persuaded to bring out a new edition, for what it has to say is even more timely today than it was a generation ago.

Tumulty wrote that the small group around Wilson resisted the idea of the trip as soon as it became known. The President had returned from Europe showing the effects of his exertions. He was suffering from violent headaches and was easily fatigued. When an attempt was made to postpone the trip Wilson would have none of it. He told Tumulty that he knew he was "at the end of my tether," but insisted that a desperate effort had to be made to win over the American people in time.

"If the Treaty should be defeated," he said, "God only knows what would happen to the world as a result of it. In the presence of the great tragedy which now faces people everywhere, no decent man can count his own personal fortunes in the reckoning."

Tumulty suggested a compromise. Set aside one week in the tour for a rest at a quiet place in the Grand Canyon. Even this the President rejected. "This is a business trip, pure and simple," he insisted, "and the itinerary must not include a vacation of any kind."

The trip got under way. As it progressed, Wilson seemed somehow to find a magical second wind that enabled him to speak three, four, or even five times a day, seven days a week. Tumulty and the President's staff marveled at his ability to mask his fatigue while talking. Never had they heard him more eloquent or more convincing. Many of the talks were extemporaneous but they all reflected Wilson's great talent for clarity and precision of thought and expression.

And Wilson's message was getting across. It was hard work, but you could see the people responding to the call for sanity and the need to put decency to work in dealings among nations. There were hopes in the President's party that the encouraging early reactions would reach a crescendo by the time the tour ended. When the President spoke at Pueblo on September 25 he was more impassioned and effective than ever. It was a longer talk than usual, and it almost seemed that Wilson realized it might be his last. As he spoke, the audience was deeply moved by what he said but they were also moved by his frail appearance. It was easy to see that something was wrong; his face clearly showed the effects of the constant strain not only of the trip but of his labors overseas for the League.

He began his Pueblo talk by saying that he had come to speak in behalf of his clients. Those clients, he said, were the next generation. He wanted to be sure that the measures would be taken here and now that would make it unnecessary for that next generation to be sent on another war errand. He spoke of the hundreds of American mothers who had come up to grasp his hand during his trip—mothers whose sons had been killed in France. They had said, many of them, "God bless you, Mr. President."

"Why, my fellow citizens," he asked, "should they pray God to bless me? I advised the Congress of the United States to create the situation that led to the death of their sons. I ordered their sons overseas. I consented to their sons being put in the most difficult parts of the battle line, where death was certain, as in the impenetrable difficulties of the Argonne forest. Why should they weep upon my hand and call down the blessings of God upon me? They do so because they believe that their boys died for something that vastly transcends any of the immediate and palpable objects of the war. They believe that wrapped up with the liberty of the world is the continuous protection of that liberty by the concerted powers of all the civilized world.

"These men were crusaders. They were going forth to prove the might of justice and right, and all the world accepted them as crusaders. Their achievement has made all the world believe in America as it believes in no other nation in the modern world."

The President spoke of his visit to a hillside near Paris, at the cemetery of Suresnes, where American soldiers were buried. He then referred to the many men in the Congress and public life who were now opposing the creation of a world society which, if all nations joined in giving it real authority, might be able to crush the causes of war, and he said he wished these men could have been with him to see those graves.

"I wish," he said, "that they could feel the moral obligation that rests upon us not to go back on those boys, but to see the thing through, to see it through to the end and make good the redemption of the world. For nothing less depends upon this decision, nothing less than the liberation and salvation of the world.

"Now that the mists of this great question have cleared away, I believe that men will see the truth, eye to eye and face to face. There is one thing that the American people always rise to and extend their hand to, and that is the truth of justice and of liberty and of peace. We have accepted that truth and we are going to be led by it, and it is going to lead us, and through us the world, out into pastures of quietness and peace such as the world never dreamed of before."

As the President spoke, Tumulty looked around and could see the impact of his words. Hard-boiled newspapermen who had sat dry-eyed through the previous speeches were now visibly moved. He looked at Mrs. Wilson and saw tears in her eyes. The thousands of people in the large amphitheater were responding.

But the tour was never completed. Late that night, the night of the Pueblo speech, Dr. Grayson, the President's physician, summoned Tumulty. The President was seriously ill. His left side was paralyzed. One side of his face was limp and expressionless. His left arm and left leg failed to respond to stimulus. The searing headaches that were an old story throughout the tour now held the President's mind in a steel-like grip.

The Western trip was over. Woodrow Wilson had fought and lost.

For at least fifteen years Americans gave little thought to this defeat. All during the twenties and into the thirties it was fashionable to view Wilson kindly but somewhat skeptically. He was a great idealist, we said patronizingly, a great idealist who never realized we lived in a practical world. The word "impractical" became his epitaph.

But during World War II and, indeed, in the years immediately preceding the war, the realization grew that Wilson was perhaps the most practical man of his time, for he had addressed himself to the basic needs —both of America and the world. He spoke of ideals, certainly, for he believed that ideals were our natural assets and, in time of emergency, our finest weapons. Our failure to act on those ideals in time resulted in countless thousands of Woodrow Wilson's "clients" going to another war.

And what about Woodrow Wilson's ideals today? There is a United Nations, and the United States has accepted the responsibilities of membership. But is the United States exercising the type of leadership in the United Nations that can yet achieve world law? There are signs that we are, as in Korea. But there are also signs that the United States is still hypnotized by the false slogans of sovereignty, still willing to shelter the fallacy that world law can operate without compulsory obligations and commitments. We are reluctant to talk about the ideal of world citizenship, although it could be the most effective salient there is against Russian ideology. When we talk about ideals we mumble them somewhat incoherently, as though they are uncomfortable on our lips.

When Wilson spoke of ideals he was not self-conscious, he did not stammer, he was not apologetic. He was representing the strength of America as he understood it and as history had confirmed it. At the heart of his convictions was the belief that vision—vision with spaciousness and moral grandeur—is not only the solvent of potential danger but the natural setting for a human community at peace.

*—September 23, 1950*


# No


A number of the nation's leading thinkers came together recently at Columbia University and asked each other why democracy should be on the defensive today throughout the world. They tried to think through the problem of giving democracy more dynamism and magnetism in its appeal to the world's peoples. What democracy needs, many of them concluded, is a dynamic ideology of its own to combat fast-moving communism.

Julian Huxley, in a recent issue of *Harper's*, comes up with much the same answer. In the long run, he says, ideological weapons are more potent than physical ones.

"The East possesses a powerful weapon in the shape of revolutionary communism," he wrote. "But the West has as yet no single ideology which unites it—only a mixture of partial ideologies—such as various brands of religion and theology, the American way of life, parliamentary democracy, the cult of the common man, and the welfare state, which more or less cancel each other out in an eddy of confusion, instead of providing a single driving force."

This summons to all-out ideological warfare is not new. It has been a recurrent theme ever since Nazism went on the march seventeen years ago, attracting or absorbing millions of people. There has been a growing realization that it is not only the pushing power but the pulling power of totalitarianism that must be understood and combated. And today, with 800 million under Communist governments compared to 200 million only five years ago, there is greater concern than ever before over the need to shine up the democratic ideal so that its gleam can catch the eyes of people now being drawn the other way.

But democracy so far has not been able to generate a comparable movement. The answer perhaps is to be found in the nature of democracy itself. For democracy in its most fundamental sense is a denial of the very elements that go into the making of a "dynamic" ideology—if what we mean by a dynamic ideology is a clearly defined and ordered system of political theory and objectives.

Totalitarianism is made to order for an ideology that is readily and unambiguously described. Totalitarianism requires a continuing supply of pat theory and dogma which cannot be examined piece by piece but which must be accepted in a neatly tied bundle. Ideology also gives totalitarianism its forward thrust toward fixed aims, with a steam-roller approach to critical forces in its path or within itself. One of the essentials of democracy, however, is its own lack of dogma. Its principal strength is not in uniformity but in diversity. It is based on the inevitability of differences—differences of people themselves, differences of opinions and beliefs, differences in methods and objectives—but differences that have to compete for public favor in the open market place of ideas. This right to differences directly violates one of the central requirements of a "dynamic" ideology: the obligation to conform.

There is an even greater difficulty than this, however, in the way of creating a positive ideology for democracy. The principal values of democracy are negative. Basically, democracy is a philosophy of magnificent restraints. Those restraints operate primarily upon government itself. There is the logical belief that power is a natural invitation to tyranny, and that therefore the only safe repository of ultimate power is in the people themselves. Only the most rigorous system of checks and balances can protect the people against the natural tendency of government to conceal its errors and increase its prerogatives.

Thus democracy is the only political philosophy that entitles and enables the individual to say "no" to government—and get away with it. Indeed, the one word most expressive of democracy is "no." Democracy says "no" to the government that would invade the natural rights of the individual or the group. It says "no" to the government that would push people around, even though this may mean that the people can push the government around. The American Constitution is more specific concerning what shall *not* be part of the structure of government than it is concerning what shall. The words "no" or "not" are conspicuous in every article and section. Nowhere are those two words more in evidence than in most of the clauses of the Bill of Rights:

ARTICLE I. Congress shall make *no* law respecting an establishment of religion, or prohibiting the free exercise thereof; or abridging the freedom of speech or of the press; or the right of the people peaceably to assemble, and to petition the Government for a redress of grievances.

ARTICLE II. A well-regulated militia being necessary to the security of a free state, the right of the people to keep and bear arms shall *not* be infringed.

ARTICLE III. *No* soldier shall, in time of peace, be quartered in any house, without the consent of the owner, *nor* in the time of war, but in a manner to be prescribed by law.

ARTICLE IV. The right of the people to be secure in their persons, houses, papers, and effects, against unreasonable searches and seizures, shall *not* be violated, and *no* warrants shall issue, but upon probable cause, supported by oath or affirmation, and particularly describing the place to be searched, and the persons or things to be seized.

ARTICLE V. *No* person shall be held to answer for a capital, or otherwise infamous crime, unless on a presentment or indictment of a grand jury, except in cases arising in the land or naval forces, or in the militia, when in actual service in time of war or public danger; *nor* shall any person be subject for the same offense to be twice put in jeopardy of life or limb; *nor* shall be compelled in any criminal case to be a witness against himself, *nor* be deprived of life, liberty, or property, without due process of law; *nor* shall private property be taken for public use, without just compensation.

ARTICLE VI. In all criminal prosecutions, the accused shall enjoy the right to a speedy and public trial, by an impartial jury of the state and district wherein the crime shall have been committed, which district shall have been previously ascertained by law, and to be informed of the nature and cause of the accusation; to be confronted with the witnesses against him; to have compulsory process for obtaining witnesses in his favor, and to have the assistance of counsel for his defense.

ARTICLE VII. In suits at common law where the value in controversy shall exceed twenty dollars, the right of trial by jury shall be preserved, and *no* fact tried by a jury shall be otherwise re-examined in any court of the United States than according to the rules of the common law.

ARTICLE VIII. Excessive bail shall *not* be required, *nor* excessive fines imposed, *nor* cruel and unusual punishments inflicted.

ARTICLE IX. The enumeration in the Constitution, of certain rights, shall *not* be construed to deny or disparage others retained by the people.

ARTICLE X. The powers *not* delegated to the United States by the Constitution, *nor* prohibited by it to the States, are reserved to the States respectively, or to the people.

This is not to say that democracy lacks affirmative values. The affirmative values are many and varied, but they all rest on a solid bedrock of restraints upon government. It is no discredit to democracy to say that restraints are not the stuff of which a dynamic ideology is made—again using the word ideology in its combative sense. Totalitarian ideology can be superimposed upon a nation, since its principal ingredient is force. But free government can never be superimposed or exported or bought over or under the counter. It comes from within or it doesn't come at all. Because of this it is never exactly the same. Since the perfect democracy does not exist, there is no absolute yardstick for the measurement of a standardized democratic government. Some democracies are further developed than others and along different lines. When America talks democracy to the rest of the world, it talks about itself, the result being that what we say is a compound of political experience and a description of American civilization. When Britain talks about democracy, it brings in the stabilizing factor of monarchy and the economic reforms of democratic socialism. When Sweden talks about democracy, it bears the authentic imprint of Swedish history.

It would be difficult, however, to get all Americans to agree that the present British government has anything at all to do with democracy. Some of our British cousins entertain similar doubts about us. And even within the United States, democracy as practiced and defined, let us say, by Senator Joseph McCarthy, is hardly recognizable alongside that of Senator Estes Kefauver. But the biggest complication of all is presented by Soviet Russia. Communist propaganda is invariably carried out in the name of democracy, too. Russia doesn't refer to herself as a Communist totalitarian state but as a functioning democracy.

For all these reasons—and doubtless a great many more—it is not likely that democracy will develop a unified, clear-cut, "dynamic" ideology. Does this mean that the free world is helpless in the war of ideas against totalitarianism? Certainly not. Our assets are in diversity. Let's put them to work. We can capitalize on the lack of any packaged dogma. We can stand for the right of peoples to say "no" to the abuses of government. We can oppose the master-slave relationship whether between man and his government or between man and man. We can make it clear that we are not in the business of attempting to export democracy, but neither are we disinterested bystanders in the struggle of people to resist totalitarian encroachments. And we can measure democracy elsewhere not in exclusively American terms but in terms that bear some practical relationship to conditions under which democracy in the rest of the world has to come into being and sustain itself.

Finally, and most important of all, we can do a great deal to prove to the peoples of the world that we can fight the threat of communism at home without frenzy and foolishness and without imitating and adopting the worst features of the ideology we profess to loathe.

—*October 7, 1950*

# They Love Us for the Wrong Reasons

They love us for the wrong reasons. During the highly successful run of a recent musical revue in Rome, the most popular number was a skit showing how the Italians under Mussolini secretly manifested their friendship for the American people. The skit featured Italians snapping to attention with the fascist salute in the presence of government officials, then promptly switching to democratic symbolism the moment the officials turned their backs. The symbolism took the form of gaping mouths with jaws swinging loosely on their hinges. The right arms, now with the palms downward, described strange vertical gyrations.

The significance of this pro-democratic symbolism escaped me. I turned to a young Italian in the next seat and asked for the favor of an explanation.

"This scene shows that we Italians were really on your side during the war and that we preferred democracy to fascism," he said. "Just a moment ago you saw them do the fascist salute. Now that the officials have gone, you see the actors chewing gum like Americans and making motions with their arms as though they were bouncing your yo-yos."

For a moment the term "yo-yo" didn't register.

"Surely you must know," my companion explained. "The yo-yo is the colored wooden spool that climbs up and down a string."

It registered. I remembered. But my own jaw began to sag at the thought that this symbolism was immediately recognizable by all Italians in the theater as a quick way of representing American democracy.

"Did I say anything wrong?" asked the young man, apparently observing my bleak expression. He smiled as though to reassure me. "The act is meant to be favorable to America," he said winningly. "We think your gum-chewing and your yo-yos are quite charming, though we are not sure we understand it."

It may seem farfetched to attach any importance to an episode originating in a musical revue where anything goes. What should be taken seriously, however, is not only what happened on stage but what happened in the audience. To the Italians there was nothing grotesque or mystifying about the symbolism. The playwright and producers wanted a sharp and quick contrast between a fascist gesture and an American gesture that would catch on with the audience, and they succeeded. In so doing they demonstrated the unfortunate truth that many of the old stereotypes about the American people persist abroad. These stereotypes are damning even when used in an uncritical context.

In Hong Kong last year the proprietor of a combination newsstand-bookstore said he wished he could get more of our terror comic books and hot sex pulps.

"Nowhere in the world are there comics as good as yours," he said, as though he were conferring the ultimate praise on America. "But it is difficult, very difficult, to get enough of these comics from your country. I have to turn away many customers."

In Hiroshima some of the young folks proudly called my attention to what at the time was the city's only neon sign. It served as the blinking crown for a new night club. When lit it looked like an incandescent infection against the dimly lit background of a still-crippled city.

"It is wonderful, is it not?" said a girl of about nineteen. "It is just like the pictures we see in the American magazines. In the room downstairs they serve drinks and cocktails. Upstairs, we have a dance hall. We play only American music and we do only American dancing—the same as you do, ballroom dancing, jitterbugging, and jive.

"The young people are disturbed," she continued, "because some of the old-fashioned people are talking of getting rid of the night club or making it close earlier each night. They are very much tradition-minded, the older people. They are deeply shocked to see boys and girls dancing together and drinking together and staying out very late. But the older folks will never do anything more than talk about it. They know they are powerless. Now it is a new day for Japan with new ideas and new customs like you have in your great and powerful democracy. We like it this way. We like your freedoms."

Not far from the dance hall was a sign advertising two new motion pictures—one American, the other Japanese. Both ads looked as though they had come off the same assembly line. The sign on the top showed a golden-haired American beauty struggling to keep a clawing maniac from divesting her of the few remaining square inches of cloth which clung insecurely to her body. The companion sign at the bottom showed a Japanese gangster, a smoking revolver in his hands, making a fast getaway.

The older folks, I was told, keep their heads down when they pass these movie placards. They are bewildered by some of the aspects of the new order and have come to regard democracy not so much as a necessary revolution in thought and social and political conduct as a revolution in manners and morals, generally for the worse. If this was the phoenix of democracy rising from the atomic ashes of Hiroshima, and if it was not to be opposed, then at least the old folks could keep their heads down in their futility and bewilderment.

In more prosperous Tokyo, comparatively speaking, young girls wore tight sweaters, short skirts, and American-style shoes. They chewed gum, went dancing, liked hot music, preferred American movies and Japanese vaudeville to the traditional Kabuki theater. The old folks blinked at this, too, but rarely tried to assert the old authority.

In a dozen other places around the world it seemed clear that the first thing some people thought of when the subject of America came up was usually the last thing we would take pride in their thinking. It wasn't that they were being deliberately critical. As in the case of the Italian musical revue, they were actually sympathetic, and, indeed, were imitating us to prove it.

But to be loved or praised for the wrong reasons is a precarious business. It is too easy for that type of acceptance or admiration to be turned into contempt. Gum, jive, jazz, tight sweaters, padded bras, yo-yos, comic books, neon lights, dance halls, and chromium trim all are part of the American story but they are not the whole story. Certainly they are not the reinforced concrete foundations on which the meaning of America rests, or the solid base on which to build our relationships with other people.

The whole story of America—a story worth the telling and worth the understanding—begins with an idea. This idea is actually the political expression of a basic law of nature—that there is strength in diversity. According to this idea, America is a place where people can be themselves. It is a human experience rather than a purely national or cultural experience. It is built upon fabulous differences—religion, race, culture, customs, political thinking. These differences, or pluralism, as the sociologists call it, are actually the mortar that holds the nation together.

According to this idea, too, there is a constant and wonderful process of shuffling, so beautifully described in Edward Bellamy's *Looking Backward*. People are climbing up and down social and economic ladders, reaching for the stars most of the time and actually getting close some of the time. An immigrant shoemaker dies happy because his son is a world-famous surgeon. A wealthy industrialist dies unhappy because his son has dissipated the family fortune and disgraced the family name. A man whose grandparents fled from Europe to America becomes a Presidential candidate.

Sometimes things, like people, get all mixed up, and the nation has a collective headache, as during an election year. But this disorder somehow works, certainly much better than the orderly and immaculate elections in which all the X's are fitted into one row of neatly arranged squares and where there are no arguments over the counting of the ballots. Sometimes persons in advantageous positions stick their hands into the nation's pockets and keep them there too long. But at least the rascals can be hunted down in public. The government cannot insulate itself from the consequences of its own errors. Shocking as the corruption is, it is not nearly so shocking as having the corruption carried on by a government without watchdogs, without an opposition party hungry to return to power—hungry, too, to seize upon anything to embarrass the incumbents.

Another barrier to continuity in corruption are the reformers, who, it develops, have far more tenacity than the crooks. Indeed, American democracy sprouts reformers the way Italy sprouts opera singers. In many respects, as Lincoln Steffens once pointed out, the reformer is perhaps the most interesting product of all.

But for all this diversity, complexity, unconformity, and informality, there is a single pulsebeat to America. It's something that doesn't make the headlines, is seldom talked about, very rarely even defined. It's the individual's determination to keep the American combination alive. The reason for it is that the individual is convinced he has a better chance of finding his answers inside democracy than outside it. He knows that basically this is his show, and he would like to keep it that way—even though he spends most of his time complaining that he is politically helpless.

If our history lays any special charge upon us it is this: that we recognize America as a human community in which government and ideologies are subordinate to a free man's nobility or meanness, or the sum total of both. And it is for this that we should take pride in being known. It is always nice to be loved, but especially nice to be loved for the right reasons.

—*January 19, 1952*

# The Book Isn't Everything

"I had the advantage of being born at a time when the world was agitated by great movements, which have continued during my long life," Goethe once wrote. "I am a living witness of the Seven Years' War, the separation of America from England, the French Revolution, and the whole Napoleonic era, with the downfall of that hero, and the events which followed. Thus I have attained results and insights impossible to those who must learn all these things from books."

There was no lack of respect for the world of books in what Goethe said. He was part of that world, but he knew that no book could tell a man as much as he had to know in order to understand his own times. Great books could define the great principles, but they could never anticipate the startling and sometimes shattering variations of the conditions and circumstances that would test or illustrate the principles. Thomas Jefferson moved with as much assurance and pleasure in the literary kingdom as any American statesman in our history. Indeed, he described books as the most important capital that any professional man could have, and said that he himself "could not live without books." Yet, looking back on his own lifetime, he could write that his years in government taught him more than he could receive in a century of book reading. Emerson put it even more succinctly when he said, "Only so much do I know as I have lived." Carlyle, for all his veneration of books, knew that compared to life itself books were "a triviality." And John Locke regarded experience as the foundation and repository of all knowledge.

Not too much is known about the life or philosophy of Thucydides, but we do know he wrote his epic *History of the Peloponnesian War* out of the conviction that none of the old writers, not even Homer, could prepare a Greek citizen for comprehending that war, which he described as "the greatest movement yet known." Nothing in the literature or the annals of Hellas, he wrote, compared with living history. As for that illustrious contemporary of Thucydides—Socrates—we read in De Vesme's fine study that Socrates never allowed his knowledge or his reading to have priority over "the only touchstone at our disposal, the touchstone of experience."

There was nothing illogical or synthetic about the humility of these great bookmen in calling attention to the limitations of the book. No book can enable us to know everything that is to be known, or feel everything that is to be felt. A book is part of life, not a substitute for it. It is not a fit subject for worship or enshrinement. It loses its charm and much of its value when accepted uncritically. No one would have been more disturbed than Aristotle if he could have known of the excessive and harmful veneration that would be accorded his ideas in centuries to come. When his works became the last words of advance knowledge, such knowledge became neither advanced nor vital. Instead of using Aristotle as a powerful whetstone for sharpening the critical faculties in carving out ever larger areas of knowledge, the early medieval scholars allowed their thinking to be dulled by literary ancestor worship.

The particular occasion for these remarks is that there are signs here and there that some of us in the book world may be taking ourselves too seriously. In the effort to increase book reading some extravagant things are being said about books. It is made to appear that nothing is happening now that has not happened before, and that the only true approach to understanding is through books. We do neither service nor justice to books by imposing upon them such omnipotence and omniscience. Many of the answers we need today are not necessarily to be found between covers. There are elements of newness in the present dilemma of man that will not readily be disposed of by required reading or ready reference. Books are not slide rules or blueprints for furnishing automatic answers. What is needed is a mighty blend of the wisdom of the ages with fresh, razor-edged, analytical thought.

Another mistake made by many of us in the book world is to make books sound so confounded good for people that you can't blame them if they would rather die than read. Even goodness can be a crushing weight when it becomes compulsory. Or we will damn books by speaking of them with hushed awe. Overawed people are sometimes the most difficult to persuade.

So far as our friends the librarians are concerned, we are afraid they have overdone the virtues of silence. Contemplation and chaos don't go together, but there is altogether too much restraint in libraries. A place comes alive when people can laugh out loud, when friends can discuss the things that concern them, and when other people can eavesdrop without too much straining. Keep the reading rooms sealed off, but make the rest of the library hospitable to the sound of the human voice. Bookshelves are not a final resting place for the written word; they are or should be traffic centers of ideas—even when the traffic is noisy. The important thing is to get rid of the feeling that services for the dear departed are going on just across the hall.

A good book is a supple and yielding thing. It is meant to be argued with, challenged, marked up. It is a battleground for ideas and should show some evidence of a fight or at least some preliminary skirmishes. It is good for igniting minds—even if the resultant illumination shows it at a disadvantage. It achieves a noble function if it leads directly to the writing of a better book on the same subject. It can never replace needed action or thought, nor can it become the be-all and end-all of a balanced and productive life.

*—March 8, 1952*

## Inside Man, Outside Man

This is a rough guess about one of the reasons behind the decline in the popularity of the contemporary novel. Too many of the characters in modern fiction leave the reader with a feeling of indifference or distaste. A book demands an emotional investment. The reader must care deeply about what happens to the people he reads about. He wants them to spring to life from the printed page, but in too many instances he feels he has been associating with pasteboards. Identification with the odd lot of characters who parade through these books is more than a strain on the imagination; it is a vast imposition.

We have at hand two dozen novels published in recent months. An inventory of the principal characters shows only a few people interesting enough to be worth knowing in real life. Most of the others add up to a thoroughly uninspired collection of psychic misfits, self-gratifying emotional cripples, whopping cases of arrested social development, or glandularly abnormal folks constantly in search of new sensations. The reader feels no special claim on his affections or on his ability to get caught up in the intricate situations in which these characters find themselves.

For all these people, the reader's principal attitude is pity. Not compassion. Compassion is a somewhat higher quality of human response. It requires a certain mutualization of the emotions, a tug at the heart. But these characters are cold and seldom reach the heart; they do little to illumine the human spirit or the sense of largeness in man. There is little of the generating power that enables the individual to transcend himself—always a valuable and valid function of literature.

If this sounds like a call for a return to the heroic novel, we should say that it probably wouldn't be a bad idea, but that is not precisely what we are writing about here. We are not asking novelists to make virtuous giants out of all their characters, or to endow them with the attributes of disguised but glamorized Horatio Alger indomitables. We don't expect them to dispense with meanness, weakness, arrested development, neuroticism. A morality potboiler is still a potboiler; the tastelessness of the brew is not removed by a constant sprinkling of sugar to increase the palatability of unsavory characters.

Our complaint is on a different level. By way of leading up to it, we make the proposition that the deepest animations of man have to do with the perennial struggle inside him between good and evil, between his desire to cooperate and his drive to compete, between his altruism and selfishness, between his sources of inspiration and despair. The great novels and plays are not necessarily those which produce the noblest characters but those which produce the most convincing evidence of this inner struggle. The salutary doesn't always have to triumph over the unsalutary to make the characters authentic, any more than it does in real life, but at least the struggle is there and the reader responds to it.

Isn't it possible that the reason Hamlet has stimulated the writing of more books than any other character in the theater is because of this very dualism? Hamlet only seems to be all things to all men; what happens is that we see more things in ourselves as the result of seeing him. The interior battleground in Hamlet is far more exciting and meaningful than the national struggle which serves as the background of the play. Similarly, when Aristophanes put people on a stage, he juxtaposed them not for purposes of external conflict but in order to reveal the far more compelling drama within. Is there a play in our contemporary theater that more effectively gets at this inner drama than Shaw's *Heartbreak House*? When the final curtain comes down, the theatergoer is left staring—not at the stage but at his own psyche.

Now, the failure of the novelist to create real people—sympathetic or unsympathetic—can often be related to his failure to deal with the inner man. The flabbiness and essential dullness of his characters are the result not of unexciting plots or situations but of flimsy and often mechanical interior stuffings. Nothing is more pronounced in fiction than the reluctance to recognize and deal with the subjective struggle of good and evil. Perhaps this is the result of a distorted relativism; perhaps too many authors would regard considerations of subjective good and evil as horribly unscientific or unsophisticated or sentimental. One suspects that some authors would rather be found dead than caught in the act of shedding an honest tear. Thus they create characters who try to interest the reader through the unusual situations in which they are placed, or through the things they do, but only rarely through the things they feel or ponder about. They are generally buffeted about by circumstances; a problem is not a challenge but an ugly plot which can be solved only through an uglier counterplot. Insight or purpose flees before the compulsions of tight little egos. Along with this is the apparent notion that the only truly worth-while experience is that obtainable through self-gratification.

Our complaint, then, is directed at the apparently increasing tendency of authors to get outside rather than inside their characters. The outside man is a type; he depends upon the bizarreness of his actions to get by, and fails. The inside man, the creature of dualism, has universal substance and has only to make visible a part of the inner struggle in order to communicate with the reader. He is difficult to create but the ability to do so is what is meant by good writing. Unusual plots are a dime a dozen; interesting people in fiction, real people, are rare and represent the highest expression of the writer's art.

*—April 19, 1952*

# Confessions of a Miseducated Man

These notes are in the nature of a confession. It is the confession of a miseducated man.

I have become most aware of my lack of a proper education whenever I have had the chance to put it to the test. The test is a simple one: am I prepared to live in and comprehend a world in which there are 3 billion people? Not the world as it was in 1850 or 1900, for which my education might have been adequate, but the world today. And the best place to apply that test is outside the country—especially Asia or Africa.

Not that my education was a complete failure. It prepared me superbly for a bird's-eye view of the world. It taught me how to recognize easily and instantly the things that differentiate one place or one people from another. Geography had instructed me in differences of terrain, resources, and productivity. Comparative culture had instructed me in the differences of background and group interests. Anthropology had instructed me in the differences of facial bone structure, skin pigmentation, and general physical aspect. In short, my education protected me against surprise. I was not surprised at the fact that some people lived in mud huts and others in bamboo cottages on stilts; or that some used peat for fuel and others dung; or that some enjoyed music with a five-note scale and others with twelve; or that some people were vegetarian by religion and others by preference.

In those respects my education had been more than adequate. But what my education failed to do was to teach me that the principal significance of such differences was that they were largely without significance. The differences were all but obliterated by the similarities. My education had by-passed the similarities. It had failed to grasp and define the fact that beyond the differences are realities scarcely comprehended because of their shattering simplicity. And the simplest reality of all was that the human community was one—greater than any of its parts, greater than the separateness imposed by the nations, greater than the divergent faiths and allegiances or the depth and color of varying cultures. This larger unity was the most important central fact of our time—something on which people could build at a time when hope seemed misty, almost unreal.

As I write this, I have the feeling that my words fail to give vitality to the idea they seek to express. Indeed, the idea itself is a truism which all peoples readily acknowledge even if they do not act on it. Let me put it differently, then. In order to be at home anywhere in the world I had to forget the things I had been taught to remember. It turned out that my ability to get along with other peoples depended not so much upon my comprehension of the uniqueness of their way of life as upon my comprehension of the things we had in common. It was important to respect these differences, certainly, but to stop there was like clearing the ground without any idea of what was to be built on it. When you got through comparing notes, you discovered that you were both talking about the same neighborhood, i.e., this planet, and the conditions that made it congenial or hostile to human habitation.

Only a few years ago an education in differences fulfilled a specific if limited need. That was at a time when we thought of other places and peoples largely out of curiosity or in terms of exotic vacations. It was the mark of a rounded man to be well traveled and to know about the fabulous variations of human culture and behavior. But it wasn't the type of knowledge you had to live by and build on.

Then overnight came the great compression. Far-flung areas which had been secure in their remoteness suddenly became jammed together in a single arena. And all at once a new type of education became necessary, an education in liberation from tribalism. For tribalism had persisted from earliest times, though it had taken refined forms. The new education had to teach man the most difficult lesson of all: to look at someone any-where in the world and be able to recognize the image of himself. It had to be an education in self-recognition. The old emphasis upon superficial differences had to give way to education for mutuality and for citizenship in the human community.

In such an education we begin with the fact that the universe itself does not hold life cheaply. Life is a rare occurrence among the millions of galaxies and solar systems that occupy space. And in this particular solar system life occurs on only one planet. And on that one planet life takes millions of forms. Of all these countless forms of life, only one, the human species, possesses certain faculties in combination that give it supreme advantages over all the others. Among those faculties or gifts is a creative intelligence that enables man to reflect and anticipate, to en-compass past experience, and also to visualize future needs. There are endless other wondrous faculties the mechanisms of which are not yet within the understanding of their beneficiaries—the faculties of hope, conscience, appreciation of beauty, kinship, love, faith.

Viewed in planetary perspective, what counts is not that the thoughts of men lead them in different directions but that all men possess the capacity to think; not that they pursue different faiths but that they are capable of spiritual belief; not that they write and read different books but that they are capable of creating print and communicating in it across time and space; not that they enjoy different art and music but that some-thing in them enables them to respond deeply to forms and colors and ordered vibrations of sounds.

These basic lessons, then, would seek to provide a proper respect for man in the universe. Next in order would be instruction in the unity of man's needs. However friendly the universe may be to man, it has left the conditions of human existence precariously balanced. All men need oxygen, water, land, warmth, food. Remove any one of these and the unity of human needs is attacked and man with it. The next lesson would concern the human situation itself—how to use self-understanding in the cause of human welfare; how to control the engines created by man that threaten to alter the precarious balance on which life depends; how to create a peaceful society of the whole.

With such an education, it is possible that some nation or people may come forward not only with vital understanding but with the vital inspira-tion that men need no less than food. Leadership on this higher level does not require mountains of gold or thundering propaganda. It is concerned with human destiny; human destiny is the issue; people will respond.

—*May 10, 1952*

# The Garret and the Masterpiece

The creative artist needs help. He has always needed help. But he hasn't always received it. Some of the reasons for this grow out of three misconceptions concerning the creative arts in general and creative people in particular.

The first of these misconceptions is the one which says that the artist or writer or musician or independent scholar does not have to be supported because, if he has something in him that deserves to find expression, it will come out anyway. Related to this is the misconception that creative people work best under conditions of personal stress.

Over the years we have been in a position to observe the ways in which authors and artists work. We know of dozens of cases in which demonstrated creative ability has been dammed up waiting the proper conditions for release, but where the conditions never materialized. We know of young authors whose first books were lavishly praised but who never had the chance to develop or test their talent. We know of young artists whose early work won prizes in exhibitions but whose spirit was broken because they could not eat blue ribbons or cash favorable reviews. Many of these artists turned commercial "just to keep going." A few of them were able after several years to resume their careers as serious painters. Most of them, however, had their feelings of romance for painting so dimmed as the result of day-in-and-out pressures that they never did make the journey back. Nor can they be universally blamed. A society which venerates material success as a social and frequently as a moral yardstick cannot in good conscience blame the artist for mirroring those values.

In any event, we must scotch the fallacy that good artists, writers, musicians, or scholars are not affected by personal adversity. For every story of a famous artist who continued to work creatively despite hunger, sickness, and misery, there are countless instances of those who stopped working when they stopped eating. Cervantes might have done more if he hadn't been demoralized by hardship. Vondel, frequently referred to as the Dutch Shakespeare, carried on as long as he could despite intense privation, then gave up. Camoëns, the Portuguese poet, receiving a complaint that he had failed to deliver verses as promised, replied: "When I wrote verses while a young man, I had sufficent food, was a lover, and beloved by many friends and by the ladies. Then I felt poetical ardor. Now I have no spirits, no peace of mind." Camoëns's former servant tried to keep him alive by going out on the streets at night foraging and begging for food.

Balzac made money and had no trouble spending it. Whatever his personal inadequacy as a budget balancer, however, we do know that he worked poorly or not at all when unable to pay his bills. Rossini was accused of prostituting his vast talent for money. He made little effort to refute the charge; it takes money to live. Christopher Smart, like any number of his contemporaries, enjoyed the benefactions of a patron. When the patron died, Smart's pension dried up and none other was forthcoming. Like ordinary mortals, he cracked up under adverse circumstances, became institutionalized, and died at the age of forty-nine.

The poverty of Pierre Corneille has frequently been exaggerated. What is true, however, is that the eminent dramatist-poet occasionally suspended his work because he was in debt. It is said that Racine once found him in a state of acute hunger, reported the fact to Louis XIV, who only then sent Corneille enough money to get going again. Isaac Disraeli, who is authority for the story, also quotes from a petition to Parliament by the Marquis of Worcester during the reign of Charles II, asking for money to finance himself and to publish his *Centenary of Inventions*. The money was not granted and the account of the inventions was lost. There is reason to believe, says Disraeli, that inventions similar to the steam engine and telegraph were among them.

Perhaps only one other poet in English literature can match Spenser's gift for perfectionism in verse. Yet Spenser died, in Ben Jonson's words, "for lack of bread." True, he died under circumstances of political strife so great that the actual cause of his death may have been obscured. But there can be no doubt that his later years were robbed of productiveness because of poverty. As he himself wrote:

> Full little knowest thou, that hast not try'd,
> What Hell it is, in suing long to bide.

and:

> To fawn, to crouch, to wait, to ride, to run,
> To speed, to give, to want, to be undone.

What emerges from all this is not the determination of the artist to create despite all obstacles but the fact that the artist has frequently been hurt or diminished because of the bland assumption that an artist is a somewhat separate species capable of living indefinitely on art and adulation.

The second general misconception is that literature or music or art, if only it is good enough, will pay its own way through public acceptance.

The contemporary refutation of this fallacy is Gian-Carlo Menotti. He is now generally regarded as one of the most gifted young writers of serious music in America; yet his work, however excellent, has for the most part failed to pay its own way. *The Medium* and *The Telephone* did not pay their own way when first produced. It was only the intervention of a few sponsors who believed in Menotti that kept the operas going.

Hundreds of American writers, painters, and musicians have benefited from the grants of foundations, the most active in which in this particular field has been the Guggenheim. Out of all these grants has come an impressive number of artistic creations which do considerable credit to both artist and foundation. There is scarcely a first-rate publisher whose lists have not been enhanced through such works, many of which the publisher himself could not have afforded to underwrite. If we make the statement that these books would somehow have been written or published even without foundation support, we may be only partially right. And to the extent that we may be partially wrong, we would have been deprived of books and paintings and music and scholarship which we would regard as serious losses.

All of the foregoing is intended to suggest three things. First, that it is not necessarily true that the creative person can create with or without vitamins. Second, that not every work of art has been supported on its merits, if, indeed, it has been supported at all. Third, that certain forms of support for the artist are degrading, demoralizing, and debilitating. They harm not only the artist but the community at large. A good artist is a prism for refracting beauty and truth; he is to be supported not because it is thoughtful to keep people from being hungry—that is the function of charity or government—but because the human community cannot live fully or joyously unless its sense of beauty is exercised and proclaimed. It is the artist's job to deal with these things of beauty in order to provide not necessarily a joy forever but a touch of loveliness that will last as long as society's capacity for beauty will last.

This brings us to the next misconception detrimental to the humanities: That great art is something which by its very nature endures, is never lost, and therefore does not have to be specially supported or protected when it is first brought into being, assuming one is able to recognize it for the work of genius that it is.

We begin with the first part of this fallacy. We pay both honor and attention to the Greeks and the Romans, as we should, but we have so far mined only a fraction of the cultural treasures of those times. This is not to say that Plato, Aristotle, Thucydides et al. were a mere sampling of an Athenian constellation as yet far beyond our historical range finders. What it does mean is that genuine classical riches have been lost not only through carelessness but through ignorance. Juvenal, Persius, and Martial have fared well, but can we say the same of Livy or Cicero or Virgil or Horace or Sophocles or Aeschylus or Xenophon or Aristophanes? It was only the sheerest accident which made it possible for Cicero's *De Republica* to come to light. This key item of Cicero's essays had served as the base for a surprinting of a tract on the Psalms and was not discovered until 1823. Another valuable Cicero essay, *De Gloria,* spoken of so glowingly by Petrarch, may never come to light; its last known address was a nineteenth-century pawnshop. Let us not forget that Quintilian was discovered in a rubbish heap in a monastery of St. Gallo; that the original manuscript of Justinian's *Pandects* was discovered in Calabria by the Pisans; that the works of Agopard were about to be used to reinforce bindings in a bookbinder's shop in Lyon when they were accidentally discovered by Papirius Masson; and that one of the original Magna Chartas, with all its fancy seals and signatures, was discovered by Sir Robert Cotton, in one hand of a tailor, poised scissors in the other hand ready to cut into the parchment for use as measuring slips. Still other instances: The manuscript of Montaigne's *Journal of His Travels to Italy* was not published until many generations after it had been written, when it was finally uncovered in a worm-eaten coffer in Montaigne's former chateau. Lady Mary Wortley Montagu's *Letters* were lost by her lawyer in his own office. Some non-legal reason, no doubt. The propensity of lawyers, publishers, and editors for this sort of thing is a historic fact, as bewildered authors and their estates can attest. But one might as soon attempt to reform the solar system as set about reforming the desk habits of editors and lawyers.

And what of the countless hundreds of other manuscripts and early editions that have rotted in attics or trunks, or that were dumped or burned and whose very existence at one time was not even a matter of record? What about the books that died as manuscripts not because of lack of intrinsic worth but because a publisher may not have had the resources or the judgment or the imagination or the confidence to accept them? What about physical difficulties in the way of publishing books and keeping them alive?

Most importantly, what about the destruction of books or works of art for destruction's sake? Clarence Day to the contrary, a good book can die—through murder and, more especially, through neglect. So far as book burnings are concerned, where manuscripts or other copies are available, the books survive. But when the destroyer is able to burn the only existing copies, the books die. As a prime example of neglect, consider Alexandria. At one time Alexandria was the greatest literary and artistic city in the world. Whether with respect to its library, its art treasures, or the creative activities of its citizens, Alexandria was a forcing house of genius. It could have been another Athens. But it wasn't. Over a period of time, the conditions of creative activity were altered or damaged. Wars, sickness, human depletion, crassness combined to destroy Alexandria. The famous library didn't die all at once. For a long period before Caliph Omar arrived on his leveling expedition the library was slowly dying of neglect—always more destructive than combustion. Incidentally, the most valuable item lost or destroyed in the Alexandrian library was the master list or catalogue file. Hundreds of thousands of manuscripts were lost; and there is no record to tell us what these manuscripts were or the subject matter they covered.

Yes, books can die of burning or indifference. And no one knows how many books which had been conceived in the minds of their authors were never written. Hitler did more than merely burn books; he burned the creators of books. There is no answer to this system of preventive cultural assassination. No answer, that is, except one. That is the inspired resolution of free men to keep alive the conditions of creative progress against all attackers—from within no less than from without.

When Hitler himself died in the great fire of Berlin, the ultimate challenge to human decency and progress did not die with him. Today, in many parts of the world, art and culture are being poured into stultifying political molds. And artistic and cultural sterilization has been practiced on numberless men of genius. No one knows what magnificent compositions within the original creative potential of Shostakovich will never be produced because in Stalin's society the worst thing that can happen to a man is not to create bad art or music but to be a deviationist. And to dozens of Shostakovich's colleagues, whether in music or art or literature, the gift of a creative potential will be meaningless as long as their work will be reviewed not by free critics but by the state itself. No state in history has known enough to do a successful job of cultural criticism. Government is difficult enough without having to take upon itself and unto itself the job of defining the good, the true, and the beautiful.

I stress this last point because the question of how best to contribute to the humanities—inside or outside the university—must not be confined to a narrow answer. Even before we contribute money, we must contribute convictions. We can put those convictions to work today in protecting a free and creative society. We can contribute our services to the fight against conformity. Contributing our decibels to the vocal fight against totalitarian suppression abroad is not enough. There is the need to contribute our voices and our energies to a mobilization at home against know-nothingism and cultural vigilantism. We can contribute the products of good sense in not allowing a free society to be destroyed by home-grown and self-appointed dictators of the public morality who expect that they have only to utter the words "anti-Communist" to qualify as leaders. The fight against communism will not be won by reducing our liberties but by enlarging them; not by imitating the Communist in his police-state psychology but by respecting and indeed exalting the strength of an open society; not by peddling slogans but by a careful understanding of what it is we are resisting and what it is we intend to keep.

It is not necessarily true that the artist or writer is an aloof figure who is disdainful of the surrounding community. When the community itself has respect for the artist, when it develops a sense of responsibility toward the creative life, we will find that the artist will need no further inducement to become an actively proud and proudly active member of that community.

—*July 5, 1952*

# The Living Language

When John Russell Bartlett published his *Dictionary of Americanisms* a little more than a century ago, he challenged a popular assumption about the development of language in general and the American language in particular.

This assumption or notion held that language tends to deteriorate under the pressure of dialect. Bartlett contended that the "natural tendency of a language is to improve." He saw dialect as an endless source of new strength. He believed that the process of natural selection would retain only the most useful expressions in each dialect.

As for the invasion of slang, Bartlett was untroubled by the perennial war between literary language and the vernacular. He refused to accept the view that in such a struggle the literary language inevitably came out second best. The language of books, he was convinced, exerted the primary influence on American English. He regarded writers as the principal protectors of and providers for a strong language. He was confident that good books would continue to be the best circulators of good words, and that they could be trusted to incorporate the best of the colloquial while rejecting the slovenly. Such slang as was absorbed into the bloodstream of the language would have a tonic effect.

Seen from today's perspective, Bartlett is vindicated on all counts. The dialects have enriched the language. Even in Bartlett's time, people were getting used to such words as ranch, lariat, lasso, fandango, tortilla, chile, mesa, canyon, and stampede from the Spanish; or bayou, levee, banquet(te), distrait, echelon, ennui, bizarre, charlatan, commode, and chiffon from the French; or chipmunk, moose, raccoon, skunk, persimmon, pecan, maize, tobacco, hominy, succotash, tapioca, canoe, hammock, moccasin, and sagamore from the American Indians. And there has been a continuing healthy accretion from the dialects ever since.

As for the supposed threat from slang or the vernacular—a threat periodically invoked by well-meaning purists—any term coming into common usage has to run a pretty long gantlet. It is not under-use that kills slang so much as overuse. Sudden and drenching popularity is as hard on words as it is on actors and authors. Slang has to survive the quick enthusiasm it generates in order to avoid the inevitable graveyard of exhausted stereotoypes. It has to insinuate itself into the language; it cannot pressure or push its way in. Many of the colloquial expressions of Bartlett's time, good enough to make his *Dictionary of Americanisms*, weren't good enough for the long haul. One never hears today such verbs as gaum (for smear), or mizzle (for abscond), or rail it (for taking the train), or shingle (for spank). Or such nouns as hurryment (for confusion), or cooling board (for mortician's slab), or chirk (for good spirits), or Hunkers (for political conservatives), or redeye (for strong whisky), or squaddy (for short and fat), or jigamaree (for nonsense).

The words that stuck were the ones that seemed to come out of nowhere, slowly. Bartlet was impressed with the staying power of what were then such colloquial expressions as in cahoots, plug-ugly, hopping mad, chisel, conniption fit, boss, heap, let up, let on, let be, make tracks, dirt (for earth), engineer, elegant, ilk, knockdown and dragout, knocked into a cocked hat, knockkneed, offset, play possum, pull up stakes, pull wool over the eyes, or row to hoe. All these are now fairly standard items of speech and writing.

On the other hand, few of the standard similes of Bartlett's time are in general usage today. As straight as a loon's leg, or as smiling as a basket of chips, or as straight as a shingle, or as dry as the clerk of a lime kiln, or as crooked as a Virginia fence, or as melancholy as a Quaker meeting-house by moonlight, or as wrathy as a militia officer on a training day— all these were part of everyday speech a century ago. A few similes, however, are still stock items of conversation: crazy as a bedbug, big as all out-of-doors, slick as greased lightning, happy as a clam at high water.

What bothered Bartlett far more than the incursions of dialect or colloquialisms were stiff-necked words created by "educated men, and particularly by the clergy." This group, he said, which "ought to be the conservators rather than the perverters of language," was responsible for such linguistic abominations as the verb to doxologize, to happify, to difficult, to donate, to funeralize, to fellowship, etc., Such hard-sounding concoctions, he believed, were only a cut above the teachings of "priggish pedagogues" who favored such impossible constructions as "I feel very badly" or "You look charmingly."

Happily for the United States, Bartlett said, it has a vigorous political system. Americans could always count on political campaigning or just the sheer mechanism of political organization to provide an endless supply of juicy, appetizing new expressions. Generally, these words were obscure regional products but were snapped up by candidates or political writers with a good ear for vivid language. Among the words or phrases thus given wide and enduring currency were: flash in the pan, cave in, bark up the wrong tree, fizzle out, lobby, gerrymander, splurge, wirepuller, fire-eater, Know-Nothing, bunkum, mileage, stamping ground, etc.

Abraham Lincoln contributed more than his fair share of Americanisms to the language; so did Andrew Jackson, Ulysses Grant, Zachary Taylor, and the two Roosevelts. And, unless we miss our guess, the current Presidential race ought to be especially productive. One of the candidates has as much fun with words as any man who ever aspired to the White House, and the other has at least thirty years of Army life behind him. Whatever the state of the nation, the American language ought to do pretty well.

*—September 27, 1952*

# Worse than the H Bomb

There is something far more terrifying about the hydrogen bomb than the fact that it has reduced the atomic bomb to a .22-caliber rifle alongside a large cannon. What is most terrifying about the hydrogen bomb is its grotesque lack of impact upon the public mind. It can rock the earth but it has yet to make a dent in our thinking. The news of the explosion was a one-day story, like a bank robbery or a love triangle or a prison break. It had its brief moment of power and glory and horror and then gave way to a crime investigation.

Is there anything more appalling than the fact that the most significant event in human history should fail to ignite human thought? Man goes into his laboratory and comes out with a device that has stamped upon it a death warrant for at least a billion persons. The device makes it possible to expunge in a fraction of a second what it has taken two thousand years to put together piece by piece. The device is not created and produced on an empty and tranquil stage. It is presented against a background of lit fuses and supercharged tensions. Yet nothing explodes in our minds. Nothing happens. It is a new bomb but it is the same world. The bomb is merely another lump in a continuing crisis; we swallow hard and go on.

Seven years ago, when the atomic bomb became a reality, there was a brief flurry of sanity. Men began to think. Something new and important was in the air. Facts were put together. Ministers, philosophers, writers, educators, scientists, and soldiers looked at the facts and struggled to make them clear to others. It seemed for a time that man's horizons were stretching. There was the inspiring possibility that people might transcend the old and puny ideas on what was required to safeguard human existence on this planet. Striking and stirring things were said about the need to liberate the world's people from the jungle of their fears. The time had come to destroy anarchy on the world level; this anarchy was far more dangerous to human peace and freedom than any amount of lawlessness within any nation.

This would mean, without question, a government of the whole. None of the objections about difficulties or differences had any validity alongside the cool fact that an ultimate challenge had abruptly crystallized. This challenge was far greater than anything that existed on a nation vs. nation basis. It was directed at and to man. It would not grow smaller by staring at it or looking past it. It fed on blindness and it got fat on delay. And it seemed to many men during that short and wonderful period of insight that the United States had the principal responsibility for leadership in moving toward such a positive goal. It was felt that no opposing nation could stop the forward thrust of the world's peoples. No force could be great enough to block a movement based on the fundamental and universal wants and hopes of the overwhelming majority of the world's peoples. Indeed, the only effective way of dealing with an aggressive totalitarianism would be through just such a massive and persistent leadership working for world peace and justice.

All this made tall sense but it didn't last very long or get very far. We had reckoned without our pygmies. They cut the big ideas down to size. They were able to do this because everyone seemed to be waiting for someone else to do something. The people were waiting for the leaders and the leaders were waiting for the people. And in this vacuum of indecision an important and dangerous thing happened. The world began to slip away from us. Our emphasis had been on things rather than ideas. We took a narrow view of power, regarding it largely in terms of destructive potential, and not quite recognizing that this particular crisis called equally for things of the spirit, for ideas with spaciousness and moral grandeur that could win the fight on the first front—the human responses of people.

We became afflicted with day-to-dayitis. What might happen next year or next month or even next week would have to take care of itself. The panorama of history behind us, offering valuable guidance, was regarded as feeble stuff and a bore. The only thing that counted was the twenty-four-hour period that comprised the now.

The first big jolt came only five years after the beginning of the Atomic Age and it happened not far from where the war ended. Korea interrupted the daily routine, and we doubled and redoubled our *physical* efforts, apparently not stopping to ask how and why Korea started and what would be required to end it. Few apparently remembered the warnings of 1945 that the trouble with a weak world organization was not only that it could not cope decisively with crisis but that this very weakness tended to invite crisis. Back in 1945 America had been urged to lead the way in the creation of an adequate United Nations force, to be recruited not on the basis of voluntary offerings but on the basis of fixed commitments. But we shuddered at the thought, for that meant a sacrifice of sovereignty. Five years later we were to lose our sovereignty and our men, too. Because we didn't quite understand in 1945 that the foundations of sovereignty in the modern world had been shattered, we were to pay the price in blood. And the lesson hasn't been learned yet.

After two years of struggle and stalemate in Korea, we still haven't come before the United Nations with the only proposal that could make sense in Korea—or anywhere else. We still haven't insisted that the nations stop their diddling on the issue of world law and that they create a common government with adequate and even overwhelming force, based on fixed and fair obligations, and built upon the principles of justice that would command the allegiance and hopes of the world's peoples. As for the plodding question, "What will the Russians do?" the only answer is that if we continue on our present course, the Russians will continue to whittle away large areas of the world and continue to keep us on the defensive. And they will continue to do this until we discover we can't win a big fight unless we have a big idea.

There is a far more vital question about Korea than the one about the Russians. It is, simply: What have we learned from Korea? The aggression in Korea would never have occurred if the United Nations before June 1950 had had at least as many men under arms as it put into the field once the aggression took place. But what about a larger crisis just ahead? Is the UN ready for that? Are we willing to support the components of that readiness, or are we going to intimidate ourselves again with the myth of sovereignty—only to lose more sovereignty and more lives?

If we are really serious about meeting the Russian threat, let us stop playing into Russia's hands. Russia wants a weak UN. Are we willing to commit ourselves to a strong one? Russia wants to retain the veto. Are we willing to abolish it? (We proposed it at San Francisco.) Russia would like to keep the UN going on a bare-subsistence level because she doesn't want the responsibility for killing it. Are we willing to help put it on a higher level? And let us not use the specious argument that we are afraid that Russia would not go along with a UN having adequate powers. If Russia will go along only with a policy leading to UN impotence, we don't retard that policy by imitating it. Indeed, it is likely that Russia will give up her intransigence only if she is convinced that the rest of the world is determined to equip the United Nations with the powers of government. Russia has little to fear from an unorganized world, however large the stockpile of hydrogen bombs which presumably she has as well. She does, however, have a great deal to fear from pressure inside her own country once a bona-fide offer is made to her to become part of a workable world society based on justice and enforceable law.

The advent of the Hydrogen Age leaves as little margin for routine thinking as it does for error. With the atomic bomb we were able to put a pretty face on the matter and talk about all the wonderful things that atomic energy could do in making a better world. But the hydrogen bomb knows no such happy equivalent. It is a tightly packaged instrument for mass human slaughter; that and nothing more. The only way we can live with it is to control it. The problem is still the elimination of war itself—not on the basis of knuckling under but on the basis of organized law for the world community.

Seven years ago, when world law was mentioned, people said it was too soon. Now, when it is mentioned, they say it is too late. It is neither too soon nor too late. If we have a voice and an idea behind it, and if what we say makes sense, the time is just right.

—*December 13, 1952*

# The Product Is Hope

EDITOR'S NOTE: *On Monday, December 22, 1952, the Court of Special Sessions in Brooklyn considered the case of Harry G. Purvis, a businessman charged with having violated a local ordinance. Atop Mr. Purvis' factory in Brooklyn was a large sign calling for world peace through world federation. The ordinance forbids advertising signs in this particular vicinity except as they might advertise the firm's own name or products created on the premises. The editor of the* Saturday Review *was called as the principal witness for the defendant. Abstracts from his statement follow. Decision in the case was reserved by the court for a later date.*

Mr. Purvis is accused of displaying a sign which is apparently advertising something without a product being available on the premises. I am by no means certain that Mr. Purvis and many millions of people like him throughout the world are unable to produce this particular product. But about this, more later.

My purpose today is to call the attention of the court to some of the factors in this case that go beyond the purely local ordinances. I have come, too, because I am confident that this court will be guided by Justice Holmes's moral yardstick. Wasn't it Justice Holmes, your honor, who said that "the law cannot be dealt with as if it contained only the axioms and corollaries of a book of mathematics"? Wasn't there also some reference to what he called "the felt necessities of the time"? Isn't this a development of the same idea of essential flexibility in Jefferson's advice to a young country that "laws and institutions go hand in hand with the progress of the human mind"? And isn't there, perhaps, an echo of all this in Justice Jackson's recent observation that the "life of the law has not been logic; it has been experience"?

It is with confidence, then, in the application by this court of essential flexibility that I should like to argue this case.

Let us consider, first of all, the man himself. Mr. Purvis, it is apparent, is an individualist—at least so far as his convictions are concerned. And, technical legalities aside, he offers a good test case of responsible individualism in America today. For Mr. Purvis is being individualistic in the best possible way. Through this little tangle of his with the law in Brooklyn he has reminded us that the big ideas in this world cannot survive unless they come to life in the individual citizen. It is what one man does in responding to his convictions that provides the forward thrust for any great movement. The basic energy behind American independence was supplied by the combined heartbeats of individual men. Today, one hundred and seventy-three years later, a great jurist, Learned Hand, can write that the "vastest conflict with which mankind has ever been faced . . . in the end turns upon whether the individual can survive."

As a responsible individual, Mr. Purvis knows that democracy is no better than the ability of its citizens to make right decisions. He knows something about the wars that have happened during his lifetime. He is being entirely realistic and practical when he says that American cities are no longer immune to direct attack; that the skies will be filled with guided missiles penetrating far beyond the speed boundaries of sound; that men may not be able to dig deeply enough into the earth to avoid the shocks of the man-made hydrogen earthquakes; and when he tells what General H. H. Arnold, chief of our air force, said in 1948: "We won the last war, and it's the last war we'll ever win. If we have another, this nation will lose. We'll lose and the enemy we fight will lose, because victory in atomic warfare is no longer possible. One nation cannot defeat another nation today. That concept died with Hiroshima. War is like fire: you can prevent a fire, or you can try to put it out, but you can't win a fire, because fire is destruction."

But Mr. Purvis doesn't rest his case on the fiendishness of war in the twentieth century. I do not know him, but I do know he is not a pacifist. If I understand him correctly, he is a Federalist. He believes there is an answer to war. It is not an answer to be found merely through disdain for war or horror of war; for it takes more than disdain or horror to make peace. Nor does he as a Federalist believe that the answer to war is to be found through appeasement. He would fight if our values were attacked because he doesn't believe in peace at any price. But he believes that an honest peace, a just peace, a peace with values is possible. He believes that such a peace is not to be had merely for the asking or the taking. As a Federalist, he knows that no peace in history has come about by itself. He knows that peace must be created; it is a specific and tangible thing; it must have a definite architecture to it.

This architecture, Mr. Purvis believes, is the architecture of federalism. It is an unfortunate commentary on American forgetfulness, your honor, that it should be necessary to define federalism for an American audience. Nothing in our history is as uniquely American as our federalism. Yet too many of us turn our backs on it.

Federalism is an approach to government based on equating power with justice, on equating force with responsibility, on equating authority with due process of law. Federalism is unity without uniformity; it is the rim of a wheel that has many spokes; it is a technique not so much for eliminating differences as for keeping differences from resulting in organized violence. It defines the areas of workable sovereignty. It assures to each state the right of self-development, but it maintains for the larger unit of all the states the machinery for operating and maintaining peace. Federalism is based upon the existence of natural spheres of authority—those retained by individual states, those given to the collective entity of the states for the greater safety of all.

In sum, federalism does not destroy sovereignty. It calls for an investment of some sovereignty, and offers a definite and important return on the investment by protecting the individual nations against attack and by freeing them of the enormous burden of piling up armaments without limit and without end.

I have a feeling, your honor, and I know that it is not customary to talk about one's feelings in presenting an argument before a court of law, that Mr. Purvis would not be here today if our history were better understood. I have a feeling that if Mr. Purvis's sign had been concerned with a familiar and popular idea or slogan, for which there didn't seem to be a product on the premises, there might not have been a trial. Suppose, your honor, the sign had expressed Mr. Purvis's hope—a hope, I hasten to add, that I personally share—that the Brooklyn Dodgers would finally win a World Series in 1953. I am certain no officer of the law would dare to invoke this particular ordinance. But it is perhaps the very strangeness of purposeful hoping in our time, this curious and paradoxical unfamiliarity with the word federalism, that made this young man somewhat suspect, as though he were trying somehow to damage the country whose history and institutions he knows so well and for which he has such devotion.

Are there not signs throughout Brooklyn, your honor, that call attention to the religion of the Prince of Peace? This is a borough famed the world over for its churches. I should be disappointed if there are not countless signs extolling His way. These signs do not come within the letter of the law regarding the availability of a tangible article or product, for they deal with things of the spirit; and yet I am certain that no officer of the law would seek to remove them.

And if it is said in rebuttal that there is indeed a product behind such devotional signs, and that this product is a thing of the spirit as meaningful and important as any tangible product, I would agree. And I would say it is good that they are not excluded because of any superficial distinctions between spirit and substance. But I would also contend that there is a spiritual product behind Mr. Purvis's sign, one that is especially meaningful just a few hours before the anniversary of an event we associate with peace on earth and good will toward all men.

Mr. Purvis *has* a product on his premises, your honor. His product is hope. His product is apparently so rare today that it can hardly be recognized for what it is. Hope, like conscience, may have its pains, but nothing is more essential to human existence. Nothing can better yield the precise ingredients for the making of a better tomorrow than hope. Tennyson tells us that there are "mighty hopes that make us men" and Thomas Fuller that "we are as great as our hopes." Each language has its proverbs which place hope close to the center of the gifts that are uniquely human.

Mr. Purvis's particular hope, your honor, is that his neighbors in Brooklyn, and indeed his neighbors throughout the world, may live productive and free lives. He hopes that war and the causes of war can be brought under control. He hopes that this good earth can be made to serve the ends of man, rather than become parched and clotted with human blood. Most specifically, he hopes that the United States will recognize that it is unnatural and evil for world man to live under world anarchy and will take world leadership in defining federalism as a sound and workable basis for world peace. He hopes that other peoples inside the United Nations will respond to this leadership and will press forward behind this great idea.

Mr. Purvis's hopes are not enfeebled because of the probability that Russia might not respond to American leadership on such a level. Mr. Purvis knows that our best chance of reaching the people behind the curtain is to hold up an idea so vital, so strong, as to start a groundswell of potentially volcanic force. For even should this big idea be rejected time and again, the very persistence with which we advance it will serve to bind together the preponderance of the world's peoples.

These hopes, your honor, can be powerful things once they are awakened in the minds of enough men. Peace—meaningful peace, purposeful peace, vital peace—constitutes the essence of the product behind Mr. Purvis's sign.

Surely, on the eve of Christmas, 1952, these hopes are worth our thoughts.

*—January 10, 1953*

# Has the Church Failed?

The paradox that troubled Albert Schweitzer was that "for centuries Christianity treasured the great commandment of love and mercy as traditional truth without recognizing it as a reason for opposing slavery, witch-burning, torture, and all the other ancient and medieval forms of inhumanity."

The paradox grows. Today, more than a generation after Schweitzer called upon the Church to act out its beliefs, Christianity has yet to deal with the greatest challenge of all—war and injustices leading to war. For centuries Christianity has extolled the idea of peace on earth, without regarding its beliefs as a mandate for dedicated action to that end. There is little effective connection between the recognition of the sacredness of peace and any vital determination to save it.

Never before have there been so many churches and so many Christians; never before has the institution of man been in greater jeopardy. Christianity has not truly involved itself in the human situation. It has become strangely adjacent to the crisis of man, seemingly content with trying to create a moral and spiritual atmosphere instead of becoming a towering and indeed dominant force in the shaping of a world congenial to man. To paraphrase Pascal, it has been wandering around the circumference instead of embracing the center. It has become one of the values we fight for instead of a force in itself. It is not regarded as the working source of wisdom and strength, but as a factor, a respected possession, a shelter for conscience. It has yet to become supremely pertinent and supremely effective in safeguarding the commonwealth of man at a time of peril so profound as to be incomprehensible to the rational intelligence alone.

Much has been said about the significance of the revolution in communications, transportation, and invention in the modern world. The gap between scientific knowledge and political institutions has been clearly seen and clearly felt. But scientific "progress" has created an even greater challenge to spiritual man than it has to political man. If science has suddenly brought all peoples within a single small enclosure, with the option to make it into a single battlefield or a single neighborhood, then it has also brought about a vast test for the world's great religions. Can religion act in behalf of the human species itself at a time when the species is unrepresented and in danger? How important is man? These are the questions that starkly confront every church and all churchmen.

The men of God share in the responsibility for the developing failure of the Church but their share is not the dominant one. No group senses its own inadequacy more keenly than the clergymen. As individuals they are starkly aware of the big paradox and are pained by it. In an age of saturating frustration, theirs is perhaps the uneasiest lot of all, for they are trying to give life not merely to religious doctrine but to the moral imagination. They are trying to impart substance, reality, and relevance to the ideas of Christ in the modern world; but their words are absorbed as tentative sound without changing the color or the shape of the walls of the mind. The ministers realize this, and struggle all the harder to create human adequacy for human crisis. But to do that it is necessary first to decompartmentalize man—to enable him to move easily and naturally from theology to action—action that is morally effective and effectively moral. And this is not a simple thing to do, even for the man of God.

The pulpit, to repeat, is not at the heart of the Christian paradox. The custodian of that pulpit knows, if anyone knows, the nature and reality of the crisis of man. He realizes that the nation today, any nation, is a feeble thing and incapable of protecting human existence and those values which make life distinctive and purposeful. Most dramatically, he can visualize the consequences of world anarchy. He can anticipate the earth shudders that will be produced by nuclear explosions. Since a single life is sacred to him, his mind must blister and burn when he multiplies one life by hundreds of millions. He must contend with the palpable fact that it took a divine cosmos more than two billion years to create the conditions for producing and sustaining human life, but it could take human intelligence less than a day to bring it all down.

As for the denominations themselves, their failure is not marked by any lack of recognition of the monstrous threat to man's estate in the modern world. Indeed, they have done everything except to act dramatically in behalf of their own comprehension of crisis.

The General Convention of the Protestant Episcopal Church; the General Assembly of the Presbyterian Church; the Methodist Church Conference; the Congregational Christian Church; the Disciples of Christ, and the American Unitarian Association have all recognized the need for action behind the principles of enforceable world law. And no statement was more searching or impassioned in behalf of these principles than that issued by Pope Pius XII two years ago.

All these declarations and statements, superb in themselves, have been milestones of analysis and intent but not the springboards for decisive action. When Father Edward A. Conway, of *America*, said that American Catholics were "giving the silent treatment" to Pope Pius's declaration, he might well have added that Christians in general have yet to mobilize in behalf of the ideals that are even more important than armaments in serving the human cause.

The possibilities for action are not cramped or confined unless we are to say belief must be protected from such vitality as may exist within it, that inspiration must be shorn of purpose, and that action is justified only if it is devoid of conviction. Certainly there is scope for religious and ethical action in the world today. We are thinking not of an invasion of the political arena or of mass movements as such or of any of the churnings usually associated with political activity. We are thinking of the gestation of vital purpose, the creation of moral imperatives that can produce vital change, the conditions for supporting vital leadership. On the level of direct action, and in a more limited sense, there is a real need and opportunity for a world parliament of religions that will address itself to the human situation in 1953. Let the great religions cease explaining their differences to each other and begin to chart the elements of basic unity that could serve as the building blocks for common action. Let all talk of separate "destinies" be recognized for the disservice to spiritual man that it is. What is at stake today is not primarily Christian civilization or Islamic civilization or Jewish civilization or Hindu civilization or any other. It is not man's particularized beliefs but his own uniqueness that counts. For what is threatened are the basic conditions that make life meaningful and purposeful. To the extent that any religion speaks only in behalf of its own interests; to the extent that it places itself above or apart from the whole, it jeopardizes its own interests and injures the whole. In order to get inside man, the Church must get outside itself.

If we argue that the possibility of convening the great religions in behalf of man is far more complex and difficult than the making of peace itself, or that even if such a parliament could be convened, it is unlikely that any action could proceed out of it, then we are arguing against the validity of religion itself in the modern world. If the Church is the custodian of the spirit of man, and if that spirit is imperiled, then responsible action is possible and essential.

*—February 28, 1953*


# Litany for Modern Man

I am a single cell in a body of 3 billion cells. The body is mankind.

I glory in the individuality of self, but my individuality does not separate me from my universal self—the oneness of man.

My memory is personal and finite, but my substance is boundless and infinite.

The portion of that substance that is mine was not devised; it was renewed. So long as the human blood stream lives I have life.

I do not believe that humankind is an excrescence or a machine, or that the myriads of solar systems and galaxies in the universe lack order or sanction.

I may not embrace or command this universal order, but I can be at one with it, for I am of it.

I believe that the expansion of knowledge makes for an expansion of faith, and the widening of the horizons of mind for a widening of belief. My reason nourishes my faith and my faith my reason.

I am not diminished by the growth of knowledge but by the denial of it.

I am not oppressed by, nor do I shrink before, the apparent boundaries in life or the lack of boundaries in cosmos.

I see no separation between the universal order and the moral order.

I cannot affirm God if I fail to affirm man. If I deny the oneness of man, I deny the oneness of God. Therefore I affirm both. Without a belief in human unity I am hungry and incomplete.

Human unity is the fulfillment of diversity. It is the harmony of opposites. It is a many-stranded texture, with color and depth.

The sense of human unity makes possible a reverence for life.

Reverence for life is more than solicitude or sensitivity for life. It is a sense of the whole, a capacity for wonder, a respect for the intricate universe of individual life. It is the supreme awareness of awareness itself. It is pride in being.

I am a single cell. My needs are individual but they are not unique.

When I enter my home I enter with the awareness that my roof can only be half built and my table only half set, for half the men on this earth know the emptiness of want.

When I walk through the streets of my city I walk with the awareness of the shattered cities beyond number that comprise the dominant reality.

When I think of peace I can know no peace until the peace is real.

My dedication, therefore, is to the cause of man in the attainment of that which is within the reach of man.

I will work for human unity under a purposeful peace. I will work for the growth of a moral order that is in keeping with the universal order.

In this way do I affirm faith in life and life in faith.

I am a single cell in a body of 3 billion cells. The body is mankind.

*—August 8, 1953*

*Many times since coming to the* Saturday Review, *I have taken to the high road. Sometimes, as in the case of the Bikini nuclear explosions or the article on Berlin which follows, I have gone in a reportorial capacity. Sometimes, as in the case of trips to the Far East or the Soviet Union, I have gone at the request of the U.S. Department of State in connection with cultural exchange agreements with other countries. Sometimes I have gone to attend special events or dedications. And sometimes I have gone for the pure enjoyment of going.*

*If it is asked how it is possible to edit the* Saturday Review *under conditions of almost perpetual motion, the answer is a combination of two things—first, an air age that makes it possible to send and receive materials within a day or two from almost any part of the world; second, a supporting staff at the home office, beautifully departmentalized, that knows its business. In any case, from the late forties and increasingly during the fifties, the editor's chair was often a seat in a plane to distant parts of the world.*

# Berlin, 1953

Let me begin by telling you about two German ladies.

I can't tell you their names; I don't know their names. Nor did I have any right to ask. They were from the Soviet zone of Germany and they were wise to conceal their identities. They feared that if what they were doing became known, they and their families might be hurt.

Their crime was a simple one. They had violated an order and had come from the East zone to West Berlin. They came because they were hungry, and they came to get free food.

I should like you to know about these ladies because you might like to know more about a situation in which it is a crime for hungry people to accept free food. When I met them, they were at one of the six free food-distribution centers in West Berlin. One of the ladies was about fifty-five, the other about forty. In common with countless thousands of other Germans from the Soviet sector of Berlin or the surrounding Soviet zone outside the city, they came because the Americans were providing emergency food packages. They knew that they could get only one package per person per month. They knew, too, that one package would meet the basic nutritional needs of one person for only one week. (Each package contained one and a half pounds of lard, two tins of condensed milk, one packet of powdered milk, one packet of lentil beans, and one pound of flour or rice.) But even this was necessary and welcome.

By word of mouth or by secret radio, the hungry people had learned the address where they would be given food. When they arrived at the factory they found an efficient and swift-moving distribution system in operation. A large area on the first floor of the factory had been cleared away; long tables had been set up, and dozens of Germans were at work unpacking the crates of food. The people moved by the tables at the rate of about twenty a minute.

Near the door was a West Berlin policeman, a tall youth of about twenty-two, who was answering the questions of anxious and bewildered people, many of whom were in West Berlin for the first time since the end of the war. To those who came without proper cards he explained that it is first necessary to have their East German or East Berlin papers checked at the nearby town hall, where food cards would be issued. One person could obtain as many as seven or eight food cards if he had that many people in his family—so long as he could prove it with their identification papers, and so long as he had the strength to carry the food away.

I was astounded to see women of sixty or seventy years make off with bundles that must have weighed sixty or seventy pounds. An elderly woman who couldn't have weighed more than one hundred pounds herself was carrying at least half her weight in two old burlap bags, one in each hand.

For an hour I had been watching the East Germans as they came to collect their food. They were of all ages. Mostly, though, they were people in late middle age or older. All were poorly dressed, some in clothes that had been patched and repatched. Even the younger people had a drab look about them. And almost all of them had come on foot. I saw at least a dozen young mothers with baby carriages.

At the beginning the crowds would average 20,000 to 30,000 people per day at this particular food center. But that was at a time when it was feared that the giveaway program might last only a few days or so. Now that the food-package distribution plan is being set up on a continuing basis, providing for one package per person per month, the East Berliners have leveled off to a steady rate of about 4,500 per day at each of the six distribution points.

As you have no doubt read, the East Berlin authorities have tried every trick in the book to keep the people in the East zone from getting the free-food packages. It is impossible to build barriers at every one of the thousands of streets which connect Communist Berlin with Free Berlin. But the authorities have tried everything else—including threats, force, and propaganda persuasion. They even sent thousands of Communists to apply for the food packages; no questions are asked by West Berlin, of course, concerning a person's political ties. These Communists would then trail other East Berliners back to their homes and inform on them.

The resultant punishment would take various forms, of which confiscation of the food package was the most lenient. In some cases people would be deprived of their identification papers, which had enabled them to move about the city. Some were deprived of their jobs.

The Soviet authorities even set up a food-distribution center of their own in East Berlin for the "relief" of 300,000 unemployed West Berliners. This plan was advertised over the radio. It turned out that the food packages were the very ones that had been confiscated from people returning to East Berlin. Thousands of West Berliners went over to East Berlin in response to the offer, collected their packages, and returned to West Berlin, where they promptly handed over their packages to the same distribution centers where the East Berliners had picked them up in the first place. There was some speculation that some of the packages might have shifted back and forth a dozen times or more. The shifting stopped, however, when the Communist authorities realized their plan had backfired.

I watched the people leave the main counters and make off for one side where they unpacked their food kits and then reassembled them in somewhat more concealed form. The women with the baby carriages were carefully stuffing their tins and packets under the mattresses. It was then that I met the two German ladies I am anxious to tell you about. They were stuffing small tin cans into pockets of their coats or into the sleeves of sweaters or coats to be carried over their arms. Other items were stuffed into oversized pocketbooks or valises or shopping bags carefully covered at the top with camouflage materials. Each seemed to have at least six food-supply units.

As I looked at these two women with their extra food parcels I knew that no matter how many sleeves and coats they filled, they wouldn't be able to conceal the fact that they were carrying American food into East Germany. I went up to them and asked if I might talk to them.

I don't think I shall ever forget their look of horror as they stared up at me, eyes and mouths open and faces taut. After a brief moment one of them said they had nothing to say. The other said there was no way for her to know that I wasn't someone who was trying to get information about them in order to report her to the Communist authorities.

Through an interpreter, Werner Shultz, I explained that I had come to observe the food-distribution plan in action. All I wanted to know was how she was going to manage all these bundles and how far she had to go.

The young policeman who had been standing nearby reassured the women and little by little they began to show confidence. After a few minutes the older woman explained her fright and caution by saying that her friends had advised her against coming, saying that the food was merely the bait in a trap and that she might endanger her entire family.

"Already we have suffered much," she said. "My husband owned a flour factory. When the Communists came in, they said he was a capitalist and took it away and made it a people's factory. They gave him nothing for the factory but they said he could work as a foreman at the shipping station for the flour. He had to take the job or there would be no work and we would have no food.

"My son, he was in the war and lost both legs. When he came home from the hospital, my husband had given him a job as accountant. Then, when the Communists took over the factory, they told my son he could keep his job if he joined the SED.* My son, he didn't want to join because of what they had done to my husband, and they took away his job and said he could have no other. They said all he could have would be his veteran's pension, which is only seventy-five East Marks a month. [About $4.]

"We have had enough trouble already."

When I asked how far they had come, they said they were from a town some seventy miles from Berlin. They had started their journey at 5 A.M. that morning, taking a train and a bus and then working their way across the city in order to avoid the checking points.

Weren't they concerned about getting all the food out of West Berlin? What about the other people on the trains and buses? Some of them might be party functionaries or informers, *nein?*

That wasn't the way it worked, they were prompt to reply. What you did was to leave the big items of food with friends in West Berlin who would carry the packages into the East zone without too much vulnerability. Besides, the homes of friends were good parking stations, and you could have the food picked up by other friends from East Berlin who happened to be going into West Berlin for one reason or another.

"Ach," she said, "there are so many ways to get the food through."

We offered to drive the ladies to their friends' home in the French

* Sozialistische Einheitspartei Deutschlands.

sector of West Berlin, and they accepted. As we drove away from the food center, the younger lady, who up until this time had been the more shy and hesitant of the two, spoke up.

"I am sorry I was so soon having to go home," she said. "This is the first time since before the war I have ridden in a private car. And never have I seen so many autos before—"

Our car swung into the Kurfurstendamm near the Wilhelm Memorial Cathedral. We passed some big department stores, their windows displaying oversized Persian rugs, attractive furniture, and stylish evening gowns.

"It is so hard to believe," she continued. "The Communists tell us that there is luxury in West Berlin but that it is all owned by the Americans, and that the new buildings and the new stores are all paid for by the Americans, who are going to make the Germans pay for it many times over with high interest. They have said that the working people cannot afford to buy these capitalist goods. But where do all these rich people come from? Everywhere I look I see people going into the stores and coming out with packages. Maybe these are not just rich people. Maybe the working people have enough money to buy these things, too.

"In the Soviet zone we have to use these"—she fished some rationing coupons out of her bag and waved them—"but even then it is no good. A spoonful of butter for one person has to last a full month.

"Not enough milk. My young boy has tuberculosis. In West Berlin you can buy butter and milk enough for your family. I will tell my husband about this."

This was the first time the younger woman had referred to her husband. When I asked what her husband did, there was an awkward pause and the women looked at each other as though trying to decide whether they ought to answer the question. I was afraid I had touched on a sensitive point and started to change the subject when the younger woman replied.

"He is a clerk who does bookkeeping and he is a member of the Communist party. But he is not a real Communist. I swear he is not a Communist. He joined because he had to. When they came and invited him to join the SED, he knew he would lose his job and not find another if he did not join. He is always thinking of his family. He joined the SED."

I looked first at one, then at the other, then asked the inevitable question. If conditions in the Soviet zone were as bad as all that, why stick it out? Why not come over to West Berlin and make a fresh start?

The question didn't go down too well.

"It is not so easy, just to come over to West Berlin," the older woman said, somewhat sharply. "I am not a young boy of nineteen who is alone in the world. If you have relatives, the only way to get out is for all to go. The ones you leave behind are the ones who will suffer. We know. We know already many people who have left to come to West Berlin and we know that the brothers or sisters or cousins and even the friends are made to pay. That is why so many know they can't leave."

Our car swung into a street in the French sector of West Berlin where the ladies were to cache their food packages at the home of a friend. Nearby was a small delicatessen. I suggested to Shultz that we stop for a moment, then invited the ladies to shop as my guests. This they were extremely reluctant to do, but Werner Shultz helped me win the argument. I noticed that the younger woman seemed hypnotized by the large bars of sweet chocolate behind one of the cases. She said her younger children had never tasted chocolate. When she was handed the chocolate bars she said she was certain her children would never forget it. Then she added that this whole experience was nothing she herself would soon forget. She spoke for both of us.

I looked over at Werner Shultz and wondered what his thoughts were. In fact, I wondered about Shultz himself, just as you wonder about all Germans you try to get to know. What were they thinking and doing back in the days when Hitler was telling them they had the right and duty to run the whole show? Did they have any knowledge of what Hitler was doing to his victims and indeed to the world, or did they merely take it in stride so long as they were on top? I asked Shultz whether he was in the war.

Shultz had no qualms about talking freely. He said he was brought up as a member of the Nazi youth organization, had been completely indoctrinated, and believed at the time that what Hitler was doing was necessary and good.

And now?

One minute, he said, there was something more to say. When he reached military age in 1942, he went into the army. The first time he fired a gun against a human being was against an American. He doesn't know whether he found the target, then or later, but there was no point in kidding me and saying, as so many other German veterans have been saying to Americans, that the only action they saw was on the Eastern front, against the Russians. He said you are brought up in a certain atmosphere, with certain ideas pounded into you, and you take your values from your society, and you do your best according to the job put before you.

"I was captured in Italy by the Americans," he said simply. "I hated it. It was a humiliating thing to be, what do you say, side-lined, when everything else was going on. But then I began to get to know the Americans and I could see a very big, a tremendously big difference between the way they acted and the way we had been taught to act. For the first time in my life I began to learn by watching them about what it means to be decent, and I had the strong feeling you get when you are part of something good. The Americans trusted me as a prisoner. They let me drive trucks for them far outside the prisoners' camp—alone. They never bullied me into doing anything and they never gave me, what shall I say, the feeling that I was part of a gang and that the gang had power and could do whatever it wanted to do.

"Well, after the war was over I wrote home to my mother and told her I hoped she wouldn't mind but that I wanted to stay in Italy and continue to work for the Americans if they would have me. She told me to stay as long as I could, for conditions in Berlin were terrible and there was little food or heat.

"The Americans let me stay on for a year, and I did a lot of things. One thing I did was to learn how to speak English. I was glad that I did because it made it possible for me to get jobs with American firms in Berlin when I came home. And now I work for the American Express Company. I do everything. I do interpreting. I drive cars. I take people sight-seeing.

"You have asked me how I feel now. I can tell you easily. Now I am trying to get to America so I can be an American citizen. One of my friends, he is a mechanic, and he met an American who has helped to bring him to the United States. His friend got him a job as mechanic in Milwaukee; he is happier than he has been in his whole life and he writes to me that maybe soon he will have enough money to help me come over, too.

"Of course, it is a complicated thing but I know I want to do it. My fiancée, she is a nurse and I think we will both be happy in America."

I asked Werner if it would be possible for him to drive me through the Communist sector. He said there would probably be no trouble in getting around East Berlin so long as he identified me as a tourist and himself as a professional guide.

Just after we passed under the massive Brandenburg Gate, now so badly scarred, we had to stop at a screening station where East Berlin police asked our purpose. The police asked for the key to the trunk of the car, opened and inspected it, then looked inside the car for propaganda materials or food packages. They seemed pleasant enough and told Shultz to proceed.

We passed the wreckage of the famous old government buildings, the libraries, and the galleries along what had once been one of the most beautiful boulevards in the world. Then we turned off Unter den Linden; Shultz wanted to show me the heart of the business and residential sections of East Berlin. We went from the main thoroughfares into the back streets, weaving around the city in order to get the full picture. The contrast between East and West Berlin was sharper, if anything, than the accounts I had read in the various news reports. It wasn't only the fact that few stores were open and that the goods they were selling seemed nondescript. Nor was it merely the fact that there seemed to have been such little real progress in cleaning up the bomb wreckage compared to West Berlin. The greatest difference was in the people themselves. Very few of them were on the streets, to begin with, and the ones you saw, on the whole, were poorly dressed. There was almost no traffic. It was a drab place.

"Surely," I said to Werner Shultz, "there must be some place in East Berlin where things are happening."

"Oh, yes," he said. "Soon we will see something big and interesting."

Then he told me about a section of East Berlin that was fast becoming the headquarters of communism not only for East Berlin but for all of East Germany. This was a large building project called Stalinstadt—Stalin City—that the Communists were very proud of. In fact, it was a city within a city, which hadn't been completed yet. The main street, however, with its large apartment buildings on each side was almost fully built, and thousands of families had already moved in.

"There's a catch to it, though," Werner said. "You just don't get into a place like that because you are without a home. You've got to prove your worth. That means you not only have to belong to the Party but must have rendered special service of one kind or another."

In a few minutes we turned into a 300-foot-wide street named "Stalinallee." It began in a large traffic circle. There were steel skeletons of tall buildings under construction around the circle. Then, starting down Stalinallee, I had the feeling I was in the middle of a Russian postcard showing fancy new building projects. The architecture was distinctly Russian; the design was rigid and geometrical, with Georgian setback effects. The buildings seemed to repeat themselves endlessly, relieved only occasionally by small open areas in the center of which would be tall statues of Soviet heroes. At the beginning of Stalinallee was a statue of Joseph Stalin molded along athletic and heroic lines.

Across the way from the Stalin statue was a combination exhibition hall, information center, and indoor stadium. I learned that it was used almost nightly for everything from sports events to public lectures, which would usually be about aspects of Soviet life or about Communist ideology.

I asked Werner whether it would be possible to visit some of the apartments. We entered the first apartment building on Stalinallee  Werner spoke briefly to the caretaker-attendant on the first floor and re :eived the name of someone on the fifth floor who might be receptive. Tl ere was a small self-service elevator.

The people in the fifth-floor apartment were cordial and responsive. The family consisted of a man, his wife, his sister, and his aged parents. There were two boys in the family, eleven and thirteen, but they were now both away at camp. I judged the man to be about thirty-eight or forty. He was dark, tall, and spare. His face was bony and intense. When he smiled, however, the hollows disappeared and his manner was winning.

The foyer was large, but the rooms were small. There were two bedrooms, a kitchen, and a combination dining room and sitting room. Window space and lighting were good. Kitchen equipment was compact, but no modern appliances such as electric refrigerators or washing machines. The furniture, both in the living room and bedrooms, was inexpensive but sturdy.

We were invited into the living room and then sat around the oak dining-room table and talked. The conversation lasted perhaps half an hour. It developed that Emil Horst was what is known as a Communist party "activist." His role in the building of Stalinstadt had been that of an assistant supervisor in charge of assignments; he would organize working teams or units. He admitted frankly that apartments had been distributed according to one's contribution to the project as a whole.

"With so many people looking for homes, it is only fair that those who help should be rewarded," he said.

"Were top-ranking members or officials of the Communist party given preference even if they had no direct part in the project?" I asked.

"That is a difficult question to answer," he said. "Leading officials of the SED [he avoided the term "Communist party" throughout our talk] of course have been given apartments. But they have all made contributions in one way or another. Even those who did not work with their hands have had important responsibilities in connection with morale or leadership or activities in the arena. But many of the apartments go to workers. They have shown wonderful spirit, the workers. It is a wonderful thing to see the way even the women will be working long after dark; sometimes they skip their meals entirely."

I asked him whether he had heard much about the United States.

Not much, he said. Occasionally he received letters from friends. He said that part of what he had heard was not very good. One of his friends was Steve Nelson, who had been put in jail because he was a Communist. He reached into his pocket and took out a letter from Steve Nelson and held it in front of him.

"This is not good," he said. "Why should the United States persecute Communists? This is not freedom."

I started to explain that the Steve Nelson case involved more than the mere fact that Steve Nelson belonged to the Communist party, but Werner Shultz headed me off, saying in English that it was better not to get into political controversy. I think Emil Horst got the sense of what Werner was saying because he smiled, then said that he had no argument with the American people; it was only the government that was doing bad things.

Such as?

"Such as setting German against German. Such as trying to make Germans think that the Soviet seeks to enslave them instead of liberate them. Or to trick them through the food packages."

He spoke evenly, without rancor or even argumentativeness in his voice. There was no doubt in my mind that he believed what he said. And he listened carefully when I tried to answer him point by point. I tried to avoid saying anything that I felt could not be documented, then told him I would be glad to send the documentary material.

Werner squirmed uncomfortably, then said in English that the easiest way to get this fellow into serious trouble would be to send him any material; it would almost automatically be branded as propaganda.

If I hadn't felt an unbridgeable gulf before, I felt it then. For a moment, earlier, I had felt confidence in the sheer fact of proximity. I had thought that a face-to-face meeting could at least serve as the means for a full exchange of ideas. Yet what separated us and placed us in two different worlds was the result of much more than distance or the inability—or ability—to sit around the same table and talk to each other. What separated us was the fact that there were boundary lines in our conversation and in our relationship that would make it impossible to pursue a fact or to forge successive links in a chain of persuasion.

If Emil Horst sensed this feeling of a sealed-in futility, he showed no sign of it. But he did want to make the point, he said, that even if what I said was true, that still didn't explain why the United States government turned down the offer of the Soviet leaders for a face-to-face meeting. Surely, he said, it will be good for the world's peoples if the world's leaders can get together to talk about their differences.

There was something almost symmetrical between his question and our own relationship. It was more than a matter of people coming together, I said; the conditions and the circumstances of the coming together were important. Surely, if the main purpose of a meeting was merely to serve as a propaganda opportunity for one side to blame the other for the failure of the meeting, then nothing would be gained. And why have a special meeting when the United Nations itself offered the proper forum for settling disagreements? And if the United Nations as presently constituted lacked the basis for reaching such agreements based on justice, wasn't it sensible to work for a stronger UN which did in fact possess such responsible powers, a UN which could command the confidence of the world's peoples? And why had the Soviet leaders opposed measures to strengthen the UN?

Emil Horst smiled and said that he didn't feel qualified to go into such complicated matters. All he could do was to have confidence in his leaders to do the right thing about such difficult questions. Besides, he hadn't been well informed about these things.

Once again I could feel the power of the separate worlds that claimed us. Emil Horst could argue only up to the point where a new frame of reference would be created; then he would stop or try to revert to the old. When a new fact was introduced which changed the old frame of reference, he would invoke the leader principle. New facts meant follow the leader, not assess the facts and help to mold leadership to meet them.

I realized the matter could not—perhaps ought not—be pursued. I changed the subject and asked him about his boys.

"Two wonderful boys," he said. "Ten and twelve. Both away at a summer workers' camp. I pay nothing. We visited them last week. They look fine. They get exercise and discipline. They taught my older boy how to ride a motorcycle. I was surprised to see how well he did it."

He asked me about my family. I gave him a brief account. It was getting late and we got up to leave. I thanked Emil Horst, who replied that he was glad I had come, and that he had tried to answer my questions to the best of his ability.

As we drove away from Stalin City Werner said: "You know what bothered me the most about our visit back there? It was what the man said about his boys. I know all about those boys' camps"—he gave an ironical twist to the last two words—"and I think I know where it all leads.

"I was a member of the Nazi Youth—just as these boys are now in the Communist Youth Organization. When I was ten I was first sent to a summer camp. Each year after that I would go back. I would get exercise and discipline. I grew away from my parents. My whole life was in the Nazi Youth. When I was thirteen they taught me how to ride a motorcycle. It was the biggest thrill of my life. And I liked the discipline. I liked the uniform and the stripes I got with increased authority.

"Then one day—I was no more than fifteen, I think—they gave me a gun. They made me feel I was going to own the world. Now look at the world we own." He waved his arm in the direction of a row of bombed buildings.

"And today it is the same thing all over again, only they change the label. Yesterday it was National Socialism, today it is People's Socialism."

It was getting dark. The sidewalks of East Berlin seemed deserted, and not too many of the apartment dwellers had switched on their lights.

Then we swung into a street leading to Potsdamer Platz, the crossroads between East and West Berlin, the focal point of the riots of the past June when East German crowds turned on the Communist police and tried to wreck one of the local Communist functionary headquarters.

In the distance we could see, very brightly, the large electric sign atop one of the West Berlin buildings on the border between the two sectors. It was an electric news board, flashing the news of the day in bright lights right into the heart of East Berlin. The few East Berliners we passed on the street did not stand still and stare at it; they're supposed to ignore it. But as they walked toward the light, they would look up at it now and then, quickly.

We stopped on the east side of Potsdamer Platz and were searched by the sentries again and cleared. In a few minutes we were in West Berlin, cruising down the brightly lit Kurfürstendamm, with its hundreds of automobiles and their flashing headlights. Countless large neon signs dominated the sky. Smartly dressed couples were dining under the canopies of the sidewalk cafés.

Flying out of Berlin several days later over the same countryside that I had seen during the days of the air lift I was still sorting my impressions. There were many elements, but some things began to stand out. The strongest of them was that no other city in history, not even ancient Rome or Athens, had within it so completely all the elements involved in the crisis of its time as does Berlin today. No other city in history has been more densely packed with conflicting historical forces; no other city has had stuffed inside it such contrasting symbols, or has been cleaved so sharply into such different worlds. And no other city has taken the shape of such a precarious fuse, with the world itself as the explosive.

The first eruption—minor in scope but titanic in its implications—had already occurred. The June riots were more than an isolated outburst. They were the escaping steam of something too far past the boiling point to cool off rapidly just by turning down the fire.

There were—and are—many visible causes behind the June riots against Communist control. These causes become apparent when you get to know the hungry people who cross over to get free food, or when you go into East Berlin itself and see the East Berlin policemen traveling in pairs armed with sub-machine guns, or when you learn about the living conditions of the majority.

The East Berliners who revolted were not physically opposed by soldiers exported from Soviet Russia. They turned against a system operated by the Soviets; but the stones they threw and the clubs they swung were directed at other East Berliners who represented the instruments of an oppressor authority. No Russian Communists fired shots or were fired upon during the riots. It was a case of German against German: those who had been imposed upon against the agents of the imposition. In this sense, the riots were only one of an increasing number of skirmishes in what is actually a civil war whose roots are not confined to Germany.

I do not say "ideological" civil war; it is much more than that. It is as complex as a human being himself. It is men preying upon other men; it is the strong undertow of an age of multiple pressures and confusions; it is a piling up of historical forces and causes so great as to resist perspective itself.

No matter how heavily we arm ourselves against the threat of communism, we will not be fully armed until we know—know much better than we do now—why men go Communist. One stereotyped half-truth that shall have to go is the easy assumption that communism is no more complicated than an empty belly. There are hungry people in East Germany who, far from turning to communism, would flee it if they could. And there are people—many of them—who have never known hunger or hardship in their lives who have enlisted on the Soviet side. The hunger theory isn't the whole story. Nor is the devil theory of communism. This is the stereotype that communism appeals primarily to the evil in man and that only evil men respond.

In Horst's case, the basis of the appeal was not evil but good. The arguments that persuaded him were not based primarily on hate. This is an important distinction that must be made between Nazism and communism. The appeal to Horst was a deeply moral one; it involved, or professed to involve, the elements of justice and generosity of spirit.

What, in particular, were the moral arguments that appealed to Horst? I cannot say precisely, but judging from what he said, and from the literature he read, I would say that he was told, and believed, that communism meant idealism, equality, service to man, brotherhood, humaneness, social justice, freedom, opportunity, hope. I have not selected, nor do I use, these words ironically. Should you say that if Horst believes this, he is a fool, I will agree with you; but I would also ask that you know what it was that fooled him, and that what threatens us is a fool's paradise.

Will Horst remain a Communist? Can he possibly maintain his illusions—with all the contrary evidence around him, with thousands of his friends and neighbors turning against a monstrous hoax? It is hard to say. A lot depends on the depth not only of his commitments but his involvements. It depends too, perhaps, on the ability of the ideology to keep him comfortable in the belief that good ends justify bad means. Finally, it depends on the pace and the process by which he is assimilated into the lie. At some point his conscious share in the guilt and his need for self-justification may become synonymous with self-preservation, and Horst may in the end personify the evil for which he now is an agent and which came to him originally in the image of a powerful truth.

I do not believe that the path by which Horst arrived at communism is the only path to it, any more than I believe that any single theory can explain the advent of communism and its march in one generation across two-fifths of the world. But of one thing I am certain. It can be defeated only with affirmative values. It is less afraid of guns and bombs than it is of courageous idealism. Communism may itself turn to guns in its desperation; but the real decision, the ultimate decision, will turn on whether we ourselves fully understand the power of hope and can make enough people believe that our commitment to hope is total and undeviating. Not hope as a slogan but hope as a product of working ideals that are literally large enough to embrace the world.

*—October 10, 1953*

# Where Violence Begins

This is about Kamilal Deridas of India, who killed his friend. The killing occurred in 1947. All his life Deridas had followed the nonviolence teachings of Mahatma Gandhi. He kept his thoughts free of fear and hate. And then one day, suddenly, he reached for a knife and slew his friend.

I met Deridas at a refugee camp on the outskirts of Delhi in February, 1951. I shall never forget the account of his experiences during India's ordeal in the summer of 1947, when the country was partitioned into three units—India proper, Pakistan West, and Pakistan East. The two sections of the new Pakistan were united politically, but they were separated by the geographic expanse of India at its widest. If you can imagine that Mexico, instead of being situated south of the United States, were to be split in half, with one part in southern California and the other in New England, then you may have a fair idea of the geographic relationship of Pakistan to India, as well as the difficulties surmounted so heroically by the Pakistani leaders in operating a unified and free government.

The background of partition is long and involved. It was the culmination of more than a century of dual struggle—the struggle for national independence against England, and the struggle for power inside India between Hindu and Moslem. Centuries ago the Moslems ruled the northern part of India. When the British quit India in 1947 there were perhaps 100 million Moslems in all of India, and more than 325 million Hindus. With partition some 65 million Moslems formed the population of the new Pakistan, the balance remaining in India. Today the population of Pakistan is more than 75 million, with close to 40 million Moslems still in India proper.

Partition and national independence were part of the same historical event. Neither was then possible without the other. But the sudden rupture of a great nation caused it to bleed hideously. The struggle for national independence had been waged for centuries but it came virtually overnight and no one was prepared for it. The new Free India had only a bare governmental skeleton with which to administer the affairs of the second most populous nation in the world. Pakistan started absolutely from scratch, having to use empty crates for government desks.

And in those early days of uncertainty and confusion people became panicky. Whatever the animosity had been between Hindu and Moslem before independence, the people had managed to live side by side. There had been recurrent violent flare-ups, to be sure, but they were not too serious. With partition, however, millions of people suddenly became jittery and insecure. A Hindu who lived in a city near the border such as Lahore wondered what was to happen to him now that Lahore was to become part of Pakistan. A Moslem who lived on the outskirts of Calcutta wondered what was to happen now that there would be a separate Moslem government in Pakistan that did not include him. The insecurity and confusion became multiplied as millions of people decided to move in order to be governed by their own group.

Then came violence. At first there were only sporadic incidents. A Moslem in Dacca, for example, would smash the shopwindows of a clothing store owned by a Hindu, claiming he had heard that Hindus were looting Moslem shops in Calcutta or Delhi. A Hindu in Calcutta would set fire to a Moslem home, in open view of a crowd, yelling that he had heard that Moslems were burning homes of Hindus who remained behind in Dacca or Karachi. Some Hindus or Moslems would try to take advantage of the national turmoil by seizing business properties or homes.

Each incident, of course, fed on rumors and led to even greater rumors. Outrages were carried out in the name of retaliation. Soon a civil war without battle lines or armies raged throughout the sub-continent. People rushed through the streets with sticks or torches or whatever could be used to kill a man.

Like millions of others who lived through the dark days of 1947, Kamilal Deridas didn't like to talk about what happened or his own part in it. It was only after we had spent many hours together, discussing the event in a general way, that he began to speak in terms of his individual experiences. I had told him that I found it difficult to understand how people who achieved so much through their belief in nonviolence could suddenly abandon that belief at the very moment of its fulfillment. How could they allow themselves to become something they had never been? Deridas's reply to my question was simple and vivid.

"I can answer you because I know how it was. I was part of it from the very beginning. I was twenty-six at the time. My wife, my two little boys, and I lived with my parents in a nice house on the edge of Lahore. My father operated an arts-and-crafts shop. Lahore was something of a world convention city. The weather is clear and good almost the entire year and there were generally meetings that brought many people to the city.

"I had many friends in Lahore—among both Hindus and Moslems. Those of us who had gone to college thought all the old antagonisms were foolish, and we were bored by the traditional hostilities of the older people. Two of my closest friends were Moslems and they were as indifferent to the old religious and cultural rivalries as I was. The name of one was Faiz; the other Ahmed.

"After plans for the partition were made in 1947 Faiz came to me and said that he was worried about talk he had heard in town. He had heard that certain Hindu homes would be requisitioned after Pakistan came into being in order to make room for the many Moslems who would be coming to the city. And our home was on one of the lists.

"My father dismissed this talk as nonsense. He said that the new Pakistan would not tolerate such outrages because there were more Moslems in India than Hindus in what was to be the new Pakistan. He said the new government would know only too well how much worse it would fare than India in any contest of seizure of private property. He told me to forget about it.

"But as the time for partition neared, and as reports reached Lahore of local riots in sections where there were mixed populations, I became very alarmed. One night Faiz came to my home through the back door and begged me to get my belongings together as quickly as I could, take my family, and flee Lahore.

"He said that there had been a secret meeting a few hours earlier in town and that reports were read which told of Hindu looting of Moslem shops in Delhi and Bombay and also that in several places Moslem women had been violated by Hindus and put on public exhibition. He said there were also reports that many, many thousands of Moslem homes had been seized by Hindu crowds throughout India. The men at the meeting were hysterical with rage and called for immediate retaliatory action.

"There were some at the meeting who cautioned against anything that might start a riot. But most of the others turned on these cautious few and shouted them down, saying they were traitors, and then the cautious few spoke no more.

"I made up my mind that we would have to leave within a week at most and began to plan a way out and also to plan some way of getting the most valuable items in our store to a place of safety. I sought the help of Ahmed, who agreed to keep the most valuable items in the cellar of his home. That night and the next night, between 1 A.M. and 4 A.M., we transported the valuables in Ahmed's car from our store to his home. It was a courageous thing for him to do. It would have meant his death if he had been discovered.

"Then Ahmed and Faiz and I met in order to make plans for us to get out of Lahore until some measure of stability returned to the city. My father was difficult to persuade about this but something terrible that happened to us two days after Faiz came to warn me changed his mind.

Our store was located in the resort section, which is the far side of the city. Early in the morning, shortly after I had opened the shop, I heard the sounds of a great commotion coming from afar. I locked the store, then rushed toward the center of the town. As I approached I saw that the looting and the burning had already begun. There was smashed glass all over the streets. Not far away I could see smoke rising from the heart of the city.

"I ran back to the store. My father and my brother-in-law were waiting. They were very agitated. My twenty-one-year-old sister had been missing since 8 A.M. It was now 10 A.M. We barricaded the store to the best of our ability, then rushed home. We never saw my sister again. That night my brother-in-law learned that she had been abducted, along with sixty or seventy young Hindu wives. We could only pray for her life and her integrity of physical self, but I feared the worst.

"That night, we left the house one by one, dressed in Moslem style, and were picked up by Faiz and Ahmed in their cars and brought to Ahmed's house, where we were to stay secretly until we completed arrangements for getting out of Lahore. It was lucky we left our house when we did. Part of it was wrecked the very next day and the part that remained was occupied.

"Our plan for leaving Lahore was a simple one. We would travel in three pony carts. After a day's travel from Lahore we would slip over the border at night and then get a train to Delhi, two hundred and fifty or three hundred miles distant. At Delhi we would try to find a place to live.

"Then one night—it was after midnight—Ahmed came to the small room in his house where we were all hiding. I could see that there was something wrong. He was almost hysterical. He had just been told that his parents had been burned to death the night before in their beds. My father tried to calm him by saying it could not be so, that Hindus would not do such a thing; and Ahmed said that there was no doubt about it. He said he knew that there were outrages on both sides; he had wanted to stay free of them, and had risked his life and the lives of his immediate family to help Hindus, and that this was now his reward—a mother and father burned in their beds by Hindus.

"My father again insisted that it was not so, and that someone had lied to Ahmed, and before I knew what was happening my father and Ahmed were quarreling and shouting at each other. I begged them to be quiet, for they were certain to rouse the entire neighborhood. But those were no days of calm tempers; we had all been without sleep and were on edge and had been infected by the ugly passions that were sweeping over the two countries. My father and Ahmed continued to shout at each other; then my father in a moment of rage said that he was certain that all Ahmed was after was our valuables which we had stored with him.

And Ahmed, insane with grief over the killing of his parents, went into a blind fury, reached for a knife, and started after my father.

"Right then something happened to me. I don't remember it clearly; in fact, I don't remember it at all, but my wife told me about it later. The sight of the knife after everything that had happened in the past few days made me lose my senses. I took a knife that Ahmed had given me earlier for my own safety. I killed him. I reached over his shoulder with my knife and I killed him.

"Right after that we left the house, taking Ahmed's car, even though it had been decided earlier that we would not use an automobile because cars on the road going to the border attracted too much suspicion. We knew the pony carts were small enough for the back roads. But now we had no choice. How we finally made the border is almost too incredible to tell. Anyway, that is not what you wanted to know about. You wanted to know how peaceable men could forget all their convictions, forget everything, and kill. I have tried to tell you.

"There are many, many thousands of people like me. No one knows how many people became killers during those dark days. What we know is that maybe 300,000 were killed; maybe half a million; maybe a million. No one stopped to count. But we do know that 12 million people lost their homes and fled in terror. Seven or 8 million Hindus. Four or 5 million Moslems. Maybe more.

"I have talked about my part in the dark days to very few people. But one man to whom I spoke had known Gandhi, and you know that Gandhi himself was killed in that terrible period during partition. And this man, who would know what Gandhi would say if he knew what I had done, told me that what had happened was not my sin alone but the sin of all the people of India and Pakistan. Gandhi made no distinction in his life between Hindu and Moslem; he loved us all. And his friend told me that Gandhi would have said that I had temporarily lost my sanity with all the others but that I should work for friendship between Hindu and Moslem as the only way of paying for my crime.

"What he said helps. It also helps to remember that when men are soldiers they kill because they are caught up in something larger than themselves.

"Perhaps you are wondering," he resumed after a minute or two, "whether these terrible things happened here in India and Pakistan only because—well, because there is something perhaps primitive or uncivilized about these people; and that this could never happen to people like yourselves who are educated and refined. One thing I surely learned during that time was that everything is swept aside in panic. I was a college man; Ahmed was a college man. College men were in the crowds that set fire to the shops and the homes. And in the Western world a high literacy rate didn't keep the German people from going in for mass murder. And there were many outrages in your own Civil War. I'm afraid I would have to say that what happened to us could happen to anyone when people are governed only by their fears. It is then that the worst elements in the society can set the pattern for society itself.

"At a time like that is when the very great men in a society show themselves. And it was then that the world really knew that Jawaharlal Nehru was fit to wear the mantle of Gandhiji. For it was Nehru who risked his life to save Moslems during the Delhi riots. It was Nehru who rushed out into Connaught Circle late at night and thrust himself between a Hindu looter and his intended victim. And it was Nehru who while on the spot ordered Hindu police to shoot at Hindu looters. And the rioting and the killing receded faster in Delhi than anywhere else—because of Nehru.

"And it is Nehru's presence in the government that has caused many millions of Moslems to stay behind in India. Both Hindus and Moslems have sinned deeply. Only in friendship can they clear those miserable stains. And Nehru is trusted by the Moslems in India. They shudder—and I shudder with them—when we think of what would happen in India if anything happened to him.

"For there is still great uneasiness in the two countries. There are many issues which are unsettled between Hindus and Moslems as the result of partition. I have had to live with my family in tents or shacks, without proper sanitary facilities, since 1947. What about our property in Lahore? Shouldn't there be some payment for our store and our home? And what about the abducted women? Pakistani have many of the same claims against India. Then, to top everything, of course, is the Kashmir dispute.

"The situation between the two countries is precarious. Zealots on both sides are trying to inflame the people. Moslem religious fanatics think Pakistan ought to wage a holy war against India and unite the entire country on the basis of Moslem rule. And we have our own Hindu fanatics who want to sweep into Pakistan and bring about reunification through force and then set up a theocratic Hindu state.

"That is why I pray that these two countries may have peace."

Deridas's story about the dark days of 1947 in India has a special meaning today for the American people. America is in a position to exercise a profound influence on the affairs of India and Pakistan. If we are wise we can contribute to the peace and well-being of both countries. If we are foolish or insensitive we can upset a precarious equilibrium and help to touch off a sub-continental civil war.

Of all the issues outstanding between India and Pakistan today none is more difficult or more combustible than the Kashmir dispute. There is no clear-cut question of right and wrong here between India and Pakistan. Anyone who has attempted to study the problem on the spot knows the difficulty of striking a balance between the claims of both parties. Similarly, anyone who has made a sensitive appraisal of the situation knows that the present prime ministers of both countries are far more moderate in their approaches, far more convinced of the necessity for and possibility of a peaceful settlement, than large segments of public opinion in their respective countries. Both Mohammed Ali and Jawarharlal Nehru have demonstrated a sense of total responsibility in opposing the growing extremist factions.

In the midst of this touch-and-go situation comes the report that America is preparing to send arms to Pakistan. The effect has been exactly what was to be expected. In India it has already strengthened the hands of the extremists who want to press for a forcible seizure of the Kashmir. It gives the Communists the most powerful weapon they have had since India became independent. It puts them in a position where they could claim leadership against what they denounce as the vacillating policies of Nehru. It enables them to exploit the passions of the militant Hindus, playing upon their fears that the religious fanatics in Pakistan would seize the upper hand and use American arms against India. It makes the entire nation fearful that Pakistan would be in a stronger position in the event of a showdown over the Kashmir.

Russia does not want peace in Asia. Russia has no way of coping with peace in Asia. Russia wants chaos in Asia. We are proposing to make her that gift.

It is one of history's most stupendous paradoxes that step by step, day by day, in the name of anti-communism we seem to be doing the very things that will give communism control over the majority of the world's peoples.

Our business in the world is the business of peace. If we are to do anything for Asia let us do the things that are in keeping with the American character. If we want to help Pakistan build real defenses against communism let us put up giant dams and power installations. Let us help her develop her farms and her industries. If we are concerned about communism in India let us fight the threat where it exists today—in the farms and villages and factories—by helping to prove to the Indian people that communism is the false answer to famine, poverty, illiteracy. We can prove that democracy is the right answer by putting democracy to work. But if we can do none of these things at least let us not set the stage for mass murder.

—*January 16, 1954*

# The Novelist's Dread of Finality

For years Hervey Allen worked on *Anthony Adverse*. At least half-a-dozen times his mound of manuscript approached a logical terminus in the story. But each time Allen veered away from the final chapter and kept on going. Finally his publisher exercised the necessary initiative, took the manuscript away, and committed it to print.

It wasn't easy to persuade Margaret Mitchell to part with the manuscript for *Gone with the Wind*. It was four or five times longer than the average novel, but she still felt it was unfinished.

In Thomas Wolfe's mind all his books were part of a single work, and that one incomplete. The works that were issued to the public he was inclined to regard as packaged carvings from the whole. His approach was that of the author who had only one story to tell and one book to write and he was still doing it when he died.

At least two experiences are shared by every serious writer. The first is the yearning or determination to write his heart out in one big book, a book that would fulfill itself and himself. The second is the dread of finality—as represented not only by his difficulty in knowing when a book is finished, but by his reluctance to part with it even after he has managed to end it. Theodore Dreiser had no distaste for publication; the reason he kept pecking away at his manuscripts long after they had actually become a literary whole was his dread of the perils of finality. A novel is a prodigious experience for the writer. It is a possessing embryo which consumes the imagination and drains the mind. But it also nourishes and replenishes even as it seeks the materials for its own needs. Thus it becomes a process of growth and change for the novelist himself. And he hates to let it go, not only because of the painful joy of creative work, with its continuity and uninterrupted purpose, but because he feels what he has done can be made better and he does not want it ever to get beyond reach.

Six years ago Ira Wolfert published *An Act of Love*. Before that he had written some fiction. His chief distinction, however, had been as Pulitzer Prize war correspondent and author who was highly regarded for the careful strength and craftsmanship of his writing. It was clear that *An Act of Love* was to be his big book. Into it he had put everything he had learned and felt as a war correspondent who had seen almost too much for one man to digest. In the book he posed the eternal human questions against the background of his own experience. He did this through the highly dramatic story of a Navy flier who was washed ashore on one of the Solomon Islands after a half-dozen flirtations with death. The flier is rescued by members of a local tribe. Among the few white inhabitants of the island are a self-exiled American planter, his wife, and their attractive daughter. The war comes to the island, which gives Wolfert a chance to deal with society as the great pursuer, destroying the prospect even of accidental escape. The struggle of a man to find the best in himself is thus juxtaposed against the world at its worst.

*An Act of Love* was more than a fair success as a published novel, but it apparently failed to provide catharsis for the author. The story and its meaning still grew inside him, and the published book was now a partial product. And the old questions came up: What happens after publication day? Does the author cease to exist? Has he been totally consumed by his own creativity? Is he supposed to create another big book out of materials that couldn't possibly be as powerful as the ones that became dominant in his life and mind? If the reception to the book is not so big as his conception of it should the author make the adjustment to a lowered station? Should he seek or synthesize for himself the potential solace of eventual recognition for his novel in terms commensurate with his emotional investment in it? Or should he coast as a novelist, recasting or re-angling his old materials, hoping that new disguises will somehow bring out the old beauty?

These are the eternal and punishing questions for the novelist. And these are the questions that lie deep behind the reluctance to part with the manuscript of what the writer hopes will be his big book. Wolfert was unwilling to create new disguises. In the months and years after the book appeared, his ideas about the novel continued to develop and mature. In this case, he decided to contest the idea of finality. He had learned some things about the techniques of the novel since his book first appeared; he had thought deeply about ways in which the same story might be more dramatically presented; and he asked his publisher for another chance. The book would carry the same title. Readers would be told exactly what had happened.

To the credit of Simon and Schuster, Wolfert was given the chance to do what almost every serious novelist who ever lived has dreamed of being able to do; to give added growth and dimension to a book apparently beyond reach. What is important here is not whether the retold version of this particular book is better than the first. It does happen to be better—much better; but the achievement here goes beyond *An Act of Love*. The achievement is demonstrated by a courageous belief, both by novelist and publisher, in the essentials of a writer's growth. Apart from this, it is altogether a novel approach to the novel. Is Hemingway satisfied with *A Farewell to Arms*? In the light of his own development, how would he like to refashion or retell the story today? What about the earlier works of Steinbeck, Faulkner, Thomas Mann, Dos Passos?

It may be argued, of course, that we are apt to get into a hall of mirrors, for there is no assurance that the authors may not wish a third, fourth, or fifth try. Whatever the risk, it may be worth it.

*—August 14, 1954*


# Are We Men or Murderers?

Something happened not long ago that made no headlines and was hardly even reported. In fact, it was all but lost in the flurry over Formosa. But it was as important as any single event in the past ten years. What happened was that the United States government quietly repudiated its historic position under which heads of enemy governments at the end of the last war were killed or punished for the crime of war. Without benefit of national debate or a vote of the Congress or even an explanation to the American people, the United States reversed itself on the principle of world law under which we had earlier declared that not nations but individuals make war and are therefore to be held accountable for war.

Before fixing our gaze on the incredible historic liability we have just incurred, let us review the background. Almost as significant as victory itself in World War II was the proclamation of a new principle, investing sovereignty in the community of nations as a whole. Under this principle it was decreed that war was a crime by individuals against the world community. Accordingly, eminent jurists from the victorious nations came together in a Four-Power Tribunal to define the principles of world law under which individuals were to be tried. Hundreds of political and military leaders from the Axis powers were arraigned, tried, sentenced, and punished. The indictment drawn up against the inner Nazi circle, for example, charged twenty-two men with (1) participating in a conspiracy to commit crime against the peace and against humanity, (2) planning and executing a war of aggression, (3) violating the rules of warfare by mistreatment of civilians and prisoners of war, (4) murdering and enslaving people because of race, religion, or political belief.

The tribunal condemned twelve high-ranking Nazis to death by hanging. Seven were sentenced to long prison terms; three were set free. Subsequently, under these precedents, and with prosecutors from the Allied nations, various other trials were held. The final score was 456 death sentences and 1,112 convictions with lesser penalties. In Japan, acting under the same legal sanctions, the United States tried twenty-eight Japanese war leaders, executing seven and imprisoning eighteen.

Supreme Court Justice Robert H. Jackson, who headed the American staff of jurists participating in the Nuremberg trials, made it clear that this country was not using the forms of legality as a cloak for vengeance. Even though there was no government of the whole to represent the human community, the community existed and possessed certain basic rights. When these rights were violated it became the responsibility of that community not only to protect itself but to invoke the mechanism of legality at its disposal against the criminals. Individuals who operated or governed aggressive nations could not escape responsibility by pretending to be merely the agents of those nations. Their decisions were the ones that led to the crimes.

Seldom in human history had there been anything as epochal as the definition and application of these principles. In essence, they laid down the basis for world law. They also made implicit the need to create a constitutional basis for the community of nations in order to enable it to deal with world criminals *before* and not *after* the damage was done. In any event, we had made certain specific commitments to basic legal and moral principles from which we could not depart without becoming world criminals ourselves. For if the decisions that were to send more than a thousand human beings to their death were to be undone, we would stand condemned under the very statutes we invoked to condemn others.

To repeat, the big challenge after the Nuremberg trials was to incorporate its basic provisions into the Charter and structure of the United Nations, which was vested with the responsibility for keeping world law and order. This meant that the Nuremberg principles would have to be codified and given the full machinery of implementation. Since aggression did not disappear with the end of World War II and since, indeed, it became essential to create within the shortest possible time the adequate means to safeguard world peace, the principles of the Nuremberg trials offered a magnificently prepared ground on which to build. If a human community did in fact exist, and if there were threats to that community, then Nuremberg represented both a mandate and a fixed need.

However, the work of drafting a code based on the Nuremberg principles went slowly in the councils of the United Nations. Finally, the issue recently came before the General Assembly of the United Nations and a preliminary decision had to be made. It was at this point that the United States opposed the arguments of the representative from the Netherlands. On November 17, 1954, Charles H. Mahoney, U.S. representative, explained the American position. There was nothing ambiguous about our statement, nothing which would enable us to avoid the condemnation of history. What we said, in so many words, was that the United States government did not wish to subject its citizens to "those regular and continuing processes of investigation, prosecution, and trial by international agencies which would be necessary for real enforcement of an international criminal code." We also said officially that "the project for a code of crimes under international law in today's world is impractical and inappropriate."

Impractical? Is it more practical to wait until a billion human lives are expunged before we decide that something ought to be done about the principle of individual responsibility? Is it practical to construct an elaborate legal mechanism in the name of justice and then to turn away from it when it fails to serve our purpose? Inappropriate? Is there anything more inappropriate than to be guilty of a double standard in the eyes of history, seeking immunity from the very legality we solemnly impose upon others? There is an equally important question that concerns Supreme Court Justice Jackson and the able corps of American jurists who worked with him at Nuremberg. Have we by our action before the United Nations converted them into murderers? If the legal basis of their work is to be dissolved, what status are they to occupy in history?

Ever since the United Nations was founded, American delegates to the United Nations have chafed under the frequent use of the veto by Soviet Russia in the Security Council. But not once have we reminded the world that we ourselves proposed the veto. Nor have we ourselves proposed that the veto be replaced with binding obligations—on us as well as everyone else. Similarly, we have made dramatic postures against aggressors and world criminals but when the hard question of individual responsibility actually comes up we ourselves have run for cover. Most perplexing of all is the presumption of our delegation in saying that the American people are not ready for the measures that are an organic part of world law and therefore world security. Has the question been put to our people? Has there been a national debate? How does the delegation know?

Is it possible that the American delegation to the UN is more concerned over the probable attacks by certain senators who fear world commitments than they are over the moral and historic significance of their reversal of Nuremberg? It is undoubtedly true that some senators will shout to the skies against the creation of a higher sovereignty. That is their right. But it is also the right and privilege of the government to take the fight to the people.

The American delegation to the UN has put the American people on the spot. Whether we get off it or not depends on whether the American people will allow their name to be used lightly in the world, even by their own government.

—February 17, 1955

# Does Anyone Have Time to Think?

We in America have been concerned for some years with the lot of underprivileged peoples throughout the world. But we have yet to do anything for one of the most underprivileged peoples of all. Ourselves.

We have more food than we can eat. We have more money per person than anywhere else in the world; with 6 per cent of the population we hold 80 per cent of the wealth. We have bigger homes, bigger television sets, bigger cars, bigger theaters, bigger schools. We have everything we need, in fact, except the most important thing of all—time to think and the habit of thought. We lack time for the one indispensable for safety of an individual or a nation.

Thought is the basic energy in human history. Civilization is put together not by machines but by thought. Similarly, man's uniqueness is represented not by his ability to make objects but to sort them and relate them. Other animals practice communication; only man has the capacity for comprehension. Displace or eliminate thought, and the species itself has as little claim on survival as the dinosaurs with the four-foot skulls and the pea-sized brains. The impotence of the brute alongside the power of the sage is represented by thought.

Consider where we in America stand today. We have been told and we have told ourselves that we have the responsibility to lead. We are asked to keep freedom alive; we are asked to find some way to prevent a war that would incinerate one billion or more human beings and twist and deform the rest. It is not a simple task. Leadership today requires not so much a determination to smash the other fellow as an understanding of the lessons of human experience. It requires a profound knowledge of the diseases of civilizations. It requires ability to anticipate the effects of actions. In short, it requires thought. But who is doing the thinking? Who is giving sustained and incisive thought to the most complicated and dangerous problem in the age of man?

Next question: Does anyone have time to think? Does the President have time to think? The daily calendar of an American President, with its endless appointments and gladhanding chores, not only excludes sustained thought but creates the kind of staccato, jangling pattern of mental activity that leads to a demand for surcease rather than study. A day on the golf links thus becomes a useful cathartic for eliminating congested impressions and helping a man to retain his sanity, but it doesn't necessarily provide the occasion for concentrated and consecutive thought.

If the President has no time to think, then who? Almost everyone in

Washington is spending so much time being strategical that almost no one is being historical. There are so many movers and shakers that there is hardly any room for thinkers.

This is not a political party matter; the churning and flailing easily cross party lines. Washington does not exist in terrible isolation. Washington can be only a reflection and a projection of the national character and temperament. If officeholders are too busy to think, do they differ from the business executive, college president, teacher, man on the assembly line, or housewife?

The paradox, of course, is that we are busy doing nothing. Never before has so much leisure time been available to so many. Leisure hours now exceed working hours. But we have a genius for cluttering. We have somehow managed to persuade ourselves that we are too busy to think, too busy to read, too busy to look back, too busy to look ahead, too busy to understand that all our wealth and all our power are not enough to safeguard our future unless there is also a real understanding of the danger that threatens us and how to meet it. Thus, being busy is more than merely a national passion; it is a national excuse.

The real question, however, concerns not the time or lack of it we provide for thought, but the value we place on thought. What standing does thoughtfulness enjoy in the community at large? What great works of contemporary literature assign importance to thought or make heroes of thoughtful men? Action, accumulation, diversion—these seem to be the great imperatives. We are so busy entertaining ourselves and increasing the size and ornamentations of our personal kingdoms that we have hardly considered that no age in history has had as many loose props under it as our own.

Everyone seems to agree, from the President down, that we have to find some way other than war to protect ourselves, support the cause of freedom in the world, and serve the cause of man. But who is giving any consecutive thought to an "other way"? We ask the world's peoples to spurn the idea of communism, and we back up this advice with the offer of guns, but what revolutionary idea do we ourselves espouse? War in Asia seems all too imminent but we talk about it as though it is some unpleasant little business at a distance instead of the curtain raiser for a war in which the big bombs will be dropped on America just as surely as they will be dropped on the enemy. Meanwhile, we are told by government that there is no real defense against atomic attack, after all. Surely all this requires some thought.

This nation of ours will not reproduce itself automatically. The meaning and the wonder of it will not be sustained by momentum alone. If we have something worth saving, as we have, somewhere in our national culture or economy we shall have to find a proper place for thought.

There is no point in passing the buck or looking for guilty parties. We got where we are because of the busy man in the mirror.

—*March 26, 1955*

## Report from Bandung

"Could you please tell me what you think of our city?" the man asked.

"It's one of the nicest cities I've ever seen," I replied.

"It is a big relief," he said. "For four months we have worked to get it ready for the conference. Do you know that every building and every home had to be painted or whitewashed? Maybe 20,000 whitewashing jobs. Every store front had to be fixed up. They even imported special goods to put in window displays but not for sale.

"Every street had to be paved or repaved or fixed up. I know. I filled in hundreds of holes myself. It is all for you; it is a big relief that you like it."

My companion, whom I happened to meet near the Dutch-style hotel where I stayed, was not a road repairer by occupation. He was an elementary-school teacher. In common with numberless other Indonesians, he had volunteered for the special task force set up by the government to prepare Bandung for the Asia-Africa conference.

Preparations involved much more than the appearance of the city. Delegations from twenty-nine nations had endless needs that had to be anticipated and provided. Comfortable quarters, compatible foods, special transportation to and from the conference sessions—all these had to be arranged. For the hundreds of "pressmen," as they were officially designated, there was the problem of all the foregoing plus the need for peak-load cable facilities and short-wave broadcasts to the rest of the world. Like soldiers in the field, each of the delegates or pressmen on the front line had to have six or seven men in depth behind him to keep him going.

From the standpoint of place and facilities, then, Bandung passed every test. Bandung is near the equator but it is on a high plateau, impressively rimmed by mountains. The temperature during the day never gets much above 80°. At night it drops to a sleep-inducing 60° or 65°.

The principal attraction, apart from the people, is the Indonesian sky. Nowhere in the world do clouds and colors combine to put on a more spectacular performance than over these serried lands. Anyone who collects memories of skyscapes as a hobby and can afford to indulge himself should settle down here for life. As a special fill-up he might take a plane ride toward sundown.

The people seem initially shy and reserved but warm up instantly on a smile from a stranger. Once they learn of your desire to be friendly there isn't enough they can do for you. Once you establish rapport with children they hold you by the arm and won't let you go. People whose earnings were only a few cents a day would offer you a place at their table.

In its external aspect, as might be expected, Bandung combines the Dutch look with the Orient. The architecture of the private homes and business buildings is unmistakably European-resort style, but the general layout of the city is somewhat reminiscent of parts of Madras—reflective in part perhaps of the large Indian population in the city.

This, then, is the city that may eventually become the capital of Asia, if the long-term visions of some of the delegates come to pass.

Easily the most remarkable thing about the Asia-Africa conference was the sense of history it represented and reflected. The nations at Bandung possessed as large a variety of political views and cultural or religious backgrounds as exist anywhere in the world; yet all the delegates seemed to feel they were part of one vast idea to which each was paying homage. The work of the conference, the public and private sessions, the general statement which required so many hours of debate and compromise—all this was actually minor compared to the symbolic significance of the event. Bandung was more important as ceremony than as conference.

The ceremony, of course, was the graduation exercises of two continents —graduation into equality in the family of free nations.

The process of breaking loose from colonial rule had been spaced out over a generation or more. The individual gains had been celebrated, but now for the first time, all at once and in a single place, more than 1,300,000,000 human beings who had achieved freedom were observing the total event. It created a sense of exultation and kinship difficult to describe to anyone who wasn't there. The historical momentum was so great that it affected almost everything that was said or done.

Thus, it was no surprise that most of the delegates had a single answer for the question put to them at the end of the conference: "What would you say was the principal significance of Bandung?" Their answer, in one form or another, "The fact that it was held." Every delegate I spoke to felt keenly the honor of having been able to represent his people at the one event toward which his nation had been aspiring for so many years. Triumphs or defeats over conference statements were lost alongside the mountainous fact that each person present gloried in the historical aura of the occasion.

The men at Bandung marked their freedom, but there was neither gloating over the event nor the eruptive release of resentment toward the former captors or governors. General Carlos P. Romulo, who emerged from the conference as one of the most influential and eloquent spokesmen for the new Asia, keynoted the spirit of the meeting when he said:

"The success of this conference will be measured not by what we do for ourselves but by what we do for the entire human community. Large as is the cause of Asia and Africa, there is a cause even larger. It is the cause of the human community in a world struggling to liberate itself from the chaos of international anarchy. In short, our cause is the cause of man.

"Fellow delegates, our strength flows not out of our numbers, though the numbers we represent are great. It flows out of our perception of history and out of the vital purpose we put into the making of tomorrow. If that purpose is stained by resentment or the desire for revenge, then this conference will turn out to be a fragile and forgetful thing. Let us therefore not seek to draw strength from hurt or heartbreak but from our common hopes—hopes that can come to life in all peoples everywhere. And if the test of that strength should be our ability to forgive, then let it be said that we were the giants of our time."

The spirit of the conference gave substance to General Romulo's remarks. Certainly, those who had loudly predicted that the conference would serve only as an intercontinental amplification system to denounce the United States in particular and the Western world in general were made to look foolish. Nor was this a "lynch party in reverse," as a few writers had blithely forecast. It was a sober event, soberly observed.

This did not mean that the conference was all sweetness and light. There were debates—plenty of them; but the dominant feeling was a desire to achieve positive results and to preserve the largest measure of unity possible.

This desire for unity was remarkable, considering the composition of the conference. As one's eyes traveled from one side of the conference hall to the other, he was aware of strong and contrasting undercurrents. First of all, of course, one looked at Premier Chou En-Lai of the People's Republic of China, as it was officially designated.* Seated nearby were men juxtaposed against him, politically and ideologically: Prince Wan of Thailand; Dr. Fadhil al Jamali of Iraq; Sir John Kotelawala of Ceylon, and Mohammed Ali of Pakistan. The apprehensions and grievances of these countries, however, were not directed solely toward Communist China. Pakistan, for example, was having its troubles with Afghanistan, with relations between the two countries at rupture point. Nor was Pakistan forgetting for a single moment its long-standing dispute with India over the Kashmir. India's own views on the Kashmir were hardly less emphatic. And, though India was not saying much about it, the long border between Nepal and China was a matter of significant concern in view of political developments inside Nepal itself.

* The desk plate in front of Chou En-Lai's seat simply read "China" at the start of the conference; several days later it was replaced by "People's Republic of China."

One's gaze shifted from Nepal to the delegates from North Vietnam and those from South Vietnam, appropriately seated far apart in the conference hall. As though the civil war between the two factions had not caused enough anguish to the people, South Vietnam now had to contend with insurrections within itself, and the danger that it might become so weakened through internal convulsions that, ironically enough, the people themselves might turn to communism in a desperate attempt to put an end to the chaos.

Not far away from the South Vietnamese sat the Japanese delegation. Not so long ago the Japanese were in military control of Bandung and, in fact, of almost all Southeast Asia. One wondered how the Indonesians felt when they went about the business of being the polite host to a nation that only a short time ago held them in subjection. Almost everywhere one looked in the conference hall, in fact, one looked at differences, large and small, relating to disputed territories, borders, economics, politics, or minority groups. Yet the sense of historical continuity was so great and the feeling of shared experience so dynamic that current differences almost seemed irrelevant.

This feeling of historical unity was the big story at Bandung, even though some of the accounts in the American press stated that the conference was split into two warring groups. According to these accounts, Sir John Kotelawala of Ceylon headed one camp and Prime Minister Nehru the other. It was made to appear that Nehru flew from one temper tantrum to another largely because of Sir John's denunciation of communism as the new imperialism at one of the early sessions of the political committee. The only trouble with those stories is that two central facts were missing:

First, Prime Minister Nehru championed Sir John Kotelawala's conference policy statement on peace.

Second, the final conference communiqué denouncing all forms of colonialism and imperialism found Premier Chou En-Lai of Communist China as the principal objector and Prime Minister Nehru as the most effective supporter. The Nehru position was adopted. Far from attempting to monopolize the spotlight, Nehru seemed to go out of his way to avoid it. Some delegates were surprised, for example, when Nehru declined to join the roster of delegates who made opening addresses at the public sessions. [Originally the conference hosts had decided against opening statements. But a number of the delegates claimed that they hadn't come thousands of miles just to sit still or applaud politely. Premier Chou En-Lai declined to vote one way or the other but made it clear that he had come to the conference with a prepared speech—just in case.]

Prime Minister Nehru's most interesting difference of opinion was not with Sir John but with General Romulo. At the closed meeting of the

Political Committee, Mr. Nehru said he was appalled at the world's dangerous drift into coalitions and military alliances, citing SEATO in particular as a disturbing manifestation of narrowly conceived power politics. Carlos Romulo rattled no sabers in his reply. He, too, recognized the danger of coalitions. But he pointed out that SEATO did not exist in a vacuum but was the result of a specific and all-too-recognizable cause: a world which had not yet been made safe from aggression. He said that the government of the Philippines would be the first to move for an end to SEATO once the United Nations enjoyed effective police powers and the machinery to ensure world justice.

General Romulo then praised Prime Minister Nehru's statesmanship in Asia, and said that the full development of the UN offered the best hope for the durable peace and stability that both Mr. Nehru and he were working for.

The final communiqué issued by the conference seems to represent a logical fusion of these two positions. It also reflects the determination of the delegates to define the largest area of common ground. In the communiqué the delegates:

▶ Stressed the importance of economic cooperation among the Asian and African nations, but also recognized that this was a world problem and that, accordingly, economic cooperation would be sought with nations outside the two areas. [This was an effective answer to those who had feared the creation of a regional economic bloc.]

▶ Recognized and praised the effectiveness of outside economic aid. [This was a far cry from a statement repudiating American support, as had been grimly predicted in some quarters in the United States.]

▶ Welcomed the offer of "the powers principally concerned" to share information relating to the peaceful uses of atomic energy.

▶ Called for strengthening the cultural ties among nations, and for removing whatever barriers existed to the fullest possible interchange of ideas, information, and people.

▶ Recognized that the cultures of Asia and Africa rested on spiritual foundations. [There was no indication here of objection by Communist China.]

▶ Supported fully the Declaration of Human Rights as set forth in the United Nations Charter. The Declaration was hailed as a "common standard of achievement for all peoples and all nations." [Premier Chou En-Lai, of China, had originally objected to any conference statement based on a United Nations principle or position. He declared that since the People's Republic of China was not a member of the United Nations, and therefore had no opportunity to participate in the formulation of such UN statements or policies, his country could not be expected to attach its name to any conference statement tied to the UN. There was general enthusiasm in the committee, however, for the UN Declaration on Human

Rights, and Chou En-Lai withdrew his objection. This was a major break in the Communist Chinese position at Bandung, for it enabled the conference to proceed to a half-dozen other points involving support for provisions in the UN Charter.]

▶ Declared its support for the principle of self-determination of peoples and nations as defined in the UN Charter.

▶ Declared its support of the rights of Arab people in Palestine, called for implementation of the UN resolutions, and expressed hope in a peaceful settlement of the issue.

▶ Advanced the candidacy for membership in the UN of Cambodia, Ceylon, Japan, Jordan, Laos, Libya, Nepal, and unified Vietnam. [The fact that the delegates did not find the People's Republic of China "qualified" for membership was one of the most significant developments of the conference.]

▶ Called for revision of the United Nations Charter in order to provide for more equitable representation of Asian-African countries on the United Nations Security Council.

▶ Called for effective international control of atomic and thermonuclear weapons and asked the great powers to reach agreement on the suspension of atomic experiments.

▶ Recommended effective and universal disarmament under the United Nations, to apply not only to weapons of mass destruction, but to armies.

▶ Denounced colonialism *in all its manifestations* as "an evil which should speedily be brought to an end."

▶ Reaffirmed the principle that all nations should have the right to choose their own political and economic systems and their own way of life in conformity with the purposes and principles of the United Nations.

These declarations, to repeat, were hardly what one might term milk-and-water propositions. In order to achieve unanimity, it became necessary for some of the states to change drastically from positions they had long maintained in or out of the United Nations. And, since both the free world and Communist China were represented at the conference, any general agreement meant inevitably that someone would have to give considerable ground.

Whatever may have been in the mind of Premier Chou En-Lai, when he first came to the conference, the fact is that he apparently changed his mind at the conference itself. Chou En-Lai was witnessing for the first time a diversity and a spirit of independence in Asia and Africa that any restless or aggressive nation would be foolish to ignore. He had to listen to at least a half-dozen opening statements by which heads of governments or foreign ministers reaffirmed their nations' determination to maintain their independence against all threats—including the threat represented by the new imperialism of world communism.

These anti-Communist declarations were not made flamboyantly or viciously. They were stated calmly and with a sense of strong responsibility. They were received by the conference in the same spirit in which they were uttered. Chou En-Lai listened carefully, now and then making notes. He was observed to make a note, too, when President Sukarno, of Indonesia, in opening the conference, invoked Longfellow's poem "The Midnight Ride of Paul Revere," adding that the inspiration of the American fight for independence had meant much to peoples fighting for freedom against outside rule. In fact, the United States, far from being lashed to any whipping post, was held up as the finest example in history of a major nation freeing itself from colonialism. Another thing that apparently impressed Chou was the frequency with which speakers at the conference would invoke the blessings of the Deity.

When it came Chou En-Lai's turn to make his opening address at the public session he discarded his prepared script and attempted to narrow the gap between himself and his critics. He tried to explain what he said were some misconceptions about the People's Republic of China. He said that communism in general was atheistic, but that his government permitted freedom of worship. He mentioned members of his delegation who held orthodox religious views and listed the many denominations, including Christianity, that were active in China. Then he asked the same tolerance for his religious "nonbelief" that his country extended to believers. One wondered whether this reassurance, like other friendly gestures, was primarily intended for the Moslem delegates.

Next, concerning the matter of Communist China's ideological differences with other nations, he acknowledged the extent of the diversity as was represented in the conference itself. But he believed that different political systems could live amicably and he said he was willing to explore the basis for promoting such amity and common ground with any delegation.

Finally, he assured the delegates that his government "had no wish to subvert the governments of its neighboring countries."

As a token of good faith, he invited all present to visit China with complete freedom of travel and investigation. "We have no bamboo curtain, but some people are spreading a smoke screen between us."

It was interesting to compare his new speech with the text of the one he discarded. While the discarded speech was fairly mild in tone, it was far less conciliatory than the one actually given. There was no doubt about the fact that Chou was listening or that he felt a need to be in tune with the dominant mood of the conference. Day by day, in fact, Chou spent increasing amounts of time with his critics. The result was that Chou was winning friends and influencing people at Bandung.

It had been supposed, for example, that Chou would oppose the demands of the Arabs for a resolution censuring Israel. India, despite its own large Moslem population, opposed the Arab demand because Prime Minister Nehru believed it unfair for the conference to denounce a nation which had been deprived of an opportunity to state its case. He pointed out that Israel had not been invited to the conference because of the objections of the Arab nations. Premier U Nu of Burma backed this position strongly, appealing to the "chivalrous spirit" of the conference in considering the censure demand. China, however, supported the Arab demand. This made a deep impression on the Arab leaders, who were as surprised as they were delighted. Thereafter, Chou En-Lai had private meetings with Arab delegations, strengthening the impression that he was trying to break the substantial wall of resistance to Communist China that seemed to be represented by the Moslem nations.

At all events, Chou En-Lai at Bandung was definitely in a giving mood. In fact, it had almost seemed for a time that it was Christmas at Bandung. There were presents for everyone. In addition to giving the Arab nations support for its position on Palestine, Chou En-Lai gave Indonesia an agreement ending the principle of dual citizenship for the Chinese minority in Indonesia. Dual citizenship had been a source of annoyance and potential trouble, for it had enabled Chinese families to live in Indonesia for generations while remaining subjects of China. Now the members of the Chinese minority would have to choose one or the other. Other Southeast Asian countries with substantial Chinese minorities were encouraged to believe that there would be no trouble in obtaining similar agreements. In addition, there were assurances against military or political encroachment. While the benefactions were being dispersed, Tatsunosuke Takasaki, heading the Japanese delegation, met privately with Chou En-Lai. Mr. Takasaki told Chou that Japan was concerned about the propaganda line of China that denounced the Japanese government as an American puppet. Chou En-Lai said his government would recognize the Japanese government as the proper representative of the Japanese people. Then Mr. Takasaki said that a thousand or more Japanese who had been captured by China during the war were still being interned. Some of them, Mr. Takasaki added, were his personal friends. Chou En-Lai didn't attempt to defend Chinese policy in this regard. He said simply that all Japanese prisoners would be released except those who were serving prison sentences for criminal acts. Even here, he said, China would permit wives or members of families to visit the imprisoned men.

For the conference as a whole came the biggest present of all. It had been hoped during the closing days of the meeting that Bandung, in addition to its symbolic significance, might make a historic contribution to world peace. Then came Chou en-Lai's dramatic announcement. Far from pressing for a conference statement denouncing the United States,

Chou wrote out three sentences in his own hand which he read to the political committee:

"The Chinese people are friendly to the American people. The Chinese people do not want to have a war with the United States of America. The Chinese government is willing to sit down and enter into negotiations with the U.S. government to discuss the question of relaxing tension in the Far East, and especially the question of relaxing tension in the Taiwan [Formosa] area."

Chou's dramatic announcement grew out of a small lunch. Among those present in addition to Chou: Jawaharlal Nehru, General Romulo, Prince Wan of Thailand, Dr. Sukarno of Indonesia, U Nu of Burma.

During lunch the Formosan situation was informally discussed. Chou agreed that the conference offered an excellent background for establishing constructive and peaceful approaches to this question. Then he asked the advice of those present about a general statement he had in mind toward that end. The response was immediate and affirmative. Chou then wrote down the gist of his position in the three sentences quoted above.

The big question, of course, was whether Chou En-Lai really meant it. I put the question to General Romulo, who had a chance to observe the Chinese premier at close range during strategic meetings at the conference as well as at small social functions. General Romulo said all the evidence pointed in the affirmative. He said he believed it would be a mistake not to give the fullest consideration to Chou's offer. Communist China genuinely needed a long period of peace, he said, and Bandung probably served as the occasion for Chou to come to terms with the world.

I put the same question in a note to Prince Wan, one of the most outspoken and uncompromising critics of world communism at the conference. Prince Wan sent the following reply:

"Yes, he really means it. He wants to get to know people with a view to entering into international life. His ready compliance with reference to the U.N. Charter came as a pleasant surprise and facilitated my work as *rapporteur*."

(When Prince Wan had been proposed originally as *rapporteur* or recording secretary of the Political Committee, Chou registered his objection—largely, it developed, because he hadn't known what a *rapporteur* was. But when Jawaharlal Nehru declined the post, and when it was pointed out how competently Prince Wan had filled the post at the United Nations, Chou backed down.)

The moment Chou En-Lai made his sweeping peace offer, the speculations of the entire conference turned toward Washington. Many of America's friends at Bandung hoped that we would do no shooting from the hip. There was a genuine sense of shock when we did exactly that, for it seemed to the delegates that we had failed to take into account the general background and staging of Chou's statement. Nothing that Chou himself said or did at the conference, in fact, bolstered his position more than the rigid, negative statement issued by our State Department.

As a result, Chou En-Lai was able to say to the delegates, in effect: "You urged me to make a friendly approach to the United States. You wanted the People's Republic of China to take the initiative in seeking a settlement of the Formosan question. But you now have another demonstration of the fact that the United States has no intention of settling this issue peaceably." Two days later President Eisenhower made it clear that America would throw no cold water on any legitimate peace offer. By that time, however, the conference had ended, and Chou En-Lai had been able to score his greatest diplomatic triumph. We had lost ground among our friends.

One of the early developments at Bandung had been the strength and eloquence of the spokesmen for the free world. That this should have come as a surprise, which it did to the United States, is an unhappy commentary on America's skimpy understanding of the East. We had been uncertain, apprehensive, and insecure about the prospect of Bandung. We had measured it solely in our own terms instead of attempting to see it in historical perspective for the grand symbol it was. We apparently overlooked the fact that there was much in our own past to link us to Bandung; and we had to be reminded of it by President Sukarno in his reference to Longfellow.

The situation, to repeat, is not irreparable. But if we are to exercise effective leadership in the world we may have to think in terms of the needs and problems of other peoples. In carrying the torch for freedom we may have to recognize that our emphasis on freedom of the individual has meaning to others only if we couple it with the freedom of a nation from outside rule. And in talking about security it might help to remember that military security has meaning only when there is something to protect.

Finally, the key to Asia and Africa is in our own history. The closer we get to the real meaning of what happened in America one hundred eighty years ago the easier it may be to understand the dominant accent of the twentieth century. The liberation of Asia, in which America figured so prominently, helped set the stage for Bandung. We still have a place in that picture.

−May 21, 1955

# Incident in India

By itself, the incident was not large or important. But it did serve to bring a nation and an age into focus for me. It happened early in 1951, but it has come to mind many times since—especially when press reports about India raise questions about the position of the Indian people in the world today.

The incident took place at a refugee camp called Kingsway, not far from the old city of Delhi. At one time, in British India, Kingsway had been a military cantonment for some 1,500 troops. After Indian independence Kingsway became one of the emergency housing centers for displaced persons. By 1951 it had been stretched to contain some 30,000 Hindus who had fled in terror from predominantly Moslem areas during the partition of the subcontinent in 1947 between India and Pakistan. Altogether some 12 million Hindus and Moslems abandoned their homes in search of safety. Of this number, approximately 8 million were Hindus, the remainder Moslems.

Both India and Pakistan did the best they could to find or improvise shelter for the refugees. Perhaps 1 million of the Hindu refugees crowded into Delhi and vicinity. Some of the early ones were allowed to move into Kingsway.

I went out to Kingsway and spoke to some of the displaced persons, most of whom had come from the Lahore section of what is now Pakistan. Many of them had been merchants or clerks. They belonged, roughly speaking, to the Indian middle class. A not inconsiderable number of them had been well educated, for Lahore was a university city. In any event, the people had left their homes or their jobs or their schools in Lahore and were now herded together in Kingsway in what had become a stark effort for survival. There was an acute shortage of medicines, especially antibiotics. Sanitation was almost nonexistent. Water was scarce. The people were hungry and sick.

"Most of us have been here almost three years," an elderly man who had been a teacher in Lahore told me. "At first, we thought we might have to stay here only a few months before new housing was found or built. But it became impossible to do anything for us because of all the thousands of refugees who came to Delhi.

"When this camp was turned over to us in 1947 it was bad enough. But there were only 5,000 of us here then. Within a year there were 15,000. Today there are 30,000. If you will see how we live, you will see that seven and eight families have to share a single room. It is not meant for human beings to live this way. But I suppose we are lucky. At least we have some shelter. There are many thousands more who do not even have this; they are living in the streets of the big cities."

I asked many questions about the camp—about the health of the people, about the food supply, about the schooling of the children. I was told that these questions were best answered by members of the Kingsway Council. These were the younger men who were now out foraging for food or fuel or searching for jobs. Those who had found jobs in nearby Delhi would not return until evening. It was suggested that I return some evening later in the week, at which time a meeting with the younger men could be arranged.

At dinner that night I told the Prime Minister about my visit to Kingsway. He was familiar with the camp and discussed it in the context of the larger problem of displaced persons in general.

"There is no full or prompt solution," Mr. Nehru said. "Even time, which is what is required, is no answer to people who suffer today. We have 8 million displaced persons. Even if we were successful in meeting the full needs of only half of them, that in itself would represent the largest such effort in history. But it would still leave 4 million. Let us go even further. If all our plans turn out right, we may within a year or so substantially improve the living conditions of 7 million displaced persons. But that would still leave 1 million human beings, some of them at Kingsway or camps like it.

"Actually, we are working on the problem constantly," he continued, "and it engages much of my thought and attention. What makes it more difficult, of course, is that the hunger and sickness are not peculiar to the displaced persons. There has been the failure of the rains for almost three years, and crops have badly suffered. But the fact that a general problem exists does not mean that we cannot do a better job than we are doing with different parts of the problem."

The Prime Minister said he would be in touch with the office of Rehabilitation Minister Jain about Kingsway and would obtain information about what could be expected there.

The following morning the Rehabilitation Minister's office telephoned to say that relief for the people of Kingsway was scheduled for some time during the year—at a minimum, three months; at a maximum, six months. The message also said there was no objection to my making this fact known on my return visit to the camp.

Early the next evening, with Kuldip Nayar, an Indian journalist, as my interpreter, and with a Sikh driver at the wheel, I revisited Kingsway.

As my car swung into the Kingsway compound I was puzzled to observe that the refugees took one look at my car, then, as if by pre-arranged signal, turned their backs and walked directly to the barracks or the huts, from which they peered at me through the narrow slits that served as windows.

After a moment or so, a young man walked directly toward me. He was saying something in an agitated voice as he approached. He was poorly dressed, wearing a faded Gandhi dhoti and a collarless shirt. I judged him to be perhaps twenty-five or thirty, though it is difficult to tell ages in India. His face was pinched and taut, and he hadn't shaved for several days. His eyes were bright, almost glazed.

At first I couldn't grasp any meaning from what he was saying, but I knew his manner to be unfriendly. Then his words came to me.

"You are not welcome here. Go away. You are an American." His voice was tense, high-pitched.

I said the obvious thing: that I felt there must be some mistake, that I had been at the camp several days earlier, and that I had been asked to return so that I might discuss the camp with members of the council.

"Yes, I have heard about your visit. You have taken advantage of our people. You made them think you were their friend. I know better. You have come here to spy on us and to say ugly things about us. We do not wish to meet with you. You are an American and you are not our friend."

He had been speaking only a minute or so. But in that brief moment, the compound or courtyard started to fill up with people. Soon they were pressing in on us, creating a din. The young man continued to speak, but I found it difficult to hear him over the crowd.

My Sikh driver, towering over the other people, pushed his way to my side, took me by the arm, saying we should leave. Kuldip Nayar took my other arm, and they started toward the car.

I remember thinking that this was some sort of weird dream and that everyone had taken leave of his senses. I pulled myself free of the Sikh and Nayar and told the young man I had come to meet with the members of the Kingsway Council.

He said I could not.

I asked him if he could tell me whether he represented the people of Kingsway. I told him I would leave if it was their wish that I do so.

People around us were shouting and shoving. The young man held up both hands and called out to the crowd to be quiet. Then he stood up on a bench and put the question to them.

He spoke in Hindu in a strident and staccato voice. Kuldip Nayar was at my side, translating. "The American wants to know whether I represent you. The American can see for himself whether I represent you."

Unable to see beyond the people closest to me, I was at least able to perceive that there was neither visible nor audible disapproval to what the young man was saying. He continued.

"I have told the American that he is not welcome here and that we do not trust him. He comes from a country which thinks it can block the march of the Asian peoples for national independence and self-respect and we must not be cowards in telling him the Americans will never succeed. They cannot stop us. No one can stop us. For more than one hundred fifty years Asia has endured the rule of the white man, who has taught us to bow before him and call him 'Master.' But we need call him 'Master' no longer.

"The white Westerners keep talking about freedom," he went on, warming up to his task. "What they mean is freedom for themselves. When the Americans talk to us about the importance of freedom they do not know how silly they sound. Did it ever occur to them that others might like freedom, too? What is it that they think we want if not freedom? And who is it that they think is standing in the way of freedom in the world?

"Has the United States, which says it loves freedom so much, been willing to help the Asian peoples to achieve the same freedom the Americans enjoy for themselves? They are a powerful nation, the Americans. If they were to declare themselves against slavery in the world and against the rule of the white man in Asia, the rest of the West could not stand against them and all Asia would be able to throw off the chains.

"But the United States will not do this, so Asia will do it the hard way and the Americans will be thrown out of Asia along with the others. Now does the American understand why he is not welcome here?"

There were some scattered cheers from the crowd, but not the strong response that the young man seemed to be calling for. I asked Nayar to request that I allowed to reply. He called out to the young man and some people in front of the crowd echoed the request.

"The American asks for a chance to be heard," the young man said. "We will hear him but I am not yet through. When we read that Indian students who visit America have to be careful when they travel in some parts of his country because they are regarded as inferior beings, how are we supposed to feel? Are we supposed to accept inferiority because God has given us a dark skin to protect us against a hot sun in an open country?

"We will not accept inferiority, and the American should know it. And we believe that any people who impose punishment on others because of color are people who do not know the meaning of freedom."

His words seemed to be hitting their mark. There were no cheers, but there was no mistaking the fact from the open expressions of the people and from the nodding of heads that these things were deeply felt.

The young man was far from through.

"For several months now the American government has been discussing sending us food to relieve the famine in India caused by the failure of the monsoons. The United States has rich lands and the people have taken good care of their fields. But America has year-round rainfall and we do not.

"When we heard that the United States might send us wheat from their vast stores which are not being used, we became very hopeful. In the past, we had been shocked to read that the United States had taken good food from its surplus and dumped that food into the sea rather than give the food to hungry people. But we were pleased and eager when the proposal was made in America that wheat might be sent to us.

"But months have passed and nothing has happened. Astonishing things have been said in the United States. It has been said that the wheat should not be sent because our Prime Minister has disagreed too much with the United States in the United Nations. What does that have to do with it? If the Prime Minister agrees or disagrees, does that change the fact that the Americans have food they do not need or that we are hungry? Does this mean that the American people believe that starvation should be used as a political weapon? Is this what freedom means?"

Then the young man began to address individual members of the crowd.

"Davidas," he said, looking at a man of perhaps thirty with a bronze tinge to his hair. "Your little boy died while the wheat debate in the United States was going on. Your other son is now hungry and ill. How do you feel when you hear that the Americans are debating the sending of the wheat because there are political differences between the two governments? Do not human beings have obligations to each other no matter what papers their governments may sign or what the votes may be in the United Nations?

"Shandar," he said, pointing to another young man up front, "you told me yesterday you were unable to bring home food for your family. Do you feel kindly about a man who comes from a country that thinks it can take advantage of our suffering in order to force its will upon us?"

After Shandar, he addressed himself to an elder known as Chatterjee, who, it was brought out, had lost two members of his family in recent weeks. Then he called out to three more. And as he appealed to each one in terms of his own experience, a strange and frightening thing was happening. He was producing a single countenance of hurt and hate in the crowd. Once again the Sikh started to pull me away. But the young man was now through and told me I could speak if I had anything to say.

Even before I could get to the bench on which the young man stood, someone was there ahead of me and had started to speak. It was Davidas, the man with the bronze tinge to his hair.

"The American will forgive me if I speak first," he said. "Sahani has asked me a question and I should like to answer it. I want to answer it by asking all of you to look at each other. What is this ugly thing I see on your faces? I see something that would have sickened Gandhiji.* I see hate. Hate for a man who has come to visit us.

"I am ashamed of what I have heard and even more ashamed because

* The addition of "ji" in India denotes friendship and respect.

of what I see. We have suffered in this camp, true, but Gandhiji was no stranger to suffering and he would not use suffering as an excuse for excuse for hate. Can anyone imagine Gandhiji saying what Sahani has just said? Can anyone imagine Gandhiji sitting and listening with the same approval as you have done to what has just been said?

"While Sahani was speaking I had to ask myself: 'Is this Gandhi's India in which I grew up? Is this all that Gandhi means to us? Is this what he has left behind—that we should find ourselves covered with hate and abusing a stranger?'

"If we remember, Gandhi taught us to think the best of people, even when they were not our friends. He taught us that if we ourselves react in hate, it is only evil that has triumphed. He taught us to accept the stranger in good faith and never to assume bad faith. And he taught us nonviolence. The words spoken by Sahani are bad and violent words and I beg the American to forgive him and us.

"Sahani has asked me how I feel when I read that the Americans are holding back the shipment of their wheat surplus for political reasons. I am hurt because of it and, when I think of my son, I find it difficult to know why human beings in one country would act that way about human beings in another country. These things are difficult for me to under-stand, for I am a simple man and I know very little about the way big nations are run and how they deal with each other. But the American who has come to us is a single American. Can any of you say that his heart is bad or that he is evil? You do not know him. You have not yet listened to him. Gandhiji knew how to listen. Gandhiji trusted the indi-vidual. Why should we not trust this American? Why should we not think the best of him?

"Some things I know about Americans. I remember very clearly that the Americans were on our side during our struggle for independence. Nowhere in the world did we have finer friends than among the American people. Can we have forgotten so soon how much these people meant to us or the inspiration of their history? Have we forgotten what Gandhiji used to tell us about America and its own struggle for freedom? I have not forgotten these things because I have not forgotten Gandhiji.

"When I ask myself: why is it that the Americans do not send us the food, I think that something must be happening that we do not know about, and I believe that the food will yet come. The Americans cannot have changed so much in a few years. I have faith in them. I believe they will send the wheat. But even if they do not, the visitor from the United States is welcome here. He is our guest and we are grateful to him for coming."

Nothing was more striking than the change in the people while Davidas spoke. They didn't cheer or applaud. He had reached them in some unde-finable way—the same way perhaps that Gandhi himself used to reach them. As the people listened to him they ceased to be a crowd and became individuals again. Sahani had played upon their resentments and fears; he had fused them into a composite personality ready to hate. But now Davidas was releasing them from their fears and their hates and they were responding to the urges of individual conscience.

What was most significant of all was that the change in them had become visible and dramatic the moment Davidas had mentioned Gandhi.

I looked over at Sahani, wondering whether he would regard what Davidas had said as a challenge. His face was still strained and he was staring at Davidas. But he gave no sign that he wished to reply. I tried to guess what was passing through his mind.

Then Nayar was tugging at my arm, saying that Davidas had told the crowd that I would now speak for myself. One thing I knew: anything I might say would be an anticlimax. I told Nayar to say that I could add nothing to what Davidas had said. Nayar replied that it was desired by the people that I should speak. He said that these were people who had never seen or listened to an American before.

Davidas was now at my side, leading me to the bench.

I am afraid I floundered badly in what I said. I didn't want to appear to be arguing my own case, nor did I wish to seem to be exploiting the favorable mood created by Davidas. Yet some of the basic questions raised by Sahani about the attitude of Americans toward the Indian people; about our general position on the struggle of Asian peoples for freedom; about the American heart—these questions remained and an American had a right perhaps to try to answer them.

It seemed to me to be necessary in anything I might say—as it had been wherever I had spoken in Asia when people were meeting an American for the first time—to make it clear that no single American, probably not even the President, could speak for all the American people. And so I began at Kingsway by telling of our astonishing diversity, the history behind it, and of the even more remarkable fact that it was this very diversity that gave stability to the country.

This meant that men could disagree yet work together. It meant that people from other lands could come to America, leaving behind them the idea that a man was limited to a fixed group or class or to the occupation of his father. The law couldn't ensure absolute equality of attitude in America, nor could it insure equality in the fulfillment of opportunity. But what the law could do was to prevent men from preying on one another. The law could recognize and support the things that helped an individual to grow and fulfil himself.

The system was not without its disadvantages, I continued. It fostered competing pressures among the people, as group after group sought favors from government, legitimate and otherwise. It even slowed up the processes of government itself, for there were many voices to be heard before national laws or policy could be created. And, sometimes, the most strident voices might sound like the dominant ones—as in the case of the debate concerning wheat to India.

No one could excuse the delay in sending food to hungry people, but it was necessary at least to explain it. Certainly it would be a mistake to assume from the prolongation of debate that the American people were turning their backs on human misfortune. Indeed, the overwhelming majority would support sending the wheat immediately—not because it was politically smart or because it would gain us a point in the Cold War but because it was the right thing to do.

I realized, I said, how absurd it was for me to ask people who needed food to exercise patience; but the issue was far from lost in the United States.

I looked directly at Sahani and asked him not to lose faith with the American people—at least not until it was known definitely that America had refused the aid.

Nor should other things be forgotten. Large and increasing numbers of Americans, such as Marie Buck and Russell Wulff and Elvira Eldridge, had come to live in India, giving superbly of themselves in towns and villages and cities, contributing their resources and their knowledge in an adventure of sharing.

Or the growing number of scientists, engineers, and health specialists who were coming to India under an Act of Congress for the purpose of responding to Prime Minister Nehru's statement of India's primary need—to make her soil more productive and to develop her technological capacities.

I had already said more than I had intended. But there was still the matter of Sahani's indictment of the American people because, in his words, we were holding back the "march of the Asian peoples toward freedom." What he had been referring to, I said I supposed, was the apparent reluctance of the American government to insist that the other Western nations completely relinquish their holdings in Asia.

Now some of these criticisms of the United States may have been based on speculations and some on fact, but I said that even before we tried to sort out one from the other, it might be well to consider something even more basic than had been mentioned by Sahani. This was America's own record with respect to imperialism. What about the documented and historical account of what we did with our own holdings? We had been imperialistic in Asia, along with the rest, and we took the Philippines for our own. But the record also showed that we left—not under pressure from the Philippines but under the pressure of public opinion in the United States. And when we did leave, there were those in the Philippines who thought we might be leaving too soon.

Apart from all this there was one thing that the people in India ought to know about America. The American people were deeply interested in them. Wherever I had traveled in the United States, I found people eager for information about India, about Gandhiji, about Nehru, and about their magnificent undertaking of national independence. We didn't know as much as we should know about India—or about Asia itself, for that matter; but in fairness to ourselves, many Asians didn't know too much about Americans either. Perhaps this was something for all of us to think about.

I expressed my thanks to Davidas and stepped down.

The crowd didn't disperse. Instead, it reformed in animated clusters. Davidas pushed his way through to my side and invited me to come to his quarters for tea. I accepted. The Sikh stayed close to the car. Kuldip Nayar joined us and we threaded our way through the crowd.

Just beyond the compound a long line was forming again. The people were waiting for their turn at filling their buckets or jars or pots. Two water taps had to serve the 30,000 people of Kingsway. Not infrequently, one of the taps would not be working properly. Today was such a day.

"Sometimes there are 2,000 people on line," Davidas said. "Sometimes they have to wait all day, for this is the only water there is. And you can understand how tempers grow short. Sometimes there is violence on the waiting line for there is fear that the water may dry up before the people get to it."

A short distance beyond the waiting people there were open latrines.

"As you can see," Davidas said, "the lack of sanitation is dangerous where people are crowded together. There is much sickness at the camp."

He pointed to an elderly woman lying on a burlap-covered bed outside one of the huts. Then he nodded with his head in the direction of a young woman lying with a three- or four-year-old child.

"Without medicines and enough food the only thing that costs nothing is to lie still."

As Davidas spoke there came to mind a crowded village I had visited not far from Calcutta. A smallpox epidemic had been raging through the village and was only now subsiding. I had spoken to a man whose entire family—wife and three small children—had been lost to the disease.

"I am sorry the sickness did not take me, too," he had told me. "Here in India we have so many people and so little food, and I sometimes think that the best thing one can do for one's country is to die and get out of the way."

I could reflect upon this definition of patriotism while walking alongside Davidas.

Soon we came to Davidas's quarters, a poorly lighted room of perhaps twelve by fifteen feet.

Davidas and his family shared this small room with four other families.

"We thought it was crowded for our own little family when we moved in several years ago," he said. "But after Kingsway filled up and the other families moved in we shared our room with the newcomers. And now we look back and almost wonder at the fact that we should ever have had this room all ourselves."

Davidas introduced me to his wife and seven-year-old son. We squatted on the floor and the tea was served. I asked my host some questions about himself. He was the son of a Lahore merchant who owned a fair-sized cloth-and-notions shop. After his father died Davidas operated the establishment. Then came partition, with its terrors and bloodshed, and Davidas and his family fled Lahore.

"What about the store?"

"Gone," he said. "Gone like all the other Hindu businesses in Lahore. We were lucky to get out with our lives. But there are also Moslems who abandoned their businesses in India and are now refugees in Pakistan. No one knows whether the refugee property situation will ever be straightened out. It is all terribly confused. I try not to think about it any more. I say to my wife we must not look back. Now we must fight to live. We have lost one son."

It was late and I got up to leave. On the way back to the car I asked about Sahani, the young man with the glazed eyes and taut face who had spoken against America.

I learned that Sahani and been a law student in Lahore. His education had been cut short by partition. The most precious personal possessions he took with him on his escape were some lawbooks. And ever since coming to Kingsway, Sahani had been studying law by himself. He was hopeful that someday he might be able to take his examination.

"Sahani is an embittered young man," Davidas said. "He is opposed to Prime Minister Nehru and the Congress party. He believes in very radical solutions. Not very many people were persuaded by him when the camp was first set up. It would have been impossible three years ago for him to have people gather around him and listen as they did today. But much has happened. People have suffered, too many of them; and now they are listening to Sahani.

"But most of them still have faith in Jawarharlal Nehru. I am one of them. I do not accept the Communist arguments against Nehru because I know how difficult are the problems Nehru has to face. The Communists say they can do better. We are told that they have set up relief stations in the villages and are keeping hundreds of thousands of people alive. But I believe Nehru when he says that the Communists are terrorists and do not really believe in freedom. We have fought for freedom. We want to keep it. And Gandhiji was opposed to communism. Gandhiji wanted Nehru to lead India. Gandhiji was proved right in what he did. He was right about Nehru."

We came to the car. Davidas became engaged in conversation with one of the elders who were there to say good-by. I took Kuldip Nayar to one side and asked his advice about something that weighed heavily on my mind. I wanted to help Davidas. I knew his family was hungry. In my pocket I had almost one hundred rupees, the equivalent of about thirty dollars. I wanted to give the rupees to Davidas, or as much as he would take. It was a delicate problem and I asked Nayar if he would put it in the right light to Davidas.

Nayar shook his head and said in a low voice that he didn't think he could persuade Davidas to take it. He said I might try, if I wished.

When I turned back to Davidas, he was looking at me in a way that made me think he knew what I had been saying to Nayar. I told Davidas it was my deepest wish that he would regard me as his friend, for that would entitle me to his help if I needed it. If I should have pain, I knew he would want to take part of that pain for his own. And what he would do for me he would have to let me do for him. Then I pressed the rupee notes into his hand.

Davidas smiled but shook his head. He said he would always regard me as a friend. And it was out of friendship that he wanted me to understand that he could not accept what I was trying to press upon him.

I said I understood, but asked that he view it as a small loan.

Again he declined, closing my hand over the rupee notes and then dropping his own hand to his side. He did it with great dignity. I admired him for it as much as I have ever admired any man for a single act, but I would have given anything to have been able to transfer those few pieces of paper from my hand to his.

There was yet one thing to be covered before leaving Kingsway. I wanted to pass along the report I had received from the office of the Rehabilitation Minister that relief was coming. I hadn't done so while talking to the people because I didn't want to exploit good news for the purpose of meeting a difficult personal situation. Also, the people had been disappointed before and it might have seemed to some that I was raising false hopes. But neither was it fair for me to withhold altogether important information that had its sanction in the Prime Minister's office. I thought it best to report the facts as fully as possible to Davidas, for I had complete confidence in him to present the news to the people of Kingsway with whatever qualification the situation required. After I did this I shook hands with Davidas, and we left.

On the drive back to New Delhi not much was said. Nayar was just as busy with his thoughts as I. For a few brief moments I had had a glimpse of the struggle and torment of a nation and its people in their fight for life. I had seen a sudden boiling up of all the elements of human and national crisis. For the refugee was the painful product of independence, yet not one of them would accept his former favored station if that would mean the loss of national freedom. The division of the subcontinent between India and Pakistan; the historic antagonisms between Hindus and Moslems; the lack of water, medicine, food; the inevitable attempt of the revolutionary, whether Communist or any other, to turn the situation to his advantage by posing as defender and champion; the vulnerability of a rich nation such as the United States when seen at a distance by people who know little about us beyond the astounding fact that we have more food than we can eat and that we are upset when other people don't agree with us—all these giant facts in the predicament of the Indian nation today and in its relations with the United States seemed to be tied together in what I had just seen at Kingsway. But there was something else I had seen.

I had seen the vast power for good in the symbol of a single man. When all the many other impressions of my visit to Kingsway were sorted and balanced, one image stood out from all the rest. It was the recollection of the change that had come over the people of Kingsway when Davidas invoked the memory of Mahatma Gandhi. Whatever the miracle of his hold on the Indian people had been while he lived, the miracle itself had survived his death. An appeal to reason and mercy and greatness in his name represented the main strength in and of the Indian people. And Gandhi had taken his mantle and given it to Pandit Nehru. That fact had a sovereignty of its own.

Once earlier, under much different circumstances, I had seen the miracle at work. It was in a village not far from where I had spoken to the man who felt the greatest gift he could give his country was to die so there would be one less mouth to feed.

I had stopped with my interpreter to chat with some children who were playing at the edge of a grove. My friend explained to the children that I came from the United States, many thousands of miles away. They were interested but shook their heads and said they had never heard of the United States. We mentioned the names of America's most famous presidents; even that drew no recognition. Then we referred to other famous names in the news about Europe and Asia. Still no response.

"You have to understand," my friend had said, "that news of the outside world is totally lacking in many of these villages. In fact, in the more remote areas of India there are people who haven't even heard of Gandhi, incredible though that may seem. But in this village, so close to Calcutta, there is no question about Gandhiji."

At the mention of Gandhi's name, the faces of the children had lighted up and they shook their heads and smiled broadly. Whatever their other shortcomings on worldly knowledge might have been, the name of Gandhi was a recognizable universe.

"Ask this youngster," I had said, pointing to a boy of perhaps nine or ten, "if he can tell me what Gandhiji means to him."

The interpreter had repeated the question. The boy had hesitated for a moment, then communicated his answer to me directly. He put his arms around my neck, and smiled, saying a few words as he did so.

"The boy says that Bapu, which means father—the father of our country—has taught him not to be afraid to show his love for other people even though they may be complete strangers. That was why he put his arms around you."

One thing remains to be said. Last year I returned to India and Pakistan. The rains had been good and the crops has come back and fewer people were hungry. America had sent the wheat; it had been late in coming but the important thing was that it *had* come. And we were sending technicians and tools to aid in the plans for industrial expansion. The community development program, to which the United States had made important contributions, offered promising resettlement possibilities. In general, conditions had improved considerably. The refugee problem was still a long way from being solved, but several millions of refugees had been relocated and were now absorbed in their new surroundings.

Shortly after I arrived in Delhi I drove out to Kingsway. What I found was not a refugee camp but an improvised housing project. The buildings were not of a permanent nature, but at least they were a vast improvement over what Kingsway had been only two years earlier.

In the compound at Kingsway where once Sahani had publicly asked an American to leave and Davidas had asked him to remain there was now a public school. It wasn't the gleaming, modern type of public school now being constructed in the United States. But it had benches and desks and blackboards. And in front of one of the classrooms was a large poster about the UN. The poster was in English and it spoke of the promise and purposes of the world organization.

I asked the teacher in charge whether he could tell me anything about a man named Davidas. He shook his head. I described Davidas as best I could and said it was important for me to find him. The teacher shook his head again. He said that the early refugees at Kingsway had long since been moved to better quarters. And there were many men with the name Davidas. Of that I was certain.

*—July 2, 1955*


# The World of John Gilbert Graham

John Gilbert Graham, age twenty-three, took air-flight insurance on his mother and then placed in her suitcase two sticks of dynamite attached to a time fuse. The mechanism worked and a plane carrying forty-four human beings exploded in flight. There were no survivors.

The shock waves of the blast were felt in the consciousness of number-less millions of people. The human mind was rocked by realization of the stark helplessness of people when an evil idea seizes a single individual. Forty-three men and women aboard the plane were totally uninvolved in the life of John Gilbert Graham. They were incidental and extraneous. Their lives were less than merely cheap; they were meaningless in his design. The impersonality of evil had become sovereign. And the ease with which the evil had been fulfilled seemed no less hideous than the evil itself.

Now take this danger and multiply it by infinity. Take the vulnerability and the impersonality and extend them to 3,000,000,000 human beings. When you do this you have a portrait of the age. We are all in the plane. The hold of the plane is already packed with the mammoth explosives and detonators. A madman at the head of a nation can touch off the first big blast and the others will go off automatically. And even without reference to the explosive cargo a struggle is going on in the cockpit for control of the aircraft.

No one disputes the consequences of the explosion. Scientists, soldiers, and statesmen do not disagree that the war would pulverize man and all his works. The man or men who set off the first explosions will themselves be shattered by the later ones. But even this fact does not serve as a suffi-cient guarantee of the public safety—any more than John Gilbert Graham, who was possessed by an evil design, was deterred by the likelihood of his arrest.

Indeed, even among some men who have been identified with habits of reasonable thinking we can see the lure of suicide. These are the men who are appalled by the ease with which the madmen could blow us up and therefore propose that we blow them up first. But since we are all in the plane no distinctions can be made between the effects of the supposedly therapeutic explosions and the effects of the evil ones. The big bombs are as impersonal as war itself and are wedded to each other and follow a united course even though man does not.

John Gilbert Graham is a monster but he is also a miniaturist. He has given us diamond size and diamond sharp an image of the world in which we live. He has spelled out on the head of a pin the predicament of our species.

As in the case of the people in the plane, there is little connection be-tween the things we do and think about and the big facts that shape our destiny. Unlike the people in the plane, however, we have at our disposal the mechanism that can detach the fuse. That mechanism is a key fur-nished by history itself. For nothing is more explicit in history than that the only antidote for lawlessness is law; the only cure for anarchy is gov-ernment. And the only safeguard against bad government is the determination of the individual to keep close enough to it so that it never becomes an end in itself.

If the world is not to belong to the John Gilbert Grahams sometime soon the central problem will have to be seen for what it is. The central problem is to tame the nation and to keep human life from becoming impersonal or extraneous. This is done not by acquiescing in national aggression or ambition, but by creating the specific instruments that can cope with it or prevent it. So far as the people of the United States are concerned our greatest strength may very well lie in the world advocacy of that idea. For our own claim on survival will be defined not by what we do for ourselves, but what we propose to do for all.

—*December 3, 1955*

## The Mission of Satis Prasad

In a village in the hills below Jakarta, Indonesia, I met a man whose name, if I recall it correctly, was Satis Prasad. He was a Hindu priest who had come to Indonesia to look into the religious situation of the many people of Indian descent who lived in the area.

"I am not what you in the West would call a missionary," he said. "My purpose here is to find out how strong the attachment is to Hinduism of the present generation. But I would in fact like to become a missionary and perhaps you can help me."

"Help you? How?"

"By telling me if it is true that the American people believe in missionaries and support their work."

"To a very large extent, yes," I replied.

"Then they would be agreeable to my coming to the United States to work as a missionary among the Americans?"

"You would like to convert Americans to the Hindu religion?"

Satis Prasad smiled. He rose to his feet and slowly circled my chair.

"No," he said. "I would like to convert them to the Christian religion. You see, there are no basic differences in the moral substance of Hinduism and Christianity. Historically and theologically, of course, each has its own distinct character. But in the moral teachings they have far more in common than most people realize. I would like to concentrate on making Americans aware of the need to believe in these moral teachings, by whatever name they go. The important thing is not what I call it but the teachings themselves."

I asked Satis Prasad several questions. First, exactly what moral teachings did he have in mind that both Hinduism and Christianity had in common. Second, why did he feel the American people were in particular need of this kind of missionary work.

"I have made a study of the similarities," he said. "It is a pity, a great pity, that the Americans know so little about the religions of other peoples. That is one thing, incidentally, I should like to help to correct. For it is unchristian not to understand one's neighbors. Let me give you just a sample of the moral teachings shared by both religions."

He produced a card. In parallel columns he had written out in long-hand passages from the Old and New Testament and on the other side similar passages from the *Mahabharata*, the epic poem of the Hindu religion. Under the Golden Rule, for example, he had copied the following:

*This is the sum of all true righteousness—*
*Treat others as thou wouldst thyself be treated*
                        —MAHABHARATA.

*Whatever you do not wish your neighbor to do to you do not*
*unto him.*                        —OLD TESTAMENT.

*Whatsoever ye would that men do to you, do ye even so to them;*
*for this is the Law and the Prophets.*        —ST. MATTHEW.

*A man obtains a proper rule of action*
*By looking on his neighbor as himself.*
                        —MAHABHARATA.

*Thou shalt love thy neighbor as thyself.*        —ST. MATTHEW.

Under "Evil and Righteousness" he had copied out:

*Love ye your enemies, and do good, and lend, hoping for noth-*
*ing again.*                        —ST. LUKE.

*High-minded men delight in doing good;*
*Without a thought of their own interest;*
*When they confer a benefit on others*
*They reckon not on favors in return.*
                        —MAHABHARATA.

*Overcome evil with good.*    —ST. PAUL's *Epistle to the Romans.*

*Overcome the evil man by goodness.*        —MAHABHARATA.

*Behold, God will not cast away a perfect man, neither will he*
*help the evildoers.*
    *The eyes of the Lord are upon the righteous, and his ears are*
*open unto their cry.*                        —OLD TESTAMENT.

*Then shall the righteous shine forth as the sun in the kingdom*
*of their Father.*                        —ST. MATTHEW.

*Then, in a religion bright with golden luster—*
*Center of light and immortality—*
*The righteous after death shall dwell in bliss.*
—MAHABHARATA.

Under the heading "Moral Conduct":

*If thine enemy hunger, feed him; if he thirst, give him drink.*
—ST. PAUL'S *Epistle to the Romans.*

*Even to foes who visit us as guests*
*Due hospitality should be displayed.*
—MAHABHARATA.

*A soft answer turneth away wrath; but grievous words stir up*
*anger.*                                                    —OLD TESTAMENT.

*Lay not up for yourselves treasures upon earth, where moth and*
*rust does corrupt, and where thieves break through and steal;*
*but lay up for yourself treasures in heaven, where neither moth*
*nor rust does corrupt, and where thieves do not break through*
*and steal.*                                              —ST. MATTHEW.

*Lay up the only treasure; do good deeds;*
*Practice sobriety and self-control;*
*Amass that wealth which thieves cannot abstract,*
*Nor tyrants seize, which follows thee at death,*
*Which never wastes away nor is corrupted.*
—MAHABHARATA.

*Straight is the gate, and narrow is the way,*
*Which leadeth unto life, and few there be that find it.*
—ST. MATTHEW.

*Heaven's gate is very narrow and minute;*
*It cannot be perceived by foolish men,*
*Blinded by vain illusions of the world.*
—MAHABHARATA.

"This is only one side of one card," he said. "Actually, the parallel teachings could fill many pages."

"But the same could be said of all the world's great religions," I replied. "The oneness of man is nowhere expressed more dramatically than in the similarity of the spiritual teachings."

"Precisely," he agreed. "But the important thing is to get people to act on the basis of these teachings. And that is why I am so eager to help save Christianity. Christianity cannot survive in the abstract. It needs not membership but believers. The people of your country may claim they believe in Christianity but from what I read at this distance, Christianity is more a custom than anything else.

"Your very way of life, your whole economy, your foreign policy, your values—surely you must see the great inconsistency between them and the teachings of Jesus. Christianity is a religion of humility, of renunciation, of sacrifice, of moral purity. It is not a power doctrine for a nation or an individual. Yet even as you flout Christ's will you call yourselves Christians. My mission will be to get you to realize what you have to do before you have a right to use the term.

"I say this not in anger. America has given much to the world and can give more still. But in recent years you have lost much strength in direct proportion as you have departed from the literal acceptance of the doctrine you profess to follow. I can think of no country in history that weakened itself more than America did when it dropped two atomic bombs on living creatures. Please do not stop me by saying that there can be no religion in warfare. When you kill without meaning, you go beyond war.

"Atomic energy transcended warfare and was the beginning of a new age on earth. You had sole possession of the bomb. Your leaders knew the end of the war was at hand. They did not tell the truth when they claimed they were trying to save the thousands of lives that an invasion would cost. All the documents which have come out since the war have proved that your leaders knew the atom bomb was not necessary to win the war. Yet they used it not once but twice. If there was an excuse for the first bomb, what excuse do you give for the second a few days later?

"These things weigh very heavily on me. Americans are my brothers. So are the Russians. But the Russians are opposed to the Hindu-Christian spiritual development of man. You at least accept it in theory, and that is why I want to come to America to see if I cannot get you to accept it in fact."

"What is it you would have us do?"

"I would ask in good conscience and in good faith that you first of all come to terms with yourselves. I would ask that you cease justifying your inconsistencies by saying, as so many of you often say, 'Of course, Christianity does not exist here in its pure form, any more than it exists anywhere in the world in its pure form; it is an aspiration and we are moving toward it.' I would ask that you not take refuge in this argument. It is a trick of reasoning and is meaningless. Can you imagine Jesus explaining away the present Christian paradox by pointing to an aspiration?

"I would ask that you either accept the teachings of Jesus in your everyday lives and in your affairs as a nation or stop invoking His name as sanction for everything you do.

"Perhaps without realizing it, you have a superiority complex. You claimed that only you could do certain things, as in science, and it turns out that you were as wrong as everyone else in history who had made claims of superiority. Mistakes like these come at heavy price.

"America has much to offer the world. But it will continue to weaken itself unless it throws off its assumptions of superiority and thinks in terms of mutuality. True strength can only be in moral principle come to life.

"One has the impression you are made uneasy by talk concerning the literal application of such principles. You are impatient, for example, with anyone who says you should re-examine fearlessly all the circumstances and aspects concerning the decision to use atomic weapons on living targets. You are annoyed by this and would prefer to drop it and forget it. But you cannot drop it or forget it. You cannot because the same faulty reasoning which led you to use it expresses itself in so many other ways and decisions. And faulty reasoning creates its own punishments.

"I want to come to America to make you try to understand that retribution is not a random divine act for a random event but something men themselves fashion out of continuing error and out of a continuing failure to see the validity of moral law in their actions. I should like to tax the Christian individual with responsibility for the group.

"But most importantly, I should like to do what I can to help America prepare itself for the big developments of the next few years. Asia and Africa are now awake. They are tearing themselves free of their bondage. They are learning how to read and write and make things. Soon they will be more powerful even than you. What will happen when America discovers that it no longer is the most powerful nation in the world? Will it become resentful and antagonistic? Will it learn how to abide the fact that it is not predominately a white man's world? It must not be a dark man's world either, and both white and dark will have to make the adjustment.

"I would like to be able to convince the Americans that their guideposts at such a trying hour can be found in their own spiritual legacy, and not in striking out fiercely and wildly in an attempt to hold back history. For I would persuade them that the greatest honor and source of pride are to be found not in the banners of the group but in human brotherhood.

"I preach. I know I preach. That is exactly what I would like to do in America. I want to be a missionary in your country. I want to help save Christianity for the Christians. How do I go about doing this? Do the Americans believe in missionaries? Will Americans welcome me?"

                                                                    —January 14, 1956

# The Poverty of Imitation

Mr. Erich Leinsdorf, the distinguished conductor, recently invited David Oistrakh, a master of the violin and a citizen of the Soviet Union, to appear as guest soloist with the Rochester Philharmonic Orchestra. Mr. Oistrakh was willing but the U.S. State Department vetoed the concert. It ruled that Rochester was out of bounds for the Russian violinist.

Rochester is neither a center for the production of fissionable materials nor a launching site for intercontinental guided missiles. The city specializes in photographic equipment, good music, and excellent education. David Oistrakh commands only the science of the violin. Yet the State Department banned his appearance. When it was argued that Rochester has cultural rather than military significance, the State Department replied that it was "retaliating" because some of the Russian cities have been declared out of bounds to American tourists.

Whom are we retaliating against? Whom are we hurting in this childish game of last tag? By depriving the people of Rochester of the privilege of hearing one of the three or four greatest living violinists, do we thereby teach the Russians a painful lesson and win a point in the cold war? Is this our idea of an intelligent and imaginative approach to the competition with the Soviet Union for world leadership? If the Communist rulers make a prodigious mistake, can we think of nothing more exalted for our own role than the imitation of error?

Congressional committees have been concerned with un-American behavior. Here is a large, clear, and fully visible specimen that we commend for investigation. It has nothing to do with secret meetings or spying or plots to destroy the government. Yet what is involved can be just as serious. We refer to an un-American smallness—an un-American shortage of the kind of moral imagination that went into the making of America and that will somehow have to be rediscovered if America and its values are to survive no matter how many atomic warheads we fashion.

It is un-American to act like frightened pygmies. Can anyone imagine Abraham Lincoln suggesting we should cope with the stupidity and narrowness of our foes by measured imitation? Does anyone suppose that Thomas Jefferson, if faced with a similar situation, would have advocated acceptance of the twisted standards of a totalitarian state operating out of fear and the collapse of a compassionate intelligence? One can hardly imagine that Dwight D. Eisenhower could have had anything to do with such puny ideas; and we can only suppose that because of illness this matter did not come to his attention.

Here was the ideal stage for dramatizing to the entire world the largeness of spirit that must flow out of the history and vital purpose of a free people. Much has been said in government and the press about the need to point up the moral factor in the democratic equation. Why could we not have used this as the occasion for opening our doors in a way that would have been in obvious contrast to the conditional parting of the Iron Curtain?

In this respect, the smallness is not the exclusive copyright of either political party. Ever since the end of the war, we have hurt ourselves by an unthinking, negative approach to the challenge of communism. Some of the leading sponsors of such a powerful idea as Point IV, for example, deprived the plan of much of its moral power when they sought funds from the Congress by claiming that this was a cheap way of combating communism and helping ourselves, instead of standing bold and firm on the proposition that this was something we should do because it was the right thing to do.

Our leaders may hold the American people too cheaply. It is not necessary to disguise good purposes and objectives in the slick clothing of national self-interest in order to win support. The overwhelming majority of the American people are not crass or cynical; they have a historical sensitivity to human needs and will respond when those needs are honestly and frankly described and tied to a plan for effective and competent action. Yet it is supposed to be smart, realistic politics to affect tough self-seeking arguments in order to achieve broad human goals. It so happens, however, that the people whom we want to help are listening too.

In place after place in Southeast Asia where we spent Point IV money, I would meet people who would ask in effect: "This is wonderful assistance you are providing; but is it true that we do not really figure in this aid as human beings, and that you are really trying to help yourselves in your contest with the Soviet?"

I met the question as best I could, but more than once I was tempted to say that actually we were all playing a game. The men who conceived of the idea of foreign aid did so out of decent impulses but found it hard to believe that enough men in the Congress could be similarly motivated. Meanwhile, the men in the Congress who were decently impelled would echo the tough arguments because they didn't feel they could appeal to the decent instincts of the people at home. And in the public debates, many of the citizens suporting foreign aid seemed content to cut themselves down to the size of their opponents by arguing the issue on the grounds of self-interest. Then, having won, they somehow expected that the recipients abroad would know it was only a game and that the real intent was noble. But it didn't quite work out that way. The others played it straight.

National policy by imitation and the negative approach to worth-while goals are exercises in national shrinkage—shrinkage in strength, shrinkage in values, shrinkage in prospects. The times cry for growth.

*—February 11, 1956*

# A Visit to Gaza

When the fighting ended in Palestine in 1948 the Armistice Commission was unable to redraw the boundaries in a way that suited all parties concerned. One of the areas thus redefined which produced the greatest tension was what is now known as the Gaza Strip. It is about ten miles wide and thirty miles long. It is a long rectangular patch with the Sinai Peninsula at the southern short end, the Mediterranean on the west, and Israel on the east and north. One way for an American to visualize this is to imagine that a narrow strip of land would jut out from Mexico into the body of California with the Pacific as the west boundary.

Geographically, then, the Gaza Strip is a freak. Politically, it is a world fever-blister. It was not incorporated into Egypt as an integral part of that nation by the Palestine Armistice Commision but was administered by Egypt. Adding to the volatility of the area is the fact that almost 200,000 Arab refugees, who fled from Israel during the fighting in 1947–1948, are now in the Gaza camps for displaced persons. The UNRWA (United Nations Relief and Welfare Agency) provided the refugees with housing, food, schools.

The Gaza Strip quickly became something more than an enclave for refugees. It became a highly combustible zone in the relations between Egypt and Israel. It was from the Gaza Strip that Egypt later began to launch its terror raids into adjoining Israeli territory. And it was into the strip that Israel sent punitive expeditions. Then, the past October, the Israeli army moved into the Gaza Strip and funneled out into the Sinai Peninsula.

Finally, the Gaza is one of the two main areas on which Israel has been seeking guarantees before giving up all the territory it had captured in the campaign. It asked guarantees from the UN that the Gaza Strip would no longer be used as a base for the hit-and-run terror raids. It wanted a guarantee, too, that its access into Elath, its seaport on the Gulf of Aqaba, would not be blockaded by Egypt when Israeli ships passed through the narrow straits on the southern end of the Gulf.

I came to Gaza because Gaza had suddenly become more than a saturation point of tension between Israel and Egypt. Gaza was now a fuse which, unless controlled, could touch off an explosion whose effects could be felt far beyond the Middle East. Of real importance, too, is the historical and spiritual significance of Gaza and the Sinai Peninsula. And the world is interested and concerned. Unfortunately, not enough is known in the outside world about the complex problems of the Gaza Strip and its refugees to enable most people to make careful judgments. For that matter, I am afraid that not enough was known about the general situation in the Middle East to support the big decisions that have to be made. As an American, I had not felt that I could see the proportion of all the parts or the perspective of the whole. And so I came to the Middle East to find out.

Shortly after I arrived in Tel Aviv I asked the authorities for permission to visit the Gaza Strip, then under Israeli military occupation. The permission was granted. David Solomon, an information officer, was assigned to escort me through the military guard posts. The first thing I wanted to do was to visit an Arab refugee settlement. I was taken to the Beach Camp, one of the largest of the Gaza camps operated by the UNRWA. As soon as I walked into the settlement, I noticed that the youngsters seemed to hold back when I smiled at them. I picked up one of them and showed him how my camera worked. Then the other children broke into wide grins and began to pepper me with their Arabic. Now and then I would hear a strident "hahloo."

The older people would glance at me and go about their business. Many of them were squatting or sitting at the doorways to the stone-and-cement quarters that had been built for them by the UN.

I picked my way carefully through the narrow lanes of the settlement, for the children by this time were swarming around me. I was afraid that some of them would get underfoot.

A young man pushed his way through the gathering crowd and addressed me in English.

"Are you an American?" he asked.

I nodded.

"How do I know you will tell the truth?"

I asked why he was afraid that I would not tell the truth. He replied that none of the people from America who visited the camp told the truth when they went home. He said they told him that they were friends but later turned against the Arabs.

Then he spoke with great intensity about conditions at the camp. He referred to the lack of sanitation and the piles of refuse that had not been cleared away. Then he told me that Arab girls had been violated by Jewish soldiers and that women had been murdered in their beds.

"The Jewish authorities have closed our schools," he said. "I am a schoolteacher and they will not let me teach. What am I expected to do? But what is worst are the attacks by Jewish soldiers on our women. They have forced their way into our homes. Do you know how important virginity is to Arab girls? Last week an Arab mother was murdered in her bed. What are we to do? Why have the Jews invaded Egypt and overrun our camp? What are they going to do next?"

When I got back in the car. David Solomon refrained from comment on what I had been told but asked me if I would care to speak to the United Nations people who were in charge of the camp and in a good position to know what was happening. I assured him of my eagerness in this respect.

After a few minutes we drove into the compound of the United Nations Relief and Welfare Agency headquarters for the Arab refugee settlements. The administrator was Colonel Roy Lucas of New Zealand. We discovered we had mutual friends in the United Nations; indeed, that two of them had been married at my home in the United States.

Colonel Lucas leaned back and spoke with complete frankness about conditions at the Beach Camp in particular and the refugee settlements in general.

He began by making it clear to me that the Israeli had taken me to the only camp in Gaza—there being a half dozen—which had serious problems or grievances.

"The over-all picture is quite good," he said. "We have no complaints to make about the cooperation of the Israeli. If you had gone to almost any other camp you would probably have heard complimentary things about the military occupation. Even here at the Beach Camp it all depends on whom you talk to. There are some troublemakers, I am afraid, and it is rather easy to get a distorted picture."

I told him about the things that had been called to my attention.

"Yes," Colonel Lucas said, "we have jurisdiction over these camps, and any such outrages as were described to you it is our responsibility to investigate. We have checked into all such charges and are continuing to do so. Up to now, we have found nothing to support them. These investigations have been more than routine. On the basis of what we have learned so far, we are unable to make any charges.

"There is, of course, a certain amount of loose conduct in all armies under battle conditions. But we have been given nothing that can be regarded as evidence. Even so, we have reported whatever protests we received to the Israeli military authorities.

"Last Friday a woman was murdered at the Beach Camp. Some of the Arabs charged that the murder was committed by an Israeli soldier when the woman resisted his attentions. This, too, we have been investigating thoroughly. We are also investigating the possibility that the woman was murdered by someone from within the camp itself. It's a fairly complicated story involving jealousy by a third party; even here, however, we have to do much more checking."

I remembered what I had been told about the lack of sanitation and the fact that the garbage was not being removed. Colonel Lucas asked me if I had actually seen those garbage heaps. I could not say that I had seen anything that would fit the particular description. He made a notation of the fact just the same.

Then I asked him about the schools and about the fact that their teachers had been removed from jobs.

He said that my general impression was incorrect. For a time after the invasion, the life of the settlement was disrupted and the schools had been closed down. But the elementary schools, which were under the jurisdiction of the UN, had been opened some days earlier. The secondary schools were under the jurisdiction of the Israeli occupation and had opened that very morning.

As for the teachers, he said that only a few at the Beach Camp had been barred from the classroom. This was because the Israeli military authorities were disturbed because some of the teachers had a record of using the classroom for indoctrinating the children against Israel. But the overwhelming majority of the teachers had received a clean bill of health and were back at school.

The conversation then took a more general turn.

First, so far as the Gaza Strip was concerned, he said that the urgent need was for some political stability in the area. The refugees were entitled to know where they stood. The Beach Camp would continue to reflect the political uncertainty at the top. If the Israeli were going to remain in Gaza, then the Arabs there would make the adjustment accordingly. But if the Egyptians were going to return, they wanted definite word on that, too. In any case, things had to be settled on a workable basis.

Turning to the long-range problem of the Arab refugees, I asked Colonel Lucas what the prospects were for genuine resettlement.

"In this kind of work you learn to resist easy solutions," he said. "In fact, there's a certain danger in glib approaches. I've heard a great many propositions but not too many of them make sense. There's no place for the refugees either in Jordan or Lebanon because of religious differences or lack of space or both. And the Israeli proposal to settle them in Iraq seems to me to be unrealistic. The country couldn't support them.

"Meanwhile, before we decide what the long-range solution is going to be, we've got some immediate problems that vitally concern almost two hundred thousand human beings. The political uncertainty I spoke of a moment ago. But things can't go back to what they were either. The sporadic warfare across the borders hardly provides the basis for stability."

And then Colonel Lucas made what seemed to me to be a fundamental point in the relations between Arab and Jew.

He said that the area could use a little more realism. There's altogether too much fantasy. He had spoken earlier about the unrealistic Jewish proposal about resettlement in Iraq. Now he spoke about the lack of reality among Arabs who feel that there must be a return to the 1947 United Nations partition proposals. He said it was sheer fantasy to ignore the existence of Israel as a state. "Maybe if enough people learn to recognize facts as they are we might have a beginning toward something workable in the area," he concluded.

A direct correction clearly exists, it seems apparent, between what happens to the Arab refugees and the creation of an enduring peace in that part of the world. When the relations between Israel and her Arab neighbors begin to make sense, then it is likely that a program with some moral thrust behind it has a real chance to be put to work. Part of the Arab world has considered itself at war with Israel since 1948. So as long as this continues, acts of war by one side or another are inevitable. But once the sovereignties of all the nations in the area are effectively accepted, the combined energies of all the peoples can be harnessed to the full development of the region. Within Israel itself, for example, large projects are under way to reclaim the entire Negev Desert. Scientists are working on plans to desalinate the water from the sea and bring it down to the desert in pipes with a diameter of more than five feet. If the Negev can be opened up, there will be space enough in Israel for a great many Arab settlers on the same terms under which 150,0000 Arabs now live in the country: citizenship and participation in its community and cultural life. And there is the prospect of similar projects throughout the entire region.

An hour after I left the UNRWA headquarters, I met Colonel Haim Gaon, the military commander of the Gaza occupation. Colonel Gaon is a native Hollander, fought with the British in the Far East and Europe during World War II, volunteered in the Israeli army during the Palestine war eight years ago, and has stayed here since. He is well-read, follows world affairs closely, and has a well-developed philosophy of life. My guess is that once matters calm down he may turn his major efforts in the direction of diplomacy and the ministry of foreign affairs.

I covered the same matters with him that I did with Colonel Lucas of UNRWA. The picture I got was substantially the same. When I brought up the matter of the schoolteachers who were not allowed to return to the classroom, he accepted full responsibility for that decision. He realized what a delicate problem it was to suspend a teacher but said that the classroom was no place for the kind of propaganda that taught young people to hate. He felt that the teacher's job was to preside over the education of youngsters and not to make recruits for terror raids.

"But you mustn't imagine," he said, "that this has been widespread in Arab schools. Out of some twelve hundred teachers in the Gaza Strip only twenty-five have been suspended."

I asked him how a teacher could go about obtaining authorization to return to the classroom. His reply indicated that he was willing to reconsider his decision if reasonable assurances could be given.

Now for the larger questions. These questions concern the Israeli attack and occupation and, in general, the intentions of the Israeli. It was largely in search of answers to such questions that I had come to Israel. When the news of the invasion of the Strip and Sinai Peninsula broke across the world last October, the volcanic shock waves were felt everywhere. It also produced stark disbelief. Israel had not been generally associated with aggressive designs or means. Even more serious was the fact that a military thrust of this nature carried with it the danger of world war. The conflict of interests in the Middle East among the world powers is such that any sudden disequilibrium could upset the precarious balance in the world itself. It seemed inconceivable that the Israeli leaders were willing to run this risk, no matter how great the provocation of the last few years.

Before and after my visit to the Beach Camp, I discussed the question with Israeli people, in and out of government. This would include members of the Prime Minister's office, the Foreign Ministry, teachers, and people I happened to meet wherever I went. I found a unity of conviction and determination that had the virtue at least of furnishing me with crisp and incisive answers.

"You've got to live here in order to understand it," the owner of one of the many bookstores in Tel Aviv told me. "Night after night the Egyptians sent their *Fedayeen* raiders across the border. Small raids. One or two murders at a time. Too small to make news in the outside world—the headlines came only when after three or four months of terror we would launch a punitive raid in force. But those of us who live here don't need headlines to tell us the meaning of terror by night. How long can you put up with this sort of thing before you're driven to end the terror once and for all?"

The day after this conversation I had lunch at a home some twenty miles north of Tel Aviv. Less than sixty feet from where we sat was the rubble pile of a stone-and-cement cottage that had been blown up by a charge of dynamite sufficient to shatter a structure five times its size. A man who had been in the house at the time was of course killed. The dynamiting had been done several weeks earlier by terror raiders.

At another of the border settlements I visited near Gaza, I met Israeli farmers who were embittered toward their government because of the inadequate protection it had afforded against raiders. It is now possible for officers of the Israeli army to show themselves at these settlements. Before last fall, they were objects of ridicule because they had been ineffective against the *Fedayeen*.

Even after seeing the effects of the terror raids, however, I was not satisfied. It had seemed to me that the Israeli and the Arabs had been caught up in a chain reaction of reciprocal terror. Wasn't it possible that each side was determined to teach the other a lesson and that each raid was in the nature of reciprocal or punitive action designed to put an end to forays by the other? I remembered reading an article in *Harper's* magazine a few years ago in which an Israeli official wrote that the only language the Arabs understood was force. The article said that unless the Israeli hit back with multiplied impact the Arabs would have no incentive to desist. I remembered, too, a conversation I had at the Bandung Conference with President Abdel Gamal Nasser, of Egypt. The Jews, said President Nasser, understood only the language of force. It was only at the point of a gun or a sword that they could be made to see reason.

There you had it. With both sides accepting the vocabulary of violence as the only medium of communication, it was inevitable that the guns would speak. In my talk with Colonel Gaon, I said I wondered whether Israel was justified in using the *Fedayeen* raids as the reason for its attack in Gaza and Sinai in view of the fact that the Egyptian terrorist activities may have been in retaliation for the Israeli raids which were in retaliation for Egyptian raids, and so on.

Colonel Gaon shook his head, then asked me calmly whether I had taken the trouble to look into the actual sequence of events.

"When one goes beyond opinion into fact, he finds that the situation is not as you described it," he said. "The record shows that the *Fedayeen* raids would go on for three, four, maybe five months without Israeli retaliation. A farmer killed one night. A *kibbutz* store-house blown up the next night. A home in the country set afire the night after that. A boy on a bicycle machine-gunned from across the border. A professor walking on a ridge road in Jerusalem killed by a long-range rifle. Week after week it happened. Then, when the demand of the people themselves became insistent, a counter-raid would be launched. It would be a grisly business, and the world heard about it, but at least things would quiet down for three or four months and the people could get some work done. This idea of yours of one raid leading to a counter-raid just doesn't correspond to the facts. If you examine the record, you will see that what I have said is true."

I did look into the record. What he said was substantially correct. And one fact is central. The Egyptian government has publicly sponsored and rewarded its raiders. It had been openly stated that the purpose was to make life intolerable for the Israeli. It had also been stated that Egypt would not rest until the Israeli state had been drowned in a sea of blood.

"What did America and the outside world expect us to do?" I was asked time and again, from Haifa to Jerusalem. "Sit back and become passive observers at our own destruction?"

At the Israeli Foreign Office, when I said I wondered whether any provocation was great enough to warrant an action that could imperil the safety of the entire world, I was told that the failure of the Israeli to act as they did might have produced even greater risks.

"We have never made the mistake of thinking that this was only an Israeli-Egyptian affair. We couldn't even if we had wanted to. There was never any doubt in our mind from the moment Egypt began receiving massive arms shipments from the Communist world that other people were involved. The size of the arms we captured proves that it wasn't Egypt alone which was going to use them. The guns alone far outnumbered the hands in Egypt that could have held them. And what about the thousands upon thousands of bed sheets that were in military storage? Were these intended only for Egyptian soldiers? Then there were the large tanks that had been shipped in from the outside. There's no doubt that this build-up represented the real risk of war—and not the action we took to get rid of it.

"The world is terribly excited and concerned about the Israeli military campaign. How is it that there was so little concern and excitement when the Communist world shipped the arms into the Sinai Peninsula in the first place? The existence of those arms, directed against us, was an act of war.

"When Egyptian army officers took command of the military establishments of Jordan and Syria, as part of a pact against Israel, what were we supposed to do? Assume that this had nothing to do with our security? When our ships were prevented from entering a body of water on which we had an important seaport, were we supposed to believe that this was in the interests of world peace? What would America have done if another nation had tried to do the same thing to her? It wouldn't have put up with it for three minutes, let alone three years. Yes, I suppose we could have won world sympathy by allowing ourselves to be attacked and overrun and liquidated as a nation. But our purpose is survival. After that, world sympathy, if we can get it.

"Someday the world may feel to its great regret that it made a terrible mistake in its handling of this matter—in forcing us to withdraw before it addressed itself to the reasons for our being there. One can only hope that it will not then be too late."

I could see his point, but I thought it important to venture the opinion that the United Nations had widespread support in its action calling for British, French, and Israeli armed withdrawal. That support was directly related to the hope that the United Nations would finally assert itself as an effective organization wherever threats to the peace were concerned. When Israel attacked in force, it was the clear obligation of the UN to insist upon and, if necessary, to compel withdrawal. The announcement that a United Nations police force would be formed was hailed as a historic and long-overdue decision. Indeed, a strong movement has developed toward setting up this force on a permanent basis. In short, the best hope for Israel is that the precedents and machinery in the United Nations will now be created that can underwrite the sovereign existence of all nations, large and small. There is still much to be done before these principles can become a working reality; but at least a start has been made.

In response, I was told that Israel would give full support to a United Nations organization which in fact and in deed could enforce world law. But it was the very reluctance of the United Nations to assume the obligations of world law in the Gaza Strip and the Gulf of Aqaba that was creating a problem for Israel. Israel didn't want to keep the territory; all she asked was that the UN itself take over and police the area in order to enforce the peace. Another thing that bothered the Israeli was that other nations which demanded that Israel obey the resolutions of the UN Assembly were spurning UN resolutions when applied to themselves.

"How is it that the UN backs down when a mighty nation like Soviet Russia ignores the demands of the UN about Hungary, yet will direct all its energies against a small nation like Israel when what Israel actually seeks is the assumption of proper responsibility by the UN itself?"

At the same time, it will be necessary for all the nations involved to develop a greater respect for the responsible authority of the UN. When the Israeli government takes upon itself to intern or expel UN Gaza employees because they are Egyptian it is acting outside its sovereign limits and is challenging the ultimate source of its own security. And when Egypt continues to make the kind of threats that preceded the last outbreak, this, too, becomes costly anti-UN business.

The heart of the problem then, whether with respect to Israel, Egypt, the Middle East as a whole, or the world itself, is represented not just by the need for peace but the need for justice. There is not a threat to the peace in the world today that does not involve a claim for justice. Arabs seek justice for those who lost their homes in the war. Egypt seeks justice against the large nations in the matter of the Suez Canal. The large nations seek justice in their relations with one another.

But where is justice to be found? So far, the United Nations has been a market place for the display of national interests rather than an agency whose structure permits it to enact and enforce law in the interests of the human community. There is as yet no overriding central allegiance to a concept larger than that of the nation itself. There is no impartial tribunal concerned with objective judicial decision or review. Each nation insists on being supreme in matters of its own security. But nationhood on this level and human survival are no longer consistent.

Great connections beyond national boundaries and religious backgrounds will make possible a common goal—a world made safe for its diversity. It is neither too late nor too soon to begin to develop a respect for such a large design. The generations ahead have rights, too.

*—February 9, 1957*

# The Desensitization of Twentieth-Century Man

It happened at the Stamford, Connecticut, railroad station. It was Sunday evening, at about 10 P.M. Some two dozen persons, among them several young men in uniform, were waiting for the express to New York.

The door to the waiting room flew open. A woman, shrieking hysterically, burst into the room. She was pursued by a man just a few steps behind her. The woman screamed that the man was trying to kill her and cried out for the people to save her. I was standing nearest the door. The woman grabbed me, still shrieking. I tried to protect her behind me. The man tried to sweep me aside to get at her. He rushed at me, caught the woman's wrist with one hand, tore her loose and pulled her through the doorway. The woman fell to the ground and was dragged by the wrist just outside the waiting room. I tried to free her wrist. The man broke off, grabbed the woman's pocketbook, and fled on foot.

We carried the woman inside the waiting room, sat her down, then telephoned the police. The woman's eye was badly cut; she was moaning. I looked around the room. Except for three or four persons who now came up to her, the people in the room seemed unconcerned. The young men in uniform were still standing in the same place, chatting among themselves as before. I am not sure which was greater, the shock of the attack that had just occurred or the shock caused by the apparent detachment and unconcern of the other people, especially the men in uniform.

The next morning I read in the newspaper of another attack. This one was carried out in broad daylight on a young boy by a gang of teen-agers. Here, too, a number of people stood around and watched.

It would be possible, I suppose, to take the view that these are isolated instances, and that it would be a serious error to read into these cases anything beyond the fact that the bystanders were probably paralyzed by the suddenness of the violence. Yet I am not so sure. I am not sure that these instances may not actually be the product of something far deeper. What is happening, I believe, is that the natural reactions of the individual against violence are being blunted. The individual is being desensitized by living history. He is developing new reflexes and new responses that tend to slow up the moral imagination and relieve him of essential indignation over impersonal hurt. He is becoming casual about brutality. He makes his adjustments to the commonplace, and nothing is more commonplace in our age than the ease with which life can be smashed or shattered. The range of the violence sweeps from the personal to the impersonal, from the amusements of the crowd to the policies of nations. It is in the air, quite literally. It has lost the sting of surprise. We have made our peace with violence.

No idea could be more untrue than that there is no connection between what is happening in the world and in the behavior of the individual. Society does not exist apart from the individual. It transfers its apprehensions or its hopes, its fatigue or its vitality, its ennui or its dreams, its sickness or its spirituality to the people who are part of it. Can the individual be expected to retain the purity of his responses, particularly a sensitivity to the fragility of life, when society itself seems to measure its worth in terms of its ability to create and possess instruments of violence that could expunge civilization as easily as it once took to destroy a village? Does it have no effect on an individual to live in an age that has already known two world wars; that has seen hundreds of cities ripped apart by dynamite tumbling down from the heavens; that has witnessed whole nations stolen or destroyed; that has seen millions of people exterminated in gas chambers or other mass means; that has seen governments compete with one another to make weapons which, even in the testing, have put death into the air?

To repeat, the causative range is all the way from petty amusements to the proclamations of nations. We are horrified that teen-age boys should make or steal lethal weapons and then proceed to use them on living creatures; but where is the sense of horror or outrage at the cheapness of human life that is exploited throughout the day or night on television? It is almost impossible to see television for fifteen minutes without seeing people beaten or shot or punched or kicked or jabbed. It is also almost impossible to pick up a newspaper without finding someone in a position of power, here or elsewhere, threatening to use nuclear explosives unless someone else becomes more sensible.

The young killers don't read the newspapers, true. They don't have to. If they read at all, they read the picture-story pulps that dispense brutality as casually as a vending machine its peanuts. In any case, the heart of the matter is that the young killers do not live in the world of their own. They belong to the larger world. They may magnify and intensify the imperfections of the larger world but they do not invent them.

The densensitization of twentieth-century man is more than a danger to the common safety. It represents the loss or impairment of the noblest faculty of human life—the ability to be aware both of suffering and beauty; the ability to share sorrow and create hope; the ability to think and respond beyond one's wants. There are some things we have no right ever to get used to. One of these most certainly is brutality. The other is the irrational. Both brutality and the irrational have now come together and are moving toward a dominant pattern. If the pattern is to be resisted and changed, a special effort must be made. A very special effort.

*—May 16, 1957*

*The most sustained and concentrated attention given by the Saturday Review in its history to any single public question was focused on the need to end the nuclear arms—before, in President Kennedy's words, the arms race ended the human race. And the one aspect of the arms race that commanded our thoughts and energies was nuclear testing.*

*Our intense concern with this question began one day in August, 1956, when a small group of professors at George Washington University in St. Louis showed us scientific papers and documents on what was then a new phenomenon—radioactive fallout. One of the research studies, undertaken under the auspices of the U.S. Atomic Energy Commission, gave figures on the increasing contamination of milk from radioactive fallout, then comparatively light. The research paper recommended that the United States obtain estimates on the cost of decontaminating the nation's milk supply. Other research papers reported on the accumulation of human bone and tissue from radioactive fallout, especially in the case of children whose bodies mistake radioactive strontium for calcium in the building process. We came away from that meeting at George Washington University with an enlarged understanding of the need to bring nuclear testing under control, quite apart from the substantial reasons growing out of the volatility of the arms race and the danger represented by the spread of nuclear weapons.*

## The Great Debate Opens

Four weeks ago the *Saturday Review* published a Declaration of Conscience by Dr. Albert Schweitzer. In it he called the attention of the world's people to the fact that the nuclear-arms race is producing a grim by-product. The test explosions are pumping large quantities of radioactive materials into the atmosphere. These radioactive materials retain high potency for more than twenty-five years. The rate of fall is irregular, depending on rains and winds. Thus, there is no way of predicting how much will fall at any one time or where it will fall or what the strength of the fallout will be. Also, the prospect is for more frequent nuclear explosions and larger ones as other nations enter into atomic production and insist on their own right to set off the big bombs as a way of demonstrating their mature military capabilities.

The main danger is represented not by external radiation but by internal radiation. External radiation is the result of open exposure. While it may do harm, depending on the extent of the dose, it is not nearly so harmful as taking radioactive substances directly into the body through food. By way of illustrating the difference between internal and external radiation, the example of the wrist watch with the radium dial may be cited. The radium dial emits a small amount of radioactivity and may be only moderately harmful. But if someone were to open the face of the watch and scrape off the radium and put it in his food, the resultant harm would be many times greater. Radioactive strontium, for example, once taken into the body through food, affects the vital nucleic acid. It also affects the bone structure, especially of young children whose tolerances to radioactive strontium are much lower than they are in adults whose bones are fully formed.

Although only a small fraction of the radioactive materials released by the nuclear explosions has come to earth so far, enough has fallen to be detected in soil, water, vegetation, and milk. The U.S. Atomic Energy Commission, in a scientific paper prepared for it but not distributed to the nation's press, acknowledged that instruments had picked up the existence of radioactive strontium in milk samplings. Indeed, Dr. Willard F. Libby, co-author of that report, recommended that the nation obtain cost estimates for decontaminating milk. The strontium got into the milk from cows grazing on land which had been dusted by radioactivity. Since that report was made, the amount of radioactive strontium in the air, in milk, in vegetation, in water has increased many times, for the largest bombs have been exploded in the past three years.

The American Congress and the nation itself are now engaged in a great controversy over this question. Serious and responsible scientists are ranged on both sides. It is important, therefore, to eliminate as much confusion as possible from the debate. The fact that radioactive strontium is released by nuclear explosions is agreed to by both sides. The fact that it can do irreparable harm to human tissue is agreed to by both sides. The fact that milk and food throughout the world contain detectable amounts of radioactive poison is agreed to by both sides.

What is not agreed to concerns the amount of radioactive strontium a human being may absorb without serious harm, and also whether, even if this harm is real, it should not be accepted as an essential requirement of military security.

On the first question—the tolerance limits—the fact is that no scientist or expert, whether he is for or against the tests, can say with certainty what the precise limits of radioactive strontium are for a human being. It is this uncertainty that gives rise to the present debate. Dr. Libby argues that he has seen no direct evidence that the amount of strontium that has fallen so far has produced any significant damage. The scientists on the other side make these points: First, that the very fact that the tolerance limits are unknown makes it essential to suspend the explosions until we are sure that great harm will not be done to people everywhere —whether those people belong to the nation which is setting off the explosions or to nations which have nothing to do with the explosions. Second, that each new item of research having to do with the effects of radiation shows it to be vastly more dangerous than was previously supposed. The Atomic Energy Commission itself recently reduced its own guess by two-thirds concerning the safety factor in fallout. Third, new research definitely indicates a small increase in the world leukemia rate is directly attributable to the explosions.

It is at this point that Dr. Libby says that any existing risk is necessary for the national security. We cannot under any circumstances afford to fall behind Soviet Russia. Also, if the United States and Great Britain give up nuclear testing, and the Russians do not, then we have jeopardized the entire free world.

This is a seemingly plausible argument but it should be considered in the light of the following facts:

1. The principal factor affecting our military security at the moment is not more bombs or bigger bombs but the method of delivering the bombs we already have. Indeed, the controversy over fallout has obscured a fact of profound importance to every American: this nation has lagged badly in the development of its ICBM program (intercontinental ballistics missile) and is believed by military experts to be substantially behind Soviet Russia in this respect. The Soviet also has submarines that can plant large-megaton hydrogen bombs off our coasts, creating radioactive tidal waves that would wash far inland. The submarines can also be used as launching platforms for direct attack against our population centers.

2. Both the United States and the Soviet Union by this time have more than enough high-megaton hydrogen explosives to destroy each other and the rest of the world. There is not a city in the world that could not be made uninhabitable by one or at most two of the large bombs. The Russians already have bombs of sufficient power to enable them, at any time they wish, to melt the polar icecap and inundate the coastal cities of America and Europe. We have already successfully tested a bomb that is 1,000 times more powerful than the one that incinerated a large part of Hiroshima. When we talk about experimenting with yet larger bombs, therefore, we are not talking about military security but about pulverization and an assault upon the planet itself.

3. For the first time in our history we are preparing for a war we have said we cannot win. For if the war should start, then, as the President and Soviet leaders have directly acknowledged, extermination is inevita-

ble. Our entire military program, therefore, can have only one objective: to prevent a major war from starting.

Our best chance of keeping such a war from starting is by maintaining a position of real leadership in the world. For as long as the majority of the world's peoples have confidence in our purposes and believe our policies are consistent with world welfare, we have the kind of strength that cannot easily be pierced.

The struggle in the world today exists on two levels—one for military superiority, the other for leadership of the majority. No one can say what military superiority consists of or how it can be maintained. But our position with respect to the majority is visible and measurable. And today we are on shaky ground so far as the majority is concerned. On the question of testing, the world feels it has a right to expect a real measure of leadership from the United States. It understands that there are two parts to the problem—what we do and what the Russians do—but it does not feel that we have scored any great triumphs of moral imagination in our own approach to the problem.

We have allowed the Russians to become the great American alibi. We have allowed them to serve as our excuse for not doing the things that plainly have to be done. If, for example, there is a moral issue involved in testing, then we ought to state it. If no nation has the right to undertake defense measures at the expense of other peoples—and nuclear explosions rob other people's air of its purity—then we have the obligation to state it.

It is not true that America is helpless in the present situation. There is no reason why we should not come before the world and say:

"We have two central objectives in our policy—peace for all the world's peoples under law, and the establishment of those conditions under which the individual human being, wherever he is, may grow and advance in freedom.

"We do not believe that an atomic armaments race is consistent with the requirements of either of these objectives. The nature of these new weapons is such that we would rather die ourselves than use them against human beings.

"So far as nuclear experimentation is concerned, there is a vital doubt about the ability of human tissue to sustain continued exposure to the radioactive substances released by these explosions. No nation has the right to take measures that affect the purity of another nation's air, water, and soil. Because of both these facts we are suspending our own tests and we are absolutely certain that world public opinion will compel all other nations to do likewise.

"The peace of the world will not automatically be assured the moment the nuclear tests are halted. But at least it helps to create a stage for the next big move, which is to go beyond a cessation of testing into reduction and control of all weapons adapted to mass destruction. And the biggest move of all is to create the conditions under which it is possible to deal with the basic causes of war. For the aim can only be a world liberated from the present anarchy."

If we would discover our greatest strength, we shall have to look in the direction of a unifying idea. People have heard enough about their capacity to rend this universe. What they are hungry for now is a way to keep this planet and man himself whole.

—*June 15, 1957*

# Clean Bombs and Dirty Wars

Almost without realizing it we are adopting the language of madmen. We talk of "clean" hydrogen bombs as though we are dealing with the ultimate in moral refinement. We use fairyland words to describe a mechanism that in a split second can incinerate millions of human beings—not dummies or imitations but real people, exactly the kind that you see around your dinner table. What kind of monstrous imagination is it that can connect the word "clean" to a device that will put the match to man's cities? Yes; what is really meant by "clean" is that we may be able to build a bomb with a greatly reduced potential for causing radioactive fallout. But to call a hydrogen bomb or any bomb "clean" is to make an obscene farce out of words.

Or we will use the term "sunshine units" to measure the amounts of radiation suffered by people as the result of nuclear explosions. Serious research reveals that any added radiation shortens life. And when a radioactive poison such as strontium-90 enters the body it gets into the nucleic acid and the bones with a risk of leukemia and bone tumors or cancers. Yet all this now goes by the name of "sunshine units." It is made to sound as though something beautiful and gleamingly wholesome were coming into a man's life. We seem to forget that this is human tissue that is involved here. Also human germ plasm. And the effect on both of added radiation is a cheapening and a damaging effect, and therefore an evil one. To use the pretty words of the nursery in connection with such an effect is to engage in a fiendish act of moral shrinkage.

The "clean" bomb became headline news recently when three nuclear scientists, under the auspices of the Atomic Energy Commission, called on the President. The news accounts of the meeting reported that the scientists asked for continuation of nuclear testing for five years. They said they needed that much more time to develop a "clean" hydrogen bomb; that is, a fission-free explosive. There was a general air of jubilation about the announcement, as though this were the deliverance the human race was waiting for. The announcement said nothing about the fact that what the world is waiting for is not a better way to make a "clean" hydrogen explosive but a better way to get rid of dirty wars.

Exactly what do the three scientists think is going to happen in the next five years while they calmly carry out their experiments? Do they suppose that everything will stand still, that the massive tensions that have been building up for more than a decade and that are now approaching the saturation point will somehow evaporate? Do they expect that the race between the Soviets and the United States will be the first to develop a missile that can cross the oceans—do they expect that this race will be called off? Do they expect that the reserves of nuclear weapons will not mount higher and higher until their very presence may create a quick-trigger psychosis? Do they think that unlimited freedom to continue unlimited testing will cause the present world anarchy to disappear?

Important though the laboratory may be to the scientists of the Atomic Energy Commission, it is not quite the whole world. The whole world is a world of movement and tempers and sudden impulses. It can't be squeezed into a row of laboratory storage bottles, no matter how neatly labeled. It can't be characterized by a single equation; at least not so long as there are people in it. And it is precisely the boiling and churning of the unpredictables that make it necessary today to bring the weapons of mass destruction under control, to define new relationships among the nations, and to make these new relationships work under enforceable law.

The three scientists do not speak for the entire government, but the circumstances of their visit to the White House may indicate that government policy may now be developing along the lines of their recommendations. If so, and we pursue a policy of unlimited testing, then the present disarmament negotiations are fruitless. For the President has previously stated that any ban on nuclear testing must be tied to a ban on nuclear armaments. If, therefore, we now insist on continued testing, it can only mean that disarmament itself is doomed.

What is most serious is that we are in effect announcing that we don't want what the world's peoples are clamoring for—specific and concerted action that can bring the big nuclear killers under control. And nothing can be more damaging to our security than to allow the idea to get around that we are not really sincere in what we have been saying officially about our desire for arms control. Soviet Russia has been charging us with insincerity. If we now confirm that charge by what we ourselves do, then we will have suffered a loss in the world that no quantity of hydrogen explosives, however "clean," can offset.

No one argues against the proposition that we can't expect to deal effectively with the threat of communism without some measure of moral influence or leadership in the world. But moral leadership means what it says. And there is nothing either moral or influential about separating ourselves from the deeply held hopes of people everywhere.

*—July 13, 1957*

## Checklist of Enemies

The enemy is not solely an atomic-muscled totalitarian power with a world ideology.

The enemy is many people. He is a man whose only concern about the world is that it stay in one piece during his own lifetime. He is invariably up to his hips in success and regards his good fortune not as a challenge to get close to the real problems of the age but as proof of the correctness of everything he does. Nothing to him is less important than the shape of things to come or the needs of the next generation. Talk of the legacy of the past or of human destiny leaves him cold. Historically, he is the disconnected man. Hence, when he thinks about the world at all, it is usually in terms of his hope that the atomic fireworks can be postponed for fifteen or twenty years. He is an enemy because nothing less than a passionate concern for the rights of unborn legions will enable the world itself to become connected and whole.

The enemy is a man who not only believes in his own helplessness but actually worships it. His main article of faith is that there are mammoth forces at work which the individual cannot possibly comprehend, much less alter or direct. And so he expends vast energies in attempting to convince other people that there is nothing they can do. He is an enemy because of the proximity of helplessness to hopelessness.

The enemy is a man who has a total willingess to delegate his worries about the world to officialdom. He assumes that only the people in authority are in a position to know and act. He believes that if vital information essential to the making of public decisions is withheld, it can only be for a good reason. If a problem is wholly or partially scientific in nature, he will ask no questions even though the consequences of the problem are political or social. He is an enemy because government, by its very nature, is unable to deal effectively today with matters concerned with human survival. What is necessary is something to tame the national sovereignties and create a design of the whole. If this is to be done, it can be done not by the national sovereignties themselves but by bold, determined, and insistent acts of the public will.

The enemy is any man in government, high or low, who keeps waiting for a public mandate before he can develop big ideas of his own, but who does little or nothing to bring about such a mandate. Along with this goes an obsessive fear of criticism. To such a man, the worst thing in the world that can happen is to be accused of not being tough-minded in the nation's dealings with other governments. He takes in his stride, however, the accusation that he is doing something that may result in grave injury to the human race. He lives entirely on the plane of plot and counterplot, where the dominant reality is represented by scoring points on a day-by-day basis. He figures security largely in terms of statistics—generally the kind of force that can be put to work in a showdown situation—rather than in terms of the confidence and good will a nation may enjoy among its neighbors in the world. He is an enemy because he sees no connection between his own authority and the need to act in behalf of the human community.

The enemy is a scientist who makes his calling seem more mysterious than it is, and who allows this mystery to interfere with public participation in decisions involving science or the products of science. His own specialized training may have shielded him from the give and take so essential to the democratic process in government. In a position of responsibility he is apt to make decisions, or to influence others in making decisions, without due regard for the fact that the ultimate power in a democratic society must reside with the individual citizen. The requirements of the laboratory may call for complete autonomy; the requirements of the government call for an informed citizenry full of prodding questions.

The enemy is any man in the pulpit who by his words and acts encourages his congregation to believe that the main purpose of the church or the synagogue is to provide social respectability for its members. He talks about the sacredness of life, but he never relates that concept to the real and specific threats that exist today to such sacredness. He identifies himself as a man of God but feels no urge to speak out against a situation in which the nature of man is likely to be altered and cheapened, the genetic integrity of man violated, and distant generations condemned to a lower species. He is a dispenser of balm rather than an awakener of conscience. He is preoccupied with the need to provide personal peace of mind rather than to create a blazing sense of restlessness to set things right. He is an enemy because the crisis today is as much a spiritual crisis as it is a political one.

The enemy is not necessarily a bad man—indeed, he may be a man of high character and considerable good will. He may be giving the best that is in him to his family and his work. But he is a dangerous man nonetheless because he is a chronic absentee from his main job. His main job is to become supremely aware of and intimately involved in the great issues of his time. In this way he may help to create a design of safety and sanity for a world in need of both.

—*July 27, 1957*

# Is America Living Half a Life?

A deep uneasiness exists inside Americans.

It is not that we have suddenly become unsure of ourselves in a world in which the Soviet Union has dramatically laid claim to scientific supremacy.

Nor that the same launching platform that can rocket a man-made satellite into outer space can send a missile across the ocean in eighteen minutes.

Nor is the uneasiness only the result of headlines that talk of trouble between Turkey and Syria and about a war that will not be limited to the Middle East.

The uneasiness that exists inside Americans has to do with the fact that we are not living up to our moral capacity in the world.

We have been living half a life. We have been developing our appetites —but we have been starving our purposes. We have been concerned with bigger salaries, bigger television screens, bigger cars—and now, with bigger missiles—instead of with the big ideas on which our lives and freedoms depend.

The danger facing us is unlike any danger that has ever existed. In our possession and in the possession of the Russians are more than enough nuclear explosives to put an end to the life of man on earth.

Our approach to the danger is unequal to the danger. What we say and what we do somehow seem out of joint. The slogans and arguments that are part of a world of competitive national sovereignties, a world of plot and counterplot, no longer fit the world of today or tomorrow.

The main need today is to find some way of making the planet safe for human life. Man has natural rights that transcend the rights of nations. He has a right to live and to grow, to breathe unpoisoned air, to work on uncontaminated soil. He has a right to his sacred nature.

If what nations are doing has the effect of upsetting the delicate balances on which life depends, fouling the air, devitalizing the food, and tampering with the genetic integrity of man himself—then it becomes necessary for people to restrain and tame the nations.

Indeed, the test of a nation's right to survive today is measured not by the size of its bombs, or the range of its missiles, but by the size of its concern for the human community as a whole.

There can be no security for America unless we can establish and keep vital connections with the world's peoples, unless there is some moral grandeur to our purposes, unless what we do is directed to the cause of human life and the free man.

It will not be enough to make bigger missiles or space-platforms. The real challenge is to come up with some ideas that can keep the missiles and push-buttons from being used to destroy the earth.

There is much that America has said to the world. But the world is still waiting for us to say the things that will in deed and in truth represent our greatest strength.

What are these things?

*First, as it concerns the peace, we can say:*

That we pledge everything we have to the cause of a meaningful peace on earth; that there is nothing that we will not give, no sacrifice that we are not prepared to make, nothing we will not do to create a peace under justice.

That we are prepared to support the concept of a United Nations with adequate authority to prevent aggression, adequate authority to compel and enforce disarmament, adequate authority to invoke justice in the disputes among nations.

*Next, as it concerns satellites, missiles, and nuclear weapons, we can say:*

That the earth is too small for intercontinental ballistic missiles and hydrogen bombs, and that the first order of business for the world is to bring both under control.

That the exploration of outer space and the development of satellites must be carried on in the interests of the entire human community through a pooling of world science.

*As it concerns nuclear testing, we can say:*

That because of grave unanswered questions relating to the effects of hydrogen explosions—especially as it concerns the contamination of air and water and food, and the injury to man himself—we are calling upon all nations to suspend their nuclear explosions at once.

That while the abolition of testing will not by itself solve the problem of peace or the problem of armament, it represents a specific danger that can be eliminated immediately. Also, that the abolition of testing gives us a place to begin on the larger question of armaments control, for there are few complicated problems in monitoring such tests.

*As it concerns our connections to the rest of mankind and to the world in which our children will live, we can say:*

That none of the differences separating the governments of the world are as important as the things that entitle all people to membership in the human family.

That the big challenge of the age is to develop the concept of a higher loyalty—loyalty by man to the human community.

That the greatest era in history is ours for the taking, that there is no arid area that cannot be made fertile or habitable, no disease that cannot be fought, no scarcity that cannot be conquered. All that is required for this is to re-direct our energies, re-discover our moral strength, re-define our purposes.

*—November 16, 1957*

## Dr. Teller and the Spirit of Adventure

No one can say exactly where sanity must take hold if human history is to continue. Madness has a way of multiplying when unconfined. Yet if a beginning is to be made, it seems logical to look for it somewhere in the area of control over those weapons that can fracture whole continents in war and that are contaminating life in peace. Beyond such controls, of course, is the need to deal with basic causes of world tensions and unrest.

One man, however, may be pivotal in blocking even an attempt at a beginning in arms control. It is the man who devised America's first thermonuclear weapon. Dr. Edward Teller has taken it upon himself to persuade the American people against the desirability even of seeking an end to nuclear testing—and such a ban is intimately connected with the entire problem of bringing the mass killers under control.

Dr. Teller's first major public activity in this connection was a visit to the White House, where he sought to remove any doubts the President may have held about the dangers of radioactive fallout. Dr. Teller told the President that he was working on what he termed a "clean" hydrogen or thermonuclear bomb. The visit is believed to have undercut whatever plans may have been in the making for a genuine effort to seek workable agreements on cessation of testing and controls over nuclear weapons in general.

The second major public activity by Dr. Teller was an article in *Life* magazine. Here he went even beyond the reported interview with the President. He declared that there was virtually no health hazard in nuclear testing. He sought to refute the 9,000 scientists throughout the world who had signed a statement making known their deep and growing apprehension over radioactive fallout. He claimed that the amount of radiation involved in nuclear explosions, in terms of its direct effect on the individual, was less than he would receive from a wrist watch with a radium dial. He appealed to the sense of adventure in the American people.

Most recently Dr. Teller appeared on the television program *Meet the Press*. Here he went far beyond anything he had said or written before. He declared flatly there was no danger to public health from radioactive fallout produced by nuclear explosions. He said that nuclear testing would have to go on "indefinitely." And he referred once again to the fact that a "clean" hydrogen bomb was not too many years away.

If this is the way Dr. Teller feels then he has the right and indeed the duty to state his case. But it is equally the duty of those who are appalled by his arguments to make their own views known.

The most startling thing about Dr. Teller's total position is that he makes claims which even the U.S. Atomic Energy Commission has specifically avoided. The Atomic Energy Commission has stated, in a committee report issued on October 19, 1957, that maximum permissible dosages for large populations would be exceeded if testing were to be continued indefinitely. Up to now no scientist, whatever his opinion concerning the present danger, has baldly stated that tests could continue indefinitely without serious risk. Dr. Teller thus sets himself against even his colleagues on the Atomic Energy Commission.

Next, Dr. Teller has chosen to ignore other specific facts in the possession of the U.S. Atomic Energy Commission:

1. In 1954 the Atomic Energy Commission undertook a research survey to determine whether the nation's milk was being affected by radioactive fallout from nuclear testing. Levels of radioactive strontium in milk were considered well under danger limits at the time. Even so, Dr. Willard F. Libby recommended that cost estimates be obtained for decontaminating the nation's milk. It would seem strange that if no danger, actual or potential, existed, as Dr. Teller now claims, it should be necessary to consider ways of decontaminating the milk supply.

2. A similar survey for the AEC in 1954 found that there were detectable quantities of the poisonous radioactive strontium in every one of twenty-four soil samples taken from farms in Wisconsin and Illinois. Because of the favorable content of calcium in the soil, it was felt that some measure of counteractive protection existed. Even so, one farm south of Chicago was not rich in natural calcium. Continued fallout could be a problem in this case, and in all other cases where the soil is not calcium-rich. There are many areas of the world where the soil is calcium-poor. We have no way of confining radioactive fallout to our own country, nor the Russians to theirs, nor the British to theirs.

3. A report for the AEC made public very recently revealed that radioactive strontium in the bones of American adults has increased 30 per cent as the result of nuclear tests. The radioactive strontium in the bones of children has increased 50 per cent, according to the same report. The reason for the additional hazard in the case of children is that the growth process utilizes calcium for bone building; and the body mistakes the poisonous strontium for calcium. This increase in strontium in the bones of human beings is now very small alongside what it will be five years from now, to say nothing of what it will be twenty-five years from now. Only a tiny fraction of the radioactive strontium in the atmosphere has

278     The Editorial Page, 1940–1966

come to earth so far. At the end of twenty-eight years the radioactive strontium in the air still retains half its strength. Every particle of radioactive strontium taken into the body is stored by the body and gains in its power to do harm with every additional particle that is ingested through food or fluid. The exposure is cumulative.

Even more astounding are the inconsistencies in Dr. Teller's position.

One of his principal reasons for continuing unlimited testing is that he is confident that eventually he can produce a "clean bomb." This is a startling way of describing a weapon with reduced radioactive fallout that has lost none of its power for incinerating millions of people. Most difficult of all to comprehend is why it should be necessary to spend billions of dollars to develop a bomb to get rid of a radioactive hazard that is supposed to be negligible in the first place.

Next, we have his remarkable statement that the peril of radioactive fallout is even less than that represented by the infinitesimal amount of radiation a man receives from the radium dial on his watch. This has disturbed some scientists who point out that, though this statement is technically true, it is important to understand that there is a difference between the effects of external radiation and internal radiation. A man can wear a radium-dial wrist watch with a high degree of safety, but if he opened the face of that watch and began to eat small quantities of the radium he would be exposing himself to diseases of blood and bone. Similarly, the external radiation from fallout so far may not be great, but when radioactive strontium gets into the body through contaminated vegetables or milk or meat it can be highly dangerous. Moreover, the amount of such strontium now in food will be increased many times in the next few years. Every little bit that enters the body is stored and represents a hazard to the bone structure particularly. There is no mention of this by Dr. Teller.

Now we come to the most important issues of all, both of which are overlooked by Dr. Teller.

We have every right to take whatever risks we wish in the pursuit of our own security. But we do not have the right—nor do the Russians, the British, or anyone else about to enter the nuclear arms race—to take risks for other peoples without their consent.

The radioactive materials put into the atmosphere through nuclear explosions cannot be confined to any given area. This means that a nuclear explosion affects all peoples—not merely the people of the nation exploding a bomb.

The real issue emerging from all this, therefore, is a simple one: Does any nation have the moral right to jeopardize the health of other people in the pursuit of its own policies? The American people fought a revolution less than two centuries ago because vital decisions concerning them were made without their consent. The issue today is even more basic for the world's peoples, who have every right to demand "No contamination without representation."

Both the nuclear arms race and the human situation itself today are spinning out of control. A start in sanity must be made at some point. Some nation is going to have to make an assertion of conscience and sanity in attempting that start. America made the first nuclear weapon. There is no reason why we can't be equally determined and ingenious in pressing for the essential controls.

Finally, Dr. Teller refers to the "spirit of adventure" and the "fearless exploration of the unknown" in connection with nuclear testing. The spirit of adventure that is most needed in our time has nothing to do with devices for disfiguring or shattering human life. If our energies and our imaginations are to be commanded by adventure, let it be in the cause of a purposeful peace.

*—March 15, 1958*

# Neither Suicide Nor Surrender

The same set of facts about the ideological struggle and nuclear terror has produced two opposing and fast-growing viewpoints.

The facts are profoundly disturbing, but at least they are visible. The Soviet Union is in a considerably stronger position than it was only a short time ago and is getting even stronger with each passing year. While the United States has come before the world with bold visions, such as the Marshall Plan and economic assistance for underdeveloped areas, our standing and influence have not been on the ascent. What we have said and done in our relations with other nations have not always reflected careful knowledge about the actual conditions in those nations. Indeed, it has sometimes seemed that we were actually playing to a domestic gallery with our foreign policies rather than to living history. We constructed a fantasy in which security was compounded at least partially of self-serving legends and myths of invulnerability and superiority.

A political and ideological conflict has been taking place in the context of a continuing military revolution. Soon big hydrogen bombs will be fitted into missile delivery systems which will bring the Soviet and the United States within fifteen minutes of each other. In the name of security, both nations are fashioning massive pulverizing weapons against which no defense can possibly exist. But the result of these weapons will be to intensify, not reduce, the existing insecurity.

Two extreme and conflicting viewpoints have grown out of these facts. One viewpoint, now openly expressed, is that nuclear war is inevitable and that the United States is not under the obligation to wait until it is hit first. According to this argument, our only chance of victory is to be the first to drop the hydrogen bomb. Besides, it is contended that the advantage of surprise attack is so great that we can almost count upon it as certain that the Soviet Union will strike the moment it is ready. Therefore, we have to hit whether we like it or not.

The contrasting viewpoint, incorrectly identified with Bertrand Russell, is that the West should submit to the Soviet Union as the best way of preventing a nuclear war that would expunge life on earth. The price of submission may be high, it is acknowledged, but it will not continue indefinitely, for communism may eventually succumb to its own weaknesses. But if war should come, then all life would be expunged.

The first viewpoint leads to mutual suicide, for it precipitates the very nuclear war it ostensibly seeks to limit. The second viewpoint leads to the annihilation of the free man, for it equates survival with surrender.

But it is false—tragically and hideously false—to say that these are the only alternatives. We don't have to be run by our jitters and drop the big bombs that could put an end to the age of man. Nor do we have to fall on our knees before a colossus in order to keep him from waging nuclear war.

What we can do, first of all, is to stop deceiving ourselves as to the nature of peace and the requirements of peace. We can recognize that peace and unfettered national sovereignty cannot go together in a world which can be circled in ninety minutes by a device that can vaporize whole cities in one blow. We can make a total commitment to the cause of a United Nations with the effective powers of government adequate to deal with the basic causes of tension and conflict.

We can emancipate ourselves from the seductive nonsense to which we have given our energies and allegiances in such large measure since the end of the war. We can decide that the most important thing in our lives is not the height and sweep of automobile tail-fins but the height and sweep of our ideas on creating a world under law.

"This is what we own, this is what we believe, this is what we can do," we can say to the world. "We make a total and unequivocal commitment to a safe world and a better one. Our preoccupation is to sustain and serve the gift of life. We state our readiness to accept and support the concept of a federated world to replace the present anarchy. We will work for such a concept to any extent that may be required."

The alternative to either suicide or surrender is still sanity.

—*April 12, 1958*

# The Men of the *Golden Rule*

Inevitably, a man is measured by his largest concerns and by what he regards as the ultimate questions. If he is troubled only by what happens to him personally, then his measurement is quickly taken and it is not necessary to use the long rule.

But if a man places a high value on life, whatever its accent or station; if he respects a mysterious but real connection between himself and the people who have gone before him and those not yet born, then there are proportions in his measure beyond estimate. In such a man, the gift of awareness has come fully alive. His perceptions are keenest when he looks inward and sees others in himself. He will fix his mind on the things that are more important to him than whether he lives or dies. The ultimate question for him has to do not with his personal immortality but with the immortality of values and meaningful life beyond his own time.

Civilizations must submit to the same measure. No society is smaller than the one that acts as though history does not exist beyond its own time and needs, or that sees no obligation to a later generation. Conversely, a society earns its place in the future by respecting the unclamorous claims of the unborn.

How, then, are we to measure ourselves and our civilization? In using the term "our civilization," we are not limiting it to one nation or one continent. Whatever the razor's edge of our own emphasis on national differences, the species of human life as a whole is now in jeopardy, for the precarious balances which enable life to subsist are now being altered and damaged. The national units involved in the life-and-death rivalries are going far beyond the requirements of mutual total destruction. The invasion of the future has already begun. Day by day, the assault against later generations is growing in size and power. Even if the present tensions do not culminate in a world-wide explosion, the killing poisons now being put into the air and into the genes of human beings will twist and cramp and disfigure later life.

Several men who are unwilling to participate in the tyranny of the present over the future have attempted to stake their lives on their ability to awaken people. They believe that the species of man is a single organism; and so they have no trouble in recognizing and acting on the fact of connection among all men. They believe that people can become aware of the implications of what is happening only as their moral senses can come alive.

These are the men of the *Golden Rule*, a thirty-foot ketch with a sturdy sail and a twenty-four horsepower motor. There are four men in the company. The leader of the group is a former lieutenant commander in the

United States Navy who is also a former state housing commissioner. The men of the *Golden Rule* set sail some weeks ago for the Eniwetok nuclear proving grounds. It was their object to expose themselves to the effects of the explosions. They put their faith not in the ability of their bodies to withstand the radioactive bullets released by the nuclear experiments but in the power of a universal response the moment the danger became real. The certainty which sustained them was that no force in the world was powerful enough to keep people from seeing the great moral issues involved as soon as these issues became visible and clear. In short, they were betting their lives that the necessary awakening would come not on the level of argument but through the strength of a symbolic offer.

The U.S. government has put these men in jail rather than have them proceed to the nuclear proving grounds. But there is no law that is being violated. The United States does not possess the ocean area from which these men are being barred. Nor does it make sense to profess to protect them against themselves: rather, it is we who need the protection they are trying to give us.

If these men are guilty of anything it is of an effort to break down the idea that the individual is forever and tragically separated from large events. They do not satisfy themselves by bemoaning the fact of an insane society bent on altering the conditions on which life depends. Nor do they crave the distinction of belonging to the last generation of man on earth. Hence, they affirm the power of the free will to shape government and to effect historic decisions.

The men of the *Golden Rule* have been called crackpots; but who among the rest of us can call ourselves sane for sanctioning the action they seek to stop? The men of the *Golden Rule* have been put in jail, but those who have arranged these hideous explosions, with their toll of lives yet uncalculated, will go free. What the men of the *Golden Rule* seek is a simple test of conscience; what the nations seek is a test of devices that can expunge human life—devices that no longer have meaning in military terms. The weapons have nothing to do with victory; what they pulverize is the future of man and with it the things that are as valuable as life itself—justice, the assertion of conscience, freedom to grow, freedom to be.

There is unlimited power in the *Golden Rule*. If we would measure it, we have only to stop shielding ourselves from the symbolic power of what these men are and wish to do.

—*May 17, 1958*

# Earle Reynolds and His *Phoenix*

In September, 1957, we received a telephone call at our home from a man who identified himself as Earle Reynolds, an anthropologist. He and his family and crew had just put in at a dock in the Norwalk harbor after an ocean voyage from Hiroshima, Japan. I recalled having read in the newspapers that Dr. Reynolds was the skipper of a tiny Japanese-made two-master and that he had astounded the maritime world by his feat in navigating a small craft so expertly over such a long distance.

Dr. Reynolds's purpose in calling was to inquire whether his three Japanese crewmen, all of whom came from Hiroshima, might visit our home in order to chat with Shigeko, our adopted Japanese daughter, from Hiroshima. We bade them come at once.

For the next two weeks we had frequent visits with Earle Reynolds, his wife Barbara, his twelve-year-old daughter Jessica, and the three young men from Hiroshima. We listened avidly to the account of their adventure in crossing the high seas in a thirty-six-foot vessel; what the daily routine was like; how they rode out heavy storms; the people and places they saw. Both Mrs. Reynolds and her daughter were writing books about their experiences. Earle Reynolds had filled several notebooks with anthropological observations he had made at the remote places they had visited.

It developed that Earle Reynolds, prior to taking sail with the *Phoenix*, had been employed for several years in Japan by the U.S. Atomic Energy Commission. He spoke favorably of the work of the AEC in carrying out special studies among the survivors of the atomic bombings in Hiroshima and Nagasaki. His own research was concerned with children who had been exposed to radiation resulting from the nuclear explosions in 1945. After completing his work with the AEC in 1954 he decided to do something he had dreamed about for years: to sail around the world in a small boat, with plenty of time for thinking, writing, and studying the cultures and customs at firsthand of peoples in out-of-the-way places as yet unconnected with the great land masses of the world by airplane or steamship. He bought a Japanese ketch of the type used generally for coastal fishing and reconditioned it for ocean-going purposes. It was christened the *Phoenix* or *Bird of Peace* in Japanese. The people of Hiroshima took a personal interest in the ship, which seemed to them symbolically to rise from the ashes of their city. An association of supporters was formed, headed by the governor of Hiroshima, and the news of their voyage was published prominently in Japan.

For the next three years, Earle Reynolds and his little band made the *Phoenix* their home as they undertook their zigzag journey around the world. And now they had put in at Norwalk, Connecticut, in order to scrape the bottom and repaint the *Phoenix*. We visited the boat and were astounded by the magic of its internal economy. It was a sort of Utopia in microcosm. It had succeeded in liberating people from the extraneous; the things it carried passed the test of absolute necessity. It was significant, I thought, that the *Phoenix* devoted almost as much room to its little library of books as it did to its kitchen equipment.

Some days later Earle Reynolds, his family, and crew came to the house to say good-by just before taking off for the remainder of their 50,000-mile journey. We could understand why they had made so many friends in Hiroshima, for they were creative and compassionate people. After they left we received letters or postcards from ports of call on their way back through the Panama Canal to Japan.

Then one day I picked up the newspaper and saw that Earle Reynolds had been arrested by the U.S. government. He had sailed the *Phoenix* into the Pacific nuclear testing zone. His boat had been intercepted by the U.S. Coast Guard more than 4,000 miles off the West Coast of the United States. The *Phoenix* was boarded by two armed men and was directed to sail to Kwajalein. A Navy destroyer escorted the little boat to the naval base. Dr. Reynolds was flown to Honolulu where he was formally charged with violating the rulings of the U.S. Atomic Energy Commission. If found guilty, he faced a possible prison sentence of two years and fine of $5,000.

What happened, I later learned, was that Earle Reynolds and his crew had put in at Honolulu on their way across the Pacific. They became aware of the fact that the skipper of the *Golden Rule*, Commander Bert Bigelow, and his crew were being tried in the Honolulu courts for violating a legal order that forbade them to leave Honolulu on their mission to expose themselves to radioactive fallout from the nuclear test explosions.

Dr. and Mrs. Reynolds visited the court and listened carefully as Bert Bigelow, an ex-Navy commander, explained why he and his colleagues felt compelled to bear witness to their convictions. Bert Bigelow made it clear he believed as strongly in the defense of the United States today as he did when he served in the Navy, but he did not believe that setting off nuclear bombs contributed either to the defense of the United States or to our moral position in the world. He condemned the Soviet Union and Great Britain for engaging in nuclear testing, presenting facts concerning the contamination of atmosphere, land, water, milk, and food.

This was not the only moral issue involved, Commander Bigelow declared. He felt that the United States had the moral responsibility to assume world leadership in putting an end to the tests. He knew that the Soviet Union was gaining much support throughout the world by posing as the champion of peace; he didn't want the United States to be put in the position of announcing test cessation after the Soviet Union had done it first. He believed that democratic governments existed for the purpose of serving the individual. He was grateful that he did not live in a totalitarian nation, such as the Soviet Union, where individual protest against high government policy was prohibited.

That was why the crew of the *Golden Rule* intended to sail directly into the atomic testing zone, willing to be hit by radioactive fallout in an attempt to prod the consciences of their fellow Americans.

The court listened to Bert Bigelow's statement, then sentenced him and his colleagues to sixty days in jail.

Earle Reynolds and his wife were listening, too.

Up to then, they hadn't thought too deeply about the issues involved in nuclear testing. But what Bert Bigelow had just said could not be disregarded in any test of sanity and conscience. The power that was now being assembled no longer had any relationship to the legitimate requirements of nations; if used, the result would not be the victory of one nation over another but the pulverization of life and the alteration of the incredibly delicate conditions that make life possible.

That night Earle and Barbara Reynolds made the most important decision of their lives: they would attempt to complete the mission begun by the *Golden Rule*. They would do it as individuals. They would make no dramatic proclamations, they would seek no organizational connections or support. They would take off in their boat and set a direct course for the testing area. One fact loomed large in their thinking. It was that the United States had decided to go far beyond its own territorial limits, marking off an area of 390,000 square miles of ocean area and then forbidding entry. Earle and Barbara Reynolds also felt that the rights of the Marshall Islanders had been set aside when these people had been evacuated from their homes in the interests of the nuclear tests.

The *Phoenix* lost little time in setting sail for the forbidden area. Eventually they were spotted by a Coast Guard boat and warned to keep clear of the testing zone. The *Phoenix* continued on its course. When it was sixty-five miles inside the zone, the arrests were made.

When they were back in Honolulu again, the government moved at once to bring Earle Reynolds to trial. No action was filed against the other members of the group. Dr. Reynolds asked for and received permission to visit the mainland to arrange for legal representation. When he returned to Honolulu, he reported to the court that his attorney would not be able to do all the preparation necessary in time for the scheduled trial, and asked for an extension of time. The request was refused and the date of trial was fixed for August 25.

A local lawyer was retained temporarily to handle the preliminary legal details. Again a request was made, and denied, for a brief time extension. The court saw no reason why this case was more deserving of special handling than any ordinary traffic violation.

Rather than participate in the defense of his client without adequate preparation, Joseph L. Rauh, Jr., of Washington, D.C., instructed Dr. Reynolds to appear at the trial without counsel and again request an appropriate delay.

On August 25 the trial was held as scheduled.

Judge J. Frank McLaughlin listened to Dr. Reynolds's request for postponement on the grounds that he was without counsel, then directed the local attorney who had helped Dr. Reynolds with the early legal details to proceed with the case. The lawyer declined to do so, out of respect for Dr. Reynolds's wishes; the judge refused to permit the withdrawal and ordered the case to proceed. This was done without any consultation between lawyer and client concerning the defense or the preparation of witnesses.

Twenty-four hours after the case was called, the trial ended. Dr. Reynolds was found guilty. He was not permitted to speak to the court. The sentencing did not take place at that time, pending a request for appeal.

The hearing on this request was held on September 18. Mr. Rauh flew to Honolulu from Washington and represented Dr. Reynolds. Judge McLaughlin refused to recognize Mr. Rauh as Dr. Reynolds's attorney, but permitted him to make the argument as an aide to the local lawyer.

Mr. Rauh questioned the legality of the AEC order closing off hundreds of thousands of miles of open ocean for any purpose. He asserted the right of individual protest in a matter of such profound moral and political significance. He attempted to show that Dr. Reynolds was deprived of effective legal counsel and due process of law.

Judge McLaughlin was unconvinced. He denied the request for a retrial and sentenced Earle Reynolds to six months in jail.

Mr. Rauh has now returned to Washington and intends to bring the case before the Ninth Circuit Federal Court in San Francisco—that is, if the money is forthcoming to enable him to do so. Pending the appeal, Dr. Reynolds's prison sentence has been deferred.

Earle Reynolds has no objection to going to jail for his convictions. But the least that is owing to him is a chance to air these convictions openly, and to have a lawyer of his own choosing fully recognized by the court.

Dr. Reynolds and his family and crew have attempted to engage in an act of moral communication with their fellow citizens. Whether or not he goes to jail, it would mean a great deal to him to know that some people were listening.

*—October 11, 1958*

# Of Nonsense and Nematodes

Nonsense is on stage and the stage is the world. A giant panda, one of the largest and most valuable of its kind, has been barred from the United States because it comes from Communist China. Zoos in this country have offered up to $25,000 for the clown of the raccoon family, but various restrictions having to do with Communist China prevent the panda from entering the United States. Meanwhile, the animal is appearing in zoos throughout Europe without any noticeable threat to the internal security of the nations involved.

In the Soviet Union one of the world's great writers committed an apparently subversive act by being awarded the world's most important literary prize. The Soviet Union of Writers was willing to put up with Boris Pasternak despite the independent nature of his work, but the moment he received the Nobel Prize he was expelled from the Writers' Union and denounced as a traitor. The implication is clear that writers in the Soviet can write about anything they wish so long as they do so with genuine mediocrity.

Meanwhile, the glossary of nonsense in the twentieth century is being constantly enriched. Now, in addition to words like "clean" to describe a supposedly radioactive-free nuclear explosive, or "sunshine units" to describe the amount of radiation exposure for human beings, we have the term "tiny" to describe a newly-developed H Bomb. A commander of the Air Force in the United States broke the good news that a "tiny" hydrogen bomb had been perfected that can be carried by a fighter plane. The bomb will of course contain the equivalent of several billion pounds of dynamite, enough to pulverize a city, but it now comes in the convenient and cozy fighter-plane size. People who are used to thinking of the word "tiny" to describe little children will have to make a minor adjustment.

It is curious to see the way nonsense is attracted to power, as though this were its natural habitat. In the Far East, the Chinese Communists pursued a combined policy of murder and mercy for one month toward the occupants of Quemoy and Matsu. Bombing and brotherhood were tied together as a unified program. On Monday the people on the islands would be shelled. But on Tuesday the shelling would cease and the people would be encouraged to entrench themselves and receive supplies. Indeed, if the food ran short, they had only to ask the mainland and it would be supplied. If this policy of now-we-will-kill-you, now-we-won't made sense to the islanders, they made no mention of it.

Almost by way of establishing a grim consistency, the head of the Chinese Communist party announced that his country could not be intimidated by the threat of nuclear war. He was willing to admit that 300 million Chinese might be killed in such a war. Even so, he said, there would be 300 million left. Something else would be left. The people would have their memories. They would have memories of the missing from among their families and friends. They would also have memories of a world that had turned against itself.

But Communist China isn't the only nation that feels obliged to pronounce such nonsense to the world. In the United States, officers of the State Department have openly declared that our main security is to be found in our willingness to risk all-out nuclear war. Fortunately, there are still a few people left in government who believe that for our safety we must look to world control of nuclear weapons rather than to nuclear stockpiles. What these people say makes sense, but the surrounding sounds of nonsense are rapidly becoming louder.

Commissioner Willard F. Libby of the U.S. Atomic Energy Commission, for example, spoke dangerous nonsense the other day to Mayor Norris Poulson of Los Angeles. Mayor Poulson was deeply alarmed about the heavy radioactive fallout that took place over his city as the result of the recent beat-the-deadline Nevada nuclear tests. He telephoned Commissioner Libby who told him, in effect, to forget it. But Mayor Poulson wouldn't forget it. The fallout had soared far beyond the danger limits set by the Atomic Energy Commission itself. There was a real threat to the health of his people. Mayor Poulson regarded what Dr. Libby said as casual and callous handling of an important problem. In any event, Dr. Libby has made it clear that his job is to make and test the bombs, and not theorize about ways in which people can counteract the effects of the resultant radiation in their water, milk, and bones.

All these incidents are not something out of the fiendish tales of a bygone era of ghouls but a characteristic feature of an age, our age, in which absolute force and absolute nonsense attract one another and are being made dominant in human affairs. The unholy alliance seems to assert itself wherever vast force appears, almost as though the very nature of the force divides the human community into the sane and the insane and confers upon the latter the privileges of rule. Indeed, there is a blighting quality to the power, for once-reasonable men who come in contact with it seemingly become transfixed by it and take easily and freely to the language of nonsense that belongs to the power.

By way of lending grim point to the consequences of invested nonsense we read a report from the U.S. Department of Agriculture which says that the nematode, a species of plant worm or parasite, carries within itself a mysterious ability to resist harm from radiation. Man, puny creature, gets into trouble when he is exposed to doses of 300 roentgens or more. But the nematode can take up to 600,000 units of radiation. Man

need not therefore fear that his nonsense will empty life from this earth.
If man doesn't want the world the nematode is perfectly willing to take it.

—*November 29, 1958*

# The Debate Is Over

The debate on the danger of radioactive fallout has ended. Commissioner
Willard F. Libby, of the Atomic Energy Commission, has now acknowledged a "real concern" over contamination resulting from the testing of
nuclear explosives.

Two recent events may have contributed to this concern. The first is
that southern California experienced a radioactive fallout far higher than
the danger line specified by the AEC. The second came a few weeks ago
when the wheat fields of northern Minnesota were dusted by an over-
the-safety-limit quantity of radioactive strontium.

The significance of Dr. Libby's present concern is related to the fact
that he is the government scientist chiefly responsible for having assured
the President and the American people in the past that the risk involved
in nuclear testing was too small to worry about. Along with Dr. Edward
Teller, Dr. Libby was one of the most influential spokesmen in blocking
any serious effort to arrive at a world-wide ban on nuclear testing *even if
inspection and enforceable safeguards could be worked out.*

It was more than three years ago that the possible danger to human
bone and tissue, as well as to food, was called to the public attention by
independent scientists *outside* the AEC. At that time Commissioner Libby
contended that the problem was negligible. One year later Dr. Albert
Schweitzer issued his now-famous "Declaration of Conscience," in which
he said that the explosion of nuclear weapons represented a violation of
the natural rights of man, threatening his health, his air, his water, and
his food. Dr. Schweitzer called on all nations to renounce the explosions
before the atomic armaments race got totally out of control, brooking
the danger either of a world-destroying war or wholesale contamination
of the atmosphere, or both. Dr. Libby's reply to Dr. Schweitzer no longer
used the adjective "negligible." This time he acknowledged that a "small
risk" was involved, but he said that the security of the free world depended on keeping ahead of the Soviet Union in the arms race.

In any event, Dr. Libby now asserts a "real concern." Those who
opposed him can take no satisfaction in the fact that they were right.
Nor does Dr. Libby's recent resignation from the AEC and the discon-
tinuation of Dr. Teller's advisory position with the AEC correct the
situation they were largely instrumental in bringing about. Even if not

another bomb is exploded, the atmosphere will carry a burden of poisonous radioactivity for many years to come. There is no known way of
washing the sky; no way to keep the strontium and the cesium from
falling like rain; no way to keep it from getting into food and milk and
thence into the bones of children where it will create radiation pockets
in the bone marrow. But we can at least try to keep the situation from
becoming immeasurably worse. The fact that danger exists is no warrant
for multiplying it.

No one can question the patriotism of men such as Dr. Libby and Dr.
Teller. No one can doubt that they honestly felt that our ultimate security
depended on the acceptance of their policies. But they are guilty, we
believe, of putting false facts before the American people in an attempt
to get those policies accepted. First, they concealed any unfavorable
information about the by-product effects of the explosions. Second, when
outside information developed, they attempted to minimize the danger.

Didn't they know from the start that the danger was "real"? We find
it difficult to believe that they did not. But we believe that they genuinely
felt that the loss of thousands of lives was small alongside the millions
of lives that they felt would be jeopardized if the Soviet Union should
seize nuclear leadership in the world. The weakness in their argument is
that the security of the United States depends on arms control rather
than on arms supremacy. Therefore, the United States should seriously
seek effective and enforceable ways of both stopping the tests and putting
an end to the nuclear arms race. But this is not what Dr. Teller and
Dr. Libby wanted—*even if a method of foolproof inspection could be
achieved.* And they have been working behind the scenes to prevent any
agreement at Geneva or anywhere else.

Why do they hold to this position? In private briefing sessions to the
press they express the view that the present large nuclear weapons practically ensure that the next war will be a suicidal one. Therefore, they
want the testing to continue to enable them to develop non-suicidal atomic
weapons. They don't say that they will donate these weapons to a potential enemy to make sure he will use them on us. Nor do they say why
they insisted on developing the suicidal weapons in the first place. There
is more than merely a collapse of logic here. There is a surrender to the
whole fantasy of absolute power in a way that would have appalled the
men at Philadelphia in 1787 and confirmed them in their view of the
danger of ever allowing men, even good and honest men, to become
more important than law in the operation of a society.

The essential problem before the American people today is not to
devise punishments for madness but to put an end to it. It may or may
not be too late to stop the nuclear arms race. Concerning that, no one
really knows. But it would be tragic to *assume* it is. At least we owe it
to sanity to make the effort. But it will have to be a large effort. It will

have to be large enough to enlist the support of most of the world's peoples. It cannot be a synthetic effort. The moral content must be clear and substantial. If we are capable of such an effort, there is a chance our nation and generation can serve history in the way it most needs to be served in our time.

*—April 4, 1959*


# An Address in Moscow

*Early in 1958 I was invited to visit the Soviet Union under the terms of the Cultural Exchange Agreement between the U.S. and the U.S.S.R. My host in the Soviet Union would be the Union of Soviet Societies for the Friendly and Cultural Relations with Foreign Countries. I was told that my duties would be minimal; I would be called upon for several lectures dealing with American literature and world affairs. I would also travel around the Soviet Union and meet with people in fields similar to my own.*

*As I thought about the invitation I wondered whether the matters I wanted to lecture about would create difficulties either for my host or myself or both. Having been told by the State Department that many of the people who would attend my lectures would be hearing an American for the first time, I wanted to make the most of the opportunity. And yet I felt it only fair to inform the Soviet authorities about the general nature of my talk in advance. For example, I wanted to be able to speak frankly about problems that had to be faced in any basic understanding or agreement between the United States and the Soviet Union. Then, since I would be appearing before the Writers Union, I felt it might be useful to present the view of American critics on the Pasternak case and, as I thought about the talk before the Academy of Social Sciences, I felt it might be appropriate to speak of the concept of natural rights, especially as reflected in the U.S. constitutional debates at the Philadelphia convention.*

*I was naturally pleased when I learned there would be no objections to these subjects and that indeed I was free to present any material I wished.*

*I arrived in Moscow on June 16, 1959. The first talk took place on June 25, 1959, before the Presidium of the Soviet Peace Committee. It was held in the large conference room of the Committee's headquarters. Members of the Presidium sat at the long conference table. Observers and press representatives sat at the far side of the room. I spoke through an interpreter. This was the text:*

It has been only a short time since I arrived in this country; too short even to make the acquaintance of a big city such as Moscow, but long enough to become aware of the extraordinary vitality, intelligence, and capacity of the Russian people.

I have also been made aware—profoundly aware—of the good will of the Russian people toward the American people, and, generally, toward peoples everywhere. Speaking personally, I can say that I have met a cordial welcome wherever I have gone. My contacts with people here have been casual, it is true, but I have seen and felt an attitude of friendliness and genuine good will.

In fact—just the other day—I asked a traffic policeman in the heart of Moscow for directions. When he discovered that I was an American, he threw his arms around me in an affectionate embrace and did all but kiss me on both cheeks. It developed that he had been in that division of the Soviet Army that joined up with the Americans at the Elbe. And so I was the beneficiary of his warm recollections.

This incident made a strong impression on me. I have been in many countries of the world, but never before have I been embraced—affectionately or otherwise—by a policeman.

The spirit of friendliness is not confined to your traffic officers, I hasten to add. I have seen and felt it in many places—on your streets and in your libraries; in your theaters and universities; in your taxis and subways.

Something else I have observed needs to be mentioned. This is the unquestioned fact that the people of the Soviet Union want peace. I don't think that anyone can visit the Soviet Union—however brief that visit may be—without being convinced of this.

It is clear beyond question that the Russian people are concerned most of all with the need to develop their nation and its resources and to build a productive way of life.

I believe these things to be true.

I ask you to believe that these things are equally true of the American people.

First of all, the American people have only the warmest feelings of friendship for the Russian people. Nothing would please us more than to feel we had complete access to one another; to share—as friends must share—our ideas, our concerns, and our hopes for a world that does justice to man and in which men can do justice to each other.

Just as the Russian people long for peace and believe in peace, so do the American people long for peace and believe in peace. This I report to you as a fact. There is hardly a city of any size in the United States that I have not visited in the past few years, talking about peace as I talk to you today. And nowhere in the U.S. have I found anything but the strongest desire to keep the world free of war, free of aggression, free of provocation, free of the bondage that can erupt into war.

You are engaged in the mighty work of building a nation; so are we. The most exciting and demanding tasks in our history are ahead of us.

The challenges that face America have to do not with the development of our physical resources alone but with the fullest possible development of our human resources. This cannot be done without peace.

Now, therefore, consider the paradox. The Russian people want peace and need peace. The American people want peace and need peace. Yet this has not been enough to create peace. Why?

This is the question I propose to explore with you today.

I do not say that I have the answers; but at least we may be able together to consider the separate parts of the problem.

Let me say here that I am grateful to the Soviet Peace Committee in Moscow for providing me with this platform. Before I came to your country I was told I would be free to speak as I wished. The invitation to visit the Soviet Union was issued under the general terms of the cultural-exchange program between our two countries.

I believe the invitation was issued in good faith, and I accepted in good faith. I intend to speak as I am sure you would wish me to speak—in absolute candor. Anything less than open and direct talk between us is actually a form of treason to the human race. People everywhere are looking for us to end the madness that could put the torch to the world itself.

Consider the power now at the call of nations. Nuclear bombs have been tested that contain the equivalent of 20,000,000 tons of TNT. Not pounds or kilos but tons.

Thousands of these large bombs exist and are now ready for use.

The human mind does not easily comprehend such power or its implications. Yet unless we manage somehow to comprehend this power we will not be able to control it.

One way of comprehending this power is to think of every city that has been bombed. Think of Leningrad, Stalingrad, Kiev, Riga, Minsk, Sverdlovsk, Kharkov, Warsaw, Lodz, Pilsen, Poznan, Berlin, Frankfurt, Hamburg, Bremen, Munich, Essen, Aachen, Cologne, Darmstadt, Dussel-dorf, Mannheim, Stuttgart, Amsterdam, Rotterdam, Milan, Turin, Salerno, Calais, Cherbourg, London, Coventry, Manchester, Birmingham, Southampton, Madrid, Barcelona, Shanghai, Chunking, Tientsin, Hankow, Nanking, Tokyo, Yokohama, Nagoya, Kobe, Hiroshima, Nagasaki.

Think of the destructive power of all these bombings. Put them all together and they still do not come up to the destructive power now contained in a single bomb that can be carried by a single plane or a single missile—against which there is no defense; no defense except peace.

Before long, missiles will be in existence that can travel halfway round the world in twenty minutes or less.

There is no defense against such weapons—no defense, I repeat—except peace.

The danger that these weapons will be used is not limited to intent. There is the danger of an accident. There could be a mistake in interpreting strange markings on a radar screen.

Neither side wants war; true; but mutual terror has a way of producing mutual tensions and jitters, and jitters have a way of producing accidents.

Surely the gift of human existence is not so base or valueless that we can afford to risk it altogether on a single throw of the nuclear dice.

This, then, is the situation in which we find ourselves at the end of some hundreds of thousands of years of human evolution, much of it glorious and lit up by brilliant achievement, but almost all of it difficult and precarious. And now we reach the point where we have used up our margin of error—where every decision must be the correct one.

For if the missiles should begin to fly and the bombs begin to fall, then it will make little difference whether the purchasing power of the ruble is greater than that of the dollar or if Soviet science can outstrip American science.

After a war Russia and American will be indistinguishable. Nuclear rubble looks alike. This kind of unity we can forego. Indeed there may be none to record the results of the madness. For it is now within our joint means not only to expunge the past and demolish the present but to shatter the future. What then do we do?

The obvious thing to do is to create a great design for survival and for the making of a genuine peace—a design to rescue the world from its present anarchy, a design for effective law and justice among nations. It would have to be the kind of design that would establish working controls not only over nuclear armaments but over war itself.

Not until such a design and such controls are created can the humans on this earth be safe. Not until then, in fact, can the commonwealth of man in the twentieth century lay claim to being civilized.

If it is obvious that a design for survival is needed, it is equally obvious that neither the Soviet Union nor the United States can create such a design by itself. Indeed, it may be dangerous for one country to carry out a design regardless of the ideas or needs of others. The peace we seek is not the peace of world domination but the peace of an interdependent diversity based on consent, justice, and the orderly processes of world law.

The necessary design for peace must be a plural enterprise. Therefore, we have to find some way for getting through to each other, some way of drawing up the ground rules for our discourse.

Yet any mutual effort requires mutual trust. And it is precisely here that the difficulty is greatest. For it is the very lack of mutual trust that has produced the runaway nuclear arms race.

One of my purposes in coming to the Soviet Union was to learn at first hand what your feelings are about American policies and our way of life in general. I am learning a great deal on this score, and intend to report fully in my journal on my return.

And now I should like to explain to you why most of our people feel as we do. I do not ask you necessarily to agree that those feelings are correct. I ask you merely to consider that those feelings exist, and what are the reasons and causes behind them.

Let us begin with the activities of the Communist parties outside the Soviet Union.

The Communist Party in the United States has been a party without honor for a very simple reason. It has managed through its actions to convince the American people that it has not been concerned primarily with the welfare of the nation in which its members claim citizenship. It has directed its main energies not toward the development of social progress in America—but toward the needs of a foreign government. It has not been open and aboveboard in its dealings with the American people. It has taken advantage of the machinery of a free society to weaken that society.

I was a member of a writers' trade union before the war in which Communists gained control. Yes, they gained control because they worked harder than anyone else, because they were disciplined, and because they had a singleness of purpose. But, once in power, they directed their main efforts less to the needs of the writers' union than to the policies of the U.S.S.R. They collected dues—some of which went into propaganda advancing the foreign policy of a government 5,000 miles away.

Now, this situation in the union couldn't last in the very nature of the case. What the union heads were doing became transparent to the majority of our members and eventually they were replaced.

America is not opposed to genuine radicalism. Radicalism is deep in our history. It is part of the national bloodstream. We were born in revolution. It was a revolution based on a clearly defined idea: That the state existed for the sole purpose of protecting the rights and freedoms that come to a man just in the act of being born.

This is a radical idea—and it has yet to be perfectly realized in the United States or elsewhere. But it is the dominant idea of our society. And there are radicals in the United States—call them persistent revolutionaries if you will—men in the spirit of Jefferson and Lincoln who will not be content until the fruits of freedom are enjoyed by all our citizens irrespective of their minority backgrounds or the pigmentation of their skins.

This kind of radicalism, I repeat, exists in the United States, and indeed exerts a powerful thrust in our development. But the Communist Party in the United States, to repeat, has never been a real part of that thrust precisely because its role has been more that of an apologist for another government than a genuine advocate of social reform. In this sense, it has done a great disservice to your country.

For the American people to have reacted as they did against the Communist Party in the United States is not unnatural. I ask you to consider your own response if the situation were reversed and a political party were able to exist here that was acting in the interests of a foreign power.

This leads to an even more fundamental point; namely, what it is that the American Communist Party was an apologist for?

In the early 1930s, the American people began to take a more sympathetic view of the Soviet Union and its system than we had done in the previous years. The United States had just extended recognition to the Soviet Government and it appeared that an important and fruitful relationship might become a working reality. But then came a series of political purges inside the Soviet Union, the extent and harshness of which produced shock waves throughout the world. It became clear that the Russian nation was in the grip of a powerful dictatorship. And, once again, great foreboding was felt in America about what was happening in the Soviet Union.

In opposing that dictatorship we were not opposing the Russian people. Indeed, we were manifesting our friendship for the Russian people.

What we said then was denied by the then existing leadership of the Russian Communist Party. But many years later the main points of our indictment were verified and substantiated by the man who now has the honor to be the Premier of this mighty nation.

The height of America's moral separation from the Soviet Union came in August, 1939, when a nonaggression pact was signed with Adolf Hitler. A few days later Germany launched the Second World War, and we were to hear from Moscow that Fascism or Democracy was a "matter of taste."

Then Hitler broke the nonaggression pact, and the Soviet Union, like the rest of the West, was engaged in a fight for its life. The magnificence of the Russian people in the defense of their homeland gave inspiration to the world. The light that was cast by the Russian people at that time will illuminate and enrich history as long as history is written.

Certainly at the end of the war the prospects for friendship between the two peoples had never been greater. But then, very quickly, a whole series of negative events occurred that made the outlook as ominous as only a short while earlier it had been bright. Mutual suspicions replaced mutual respect. Common hopes gave way to common anxieties. The Cold War set in.

I repeat once again that I recognize that you feel there was much in American policy that contributed to that situation. Let me, in return, put before you the American feeling about what was happening at the time. I do this not for the purpose of reopening old sores but for the purpose of getting at the sources of present fears and resentments, the better to do away with them.

There was a series of events after the end of the war, as I say, most of them having to do with the functioning of the United Nations, especially as it concerned the veto in the Security Council. No single one of these events by itself was in the nature of a crisis but the accumulation of them was not favorable to the cause of American-Soviet friendship. Then came a major setback of historic proportions. I refer to the sudden change in the status of Czechoslovakia and to the suicide of Masaryk, whose name had become such a symbol of independence in that nation.

Increasingly, thereafter, the situation of the Central European nations forced itself on the consciousness of the outside world. Then, like a suppressed volcano, giant eruptions took place—in East Berlin, in Poland, in Hungary. I was in Berlin that summer and I ask you to believe that this was nothing impulsive, accidental, or unimportant. It was a genuine reaction to an intolerable situation. And now, day after day and week after week, countless hundreds and thousands of East Germans are fleeing to West Germany by way of the West Berlin gateway. This, too, I am able to report to you first hand, for I have been at the gateway and spoken to the people as they came. Just in 1958 alone, a total of 9,200 scientists, doctors, professors, writers, engineers, students, and professional people crossed the line.

Again, in the past year, I have had occasion to be in Poland three times. I had a chance to talk to people in many walks of life—students, professors, workingmen, writers, scientists, store clerks. It is important for the Russian people to know that a terrible wall of resentment exists in Poland against the Soviet Union. There was a dramatic demonstration of this less than three years ago, when the Poznan riots touched off upheavals that spread from Poland to Hungary.

There was both shock and revulsion not only in the United States but throughout a large part of the world—in India, Japan, Southeast Asia, and not only the West—when the Hungarian revolt was violently put down and when Soviet tanks and guns went into action.

Following these incidents, there was a liberalization of controls. But, today, once again, the pressure of uneasiness and resentment is mounting.

Having just come from Warsaw, I believe that the Polish people want complete and unconditional national freedom. I welcome this chance to convey this information to you at first hand.

Now, all these events, as I say, figure in the present atmosphere and in the face-to-face position in which our nations find themselves today. As against this, however, there are a number of recent positive factors, high among which is the liberalization of foreign affairs under Premier Khrushchev and the willingness to explore direct approaches to the making of a durable peace.

I might also mention here that the recent Communist Party Congress made a re-evaluation of basic policy that is of the utmost affirmative importance in increasing the chances for peace. I refer to the fact that Communist authorities and philosophers no longer believe that war is inevitable in the nature of capitalism. This modification of Marxian thought can be a prodigious factor in favor of the mutual great design for survival.

The will to peace exists strongly in both East and West, and it may be that the world will soon have another chance to make the human common-wealth reasonably safe for itself. It is doubtful, however, whether the national governments can do the job by themselves. Indeed, the peace of the world is much too important to be left to governments. If the peace is to be real, people everywhere will have to speak up. For what has to be created today is a structure of world law to which the nations themselves must submit.

What kind of structure? First, the kind of structure that does not require unilateral acts by nations for keeping the peace. It should have the authority to carry out a ban against nuclear testing, for example, and make the ban stick. It should do this by having the right and the author-ity to inspect and enforce.

Second, it is not enough just to stop the tests that are contaminating the air that belongs to all peoples. The structure of world law that is needed should be applied to the existence of nuclear weapons themselves. The manufacture and possession of these planet-shattering explosives should be outlawed—again on the basis of ironclad safeguards, for neither the United States nor the Soviet Union will feel secure if there are any loopholes in an enterprise so vital to their survival.

Third, the great design should be able to underwrite the security, sovereignty, and independence of all nations, large and small. It may be that the Soviet Union has felt compelled to hold on to the Central European nations as a possible buffer against the West. In this case, a structure of world law strong enough to underwrite the security of the Soviet Union should provide the reassurance and guarantees the Soviet leaders may feel they require in order that the Central European nations may regain complete autonomy.

The same would apply to the question of a rearmed Germany. The prospect of a Germany armed with nuclear weapons is a somber one indeed. Yet if the present power vacuum in Europe can be eliminated through adequate security guarantees under enforceable world law, then the way for long-range pacification of Germany and a peace treaty may be cleared.

Where is such a structure to come from? How will it be made?

We must begin with what we have. The United Nations now exists. It has done remarkable things and it has earned the gratitude of the world's peoples. But the United Nations cannot now underwrite the peace. It cannot carry out an enforced ban on nuclear weapons testing or on nuclear weapons themselves. It cannot underwrite the security of the large nations.

Therefore, the job before us is to make of the United Nations what it most clearly must become—a world agency strong enough and responsible enough to get rid of the present world anarchy and replace it with workable world law.

No more difficult task has ever faced the human intelligence and human conscience. But what other hope is there? Is there hope that peace can be achieved through balance of power, or through nuclear stockpiles, or through muscular exercises of national sovereignty? Something beyond the nations is now necessary. It will have to be real. It will have to be universal. It will have to be just.

Therefore, let us demand what we properly need and rightly deserve. Let us ask for a revision conference of the United Nations. Let us ask for a fresh start. Let us ask for an end to competition in destructive capacity and a beginning of the finest competition the world has ever known. I refer to a competition between the Soviet Union and the United States in what each nation has to give the world's peoples—not just in tangible offerings but through the power of example. This is the kind of competition that belongs to a great design and that can help to make our earth not only safe but fit for human life.

I address you now as fellow human beings in the human family, and not as the citizen of one nation confronting those of another. We have the gift of life. We have the faculty of reason. We are part of one another. We can have peace.

*The audience was politely attentive, except for several minutes during that part of my talk when I spoke about the American Communist Party and the situation in Central Europe. One of the Committee members started a brief flurry of disagreement, in which he was joined by two or three others. I stopped my talk for perhaps thirty seconds, the chairman called for order, and the talk was uninterrupted until it was completed.*
*The questioning following the talk was strong and pointed, but orderly*

*and respectful. There was general resistance to the idea of a "structured peace," the feeling being that if the U.S.A. and U.S.S.R. agreed to live peaceably with one another, nothing would be needed in the way of an authority that would have jurisdiction over nations in those matters concerned with a common security.*

At this point I advanced the idea that it was unreasonable and perhaps even unhistorical to expect that any agreements other than enforceable ones could provide security to either nation. Therefore the essential question concerned the nature of enforceable agreements. This in turn pointed to world organization—hopefully the U.N.—as the structure within which enforcement procedures might best be worked out.

The general reaction to my reference to the American Communist Party was that what I said was irrelevant. What the American Communist Party did was a matter between itself and the American people; the Soviet Union was not responsible. I then stressed that it was precisely the evidence of the binding tie that created the problem in the first place.

There was not too much questioning about my references to Poland and Hungary, other than the general comment that the peoples of those countries enjoyed self-determination. I begged my auditors to consider that the peoples of those countries did not agree that they enjoyed self-determination, whatever the official statements might be to the contrary. In any event, I urged the questioners to visit Poland and Hungary in order to see for themselves. I repeated that my sole purpose in bringing up this matter was to put before them in complete good faith some facts that I had been able to verify for myself.

Considerable criticism of American foreign policy was reflected in the questions, especially in connection with public statements or testimony by American military leaders on the readiness of our military machine to destroy the Soviet Union. Other statements by Americans of a preventive-war nature were termed provocative and dangerous. If the United States really wants peace, the comment ran, why does it talk war in this way? Why do American magazines such as *U.S. News & World Report* run large maps showing how the United States will bomb the Soviet Union?

I asked the audience to recognize that a different yardstick had to be applied to such statements from the yardsticks customary in the Soviet Union. In the Soviet Union, any military or political official who made a pronouncement on world affairs could properly be considered to be reflecting government policy. This was not necessarily true of the United States. An editorial in *Pravda* could be construed in an official light; not so an article or editorial in an American magazine. In any event, there were Americans, many of them, who did not hesitate to denounce loose and inflammatory talk of the kind that had been mentioned. Indeed, countless numbers of Americans, public and private, openly criticized various aspects of American foreign policy with which they disagreed. Without being disrespectful, I said, I thought it proper to point out that I knew of not a single instance in which government policy was publicly questioned or criticized in the Soviet Union. Was it not essential, I asked, for such criticism to be possible on both sides if the governments were going to arrive at a fair and reasonable basis for a peaceful relationship?

I said that my questioners were certainly within their rights in taking exception to the provocative reports they had just quoted. But were they not also aware that the United States Senate had passed a resolution calling for effective agreements to end nuclear testings? Also, was any American action on the question of peace more significant than President Eisenhower's prompt rebuke of Britain and France after the attack on Egypt three years ago and his insistence that we did not believe in two sets of laws—one for our friends, the other for our opponents?

A. V. Karev, the General Secretary of the All-Union Council of Baptists, said he completely accepted the sincerity of the speaker and believed that a program for peace was attainable on the basis of the exchange of ideas that had taken place. He said he didn't want the present occasion to pass, however, without giving voice to something that had been troubling him for many years. This was Mr. Truman's decision to drop the atomic bomb on Hiroshima. He, Mr. Karev, was a Baptist. He knew that Mr. Truman was a Baptist. Mr. Karev said neither he nor his fellow Baptists in the Soviet Union could understand how a good Baptist like Harry Truman could drop an atomic bomb on human beings.

I replied that it was fair to say that Mr. Truman's decision to drop the bomb was not made as a Baptist but as a President. While a number of Americans openly criticized President Truman for having made that decision they recognized that he had made it in the context of a war situation the very nature of which caused many religious precepts to be set aside.

Archbishop Nikodim then asked for the floor. He said he was certain from what I said that the speaker's desire for peace was as deep as his own or that of anyone present. He said he felt that a number of important points had been raised that helped to clear the air for the major work of building a lasting peace. He asked that the speaker, when he returned to the United States, would carry a message from the religious community of the Soviet Union to the American people—a message that would stress the basic fact of brotherhood between both peoples. It was not necessary, he said, for either people to embrace the ideology of the other in order to have peace. All that was necessary was for both peoples to remember that the peaceful words of Jesus Christ applied to all men.

Mr. Kotov, the General Secretary of the Committee, asked if there was any specific way in which citizens in both countries might work together for the peace both nations needed.

One thing we might do, I responded, was not only to make known our desire for peace but for each of us to prod his government to do those things that made for peace. Another thing we might do was to hold a conference of scientists and experts to consider some of the obstacles that had come up at the nuclear talks in Geneva and see whether, on a non-political basis, we might indicate some approaches to meaningful agreement on the technical questions. We could also come together in calling for the United Nations to be strengthened in order to deal effectively with problems of war and peace.

Mr. Kotov said he would like to pursue these suggestions with me further and the meeting ended.

Was the meeting a success? It was not a success in terms of reaching large numbers of people. The Soviet press, which was amply represented at the meeting, published nothing about the talk the next day. Moreover, the censor's office did not clear stories about the talk filed by foreign correspondents.

In terms of the direct exchange of ideas, however, I do not consider that the meeting was a failure. I had hoped to be able to convince some persons, however few, that not all critics of Soviet policy were war-mongers; indeed, that it was necessary to construct a platform outside the give-and-take of power politics—a platform where the needs of all peoples rather than those of one or two nations can be taken into account. Finally, I wanted to test the proposition that there is a natural allegiance among men to a human society if the cause of that society is made real and visible.

In all these respects, I had no reason to be discouraged. For while the meeting itself may have yielded no striking results, in the days following the meeting individual members sought me out to discuss seriously and eagerly some of the viewpoints I had attempted to put before them. They were interested, responsive, constructive. I found this significant and rewarding.

—July 25, 1959

# A Toast in Georgia

It had been raining hard all day. When the ground drank its fill, the water ran down from the hills and collected in the valleys. It came sluicing across the roadways, mud-colored and heavy. The sky hung low with its burden.

We had been driving from Tbilisi (Tiflis), capital of the Georgian Republic of the U.S.S.R., down near the southern corner where Europe and Asia meet in the Middle East. We were on our way to a State farm about 120 miles from Tbilisi, not far from the Armenian border.

Then we ran into trouble.

About three hours out of Tbilisi, the driver came to a turn in the road at the bottom of a hill. He stopped the car and shook his head. The bridge was out.

Ordinarily, this would have presented no problem. For the river bed had been dry since last winter; the area had been without sustained rainfall for some months. Cars could drive across the rocky floor. But now, with the flash floods, the racing waters were cutting deep channels as the river sought to restore itself.

It was almost dark by now, but I could see the outlines of a stalled truck. It had tried to make a run for it but had strayed wide of the rocky bottom, and lodged itself in the mud. And now a companion truck was gingerly maneuvering into position to attach a tow line.

Several other automobiles ahead of us had come to a stop on this side of the river bed and were pointed in various directions. Their drivers were consulting—sometimes arguing—about whether to attempt the crossing and, if so, where the high ground was likely to be. So long as the cars could stay on the rocks and find a place where the current wasn't higher than the floorboards, they could probably make it across the river bed— or at least this seemed to be the consensus.

What troubled me was that there were at least four separate channels between us and the other side. Besides, even without the flash floods, the size of the rocks and the depth of the ruts demanded respect from a mere automobile and its riders. I suggested politely to my interpreter that it might be prudent to turn back.

My traveling companions consisted of Igor Alexandrov, my interpreter, a Georgian professor of history, and our Georgian driver. When I made the suggestion, Igor looked at me reproachfully. "You may have forgotten that a Georgian is driving this car," he said. He didn't even bother to translate my cautionary notes.

What Igor had said about the Georgians was far from being a conversation piece. For century after century, Georgians had to fight for their homes and their lives—against Genghis Khan, Mongols, Turks, Persians, Romans, and Germans. Now the only problem was that a puny bridge was out and torrential rains were opening up large sluices on the river bottom. Child's play.

I gasped when I saw one of the cars head out for the other side. The driver swung north up the stony floor, driving very close to the first channel. Then he found what he was looking for and angled sharply into the stream. The men from the other cars watched intently as the pioneer auto plunged ahead. The water rose above hub caps but no higher. Then the car emerged from the torrent and the driver reversed his field, repeating the process with the second stream, and then was lost to sight around a bend in the river bed.

"Our turn next," our Georgian driver said.

All I could think about as we neared the first torrent was an experience I had had in Los Angeles several months earlier. The city had been hit by flash floods. I was in a taxicab on my way to the airport at the time. When we approached the intersection where Sepulveda Boulevard crosses Slawson Avenue, the cars were backed up for several hundred yards. The intersection was under two feet of water. My driver asked whether my airplane connection was an important one. I told him about a lecture in San Francisco that noon. He thereupon pulled out of the line of waiting cars and hit the current in the wake of a large truck. We got halfway across the intersection when the water sploshed in over the floorboards. The engine died without even a damp cough. The taxicab driver took off his shoes and socks, rolled up his pants, got out of the cab, and ordered me to get on his back. He would carry me to the other side, where cabs were available; he figured I could still make my plane if we moved fast. I did as ordered. The driver took two steps, lost his footing, and the two of us fell smack into the water, rolling over several times before we were able to struggle to our feet. I missed the plane.

Now, four months later, it suddenly occurred to me that my Los Angeles cab driver may have been a Georgian. In any event, the California episode inevitably came to mind as we followed the path of the pioneer car. The big difference, of course, was that this time we were up against no deadline. We could just as easily arrive at the State farm the next morning. But, as Igor had pointed out, we were the guests of Georgians and an element of challenge was involved in the present situation.

My apprehension gave way to exalted admiration for the driver as he successfully forded the first three currents. Muddy spray splashed up over the motor hood. Rocks were spinning off the tires and made banging noises against the underside of the car. Yet we kept moving. When we came to the fourth stream, the rear wheels hit some mud and we came to a stop.

I wondered how long the car could stay upright if the water rose any higher. The heavy rain and the harsh winds were unabating. It was now dark. Far ahead of us, I could see the tail-lights of two stalled cars. There were no cars behind us. Our Georgian driver spit lightly on his hands and took firm hold of the steering wheel. He got the car to rocking. Then he grunted triumphantly when the tires caught on a reverse thrust. We kept backing out until we could feel the rocks banging against the floorboards again. Then the driver made two or three large circles, hit several streams in low gear at a fairly high speed, emerged from the river bed, found the black-top road, and proceeded on our way.

No one said anything. I looked over at Igor and whistled softly in mixed relief and stark awe at the driver's feat. After a minute I told Igor to congratulate him for me.

"I'll congratulate him on pulling us through safely," Igor said, "but I'll have to do it tactfully. You've probably lost your sense of direction. We never got across the river, after all. The driver gave up on the last stream and decided to retreat. We're on the road back to Tbilisi again. I don't want the driver to think we're being sarcastic."

Going or coming, it was good to be dry. But it was also late, very late, and it was still raining. Surely we were not going all the way back to Tbilisi tonight. Even before I could put the question for translation, the Georgian professor told the driver to stop. Then the professor went into a farmhouse to do some telephoning in an attempt to arrange a place for us to spend the night.

While waiting for the professor, I made some inquiries about our car, which was Russian-made. It had performed remarkably—almost miraculously, in fact. It had been both nimble or sturdy when it had to be. The brakes hadn't locked after being submerged; the springs had held up under terrific pounding; the traction and balance were excellent; there had been no overheating despite the long strain of climbing and raced motor. Besides, I learned from Igor that the stream had in fact been higher than the floorboards but the car had been so engineered that it would be hermetically sealed with the closing of the doors and the trunk compartment. It was not a large car by American standards but it could carry five or six passengers in genuine comfort, if not luxury. Besides, it possessed a feature missing from most American cars for the past six years: it was built for people with legs. My knees were not at my chin or pressed against the rear of the front seat. I could stretch my legs normally and comfortably or cross them. Nor did the driver's legs hit the steering wheel when he raised his foot from accelerator to the brake. There was no mountainous floor ridge dividing the car into two parts and making second-class citizens of the poor souls who happened to be sitting in the center.

I learned from Igor that the car was a Volga make and sold for about 30,000 rubles—or $3,000 at the standard rate of exchange inside the U.S.S.R. Comparatively few were available for private sale to individuals; most of them were now allocated for taxicabs or organization use. But once the heavy official demand receded, it was planned to offer the car for general sale. This might not be for several years, however.

Could many persons afford it? The answer is emphatically in the affirmative. One of the most significant facts about the Soviet Union today is that the Russian people are enjoying a wave of comparative prosperity unlike anything they have known in their history. At least fifteen of the forty years since the Revolution were spent in war or reconstruction from war. Almost 20,000,000 people lost their lives in the Second World War. Dozens of cities and hundreds of villages had to be completely rebuilt. But during the past three or four years, the nation has been able to make the transition from war reconstruction to general development. It has been producing all sorts of goods—all the way from heavy trucks and tractors to luxury items—in vast quantities and of high standard.

Indeed, the Soviet Union today is on a production kick. People talk production and think production—new methods of increasing output or possible refinements—with a zest and a persistence that an outsider would suppose they had reserved for Marx, chess, or the classical ballet.

Meanwhile, incentives are offered for production gains, generally in the form of bonuses that in many cases double regular salaries. This has figured largely in a prodigious increase in the national income. As a result, one of the significant aspects of the Soviet economy today is the substantial purchasing power of the average consumer. People have money—a great deal of it—and they are ready to spend it on major purchases. At the present pace of private accumulation of capital, the market for private automobiles by 1965 may have to be reckoned in the hundreds of thousands and possibly even millions.

Little wonder that a parked new American or European car in front of a Russian hotel would attract large crowds and make for animated and analytical discussion sometimes lasting far past midnight. The Russian people are car-conscious today and can hardly wait to get their hands on one they can call their own.

This digression is prompted by the part played by the Volga in getting us safely through our bout with the rocky river bed. Back to the main story.

The Georgian professor was gone about half an hour. When he returned, he brought with him the head of the local community, Mr. Shakeo Gochiashvili, whose job corresponded to that of mayor. The community itself was a collective farm, the main product of which was grapes for winemaking.

The Mayor greeted us most cordially for a man who, it developed, had been roused from a deep sleep. He led the way to a narrow lane off the main road. A very short distance up the lane we came to his home, a two-story, bungalow-type frame house. An outdoor wooden stairway led up to the living quarters, where we met the Mayor's wife. She most graciously assured us it was a privilege to offer us a place to spend the night. I asked about the rest of the family and learned there were two children—a girl of ten and a boy of six.

The house itself was simple, almost spare, in design and construction. The main living quarters were on the second floor and consisted of a living room, a dining room, and two bedrooms. The kitchen, storeroom, and utility space were located on the ground floor. There was an all-purpose sink in the living room. An outhouse was located about 100 feet from the house.

The Mayor was like a character out of a novel about early New England: quiet, almost shy, but he carried on his small frame a granite-like quality of strength. You had the feeling that he came by his job through no accident. His wife was careful to stay in the background, generally saying anything she had to say through him. She had correctly assumed we had had no dinner and, though it was now past 11 P.M., she had already started to prepare a meal.

While waiting for dinner, the Georgian professor and I played chess. I was lucky enough to gain a rook as the result of an accepted Danish gambit when the game was adjourned in response to the call to table. The Mayor's wife did not sit down with us but the Mayor did and he proceeded to eat the full meal, as the custom dictates. The dinner party numbered five, including our Georgian driver. The dinner was a feast, the main course of which consisted of roast chicken and scallions. But the principal feature of the dinner was the wine toasts. In keeping with Georgian traditions, a meal among friends is an occasion for good spirits and camaraderie, the symbol of which is the toast.

True to tradition, the Mayor offered the first toast—to the parents of all present and to all the sacrifices they had made for us in life, to their nobility, their thoughtfulness, and to their everlasting honor. Igor whispered to me that this was an important toast and meant bottoms up. A few minutes later, again in keeping with tradition, the Mayor offered a toast to his wife, who was peering at us from behind the curtains of the next room. She was a good woman, he said, and this toast was to her health and long life.

The wine was delicious, but I suddenly began to wonder about my capacity. And well I might, for before the evening was over, thirty-one toasts were to be offered. Bottle after bottle was opened. There were to be toasts to all present. (Personal toasts to friends at the table are standing toasts and are a bottoms-up occasion. Toasts to those absent or to institutions are sitting toasts and sipping is permitted.) Each person is expected to offer his share of the toasting. On this night, there were at least fifteen personal toasts—a toast may be repeated if offered by different persons.

The two finest toasts of the evening were offered by the Mayor. One was to the men who work the land, who understand nature and love her, and who supply nourishment to all. He also proposed a toast to peace and to the wisdom and good will by leaders in both countries that would make peace possible. I followed with a related toast, to the determination of peoples to play a full part in the making of such a peace and in bringing about justice that would make peace worth-while.

The Mayor held out his hand. I reached for it as best I could under the circumstances, shook it firmly, and everyone was happy, for the problems of war and peace had been resolved. What the world needs, I thought, was some good Georgian wine.

It had been a long dinner, made long not by the toasts but by the need to do extra translations. Georgians speak their own language and hardly any Russian. Igor understood English and Russian but no Georgian; the professor understood Georgian and Russian but no English. I understood neither Russian nor Georgian and the Mayor neither English nor Russian. For the Mayor to get through to me or me to him, it was necessary to be toasted in three tongues. This must have produced some interesting variations; it also took a deuce of a long time, especially when we began to trade similar stories from different cultures.

At three A.M., well-fed, well-toasted, and well-translated, we rose slowly from the table. Igor and I were shown to the main bedroom. When I protested that the Mayor and his wife were giving us their own beds, Igor shushed me by saying we must not argue with any aspect of Georgian hospitality. I yielded. It had been a long day.

A few hours later, the air of the farm was riddled by the pronouncements of roosters—countless thousands of them just outside the window, or so it seemed to a man just settling down to a sustained sleep. I heard the Mayor, in a stern whisper, admonish his little boy to be quiet; if he said anything to the roosters, they paid no attention. Unwritten farm laws are the same all over the world, one of which has to do with getting up on time. This we did, although I noticed that the veterans of last night's valiant wine marathon were still gasping for breath.

After a brief discussion, it was decided we would stay right where we were, at this particular collective farm, rather than push on to the State farm. This decision pleased me, for it gave me a chance to make some unscheduled observations. Moreover, I was eager to see how an average collective farm operated. The difference between a State farm and a collective farm is that the latter is run by the farmers themselves, who make the decisions, take the risks, and receive the profits, whereas the former is owned by the State, which hires farmers and pays them salaries. State farms are among the most modern in the world with respect to equipment and techniques. Collective farms are generally as modern or efficient as the farmers wish to make them or are able to make them. Since there were many more collective farms than State farms and since they played a larger part in the general economy, I felt the change in our plans would not be unprofitable.

The Mayor had arranged for us to meet with the officers of the local collective, including the chairman, vice-chairman, controller, and chief agronomist. The meeting turned out to be something in the nature of a briefing session, in which I received answers to questions.

I learned that the community or township had been named after Stalin, the best known Georgian of them all. The collective farm itself was called Shroma, which means toil in Georgian. The farm had been organized in 1926. Fifty peasants in the area, all of them poor, had come together to create a collective farm under the State enabling laws. Their application was approved and the Government allotted them 2,600 hectares. The State retained ultimate ownership of the land but the peasants were given indefinite operating rights. Land cannot be bought or sold in the Soviet Union; it is assigned.

The number of farmers working on this particular farm grew from the original fifty families to the present 650 families. This means a total present population of about 3,000.

How does the collective farm actually work? Through the case history of a single farmer, Ivan Tschliouri, I learned something about the functioning of the enterprise.

Ivan Tschliouri is thirty-six. His family includes his wife, his mother-in-law, his seven-year-old son, and his four-year-old daughter. Ivan grew up on a farm but most of his scientific knowledge about modern methods of farming he learned from a correspondence course supplied by the University at Tbilisi. Ivan didn't study marketing—and he didn't study distribution. He didn't have to. He is not expected to be a salesman or a negotiator. All that is expected of him is that he will do a good job of growing grapes. He has no worry about laws of supply or demand or about plunging or skyrocketing prices. The Government guarantees in advance to buy as many kilograms of grapes as he is able to coax out of the vine. He doesn't even have to deliver the grapes to a Government station; the Government comes and gets them.

Ivan and his family live in a small four-room cottage. There are no modern conveniences in the house, such as a water closet or shower or steam-heating, nor are there luxuries such as an electric dish-washer or clothes-washer or dryer, or television, or high-fidelity equipment. Nor does he have a car of his own.

Not that Ivan cannot afford these conveniences and luxuries. He can, and with abundant cash to spare. And, two or three years from now, he may be able to begin to obtain some of them. Right now, Soviet industry is turning out the lathes and the machines that will go into more factories for making such consumer goods in substantial quantities.

Meanwhile, Ivan is putting his money in a savings bank, for which he gets 3 per cent interest. As a holder of a savings book, he is also entitled to participate in periodic lotteries, in which there are thousands of prizes ranging all the way from a cash gift of 100,000 rubles or a fully furnished home to a bicycle or an umbrella.

Ivan's expenses are not high. He buys clothes for his family, furnishings for the home, newspapers, magazines, books, etc. The family goes to the cinema or sees a traveling opera company or jazz band, for which Ivan pays about two rubles per ticket.

Ivan owns his own cottage, made possible two years ago by a community-government loan of 10,000 rubles. Next year, he will have to start amortizing the debt over ten years. This will come to about 1,000 rubles, or $100 a year. He grows much of his food on a small plot of land that is available for his own use and that is independent of the land he works as a member of the collective farm. He also owns his own cow, for which he paid 1,700 rubles; a horse, which cost him 1,000 rubles * when it was a colt; a pig, seven sheep, and about sixty-four chickens. In these possessions, he stays within the prescribed limits. Individual farmers may not own more than one cow, one horse, one pig, ten sheep. No limit on poultry.

He has no medical or dental or hospital expenses. He pays no direct Government taxes—national, state, or local. He has no membership dues or organization fees. He is not expected to contribute to any funds for new equipment or facilities required by the collective farm.

Most significantly, he has no working hours. His income from the collective farm is based on completed "job units." A "job unit" may represent any number of things. It could include maintenance of machinery; care of livestock; road-building or repair; tilling a certain amount of land, and, most important of all, producing a large grape yield.

No limit is fixed on the number of job-unit credits a farmer may accumulate during the course of a year; but each farmer is expected to turn in a minimum of 150 units a year. For each completed job unit, a farmer is credited with twenty rubles. Thus, the minimum yearly income of a farmer would be 3,000 rubles a year, while the maximum would be determined only by his own capacity. Generally speaking, a single job unit can be completed in six to eight hours. Most individual farmers average about ten units a week. Thus, storing ten tons of wheat might be worth, say, five job units. Planting and harvesting ten kilograms of grapes might be worth four units.

Both Ivan and his "team leader" keep account books in which the job units are carefully recorded. If there is any discrepancy, Ivan can ask for a review by the Executive Committee of the co-operative.

Ivan's wife and mother-in-law frequently join him in the fields or in special jobs. Each one has an account book of her own. Thus, with three members of the family at work on the farm, Ivan was able last year to turn in one of the highest number of job units in the entire collective farm. The account books of the Tschliouris showed that they completed just over 1,000 job units, for which they received a combined total of

* When I asked about the average cost of a horse, the Mayor grinned. "It's the same all over the world," he said. "There are no standard prices. There are only good horse-traders and stupid ones."

20,000 rubles. Of this amount, Ivan received 17,000 rubles in cash, one ton of corn, one-half ton of wheat, and fifty kilograms of cheese. The farm produce given him is computed at the Government or wholesale selling price. If Ivan wishes to sell this produce on the open market, he may receive much more than the 3,000 rubles represented by the difference between the cash given him and his original job-unit credit. No one will ask him any questions about any cash he received as the result of his private sales, whether with respect to farm goods paid to him or that which he grows himself on the portion of land reserved for his own use.

All this is apart from bonuses. If Ivan exceeds his individual quota, working as a member of a "team," he is eligible for a bonus. Last year, Ivan was given a quota of seven tons of grapes to be produced on a single hectare. He produced ten tons. When the collective farm sold the grapes to the State, Ivan was credited with a cash bonus of 3,200 rubles, representing 20 per cent of the amount received by the collective farm for the extra three tons Ivan turned in.

Ivan likes to travel, and expects sometime soon to gratify his wish to be able to see far-off fabled places like Moscow and Leningrad. He expects to fly the Tupulev jet to Moscow and Leningrad this summer. The distance is about 1,000 miles; the flight takes less than three hours. Ivan's ticket will cost him about $70 for the round trip. (Jet transportation in the Soviet Union is practically standard for all long-distance flights, and is the cheapest in the world.) Ivan would also like to spend some time with his family, maybe in a year or two, at a resort on the Black Sea Coast. If his doctor says that he or his wife need a rest for their health, Ivan will find all sorts of health facilities open to him at any one of a number of places like Sochi or in the Crimea. The collective farm will pay 70 per cent of the cost of the health resort and travel; Ivan will pay the balance.

It has been only comparatively recently that Ivan has been able to think seriously about seeing the rest of the Soviet Union. He has not always been so prosperous as now. For many years the Government did not pay enough for the grapes; it had been hard work, very hard, and the rewards seemed small. But a few years ago, there were many reforms. The Government prices for farm products were doubled and tripled. There were many new incentives. Another important development was that the Government no longer required the collective farmers to rent their tractors and trucks and heavy equipment from the State tractor stations. Now a collective farm can buy its own tractors or trucks. Last year, the Shroma Council decided to buy ten tractors and two combines. Collectively, the farmers now own eleven trucks and two passenger cars. One of the cars is used by the chairman of the Council; the other is available to the farmers themselves. Now, twenty farmers have filed application to buy private cars when they are available. They may have to wait for five years or more.

The farmers make their collective decisions—election of officers and members of the Council; whether to buy new equipment and how much; what their quotas for the new year are to be; whether to admit new farmers to the collective, or how the money paid by the Government for the collective yield is to be divided, etc.—at full sessions. Since there are more than 650 families, and since some families number three farmers, this can mean that 1,200 or more people come together to take part in the decisions. Sometimes the meetings are held outdoors; during bad weather they may be held in the community sports arena. These full meetings occur five or six times a year.

The actual governing body, or Representative Council, is elected by the full group for a period of two years. It consists of the chairman, vice-chairman, treasurer, and elected representatives; it meets twice a month and handles the operational functions in addition to making necessary interim decisions. They may decide to replace a tractor, or consider a complaint by one of the farmers concerning a mistake in the computation of his work units, or arrange for entertainment, etc. (The moving-picture house shows films daily. Every once in a while, a symphony orchestra will be brought to Shroma; at other times, the farmers and their families may see a traveling dramatic company or a magician. Or the university at Tbilisi will make available professors for lectures. Then, of course, there are always the wrestling matches. Georgians believe they have the toughest wrestlers in the world; it might be risky, though instructive, to argue the proposition.)

The cost of a movie is a couple of rubles. For more serious entertainment, such as a symphony, the price may run up to five rubles (fifty cents) Depending on the desirability of the seat. Ivan and his family go out on an average of two evenings a week. He doesn't go to the lectures, generally, preferring to read. He likes novels, mostly Russian and American. He has read translations from many books of Hemingway, Steinbeck, and Jack London. Some years ago, he liked Mark Twain but now finds himself interested in the more serious American novel. His favorite author, of course, is Shota Rustavelli, the Georgian national poet and hero, who occupies a station of reknown akin to a combination of Shakespeare and Dante. Ivan says he has memorized maybe 100 poems by Rustavelli, who writes so lyrically of the struggles of the Georgian people and the enchantment of their wondrous land. For his books, Ivan pays about eight to ten rubles for bound volumes and a little less for the classics.

Ivan is not too much interested in ideological questions. He knows about the general ideas of Marx, of course; but he realizes there have been many changes in the applied form, especially in recent years.

After completing Ivan's case history, the Mayor and Chairman escorted us on a tour of the collective farm—through the vineyards and the wheat and corn fields, the chicken houses and the cow barns. The equipment seemed to be divided between the very new and the dilapidated. As a whole, it was not what one would call a highly modern establishment, according to American standards, but that it was busy and productive, there could be no doubt.

(Subsequently, I learned that there is a considerable range in the productivity and prosperity of collective farms. In some places the farmers still don't seem to take to the idea, or the land itself may be poor, as in the hilly or mountainous areas. But most of the collective farms seem to be doing well, especially since the Government's action in upping the prices for farm produce so sharply in the past three years.)

It goes without saying that we had another big meal at Shroma before we left, in which fluency and fluidity came together beautifully and insistently during the noble toasts. Once again, there were the standing toasts and the sitting toasts, the bottoms-up toasts and the sipping ones. Once again, too, the world became most tolerable. We had no trouble in agreeing that if a summit conference is held, it should be in Georgia. Shroma wine, of course.

—*August 8, 1959*


# Peace without Panic

Something is troubling the American people. It is unpleasant to think about and awkward to talk about. Even to raise the question can produce profound uneasiness. The question is whether we can afford peace. Lending grim reality to this question is this headline in a recent New York newspaper: "FEAR OF PEACE DEPRESSES MARKET."

Or the following prominent billing on the cover of a national weekly magazine: "WHAT PEACE WILL DO TO YOU."

No one in his right mind wants war. Yet more and more people seem to feel we need the threat of war. There is underlying fear that the national economy would come apart at the seams should real peace break out. The nation has been engaged for so long in the business of preparing for war that it has become part of our economic metabolism.

Even more significant than the economic adjustment has been the psychological adjustment. Somehow the notion has become general that we can never be prosperous unless we continue the present program. The notion becomes dangerous to the extent that it may rob us of an essential intensity in thirsting for peace or questing for peace. It is dangerous because it assumes that a course of action is without logical consequences. It is dangerous because it may cause us to be indifferent or mute if a genuine opportunity should develop to bring the means or the causes of war under control.

It will not suffice to dismiss the discussion on the grounds that national security demands continual and expanded arms development. The issue, to repeat, is this: Are we afraid of peace if we can have peace—the kind of peace that is consistent with national security? For if this is our underlying fear, we can mark it as certain that there will be no peace. Nor will the trend stop there. A moral failure is a galloping thing. We cannot expect that dependence on war equipment, even when circumstances permit the exploration of a different course, will be without a whole chain of destructive effects.

If we are in a position today—as we may now well be—to reduce and eliminate the dangers of nuclear war, then we should leap at the prospect even if we are convinced it would produce the worst depression this world has ever known. Indeed, only as we demonstrate our readiness to sacrifice for a just and workable peace do we qualify ourselves for the peace-building task.

This much out of the way, we can consider the economic problem. There need be fear of economic collapse only if we are completely blind to the opportunity surrounding us. What is the thing we dread? We dread that the wheels of our factories will stop turning, the energy of our transistors be stilled, and the circulating power of the defense billions be cut off. We dread the cutoff because we know nothing to take its place. Are we so sure of this? If we have to spend 60 billions a year on an arms program to keep our economy afloat, we can spend at least that much on things we really need, some of which might even brighten up this planet for most of the people who live on it.

Let us announce to the world that as soon as the United Nations is fully capable of taking over the international security function, we will be prepared to embark on a ten-year program seeking the following objectives:

1. The manufacture of 100 million prefabricated three-room homes, for shipment to and assembly in those countries, principally in Asia and Africa, in which homelessness is a major problem.

2. The construction of community development projects for relocating the major refugee groups in the world, be they Arab, Pakistani, Indian, or whatever, so long as the necessary land is contributed by the respective governments.

3. Large-scale hydrolectric power projects, irrigation projects, road-building projects, health-center and hospital-building projects in other countries on the basis of long-term credits.

4. Use of our agricultural surpluses to help meet the stark fact of hunger that now affects at least one-third of the world's peoples.

So far as the United States itself is concerned, we can launch a program to build at least 25,000 new elementary and secondary schools; to build at least 500 new teachers' colleges; to provide new equipment or facilities for 1,500 colleges and universities; to build at least 10,000 miles of much-needed new Federal highways; to enlarge the plants and facilities of 25,000 hospitals; to carry out an air-decontamination program to get rid of poisons resulting from industrial gases, automobile fumes, and radio-active fallout; and to restore the eroded or eroding lands of the Midwest and West.

Such a program would easily take up the slack left by a substantial reduction in manufacture of weapons of mass destruction.

It will be argued, of course, that the country couldn't possibly afford to spend so much. The answer is that we are already spending that much. Then it will be argued that where our security is concerned there is no choice. The answer is that our security depends even more on creating conditions of stability and progress in the world than on turning out weapons of absolute destruction.

In any case, the problem lies not in any laws of economic determinism, but in our values and our purposes.

*—November 14, 1959*

# Don Pablo

San Juan, Puerto Rico

Pablo Casals is regarded by the people of Puerto Rico as one of their leading assets, along with one of the most attractive climates in the world, a bountiful sun, a view on the sea, and a congenial system of taxation. They know him as one of the great men of his age—not just for his musicianship but for his warmth as a person and as a citizen at large of the twentieth century.

Don Pablo lives with his wife in an attractive villa near the sea on the outskirts of San Juan. The fact that he is now eighty-three and is not in the best of health may have caused him to reduce his concerts and his public appearances but he still works intensively with his music; he is still very much a part of the world. He sees and feels no separation between human creativity and human freedom.

Music helps to express the human spirit, helps to knit man together and make him whole. But the habitat of society must have a wholeness, too, if it is to serve man well. Therefore, there must be no disconnection between the arts of man and his institutions.

Don Pablo is a giant among men in spirit and creative stature, but physically he is delicately built, almost frail. He is buoyantly sympathetic in manner, managing to involve himself very quickly in the concerns or problems of his friends or visitors. His responses are unhurried, genuine, full. He showed me some of his original music manuscripts by Bach, and he remarked that Bach meant more to him than any other composer.

This was only one of several things he had in common with Schweitzer, I observed.

"My good friend Albert Schweitzer shares with me the belief that Bach is the greatest of all composers," Don Pablo said, "but we like Bach for entirely different reasons. Schweitzer sees Bach in complex architectural terms; he acclaims him as a master who reigns supreme over the great and diverse realm of music. I see Bach as a great romantic. His music stirs me, helps me to feel fully alive. When I wake up each morning I can hardly wait to play Bach. What a wonderful way to start the day."

If Bach was his favorite composer, what piece of Bach, then, was his favorite composition?

"Strangely, it is not a piece by Bach," he said. "There are many compositions by Bach that I cannot live without, but the piece that means the most to me was written not by Bach but by Brahms. Here, let me show it to you. I have the original manuscript."

He took down from the wall, where it had been framed behind glass, one of the most valuable music manuscripts in the world now in private hands—Brahms's B Flat Quartet.

"Interesting, how I happened to acquire it," he said. "Many years ago I knew a man who was head of the Friends of Music in Vienna. His name was Wilhelm Kuchs. One night in Vienna—this was before the war—he invited several of his friends for dinner, myself included. He had what I believe may have been the finest private collection of original music manuscripts in the world. He also owned an impressive collection of fine musical instruments—violins by Stradivarius and Guarneri among them. He was wealthy, very wealthy; but he was a simple man and a very accessible one.

"Then the war came. He was in his eighties. He had no intention of spending the rest of his old age under Nazism. He moved to Switzerland when Hitler moved into Austria.

"After the war I went to see him in Switzerland. He was then more than ninety. I was eager to pay my respects. Just seeing him again, this wonderful old friend who had done so much for music, was to me a very moving experience. I think we both wept on each other's shoulder. Then I told him how concerned I had been over his collection of manuscripts. I had been terribly apprehensive that he might not have been able to keep his collection from falling into Nazi hands.

"My friend told me there was nothing to worry about; he had managed to save the entire collection. Then he went and got some items from the collection—some chamber music by Schubert and Mozart to begin with. Then he placed on the table before me the original manuscript of the Brahms B Flat Quartet. I could hardly believe my eyes. I stood transfixed. I suppose every musician feels that there is one piece that speaks to him alone, one which he feels seems to involve every molecule of his being. This was the way I had felt about the B Flat Quartet ever since I played it for the first time. And always I felt it was mine.

"Mr. Kuchs could see that when I held the B Flat Quartet manuscript in my hands it was a very special and powerful emotional experience.

" 'It is *your* Quartet in every way,' Mr. Kuchs said. 'It would make me happy if you would let me give it to you.' And he did.

"I couldn't thank him adequately then, but I did write him a long letter telling him of the great pride and joy his gift had brought to my life. When Mr. Kuchs replied, he told me many things about the history of the B Flat Quartet I had not known before. One fact in particular stood out. It is that Brahms began to write the Quartet just nine months before I was born. It took him nine months to complete it. We both came into the world on exactly the same day, the same month, the same year."

As Don Pablo spoke, he seemed to relive the experience. His features, unmarred by any hard lines, were so expressive that his words seemed merely to confirm the image. Indeed, his face had the dramatic power of a full Ibsen cast.

I asked Don Pablo whether any other individual compositions had special meaning for him.

"Many pieces," he said, "but none that I felt owned me and expressed me as much as the B Flat Quartet. Yet, when I get up in the morning, I can think only of Bach. I have the feeling that the world is being re-born. Nature always seems more in evidence to me in the morning. And when I come back from my walk I always sit down at the piano and play Bach—generally the *Wohltemperirtes Klavier*. Here is the passage I like."

He went over to the piano and began to play. I had forgotten that Don Pablo had achieved proficiency on several musical instruments before he took up the cello. He hummed as he played, then said that Bach spoke to him here—and he placed his hand over his heart.

"There is one other piece I must tell you about. This one, too, has special meaning. I think it is the piece I would like most to hear again during my last moments on earth. How lovely and moving it is, the second movement of Mozart's Clarinet Quintet."

Don Pablo played it. His fingers were thin and the skin was pale but they belonged to the most extraordinary hands I had ever seen. They seemed to have a wisdom and a grace of their own. When he played Mozart, he was clearly the interpreter and not just the performer; yet it was difficult to imagine how the piece could be played in any other way.

After he got up from the piano he apologized for having taken up so much time in our talk about music instead of discussing the affairs of the world. I told him I had the impression that what he had been saying and doing were most relevant in terms of the world's affairs. In the discussion that followed there seemed to be agreement on the proposition that the most serious part of the problem of world peace was that the individual felt helpless.

"The answer to helplessness is not so very complicated," Don Pablo said. "A man can do something for peace without having to jump into politics. Each man has inside him a basic decency and goodness. If he listens to it and acts on it, he is giving a great deal of what it is the world needs most. It is not complicated but it takes courage. It takes courage for a man to listen to his own goodness and act on it. Do we dare to be ourselves? This is the question that counts."

*—December 12, 1959*

# A Most Remarkable Young Man

Nowhere in the world have I met a more remarkable man than Ved Mehta. Certainly I know of few persons who are better adjusted or who come closer to tapping the vast potential of a human being.

He is a young man, a very young man, and he is blind.

I first heard of Ved Mehta from his father in New Delhi in 1951. Dr. Amolak R. Mehta was Deputy Director General of Health Services with the Indian government. He came to call on me at the home of a mutual friend and he spoke of his young son, then fifteen. Dr. Mehta said that Ved was attending a school for blind children in Little Rock, Arkansas. He hoped that when I returned to America I might have occasion to see him. He explained that he had sent his son to the United States because of the unfortunate station of a blind person in India.

"There is too much of a disposition in Asia to assume that a blind person must be doomed to the life of a beggar or a cane-chair maker," Dr. Mehta said. "I want my son to have as normal a life as possible. I don't want him to weave baskets or feel that he is condemned in any way to the things that blind people are usually trained to do."

I learned from Dr. Mehta that Ved became totally blind at the age of three, following a severe attack of meningitis. At the age of five he had been sent to a school for the blind in Bombay, operated by Americans. In accordance with Dr. Mehta's instructions, the child was taught to recognize and develop his own potentialities. He learned Braille, of course, and arithmetic on an abacus. He also learned how to speak English. But when Ved was eight, he had gone as far as it was possible for him to go at the Bombay school and was sent home.

Dr. Mehta tried unsuccessfully for several years to send Ved to a school in Europe or the United States. The headmasters seemed to feel that the problems of adjustment for any Asian child in the West were substantial; for a blind boy, they would be insuperable. Ved himself wrote countless letters of application; the twenty-ninth was to a school in Arkansas and it produced a favorable response.

After I returned from India, I entered into a correspondence with Ved, whose letters were surprisingly mature for a boy in his teens. They were clearly the work of a resourceful mind. What impressed me particularly was his supple use of the English language.

I met Ved for the first time in the spring of 1952. He came to our home with his father, then in the United States as a visiting Fulbright professor. There was nothing about Ved that suggested a handicapped person. He used no cane. He had no seeing-eye dog. He didn't wait for people to lead him from one place to another. Not once did his father take him by the hand. Yet he moved about easily. He was not self-conscious about his blindness. He put my children at ease when they awkwardly tried to hide their curiosity, and he answered their numberless questions with the sincerity and gentle humor that appeal to a child's mind. I found myself as fascinated as the children, especially when Ved demonstrated how he avoided bumping into walls or objects without the use of a cane or out-stretched arms.

Thereafter, at least twice a year, generally at Christmas and during part of the summer vacation, Ved would come to visit us. Sometimes he would arrive after hitchhiking from the West Coast, where he had en-rolled in Pomona College in the fall of 1952. I was terrified at first when I thought of this blind boy at the mercy of the juggernauts of the high-way. But I remembered that his father had once told me that Ved would never attempt anything beyond his capacity. Apparently this meant he could do just about everything, for his capacity seemed limitless.

Three years ago I was toying with the idea of learning how to play chess. Some friends had gone to the trouble of familiarizing me with the game. But it was Ved who gave me the working demonstrations. His fingers danced lightly but surely over the pieces as he instructed me in the subtler strategies of the game. And when I was up against other players, we would announce each move and he would follow the entire game in his mind.

Once we went to New York together by train. He stayed close to me when I walked up to the ticket counter and when we went out on the platform. I could tell he was memorizing distances and positions. When we arrived at Grand Central Station I escorted him around the mammoth terminal, pointing out the ticket counters and the various exits. After this, he went into the city by himself, navigating in and out of Grand Central with relative ease. He seldom bumped into anyone or anything.

It was astounding to see Ved handle himself in traffic. He had figured out the clicking sounds of the traffic lights and he could tell by the racing of the motors or the shifting of gears when the lights had turned green again. He was careful, too, to stay close to other people while crossing, being able to judge from the sounds of their footsteps how fast he had to move to keep clear of cars making right-hand turns.

I was mystified by the way his foot would rise to meet a curb; he also knew exactly when to step down. It was baffling, too, to see the way he would stop short in order to avoid bumping into a person. Or he would shift his direction suddenly in order to walk around a telephone pole or a crate on a sidewalk. It was almost eerie to see him walk between cars in a crowded parking lot and find our car unaided. It almost seemed as though he operated on some sort of built-in radar.

When I spoke to Ved about this his explanation was simple and matter-of-fact. It was a number of things in combination that enabled him to "see."

First of all, there was the matter of skin sensitivity. He had been able to develop, over the years, a sensitivity to subtle changes in the movement of air. Just as the eye picks up light when reflected from a surface, so his skin would pick up changes in air pressure when he was near objects, or when there was even the slightest change in elevation. The air felt one way when he came to the foot of the stairs, another way at the head of the stairs. If I walked behind him he would wait for me to catch up. His skin would feel the difference between the interruption in the movement of air caused by a parked passenger car and a parked truck. At my prodding he demonstrated this for me once by walking close to the curb of a street filled with parked vehicles, and he would identify them according to whether they were cars or trucks, and frequently he would add "rather large truck" or "pretty small car."

He could also tell, when we walked on a city street, his distance from the buildings. Whenever we passed an office building with a large recessed entranceway, his skin would be able to record the fact.

Closely related to his "skin vision" was his hearing perception. It wasn't that his hearing range was far beyond the normal; his acuteness lay in his ability to make sharp distinctions between various sounds and to relate them to certain experiences. The sound of a person's footsteps usually would give him a clue to age, sex, and disposition. Sometimes when I would come back from the city, he could tell by my step and voice what kind of day I had had. Or he would say that I "looked" as though some exciting things had happened to me. But he never gave the impression of demonstrating his skills just to make his presence felt.

His memory was another prodigious asset. Once you escorted him around a house, however complicated, the number of steps from one room to another and the size and position of the furniture became permanently fixed in his mind. Shortly after we moved into our new home Ved came to visit us. The first day he was there I arrived from the city late at night. I had no key and was fumbling at the door. Ved came down from his room on the second floor to let me in. He found his way unerringly to the door, handling the complicated latch with complete ease. Then he snapped on the lights for my convenience. After an exchange of pleasantries, he reminded me to turn off the lights, and he went upstairs to bed.

All these three highly developed senses—skin sensitivity, hearing, and memory—were involved every time he traveled by himself, whether getting on or off a train, or crossing a busy thoroughfare, hitchhiking on a crowded highway, or riding a bicycle. I was astounded when Ved said casually that one of his hobbies was bicycle riding. He demonstrated by borrowing my eldest girl's bicycle. He made perfect circles in the driveway, avoiding the parked car and the low-spreading branches of a pine tree. He sat high and straight on the bicycle, his head perfectly still and his face flushed with pleasure. I noticed that he would almost come upon an object before he would veer away from it.

Ved explained by saying that, first of all, he was familiar with the size and shape of the driveway. Then it was just a matter of operating within his memory and depending on his skin vision to keep clear of other vehicles or objects.

Did he ever fall? I asked. Many times, he said. Once, while he was bicycling to school, a heavy truck rumbled past. The volume of noise deafened him momentarily and the pressure of the air disrupted his skin sensitivity and he became truly "blinded," with the result that he lost his equilibrium. The bicycle jumped the sidewalk and rammed into a pole.

Another time he walked into an open manhole.

Then there was the time he was walking rapidly with some college friends. They were talking excitedly about various things. A truck thundered past, blocking Ved's senses. He walked into an iron lamp post, laying open his forehead. After he recovered, he made up his mind that the next time a sudden heavy noise occurred he would stand still until he knew exactly what he was doing.

His body contains the scars of numberless falls, all incurred as an inevitable part of his development. He lost his front tooth as a result of a hard spill while roller skating as a child. Today bumps and falls are infrequent. Sometimes he bangs his kneecap against a fire hydrant projecting out from a building. This doesn't bother him for he knows that the same thing happens to many people whose vision is perfect.

Ved graduated from Pomona last year with top honors and a Phi Beta Kappa key. He enrolled in courses at Harvard and then received a fellowship at Oxford. He is interested in English literature, government, and history. For a while he had thought he might study law, so that he could go into government service on his return to India. But he felt that the Asian notions about a blind man's limitations might put a ceiling over his possibilities. And so, increasingly in recent years, he has been thinking about writing as a career when he completes his studies at Oxford.

He had the good fortune to meet Edward Weeks, the editor of *The Atlantic Monthly*, while the latter was on a lecture tour in California. Mr. Weeks was immediately captivated by Ved's grasp of situations and his ability to communicate. He encouraged Ved to write. When Ved came East to go to Harvard, Mr. Weeks provided invaluable help in developing the manuscript of a book that would deal with the two worlds of India and America.

Ved has never learned how to write in longhand. He can sign his name, but that is about all. He can, however, use a regular typewriter. He also works with a tape recorder, dictating for many hours at a time, then turning the tape over to a friend for transcription. For almost two years Ved typed or dictated or corrected the transcripts of his book.

A month ago Ved came out to see us in the country. A special-delivery package with a Boston postmark was waiting for him. He opened it carefully. It was the first copy of his book, *Face to Face* (Little, Brown, $4.50).

Ved handled the book carefully, running his fingers over the jacket, judging the thickness of the volume, and feeling the texture of the paper. He asked me to describe the jacket to him and the typography of the book. I told him it was a most impressive piece of bookmaking and that he had every reason to be happy with it.

He smiled, then said that it felt strange to have written a book which he was totally unable to read. Strange, but wonderful just the same, he added. He wasn't sure whether he would want to have someone read it to him; perhaps he would wait and see.

*Face to Face* is as perfect a reflection of its author as any book I have ever read. It is straightforward, dignified, appealing. It has a great deal to give to anyone who comes to it, for it is in many ways a mind-stretching experience. Ved Mehta neither exploits nor skirts around his blindness in his account of growing up in India and in coming of age in the United States. He treats it the way he lives it—as a natural part of his life. He describes it without making it central in his story; at the same time, he faces up to such aspects of blindness as may interest the reader.

The principal value of the book, however, is in its insights. It is easily one of the three or four best accounts I have seen of life in India during the historic period immediately leading up to independence. And its account of the turbulence and violence in India at the time of partition helps to close one of the great gaps in the knowledge of most Americans about a large part of the rest of the world. Our age has no shortage of drama in the large; it is possible for even large dramatic upheavals such as the partition of India to be obscured at a distance. *Face to Face* makes it possible for Westerners to see the period in its full and living dimensions.

It is in Ved Mehta's observations of life in the United States, however, that he enables us to see things we may never have seen before. He takes America in his stride, but it is a most original stride; and through him we have an access to ourselves that we never knew existed. He writes about Americana—all the way from the subway and Coney Island to life in the Deep South or on a college campus in California—with a sense of color and beauty. He has crossed the United States fourteen times and been in thirty-seven states.

"Of course, when you are blind, you miss the scenic part," he writes. "That is to say, you miss the view of a snow-clad peak, the impression of skyscrapers lined up shoulder to shoulder, a vast stretch of range, with cows milling about, or the way a city looks from a plane when draped in a thin veil of clouds. You become, however, more conscious of smells, the gamut of accents, or the unusual names streets have in some cities. But what you remember most of all . . . are the people you encounter, even the ones you meet only for a moment on the street corner or sitting at a counter, or the kind driver whose motor you can hear coming faster and faster while you suspensefully wait to see whether he will pass you by like the one before him or stop. You remember vividly the moment when a car slows down, and a voice says, 'Hey, feller, want a ride?' "

There is also the description of his experiences with his new American friends at school and his involvement in a new kind of life. His sensitive handling of and response to challenge on the level of friendships with young Americans, boys and girls, is among the impressive achievements of his book. His story, of course, is not complete. The basic conflict, such as it is, between his two worlds is not yet fully defined and cannot be until he returns to India. In the meantime, we have a book that is enormously appealing and that will be widely read. I readily admit my bias. But it is the kind of bias that is proudly shared. For *Face to Face* is a remarkable book written by a most remarkable man.

—*October 17, 1957*

*Ved Mehta is now a staff writer for* The New Yorker. *His books include:* Face to Face; Fly and the Fly Bottle: Encounters with British Intellectuals; Walking the Indian Streets; *and* The New Theologians.

# Two Projects

*In 1949, the* Saturday Review *undertook a "Moral Adoptions" project in Hiroshima for the care of some 400 children who were orphaned by the atomic explosion. Readers of the magazine, responding to the appeal of the editorial page, "adopted" the children at a distance. Their support made it possible to build new orphanages and to enlarge old ones. The "parents" corresponded with their foster children and with the heads of the orphanages. In addition to contributing to the general support of the orphanages, the Americans made it possible for the children to receive special educational training. Eventually, most of the orphans went to college or vocational schools under the Moral Adoptions plan.*

*A related project in Hiroshima undertaken by the magazine was medical and rehabilitative in nature. The focal point of this program was the treatment of young girls who had been disfigured or crippled by the bombing. The project began in 1953 and continued for four years.*

*The "Hiroshima Peace Center Associates," referred to several times in this section, was formed by the editors as the operating American agency to administer the Moral Adoptions program and the program for treatment of the Hiroshima Maidens.*

*A second major project undertaken by the magazine concerned the "Ravensbrueck Lapins," a group of Polish ladies who had been used as medical guinea pigs by Nazi doctors during the Second World War. Aided by the experiences of treating the Hiroshima Maidens, the magazine brought the Polish ladies to the United States for medical, surgical, and psychotherapeutic treatment.*

*The following two sections are drawn from articles and editorials appearing in the magazine describing both these programs.*

## The Hiroshima Maidens

It was at the Nagarekawa United Church of Christ in Hiroshima that I first met the "Hiroshima Maidens." Kiyoshi Tanimoto, the American-educated Japanese Methodist minister and one of the central figures in

John Hersey's *Hiroshima,* had often referred to the Maidens in his letters to me following my 1949 visit. When my wife Ellen and I arrived at the Hiroshima railroad station in August, 1953, he met us and spoke of the predicament of the Maidens.

The girls, some sixty in number, had drifted together out of common experience and common loneliness. All were survivors of the experience in Hiroshima on August 6, 1945. All were badly disfigured or crippled by the heat and blast of the bomb. Most had been young schoolgirls at the time. As they grew older, they became separated from the kind of expectations that light up the world of teen-age girls. The prospect of marriage and children was almost nonexistent.

Adding to this sense of alienation was the fear of being seen in public. The tendency of human beings to shun and even subconsciously to resent human beings with deformities is strong in Japanese culture. The Maidens had no sense of ease in moving about the city during daylight. A few of them had jobs—generally in social welfare activities, such as the School for the Blind. Most of them, however, stayed at home.

Dr. Kiyoshi Tanimoto became their crusader and benefactor. He brought them together, gave them things to do, individually and collectively, and provided focus for their lives. Plastic surgery as a disciplined branch of surgery had yet to be developed in Japan.

All this Kiyoshi Tanimoto made known to Ellen and me on our way from the railroad station to the hotel. He asked whether we would come to his church to meet the girls. We agreed.

The Nagarekawa Church had been partially destroyed by the bomb. Tanimoto had personally supervised the rebuilding. It was a modest structure, brick and stucco, not unlike the type of small church building one might find in the United States. The basement had a fairly large meeting room. It was here that we met the Maidens.

There were perhaps thirty or thirty-five of them. They sat quietly on the hard benches. Each of them came forward as Kiyoshi Tanimoto introduced them, giving a little background. Then he interpreted as the girls spoke of their experiences.

Dr. Tanimoto said the girls had read about advances in plastic surgery in the United States and hoped for the miracle that would enable them to come to America for the operations that might return them, at least to a small degree, to a normal life.

I watched the girls closely as they spoke of their hopes about coming to America. There was something akin to a sense of transport in their voices. I knew I would have to be careful about creating false expectations, so I said I had no way of knowing whether what they wanted to do could be done. At any rate, I would stay in touch with Dr. Tanimoto and tell him what I learned after my return to the States.

It was almost two years before the preparations were completed.

The natural agency in the United States to handle this project, we felt, was the Hiroshima Peace Center Associates, Inc., a group of Americans interested in Hiroshima who had administered the Moral Adoptions Plan. The HPCA board agreed to sponsor the new project.

But during the first six months after our return from Japan, things went slowly—dismally so. We went to foundation after foundation, seeking money for doctors, surgeons, hospital care, home care, transportation. And foundation after foundation turned us down. One was fearful that if one of the Maidens died on the operating table the foundation would be held responsible. Another was concerned about the political views of the girls and was reluctant to furnish ammunition to some future congressional investigating committee. Still another felt that, unless all the Hiroshima victims could be cared for, it might be a mistake to do something for any single group. Any number of foundations expressed sympathy, but said their charters did not provide for mercy projects of this particular nature.

Dr. William M. Hitzig, my personal physician and friend, brought the project to the attention of the director and board of Mt. Sinai Hospital in New York, with which he was affiliated. As a result of these discussions Dr. Arthur J. Barsky, one of the nation's most prominent plastic surgeons, agreed to take charge of all operative work, assisted by his staff. The Mt. Sinai Hospital volunteered to supply operating facilities and hospital bed care free of charge. The contribution of the surgeons and hospital was both substantial and heroic, since four or five operations per patient might be necessary, and each girl might have to spend four to six months in the hospital. It would be a year before the party could return to Japan.

A special committee of the American Friends Service Committee was created to map out a program for the girls when not in the hospital. The girls were to live in American homes, share family activities and responsibilities, and receive special education or training that might be useful in making them self-sufficient on their return to Japan. Mrs. Jeanne Lewisohn, who had served as volunteer executive secretary of the Orphans project, now agreed to act as coordinator for the Maidens.

But the transportation problem held up the project for more than a year. We tried the airlines, only to run into official regulations concerning free passage. We went back to the foundations, with no greater success than before. Then Miss Janet Tobitt, one of the "moral adoptions" parents who had recently returned from a year in Japan, suggested that Mr. Kiyoshi Togasaki, resourceful president of the *Nippon Times*, English-language newspaper of Tokyo, might be persuaded to work on the transportation problem. It turned out to be an inspired idea. After exploring every approach, Mr. Togasaki arrived at a solution as ingenious as it was effective. He went to General J. E. Hull (U.S. Army, Far East Command) and asked whether the U.S. Air Force would fly the girls. After being supplied with detailed information about the project, General Hull said yes. Pan-American World Airways agreed to fly the Maidens back to Japan.

In Hiroshima, Mr. Togasaki met with Mayor Shinzo Hamai and Dr. Tanimoto, who felt that the American doctors ought to come to Hiroshima to pass on the girls being screened for the trip. They would have to rule out girls suffering from tuberculosis or other diseases that would make their coming to the United States inadvisable. Also, they believed that everything ought to be done to avoid sending any Maiden unless there was a reasonably good chance that her disfiguration might respond to surgery.

Another suggestion made by Mr. Togasaki was that two or three Japanese surgeons be permitted to accompany the party to the United States in order to study American plastic surgery techniques at first hand. Then, on their return to Japan, the surgeons could work with other sufferers.

These suggestions were readily accepted by the American committee. Both Dr. Barsky and Dr. Hitzig seemed startled when they were asked to give up a month's practice in addition to paying all their own expenses in Japan, but they agreed to undertake the trip if we would accompany them. Mt. Sinai Hospital offered full hospitality to the Japanese surgeons accompanying the Maidens.

This, then, was the way the venture finally took shape—as a nongovernmental, volunteer citizens' project to bring the girls to the United States for the finest kind of treatment that modern medical science had to offer.

The project group assembled in Tokyo in April, 1955.

News of the project had been prematurely published in Japan. Thus, weeks before we arrived in Hiroshima other Maidens had presented themselves to the local committee for consideration. By the time we arrived there was a total of forty-three. The project had been set up originally to accommodate approximately twenty.

Nor were we prepared for the fact that the project had become page one news, with the press requesting daily briefing sessions. The Japanese press was constructive and friendly, although the questions were often severe. Why were we *really* doing this in the first place? Who was putting up the money? Was there anything to the story that the United States government was secretly sponsoring and paying for the project, as a means of building good will to offset the bad impression created by the radioactive fallout on the Japanese fishermen following the now-famous test explosion the previous year? What about the rumor that the project was only a façade for a sideshow group which planned to take the girls on a coast-to-coast exhibition tour of America at a fancy admission charge?

Most of these questions, of course, were quickly and easily disposed of and were seldom repeated at later press conferences. The newspapers got behind the project and gave it strong support. But two questions persisted, and for a good reason. We didn't know the answers ourselves. One question: Why were we *really* doing this? The other: What about those who couldn't come to the United States?

The first question was difficult because the key to it was probably lodged deep within our subconscious. We searched our minds in long discussions late each night and didn't spare each other as we probed for answers. As individual citizens we no doubt felt a strong personal responsibility for the first atomic weapon to be used against human beings. Yet didn't the very nature of war place it beyond the control of the individual, whether with respect to the sufferer or the person who is inflicting the suffering? The feeling of guilt, while real enough, was not the whole answer and we knew it.

Was there something in the personal experience of each of us that might furnish a clue? One of us, it developed, had a father who was also a physician; the sacrifices made by the father in caring for people who were too poor to pay left both a strong impression on the son and a feeling of debt to his memory. Perhaps this project was a small payment on the debt. Another one of us had experienced a serious illness as a child. He had been aware that he might never reach adulthood; now, many years later, with his health completely regained, he felt his life was something of an unexpected dividend which he perhaps wished to share. The third member of the trio made no bones about the fact that a feeling of usefulness gave him his greatest satisfaction in life.

All this seemed too personal for public discussion. Finally, we told the newsmen we doubted that we knew the answer ourselves. As it concerned the Maidens, each of us happened to be in a position where we might be of some help and we were responding as best we could, simply because we wanted to. Apparently the answer registered. The question never came up again.

In attempting to find an answer to the second question we went directly to the Maidens themselves. Were we justified in starting such a project, we asked them, when we had only limited means at our disposal? Should individual citizens undertake a task such as this, in view of the fact that they would leave a large part of the problem untouched? Would it have been better to leave the matter to government? What could we say to the girls who couldn't come, either because they were medically unable to do so or because we lacked the means to take care of them? And how could we ease the burden of those who were selected, for their hearts would be heavy with the knowledge that their own selection meant that others could not go?

The answers from the Maidens were to be found in everything they did and said during the days we were in Hiroshima. They were the ones who cheered us up. We had come prepared to be lively in manner in order to lighten the strain of the medical examinations. We wanted to eliminate any aspect of competition between the girls in our dealings with them. But the girls had anticipated our apprehensions. There was nothing hesitant or pathetic about their manner. Their spirit was independent, alert, gay. The doctors didn't have to put on a professional act of being cheerful and reassuring. Within a day after meeting the girls they had caught the contagion of ease and pleasantness radiated by the Maidens.

The examinations themselves were facilitated by the local hospitals. The American Bomb Casualty Commission stood by with whatever medical resources might be necessary. The three Japanese doctors who had been selected to travel to the United States with the Maidens for the purpose of observing modern reconstructive surgical techniques were on hand to help. The Maidens sat on benches in the corridor outside the waiting room chatting happily among themselves.

On the evening before the final selections were made the Maidens went to Mr. Tanimoto's church for special services. The doctors and I were not present, but we learned later what had happened. Each of the girls had a prayer to offer. Most of the prayers had two parts. The first part was for the American doctors, that they might know no anguish for not being able to take all the girls, and that they might understand that the girls themselves understood. The second part of the prayer was that those girls who were selected would know no anguish because others would be left behind.

The following morning some additional decisions were reached besides the ones relating to the final selections. The biggest of these was that the project would not end with the group selected to go to America. We decided that once we returned to the United States we would arrange for the care of those who were left behind. This meant that American doctors would have to be sent to Hiroshima, where they would have to stay for a considerable period in order to provide treatment in this city. Dr. Barsky quietly said he was going to work personally toward this end. It developed that Dr. Hitzig had independently come to the same conclusion.

The next decision concerned Nagasaki. While the problem there was not as great as in Hiroshima, the problem did exist. A message was sent to Pearl Buck, one of the sponsoring members of the American committee, asking whether Philadelphia surgeons and hospital facilities might be available for another group of Maidens. Before the expedition left

Hiroshima Miss Buck sent word that Philadelphia was ready and willing; thus the machinery was set up for a similar project in Nagasaki.

The final decision concerned the Hiroshima Maidens themselves. Out of the forty-three girls twenty-five had passed the medical examinations. Rather than attempt to cut the list to the original twenty, it was decided to take the full twenty-five. Individual letters were written to the entire group of forty-three. The Maidens selected to make the trip were asked, though we knew this to be superfluous, to make a special effort to encourage those who were to be left behind. The Maidens who were rejected for medical reasons were given no promises, but it was made clear to them that the doctors intended to explore the possibilities of future treatment within the city.

Several weeks before the twenty-five disfigured Hiroshima Maidens arrived in the United States the Quakers in the New York area held meetings to discuss the hospitality problem. Since the surgical work would be spaced out over a period of a year or more, with only four girls in Mt. Sinai Hospital at the same time, the Quakers had agreed to provide for convalescent care, for transportation to and from the hospital, for sightseeing and entertainment, for vocational guidance in many cases, and for attending to whatever other needs the girls would have during the year.

At the Friends' Meeting House in Wilton, Connecticut, where one of the advance planning sessions took place, someone got up to oppose the whole project. He said he had lived in Japan for a number of years and was therefore in a position to offer firsthand advice. He said he did not wish to disparage the desire of the Friends to open their hearts and homes, but he felt that the sponsors of the project had very little realization, apparently, of what was ahead of them. He then presented three specific objections.

First of all, he pointed out, the Japanese girls undoubtedly would become homesick after only a few days in their new surroundings. Having been uprooted so suddenly from one civilization, they could not be expected to make the adjustment to a different world.

Second, he said, the food habits of the Japanese were so rigid that the girls could not be expected to adjust to American food.

Third, he continued, the girls would probably suspect the motives of the American families who cared for them. It was very difficult for Japanese to comprehend pure altruism, since so very little existed in Japan among people who are not tied together by family bonds.

Having made these three objections, the speaker sat down. Almost instantly one of the Friends rose to offer his home for two of the girls. He said he had never been to Japan but could not believe that an act of friendship could be as complicated or as hazardous as had just been described. Besides, he added, the girls were definitely coming to America and he didn't want the Wilton Center to throw a damper on the entire project. The Friends accepted his offer.

On May 9, 1956, the twenty-five Maidens arrived in New York. They looked uncertain and scared as they emerged from the plane on an unseasonably chilly day and huddled together at the foot of the steps. For most of them, it was the first time on foreign soil. Ahead of them was the great unknown—the surgeons, the hospitals, the strange houses. They carried their wardrobes, most of them, on their backs.

After a brief period of sight-seeing and adjustment, the girls began their appointments with the surgeons. Six weeks later, at the first of a series of summer reunion picnics held for the visitors by their "American parents," I met the Wilton Quaker who had stood up to answer the objections of the expert on Japan, and I asked him about his experiences with the Maidens.

"When the girls moved in," he said, "we looked for signs of homesickness or dissatisfaction over food or uneasiness in their general attitude toward us. The first week was too good to be true. The second week was even better. Here it is six weeks, and not a single one of the dreadful calamities that had been predicted has come to pass. We thought perhaps we had an exceptional pair; and so we checked with other friends in the metropolitan area. Almost everyone else had the same report. The girls couldn't be more cheerful or more delightful as guests. 'Guests' really isn't the word for it. They're really members of the family.

"So far no homesickness. And they love American food, especially frankfurters. We've gone sight-seeing together—to the United Nations, to the museums, and to places in New England. We've gone to concerts and baseball games. My wife and I couldn't be more grateful. I don't know how we're going to part with them."

I learned that that Quaker and his wife, in preparation for the girls' arrival, took lessons in Japanese. Then, at least once a week after the Maidens came, the parents invited a Japanese friend from a nearby town for dinner.

Almost all the "parents" remarked on the ease with which communication was possible across the language barrier. Couples with children told of the devotion between the Maidens and the infants. One of the most familiar sights at the reunion picnics was that of a Maiden with a small child in her arms.

It early became apparent that the non-medical side of the project was as important as the medical in any evaluation of the record. The girls were superb good-will ambassadors from Japan. In community after community they won the affections of all those who met them. As a group, they were not self-conscious about appearing in public, nor were they reluctant to do the things that come naturally to young Americans of the same age. They assiduously studied the English language and managed quite well when they navigated by themselves.

"If you asked me what I expect to remember most about their visit to our home," one of the Friends told me, "I should say it was the laughter they brought with them and shared with us. We had feared we might have to make a special effort to keep things from becoming too grim or restrained in the presence of disfigured persons. But these girls have a warmth about them and a gift for laughter that created an entirely different and certainly much more welcome atmosphere than the one we anticipated.

"One night, for example, after the girls had been with us for perhaps two weeks, I looked up at the clock and said to them: 'It's time for you chicks to get to bed.' Out came the dictionary. They found the word, then looked at each other incredulously for a split second before each pointed to the other and said, 'We chickens!' They started upstairs, peep-peeping and making clucking sounds. My husband joined in the game by crowing like a rooster. The girls dissolved in laughter. Two nights later we went to the movies. There appeared on the screen the inevitable Pathé-RKO rooster immediately preceding a newsreel. Immediately one of the girls pointed to the screen and called out the name of my husband. I think almost half the theater joined in the laughter."

Most of the parents spoke of these humorous episodes when talking about the girls. But they also cited something else: the Maidens' highly developed esthetic sense.

"The girls had apparently been exposed in Japan to all the usual stereotypes about the United States," one of the Quakers said. "They had heard a great deal about American materialism and gadgets. When they discover at firsthand that there is much more than this to America their joy is great. They admire the pride of Americans in their flower gardens or in the arrangement of flowers in the home. They see Americans who have hobbies or who are talented in handicrafts or knitting or dress-making or painting or who love good music as much as sports, and they are deeply pleased and impressed. When these girls return to Japan they will be able to talk about a much more accurate America than the people they see on the screen."

The relationship between the Quakers and their guests was the typical family one. The girls assisted with marketing and household chores and they shared in the family pleasures. As a whole they were remarkably free of illness. The Maidens thrived despite the emotional and physical strain of their surgical experiences. In the first six months of their stay they underwent a total of one hundred and twenty-nine operations. Dr. Barsky and his staff slowed up the pace during the summer because of the discomfort to patients in abnormally hot weather. But the schedule was soon stepped up again.

In most cases the surgery was extraordinarily complicated. It was not just a matter of cutting out the diseased part and then closing the excision. A keloid scar or a high thermal burn scar called for painstaking tissue reconstruction. The process of regeneration was long and difficult; massive skin grafting required endurance by both patient and doctor.

Following a skin-grafting operation the area receiving new skin sometimes has less lingering pain than the "donor" area from which skin has been taken. Realizing this, a "parent" who was bringing her girl to the hospital for a second operation asked to see Dr. Barsky, with a proposal she begged him to take seriously. She wanted to give her own skin for the girl and had made arrangements to stay at the hospital as long as necessary for this purpose.

Dr. Barsky said he would have given anything to accept the offer. But skin from one person cannot be permanently grafted to another, except in the case of identical twins.

On August 6, 1955, the tenth anniversary of the bombing, many of the Maidens gathered together in New York for specially arranged short-wave telephonic communication with their families in Hiroshima. Each girl took her turn in reporting her experiences in the United States. In the midst of one of the conversations a girl began to weep.

"It is not only because of my happiness that I cry," she said. "I cry because I am holding the telephone with my own hand and you cannot see it. I can move my elbow—like this—and I can move my fingers very easily."

The girls were free of the many misconceptions about plastic surgery that apparently existed in both the United States and Japan. They were told at the start that plastic surgery could not give them new faces or make them beautiful. It could work wonders in restoring facial functions —replacing eyelids that were burned away; reconstructing portions of the face such as lips that do not move properly; facilitating jaw movements and thus improving speech and mastication; removing much of the pulpy mass left by burns or radiation; liberating neck muscles which prevent a head from turning. The girls knew the value of being able to use fingers that had been bent back on their wrists or twisted out of shape, or of being able to eat without being fed, to bend one's head toward the plate, to turn it to take part in family table conversation, or to hold it erect, physically and symbolically.

Generally speaking, then, the surgical work fell into two categories. One involved direct treatment of the disfiguration; i.e., amelioration of the large facial scars. The other involved reconstruction of faces, hands, arms, or legs, replacing the destroyed surface tissue.

Shortly before one of the girls was wheeled into the operating room she asked an interpreter to give this message to Dr. Barsky. "Tell Dr. Barsky not to be worried because he cannot give me a new face," she said. "I know my scars are very, very bad and I know Dr. Barsky is worried because he thinks I may expect that I will be as I once was. I know that this is impossible; but it does not matter; something has already healed here inside."

Tomoko Nakabayashi, one of the Maidens, died in June, 1956. Her heart stopped following a surgical operation. Two previous operations on her arms had freed the restricted movements caused by injuries sustained during the atomic bombing. This third operation, for the purpose of removing some scar tissue, was one of the most minor of all that were performed on the twenty-five Maidens.

Fifteen months earlier in Hiroshima, when the girls were being selected for the trip to the United States, Tomoko's father had urged her to present herself for consideration. She had no facial disfigurement, as did most of the other Maidens, and she was reluctant to fill one of the twenty places in the quota set for the project. She yielded to her father's urging, at least to the extent of submitting herself for examination. The doctors told Tomoko they believed they might be able to restore the full use of her arms and hands. Besides, the quota was being enlarged to twenty-five; Tomoko qualified and her parents were overjoyed.

Even after the Maidens arrived in the United States, however, Tomoko Nakabayashi seemed self-conscious and uncertain. She wore long gloves to conceal the injuries to her hands and arms. And she was troubled.

"What I still don't understand," she told Helen Yokoyama, the nurse-interpreter-confidante-chaperon who had accompanied the girls from Hiroshima, "is why the Americans are doing all this. Back in Japan I was told that the Americans have a guilty feeling about dropping the atomic bomb and that this is the only reason."

Mrs. Yokoyama said that, while many Americans felt deeply about the horrors of atomic warfare, this was not the only reason for the project. They were helping the girls because they felt it was in their power to do so.

"Suppose," Helen Yokoyama said, "that some people have a philosophy of life which enables them to regard all human beings as belonging to a single family. The same love that members of a family feel for one another can be felt by these people for all others, especially for those who are terribly in need of help. Is this not possible?"

"You mean these people are helping me because they love me?"

"I believe they do," Helen replied.

"Perhaps they really do," Tomoko said. "But I am not sure that I can love them. I was brought up to believe that these people were our enemies. And the war ended for us in a way that made it difficult for that feeling to change. No; I am afraid I cannot return the love. It is difficult enough to try to accept it."

But as the months passed, Tomoko's unbending seriousness, her skepticism, and uncertainty began to change. When the girls had their reunions she appeared less reluctant to talk of the interesting things that were happening to her. And when, after her first operation, she knew that she would have the full use of her arms again, her entire outlook seemed to brighten.

Tomoko had a natural artistic flair, especially in the field of fashion design. Walter and Pauline Bishop, her American "parents," enrolled her in design courses and were delighted when school officials confirmed the fact that Tomoko had considerable talent. They said she was one of the most promising students to come to their attention in a long time. Later the Parsons School of Fashion Design offered Tomoko a scholarship that would run into 1957 and advised her to plan to pursue her studies after graduation, perhaps in Paris.

When she went into the hospital for the second operation on her arms she told Mrs. Yokoyama that she felt a totally new personality had been hidden inside her and was only now coming to life.

"I think maybe the reason I felt the way I did when I first came here was because I had never before known real happiness. And it is not difficult to love the Bishops. It is difficult not to."

The second operation was completely successful. Not only was any remaining rigidity removed but the long ridge of discolored flesh on one arm was now hardly visible. There remained an unimportant white scar on the inside of her right forearm.

The change in Tomoko brought joy to the other Maidens. Her relationships with the group were now completely relaxed and unreserved. She came to the regular reunions to share her enthusiasms instead of apprehensions. Meanwhile she had won a reputation among the girls for sound and responsible judgment. When, only a few weeks before her death, it came time for the girls to elect new officers, Tomoko was one of the two chosen as co-spokesmen.

When Tomoko came to the hospital for a routine checkup several days later, she told Mrs. Yokoyama that she felt perhaps she ought to have another operation to remove the white scar on the inside of her arm. Dr. Bernard Simon told Tomoko he would be glad to perform the minor surgery if she really desired it. She thought about it for several days and decided that she did.

The day before the operation she checked in at the hospital. She seemed somewhat pale, and when the other girls asked how she felt she admitted to some pain but insisted that nothing be said about it to anyone.

The morning of the operation she said she felt fine. The operation began early in the afternoon. At 3:45 P.M. I received a call from the hospital asking that I come immediately. Tomoko was in a respirator in the recovery room at Mt. Sinai. Through the slightly opened door I saw a battery of doctors around the long steel-and-glass tubular device in which Tomoko lay. I could see Dr. Simon, Dr. Hitzig, Dr. Fujii, Dr. Takahashi, and four or five others whose names I did not know. Among the half-dozen nurses working around the respirator I saw little Lonnie Miller, the project nurse, who was deeply loved by the girls.

Dr. Simon came outside. He said that Tomoko had stopped breathing just after the operation but that the mechanical lung of the respirator was now keeping her going. Everything that could be done for her in a great hospital was being done.

A few minutes later Dr. Hitzig came out to explain more fully. Technically, it was a case of "heart arrest under anesthesia." In such a case the surgeons have but a few minutes to open the chest wall and work directly on the heart. This they had done, massaging it until it had started its beat again, supplementing their action with a defibrillator, a device that helps electrically to activate the heart.

For almost six hours the doctors worked and kept watch over Tomoko. Nurses who were scheduled to go off duty at 4 P.M. begged to be allowed to stay. On top of the respirator was a gauge with its black arm swinging inside a narrow range. Underneath the respirator were the bellows, making it possible for Tomoko to receive the oxygen.

During these six hours there was much to think about—Tomoko herself and her parents in Hiroshima; about the effect, if the worst happened, on the surgeons who had labored through one hundred and fifteen operations so far without a single defeat; about the effect on the people of Japan, who had indicated so much responsive interest in the entire project; and, finally, about the effect on the other Maidens in the hospital and in homes throughout the metropolitan area. There were now only some twenty operations remaining. What would happen if the girl scheduled next for surgery were to decline? Would the entire project collapse? But even more insistent was the thought that kept coming back to me—that I had started in motion something that resulted in what was now happening to Tomoko.

All this time various specialists kept going in and out. Miss Miller, looking frail and fatigued, said that the heart was still beating, very irregularly, and that Tomoko's body was fighting back as hard as it could.

At seven thirty Father Gerald Keohane, of St. Francis de Sales, arrived to administer the last rites.

At twenty minutes past nine I opened the door and looked in. The bellows were still going and the black hand in the indicator was moving slightly. Dr. Simon was standing over the respirator. Then he looked up and shook his head. After another minute the indicator stopped.

Dr. Fujii came out, his arm around Dr. Barsky. Dr. Takahashi put his arms around Dr. Simon and Dr. Hitzig. I went down the hall and telephoned Walter Bishop at home. Then I sent a long cable to the parents in Hiroshima and to individuals in Japan who were cooperating in the project. Dr. Barsky, Dr. Hitzig, and Dr. Simon, with hospital officials, drew up the official statement concerning the cause of death. Helen Yokoyama went downstairs to tell the other girls.

The next morning I returned to the hospital to see the Maidens who were recuperating from their various operations. Their grief was great but so was their compassion. I had come to console them but it was they who did the consoling. And they wanted the doctors to know how deeply concerned they were for the suffering felt by them. Atsuko Yamamoto kept saying over and over that they knew it could not be helped and that we must not worry about them. Shigeko Niimoto was writing to the doctors and to the Quaker parents.

The girl whose name was next on the schedule for surgery was Masako Kanabe. Masako arrived at the hospital with her little suitcase and asked Helen Yokoyama to inform the doctors that she was ready—immediately, if they wished—to have her operation. And please tell the doctors, she said, that there wasn't a girl who didn't feel the same.

When I think back on the Maidens in America, I think of their experiences in the hospitals, but I also think of their triumphs. For example, I think of the nurses' aide graduation exercises at the Manhattan Center of the American Red Cross. Some of the girls had completed a special survey course in nursing and were now to receive their diplomas. They sat with their American "parents" radiating well-being and a sense of inner ease. They were neatly and attractively dressed: their hair and make-up were American college-girl style. Each girl walked up to receive her diploma and returned to her seat with that look so well known to parents at graduation exercises—an expression compounded both of individual achievement and satisfaction at discharging one's obligations as part of a group.

I think, too, of the farewell party given by the New York Friends Center four days before the scheduled departure for Japan. Some three hundred Friends and friends of Friends came to pay their respects to the girls. Among the Americans were the families with whom the girls had lived in communities near New York. Although most of the girls had changed homes four to six times during the year, the ties to the American families had grown strong and deep. Given their choice of things to do, most of the girls preferred to stay home as long as the family was there, too.

At the Friends Meeting House the girls heard Arnold Vaught, executive director, C. Frank Orloff, senior vice-president, and Ida Day, hospitality coordinator for the Friends, speak of their feelings about the project. A single theme ran through their talks. The purpose of this meeting, they said, was to thank the Maidens for one of the richest and most meaningful experiences of their lives.

Downstairs, at the reception following the meeting, the "parents" exchanged notes with one another about their experiences during the year. One of them told of the time her girl returned from the hospital following a second operation that freed her fingers from the contractions and deformation caused by the burns. The girl went upstairs, got a drawing pad and pencil, went outside and sketched the landscape in front of the house. In the days that followed her interest in art continued and her proficiency increased. A nationally known artist who lived nearby said the girl showed considerable promise; a scholarship was arranged at one of the country's leading art schools.

Another Quaker could speak of a similar experience. Reconstructive surgery had been successful and her girl took up drawing and painting. A scholarship was provided at a local art association. After a few months the girl did a painting that was sold on its merits at the fall sidewalk show of the Friends. The girl asked for the privilege of turning the money over to the Mt. Sinai Hospital, and the offer was gratefully accepted.

Then there was the story of another girl who was determined to learn Braille typewriting so that she might work with the blind after her return to Japan. Each of the Maidens was given a small monthly allowance for pin money. This girl had saved every cent in order to make a gift of a Braille typewriter to a Hiroshima school for the blind. She had also developed a remarkable proficiency in English, discussing with her "parents" matters such as religion in America, the structure of government in the United States, and the philosophy of a democratic society.

One of the Quakers had a friend who was a professional maker of jewelry. Twice a week she gave two of the girls lessons in ceramic jewelry making; on their return to Japan they hoped to buy a kiln and other modest equipment. Samples of their work had been sent to Hiroshima in order to ascertain the possibility of a market for it. What especially impressed the teacher was the girls' abilities in original design.

Another girl was looking forward to a job in an importing firm. Before she left Hiroshima she had been told that if she could learn to type in English she would be offered a highly responsible secretarial job on her return. Her American "parent" enrolled her in secretarial classes in the local high school. After only a month or so school authorities informed the parent that the girl had received the highest grades in typing in the class. These grades were maintained despite long absences in the hospital.

The girls experienced the feeling of acceptance and affection and of being able to develop their abilities to the utmost. The same girl who had told the surgeons early in the project not to worry about the fact that they couldn't give her a new face because "something has already healed here inside" later volunteered to forego additional surgery in order to spend more time at school. She pointed to her head. "What it knows inside will be more important than what it shows outside."

A few weeks before the first group of Maidens returned to Japan, Dr. Hitzig arranged a full day's outing for the girls and their American families, including a boat trip around the island of Manhattan, as guests of the New York City Police Department, a dinner party at a New York restaurant, and reserved seats at a night game between the Giants and the Dodges.

Baseball being as much a national pastime in Japan as it is here, the girls did not have to be briefed about what was happening on the field. When Sandy Amoros broke a tie in the fourth inning by blasting a triple against the right-field screen, the girls leaped to their feet in unrestrained joy. And as the Dodgers continued to pile up runs it almost seemed as though the universe was exploding with glee.

The few Hiroshima Maidens who favored the Giants never despaired. In the ninth inning the first two Giants went down in order. Then Don Mueller singled to left. Even before the ball was returned to the infield the Giant-supporting Maidens were on their feet.

"Here we go! Here we go!" one of them shouted.

"Yoshie," I said, "it is the ninth inning and the Giants are six runs behind."

"But there are only two outs," she sang back. "Here we go! Here we go!"

In November of that year I boarded a Pan-American Airways Clipper with the thirteen other Hiroshima Maidens who were returning to Japan after eighteen months in the United States. (One of the Maidens was still in New York, the recipient of a scholarship at the Parsons School of Fashion Design. Another had been swept off her feet by a suitor, was married, and settled in California.)

From where I sat in the rear of the cabin I could survey the entire party. I could hardly believe my eyes, for two rows of seats had been converted into a hairdressing establishment. Suzue Oshima, now a professional beautician after a full course in the United States, had set up a miniature beauty parlor with the aid of a stewardess. Her first customer was Mrs. Richard Day, representing on this homecoming trip the American Quakers with whom the girls had lived. Among those waiting in line, in addition to the girls, were Mrs. Helen Yokoyama, Miss Lonnie Miller, and Jeanne Lewisohn.

Suzue's fingers were incredibly deft; they had been twisted and limited in mobility when she first arrived at the Mt. Sinai Hospital for surgery. I was enchanted as I watched her set hair and put it in curlers, with full command of fingers and hands. The few males in the cabin were totally ignored as the females went about with their hair pinned tight to their scalps. I am certain that Pan-American Airways can report many unusual incidents in the air over the years, but I doubt that any other line in the history of aviation could boast of a long line of women waiting to have their hair set at 20,000 feet.

Suzue was returning to Hiroshima with modest capital provided by the Quaker Meeting in Fairfield, Connecticut, to help her set up an establishment of her own called the "Darien Beauty Shop," with a framed letter in the window from the Mayor of Darien wishing Suzue well and saying how proud the people of Darien were to have had her among them.

After ten operations in the United States some of Suzue's facial scars were still visible. Suzue, however, could be called disfigured no longer. She had poise, purpose, confidence. You could see it in the way she went about her work. When someone near her in the plane said something amusing, Suzue reacted with the ease of a person who knew she had a place in the world.

I turned from Suzue to look at Michiyo Zomen, whose left arm had been bent and rigid when she arrived in the United States. Now, her surgery completely successful, she reached across the aisle with her left arm to pass an American magazine to a friend. On this flight Michiyo had been writing letters in English to her American families. This meant more to her than the free movement of her left arm. In the United States she had studied English and typing, both skills much in demand in Japan, and there was a job waiting for her as clerk and secretary at the Prefectural Government in Hiroshima. Michiyo was one of nine girls who returned with American typewriters to be put to work.

Then I looked at Shigeko Niimoto who, if this group had had an official cheerleader, would have been instantly elected. She had the bounce and joyous alertness of a character out of Dickens. In many ways her disfiguration represented the most difficult challenge to the American surgeons. Much of the skin on her body that ordinarily would be used for grafts had been deeply burned. Even so, the surgeons were able to reconstruct the lower part of her face and neck and improve its contours. The skin used for the grafting and reconstruction lacked the natural color and texture of the rest of the face, but it was helped by special facial creams supplied by Lydia O'Leary of New York.

Shigeko had five operations in New York, two of which liberated her fingers. She demonstrated a most promising artistic talent and also learned enough at the hospital to want to qualify as a nurse's aide. This had been her ambition ever since she was a child when she had seen what happened when medical attention was lacking.

There was a flurry of excitement in the plane when the stewardess handed out Japanese immigration forms and the girls had to consult their passports. Emiko Takemoto took one look at her Japanese passport photograph and let out an astonished squeal. "It is someone else," she said. "They will never let me in again!"

Soon the girls were exchanging their passport pictures and exclaiming with the kind of surprise generally reserved for excursions to the attic for the purpose of being alternately delighted and horrified by old photographs. Yoshie Enokawa rushed back to show her passport photograph to Drs. Barsky and Simon, the American surgeons, and to the medical consultant of the project, Dr. Hitzig. "So much difference," she said. The other girls followed her lead, and the surgeons winked at each other over the explosions of pleasant self-discovery.

The surgeons were proud of their work, but they realized that people seeing the girls for the first time might wonder whether any surgery had been done at all. Indeed, only the night before, at the airport in Honolulu, a passer-by had inquired whether something could be done surgically to help the girls. The surgeons winced and said nothing. When they accepted the assignment eighteen months earlier they had known that people would expect miracles—and they had none to offer. But the Hiroshima Maidens understood this; they were elated by the improvement and that was what counted.

The girls knew, and didn't hesitate to talk about it, that in many ways they were not the same persons who had left Hiroshima. It wasn't merely the improvement in their facial appearances, or the full use of their arms and hands, that made the difference. There had been a creative growth in their response to life and to other people, their ability to give and take emotionally. When you looked at them they no longer seemed to blink back from a half-lit world.

The big thing was that they could circulate freely—not only physically but emotionally. They no longer felt they were cut off from the main stream, no longer awkward about the right to feel the joy and pain of others as their own. I recalled something that Shigeko Niimoto had said some months earlier. "Operations very important. But, more important, I belong to everybody. I feel also everybody belongs to me."

This confidence in being able to move easily in the great human market place was demonstrated during a stop in Tokyo, before the girls emplaned for Hiroshima. A luncheon reception for the entire party was given by the Japan-America Society, one of the most influential and cosmopolitan groups in Japan. Several hundred people attended, among them foreign correspondents, leaders in government, religion, education, industry, labor, communications. Instead of huddling together as a group, as they would have done a year earlier, the girls distributed themselves among the various tables, putting the other guests at ease and taking a gracious part in table discussion.

Following the lunch came the formal speeches. The girls designated Michiyo Zomen as their spokesman to make the appropriate acknowledgments. This was the same Michiyo Zomen who, when I first met her, was so shy she spoke in anguished whispers. Even now, as she stood in front of the microphone, I could see her trembling, and when she started to speak she did so with pained hesitation. But she held her head high and said what she felt.

She talked about the things the girls would never forget—living with American families they came to love and who had loved them; the adventure of going to school in America and being part of small community life; the care given them by the doctors.

Then she held out her arm.

"I hold out my arm to you," she said. "This is not a simple thing. It means much to me to be able to do this. For years my arm was bent like this"—and she folded it at the elbow—"and then in America they gave my arm back to me."

Again she held her arm open to the group.

"This is what you see," she continued. "What you do not see is the heart that is so full. If the heart could speak it would tell you about this feeling that we girls all now know."

Some four hours later we were in General Hull's plane en route to Hiroshima. I was sitting next to Michiyo Zomen and saw her face light up when the pilot announced we were flying over Hiroshima. You could almost feel the human electricity crackle through the plane. The returning Hiroshima Maidens eagerly pressed against the windows, each wanting to be the first to pick out the city from the air. I have no way of knowing whether we flew over the same spot that had changed the course of history eleven years earlier, or whether the girls pondered the significance of the two U.S. Air Force planes of 1945 and 1956. The girls said very little as they peered intently through the windows at the blinking lights below.

Then the plane passed beyond the city on its descent to the Iwakuni Airport forty miles away. When it rolled to a stop the door swung open and we stared at a modest portion of pandemonium. Reporters and photographers and newsreel cameramen were perched on a scaffolding at the foot of the stairs to the plane. Beyond them was a cheering throng. Here and there we could discern the faces of the Maidens who had returned to Hiroshima several months earlier. As each girl came off the plane she was eagerly grasped by relatives and friends. For fifteen minutes the rejoicing and embracing continued. In the midst of the confusion the Mayor proclaimed his welcome over the loudspeakers.

At the far side of the crowd I spotted little Yoshie Harada of the earlier contingent of Maidens. Yoshie owned the distinction of being the first girl of the group to marry. She pushed her way through the crowd, her husband in tow, then proudly introduced him. I looked at Yoshie. She had grown up since I had last seen her. She was now a young woman, and, quite obviously, a supremely happy one. She pulled at my coat so that she might whisper in my ear. "We have something to tell you," she said. "That's all right, Yoshie," I replied, after taking one look at her embarrassed young husband. "I think I know."

Each of the Americans in the party was pulled and tugged in different directions. Each girl had parents or relatives to introduce. Then, of course, there were the reunions with the first group of Maidens.

Willie Togashi, the Mayor's interpreter, told me that Mrs. Nakabayashi, whose daughter Tomoko had died during surgery, was sitting alone in the airport waiting room. We managed to work our way through the crowd to her side. For months I had tried to prepare for this meeting, planning what I would say to the parents of the girl who died while under our charge. And now, when the moment came, I lost the words. Then, just as months earlier the Nakabayashis had wired their heartfelt condolences to us even before we could write fully concerning what had happened, so now Mrs. Nakabayashi eased the pain of my awkwardness. She pressed her hands over mine and told me it was not necessary to say anything and how happy she was that we had come. I think she knew that our purpose in coming to Hiroshima was not only to escort the Maidens and to explore the surgical and medical needs of other citizens, but to pay our respects to the parents of Tomoko and to answer any questions they might have about what had happened. But in the warmth of her hands she made me understand that no explanations were needed. She apologized for the fact that Mr. Nakabayashi had not come to welcome us; he was ill, but he had asked his wife to say how grateful he was that we had arrived safely and that his every thought was for our health and well-being.

When the loudspeakers announced that the buses and cars were leaving for Hiroshima, I saw Mrs. Nakabayashi to a car provided for her by the Mayor, then rejoined the others. A long array of buses and cars had been commandeered by the city for the large number of well-wishers who wanted to greet the Maidens, and the procession started off on its two-hour ride to Hiroshima. The vehicles drove directly to the Cenotaph in Hiroshima, the memorial monument for the 230,000 people who had lost their lives in the explosion.

Hiroko Tasaka, representing the Maidens, placed a wreath under the arch.

Then the Americans went to their hotel and met briefly with the four Japanese doctors who had been brought to the U.S. to observe techniques in plastic and reconstructive surgery—Dr. Tomin Harada, Dr. Goro Ouchi, Dr. M. Fujii, and Dr. Sadam Takahashi. We reviewed our schedule for the week, giving top priorities to a visit with the Nakabayashis and to consultations with city officials and local medical authorities on a new joint Japanese-American program for survivors of the atomic bombing who required medical and surgical treatment.

A supplementary schedule was worked out to enable Mrs. Day and Miss Miller to spend considerable time with the girls and their families. We were especially anxious to help the girls make the necessary adjustments —psychologically, socially, economically. As Mrs. Day said: "It's asking a great deal of a girl who has lived in prosperous America with all its advantages and openness to go back to poverty that is the lot of the average Japanese. And think of the big difference in the customs of the two countries."

But just as our earlier fears about the difficulty of adjusting to a strange culture were quickly dispelled, so now our worries about readjustment proved to be unfounded. The girls themselves seemed to sense our apprehension, for the very next morning, when we came down to breakfast at the New Hiroshima Hotel, they were all waiting for us in the lobby—all of them dressed in their best Japanese kimonos and sandals. It was as if they were saying to us:

"You see, there is really nothing to worry about. We are back in Hiroshima and it is still home to us. This is where we belong and where we are going to stay—and it is right that it is this way."

The next night, at the same United Church of Hiroshima where three years earlier the girls and Dr. Kiyoshi Tanimoto had met us to discuss their dream about coming to the United States, they congregated again to review what had happened. In addition to the returning Maidens were most of the eighteen disfigured girls who had failed to pass the screening examinations conducted in 1955.

Hideko Hirata, whose high spirits had impressed all who knew her in the United States, got up to say, Quaker-meeting style, that there were no sharp lines or divisions in her life as the result of her experience.

"Each nation has its own advantages," she said. "In the United States we were part of a wonderful way of life and we saw and did many things different from Japan. We grew because of it. But now we are back in Japan and we see our own country with fresh eyes, and we see many advantages we never saw or understood before. And so I hope to make comparisons between the two countries. Each has its own blessings. How fortunate we are to know both."

Hiroko Tasaka, who called herself the "champion surgery girl" because she had had the largest number of operations in the United States of any of the Maidens—eleven—spoke of a visit to the Metropolitan Museum of Art in New York. She was walking from one exhibition room to another when she suddenly came upon several display cases of Japanese art.

"I was fit to burst with pride," she said. "I stood there a long time. And then some American students walked by and looked at the exhibit and seemed to like it. And I had all I could do to keep from putting my thumbs under my arms with my fingers outstretched and saying to them:

'Isn't it wonderful? That art you are looking at is from my country. And I am Japanese.'"

The girls who had been unable to come to the United States listened hungrily to the adventures of the returning Maidens. Then Misako Matsubara, one of "The Eighteen," as the girls who had stayed behind were known, stood up.

"It is such a wonderful world you have been telling us about," she said to the other Maidens. "Ever since you left we have been reading your letters and talking to your families. The wonderful picture would grow and grow. And our prayers each night got larger, too. We prayed so loud we were certain the Americans would hear us across the oceans and cause our dreams to come true. Now we look at the beautiful new dresses and coats of the girls who have come back and we see new light in their faces and we wonder if these things will ever happen to us."

It was difficult for us to say right then that the same medical reasons which prevented the Eighteen from coming to the United States in the first place still stood in the way of their dream. But the next day we asked Mr. Tanimoto to take us to visit Misako Matsubara so that we might tell her exactly what was possible. He took us to a small, dingy store front not far from the center of town. Inside was a home for blind children. Despite its obviously impoverished condition—cracked walls, poor lighting—it was clean and tidy. Misako worked here. In a small-sized room on the second floor blind tots no older than four or five played with each other by running around in circles. Every once in a while Misako would put up a deflecting hand to keep them from running into a wall. Then the children became aware of our presence and they were steered in our direction so they could kneel and bow in the most courteous Japanese fashion.

In an adjoining room a blind older girl of about twelve was practicing on a samisen, the Japanese three-stringed guitar. She was extremely talented, and Misako took pride in her accomplishment. Then we went into a small classroom where Misako pointed in awe to a new Braille typewriter, one of two brought back from the United States by Masako Wada and Keiko Kawasaki, two Maidens in the first contingent. The typewriters were working miracles in the education of the youngsters.

The tour of inspection over, we went downstairs for a frank talk with Misako. We explained that nothing was more difficult for the American doctors when they first came to Hiroshima than to be compelled to leave some girls behind. But we had all come back to assure the Eighteen that we now had the means to provide for their treatment within the city itself. Dr. Harada and his colleagues, who had gone to the United States as part of the project, would now start at once in their treatment of the Eighteen. We told Misako that all expenses, inside and outside the hospital, had been provided for.

Misako's fingers had been badly twisted and her arms badly scarred as the result of the explosion. We told her that while her hands would not be so beautiful as they once were, they could be made to function fully.

As for the experience of living with an American family and taking part in American community life, we said frankly that this would not be possible. But we told Misako that Quaker families would be happy to adopt her at a distance, would help provide such vocational training as might be useful, and would send her clothes and other things from time to time.

What we said was intended for all the Eighteen, and we wanted Misako to tell the others.

She replied that this was more than she wanted or felt she deserved. She had gone to bed with a heavy heart the night before after returning from Mr. Tanimoto's church, because she allowed herself to be carried away by wonderful visions; but she understood that some things were not to be. And what had now been told her, she said, was more than she could have wished for.

We rode back in silence from the school for the blind children, regretting that we couldn't give Misako what she had dreamed about and fully deserved. Yet some things, at least, were possible. These were carefully explored with the Mayor and with the Atomic Bomb Patients Treatment Council, a quasi-official group of local surgeons and hospital officials with the Mayor as chairman, not to be confused with the Atomic Bomb Casualty Commission, a research and investigatory group set up by the United States government for the purpose of studying the effect of atomic bomb radiation on human tissue. ABPTC could study and treat, with the emphasis on treatment. ABCC could only study, though it made the results of its examinations available to local physicians who used it as material in their own treatment.

In our meetings with the Atomic Bomb Patients Treatment Council we made it clear that we were not attempting to superimpose our ideas concerning treatment in any enlargement of the original project. We wanted to offer such cooperation as might be required and as might be within our means. One thing, however, was firm in our minds. We had made a specific commitment to the Eighteen, and we hoped that the ABPTC would be willing to consider treatment of this group as the first phase of any continuing program. We said that we were prepared to underwrite this phase with contributions left over from the original Maidens project.

The Mayor assured us that ABPTC would be willing to work at once with the Eighteen, and that a budget for this purpose was already being prepared.

We then proceeded to more difficult questions:

First, what could be done for other people in Hiroshima who needed surgical and medical treatment? How many were there? What had been happening to these cases? What was required to treat them?

Second, was there any way we could help establish plastic and reconstructive surgery in Japan on a specialized basis? Should this be done through medical schools or hospitals or both?

Concerning the first question, Dr. Tomin Harada went to the blackboard and began to write down some figures. He started with the fact that the population in Hiroshima at the time of the bombing was approximately 340,000, including military troops stationed in the city and people from nearby areas who were assisting in the construction of fire barriers. The survivors in the city numbered 98,102—meaning that considerably more than 200,000 persons had been killed.

Of the survivors, approximately 30,000 were within the area of potential radiation damage. Of these 15,037 had presented themselves to the Atomic Bomb Patients Treatment Council for examination and possible treatment. As of the present moment, ABPTC said that 1,575 of this number ought to be treated within the near future. These cases were broken down as follows:

*Radiation and internal medicine cases,* 931.

*Cases requiring plastic and reconstructive surgery,* 644.

Dr. Harada spoke frankly of the fact that ABPTC would continue to do all within its power to provide surgery and medical treatment, but additional specialists were needed. Also, the ABPTC was operating under limited means. Formerly, he continued, there had not been much enthusiasm among the Hiroshima surgeons for suggestions that American specialists be invited to join in the work. But the experience of the Japanese surgeons working with Dr. Barsky, Dr. Simon, and Dr. Kahn was so favorable that the position of ABPTC had now completely changed. There was now strong support for any surgeons who might be recruited for this purpose by Dr. Barsky and his associates.

As for the second question—the establishment of plastic and reconstructive surgery in Japan on a specialized basis—it was felt that it might be useful to have qualified Japanese surgeons come to the United States for much longer periods of time and with specific university commitments. On their return they would both teach and work in hospitals.

The sum involved for such undertakings would be considerable, as we emphasized at the time. But we promised to attempt such fund raising as might be required. The entire program would take a minimum of three years. In an effort to anticipate the kind of problems that would be involved, Dr. Barsky and Dr. Simon examined a cross section of cases requiring surgery, and Dr. Hitzig did the same with radiation cases.

One of the most heartening developments of the trip to Hiroshima was the unqualified offer of cooperation made by Dr. Robert Holmes, head of the U.S. Atomic Bomb Casualty Commission. Dr. Holmes described the work of the ABCC as well as the facilities that might be available to us in any general project for the treatment of Hiroshima survivors. This was a towering asset when the program got under way.

When I think back on all the things that happened during a busy week in Hiroshima, one picture stands out from all the rest. It is of the visit to the Nakabayashis.

The Nakabayashis lived in a small, frail house at the end of a narrow lane. They had decorated their home for our coming, concealing large cracks in the walls with freshly laundered bedsheets that lined two sides of the room. In the center of one wall they had constructed a little shrine for Tomoko, and the mourning candles were burning. There were pictures of Tomoko sent from the United States by her American Quaker parents, Walter and Pauline Bishop.

We crowded into the small front room and sat on the *tatami*. Mr. Nakabayashi had prepared a short and deeply moving speech about Tomoko and the great joy her experience in the United States had brought to her. He wept as he spoke. He was not well; a stroke several years earlier had paralyzed his right side.

Mrs. Day acknowledged his greeting and conveyed the affectionate good wishes of the Walter Bishops. She told of the love Tomoko had for them and they for her. Each of the Americans then spoke briefly.

Mrs. Nakabayashi thanked us again for coming. She apologized for her tears and for the tears of Mr. Nakabayashi.

"Please know," she said, "that our tears are not tears of grief but of gratitude."

Then Shigeko Nakabayashi, Tomoko's twenty-year-old sister, began to bring in hand-carved models of sailing ships on which Mr. and Mrs. Nakabayashi had worked for many months during every spare moment they could find. They were scale models of the Spanish galleons that took part in Columbus's voyage to the new world.

"It would make us happier than we could say if you would accept these little ships as very inadequate gifts from us," Mr. Nakabayashi said.

We left the Nakabayashis and went back to our hotel, each of us convinced, no doubt, of his own inadequacy in trying to take it all in. We had gone to offer solace for a lost life that had been entrusted to us. What we found was more than complete understanding; we found the kind of human warmth that created a sense of lasting kinship.

We drove through the streets of a city that was regenerating itself, with very little remaining evidence of the fact that eleven years earlier it had been reduced to an open smoke-filled plain. But none of the regeneration we saw around us meant more to us than the human nobility we had just found in a small house at the end of a narrow lane.

We had also learned something about the ease with which men can build bridges to each other when the strands are woven of compassion. What the Nakabayashis represented could be understood and felt everywhere.

When I returned to Hiroshima in 1964, Mayor Shinzo Hanai was back again at City Hall. We drove around a city that had seen strong change since my last visit. Wide, tree-lined boulevards dominated the area. The Exposition Building, retained as a symbol of the bombing, was still identifiable from the air but all around it were bright, sturdy, modern business buildings. Off the main streets I could see the crowded living areas and public markets. And Hiroshima's trade-mark, its fabled rivers, cut into the city like outstretched fingers pressed into sand.

Mayor Hanai said the population was now higher than it was before the bombing—close to a half million against 400,000 before August 6, 1945, when over half the population was killed. As we approached the heart of the city, I observed dozens of glass-and-concrete office buildings recently built or under construction. The air was filled with the staccato, stuttering sounds of steel riveting and ironworkers. The rising skeletons of the new buildings were covered with large colored plastic sheets, protecting construction crews against wind and rain.

The big change in the city, however, was represented not by broad avenues or modern buildings but by people. Their faces were no longer dominated by harrowing memories; they didn't walk as though out of the past. A new generation had come of age since the bombing, a busy generation with work to do and a living to make. The fact that most of the citizens in Hiroshima today are young people is the key to its personality and its psychological horizon.

The Mayor said that he now found himself preoccupied with the conventional problems of a mayor's office—social welfare services, expanding educational facilities, taxation, trade, etc. Hiroshima still had a fairly substantial population of *Hibakusha*, the term used to designate people affected by the bombing, and the Mayor had a strong concern for their needs; but his job, on the whole, was no longer predominantly that of a disaster-area administrator.

One of the milestones in the personal and psychological recovery of Hiroshima, he said, had been the passage of national legislation in 1957 providing free medical and surgical attention for all atomic-bomb survivors in need of it. Until that time virtually the entire burden had fallen on the city's own private and public medical facilities, plus such voluntary help as was made available from outside. The Hiroshima Maidens project helped to focus Japanese attention on the moral obligation to provide adequate care for survivors.

Mayor Hanai said that the consciousness of Hiroshima's place in history was still a prime fact of life but no longer an obsession. There was far less disposition than there had been ten years earlier to display or exploit personal and municipal scars. The atomic bombing, like life itself, had become matter-of-fact, and the sense of any special destiny or mission seemed to have diminished in Hiroshima.

As in four earlier visits to Hiroshima since the end of the war, I was impressed most of all with the absence of antagonism toward the United States, whether on the private or the official level.

A decade or more earlier there had been some feeling that the U.S. Atomic Bomb Casualty Commission, with a large establishment in Hiroshima, was less interested in the health of the survivors than in compiling statistics. The criticism was largely the result of ABCC policy in examining but not treating bomb victims. This policy was the result not of official indifference to the medical needs of human beings but of reluctance to interfere with the practice of Japanese medicine.

Negative feelings produced by the no-treatment policy were largely dissipated by two developments. First, ABCC was able to enlist the cooperation of the city's physicians and surgeons in working out a program under which the diagnostic reports and laboratory facilities were made available to the personal physicians of survivors. Second, the 1957 legislation providing free treatment for atomic-bomb victims gave a boost to the moral climate. In any event, ABCC had long ceased being a favorite target. The value of its work—not just to Hiroshima but to the human species as a whole—is now being increasingly recognized.

Among the major findings of ABCC so far has been the discovery of a direct connection between the nuclear explosions and a significant increase in the incidence of leukemia; evidence of a 100 per cent tumor increase in survivors within 1,500 meters of the bombing as compared to the non-exposed population; observance of "a significant loss of visual acuity" in youngsters aged seven to ten who were in the critical zone and an increase in microcephaly—smaller heads than normal with a corresponding increase in mental retardation—in children who were in embryo at the time of the explosion. These are only a few of the particularized studies carried out by ABCC with the full cooperation of the Japanese National Institute of Health.

In attempting to assess these findings one basic fact must be taken into account. The bomb dropped on Hiroshima was small, as nuclear bombs go; it contained the destructive equivalent of about 20,000 tons of TNT as against the 20 million tons of TNT in larger bombs tested later. Moreover, the radiation in the Hiroshima bomb was incidental to its blast-and-fire effect. Later bombs have been produced expressly for their radiological effects. And it is not now possible to give civilian populations assurance that, in the event of a major war, only one bomb will be dropped on each city. Another limitation in the study of Hiroshima's experience is that it doesn't tell science anything about the phenomenon of fire storms resulting from thermonuclear explosions.

Even so, the research projects of ABCC are developing a large and important body of information about human health, the benefits of which will apply to all people. Indeed, it is doubtful whether anywhere else in the world is there now being gathered more data on human health in general rather than radiation disease in particular.

Hiroshima citizens who come to ABCC for periodic examinations are aware of their important contribution to the world's supply of medical knowledge. Dr. Tomin Harada, who participated in the Hiroshima Maidens project, believes that this awareness has had a tonic effect on the outlook of many Hiroshimans.

"It is hard for anyone who has been through the bombing to believe that any good can come out of it," he said. "But the one thing the people have hoped for is that the rest of the world might learn a little from what happened here. This is happening in medicine and it gives us some satisfaction. And we are hopeful that the political lessons may be even more instructive."

In 1964, although close contact had been maintained with both the Maidens and the leaders of the orphanage program in Hiroshima, it had been almost seven years since our last visit to the city, and we were grateful for the opportunity to renew old friendships.

Soon after we arrived we were submerged in an affectionate tidal wave. Hideko Sumimura, the youngest of the Maidens and hardly more than a child herself at the time of her arrival in the United States, now met us with two babies of her own. Terue Takeda came with her three children, Yoshi Harada with two, Suzue Oshima with two. This earth contains a substantial number of wonders, but few of them can compare with a Japanese infant fully swathed in traditional Japanese dress. After a generous round of baby-bouncing and baby-kissing, we concluded that running for political office wasn't so bad as we had thought.

The term "Maidens" was now largely symbolic. Many of the girls were married, and they had a total of sixteen children. Fifteen of the twenty-five girls who made the journey to the United States were now living in Hiroshima; five were in other parts of Japan; two were living in the United States.

One of the girls, Toyoko Minowa, was an expert fashion designer and dressmaker with a small establishment of her own in Tokyo. Miss Minowa had helped train several other Maidens for careers of their own. Emiko Takemoto and Michiko Yamaoka were teaching advanced classes in design and dressmaking in Hiroshima. Yoshie Enikowa operated a small yarn and knitting shop, with occasional help from Chieko Kimura, who would have liked to spend more time at the store but had to care for her mother, who was extremely ill. Masako Wada had a job as case worker at the Hiroshima Christian Social Center and was involved in community relations work.

Suzue Oshima was still chief beautician at the beauty parlor established with the help of her American friends, but her husband and two little girls now represented primary responsibilities. Miyoko Komatsu was employed at the city hall as social worker and interpreter. Takako Hurada worked in a similar capacity for the Prefectural Government in Hiroshima. Michiko Zomen was in vocational guidance work. Atsuko Yamamoto had worked variously as a telephone operator, receptionist, and business executive. Masako Kanabe was studying ceremonial wig-making and had been asked to become the manager of a new Tokyo beauty parlor specializing in preparing young women for marriage ceremonies. (Shigeko Niimoto, who studied practical nursing in the United States, was now in Darien, Connecticut, helping to care for the distinguished photographer, Margaret Bourke-White, who was suffering from Parkinson's disease.)

It is difficult, and perhaps not too consequential, to attempt to assess the significance of the projects involving the orphans and the Maidens of Hiroshima. Comments made by two of the Maidens, however, are perhaps pertinent.

"Our problems are really good problems," Toyoko Minowa said. "They are the problems of most people. Before, our problems were mostly special problems. They were the problems that came from being apart from other people. Now they are the problems that we share with most other people —how to make a living, how to meet ordinary responsibilities, how to care for other people. It is a blessing to have such problems."

And Michiko Yamaoka said she had come to the United States to have something done about the terrible disfiguration of her face. This was done, and it made a profound difference. But she hadn't realized that something even more important was going to happen.

"I came back with a new heart. It is more important than anything physical. And it has made for me an entirely new life."

## The Ravensbrueck Lapins

One day in 1957 a tall, attractive lady came to the offices of the *Saturday Review*. She spoke to me of events my mind could not fully accept. I found it hard to believe that what she described was not a glimpse into the bowels of an imaginary hell but was part of our age and part of our world.

The human mind is capable of prodigious feats of learning and invention, but it has difficulty in sustaining painful ideas. The painful story Caroline Ferriday spoke to me about occurred during World War II. The story had been told during the Nuremberg trials, but it had been lost in the bewildering array of crimes considered by that tribunal—all the way from the planned liquidation of whole nations and peoples to individual outrages. In fact, the sheer weight and repetition of the horror expressed by Nuremberg produced a certain monotony. The news tended to trail off. As a result, some of the evidence never fully registered on the public mind in the outside world.

The story told to me by Caroline Ferriday concerned medical experimentation on human beings. Acting on specific authorization from their government, Nazi doctors during World War II carried out various forms of medical and surgical tests on concentration-camp victims. Most of the experiments were dangerous; all were performed without the consent of the victims.

In one set of experiments attempts were made to transfer encephalitis from monkeys to human beings.

In another set, legs or shoulders were amputated to see whether it was possible to transplant them from one human being to another.

Some experiments were for devising new ways of getting rid of political opponents through what was made to appear to be natural death. The intended victim was exposed to virulent germs that would produce fatal diseases within a month or so.

Other experiments had to do with producing highly efficient forms of quick death. One such technique involved the injection of gasoline directly into the veins.

Still other experiments, carried out in the name of military necessity, were concerned with the effects of high-altitude exposure. Persons were put in decompression chambers, with conditions simulated to correspond to altitudes up to 69,000 feet. By cutting open the cranium and heart of a test person, changes in the blood and brain could be observed. Between 180 and 200 victims were forced to submit to the high-altitude experiments.

Related experiments, also conducted in the name of military necessity, had to do with the effects of exposure to prolonged freezing. The object was to see how low the human temperature could be made to drop. Victims were kept in freezing water. Temperatures as low as 79.5 in the stomach and 79.7 in the rectum were recorded electrically. The medical conclusion here was that once the body temperature dropped below 82.5, treatment was fruitless. Close to 300 persons were used for these experiments.

New drugs were also tested. At the Ravensbrueck concentration camp seventy-four Polish girls were used to test the power of sulfanilimide preparations in combatting serious infections of the type that might develop from unattended battle wounds.

For this purpose the girls' legs were cut open and the bones broken or shattered. Highly potent bacilli or gangrenous materials such as glass or dirt were sealed into the wounds. Then, after the girls developed raging fevers, the sulfanilimide drugs would be used for emergency control.

The Ravensbrueck girls were also used for experiments in muscle and bone transplantation.

It was a mark of my own forgetfulness or ignorance or both that I did not know of this problem until Miss Ferriday's visit. It developed that Miss Ferriday had concerned herself for some years with deportee problems. She said that the women victims of the medical experimentation were known as Ravensbrueck Lapins. "Lapins" is the equivalent for human guinea pigs.

Some months earlier Miss Ferriday had met one of the Lapins, Mrs. Helenka Piasecka, who had left Poland in 1946 and whose husband had died in a concentration camp. Mrs. Piasecka had had the good fortune to be flown to France, where prompt treatment saved her life. Eventually she came to the United States and was now a teacher in the public schools in Cleveland.

Year after year, Mrs. Piasecka had attempted to get help for the Lapins in Poland. Above all, she had tried to initiate the kind of action in the United Nations that would bring pressure to bear on Germany. Germany had accepted its responsibility to pay compensation and pensions to thousands of concentration-camp victims. But the Ravensbrueck Lapins were overlooked.

After meeting Mrs. Piasecka, Caroline Ferriday went to work. She pursued every possibility. She attempted to get help on the diplomatic level. She sought the help of foundations. Finally, she heard of the project that had brought twenty-five disfigured girls from Hiroshima to the United States for plastic and reconstructive surgery. It occurred to her that the same volunteer group might be reconstituted in behalf of the Ravensbrueck Lapins.

Caroline Ferriday spoke calmly but eloquently about the present needs of the Lapins, about the experiments that had crippled or enfeebled many of them, and about her hope that we might be able to act in their behalf.

As I listened to her I experienced a personal problem in comprehension. The terms "surgical experimentation" and "test persons" were morally and mentally indigestible. Only after some reiteration did I begin to get down the import of what I was being told.

Inevitably, the question that came to mind was whether there was actual proof of the medical experimentation. After all, atrocity stories and war invariably march together—not always on solid ground. That night

I went to my study and took down the books and periodicals dealing with the Nuremberg trials.

It was all there. The trials had quickly established that large-scale medical experimentation had been carried out on human beings in 1942 and 1943. Nazi records, letters, and documents furnished all the proof that was necessary. The purpose of the trials was to identify the German doctors who had taken part in the experiments.

The Nazi doctors did not deny that they were involved. They sought only to disclaim personal responsibility, on the grounds that they were under orders from superiors. The Nuremberg trials concerned with medical experimentation ended on August 20, 1947. Several hundred doctors had participated in the experiments; only twenty-three had been brought to trial. Fifteen were found guilty. Of these, seven were hanged. Five received sentences of life imprisonment. Four received light prison terms. Seven were acquitted and freed. Going through these records, I came across detailed references to the experiments on young Polish women at the Ravensbrueck camp.

That night I didn't sleep too well.

The next day Miss Ferriday returned to the *Saturday Review* and deposited a bundle of papers on my desk. These consisted of case histories of each of the fifty-three survivors. Most of them had been in their teens or early twenties at the time of the experiments and were now in early middle age. Three of them were graduates of medical schools, two of dental school. Two were pharmacists. One held a chair in regional geography at a Polish university. Another was a teacher in grade school. Several of them were office workers. The majority were unable to work because of illness or debility. Almost half were unmarried.

In examining the medical records it became apparent that the ordeal of test surgery had left the women with a wide legacy of physical infirmities and diseases. Most of them now suffered from various forms of cardiac illnesses, of which chronic myocarditis was the most frequent. Osteo-mylitis, pernicious anemia, hepatitis, tuberculosis, hypertension, cystitis, rheumatism, asthma, and a wide variety of reactive neuroses—these were the other medical burdens. All this, of course, in addition to the handicap of legs from which muscles or sections of bone had been removed, making locomotion difficult and painful.

What I had seen in these records was enough to induce me to call a full meeting of the Hiroshima Maidens group. As I spoke to them about the Ravensbrueck Lapins I could almost hear the echoes of what I had said some years earlier following a trip to Hiroshima, when I first described the needs of the Maidens. In fact, as I looked around the room I could see a somewhat pained here-we-go-again expression on the faces of some of my friends. But Miss Ferriday's papers were then passed from person to person, and the impact was clearly visible as each read the case histories and looked at the photographs.

The first question that came up was: Why were these medical experiments conducted? What did the German doctors learn that could not be obtained through other means?

The answer, established by the Nuremberg trials, was: nothing. Not a single cure or research fact of practical value had been gained. The experiments had been conducted without adequate controls; indeed, the theoretical basis of most of the tests had been pseudoscientific. Dr. Andrew C. Ivy, American medical scientific consultant at Nuremberg, had declared that "the greatest of all medical tragedies was further magnified by the fact that the experiments added nothing of significance to medical knowledge."

Couldn't the doctors have refused to engage in these experiments, standing on their obligations to their profession? This, too, had been asked at the Nuremberg trials. Dr. Bernard Simon pointed out that, as a result of the actions of the Nazi doctors during World War II, the World Medical Association in 1948 enacted the first change in the 2,000-year-old Hippocratic oath. Now the new doctor is called upon to swear that he "will maintain the utmost respect for human life from the time of its conception. Even under threat, I will not use my knowledge contrary to the laws of humanity."

The meeting then considered the particular needs of the Polish ladies. The more we discussed the problem, the more uncertain we were as to how we might best help. The Polish ladies were now middle-aged, most of them. Some of them were married. Would they want to come to the United States? Even if they did, was there anything that American doctors or surgeons could do for them that could not be done for them at home, assuming the means were available?

It was for the purpose of getting as many answers as possible to these questions that the group authorized me to go to Poland. Two weeks later I was on my way.

As I approached Warsaw from the airport I was stunned by the raw evidence of bombing from the war—still starkly visible after thirteen years. Not since Berlin in 1948 had I seen so many empty shells of buildings. When I commented on this to my Polish driver, he was amazed and said I should have seen it in 1945, when the entire city was one mass of charred and smoking rubble.

We neared the heart of the city. Rising from the surrounding bleakness was a massive white skyscraper. The driver called my attention to the fact that it was some forty stories high, was called the Palace of Culture, was modeled after Moscow University, and was a gift to the Polish people from Joseph Stalin.

"Of course," he said wryly, "we paid for it."

As soon as we arrived at the Hotel Bristol and checked in, I started my telephoning. Miss Ferriday had given me the addresses of the ladies and also the names of the officials in an organization called ZBOWID, the association for concentration-camp survivors. After almost three hours of fruitless efforts to reach people by telephone, I gave up.

The next morning the American Embassy offered its assistance and helped arrange for the service of an interpreter, Mrs. Maria Frubowa, who suggested that the best way to get in touch with the Polish ladies would be to call on them.

I went over the list of Ravensbrueck Lapins and selected several names for my initial visits. The name that headed the list was that of Jadwiga Dzido-Hassa. She had been in direct correspondence with Caroline Ferriday; her letters had been crisp, clear, purposeful. Her injuries were among the most serious of the group, and she had kept a precise record of what had happened.

I took out of my brief case and reread part of the Nuremberg trials transcript relating to Jadwiga Dzido-Hassa. The prosecutor was Alexander G. Hardy, of Boston. Miss Dzido was the witness. From the transcript:

Q. Were you ever operated on in the Ravensbrueck concentration camp?
A. I was operated on in November, 1942.
Q. Now . . . will you kindly tell the Tribunal all that happened during that time?
A. That day the policewoman—camp policewoman—came with a piece of paper where my name was written down. The policewoman told us to follow her. When I asked her where we were going, she told me she didn't know. She took us to the hospital. I didn't know what was going to happen to me. It might have been an execution, transport for work, or an operation.
Dr. Oberheuser appeared and told me to undress and examined me. Then I was X-rayed. I stayed in the hospital. My dress was taken away from me. I was operated on 22 November, 1942, in the morning. A German nurse came, shaved my legs, and gave me something to drink. When I asked her what she was going to do with me, she did not give me any answer. . . .
Q. Witness, how many times were you operated on?
A. Once.
Q. When Dr. Oberheuser attended you, was she gentle in her treatment of you?
A. She was not bad.
Q. Do you remember what time your friends were called to be operated on in August of 1943?
A. Yes. In the spring of 1943 the operations were stopped. We thought we could live like that until the end of the war. On the 15th of August a policewoman came and called ten girls. When she was asked what for, she answered that we were going to be sent to work. . . . We didn't want to let our comrades out of the block. The policewoman came, and the assistants, the overseers, and with them Binz. We were driven out of the

block into the street. We stood there in line ten at a time and Binz herself read off the names of ten girls. When they refused to go because they were afraid of new operations and were not willing to undergo a new operation, she herself gave her word of honor that it was not going to be an operation and she told them to follow her.

We remained standing before the block. . . . The camp police arrived and drove our comrades out of the line. We were locked in the block. The shutters were closed. We were three days without any food and without any fresh air.

The first day the camp commandant and Binz came and made a speech. The camp commandant said that there had never been a revolt in the camp and that this revolt must be punished. She believed that we would reform and that we would never repeat it. If it were to to happen again, she had SS people with weapons.

My comrade, who knew German, answered that we were not revolting, that we didn't want to be operated on because five of us died after the operation and because six had been shot down after having suffered so much.

Then Binz replied: "Death is victory. You must suffer for it and you will never get out of the camp."

Three days later we learned that our comrades had been operated on in the bunker.

Q. Now, Witness, how many women, approximately, were operated on in Ravensbrueck?

A. At Ravensbrueck, seventy-four women were operated on. Many of them underwent many operations.

Q. Witness, were any of these victims asked to volunteer for these operations?

A. No.

Q. Do you still suffer any effects as a result of the operation?

A. Yes.

In Jadwiga Dzido-Hassa's letters to Caroline Ferriday it was clear that she considered herself among the fortunate ones. Some of the girls had been subjected to repeated experiments. Wladislawa Karolewska, for example, had six operations in rapid succession. An excerpt from Miss Karolewska's testimony at Nuremberg:

A German nurse then came and gave me an injection in the leg. After this injection I vomited and grew weak. I was then placed on a wheeled stretcher and taken to the operating room. There Dr. Schiedlausky and Dr. Rosenthal gave me a second intravenous injection, into the arm. Shortly before I saw Dr. [Fritz] Fischer leave the operating room. He was wearing surgical gloves.

I then lost consciousness and when I awoke I noticed that I was in an ordinary hospital room. . . . I noticed that my leg was in a cast from ankle to knee. The pains in the foot were very severe and I had a high fever. I also noticed that my leg was swollen from toe to hip. The pains increased more and more and the temperature rose, too, and the next day I noticed that some fluid was draining from my leg. On the third day I was placed on a wheeled stretcher and taken to the dressing room. There I again saw Dr. Fischer. He wore an operating gown and had rubber gloves on his hands. A blanket was drawn over my eyes and I did not know what was done to my leg. But I felt great pain and had the impression that something was being cut out of my leg. Present were Drs. Schiedlausky, Rosenthal, and Oberheuser. When the dressing had been changed, I was taken back to my usual hospital room. . . . Two weeks later we were all again taken to the operating room and placed on an operating table.

The dressing was removed and for the first time I again saw my own leg. The incision was so deep that I could see the bone itself. We were told that the Hohenlychen physician, Dr. Gebhardt, would come to examine us. We waited three hours for his arrival while lying on the tables. When he came a sheet was spread over our eyes. . . . Then we were taken back to our rooms. On September 8 I was sent back to the block. I could not walk. Pus flowed from my leg and I was unable to walk. In the block I stayed in bed for a week. Then I was again called to the hospital, and since I could not walk my fellow inmates carried me. In the hospital I met a few of my fellow prisoners who were there after the operation. I was sure I would now be executed. For outside the hall I saw drawn up the ambulance used by the Germans to take away persons selected for execution. We were taken to the dressing room, where Drs. Oberheuser and Schiedlausky examined our legs. We were again put to bed.

That same afternoon I was taken to the operating room and the second operation on my leg was performed. . . . I woke up in the ordinary hospital room. I felt still sharper pain and was running a temperature. The symptoms were the same. The leg was swollen and full of pus. . . .

On our way to call on Jadwiga Dzido-Hassa we passed through what had once been the Warsaw Ghetto, into which some 450,000 Polish Jews were sealed shortly after the war began. The area was leveled. A dozen or so persons survived.

Almost all the Ravensbrueck Lapins, I recalled, were Catholic. Few Jewish girls from Poland lived to tell the story of their concentration-camp ordeals.

"Don't be surprised if you have some difficulty in exchanging views with these ladies," Mrs. Frubowa said just before our car drove up to the four-story housing development where Mrs. Dzido-Hassa lived. "After all, the outside world has shown very little interest so far in what has happened to us. Germany today is the most prosperous nation in Europe, but this country, which Germany overran and razed, is still struggling to get back on its feet.

"You must understand that the last war wasn't the first time the Germans spread death through Poland. This is what our history has been full of. We love our freedom. I think we have proved that. But there is the feeling that people on the outside don't really care very much. You will probably find this feeling especially strong in the case of the ladies who suffered in the surgical experiments fifteen years ago and are still waiting for help."

We climbed the stairs to Mrs. Dzido-Hassa's apartment. An elderly lady came to the door and said that Mrs. Dzido-Hassa was working and would not be home until late that afternoon. Mrs. Frubowa and I then drove to several other addresses on our list. In each instance there was either no reply or the person we sought was not at home. We left messages and returned to the hotel.

Shortly before six that evening the telephone in the room rang to announce that two Polish ladies had arrived. When they came upstairs I was delighted to learn that one of them was Jadwiga Dzido-Hassa. She had an alert and compassionate face. There was a sadness around the eyes but her manner was gracious and cordial. I judged her to be just under forty. Apart from the fact that she walked with a slight limp, I could not have detected anything wrong with her.

The other lady, Mrs. Stanislawa Czajkowska-Bafia, of approximately the same age, was shy but gracious in manner. She was earnest without being intense. I saw no limp or other visible infirmity.

Acting on the advice of Mrs. Frubowa, I approached the subject slowly and carefully. I noticed that Mrs. Frubowa, in interpreting, was doing everything possible to win the confidence of the ladies. After I completed what I had to say, the response was slow in coming. The ladies looked at each other and seemed reluctant to speak.

Mrs. Frubowa turned to me. "I am sorry to have to tell you this, but I am afraid that it may be of no use. These ladies have used up all their hope. I don't think they believe the offer of help is true. As I told you earlier, you must understand how strange it must sound to them after all these years when someone comes from the United States and holds out his hand. I honestly don't think they believe what you say is real."

Mrs. Frubowa suggested to me that I might develop more fully my own motives. Was I doing this out of hate for the Nazis or what?

I told the truth; namely, that the accounts of medical experimentation on human beings by the Nazi doctors produced revulsion in me but not hate. After reading the Nuremberg transcripts my feeling was one of sickness and shame for being a member of the human race. It was too easy to seek catharsis by hating the Germans; the big problem was to make peace with oneself for belonging to the same species. The stain was large enough to include us all.

The ladies said that the question for them today had nothing to do with hate or revenge. What bothered them was that both the wounds and the accounts were still open. The German government had agreed to pay compensation to concentration-camp sufferers. But the Ravensbrueck victims had been ignored, despite repeated appeals. They were now getting a small amount out of the regular social welfare fund operated by the Polish government; but they would know no peace until Germany met its obligations.

"If the Germans pay us—as they are now paying others—this will not cause our serious illnesses to disappear. But it will at least relieve us of the terrible indignation we feel at the continuing discrimination. Some of us are ill, very ill, and may not live much longer. We would like to see justice done before we die. Can you possibly understand how we feel?"

Yes, one could understand. The episodes at Ravensbrueck were still unfinished business for the ladies and would remain so until an acknowledgment of responsibility was made. It would be a thin form of justice but it would be symbolic and would help close the psychic wound. One way our group might help would be to bring this matter to the attention of our own government for the purpose of making representations to the German government at Bonn. (Officially, there was no way the United States could make representations to the East German government.) Or the United States might reactivate the issue before the United Nations. In any event, if what was needed was a hot poker to prod some consciences, we could at least attempt to heat up the coals.

Next, I asked whether the ladies had any wish to come to the United States for medical or surgical treatment. I emphasized that we had no way of knowing whether this was actually possible; but we would be happy to work immediately toward that end if they wished us to do so.

Mrs. Dzido-Hassa and Mrs. Czajkowska leaned forward in their chairs as I spoke, and I thought that I could read the stirrings of hope in the sudden way they looked up, in movements of their eyes and lips. Mrs. Frubowa's own voice seemed to catch the new animation as she interpreted. Then, after a moment or two, the sparks seemed to die out.

"It sounds fine; but again I am afraid it may be very difficult," Mrs. Frubowa said. "I think the ladies are worried because they don't want the ZBOWID officials to think that they are going outside the authority of ZBOWID, which has been looking after their claims at Bonn. I ask you to understand what authority means to a people who have had the experience we have had."

We assured the ladies that ZBOWID was central in our thinking concerning any plans to help them; indeed, we had an appointment with the ZBOWID officials the next morning.

At this they brightened again. Over tea and crackers we turned from the business at hand to lighter conversation. I was happy to see that they were now relaxed. I thought, too, I could detect the fact that defeat was not altogether sovereign in their lives.

ZBOWID, the Association of Concentration Camp Survivors, was located on the second floor of a small office building on one of the busy side streets of Warsaw. We were ushered into the office of the director, Mr. Fuksiewicz, a vigorous, pleasant man who asked us to sit down at a small conference table, where we were soon joined by two other officials.

The meeting quickly established that the overriding objective was to get the German government to accept its responsibility toward these women. Numerous attempts had been made, with no success. On one occasion the German government said it would acknowledge no responsibility to political prisoners. The ladies were so designated because they had belonged to the Polish Home Army—membership in which was now a badge of high honor among the Polish people. The big legal stumbling block was that the Federal Republic of Germany had no diplomatic relations with Poland and therefore no basis for dealing with Polish citizens.

ZBOWID was now engaged in making another direct appeal to the German government; meanwhile ZBOWID sent the Lapins small monthly allowances. The Polish government was increasing its own social welfare payments, but the combined purchasing power of allowances plus payments plus salaries (for those who worked) was under twenty dollars a month.

When the discussion turned to other ways the women might be helped, the officials thought it would be an excellent idea if some of them could be brought to the United States. They felt that the combination of medical treatment and a change of atmosphere would make a big difference in their health and outlook.

In terms of reconstructive surgery, the officials weren't certain how much could be accomplished at this late date. Some cases were definitely beyond repair. They cited the case of an eighteen-year-old Polish girl who was an infant at the time she was in the concentration camp. The German doctors had used her for practice surgery. They operated on her lower digestive tract, rerouting the descending colon and establishing terminal eliminative facilities through an artificial aperture in her side, near the waist. It was doubtful whether surgery could ever restore her to normalcy.

But it was agreed, by the end of our meeting, that a committee of Polish doctors would be created to reexamine the ladies and determine which ones might be helped by treatment in the United States. Then, after this initial screening, some of the American physicians would come to Warsaw to discuss the cases with the Polish committee and to determine their own ability to improve the ladies' health.

Within a few weeks after my return to America from this trip to Warsaw, the Lapins began to realize that there might be a genuine basis for hope. It was established that Poland would grant them passports and that the American Embassy in Warsaw would issue visas. Meanwhile, clothing contributed by readers of the Saturday Review was shipped to the

Lapins. The same was true of medicine. The ladies began to hear directly from people in many part of the United States.

Something else was being contributed in substantial amounts, mainly by readers of SR—money. An article about the Lapins in the magazine had included a reference to the fact that funds would be needed. The response was electrifying in its generosity.

The next step, in September, 1958, was to send over Dr. Hitzig and his medical team. Out of the fifty-three Ravensbrueck Lapins, the names of thirty-five were put on the list of those to come to the United States. Of the eighteen who were passed over, most were either not well enough to make the trip, or had family responsibilities that could not be delegated.

Could the Lapins take heart from the kind of experience they would have in the United States? As in the case of the Hiroshima Maidens, the apprehensions of the American volunteers may have been deep but they were not long-lasting.

Of the thirty-five ladies involved in the project, twenty-seven arrived in New York in December, 1958, and the rest followed in March. In the early weeks after their arrival, a few of them had difficulty in the new environment. But most of these cases righted themselves nicely within a month or so.

Every effort was made to individualize the care of the ladies. We didn't want them to feel that our concern was primarily for the group as a whole, or that they were being given depersonalized benefits. Accordingly, it was decided to send them in units of twos and threes to different communities around the country. This was made possible through volunteer committees in Boston, Philadelphia, Baltimore, Buffalo, Birmingham, Detroit, Fall River, Cleveland, Denver, Tampa, Phoenix, Los Angeles, and San Francisco. When not actually in the hospital, the ladies lived with local families and took part in community life. They also pursued their professional interests and, if they so wished, studied English.

Few of the ladies remained in a single community. Many who spent the early part of the winter in Northern cities such as Boston or Detroit had a chance to get suntanned in Tampa or Los Angeles. Where possible, the central committee tried to utilize the unique features of a locality in determining where the ladies were to be sent. Krystyna Wilgat, for example, was interested in geology and geography. After a preliminary period in New Canaan, Connecticut, she went to Phoenix, Arizona, where the local committee arranged for special field trips and for the use of facilities at the state university. Joanna Szydlowska possessed genuine talents as sculptor, carver, and maker of jewelry. She spent most of her time in New York and California, where she could visit the museums, shops, and galleries. Another artist, Anna Zieleniec, was a talented illustrator of children's books. In California she had the kind of natural setting congenial to an artist. The ladies whose work involved medicine or science were given opportunities to study and observe as their time and energies permitted. Wladyslawa Lapinska went to Cleveland to stay with her sister, Helenka Piasecka, now an American citizen.

Most of the surgery for the project was done in Boston by Dr. Jacob Fine at the Beth Israel Hospital. Several of the operations in Boston were for the removal of neuromas caused by the surgical experiments on the legs. Detroit was exceptionally strong in psychiatric facilities available to the ladies. One of the ladies was sent to the National Jewish Hospital in Denver, which enjoys world-wide renown for its treatment of tuberculosis patients.

In the case of almost every one of the ladies extensive dental work was carried out, producing a considerable change in their appearances. Another factor contributing to their attractiveness were the new wardrobes they got in the United States. Some, in fact, were almost regally outfitted by the local committees. One of the ladies, seriously underweight when she arrived, could boast of an eighteen-pound gain in her first six months in America. Several others, somewhat overweight when they came, went on a high-protein diet and could boast of appropriate reductions. One of the youngest of the group received two marriage proposals within three months of her arrival, accepted one of them, and was married in April, 1959.

Where did the money for the project come from? The National Catholic Welfare Conference provided monthly allowances for the ladies. The Danforth Foundation and the Albert A. Lasker Foundation gave key grants. The bulk of the funds came from individual contributors, many of them SR readers.

The Polish ladies spent six months in the United States, climaxed by a cross-country sight-seeing tour in the weeks preceding their return to Poland. The members of the project's national committee arranged for the entire group to meet in San Francisco and then see America by chartered bus en route back to New York.

When the bus stopped at a little Nevada town called Las Vegas the ladies were dazzled by the bright lights and wide-open gambling casinos in the hotel lobbies. They stood at a respectful distance and observed the busy slot machines and gambling tables. Then Maria Kusmierczuk stepped forward, inserted a nickel in the cheapest machine, pulled the crank, and watched the whirling discs intently. Suddenly the machine began to emit loud, clanking, shattering noises.

"I better get out of here fast; I've broken the machine," the startled Maria exclaimed. The machine wasn't broken, just busted. Maria had hit the jackpot. "Americans are so sweet to us," she said.

As the bus rolled eastward on its way toward New York one of the ladies observed: "Such an interesting state, Texas. So large it has many towns with the same name. In the last two days I counted maybe a dozen villages with the name Tessakow or Soonakow."

Val Janta, interpreter and traveling secretary for the group, said she had failed to notice the coincidence. Within a few minutes there was an exultant cry.

"Look, quick! See the sign. We are in Tessakow again."

Mrs. Janta's attention was directed to a swinging sign at the only service station in a small town. The sign advertised "Texaco." Mrs. Janta smiled as she dispelled the confusion. Thereafter, whenever the bus passed a Texaco or Sunoco station, the Polish ladies would laughingly recall the episode.

This wasn't the first time an American sign had given the ladies some difficulty. Some weeks earlier one of them had answered a question I put to her by saying she had stayed at a fine hotel called the "Yewcah." This puzzled me until I learned that she was referring to the YWCA.

Apart from such delightful misconceptions the ladies made remarkable progress in their English studies. "Now, not you nor I will have terrible time speaking French to each other," one of them said to me. "We will speak English and only one of us will have terrible time."

Apart from observing the scenic wonders of America, the ladies had a chance on their cross-country trip to meet Americans at work and at play in small towns and large cities. "How I would like to give each of these people as much as they have given us," Joanna Szydlowska told Alexander Janta, with whom she stayed in New York.

When the chartered bus arrived in Washington the ladies discovered that they had become front-page news. The reporters from the Washington newspapers were especially interested in the question of pensions and compensation from Germany. So were a large number of senators and representatives. Senator Jacob Javits of New York was host to the ladies at a special lunch in the Senate dining room. Toastmaster of the occasion was Congressman Thaddeus M. Machrowicz, from Michigan, who had been close to the project from its inception.

After lunch the ladies visited the gallery of the Senate and observed the lawmakers in action. Then they gasped with delight when Senator Frank Carlson of Kansas, a friend of the project from the start, called the attention of the Senate to their presence. Senator Muskie, of Maine, was recognized and spoke of his own Polish ancestry. His father had come to the United States to escape tyranny. Against this background, the Ravensbrueck Lapins project had special meaning for him. "All America," he added, "has been touched by the story of the ladies."

In all, eight senators took the floor to pay their respects to the Polish ladies and to express the hope that the obstacles to recognition by the German government would be cleared away. When the ladies left the

Capitol building, one of them said that they had never before felt so confident of their cause.

When, on June 8, 1959, the ladies took off on a Pan-American Airways flight from New York on the first leg of their flight to Warsaw, they had completed the main part of the project that brought them to this country. One important piece of unfinished business remained, however. Germany had not yet agreed to extend to them the same compensation granted to concentration-camp victims from other countries. The ladies appointed me their legal representative to negotiate with Germany; as United States citizens, we did not come under Germany's ruling that it could not deal with individuals in an unrecognized country. We entered into direct discussions with German Embassy officials in Washington; they were most cordial and assured us that sympathetic consideration was being given to our request.

An interim gesture was made. At the time of the Lapins' departure for Poland, West Germany sent a check for $27,000 to the American sponsoring group as a contribution toward the medical costs of the project. The money was put in escrow pending final determination of the appeal for full compensation. We had the good fortune of obtaining the services of Mr. Benjamin Ferencz, a specialist in international law, to pursue the case directly with the German government. Several trips were made to Bonn; persistent efforts were made to clear away all the obstacles, legal and otherwise, that might be involved.

In the summer of 1961 the good news finally came that full compensation would be paid. Each of the ladies would receive between 25,000 and 40,000 DM, which would equal $18,750 to $30,000. The International Red Cross would handle the payments and help to determine the amount of compensation in each case. More than one hundred other medical experiment victims behind the Iron Curtain would enjoy the same benefits.

We went to Warsaw that summer to share the good news and to consider remaining problems. The ladies who met us at the train station were to our mind one of the most attractive and exciting groups of women we had seen anywhere in the world. They had prettied up for the occasion and were a laughing and waving company as they swept toward us on the platform.

We spent many hours together during the next few days. In most cases, the news about them was good, very good. Several had been able to obtain new housing accommodations and gloried in the privacy. One of them, an artist, had obtained important new commissions. Some of their husbands had found better jobs; one of them had recently received a doctor's degree in law. There was some bad news. Two of the ladies had not been well. Some were looking for better jobs. On the whole, however, it was a far different group from the one I had first met almost three years earlier.

There was profound satisfaction, of course, that their battle of sixteen years for recognition from Germany had been won. Not that any of them could ever be "compensated" for the years at Ravensbrueck, or the torment of the operations and the raging infections, or the long years of difficulty that followed. But at least the reality of their ordeal was no longer ignored; at least they were being included in benefits, however small or large, available to victims from other countries. Their anguished memories were not for sale, but at least the anguish did not have to be compounded.

After we discussed the yardsticks for determining payment in each case I brought up the matter of the $27,000 that had been kept in escrow pending final settlement. The $27,000 belonged to the ladies. How did they want us to give it to them—divided into equal parts or sent to the group as a whole?

Bogumila Babinska-Dobrowolska spoke up. "We have made a decision about the $27,000," she said. "We know you will have other projects. We know that always on your projects you have had to work without money. Now you will have something to start with. This will make us very happy."

It was one of the most stirring moments I have ever known, and I let the ladies know it. But I couldn't accept the money, and said so.

"We do not like to disagree with you," Bogumila said, "but our minds are quite made up. You will use the money in any way you wish. This is definite; we will not yield."

This gave me the opening I needed. Since they had just given me absolute power to do anything I wished with the money, I was now prepared to tell them of my decision. We would set aside $5,000 for a possible new project, the nature of which was to be determined on a mutual basis. Half the balance—$11,000—would be set aside as an emergency fund—whether for illness or extreme hardship—for the ladies and their families. The other half would take the form of a "Fun Fund." Because of exchange complications, it was difficult for Polish citizens to visit Paris or London or other foreign places. This fund, therefore, would be for the unabashed purpose of providing holiday opportunities abroad. It was not easy to obtain assent to this decision, but the point was carried.

In December, 1962, I dined once more in Warsaw. The ladies met me at the railroad station and made me their guest at a regal banquet in the city's leading hotel. It was four years to the day since they had arrived in the United States, and I thought back to the way they had looked then—tremulous, emotionally and physically drained. But now, as I looked around the long banquet table, the ladies were attractive, confident, radiant, full of interest in life. They spoke of things they were doing and hoped to do. They glowed when they spoke of the occasional visits to Warsaw by Americans with whom they had lived in the United States. And they made it clear that they were grateful to be able to meet their own problems without turning elsewhere for help.

"Do you know what sustained us in those days at Ravensbrueck?" one of these women had said to me in Warsaw four years earlier, on the day before their departure for the United States. "We wanted to live long enough for the world to know. We were afraid that there would be no survivors, no one left to tell. . . . The pain and the fever were bad. Far worse was the agony that came because these things could happen without anyone outside ever knowing about them."

But now Jadwiga Dzido-Hassa, the first of the Ravensbrueck Lapins I had met in Warsaw five years before, spoke to me of the psychological change in the ladies. "Why are we wealthy?" she asked. "We are wealthy because we know that whatever happens in the world we now have real friends. This is what counts. We have emotional security and it is a wonderful thing. To have people close to us gives us a feeling of warmth and well-being and we think about it and talk about it all the time."

When I asked the ladies at the dinner what they would do if they had a magic wand, the answer came back without hesitation. They said almost with one voice that what they wanted was a world free of fear, free of brutality, free of war. As Irene Backiel said: "If I had a magic wand, I would try to make all people wise enough to make a better world. With this magic wand I would abolish all frontiers, do away with all deadly devices, and introduce human beings to the real meaning of love and harmony. Nobody in this wonderful land of mine would have to worry about telling children about their murdered or tortured parents or grandparents or about death camps and destroyed cities. And people would spend their energies developing human wisdom."

# The Sixties

*Attaching labels to decades is a precarious business. History tends to resist tidy chronological compartmentalization. The problem, for example, of rehabilitation and recovery after World War II ran through the latter half of the forties and through most of the fifties. The crisis in Vietnam in the sixties cannot be considered apart from the breakup of French control in the mid-fifties. In terms of historical perspective, it is possible that the unique feature of the early sixties was the interaction of three men—Kennedy, Khrushchev, and Pope John. It would be difficult to find three men of more diverse background and character, but they were able to come together out of a common purpose, providing a new turn and thrust to world hopes—at least for a time. And then, quite suddenly, they were gone. In fact, the mid-sixties were significant for the departure of many of other key figures of the age—Churchill, Nehru, Hammarskjöld, Schweitzer, Stevenson. They left behind a glimpse of the possibilities of human intervention in world affairs. And they dramatized the fact that the greatest need of all—in the sixties as in the forties—was for a design for a workable peace, and a way of promoting justice in human affairs. The fuses were increasing in number, whether they went by the name of Laos, Vietnam, Berlin, the Congo, or the Middle East. The editorials and articles in this section deal with this extension and enlargement of the persistent problems—and also the promise, however elusive, of a safer world.*

## The Box Score Is the Thing

Someone in the party called for quiet. He had turned on the radio at the beginning of a special news announcement. The guests, about twelve in number, had come into the living room from the dinner table; they leaned forward expectantly.

The news announcer said that Mr. Khrushchev had told the Supreme Soviet that the size of the Red Army was being reduced and that a fantastic new weapon was being developed. The announcer proceeded to speculate on the nature of the weapon. He said it was probably a speedier super-missile, one that could carry several hydrogen bombs at a time, with a separate drop feature. This would enable the Soviet Union to destroy at least twice as many cities in half the time. The old Soviet ICBM, the announcer continued, required twenty-five to thirty minutes to make the journey to the farthest reaches of the United States. The new machine, he surmised, could make the trip in ten or twelve minutes.

In the general parlor conversation that followed, several members of the group saw no particular reason for apprehension. One of them pointed out that the U.S. Atlas missile was now operational. It was poised at this very moment in California for use at the flick of a switch. It contained an H-bomb in its belly. Even if it would take the Atlas a few minutes longer to reach its target than the Russian missile, and even if it could carry but a single explosive, it could wipe out any city on the face of the earth.

Someone else said he was certain that it would be only a matter of time before the United States, too, developed a missile that could carry four or five hydrogen bombs at one time, with its own separate drop feature. After discharging its last bomb, it could be made to return to the U.S.A. for another nuclear payload. Or so he surmised.

Another member of the group referred to our radar tracking stations in Greenland and elsewhere; he said that even if we had only ten minutes' notice we could probably alert several millions of people in time for them to get into underground shelters.

This led someone to say he deplored all the talk about the extermination of the human species in a nuclear war. It would be impossible to kill everybody. Enough people would be left to whom victory or defeat would greatly matter. Talk of extinction had the effect, he declared, of weakening our military posture in the world.

And so it went. I mention the conversation not because it is unusual but because it isn't. Wherever one travels in the country he can find ample interest in nuclear issues on the competitive level. But it is a little more difficult to find comparable interest in questions concerned with the hard business of preventing a nuclear war or in the problem of arms control, or in the need to develop the United Nations as a world lawmaking agency. The dominant concern seems to be less directed to moral questions—whether, for example, the nations have any right to contaminate air and water that belong to other peoples—than to questions involving supremacy or superiority.

The box score is the thing. The national ego seems to be becoming more important than the national conscience. There is more talk about "posture" than about purpose. We seem more concerned about giving a good account of ourselves in a nuclear war than about giving a good account of ourselves to the next generation.

Similarly, the argument against nuclear war is supposed somehow to lose its sting if it can be proved that some people will raise themselves from the rubble and go on with the business of living.

What is happening, of course, is that we are making our peace with lunacy. We are coping with enveloping madness by becoming part of it. We fiercely preserve all our competitive instincts, but casually relinquish our ability to reason and make essential moral judgments. We take in our stride dangerous nonsense we have no business taking in our stride. We detach ourselves from the lessons of history; this, in turn, makes it even easier to detach ourselves from a cause-and-effect approach to the future.

If a historian should be among the survivors of another war, he would have no shortage of material for his chapter on the way attitudes led to consequences. He would find it significant that the catastrophe did not overtake peoples without warning, and that almost everyone had a vivid idea that something was wrong and that the means were at hand for decimating the human race and scattering the architecture of human civilization. The historian would find it remarkable that the knowledge of all this did not produce wisdom, and that the finest communications system ever devised in human history did not produce either a basic understanding of the issues or the desire to act on them.

More than anything else, perhaps, the historian would find it appalling that even among those people who should have known better there was a curious sense of paralysis, a feeling that the individual was basically helpless and unconnected to great events and decisions. The reason this would appall the historian is that serious thinking is a force in itself. Nothing is more powerful than an individual acting out of his conscience, thus helping to bring the collective conscience to life.

—*January 30, 1960*


# It Looks Pretty on the Outside

The nation's largest city is to have a new concert hall. Plans now going forward call for the erection of a $10,600,000 palace that will probably be hailed as one of the most striking examples of architecture in the modern world. The Philharmonic Hall will be part of the mammoth new cultural community in New York City known as Lincoln Center for the Performing Arts. The estimated total cost of the Center is now $100 million.

There's just one thing wrong with the new concert hall, as Mr. Kolodin has pointed out in these pages. It is designed for posterity but not for people. It is magnificent as a structure but deficient as a place for music lovers. There aren't enough seats. The presumption must be that the planners felt the basic architectural conception would be defeated by a large seating capacity. Hence, only comparatively small audiences will be able to enjoy music in one of the most important concert halls in the world. The plans call for a capacity of about 2,500 as against 2,760 for Carnegie Hall, or 3,200 for the Royal Festival Hall in London, or 2,500 plus 1,000 standees for the Teatro Colón in Buenos Aires, or 2,800 for Milan's La Scala.

As for standees, that vertical elite of music lovers whose bank accounts may be flat but who have a soaring awareness of good music, they are out in the cold altogether. Perhaps it was believed that there was something inartistic and untidy about people breathing hard on one another as they crowded around the sides and back of an otherwise majestic auditorium. Nor do the announced plans provide a special gallery for students or people of modest means.

Even if the new concert hall were to be acclaimed as the Eighth Wonder of the World, it must be regarded as a failure if it fails to meet the dominant need of the community it must seek to serve. That need is for an auditorium acoustically excellent and large enough to accommodate a minimum of 4,000 people. If there is a reason why such a house cannot also be artistically satisfying we have not heard of it.

We mention this not only because it is important in itself but because it is unhappily symptomatic of other areas of default, minor and major. Appearance seems to be triumphing over essentials. There is a passion for the external. For at least ten years automobile designers have competed with one another in taking room away from the passengers and donating it to a rear trunk. Baggage rides in splendor, but people are cramped. The idea seems to be, not how much maximum comfort can be provided for the human frame, but how much overhang can be built onto a steel frame. Numberless new skyscrapers in the form of glass boxes have been erected of such a gross sameness as to create a massive total monotony, thus defeating the very purpose of departing from the heaviness of brick and concrete. From the outside the new structures suggest light and airiness, yet most of them have sealed-in windows, exposing the tenants to all the hazards of imperfect ventilating systems and absentee servicemen.

What has been happening, we fear, is that too many architects and designers are succumbing to the malaise of twentieth-century specialization. The scholars are publishing for scholars, the scientists are talking to scientists, the poets are writing for poets, and the architects are designing for the approbation of their fellows. We need to remind ourselves that many of the greatest works of art and scholarship have not been detached from the grand concourse of human contact and appreciation. It is not enough that an object look pretty from the outside. Does it meet the basic need set for it? If it is a building, can it be lived in? If it is a conveyance for people, does it have a place for their legs? If it is an auditorium, are there enough seats to meet the community need, and can the people see the stage and hear the sounds that come from it? Monuments are not enough. The Egyptians had the pyramids, but the Greeks had the ideas.

Even in the midst of external architectural splendor we must not forget that there is such a thing as the art of living. People have minds, bodies, appetites, needs, responses, tropisms, aspirations, expectations, apprehensions. There is nothing inartistic or demeaning about creating for this complex. The true artist enables people to experience beauty— beauty of a depth they might not experience otherwise. In this way, the artist ennobles and serves the creative spirit without which a genuine culture is impossible. Culture is not just a dialogue between specialists or critics. It involves people and the whole magical process of advancing the human situation and helping to shape the creative audience.

Curious things happen when objects come first, people second. On a front far removed from the cultural one—light-years in fact—it was learned the other day that the Americans and Russians had agreed to regard Antarctica as being out of bounds for their nuclear military activities. This is fine for penguins, but what about people who live in the populated zones? Another announcement revealed that a new pro-civilization weapon is being devised. This is a neutron bomb. It will kill people but the buildings will be unharmed. Here, then, is the ultimate monument. Man is no more but his machines are intact. All that remains is to devise a machine that can worship the memory of man, weep over his passing, and thrill to the elegance of the empty glass boxes leaning against the sky.

—*February 6, 1960*

# Education against Helplessness

In traveling around the United States, I have been made aware of a melancholy tension. The questions people ask are not related to their personal incomes or the need to find better ways to amuse themselves. They want to know how to overcome their sense of personal futility on the big issues. They have a sense of peril; they know that the fuse points of a world nuclear explosion have multiplied; they know that the giant pieces of a seeming inevitability are falling into place; and they feel impotent. In sum, the malaise is helplessness. This is the great American problem of 1960, not the steel strike or inflation or farm subsidies or TV quiz shows. The individual would like to become relevant but doesn't know where to take hold, or what to do even if he could take hold.

In the time of Pericles the answer was simple enough. If you were a citizen you went down to the Assembly and stated your case. And if you weren't a citizen you stayed on the side lines and took your chances. In the time of Jefferson, the kind of large problem that was apt to concern you could be brought before a town meeting or a state legislature. But today's world is far less cozy and outlets for concern are far less accessible. The very size of the problem creates its remoteness from the individual. He feels connected to the danger but not to the means of meeting it.

Whatever the worries of the Athenian citizen, or the citizen of the Revolutionary and Constitutional period of American history, the one problem that was not primary in his own time was human destiny. The question of human destiny may have engaged the philosophical intelligence; it was most certainly a key question in theological thought. But it was not a pressing issue for the individual citizen. Today it is the central issue to which all others are surbordinate. Yet even the individuals who recognize it as the central issue are uncertain about their own ability to become relevant, to help. The means are now at hand for purging the earth of life in human form, or, failing that, for lacerating it so severely that joy will be separated from the human heart; but the individual who wants to do something about it feels cut off and paralyzed.

There can be no more important education today than education for personal effectiveness and a sense of connection with big events. A truly educated person is one who has reasonable knowledge, if not command, of his environment, who performs those acts that are relevant to his well-being and the well-being of the people around him, who is able to think about and to anticipate the effects of causes, and who can help to control the effects by helping to deal adequately with the causes. However impressive a man's acquisition of worldly knowledge, however proficient his ability to marry theory to technique, if he cannot use his thinking ability and his skills to work for a safer and better world, his education is incomplete and he is in trouble.

Naturally, educators cannot be held responsible for a world they never made. But the problem is not any smaller because of this fact. How, therefore, do we go about educating against helplessness? What courses of study do we develop to relate a man to the making of a durable and structured peace? How do we go about establishing for the individual the relevance and urgency of what only a few years ago were regarded as ultimate issues?

With respect to the first question, it is doubtful whether just an extension of civics and citizenship courses will be enough. An individual needs instruction in the techniques of action and decision. He needs to be convinced that individuals and groups changed history in the past—and to learn how they did it. He needs an awareness of the fact that vital fractions have moved whole societies—and that the essential ingredient had something to do with the inspiration by which a man comes to recognize his own possibilities for effective action. Surely in the lives of men who have been able to harness this power there may be essential nourishment for people who are starved for purpose.

De Tocqueville concluded his study of America with the observation that "It is true that around every man a fatal circle is traced beyond which he cannot pass; but within the range of that circle he is powerful and free."

That circle is the natural arena of individual effectiveness. An individual may not be able to write legislation for the entire nation, but he can certainly make his concerns intelligible and important to the people around him. He can learn how to find essential information and how to evaluate it. He can learn how to appraise organizations and invest himself in the ones he can trust. He can communicate his concerns to the group of which he is a part. In all these respects the school need not stand aloof. It can provide the central lessons. What, after all, is a democratic civilization except a congeries of viewpoints leading up to a consensus? Not every individual may be able to have his viewpoint govern that consensus but that is part of the democratic chance. Each idea is an entry; it calls for vitality and staying power of a very high order.

One thing is certain: even the biggest idea has to have enough people behind it to give it any forward motion. The school isn't called upon to invent ideas or to take responsibility for their outcome; but it can certainly impart knowledge about the processes by which ideas move from one point to another.

Much of what is discussed here is already being done in some places. It will also be recognized, however, that the new approaches are far from being universal and that our national school system as a whole has not yet gone through the door. The fact that it is approaching the door gives rise to great expectations.

—*March 19, 1960*

# Of Death and One Man

Caryl Chessman is scheduled to die in a few days.

Many others will die during this time—perhaps hundreds of thousands throughout the world. Yet the troubled attention of a large part of humankind is fixed on this one event. The reason for it has to do with the word *scheduled.* A man may die of illness; he may die of accident; he may die of old age or starvation or heartbreak. But the idea that a man can be *scheduled* to die—this is what jabs at the collective mind and causes it pain.

National boundaries, conflicting ideologies, differences of languages and customs and cultures—all these are transcended when a natural law is violated. And the most fundamental of these natural laws is that no agency has the right to schedule another's death.

The proof, indeed, that a human society or community does exist is furnished by the near-universal assertion of conscience on this issue. Members of various European parliaments have appealed to the U.S. State Department. Belgium's Queen Mother has made a plea direct to Governor Edmund G. Brown. Throughout South America people have committed their energies and voices in the case. In Brazil alone 2 million people have put their names on a letter protesting the scheduled death.

An attempt has been made to attribute this outpouring of concern to Caryl Chessman's own publicity wiles. It is said that he has used his four books and the resultant profits to light bonfires of protest in his favor throughout the world. Certainly Chessman has succeeded in making his case visible and dramatic. But something basic is at work here that cannot be explained away just by reference to publicity techniques. What has happened is that people are responding to the most important question involved in the relationship of an individual to his society. When society decides it has the right to kill, then all the members of that society are bound up in the decision. All men are linked to the hand that pulls the final switch, and all must accept part of the responsibility.

The world-wide protest is not unnatural. What would be unnatural and frightening would be the absence of such a protest. For the great hope of the species is that there be complete freedom of movement in the moral arena, and that men make their way easily and effectively to the side of those who need help—however great the original wrong.

It is possible, too, that the world concern is a deep reflection of an anticipatory wisdom on this issue. The people of California will have the opportunity this fall to vote on the question of capital punishment. If, as seems likely, the vote will be to abolish capital punishment, and if Chessman will have died in the meantime, then the stain of the event will be great indeed.

Most of the issues in the case itself are side issues. Even so, they add to the feeling of uneasiness. Chessman has known the agony preceding death nine times. All the extreme torment that society feels justified in inflicting upon a criminal has been repeated time and again.

Another side issue concerns the technicalities involved in the original sentencing. The man committed no murder and was not accused of murder. He is accused of forcing a woman to satisfy him in an abnormal sex act. Rape in the usual connotation did not take place.

A clamor went up for the severest penalty possible. The particular sex crime did not call for the death penalty. Kidnaping, however, is a crime punishable by death. The fact that the criminal had ordered his victim to move from one parked car to another a few feet away for the purpose of carrying out his intentions was the legal technicality by which the charge of kidnaping was applied.

Another side issue concerns the fact that Chessman has continued to assert his innocence.

Still another side issue has to do with the character of the man. He has been described as impossibly egotistical, vicious, and unrepentant, all of which may be true. A similar side issue, equally irrelevant, is the contrasting statement that he has had a complete rehabilitation and is prepared to live a constructive life in society.

All these are side issues because, even if they did not exist, the central and overriding issue would lose none of its validity. That central issue is whether the proper way to deal with criminals or the mentally sick is to kill them. And the line that divides the criminal from the mentally sick is becoming thinner all the time.

The fact that other men are now under death sentence does not weaken the case for saving Chessman. He has become the ultimate symbol of a long-deferred question. It is not necessary to applaud this man or even to believe in his innocence in order to believe that the question he poses can be deferred no longer. It is necessary only to believe in two concepts. One concept is that death has nothing to do with punishment. The second concept is that society is not an abstraction but an assemblage of individuals, each of whom accepts a portion of responsibility for the acts of his group.

Governor Brown has declared he does not wish to carry out the death sentence but is compelled to do so by legal machinery. But the California Supreme Court, acting in an advisory capacity, can recommend to the Governor that the death sentence should be commuted to life imprisonment without parole. This would keep the larger question open until the people of California decide it by ballot.

World public opinion enabled Governor Brown to postpone the march to the gas chamber some weeks ago. The proper address today to which new communications should be sent is the California Supreme Court, State Building, San Francisco.

There are no technicalities in the world that cannot be cleared away with the resonant sounds of public concern. And the public is essentially the magnification of the individual.

*—April 23, 1960*

# Notes on a Changing America

Would the Golden Age of Athens have been entitled to that designation without its architectural wonders? Probably not. However towering its achievements in art, poetry, drama, and philosophy, early Greece derived a large part of its historical majesty from its consciousness of design, its awareness of the relationship of form to beauty, and its ability to translate stone into a living and enduring concept.

Today the United States is involved in a mammoth enterprise of expansion and rebuilding. And already there are claims that American civilization is in the midst of a Golden Age of its own. So far as architecture is concerned, it is reasonable to ask whether our new buildings and civic projects justify such an exalted prospect.

The verdict depends, of course, on where we look. The picture is mixed. The report is bound to be discouraging if we begin with cities such as Los Angeles, which have a random and sprawling approach to the future. Fortunately, however, cities such as Pittsburgh, Philadelphia, and Detroit seem to be looking at the problem whole and have a definite idea about where they want to go.

Pittsburgh is a good example of an architectural concept being applied to a difficult challenge. For what was once a vast pile of thick, grimy concrete at the bottom of a smoke pall has been opened up and replaced by a total architectural concept. It is clear that the designers took the trouble to ask what Pittsburgh was supposed to represent. The result is that the symbolic strength in the face of the city no longer depends on the old medieval-fortress look. The power of Pittsburgh speaks today in uncluttered, long, straight lines. Shafts of aluminum or steel climb the sky in clarity and muscular splendor. The spacing of the buildings is obviously part of a grand plan and not a blind stroke of good fortune. The new highways, bridges, and roadways in general bear some relationship to the primary purposes of transportation and the emerging form of the city itself.

What about the fabled smoke of Pittsburgh? Gone. Judging by the evidence, it's been bottled up and shipped to New York, now rapidly becoming the smokiest and perhaps smelliest city in the United States. The dirt in the air of New York may not be readily apparent at street level, but fly low over the city or look down at it from the upper stories of a very tall building and you see a densely shrouded area; you wonder how New Yorkers manage to endure such a fearsome concentration of gas, smoke, and dust. Meanwhile, the same city officials who issue proclamations against industrial smoke say very little about New York City's own incinerators, which spew out bulging mushrooms of dense smoke over a large part of Manhattan and beyond. The heavy black breath of the power companies on mid-Manhattan is a perennial victor over a clear day. All this doesn't even begin to take into account the emanations from the top sides of buildings and the backsides of cars.

New York—or any other city, for that matter—can never expect to enjoy a Golden Age with its lungs permeated with soot. The city's physical beauty, such as it is, is now largely dependent on window washers. Almost all the new buildings are encased in glass. This makes for some striking effects when the glass is clean and an appalling monotony when it is not.

New York possesses some powerful items of distinction in any national inventory of architectural assets. The United Nations building, the Lever Brothers building, the Union Carbon and Carbide building, the Seagram building, the Steuben Glass building—all these say something to the advanced esthetic sense, especially the two last-named buildings. But then there are dozens of other glass-encased structures which are uninspired and grossly imitative to the point of seeming to have originated in a bulk catalogue. The rationale behind them would appear to be that design is unimportant so long as the sheathing is made of glass with occasional metallic trim.

One of the principal points of difference between the Seagram type of building and the usual glass-fronter is that Seagram has the courage to give the public some elbow room. Instead of exploiting every inch of space for commercial purposes, Seagram provides an air of grand relief to the surrounding stone canyons with its off-sidewalk concourse, in itself a thing of beauty.

As against this—and illustrating the contradictory movements in New York—is the announced plan to install bowling alleys in the interior space of the south waiting room of Grand Central Terminal.

Next to the railroad terminal in Rome, New York's Grand Central is probably the most magnificent station in the world. Now it appears that the vaulted ceiling of the waiting room is going to come down, down, down—all the way down from its present sixty feet to within fifteen feet of the floor. According to the plan, the air space is going to be used for three floors of bowling alleys.

What Americans need—especially New Yorkers—is not less horizon in their lives but more. Already Grand Central Station at eye level has been converted to something of a bazaar, with its many commercial displays and signs. Indeed, things got so bad a few years ago that they even tried to bombard commuters and travelers with loudspeaker commercials. Fortunately, the management was shamed into abandoning its decibel attack on the public. But now comes something even worse. They're dropping the ceiling on the poor wayfarer.

What the legal rights of the public are in this situation we do not know. But we intend to find out. The *Saturday Review* has asked its lawyers to explore the possibility of a taxpayer's suit to enjoin the management of Grand Central from going through with its space squeeze. The people of New York donated the valuable land on which the railroad trains operate. They are part owners of the terminal and are entitled to be heard before it is converted into a forcing house for claustrophobia. A few feet of space above a man's head, especially in a crowded place, is little enough recognition of his need to look up now and then. A decent respect for the upturned eyes of mankind should establish some restraint upon those who cannot bear to see a single cubic inch of space remain uncluttered or unexploited. Some people would probably hang billboard signs on their grandmothers if they thought they could get away with it.

As we say, the face of America is changing. Whether these changes will become a valid part of an American Golden Age depends not just on the esthetic power of a series of individual architectural units, but on a large architectural concept. Relationships are still important. It would help, too, if a distinction could be made and maintained between the use of space and the invasion of space.

*—December 17, 1960*

# Tom Dooley and His Mission

From the inside of St. Mary's Church in Vientiane, Laos, I could see through the side door to the pocked and charred area beyond. Only a few weeks earlier the war had come this way and a dozen or more of the stilt-and-bamboo houses had burned to the ground. From outside the church, too, came the mixed sounds of the hacking coughs of old people and the staccato bragging of roosters. And at the back of the church, standing in the open doorway, were five bicycle rickshaw boys, caps in hand. They were peering over the heads of the congregation to the altar, where Father Matt Menger was offering requiem mass for Tom Dooley.

Inside the church were forty or fifty people, divided equally between Laotians and Americans or Europeans. Sitting in the front row at the right were three Laos government officials and the counselor to the U.S. Embassy. In the front two rows at the left were four mission priests, one of whom played the organ, and six white-robed nuns, who sang mass.

Father Menger spoke of Dr. Tom Dooley, his work, his beliefs, and the legacy he had left behind in Laos. He told of Dooley's last visit to St. Mary's, at 5 A.M., just before he left Vientiane for the last time. And he related events that emphasized Dooley's spunky and boyish qualities. Father Menger concluded by praising the work of MEDICO, whose name is synonymous with Dooley, and he prayed that MEDICO's work would continue and indeed expand in line with Dooley's own ideas.

After the services, people stood outside in small groups for several minutes and exchanged reminiscences. Some of them wondered whether anyone would carry on Tom Dooley's work. Others speculated on the immediate fate of the two Dooley hospital stations in Laos if they should be overrun by Pathet Lao forces in the northwest.

For the time being, at least, both hospitals are safe although they are functioning with reduced personnel. The hospital station at Muong Sing, in the remote northwest corner of Laos, only a dozen miles from the Chinese border, has already been evacuated of all American personnel. The administration of the hospital has been turned over to Dooley-trained medical attendants. The second hospital, more recently established in the western corner of Laos, is only a few miles from the Thailand border; evacuation procedures have already been worked out with the Thailand government and with the hospital staff, to be put into effect on short notice. Dr. Donald Wintrob, an American, is still at his post and has instructed Laos medical attendants in the problems of independent administration.

All this is completely consistent with Dooley's own ideas. His intention from the very start was to set up a series of medical posts and turn them over to local communities. He was aware of the stern limitations involved in medical practice by field-trained personnel. In fact, much of the criticism directed against him by members of the medical fraternity was on the grounds that the quality of such medical services was bound to be atrociously low. What these critics failed to see was that many thousands of lives could be saved even on a low level of medical training. Infant mortality in Laos is more than 50 per cent. By introducing simple hygienic procedures, Dooley was able to save countless numbers of children. Similarly, hundreds of Laotian women who might have died in childbirth have been saved because Dooley-trained midwives knew something about modern obstetrical techniques and recognized the importance of washing their hands. Dooley also trained his Laotian assistants to treat malarial victims, whose number in Laos is legion. They also are trained to make tests for tuberculosis and other local diseases and to administer the indicated drugs. Apart from this they are excellent first-aid attendants and can help avoid dangerous infections.

It is perhaps significant that many of Dooley's medical critics have not come forward with alternatives; neither have they volunteered to give up their own careers to serve at any of the local jungle stations that would be turned over to local personnel. The basic fact to keep in mind is that only one fully-qualified doctor was available for the entire population of Laos at the time Tom Dooley and his mission first came to Laos. There were, however, thousands of witch doctors who made their full contribution to the high death rate, especially among women in childbirth. The proper comparison, therefore, should be between medical attendants and witch doctors, and not between medical attendants and diploma-bearing skilled physicians. Dooley was not just a doctor. He was an educator. And he knew that the success of an educator was to be measured by his ability to teach others how to pass their knowledge along. According to such a yardstick, Dooley may well have been one of the most useful teachers of his time.

Another criticism pointed at Dooley was that he himself was rather crude in his medical techniques. Dooley generally smiled when this charge was raised.

"They accuse me of practicing nineteenth-century medicine," he would say. "They are absolutely correct. I do practice nineteenth-century medicine, and it doesn't trouble me. And when I turn over a station to Laotian personnel I am sure it will be eighteenth-century medicine. This offers at least a little service to people who are living in the fifteenth century."

Like Albert Schweitzer, whose life and work were the inspiration that propelled the young doctor in the direction of Laos, Tom Dooley had to withstand the criticism of those who were appalled by the physical appearance of his "hospital." And, like Schweitzer, he was wise enough to know that a gleaming modern hospital in the jungle would be a waste of money; it would frighten the frayed shirts off the backs of the villagers who had never before seen anything larger than a double-sized shack.

"My purpose is not to treat Americans in a marbled hospital palace in downtown Manhattan," he once said. "My purpose is to bring some help to people who wouldn't have it otherwise. And I want to use every cent I can for services and basic facilities. I certainly don't want to build a mirror image of an American hospital. I have no desire to mimic someone else's staff." On a nonmedical basis, Dooley had the book thrown at him because of his personal manner. They said he was addicted to short cuts, got in the way of established authority, was too arbitrary, was a little too flamboyant, and was not above self-advertising. The answer, if an answer is needed, is: so what? What is important about Tom Dooley is that he tried to meet the highest need of his age or any age, which is for a sense of connection between man and man. Of course he cut corners; he had to. As Schweitzer has frequently said and as Dooley himself has repeated, anyone who has a genuine desire to serve cannot expect people to roll boulders out of his way. Even if Dooley's mission in Asia were a total failure, which it is not, he would have valid claim to greatness because he made it possible for many thousands of people to be rescued from the cynicism and dry-eyed attitude that regards service in the cause of man as mawkish ostentation. Dooley was supremely relevant in a moral cause. He could have been the world's most temperamental man and this would not have detracted by the thinnest sliver from the magnificence of his ideas and his work.

Tom Dooley liked to refer to Laos as his home. "I want to get home before Christmas," he said after he had been operated on for cancer of the lung in New York in the fall of 1959. And again in November, 1960, when he collapsed in Hong Kong and had to be hospitalized, he insisted on returning to Laos to be with his staff at Christmas. He lied his way out of the Hong Kong hospital even though parts of his vertebrae had been eaten away by cancer. He got as far as Bangkok the week before Christmas and arranged for a plane to fly him to his hospital station at Ban Houei Sai. He almost made it. But the poison was now galloping through his body. For almost five days at Bangkok he could take nothing except a few sips of tomato juice. And still he insisted he was able to fly to Ban Houei Sai.

The day before Christmas, Dooley announced he was ready to go. They carried him out to the airfield but he passed out before they could get him into the small plane. And soon they took him back to Bangkok. Most of his wish was fulfilled, however. The doctors on his staff flew down to Bangkok and spent Christmas day with him. This had a tonic effect. He joked with them in a semblance of the old Dooley and teased Dr. Estelle Hughes, the only woman doctor on his staff, and in all Laos, for that matter. He said he was going home for mechanical repairs. The next day he was bundled into a Pan-American jet in which a comfortable bed had been improvised out of two seats.

The news of his death reached Laos only a few hours after it happened. Wars don't stop because one man dies, but all those who heard of Dooley paused to think about a young American doctor who had a big idea and knew how to bring it to life. There can be no question that his work here will be sustained and indeed enlarged.

*—February 4, 1961*


# Report from Laos


Vientiane, Laos.
The soldier ran down the street spraying machine-gun bullets into the shops and homes. A small white cloth pinned to his shoulder strap identified him as a member of the loyalist force.

Five minutes later the same soldier returned, working the same targets with his machine gun. This time the cloth on his shoulder identified him as a rebel fighter.

Much of the fighting in Vientiane was completely without direction or design. Men, individually or in groups, would go charging through the city on foot or in jeeps, using up their ammunition, then return to the supply depots for more. A shoulder cloth was often regarded not so much as identification as a shooting license. Some soldiers who lost their original identifying cloths would grab for the first new cloth they could find, regardless of color.

It wasn't so much a matter of armed men going berserk. Many of them had no clear idea of the side they were on, or even what the shooting was all about. They hadn't volunteered to commit themselves to one cause or the other. They were in the Laos army. There had been a bewildering series of coups and counter-coups. When part of the army broke off in one direction, the men in the ranks followed new orders. The same was true when a commander defected or when his replacement was in turn replaced. The most tangible fact to many of them was the gun in their hands.

If the men who did the shooting—wild, purposeless shooting—didn't fully understand what was happening or what they were expected to do, the people of Laos were no less stricken with confusion. I spoke to dozens of them—shop owners, bicycle rickshaw boys, small farmers, mothers—and could find very few who knew the sequence of events leading to the present situation or, indeed, the correct nature of the conflicting forces. Most of them were numb or detached. They would go about their lives as best they could, certain only that they had little connection with the big questions that shaped their future.

I wasn't in Laos long enough to find any of the answers—or even to take full inventory of the questions. One fact, however, was clear enough. Laos was the revolving door of Southeast Asia. It opened directly into China, Burma, Thailand, Cambodia, North Vietnam, and South Vietnam. What happened to Laos also affected the future of India, Ceylon, Malaya, Japan, and the Philippines. If Laos fell under Communist control or influence, the pressures on Southeast Asia would be punishingly increased.

Another prime fact was equally clear. Laos was a world fever-blister which could spread into major war. The vital interests of the United States, the Soviet Union, and Communist China came thumping together in Laos. The major powers were landlocked with their commitments. Meanwhile, many of the main elements of potential major war were beyond their control. Even though there seemed to be general recognition that Laos should not be allowed to become a nuclear torch, no one knew exactly how to put the limiting factors to work.

In fact, anyone who wants to understand the Laos situation must be prepared to put together a weird assortment of pieces spewed out over a wild landscape. History here is not a progression of events but an accumulation of tumbling paradoxes and broken facts. Indeed, if you want to get a sense of the universe unraveling, come to Laos. Complexity such as this has to be respected. And this is precisely part of the problem. There is a tendency, in dealing with Laos, to develop a desperate passion for the recognizables. Out of the pounding confusion comes a groping for familiar notions of a world divided into just two camps; a world of good and bad, with blazing lights to distinguish between the two.

But Laos won't accept such tidy conventions. It persists in retaining its elusive multiplicities. And any policy that attempts to synthesize simplicities out of the multiplicities in order to deal with them will end in frustration or defeat or both.

Six facts are central to any understanding of the situation in Laos or a policy directed to it.

The first fact is that Laos is not a nation, as the term is generally understood.

The second fact is that the people of Laos are not homogeneous, as the term is generally understood.

The third fact is that Laos doesn't have a recorded history, as the term is generally understood.

The fourth fact is that Laos is not a democratic society, as the term is generally understood.

The fifth fact is that the fighting in Laos is not primarily a civil war, as the term is generally understood.

The sixth fact is that there are now no means for terminating hostilities, as the term is generally understood.

Begin with Fact Number One. Laos, basically, is three kingdoms. It was part of French Indo-China before World War II, achieving only nominal unity as a French protectorate. The French were never involved in the affairs of Laos in the same sense as were the British in India. They built a few roads, trained a handful of civil servants, established a skeletonized public service, and that was about it. They undertook very little development of natural resources. Their stake in Laos was more geographic than economic or political.

At the end of World War II, France sought to re-establish its hold over Indo-China. But independence movements in the various units of Indo-China—particularly in Vietnam—made this impossible. The independence movement in Laos never assumed the force or unity that it did in neighboring Vietnam, but it profited from what was happening in Vietnam just the same. The Geneva agreements ending the war in Vietnam also brought to an end whatever lingering control the French had in the other units of Indo-China, Laos included.

The strategic and geographic importance of Laos did not cease with its independence. Far from it; it just meant that someone else would have to worry about Laos. That someone was the United States. This part of the story we save for later.

Here we consider Fact Number Two, which is that Laos is not a homogeneous society, as the term is generally understood. Native Lao account for only 50 per cent of the population. They are originally of varied Thai stock. The Thais of Laos today are divided according to Black Thai, White Thai, and Red Thai. Almost totally separate are the mountain tribes, whose customs and habits have changed very little in the past two thousand years. Among these primitive tribes are the Kha, who migrated from Indonesia; the Meo, of Mongoloid origin; and the Lolo and Muong, who are believed to have come from China. In addition, there are mixed strains with origins in Malaya or Burma or India. In fact, a large part of Laos shows even stronger cultural relationships with India than with China.

In any event, there is no sense of ethnic unity and very little sense of nation. Loyalty to the tribe or the local grouping generally comes first. Some of the mountain tribes are not only cut off completely from the outside world; they are hardly aware of the existence of other tribes less than fifty miles away. Communications are nonexistent in the modern sense; they are primarily a matter of a tongue and foot.

This brings us to Fact Number Three, which is that Laos has no recorded history, as the term is generally understood. There is no indication of a written language among the early migrants. Such oral history as exists is largely mythological. There is the legend, for example, that the first settler of Laos arrived with two wives on a divine mission. He plunged a hot iron into a pumpkin and out poured all the people and things that go to make up a country. In due course, the settler had seven sons, each of whom went to a different part of the country to found a kingdom. Thus, according to legend, began the royal kingdoms.

Along about the thirteenth century factual evidence began to accumulate. Writing skills, showing strong Indian influence, were supposed to have been developed at this time. There are sparse accounts of fratricidal wars among the original seven kingdoms.

By the end of the eighteenth century the seven kingdoms had been reduced to three. The colonial powers of Europe began to take an interest in Asia about this time, but Laos, landlocked and remote, managed to elude their interest. Not until 1883 did the French become involved in Laos, and then only in connection with their larger concern with Indo-China. By 1904 France had established its protectorate over Laos, consolidating the monarchies.

Even under France, most of Laos was totally devoid of contact with the outside world. When World War II came and Japan replaced France as the outside controlling power, countless thousands of mountain tribesmen were unaware of the fact—or even that France had been there in the first place. They continued to live as they had done for almost two thousand years.

At the end of World War II, the independence movement spread through Indo-China. It was not until 1953, however, that a treaty was signed with France under which the Kingdom of Laos received full autonomy and national sovereignty. French supervision of government departments and civil services was completely withdrawn. The little monarchy was now completely on its own.

We come now to Fact Number Four, which is that Laos is not a democracy, as the term is generally understood. Laos has a constitution under which the king holds ultimate power. Universal suffrage is assured but near-universal illiteracy slows up the democratic process. Moreover, the various tribes take a keener interest in local feuds than in national affairs. A national assembly of fifty-nine members makes the laws, but only a portion of the population ever hears of them. The Prime Minister is the operating head of government, appointed by the king. In turn, the PM appoints a cabinet which the asembly must approve.

Some ten political parties vie for public favor, the most important of them being the Rally of the Lao People. The RLP is a consolidation of several other parties and still reflects the separatist psychology that went into it.

The Pathet Lao is a political force without being a political party. It is Communist or pro-Communist in most of its leadership, though not necessarily in membership. It has no representation in the National Assembly, although various schemes aiming at national unity or at least at coalition have been made in that direction.

The Pathet Lao emerged as a powerful factor in the affairs of Laos during the struggle between the French and the Vietnamese. Operating in the north in close proximity to Vietnam, the Pathet Lao drew both material and ideological support from over the border. By 1953 the Pathet Lao arrogated a "government" to itself in the northern area of Laos and began to extend its dominion and influence. Fighting between the PL and government forces was far more limited than between France and Viet Minh but it threatened to dislocate the country nonetheless.

When the war between France and Vietnam was ended by the Geneva Agreements of 1954, the fighting between the Laos monarchy and the PL was halted as well. The purpose of the Geneva Agreements was to bring peace to all Indo-China. Generally, the agreements sought to recognize the military and political realities as of July, 1954, when the fighting stopped. Vietnam was formally divided, north and south. In Laos, the Pathet Lao held on to its two provinces in the north, Phong Saly and Houa Phans. However, the Geneva Agreements called for general elections in 1955 for the purpose of reintegrating the two provinces.

Another key provision of the Geneva Agreements specified that the shipment of arms by outside powers into Indo-China was to cease.

This sets the stage for Fact Number Five, which is that the present conflict is not a civil war, as the term is generally understood.

A civil war is usually a domestic conflict involving two contending forces. It is possible to identify at least four principal domestic factions in the current struggle. Moreover, five major powers—the United States, France, Great Britain, the Soviet Union, and Communist China—feel directly concerned by the events in Laos and are trying to shape them. Among the smaller nations, North Vietnam, South Vietnam, and Thailand are involved.

The principal domestic factions involved in the civil war are as follows:

1. The government organized by Prime Minister Souvanna Phouma—moderate, neutralist. No longer recognized by the United States or King Sisavong Vong. Attacked in September, 1960, by:

2. General Phoumi Nosavan, usually referred to as right-wing leader. Now officially recognized by King and strongly supported and supplied by USA. Opposed by:

3. Captain Kong Le, the most prominent military leader among those now battling General Phoumi, is an ardent nationalist who formerly served under Prime Minister Souvanna. Now identified with:

4. The pro-Communist Pathet Lao, highly unified and disciplined political and military force, which in turn receives North Vietnam arms and supplies, a large part of which is Russian in origin.

These factions didn't spring into being overnight. Behind them is a long background of national political instability and upheaval. Following the Geneva Agreements of 1954, Laos experienced wave after wave of change in government. These changes didn't affect the royalty: Laos remained a kingdom. Nor did the changes, up to a few months ago, produce serious violence, even though many of them took the form of *coups d'état*. What generally happened was that someone connected with the army would install himself and his staff in the government offices. The existing officials, finding their posts occupied and having no immediate prospect of throwing the rascals out, would generally withdraw and await a more propitious moment for a counter-coup of re-investiture. The King would be notified of the change and in due course would accord recognition.

Recognition by the United States was also essential as a practical matter; ever since 1955 the United States has substantially underwritten the government of Laos. Indeed, the United States has directly paid the salaries of the entire Laos army most of the time since 1955, in addition to training officers and furnishing uniforms and weapons. It was charged that this was a violation of the clause in the Geneva Agreements of 1954 prohibiting shipments of military equipment into Laos, or military intervention in general. The United States reply was that it had been legitimately requested by the Laos government to assist it in its internal security problem, which was not inconsistent with the Geneva Agreements.

Be that as it may, the United States was the main source of support for the government of Laos, through the various coups and changes since 1955. Altogether, the United States has spent $325 million in that enterprise, all but approximately 20 per cent of which has gone into military spending. On the non-military side, the U.S. program initiated or supported special projects in the fields of public health, education, resource and industrial development, agricultural improvement, and public works. Not all the projects have had high visibility: some were of a long-range nature in which potential benefits might not be apparent for many years to come.

Inevitably, a substantial portion of the money allocated to Laos was spent by the Laos government itself. American officials in the area today make no bones about their dissatisfaction with the way these sums were handled by the Laos government or its personnel. Indeed, accusations of wholesale corruption and dishonesty in the use of American funds have figured largely in some of the government coups. One effect, of course, was to weaken the base of public support for our program. If what the United States was doing was predominantly identified with failure or corruption, even indirectly, our presence in Laos was bound to be resented.

In terms of integrity and stability, it is possible that none of the many governments that existed in Laos during the past five years had more to commend it than the government of Prime Minister Souvanna Phouma. Souvanna was a moderate who believed in the fullest measure of Laos independence at the earliest feasible date. He was a neutral in this sense. He was opposed to Communist inroads, whether on the national or political level. He successfully resisted pressure on his government to recognize Communist China. At the same time, he was rather independent in his dealings with the United States.

British and French officials in and near Laos welcomed the neutralist stance of Souvanna Phouma. They believed it was far and away the best the West could expect under the circumstances and that we were lucky to have a government opposed to Communist incursions even though it meant we ourselves might be stung occasionally by the policy of independence. Another fact that weighed heavily in the thinking of the British and French was that they wanted to avoid a situation in which Laos might become another Korea. They were convinced that Communist China would not intervene against the moderately pro-Western government of Souvanna Phouma, even though Souvanna was not kindly disposed to communism in general or the People's Republic of China in particular. But they felt the Chinese could not tolerate, on security grounds alone, a blatantly pro-Western and anti-Chinese government in Laos.

The United States was caught in a crossfire of conflicting pressures. South Vietnam and Thailand were pushing us in exactly the opposite direction from the British and French. The South Vietnamese and the Thais wanted no ambiguity about the complexion or nature of the Laos government. They wanted the most powerful anti-Communist government they could get. Since Thailand was the hub of the Southeast Asia Treaty Organization, which figures so largely in American global strategy, the United States had to be careful about antagonizing its regional friends.

This conflict of interests came to a head late last summer after several months of political crisis in Laos. Laos General Phoumi Nosavan, son-in-law of the Prime Minister of Thailand, put in a direct bid for United States support. He promised decisive action in coping with the Pathet Lao in the north. Whether or not he got the assurances he was looking for from the Americans, he moved with force against the Souvanna Phouma government. The civil war was on.

Both General Phoumi Nosavan and Souvanna turned to the United States for help. Neither could have carried on the fight for very long without us. The United States decided to help both. In fact, the United States was in the curious position of furnishing the payroll for both armies. We would send the money to a central paymaster each payday and the civil war would be suspended in the particular location while emissaries from both Souvanna and Phoumi collected their respective allotments.

Then, for a period of ten days last October, we paid neither side. When we resumed, the bulk of the payments went to Phoumi Nosavan. Souvanna struggled to hold his government together against the combination of our dwindling support, the defections of some of his ministers, and the dramatic emergence of Captain Kong Le as a leader of the anti-Phoumi Nosavan forces. This time Souvanna made it clear that if we wouldn't help him save his government, he would turn to the Soviet Union Significantly, he didn't say he would turn to Communist China, whose armed presence in Laos under any circumstances he didn't want.

Whether or not the United States thought Souvanna was bluffing, he didn't get the help he sought. Souvanna made good his ultimatum. He called upon the Soviet Union for help. Soon thereafter the help arrived— at first kerosene, then guns. The arms were flown into Vientiane in clearly marked Russian planes. The Russians saw no reason to hide what they were doing. They were sending help to a government the United States itself had regarded as the legitimate governing body in Laos. The United States had formerly justified its military aid to the Souvanna government, despite the 1954 Geneva Agreements prohibiting arms shipments, on the grounds that it was meeting the proper request of a legitimate government. Now the Soviet Union blandly gave the same reason, almost word for word.

Meanwhile, the British and French felt that our failure to support Souvanna had opened the door to the Russians, who didn't hesitate to come in. Again our Western allies stressed their position, which is that the interests of the West would best be served by an independent, strong, neutralist government in Laos. They didn't seem to feel that Phoumi had enough popular support to govern effectively.

In any event, the civil war broke wide open. The fighting in Vientiane that took place last December was only one of a series of somewhat disconnected military actions. When Captain Kong Le tried to capture Vientiane, he met resistance from some ex-Souvanna forces and soldiers now under General Phoumi Nosavan. To say the least, the situation was confusing. All factions wore American uniforms. Hence the need for the white and red arm bands. All this went into the making of a wild and chaotic week or so in Vientiane. One hundred people were killed.

In due course Captain Kong Le's forces retreated from Vientiane and apparently fanned out in the countryside north of the city. There are no front lines in the common sense of the term. In fact, the country is not divided north and south between two well-coordinated fighting forces in battle array. Some of the battles that figure in the news might not involve more than eighty or ninety men on both sides. Pockets of guerrillas account for a large part of the total action.

Hard news is difficult to come by. I attended a Laos government press briefing session. The officer in charge told of a major intervention by troops from North Vietnam. When asked if there was definite proof of such intervention, he replied that government forces had come upon thousands of chopsticks and the carcasses of dead dogs. Since the Lao don't eat with chopsticks and since they eschew dogs as food, the evidence of North Vietnam intervention was clear.

Regardless of the somewhat meandering quality of both the official news and the war itself, one thing is clear enough. Most of the main factors that could lead to a major world war are bunched together in Laos; some of these factors are getting beyond control.

This brings us to the sixth and final fact about Laos, which is that there are now no specific means for terminating hostilities, as the term is generally understood.

Many key American officials now in the area take a common-sense approach to the Laos situation. Privately, they agree with the British that the very best we can expect—if we are lucky enough to get it—is the kind of neutralist government that we had when Souvanna was in power. This time, however, it would not be reasonable to expect that the United States could have even the modest amount of influence it once had with Souvanna.

I was encouraged, in talking to these American officials, to find a present determination to do everything possible to limit the conflict. There is genuine realization of the danger that Laos could become another Korea, presenting military difficulties for the United States that would make

Korea seem like a mild undertaking by comparison. And there is the gravest apprehension about the possible involvement of Communist China.

So far, Communist China has seen fit not to jump into the Laos crisis. The British interpretation of China's response to the varying situation in Laos so far has been confirmed by the events.

One combustible situation affecting Communist China hasn't yet hit the headlines but might do so at any moment. What makes this particular situation all the more precarious is that it also involves Nationalist China.

At the end of China's Civil War part of Generalissimo Chiang Kai-shek's Nationalist Army mysteriously disappeared. Some time later it became known that the men had taken refuge in Burma. There were some difficulties with the Burmese government at the time; according to some of the reports, Burma insisted that most of the troops evacuate. Half the force of 12,000 men (many with families) left for Formosa; the others remained and dug in.

There were some vague reports a few weeks ago that fighting had broken out between Burmese forces and the remnants of the Chinese Nationalists. Then I happened to learn that several wounded Nationalist soldiers escaped over the border to Laos, where they turned up at the Tom Dooley hospital. They reported violent fighting in Burma involving several thousand men. When asked how the Chinese Nationalists were being supplied, they replied that much of it had been coming in regularly by air lift via the southeastern route.

Obviously, not enough is yet known about the nature and scope of the fighting between the Burmese and the Chinese Nationalists to assess its explosive significance. However, if the fact of an air lift is true, the hazardous nature of such a project is clear enough, both because of the purpose it serves and the difficulty of threading an air needle to avoid flying over Chinese territory.

One specific fact of hope in the general situation is the clear evidence that the United States now is attempting to apply the brakes in Laos. Brigadier General Andrew J. Boyle, new head of the American military mission to Laos, has stressed the fact that we are strictly limiting the kind and quantity of military equipment now being furnished to Laos government forces. The one thing we want to avoid, he emphasized, is getting into an escalator arms competition with the Russians that would lead to each side stepping up the potency and numbers of weapons. Certainly there is no intention to introduce small tactical nuclear weapons, much less large ones.

If the supply competition with the Russians can be brought under control—and it may well be the only place that affords any handle, however slippery—then there is a glimmer of possibility that some military stabilization may be effected. It is inevitable that the UN or some international commission, or both, would have to figure prominently in such an interim solution.

Obviously, an interim solution isn't going to be good enough, as the Geneva Agreements of 1954 proved. The major nations, including the United States, didn't feel that their vital security interests in the area were adequately served by those agreements and proceeded to take unilateral measures. This illuminates the fundamental contradiction in our foreign policy. Our security interests are interrelated and world wide but our peace-making measures are piecemeal and regional. We put more into NATO and SEATO than we do into the United Nations, yet both NATO and SEATO have been unable to provide regional security precisely because there is as yet no real foundation for world security. We find ourselves whipsawed from one crisis zone to the other in the world, straining our resources for each one, but not addressing ourselves adequately to the central need for a world organization that alone can deal with the causes.

Finally, our policy toward Laos hasn't sufficiently taken into account the fact that the people of Laos happen to own their own country. The big problem is how to give it back to them. The Laotians may be illiterate and backward, they may be living in the third century, but this is their right. In any sane world, which is to say a world under law, the people of Laos could go their own way without making us or anyone else nervous about military or regional security. World law may be the most difficult achievement in human history but it happens to be the price of freedom and peace.

*—February 18, 1961*

# Confrontation

Americans who come to Southeast Asia fortify themselves with all sorts of pharmaceutical armor. Their little vials are like prancing medieval steeds; they carry their owners into battle against all sorts of marauding bacteria. One disease, however, the intrepid little pills cannot conquer. The disease goes by the name of compassion fatigue or conscience sickness. When it strikes, it produces a violent retching of the spirit with an accompanying severe upset of the moral equilibrium. At first the eyelids stretch wide open, then they narrow in a desperate effort to seek cover from an abiding reality. There is no prescription except to tell the victim to lower his gaze, then bundle him gently and send him home.

Over the years, on various trips to the Far East and Middle East, I have watched the newcomers as they arrived. At first there would be the full flush of exciting response to a powerful new experience. They would be caught up in the dramatic discovery of conspicuously different cultures. But then something would happen. They would be confronted by the evidence that, for the most part, the world is not congenial to life in human form. Conditioned by a society of abundance, the newcomers would be plummeted out of the sky into an area where the primary mystery of life is not how it originated but how it is sustained. The newcomers would see men harnessed to wagons like dray horses; they are by far the cheapest form of hauling power available—cheaper than bullocks or horses and infinitely cheaper than trucks. Besides, human fuel requirements are far less costly than either engine or animal.

The newcomers would also see ten or twelve people or more sharing a single room—sometimes a shanty made of old crates or discarded tin. Some people either couldn't afford the flimsy crates or, finding them too crowded, would set up their frayed bedrolls in the streets. An American who worked for the U.S. Information Service in Calcutta told how shocked he was to stumble at night upon the sleeping form of an Indian on a sidewalk—and then to recognize him as one of the clerks who worked on the next floor.

To be sure, not all Americans are affected by compassion fatigue or conscience sickness. Many of them manage to make the adjustment. As would be expected in some cases, the initial blisters on the sensitivities become hardened, even calloused, through constant exposure. A few newcomers, however, achieve the seemingly impossible. They succeed in retaining their sensitivity without narrowing their field of vision or turning away from life disfigured by hunger. The secret of their adjustment lies in their ability to attach themselves to a useful enterprise. They make important connections with the surrounding reality. They invest themselves in the human situation as they find it, working in the social services on the personal level or through the established agencies. They find their energy in a sustained purpose.

Soon countless thousands of Americans will be serving in remote places in the world as part of the President's Peace Corps. The success of their mission may depend less on their specialized training than upon their view of life. Their highly developed skills will be meaningless unless their emotional and philosophical equipment is right for the job. This does not mean that the highly sensitized individual need not apply. On the contrary, a capacity for sensitive response is a prime qualification. But it should be the kind of sensitivity that leads neither to the softness of retreat nor the hardness of acclimation. Instead, the proper sensitivity will find its outlet in the work itself, deriving its sustaining power from the fact of an attack on a difficult human situation. The key is confrontation and not solution.

Indeed, nothing is more essential than the need to separate one's assignment from the total problem. I met a young American who decided to quit India after only five months of service with a U.S. agricultural mission. "It's no use," he said. "You help one man only to discover fifty men standing behind him. Then you help fifty men and five thousand suddenly appear. You help the five thousand but what do you do about the 5 million behind them and the 50 million to follow? At some point along the line you decide it's hopeless."

Another American, an expert in housing, confessed that he, too, was about ready to give up. "Few nations in human history have made more progress in putting up new housing units than India," he said. "Last year perhaps 6 to 8 millions of people were able to move out of the impossibly overcrowded rooms and into decent quarters. But during the same time 10 million people were added to the population. The result is that the country is at least 2 million people worse off than it was a year ago. Can you imagine what the deficit will be ten years from now? How can you help but be discouraged?"

A young American doctor attached to a hospital in Bombay said he was doing everything he could to hold fast to his original purpose in coming to India. "I just wasn't psychologically attuned to the problems I would have to face. Back in the United States a doctor never has to ask himself: 'Why try to keep this baby alive?' He concentrates all his knowledge and will power on the need to save a child and give him a chance for a normal life. But here, in India, maybe two or three hundred million people will never experience a single day free of hunger or sickness in their entire lives."

The fallacy in the reasoning behind these various positions is that each man wanted the evidence of some visible amelioration of the total problem before he could justify his own efforts. Another mistake, perhaps, was that each man underestimated the power of his own example to set others in compassionate motion. Each of these men was part of a total process of creative effort, the nature and scope of which were not wholly visible but were real and genuine nonetheless.

Finally, no one man involved in the vast and infinitely mysterious enterprise of reducing human pain really knows enough about the intangibles of social interaction to be pessimistic about the future. Progress proceeds out of elusive but vital fractions. Sudden spurts in the condition of a society come about as the result of small achievements with high symbolic content. The probability of such an upturn may be slight in any given situation. No matter. No one can take the responsibility for assuming it cannot happen. To do otherwise is to hold history in contempt. "I have tried," said Augustine, "to find the source of evil and I got nowhere."

It is absurd to attempt to define the conditions under which a man's discouragement or despair may be justified. An individual's sensitivities are as personal as his peristalsis. Yet it may not be unreasonable to point out that the acceptance of defeat in many cases may be premature. Much depends on the role an individual essays for himself. If he will be satisfied with nothing less than a visible and measurable result in a great cause, he may have to defer his triumph. But if he has a sense of total involvement and engagement to the point of personal mobilization, then this is all that can be expected; this is all that counts in the moral reckoning.

Compassion is not quantitative. Certainly it is true that behind every man whose entire being cries out for help there may be a million or more equally entitled to attention. But this is the poorest of all reasons for not helping a single man. Where, then, does one begin or stop? You begin with the first man who puts his life in your hands and you continue so long as you are able to continue, so long as you are capable of personal mobilization. How to choose? How to determine which one of a million men surrounding you is more deserving than the rest? Do not concern yourself in such speculations. You will never know; you will never need to know. Reach out and take hold of the one who happens to be nearest. If you are never able to help or save another, at least you will have saved one. Many people stroll through an entire lifetime without doing even this. To help put meaning into a single life may not produce universal regeneration, but it happens to represent the basic form of energy in a society. It also is the best of individual responsibility.

Albert Camus liked to quote Emerson's assertion that every wall was a door. "Let us," said Camus, "not look for the door and the way out anywhere but in the wall against which we are living. . . . Great ideas, it has been said, come into the world as gently as doves. Perhaps, then, if we live attentively, we shall hear, amid the uproar of empires and nations, a faint flutter of wings, the gentle stirring of life and hope. Some will say that this hope lies in a nation; others, in a man. I believe, rather, that it is awakened, revived, nourished by millions of solitary individuals whose deeds and works every day negate frontiers and the crudest implications of history. . . . Each and every man, on the foundation of his own sufferings and joys, builds for all."

*—March 25, 1961*

# The Many Facets of Leo Szilard

When a mutual friend telephoned some months ago to say that Leo Szilard was dying of cancer in a New York hospital, I rushed up to see him. Halfway down the hospital corridor I heard a voice clearly identifiable as Szilard's. The door to his room was partially open. I peered in and blinked. Szilard was out of bed. The top of the bed had been converted into a working desk suffocated by papers, scientific journals, and manuscripts. Szilard was seated on a straight chair against the side of the bed, one hand holding the telephone receiver, the other making notes. He was giving orders to someone about his X-ray treatments.

He looked up and grinned, then motioned me to a chair on the other side of the bed. I carefully took a mound of papers off the chair and looked around the room for a place to put them. The chest of drawers was already buried under print. So was the night table. Part of the floor along the window was lined with tracts of various sorts. I put the papers back on the chair and sat on them.

I watched Szilard as he characteristically set someone straight on the other end of the phone. He was thinner, much grayer than I had last seen him but he had lost none of his high carbonation. I realized that Szilard regarded his own fight for life as incidental to the main one: the fight for peace. He was one of the three or four scientists most responsible for the liberation of atomic energy; in fact, he and Fermi held the first patent issued on the atomic chain reaction. It was he who made known to Einstein the practical possibility of an atomic explosive. This led to President Roosevelt's historic executive order that resulted in the Manhattan District Project. When the war ended, Szilard began a crusade that was to dominate all his thoughts and action. It was a crusade to head off a world atomic armaments race and what he feared would be the ultimate and almost inevitable result—the nuclear laceration of human society. He was like an idea factory, turning out all sorts of intricate notions and schemes for keeping the arms race from putting an end to the human race. Through it all he never lost his effervescent manner or the zest for laughter. But now time was running out—for him and for the crusade that was so important to him.

He finished his phoning, then grinned again.

"These radiologists don't know X rays," he said in feigned despair. "I find myself having to give a course in radiology to these fellows. Anyway, I'm the chief consultant on my own case. It's quite fascinating."

I asked how he felt.

"Fine. Say, have you heard the story about Senator Margaret Chase Smith? It seems she was asked by a reporter how she would like to be President and told the reporter the question was too hypothetical to be taken seriously. 'Come, now,' the reporter said, 'this is an age for new traditions. We may not be far away from the time when a woman will be President.' Senator Margaret Chase Smith still refused to comment. Finally, the reporter said: 'Very well, Senator, suppose you wake up one morning and find yourself in the White House, what would you do?' Replied Margaret Chase Smith: 'I'd apologize to the First Lady and go home.'"

Szilard let out a roar of delight at his own story, told two more, exulted over the fact that he had found an English secretary who knew how to take telephone messages and could spell. He read a passage from a new proposal he had just written having to do with the confrontation between the U.S.A. and U.S.S.R., reported on some mutual friends he had seen, and told another story.

I found myself adding to the laughter that was reverberating through the hospital corridor. What was happening was clear. Leo Szilard was not only running the doctors; he was running his visitors, creating the mood, governing the conversation. He proceeded to talk about his own plans. Victor Weybright, of New American Library, wanted him to write his memoirs. He was also toying with the idea of bringing together some satirical stories and offbeat essays he had written for private circulation over the years. There was a long piece, dealing with the nuclear race, he wanted to do for the *Bulletin of Atomic Scientists*. And he was behind in his mail. I looked again at the wild profusion of working papers on the bed, dresser, table, and floor; it would take him at least three years to get caught up. With a working schedule like this, cancer would have to wait.

That visit to the hospital was a year ago. Since then Leo Szilard has been more active than ever. He frequently abandons his hospital room altogether to see people or run his own errands. When he isn't running around he is on the telephone, working on his many scripts, getting people involved in complicated schemes to rearrange the destinies of nations.

One of the writing projects has now materialized: *The Voice of the Dolphin and Other Stories*. As already indicated, these were written for personal pleasure and the amusement of his friends. They represent just one side of Szilard. How many other sides there are to him no one knows, not even Szilard. He is without question one of the dozen greatest scientists of the age, his work embracing nuclear physics, chemistry, microbiology, biology, and radiology. The restless inventiveness of his mind knows few modern counterparts. One invention on which he has been working has so far eluded him. He is racing against a deadline to achieve it. The invention is peace.

*—April 19, 1961*


## Put Poets into Space

The idea of man in space is an explosion in the imagination. It shakes free the sense of wonder; it cracks open a vast area of the human potential; it confronts the intelligence with the prospect of an encounter with the infinite. But it also adds to the terror. Not terror from what is un-known about space but from what is known about man. These cosmic vehicles are the forerunners of space platforms carrying loaded nuclear pistols pointed at the head of man on earth. A great ascent has taken place without any corresponding elevation of ideas. Man has raised his station without raising his sights. He roams the heavens with the engines of hell.

No other human being who ever lived was able to see more of the world than Yuri Gagarin. No other human being was ever in a better position to reflect on human destiny. Yet at precisely the moment that he should have been asserting the cause of man he was asserting the cause of the nation. The one thing on earth that most needed to be left behind —the sense of the tribe—he had carried securely with him. A magnificent new vantage point was not enough to offset an old perspective. Into the center of the focused view came the national flag.

This is not to say that there is anything wrong or unnatural about a surge of national pride over such an event. Nor is it strange that the re-action in the United States should have been registered so largely on the level of the national ego, with assurances from government that we were not too far behind. In the context of a struggle for world balance of power, for prestige, and for pre-eminence, every gain is bound to be posted on the competitive scoreboard. But at some point the human race must have its innings. An assessment must ultimately be made in terms of human development. In the end, it is not the nation but man who will have to account for the record of life on earth.

The heart of the problem is that the earth dwellers, whether they live in eastern or western hemispheres, have not prepared themselves ade-quately for the journey into space. We have directed our attention to machinery rather than motives. We have been concerned with blast off when we should have been thinking about basic purpose. In a more gen-eral sense, our education bears all the marks of specific earth gravity. We have been part of the cosmos but we have tended to regard it as scenery rather than a total abode. Copernicus, Einstein, and Shapley notwith-standing, man still sees man as the center of the universe. We have cheapened our gods by cutting them down to accessible size and sepa-rating them from a concept beyond infinity. It is as though we had been preparing for Beethoven by listening to hyenas.

The journey into space is, or should be, a sublime experience. The selection of astronauts ought not to be confined to men in the military or in technology. Why not poets, philosophers, or theologians? If it is said that space has stern physical requirements, the problem can be met. There are strapping fellows among those who have demonstrated their capacity to think creatively and who have some convictions about the nature of man. One of the prime requisites for an astronaut is not just his ability to follow a specified procedure and to take measurements but to be able to be at one with a new environment. A space ship requires true perspective. This is nothing that can be imparted in a course on astronautics; it comes with the responsible development of intellect and insight. A respect for the human spirit may be even more important than a knowledge of centrifugal force. Moreover, a certain artistry is called for when man proposes to range the universe. It is an artistry both of personal response and ability to communicate. For when the astronaut returns to earth his message should be more than an excited series of remarks on a fabulous journey. The returning messenger should have the ability to impart a sense of great new connections that may transform life as we have known it.

Such men as Paul Tillich, Reinhold Niebuhr, Lewis Mumford, and Robert Frost may be too old to withstand the rigors of training for such an assignment, but at least they ought to be consulted on the younger men who may be equal to the job. In the meantime, the rest of us can try to prepare ourselves to accord a full measure of comprehension to the dimension of a new age. There is something else we can do. We can try to chart a direction for human survival with at least as much concentration of effort as we are putting into a trip to the moon.

*—April 19, 1961*

The "Dartmouth Conferences" were a series of unofficial meetings between private citizens of the United States and the Soviet Union. The first meeting took place at Dartmouth College in Hanover, New Hampshire, in October, 1960, with President John S. Dickey as host. The second meeting was held in the Crimea the following June. The third took place at Phillips Academy in Andover, Massachusetts in October, 1962, at the time of the Cuba crisis. The fourth was held in Leningrad in July, 1964. All the meetings were sponsored by the Ford Foundation, with the Johnson Foundation of Racine, Wisconsin, participating in the underwriting of the Leningrad Conference.

The series of meetings grew out of my visit to the Soviet Union in 1960 under the auspices of the cultural exchange between the two countries. While in Moscow, I suggested to Soviet writers, academicians, and scientists that the exchange program, which both countries believed to be in their mutual interests, would be substantially advanced by roundtable discussions between non-government leaders in both countries.

The response to this suggestion was generally favorable. It was made clear, however, that this was a matter for decision by the Soviet government. I was advised to make a formal proposal but not to be discouraged *if I received an initial turndown. Sometimes, I was told, a refusal might be the result of temporary factors or a desire to test my seriousness of intent. In the event of a turndown, I would do well, they told me, to renew the request.*

*The advice was excellent. It took four or five initiatives before an affirmative response was received.*

*The following accounts of the Dartmouth Conference series appeared over a period of five years—1960–1965. They appear here in sequence.*

# Dialogue with the Russians

*Moscow*

A Russian, looking somewhat distraught, rushed up to me in the Moscow railroad station and asked if I could tell him the number of the track for the train arriving from Kiev. Unfortunately, I could not. The only point of this little incident is that it probably would not have happened a few years ago. At that time, an American was clearly identifiable—generally by his shoes. Also, perhaps, at the upper end by a somewhat wide-eyed look—especially if he had just arrived himself.

Today, however, it's becoming increasingly difficult to tell Americans from Russians at a glance. Many male Muscovites now dress in the same approximate fashion as Americans—slacks, sports jacket, English-style shoes. Haircuts are generally in the American, rather than Continental, manner. Still another key fact is that so many Americans have visited all parts of the Soviet Union in the past few years that they have become absorbed in the general background.

More and more, Russian designers are looking to America—whether for styles in clothes, motorcars, or industrial products. Russians today only rarely cluster around parked American cars to observe the bulging rear decks and tail fins. Now they have rakish cars of their own, and it is interesting to see them admiring the new front grillwork, the splash and flash of the chromium dancing in their eyes.

Similarly, Americans in the Soviet Union today no longer blink when they see everyday people going into banks to make deposits or withdrawals or conduct transactions usually associated with a mercantile society. Nor are they any longer astonished by shops selling jewelry or electric razors or washing machines. Or by the forest of television antennas rising from the rooftops. Or by hotel dance orchestras playing a high quality of American jazz—sweet, cool, or hot. Or by Russian teenagers with Elvis Presley duck-tail coiffeurs. Or by the massive and ornamental skyscrapers. Or by women bricklayers, streetcar conductors, and ditchdiggers. Or by the existence of upper, middle, and lower classes in Soviet society.

Five years ago or less, a sense of elemental discovery seemed to be involved in even the most cursory meeting between Americans and Russians. It was as though the sheer fact of ideological and national separation had created two starkly distinct physical forms. Each tended to observe the other as though making a massive effort to penetrate a biological riddle. All this is no more. The staring phase of American-Soviet relations his ended. The serious dialogue phase now begins.

Conversations between Americans and Russians these days are increasingly free of the hackled tones that only recently seemed to be standard discoursing procedure. Certainly there is much less disposition to proclaim or perform in private talks; national destiny no longer seems to hang on every word. Only two years ago, as an icebreaker in the cultural exchange program, I was involved in a formal confrontation with the executive committee of the Soviet Union of Writers. I recall my impatience to enter the lists. And I just as vividly recall the zest of the Soviet writers in taking me on. We met at the offices of the Writers Union. The affair was stiffly formal; I had the feeling we were trying to make noises like hardened foreign office spokesmen. I presented a series of demands calling for observation of copyright with respect to publication of American books in the Soviet Union. I made no attempt to conceal my indignation. The counter-arguments were equally strong. I was informed that until such time as parity in publication of Soviet books in America was achieved there was little likelihood of a change in policy. At least a dozen other reasons were marshaled to justify the Soviet position. At the end, we all bowed stiffly or its equivalent, and went our separate ways, utterly convinced of the obtuseness of the other fellow.

Almost two years to the day later—which is to say last week—I returned to the office of the Soviet Union of Writers. This time, however, I didn't have the sense that I was entering the arena of mortal combat with an extraplanetary species. I still felt as strongly as I ever did about the business of issuing books without consent or contract. But by now the element of primitive challenge had gone out of the exchange between Americans and Russians. Besides, many of the Soviet writers had visited the United States under State Department auspices and I had entertained some of them in my home. One of them had debated with me on American television; it was a fairly rough exchange but we came out of it good friends. At any rate, we were no longer viewing one another across a flaming gap. We had even reached the point where a case could be argued on its merits. And so, when I went to the offices of the Writers Union in Moscow a few days ago, we could exchange ideas as common members of a literary community and not as national gladiators. When I raised the problem of respect for American copyright, I did so in the context of a problem that concerned the writing profession as a whole. I made no elaborate pronouncements. I said I was aware that genuine difficulties lay in the way, involving intricate matters of trade balances and currency exchange, but that I was certain that all those present would recognize the validity of the basic principle that a writer's work was his own.

The response was most encouraging. The members present offered no rigid defense of the practice of bypassing copyright. As they spoke, it seemed clear enough that they were prepared to accept the principle of consent and contract. They said simply that they hoped their government before long would come up with a plan that could meet the difficulties, yet do honor to the principle I had defined. They asked that American writers recognize that this could not be done overnight but that at least a sincere effort would be made. I said I was most pleased with their assurance and that I could understand the need for patience. Then we went on to discuss writing and editing problems that existed apart from national difficulties or issues. It was a fruitful meeting; when I left I was not mumbling to myself.

On the basis of this and other conversations with other people prominently identified with publishing in the Soviet Union, I would state it as a reasonable guess that the entire question of copyright observance is being carefully examined by high policy makers in the Soviet Union. It would be a mistake to expect that all theoretical accumulated back royalties will be paid or that the rate of new royalty, if established, would be more liberal than that of most European countries, where it is strikingly low. But at least the general principle of copyright plus payment may be recognized, and this is a change of considerable consequence—not just in publishing terms but as possible reflection of a loosening-up process in the Soviet Union.

In any event, it is possible to have personal rapport with Soviet citizens on a far more effective level than seemed likely just a few years ago. For example, last fall a dozen Soviet individuals, eminent in scholarship, science, and the arts, came to the United States to meet with their opposite numbers. This was the first time that a group of private Soviet citizens had left their country to discuss key questions usually reserved for officials. The questions covered the wide range of Soviet-American relations in particular and world peace in general. The U.S. State Department had been informally consulted and interposed no objection to the meeting.

For a full week, the Dartmouth conference examined the major issues between the two countries. Major positions were not substantially altered; there were no expectations in that direction by either side. But the important thing about Dartmouth was that lines of effective communication were opened up. Human relationships were established. Each position had the name of a man attached to it—someone who would sit next to you at the breakfast table, enjoy a stroll with you on the campus, swap humorous or not-so-humorous stories, go over family pictures together, and marvel at nature's fall bouquet. The hope, of course, was that a different frame of reference might be established—that problems would be considered not solely according to the national interest but according to their human interest. That aim might not have been fully achieved but at least there were moments when the common shock of human recognition seemed apparent.

It was possible at Dartmouth to exchange conflicting ideas without table pounding or loss of tempers. And it was also possible to agree on the need to enlarge the exchange in order to bring public opinion of both countries into the dialogue. On one point all were agreed: they wanted more. The next conference would be in the Crimea.

A few days after the Dartmouth Conference ended, George F. Kennan, one of the participants, met with some of his American colleagues and told of the impact the meeting had had on him. He had served in the Soviet Union for more than two decades. During all that time he had sought every opportunity for a frank exchange of views with Russians of genuine intellectual substance. But he had to wait until he came to Hanover, New Hampshire, to fulfill this aim. He said he hoped the Americans were aware of the unusual nature of their mutual experience. Ambassador Kennan was reassured on this point.

This, then is the general background of the Crimea conference, just concluded. It was somewhat larger than the Dartmouth meeting, in terms of participants. The informality was perhaps proportionately reduced; even so, there were ample opportunities for direct exchange. Several outings provided the occasion for creating the kind of relationship not always possible across the conference table. Incidentally, at Dartmouth, the Americans sat on one side of the table, the Russians on the other. At the Crimea conference, the groups were interspersed. This facilitated open rather than vis-à-vis discussion.

In a sense, the Crimea meeting may have been more businesslike than Dartmouth. Perhaps it had to be. The agenda was a full one and a great deal of homework had to be accommodated in discussion. Each subject was introduced with at least one formal presentation. Hence there was not so much free-wheeling as at Dartmouth. But the questions were certainly considered in greater depth and the various complexities attending each of them were delineated in sequence and proportion.

The conferees tried to stay away from stereotypes. Pat phrases and slogans were avoided in the final joint statement. Also, as at Dartmouth, the significant thing about the Crimea meeting was not just what came out of it, but that it was held. The effort was not to eliminate all differences but to define them with precision so that at least one would know where to take hold, given a real opportunity to do so.

In any event, the essential point about the conferences is that it is now possible to have a personal relationship between Americans and Russians in a way that might eventually yield fruit in terms of far broader exchanges. Obviously, one would be foolish to expect to go plummeting into the Soviet Union and pluck intimate relationships like spring tulips. In this, as in all important matters, proper cultivation is necessary. Moreover, there is still a general reserve in the population as a whole about becoming too involved with foreigners. To be sure, people respond generously—indeed, there are few places in the world where Americans feel greater warmth toward them in everyday contacts—but genuinely deep rapport leading to long-term associations is not yet a wholesale matter. It may be that the conditioned reflexes of many years are not easily set aside. It is also possible, perhaps probable, that on the broad operational Party level many of the old resistances are slow to change. Even so, the fact that change of this nature is occurring at all is promising and important.

Another hopeful indication is that, increasingly, people no longer feel obligated to sound like walking advertisements for their society. Occasionally, but not invariably, you will find Russians who seem relaxed about both achievements and shortcomings and who seem willing to describe the situation for what it is. The other day I visited a collective farm not far from one of the large cities. The individual homes of the farmers were sturdy and attractive; the community center building was highly functional; the equipment looked good. In a matter-of-fact way, my Russian friend told me not to think that this farm was a working sample of the collective units around the country. It was far above the average, even though it was not unique. Attempts were being made to raise the general level along lines worked out at this particular farm and various others like it. But it would be a long time before the countryside would be dotted with such modern establishments. I couldn't help reflecting that a few years ago no such qualifier was likely to be volunteered. If anything, the visitor was apt to be Potemkinized; that is, an attempt would be made to convince him that the model village or development was the standard one.

The answer, perhaps, is that the attempt must be made to keep open the lines of communication regardless of tangible results. At Dartmouth and in the Crimea, at least, it was possible to maintain a relatively free flow of ideas. For example, the Americans were able through detailed discussion to develop the position that it was unreasonable to expect a nation to disarm if the conditions that caused it to arm in the first place remained the same. Disarmament, to be effective, must be coupled with a genuine attack on the fundamental causes of insecurity among nations. And this required a structured peace.

The Soviet participants displayed keen interest in the American emphasis on enforcement procedures for disarmament and on a world rule of law. They interposed no objection to adequate inspection and control in connection with genuine disarmament. Then they explained at considerable length their apprehension lest legitimate inspection procedures for disarmament be made the occasion for all sorts of illegitimate purposes.

Out of this discussion came substantial accord on the need for adequate inspection and control strictly confined to comprehensive disarmament, and on the need to consider all the elements involved in the making of a durable peace.

In a real sense, the meetings also helped to clarify various aspects of Soviet thinking on the big questions of war and peace.

First, the nature of nuclear war has drastically reshaped old Marxist positions. Until just a few years ago the Soviet leaders accepted the traditional Marxist-Leninist view that war was inevitable because of the inherent nature of capitalism. The full implications of the inevitability theory in the context of a nuclear war did not alter Soviet dogma. At first, the Soviet people were told that capitalism would perish in a nuclear war but that the Soviet Union was well able to withstand that kind of assault. More recently, however, the government position has taken the nuclear reality into account. Statements are no longer made about only capitalism perishing in the next war. The Soviet leaders now recognize that their own chances of effective survival are small.

One of Khrushchev's main themes has been domestic reconstruction and development. Under his prodding, tens of thousands of large housing developments have been, and are being, built. Hundreds of large new power plants and industrial developments have been put into operation. Having addressed himself to remaking the face of the Soviet Union, Mr. Khrushchev has no desire to see it disfigured in an atomic war. Hence the intensive policy directed at reducing the war threat and the modification of Marxist dogma to meet the new realities.

Not everyone in the Communist world goes along with this new interpretation. Communist China, for example. Here, too, practical factors govern the theory. China is comparatively unindustrialized; it is still predominantly an agricultural society. It has a mammoth population. Chinese leaders have openly declared that they could lose two or three hundred million in a nuclear war. The pressure to reinterpret Marx on the inevitability of war is not overwhelming. In fact, the new Soviet policy on this question has served as the basis for a severe doctrinal dispute inside the Communist world. For the same reasoning that leads to the modification of the inevitability theory must lead to a conciliatory approach to the capitalist West in order to reduce the danger of nuclear war. Mao Tse-tung believes that such efforts are fruitless and, indeed, are filled with perilous heresy. He has said so. The effect of this on Soviet leaders is to make it all the more necessary to prove they are right. For, if they are wrong, then there is the grim prospect that the ideological leadership of world communism might shift to Peking.

The American people may think that Nikita Khrushchev may be the summing up of all that is horrendous in the modern world. We are in error, however, if we suppose that the present leadership in the Soviet Union couldn't possibly be worse. It could be worse. It could be a great deal worse. From the standpoint of America, a change in the leadership of the Soviet Union toward Peking could make a big difference in terms of the large factors that affect American security.

This does not mean that Mr. Khrushchev has lost, or intends to lose, his standing as a prophet of the ultimate triumph of socialism. His position is that this triumph will be the result of inexorable historical forces. The many new nations coming into freedom from outside rule will have to find some way out of their near-total poverty, illness, and illiteracy. They have to do this in a fairly short period of time. They have to industrialize. The notion that a free capitalist economy can be relevant in such situations Mr. Khrushchev finds rather remote.

To the extent, therefore, that the future belongs to the majority; to the extent that the majority will insist on being adequately fed, housed, and educated in their own lifetimes—to these extents Mr. Khrushchev believes that the future belongs to socialist techniques. He is completely empirical. Certain problems exist; experience has demonstrated a good way of meeting these problems. Mr. Khrushchev believes the good way to be his way. He also believes that the United States will fail in its bid for the support of African and Asian peoples for two reasons. First, the United States has been too closely identified with its former European masters. Second, the U.S. economic philosophy does not fit the needs or capacities of the under-developed peoples.

Such, at least, is the general nature of the challenge, as it would appear to take shape when viewed from an on-the-spot perspective. The challenge may be large, it may be complex, but it is not beyond comprehension or response.

What it requires, most of all, is recognition that we have to put at least as much resources, intelligence, and conviction into the nonmilitary effort as we have been putting into the military one. Certainly we need not be defeatist. American power begins with moral imagination. It comes forward in a straight line from the idea that the state exists for the purpose of serving man, and that this service is related to individual freedom and growth. But American power need not cease with the advocacy of these ideas. It can make them relevant in today's terms, in terms that fit the majority.

In short, the United States can commit itself to the idea of a fully developed United Nations—capable of enacting justice, capable of enforcing world peace under law, capable of utilizing the world's resources for the world's good. Such a goal may not be immediately realizable. However, just to define it as a goal and to seek commitments to it may create a new direction in human affairs. A sense of new direction is at least the beginning of better things.

*—June 24, 1961*

# Notes from the Crimea

The two most persistent questions put to me since returning from the Crimea conference were, first, whether the Americans were able to make any impact on the Russians, and, second, whether the Americans learned anything they did not know before.

Obviously, each of the participants will have to answer for himself. My own response would be affirmative on both counts. First, with respect to impact: Much of it occurred on the personal level. Previously, it had not been possible for individual Soviet citizens to have the kind of intensive, sustained discussions with Americans that took place in the Crimea and at Dartmouth College some months earlier. If prominent Russians were able, for the first time, to have unobstructed access to Americans in an atmosphere permitting uninhibited exchange of ideas, then the exchange also made it possible for Americans to get together with Russians on more than a perfunctory level. Most Americans who have been in the Soviet Union—whether in the foreign service or for news-gathering purposes or as tourists—have spoken of the rarity with which they have been invited to private homes, or the rapidity with which even the most promising social contacts tend to flake off. After a while, the lack of genuine rapport produces a sense of being cut off, of pressing one's nose against the window of a remote and inaccessible society.

The Dartmouth Conferences were making possible a full, direct exchange with Russians of intellectual substance. The benefits of the new access were therefore mutual.

What kind of impact? I tried to observe the Russian participants carefully as they came in close contact with Americans prominently identified with the capitalist economy—men such as Gabriel Hauge, chairman of the Finance Committee of the Manufacturers Trust Company and former economic adviser to President Eisenhower, or Senator William Benton, founder of a large advertising agency and publisher of the *Encyclopaedia Britannica,* or Shepard Stone, of the Ford Foundation. Or such a man as Arthur Larson, author of *A Republican Looks at His Party,* former special assistant to President Eisenhower. Or a leading American critic of Soviet philosophy and policy such as Philip E. Mosely, of the Council on Foreign Relations. Or Americans with a strong background in foreign affairs such as Joseph Johnson, of the Carnegie Endowment for International Peace, or Robert Bowie, of the Center for International Affairs, Harvard University. Or academicians such as Erwin Griswold, dean of the Law School of Harvard University, or Lloyd Reynolds, chairman of the Department of Economics at Yale University, or Professor Louis B. Sohn, co-author of *World Peace through World Law,* or Professor George Fischer, of Cornell University, whose knowledge of the Russian language and culture gave him an important advantage in direct communications. Or authors and experts such as Margaret Mead and Stuart Chase. Or a world-famous personality such as Marian Anderson. Or a religionist such as William Loos, of the Church Peace Union.

My guess is that the impact was considerable. For example, at one point in the Crimea conference, the discussion took a philosophical turn. One of the Americans spoke simply and eloquently about the primary place that a good society must accord the creative life of the mind, and of the need to keep the material things from obscuring the importance of good books, music, art. At dinner that night, several of the Russians said privately that they had been moved by this statement of a personal philosophy. Another instance: the entire conference group attended a public folk-music festival one evening. Marian Anderson was recognized and was brought to the platform. She didn't sing. She did something far more important. She spoke. What she said took perhaps no more than a minute. But the largeness of the human spirit reflected in her words and in her person became a dramatic fact of powerful dimension. I looked around and saw a large audience affected emotionally as I had seldom seen an audience affected before.

On the other side, the Americans were pleasantly startled to hear a Soviet economist make a most persuasive case for the resiliency of the American economy and its ability to withstand dislocating pressures; in particular, the fact that American capitalism was not dependent on military spending. This was a far cry from the traditional Marxist view with its emphasis on the inevitability of depression because of capitalism's inability to produce for peace as it produces for war. Similarly, one of the Soviet scientists made a striking presentation on the possibilities now opening up in science for meeting hitherto unsolved problems.

What was learned of value that was not known before?

Perhaps few new specific facts of overriding importance were developed. But the thinking behind these facts was made clear in a much fuller way than previously seemed apparent. Certainly the Soviet participants were able to observe that the cause of freedom with the Americans was not just an intellectual bauble or a political slogan but a genuine fact tied to genuine commitment. Also, there could be no mistaking either the importance attached by the Americans to peace or their insistence that the peace had to be a durable one, involving hard facts of structure and enforceability. For their part, the Americans came away with a detailed understanding of the underpinning that supports fundamental Soviet policy and strategy. Here were some of the main props as this observer appraised them:

1. Questions affecting the national *prestige* may be at least as important to the Soviet Union as traditional Marxist or ideological questions.

2. Marxist dogma does not automatically harmonize with necessity on the national level; in such cases, the national necessity tends to prevail.

3. The Soviet leaders have not given up their belief in the ultimate triumph of socialism, although the nature of that socialism may be considerably different from the textbook definitions.

4. This ultimate triumph will come about, Soviet leaders seem to believe, because the United States in particular and the West in general have little or no rapport with the broad historical upheaval now affecting the majority of the world's people, especially in Asia, Africa, and Latin America. Many of these peoples live in a condition of economic feudalism. The inability of the United States to come forward with any dynamic program of economic and social reform that has relevance for most of the Asian, African, and South American peoples will cost the United States any leadership position to which it now aspires. In short, there seems to be a belief that the United States will default on the leadership level because it is not advocating an economic and social philosophy to go along with political freedom.

5. The socialist world believes it can beat capitalism at its own game; i.e., it believes it can undersell the United States in the world markets. Already Soviet-produced oil is being offered in some places at less than the American price.

Obviously, nuclear war cannot be regarded by Soviet leaders as the means of pursuing these objectives unless suicide is regarded as a means to an end. The same is also true of the United States. If the United States is seriously concerned about the challenge, it will put at least as much effort and intelligence into the nonmilitary effort as it has into its war preparations. Indeed, the military approach alone inevitably leads to a dead end.

We are already in the stage of overkill. Additional overkill will not decrease the present insecurity. We need a program literally ablaze with moral imagination and thrust, one that aims at nothing less than the reshaping of human society in the making of a better—and also safer—tomorrow for the totality of mankind.

—*July 1, 1961*

# Experiment at Andover

For seven days, while the Cuban crisis was at its height, some two dozen prominent citizens from the United States and the Soviet Union met in a paneled trustees' room of a New England preparatory school. They were taking part in an experiment to determine whether it is possible for knowledgeable people from both countries to talk about the explosive issues between their nations without having the meeting go up in a shower of sparks.

Each news bulletin added to the tension and sharpened the anxieties. At the end of the week, the participants emerged from their long sessions clearly fatigued but just as clearly rewarded, for they had proved it was possible to have a candid exchange of views on fundamental issues, holding back nothing and rigorously examining everything. And they all agreed they wanted the dialogue to continue.

The fact that the meeting took place against a background of what seemed for a time to be an impending thermonuclear war was purely accidental. The date for the conference had been fixed many months before and was, in fact, the outgrowth of two previous meetings, the first at Dartmouth College in October, 1960, and the second in the Crimea in May, 1961. Both of these meetings had been successful, not in terms of agreements actually reached but in terms of the ability to clarify opposing positions, to submit to rules of order in debate, to subject facts to cross-examination, and to develop personal relationships that could be fruitful beyond the conference table.

Some of the participants, especially at Dartmouth and the Crimea, previously had had substantial experience in the foreign services of their governments. They discovered that the process of coming together informally and unofficially made it possible for them to engage in the kind of full, intimate discussion that had only rarely been possible in their official stations.

But neither the Dartmouth nor the Crimea meetings took place under circumstances as somber and as unsettling as existed at the meeting in Andover a few days ago. Within a day after the Soviet participants arrived at International Airport in New York, the Cuban crisis was in the headlines. Three days later, just after the group assembled at Andover, the radio was crackling with news bulletins about an imminent statement of major importance by President Kennedy. That same night, the President went before the television cameras and the microphones to announce a blockade of all military shipping into Cuba. The delegates from both groups watched the announcement on a TV screen; the tension and the uncertainty in the room were palpable and acute. The fact that their two nations were apparently on a collision course now created an atmosphere of gravity for their experiment that none could have anticipated and all could dread.

Shortly after the President's announcement, the delegates went to their evening session in the trustees' room, which had been equipped with IBM simultaneous translating equipment. The Americans were mindful that their Russian guests, 5,000 miles from their homes and families, were probably wondering whether they ought to leave the United States while there was still time to do so. It is possible that the Soviet visitors wondered whether the Americans felt there was any use in proceeding. At any event, the co-chairman of the Soviet delegation began the meeting by asking tactfully whether the Americans wished to go on with the conference. The American co-chairman said there was only one way to find out. He asked for a show of hands of those who wished to continue. Without the slightest hesitation, every hand went up.

During the course of the week, the Cuban situation gave rise to the most detailed, direct exchange of views. There could be no doubt that all the elements of the problem, including many which had been crowded out of the headlines, were fully presented. Blunt questions were asked and just as bluntly answered. One of the items on the prepared agenda had to do with the role of the United Nations in dealing with tensions, and with the place of world law in the establishment of a durable peace. It was inevitable that the relevance of this topic to the Cuban crisis should have been stressed by some of the participants.

Other topics vigorously discussed included the problem of achieving general and complete disarmament under iron-clad safeguards; the responsibility of the large nations in undertaking a cooperative program for assisting countries in need of economic development; the problem of maintaining peaceable relations while maintaining diverse political systems; and ways in which the access of each country to the other could be kept open in economic, scientific, and cultural relations.

On some days the sessions ran from early morning until late at night. Each topic produced a substantial supply of information, not all of it familiar to most of the participants. And, as might be expected, few statements went unchallenged.

Where facts were incontrovertible, positions gained in proportion. Suggestions were made for constructive improvement, especially in the area of cultural relations, and a number of them had no difficulty in reaching concurrence.

Perhaps the most interesting development of the experiment was that, paradoxically, the delegates drew closer together on the personal level even as the issues that separated them grew more intense. The international crisis deepened and the debates at the conference table were correspondingly sharper, but the personal rapport mounted from day to day. Whether this was because the participants were becoming increasingly aware subconsciously of their underlying membership in a human commonwealth, or whether, as they came to know one another, they yielded to the magnetic pull of human gravity, it is difficult to say. One thing, however, is certain: by the end of the week there was no awkwardness or strain in raising any question, however severe, or in venturing a response, however pointed. It was possible to be forthright without being caustic, impassioned without being abusive, severe without being cutting. You could disagree and still retain your respect for the person you were disagreeing with. Just in the process of working and living together, those at the conference had been able to transcend what until then had been their purely national identities, and were recognizing the implicit existence of a human agenda for their deliberations.

Moreover, there seemed to be a sense among the participants that they were sharing in a privileged experience at a critical time. Andover was probably the only place in the world where so many Americans and Russians, albeit unofficially, were talking things out together on virtually a day-and-night basis. This increased and enhanced their sense of somber responsibility. It made many of them recognize, too, that they were there not just for the purpose of proclaiming but for the purpose of legitimate self-examination.

*—November 10, 1962*

As at Dartmouth and the Crimea, some of the most memorable incidents took place away from the conference table. During one of the infrequent recess periods, the Soviet delegation went off to see some of the sites and memorials of the American Revolution. As they approached the monument at Bunker Hill, but before the inscription at the base of the monument was visible, the oldest member of the Soviet group took off his hat and began to move his lips. Those very close to him heard him recite the famous lines from Emerson:

> "By the rude bridge that arched the flood,
>   Their flag to April's breeze unfurled,
> Here once the embattled farmers stood
>   And fired the shot heard round the world."

## II

What was learned? Obviously, each participant carried away with him his own set of observations. For ourselves, what struck us most forcibly about the conference was the need for a "judge" or impartial outsider to preside over the meeting. Not that any bias was shown by the American and Soviet individuals who alternated in the chair. The chairmen followed parliamentary procedure and saw to it that everyone who wanted to speak was given a turn. But there was no one in a position to apply the rules of evidence; no one who could ask for additional facts or who could rule that certain statements were immaterial or inadmissible; no one, in short, who could apply objective criteria to the arguments offered by both sides.

The absence of such a magistrate did not mean that the discussions were without value. Far from it. The fact of confrontation alone was an important one. Conceptions and misconceptions could be rigorously examined. Each side had a beneficial cathartic experience in being able to talk to the other directly. But there was no way of moving systematically toward an objective determination or decision, no way of establishing a point beyond cavil or contradiction, no way of pursuing a line of argument through to its logical conclusion and having it accepted as a fixed point in the total discussions.

A judge or impartial authority might have called attention to the fact of an occasional double yardstick. There was a tendency—natural enough and perhaps even inevitable—for participants to measure the actions of their own country according to the stern requirements of national security and safety. The action of another nation, however, would generally be measured on a more objective basis.

The presence of an authoritative third party might also have made it possible for each side to give essential ground without feeling it had sacrificed any portion of the national honor. In the absence of a presiding magistrate, men do not easily relinquish positions affecting their vital interests. Moreover, there is a tendency for a group to close ranks against outside criticisms or claims, on the principle that one's nation is automatically right when its vital interests are questioned.

Only an impartial authority can deal with the deadlock that results when two such sets of vital interests rest on contradictory claims.

If this general principle has validity for a private conference, it is no less valid for official negotiations. In fact, we came away from Andover with an enlarged appreciation of the difficulties involved in direct discussions between the United States and the Soviet Union. Obviously, everything must be done to keep open channels of direct communications between the two countries on the highest levels. But if official negotiations are to be more fruitful than they have been in the past, it may be useful to consider the fundamental flaw in the framework of the meetings.

This flaw is represented by the absence of any machinery for decision or determination. Since 1948 there have been at least fifteen official bilateral negotiations between the United States and the Soviet Union, generally on the subject of the nuclear arms race. The fact that effective agreement on the most important matter in the world has not come out of these meetings cannot be attributed primarily to differences in the opposing positions. During the course of all these negotiations, both sides have made virtually identical proposals. However, these proposals have been made at different times and there has seldom been a synchronization of position. The main obstacle to agreement has been the lack of someone in authority who could dispose of all extraneous points or objections and apply objective criteria to all the factors involved in reaching an effective agreement.

In short, no major nation can reasonably be expected to make any concessions where its interests are concerned. It becomes necessary to dictate what such concessions are to be, based not on arbitrary rulings but on the application of reason and law.

The surprising thing about contemporary human society is that it has laboriously worked out techniques for resolving disputes among citizens but then completely sets these techniques aside for resolving disputes among nations. The machinery of law is the only effective means developed during history for dealing with private conflicts of vital interests, but the machinery of law has yet to be created for dealing with conflicts when they reach national and nuclear proportions. Against this background, no man can regard himself as civilized or educated so long as he is detached from this particular lesson of history.

The United Nations represents the best existing hope that objective criteria, or law, may yet be applied to the volatile disputes of nations. If that hope is to be realized, the amount of energy and concern put into the UN will have to be at least as great as the energy and concern now being put into perfecting the means for ending life on earth.

*—December 1, 1962*

## III

The Soviet visitors, many of whom were seeing the United States for the first time, were endlessly fascinated by life in America. That it was different from their preconceived notions was clear enough.

"Yes, things in America are not as we expected," a member of the Russian delegation observed. "The people here are gentle, friendly, home-loving, and honest."

"What had you expected?" we asked.

"I'm not sure," he replied. "I suppose I expected people to be tense, short-tempered, and, to be candid, rather crude and belligerent. Do you know, I haven't seen a single fist fight in the streets or in the inn since we arrived. Nor have I seen a single drunk. And your young women are modest in manner and dress and not at all cheap."

"Where did you get such ideas?" we inquired.

"I got them from your movies and magazines and books," he said. "Why do your playwrights and authors insist on slandering your great country? Almost every motion picture we see about the United States does serious discredit and harm to your people. You are made to seem very vulgar and materialistic, as though you had no interest in the deeper things of life, which I now know is not true. Everyone in the movies seems to be stealing from the next fellow—either his money or his job or his wife. And everybody seems to be only a straw away from punching the next man in the face. A terrible business—and all so untrue. Why do they do it?

"I read as many books about America as I can find," he continued. "They are far more responsible, of course, than your movies, but I still think the writers of these books do not do justice to your country and its people. Your writers make it appear that the United States is filled with people who are neurotic or oversexed or who suffer from infantile emotions.

"It is not at all like that, and it should make the decent people of your country very angry. I just can't understand why you permit this sort of thing to happen. One of the first things I did after I arrived in New York and got cleaned up at the hotel was to go for a walk. On the corner, I saw an open-air store—I think you call it a newsstand. There seemed to be hundreds of magazines on display. Please do not think me critical, but most of those magazines were outrageously indecent. It creates the impression that the only things the American people are interested in are violence, drunkenness, and cheap women. It didn't take me long to find out that this is not the case. But I still don't understand why so much of your printed material, like your movies, should glorify the worst things about America and not your best.

"As I say, these are the things that bewilder me about the United States. How do you explain them? Frankly, I would like to know."

I said, first of all, that I was glad he was now having this opportunity to see the United States and its people at firsthand, because nothing was more difficult abroad than to convince people—not just Russians but people everywhere who had never been to America—that life in this country was not at all what it was made to appear to be. The movies were clearly the worst sinners in this respect—not so much of a problem perhaps as they were ten years ago, but still the number-one source of misinformation, distortion, and defamation. But it would be equally difficult to say that many of our books and magazines gave a fair reflection of life in the United States. And there were many Americans who were outraged by the constant emphasis on casual violence in pictures and print.

Yet most Americans believed, I added, that the obvious correctives would, if anything, be even worse than the abuses. If motion-picture producers, publishers, editors, and writers were ordered, arbitrarily or by law, to avoid misrepresentation or distortion, then the result would be totally unacceptable. Americans wouldn't trust their own government to operate a system of censorship or control—even for the purpose of protecting their country's good name. Words and ideas, unlike meat and drugs, cannot be inspected for public consumption. The certain danger is that, in the attempt to guard against what is undesirable, the government will try to define what is desirable. And the moment a government is given the power to proclaim correctness in ideas, that power becomes a monopoly, the unhappy ramifications of which will extend into almost every aspect of life.

In any event, I suggested to the Soviet delegate, it would be a serious mistake to assume that *all* motion pictures or books or magazines were committed to the proposition that Americans were crude, cruel, callous, culture-hating, neurotic, sexually obsessed, or irresponsible. A very impressive list, both in size and substance, could be drawn up of films or publications or books which provide a balanced, representative account of life in America. Certainly our Soviet visitors' favorable firsthand impressions would be amply confirmed by the works appearing on such a list.

In any case, I was glad the question had been raised, for it was a reminder that the principal problem confronting the image of America abroad is caused not just by hostile propaganda but by the limited and damaging view Americans take of themselves.

*—December 15, 1962*

# More Talks with the Russians

For six days last month some thirty Americans and Russians sat around a large table in Leningrad and had a frank talk on the outstanding issues between their two countries. The subjects discussed ranged from differences over disarmament to difficulties in carrying out the cultural-exchange program between the two countries.

The American delegation to Leningrad included Charles Frankel, professor of philosophy, Columbia University; Dr. R. Buckminster Fuller, architect and inventor, Southern Illinois University; Professor John Kenneth Galbraith, economist, Harvard University; and former U.S. Ambassador to India; Mrs. Elizabeth Koontz, president-elect of the Department of Classroom Teachers of the National Education Association; Dr. Francis V. Lloyd, Jr., psychologist, University of Chicago; Professor Franklin A. Long, vice president of Cornell University; James Michener, author; Dr. Franklin Murphy, chancellor of the University of California at Los Angeles; Leslie Paffrath, president of the Johnson Foundation; David Rockefeller, president, Chase Manhattan Bank; Professor Marshall Shulman, the Fletcher School of Law and Diplomacy; Norton Simon, industrialist and art collector; Shepard Stone, vice president of the Ford Foundation; Dr. Paul Dudley White, cardiologist; Professor Arthur Larson, director, World Rule of Law Center, Duke University; and myself. Arthur Larson and I served as co-chairmen of the American delegation.

Co-chairmen of the Soviet delegation were Alexander Korneitchuk, distinguished playwright and chairman of the Ukrainian Supreme Soviet, and Evgenii Fedorov, meteorologist and director of the Hydrometeorological Service Department, U.S.S.R. Academy of Sciences, and former member of the Soviet delegation to the Geneva disarmament talks. Among other Soviet members were: Nikolai Blokhin, president, U.S.S.R. Medical Academy; Sergei Gerasimov, leading film producer; Alla Masevitch, deputy chairman of the Astronomical Council of the U.S.S.R. Academy of Sciences and director of satellite tracking operations; Nikolai Orlov, director, Economic Research Institute; Boris Polevoi, novelist and editor of *Youth* magazine; and General Nikolai Talensky, member of the editorial board of *International Affairs*.

The Leningrad meeting took place in a huge, crystal-chandeliered ballroom of a pre-Revolution mansion now called the House of Architects. Each delegation had its own interpreters; electronic microphones and earphones were used for simultaneous translation.

Four years ago, when the talks began at Dartmouth, it took at least two days for the strangeness to wear off. At that time, most of the participants had never met in American-Soviet face-to-face discussions. At Leningrad, the conferees were the beneficiaries of the momentum created by the previous meetings.

There was still some sense of a carryover from the atmosphere of the Andover meeting of October, 1962, which coincided with the week of the Cuban crisis. At that time, both sides were staring down the gun barrel of nuclear war. The effect was not one of intensified hostility; quite the contrary, a mood of heightened awareness and responsibility predominated. There was a realization that both nations were dealing not just with great national stakes but with the issue of human life on earth.

The Leningrad meeting retained enough of this mood of ultimate concern to provide a useful perspective on those things nations must do together, whatever their ideology. In many respects, this ability of men to break out of their national casings and to undertake a common task may be even more significant than any of the items covered on the agenda. Not that these items were in any way minimized during the discussions. There was plenty of hard talk on both sides on matters of vital interests. But there seemed to be a growing awareness that beyond the hard talk, the two countries, if only in their own self-interest, had to find a sensible and workable way to keep their differences within non-combustible limits.

As in the previous meetings, the main impact of the conference was registered by the delegates as individuals—at or away from the conference table. For example, toward the end of the week, one of the Soviet delegates came up to David Rockefeller, who had impressed the conferees with his genuine friendliness, modesty, knowledgeability, and fairness in debate.

"Mr. Rockefeller," the Soviet professor began, "maybe you do not know it but I am an old Bolshevik. I go back to the very early times—even before the revolution. You know, Mr. Rockefeller, many times since our revolution I have asked myself: 'Why don't the masses of American workers revolt against their capitalists?' Now I have met you and now for the first time I know."

Whatever the disagreements at the Leningrad conference, there was a unanimous feeling that the meetings should be continued.

—*September 26, 1964*

Americans and Russians involved in conferences or negotiations—whether on the official or unofficial level—are in substantial agreement at least on one point. This has to do with the need for each country to have the most precise knowledge and understanding of those areas of ultimate sensitivity affecting the security of the other. A precarious equilibrium is all that is now keeping alive several hundred million Americans and Russians, not to mention 3 billion human beings outside both countries who most certainly would be affected by any miscalculation and the consequent chain reaction of nuclear horror.

The most obvious instance of an inadequate assessment by one side of the other's eruption threshold is, of course, Cuba. The Soviet Union grossly miscalculated the American response to the presence of missile sites on Cuban soil. The result was the most intense crisis since the end of World War II.

In talking to Soviet representatives today, there can be no doubt about what constitutes the Soviet Union's point of ultimate sensitivity: Germany. At the Leningrad conference recently, the one subject that was most on the minds and tongues of the Soviet delegation had to do with Germany;

in particular, a Germany with access to nuclear triggers through NATO. More formally, the subject goes by the name Multilateral Force—a plan still in the discussion stage for putting atomic muscle into the NATO military machine.

On all other subjects discussed at the Leningrad conference table—Vietnam, Laos, the Near East, Central Europe, Africa in general or the Congo in particular—the Soviet delegates showed flexibility and, in two or three areas, seemed willing to concede important ground. But on the subject of Germany there was almost a chemical reaction or, in the favorite phrase of Soviet students of behaviorism, a conditioned reflex.

A blending of the Soviet opinions expressed on this subject would take approximately the following form:

"If you understand nothing else about us, try to understand this: By this time we think we know Germany. We have learned, as you say, the hard way. Twice we have learned what happens when Germany gets weapons. At first, everyone is reassured in the sweetest words that a powerful Germany represents no danger to anyone. But the theory always seems to break down—no matter how democratic and intelligent some of the government leaders may be. And somehow the moderates have a way of being replaced by militarists or madmen or both. We know. We have twenty or thirty million dead to show for it in two wars. Go out on the streets here in Leningrad and talk to people. Try to find someone who didn't lose someone close to him. Try to find someone past the age of twenty who doesn't remember the starvation and the cold after Leningrad was cut off and besieged in the last war.

"Forget what government leaders say. Just listen to the people. You think our leaders can tell the Soviet people to do anything and that the Soviet people will blindly follow? Do you know what would happen if the Soviet leaders told our people that they approved of a plan to give German militarists a chance to put their hands on nuclear weapons? There would be an outcry the like of which you never heard.

"But what puzzles us most is how you Americans deceive yourselves into believing you are not putting yourselves in the same jeopardy we would be in. Do you think Germany is content to accept her defeat in World War II? Do you suppose that her militarists aren't waiting for the day when they can smash back at her old enemies? Not just us but the capitalist West, the United States especially.

"All right, you may think that Germany is different today and that there is no longer a problem. For our part, we hope you are right. We hope Germany is completely reformed. We will be congenial and cooperative in everything that Germany does that is different from the old militaristic ways. But at the same time we know enough not to take everything for granted. New faces with old ideas can come back to power. And you will be making a great mistake if you think we will stand by idly while

German militarist fingers are given a chance to get close to nuclear triggers, however the reality may be disguised in the form of NATO or anything else.

"Finally, we don't understand you when on one hand you talk about the great danger represented by the spread of nuclear weapons and on the other hand propose to create a situation in which a number of nations, Germany most prominently among them, could under certain circumstances have access to nuclear explosives."

The response of the Americans was equally vigorous. In general, it ran along the following lines:

It was inaccurate and indeed absurd to assert that the United States was eager to make atomic force available to Germany. The Americans agreed it was essential to do everything possible to prevent the dissemination of nuclear weapons—whether to Germany or anyone else. But recognition of this fact couldn't stop Germany or any highly industrialized nation from making these weapons by itself. Under the Multilateral Force, Germany would forego the manufacture of such weapons. The authority over these weapons would rest in the hands of a supreme command. Germany, of course, as part of the supreme command, would be involved in major decision making. But there was every intention to retain the ultimate decision-making where it is now; namely, in the White House.

As for Germany in general, the Americans said it was important not to allow themselves to be so dominated by past history that we are unable to put new facts to work. Whether Germany becomes a major threat depends perhaps even more on factors outside Germany than inside Germany. If there is no progress toward a basic, durable settlement of the major problems between the United States and the Soviet Union; if better machinery is not devised for maintaining peace; if nations have no security except that which they think is available to them through raw force—then the inevitable disintegration will set the stage for the return of German militarism on a scale frightening to contemplate.

Our main job, therefore, the Americans continued, was to get on with the essential business of peacemaking, taking whatever steps are open to both countries, however modest these steps might appear to be in total perspective.

The Soviet response to this line of reasoning was that, while they could agree with much of what we said about the need for a general political settlement, they felt the Americans were over-optimistic and, not to be too unkind about it, perhaps naïve concerning Germany's willingness to contribute to the basic conditions of stability in Europe. One of the Soviet delegates had recently returned from Bonn where he had had frank conversations with Chancellor Erhard. In response to a direct question about Germany's territorial aims, Chancellor Erhard said that Germany recognized none of the geographical changes that had come about as the result of Germany's defeat in World War II. The implications of this to the Soviet delegates were staggering, for it meant that Germany wanted to return to her 1938 borders. It meant, too, that those whom the Americans regarded as moderates were proposing to return to the geographical Germany of Adolf Hitler. This territory involved large chunks of Poland, Czechoslovakia, and the Soviet Union. How would this contribute to European or world stability, the Soviet delegate wanted to know.

As for the argument that Germany could probably manufacture nuclear weapons by herself anyway, one of the Soviet delegates, a retired general, said that such capability could not be quickly pursued or highly developed without outside help. Problems of nuclear testing and complicated manufacture reduced substantially the danger represented by Germany as an independent nuclear force. With the kind of nuclear weapons available to NATO, however, an entirely different situation was created.

What the Russians basically feared, they said, was not German access to NATO nuclear weaponry per se so much as Germany's ability to commit the United States by taking certain initiatives of its own. Here, too, the Americans attempted to make the point that the Soviet delegates were confining themselves to a rather narrow band represented by the potential uses of German military power instead of taking into account all the surrounding factors that had a dominant bearing on whether Germany would be a source of stability or upheaval in Europe.

The important issue here is not whether the Soviet representatives—or the American representatives, for that matter—are responsive to logic, to the lessons of history, and to new facts. What *is* important and controlling is that there is nothing that we or anyone else can do to convince the Soviet people that a militarily powerful Germany does not represent a blazing threat to their existence. To repeat, this is their point of ultimate sensitivity, their final dividing line. We should continue, of course, to do everything we can to relieve them of the burden of such fallacies as may be involved in their position. At the same time, however, we would be making a critical mistake if we did not recognize the seriousness of any miscalculation on this matter. In today's world, the governing facts are not always tidy and logical, but they are the facts that spell the difference between life and death.

*—October 10, 1964*

# Shelters, Survival, and Common Sense

In home after home throughout the country, the question of fallout shelters has become a profoundly important and perplexing issue. The danger of thermonuclear war has become real enough—indeed, it has been given a razor's edge by the Berlin crisis—so that people are compelled to think seriously about protecting themselves and their families in the event of atomic attack. However grisly shelters may be as a subject for home conversation, parents are earnestly discussing and exploring the matter in terms of their responsibility to their children.

The purpose of this editorial is not to argue against fallout shelters per se. No one can quarrel against a decision by a citizen to prepare today against possible dangers tomorrow. But at least he is entitled to full and factual information before making up his mind. Indeed, he has the right to be protected against dishonest assurances of complete protection when no such assurances are possible or morally justifiable. And we can certainly quarrel with the idea that the family fallout shelter is a fit subject for exploitation by fast-buck operators.

The key fact, the dominant fact, in modern warfare is that the civilian will be the prime target. Every bit of scientific ingenuity will be mobilized and directed against him—wherever he may turn. All the inventiveness that has found a way to kill a city with a single explosive and that has devised a vehicle to carry a cargo of death from one continent to another in fifteen minutes—this inventiveness will not retire because people are going to burrow into the earth. Modern war intends to hunt down the civilian wherever he is, suffocating him or paralyzing him or driving him out into the open. No ventilating system has as yet been made available that can guard against gases that produce heart sickness, or disease germs that spread cholera, anthrax, plague, diphtheria, tularemia, brucellosis, typhoid fever, influenza, dengue fever, smallpox, pneumonia, amoebic dysentery, malaria, Rocky Mountain fever, Q fever, undulant fever, typhus —all of which are now in the arsenals of the major powers and primed for instant use.

Consider first of all the problem of ventilation. When a hydrogen bomb goes off, it produces firestorms over a vast area. A ten-megaton thermonuclear explosion will set loose firestorms over an area of 5,000 square miles. Oxygen is consumed by firestorms. Shelters may be equipped to cool off the air but they can't bring in air if none exists. Unless manufactured oxygen is made available, shelters in the areas affected by firestorms will become suffocation chambers. The need for manufactured oxygen has of course been considered but the difficulties of providing it on a mass scale are regarded as insuperable. Moreover, its volatility under such circumstances makes it a serious risk in its own terms.

The next major factor to be considered has to do with location. The problem of shelters is different in a city from what it is likely to be in the outlying areas. The principal problem in the city will be getting into a shelter in the first place and getting out of it in the second place. It is by no means certain that an attack will be preceded by warning. In fact, the factor of surprise is a molecular part of the make-up of missile-cum-nuclear war. And, even if warning should precede rather than follow an attack, it would be in the order of minutes. Evacuating a city is beyond possibility. Even getting people into cellars is a questionable enterprise. The idea that people in office buildings could take cover by clustering together in the hallways or stairwells or cellars has no validity in a situation involving multiple use of megaton nuclear bombs. The purpose of a thermonuclear bomb is to pulverize a city and all the people in it; as many such bombs as are required to execute that purpose will be used.

For those city dwellers who are able, despite the limited warning time, to take refuge in deep city shelters, the principal problem will be getting out of them—because of the tons of spilled brick and rubble overhead. Testimony before Congressional committees has made it abundantly clear that thermonuclear attack on cities would leave few survivors. In fact, military calculations of 80,000,000 American casualties in event of nuclear attack are based largely on the virtual annihilation of metropolitan populations.

The danger in the suburban areas will be represented not so much by blast as by firestorms and radiation. It is undoubtedly true that some lives can be saved in suburban shelters, assuming ventilation and disease germs will not be critical factors. But it is most certainly untrue that the reduced radiation after only a few days will necessarily subside to safety levels. Most of the radioactive materials released by a thermonuclear explosion are short-lived, but a few, like radioactive strontium and radioactive cesium, retain their killing power over many months. Even more important is the fact that present nuclear stockpiles have high versatility. Some bombs are packed with long-lived radioactive bullets that are designed to stay close to the surface of the earth for a long time.

Most of the specific inadequacies of shelters in cities and suburbs do not apply to country shelters. The main danger in country areas is the generalized one; that is, everything depends on the number of and nature of the bombs used in general attack. If upwards of 25,000 megatons of nuclear explosives are used in a major war—and the United States alone possesses far more than this amount, according to Congressional testimony—the long-term risk to all life in the northern latitudes will be a critical one. Secretary of State Dean Rusk has said that far more nuclear power is available than the entire human race could sustain.

However, no one now knows exactly how much nuclear megatonnage will be exploded in a major war. So long as there is even a small chance that the megatonnage will fall far short of maximum possibilities, a country dweller may feel justified in taking the shelter gamble. But at least he will not be kidding himself about his chances. For the urban dweller, whose city is a nuclear target, however, the chances may be too slight to warrant calculation, even though a fraction of the megatonnage available will be used. It doesn't take too many hydrogen explosives to expunge the cities. And anyone who lives within fifty miles of a major city is vulnerable to the effects described above.

Basically, therefore, the entire question of shelters is a personal one. The individual must make up his own mind based on his own best understanding of the range of probabilities in a nuclear war and his own philosophy of life. But it is unconscionable and contemptible to kid him, or to lead him to believe that 97 per cent of the people in shelters can be saved, or that life inside shelters can somehow be made glamorous, or that Mary Jane will be able to call her friends on the telephone, or that, after the attack, life will be resumed as usual. Life will not be resumed as usual. Those who survive will embark upon an ordeal unlike anything the human race as a race has ever known. The supply of uncontaminated food will run out; even the rain will be poisoned.

When the survivors crawl out of their holes they will not be looking at the world they knew. The crust of the earth will be burned and clotted; anything that stands, whether a tree or a structure, will be charred and skeletonized. There will be no communications, there will be no hospitals, there will be no institutions to attend to the needs of human society. This is what nuclear war is. No deodorizing can change the fact.

Not all the advocates of shelters believe that shelters will provide the advertised protection. Their position is strategical and political rather than scientific. That is, they believe that it is important for the enemy to know—as in the case of the present Berlin crisis—that the American people have the will to fight a nuclear war. And a widespread shelter program may be considered evidence of such. Moreover, they believe that, if we can get enough people underground at the time of an initial attack, we may be able to destroy the enemy utterly before he has time to attempt a second strike. This may leave us with enough people to carry on the work of rebuilding a nation.

The trouble with this strategical approach is that it works both ways. An enemy, determined to destroy this country in a first strike, may respond to the mass shelter program by polishing even further his surprise-attack capabilities.

Finally, if the case for shelters has any logic, it should become a government function. The government should plan a national program in line with its Constitutional responsibility. Moreover, if we are to take the need for shelters seriously, all our plans should be tied to the absence of warning time. This means that *deep* (perhaps 400 feet or more) mass underground shelters should be built from one end of the country to the other. They should be capable of growing their own food. They should have practically everything underground we now have above ground. They should have communications systems, hospitals, libraries, cultural centers. Most important of all is the fact that we should move into them immediately, for there will not be enough time to get into them once the bombs fall.

In short, if we take nuclear war for granted and wish to protect ourselves against its effects, we have to be prepared very soon to abandon our natural environment. There is no assurance, however, that the various groups linked together by the underground system would not find some way of getting at one another to do murder, if one group has something that another wants.

The time to make a stand is now, not later. The answer to nuclear war is a genuine peace. The answer to drift is direction. The answer to insanity is sanity. If the energy, money, and resources now going into shelters were to be put to work in the making of a better world, we would do far more to safeguard the American future than all the underground holes that could be built in 1,000 years. And if we are serious about shelters, let us make the United Nations into a shelter broad enough and deep enough to sustain an enforced peace under law.

The war has not yet begun. Freedom, however abused, still exists. Perhaps we can use that freedom to rally enough peoples around the idea of a world under law. President Kennedy's talk before the United Nations stated the problem and pointed to a way out. If enough Americans are willing to commit themselves personally to the support of the President's proposals, it might make a difference, a very big difference.

In Las Vegas, the head of the local civil defense agency recently called for a militia of 5,000 men to protect residents in event of thermonuclear war. The men would be trained to crush an expected invasion—not from foreign shores but from Southern California. It is believed that Los Angeles, as a major city, would be under direct attack. Survivors, warned J. Carlton Adair, the Las Vegas civilian defense official, "would come into Nevada like a swarm of locusts." Obviously, they would have to be repulsed.

In a less organized way, other Americans are now preparing to kill Americans. A Chicago suburbanite, according to *Time* magazine, intends to mount a machine gun at the entrance to his fallout shelter and blast away at shelterless neighbors who might try to get in out of the radioactivity. Countless other Americans may be making no open declarations about their intentions but they are calmly going about the business of equipping their shelters with guns or tear-gas devices, just in case desperate neighbors might want to poach on their preserves during or after an attack. Some are now preparing their children psychologically to accept the murder of their playmates. All this goes under the heading of civil defense.

In Hartford, Connecticut, at a private meeting of local residents who had come together to consider civil defense problems, one citizen advised his neighbors that firearms were standard equipment for shelters, along with stocks of food and medicines. People who are wounded or suffering from radiation will run around like madmen trying to find shelter, he warned. And, since there will be only so much water and food for one's own family, the intruders will have to be turned back even if it means shooting them. A woman who lived next door to the citizen who had just given this advice had a question.

"John," she said, "you and your family have been our closest friends for ten years. Do you mean to say that if this city was bombed and my baby and I were caught in the open, and we were hurt, and came to your shelter you would turn us away?"

John nodded in the affirmative. His neighbor pressed the point.

"But suppose we wouldn't turn away and begged to get in?"

"It would be too bad," John said. "You should have built a shelter of your own. I've got to look out for my own family."

"But suppose we had built a shelter of our own, yet were caught by surprise, being out in the open at the time of an attack, and we discovered that the entrance to our shelter was covered with rubble and we had no place to turn except to you. Would you still turn us back?"

The answer was still yes.

"But suppose I wouldn't go away and kept trying to get in. Would you shoot us?"

John said that if the only way he could keep his friend out would be by shooting her and her baby, he would have to do it.

In doing so, he could claim spiritual sanction. He referred to a recent issue of an important religious journal which presented a "code of ethics" of Christian morality designed to anticipate difficult questions that might arise in shelters. One point in the code advised the Christians to "think twice before they rashly give their family shelter space to friends and neighbors or to the passing stranger." Finally, the Hartford citizen could cite Civil Defense Coordinator Keith Dwyer's pronouncement that there is "nothing in the Christian ethic which denies one's right to protect oneself and one's family."

People speculate on the horrors that would be let loose by nuclear war. It is not necessary to speculate on such horrors. Some of the worst horrors are already here. The transformation today of otherwise decent people into death-calculating machines; the psychological preconditioning for an age of cannibalism; the wholesale premeditation of murder and the acceptable conditions thereof; the moral insolence of those who presume to prescribe the circumstances under which it is spiritually permissible to kill one's neighbors; the desensitization of human response to pain; the acquiescence in the inevitability of disaster; the cheapening of human personality with its concomitant of irresponsible fatalism—all these are part of an already existing, fast-swelling chamber of horrors.

It will be said that shelters and everything that goes with them are basic facts of nuclear war that do not disappear because we find them unpleasant. But this assumes there is no alternative. It assumes that everything has been done to prevent the holocaust from occurring in the first place. It assumes that we have no obligation to anyone except ourselves. Not until the individual declares a moratorium on the inconsequential in his life and invests himself fully in the effort to achieve a just and enforceable peace; indeed, not until the nation itself commits its moral energy, intelligence, and resources to a massive attempt to bolster the United Nations and give it appropriate powers of world law, however rigorous the opposition—not until these basic things are done is there warrant for defeatism. And even if these things are not done, there is never a warrant, social or spiritual, for cannibalism.

If we are truly interested in safeguarding this nation and the human values that go with it, we will scrutinize and memorize the nuclear facts of life. As a nation, we didn't fully understand the implications of these facts when we dropped the bomb on Hiroshima; we don't understand them yet. We have never quite comprehended that the use of such weapons constitutes a form of race suicide. It is impossible for any nation to wage nuclear war against another nation without also waging war against the human race. The winds are the conveyer belt of mass death. The nuclear gun contains three barrels: one is pointed against the enemy; a second is pointed against people who are not enemies; a third bends back completely and is pointed squarely at the holder.

An American demonstrates his patriotism not by pressuring for nuclear showdowns or by fast-and-loose talk about dropping hydrogen bombs but by tapping and putting to work the deepest wisdom the history of man has to offer. A new kind of force must be created which, when fully used, can safeguard this nation and its freedom and make a contribution to world peace in general. Military power no longer can accomplish that purpose.

President Kennedy's speech before the United Nations has the initial elements of that new kind of force. He made it clear that there is no security for anyone in a spiraling arms race; he called for total disarmament under adequate safeguards; he connected the need for disarmament to the need for establishing the institutions of world law: in short, he summoned the American people to a peace race. The full potential force of these words will be converted into a working program when the American people respond with depth and vigor. Earnest discussions among neighbors about their part in giving vital support to these ideas today may offer far more realistic protection for their families than shotguns for shooting down neighbors on a dreadful tomorrow.

If the battle for sanity and against cannibalism is lost, it will not be because of the inexorability of history but because men became so fascinated with the face of death that they lost hold of the meaning of life and the power inherent in it to shape its destiny.

The principal objections to the preceding two editorials on fallout shelters came from those who said we missed the main point. They did not quarrel with the facts we advanced about the possible inadequacy of shelters. Their argument was directed to an issue completely separate from shelters per se. This is what they said:

"The question of shelters is related to the war of nerves with the Soviet Union. The United States can afford to retreat no longer. If we back down on Berlin, it would be only a matter of months before an even larger threat would confront us. Therefore we have to make credible to the Russians the fact that we are prepared to fight for Berlin. We must mean it. We must not let them think we are so terrified of nuclear war that we don't have the nerve to fight. The Russians are scrutinizing us carefully for softness. If they see that the President really means business and is prepared to fight a nuclear war, and if they see that the American people are taking the possibility of nuclear war seriously and are not afraid to face up to it, they may not want to push us too far on the assumption we are bluffing. And a nationwide shelter-building program is the best evidence we can give them that the American people have the will to fight and endure a nuclear war.

"This is the whole point about fallout shelters. The facts in SR about firestorms and craters and suffocation hazards and bacteriological warfare may be true but they are irrelevant. In fact, they are dangerous. They are dangerous because they may dissuade people from building shelters. If this happens, it weakens our posture in dealing with the Russians."

The foregoing is a literal statement of the "credibility" theory. It is held by certain officials on the state and national levels. There is the candid admission that fallout shelters might not provide the protection as advertised, but the efficacy of the shelters is secondary to a strategical purpose. If one asks why this strategical purpose is not made clear to the American people as an intrinsic part of the argument for shelters, the answer one receives is that the people might not find it persuasive. It is felt they are not sufficiently sophisticated in complex questions involving strategical purpose and that only the hard line about personal and family safety is likely to work.

In a dictatorship, this kind of manipulation of public action and opinion might have some standing. In a free society, it is grotesquely out of place, and its advocates should be made to debate their propositions. It represents a surrender to the cynical view that only the few know what the many must believe and what they should be made to do. In this philosophy people cease to be people. They become pawns on a grand strategical chessboard to be deployed or sacrificed at the chessplayer's discretion. The American people may or may not agree with the reasoning of those who want to convince the Russians the United States is willing to fight a nuclear war, but they will not accept the proposition that they must become pawns in such an enterprise. Nor can they be expected to concur in the notion that their possible opposition to the credibility theory means they are unsophisticated about the complex problems of national survival.

Two issues are alive here. One is the irresponsibility and arrogance involved in a deliberate program of deceit and manipulation seeking to accomplish purposes that are not fully and directly stated. The other issue concerns the nature of the basic objectives and the quality of the reasoning behind them. The first issue needs no further exposition. We therefore proceed to the second.

The trouble with the credibility theory is that it makes the wrong things credible. It succeeds in convincing an enemy only that he must improve his nuclear capability to whatever point is necessary in order to cancel out a counter-move or possible advantage. Would United States policy makers change their position on Berlin or any other vital issue if the Russians began to build underground shelters both to prove to us that they really meant business and to increase their chances that some fraction of the population might survive after a nuclear war? Certainly not. Far from backing down on Berlin or any other issue involving our vital interests, we would make counter-moves to block or frustrate the Russian strategy. Our military people would resolutely produce nuclear weapons with ground-hugging, long-lived radioactivity characteristics. They would step up the production of firestorm-making nuclear bombs for the purpose of consuming the oxygen and driving people from the shelters into the radioactive open. In short, we would regard the Russian strategy as a feeble ploy and hold fast to our position. Yet we expect that the Russians will be deflected or influenced by strategy that would not move us.

The big need today is not to make credible to the Russians that we are only a feather's touch from nuclear war, but to make credible to the world's peoples that the United States has the wisdom to match its power. Any major war between nuclear nations is also a war against the human race. It is impossible to confine the lethal radiation to the war zones. Since all people are involved, it stands to reason that we need to make credible to them our awareness of their rights and our sense of total responsibility in the pursuit of our vital interests.

We will never achieve true security in anthing we do with or to the Russians. True security cannot be bought or contrived with nuclear power or with threats to use it. True security will be achieved in direct proportion to the reduction and elimination of anarchy in the dealings among nations. A country that commits itself fully to this objective and that pursues it with all the imagination and vigor at its command will be fashioning the only real protection available to it in the modern world.

—October 21, October 28, and November 4, 1961


# Report from the Congo

After I cleared customs at the Léopoldville airport, I asked an official where I could convert American money into Congo currency.

"Come with me," he said. "I'll take you to a money-changer who will give you twice the official rate."

"Isn't it illegal?" I asked.

"Don't worry about it," he replied. "It's much more illegal in the city. There they give you four times the official rate."

On the way into Léopoldville, I asked the Congo driver what conditions were like in the city.

"Who knows?" He shrugged. "I haven't been there since this morning."

I remarked that things appeared to be fairly quiet.

"Monsieur," he said, "it's the kind of quiet that comes from having people leave a place of trouble. The white ladies and gentlemen, many of them, they have gone away."

As we drove into the heart of Léopoldville I could compare it with recollections of a previous visit in 1957. At that time Léopoldville was one of the most impressive and spirited places I had seen anywhere in Africa. Africans and white people mingled freely. The atmosphere was vibrant, cosmopolitan. I observed many Africans reading newspapers and magazines, reflecting a far higher literacy rate than existed elsewhere on the continent. They were also better dressed than most other Africans. Almost all the children in the city wore shoes—most unusual for this part of the world. The buildings in the business section had clean, modern lines and were well spaced. All in all, it vied with Nairobi for the distinction of being the most attractive city in Africa.

On the surface, at least, the Belgian Congo appeared to justify its reputation as a trouble-free zone in a continent rapidly becoming a cauldron.

Now, five years later, it was difficult to realize I was in the same city. Much of the life seemed to have gone out of Léopoldville. Most cosmopolitan centers come into their own only when the sun goes down and the lights begin to sparkle. But Léopoldville at dusk seemed like a deserted city. Almost all the shops were closed. There were hardly any strollers. The few white people I saw were in cars.

The questions I had brought with me to the Congo became more insistent. Why had this place, which only a few years ago had seemed to so many observers to have so much built-in stability, suddenly come apart at the seams? Was it possible to make sense of the swirlings and churnings of all the different factions that dominated the news from the Congo? Why had the Congo, remote and relatively undeveloped, become a dangerous and explosive arena in which the conflicting interests of at least a half-dozen major powers and many more smaller ones were close to the point of explosion? Would the Congo become another Korea, with the United States and the Soviet Union engaged in a military showdown? If so, could a general nuclear war be averted? What about the role of the United Nations? What was the Katanga situation all about? The Congo had already cost numberless lives, including Dag Hammarskjöld's; how high a price would have to be paid before a normal beat could be brought to the heart of Africa?

An in-and-out flying visit to the Congo is obviously not enough to supply responsible answers to such questions, but at least it can provide some useful clues. It can also make known the general outlines of the plot and serve to identify the cast of characters.

Perhaps the best way to begin is by putting the Congo in a historical setting. It is one of the unhappy facts of history that the acquisition of independence has not always led in a straight line to an ordered and functioning society. Indeed, a period of disintegration seems almost to be a natural consequence of liberation. From 1783 to 1787 the American states were in a condition of virtual anarchy, following the War for Independence. The victory against Great Britain led to anything but domestic tranquillity. Powerful separatist movements took hold. It was only when men such as Washington, Hamilton, Madison, and Jay came together at Philadelphia that a design for a central federal government began to take shape.

France in 1789 fell into the wildest disorder. The struggle against the monarchy set the stage for a widespread condition of lynch law. Similar chaos existed in Germany in 1848. The annals of Italian history are disfigured with such disruptive experiences. India achieved its independence in 1947 through passive resistance and nonviolence, only to slide into wholesale communal bloodshed, resulting in the death of hundreds of thousands of Hindus and Moslems, with 12 million people left homeless.

It would indeed be remarkable if, against the long background of outside rule and a master-subject relationship, the African peoples were to run counter to history in passing from colonialism into freedom. In fact, what is most surprising about Africa is not that the upheaval and violence have been so pronounced but that, everything considered, they have not been even more acute.

In the case of the Congo, for example, the predictable ordeal following independence was intensified by divisive forces within the country itself. First of all, the Congo was never a political or cultural entity. Belgium was the governing colonial power, but the people of the Congo belonged to six regional or provincial units, which in turn were divided into districts and territories. The territories were divided into hundreds of chieftaincies. Cutting across all these were the ethnic or cultural groupings. There was little or no sense of nation or national goals. The Congo, to the Congolese, was a world defined and operated by the white outsiders.

Most of the independence movements of Asia have been accompanied by a powerful nationalistic thrust. Freedom was sought not just as an end in itself but as the means of achieving a unified national society. In the Congo, by contrast, independence pointed not to national unity and consolidation but to an internal struggle for power and for regional autonomy. In four of the six provinces or regions, local leaders were leaning away from the center. In the rich southern province of Katanga, forty-year-old Moise Tshombe was bidding for complete separation. In the Oriental province in the northeast, Antoine Gizenga advocated national unity but only on the basis of substantial authority for the regions, which would become republics. In the central province of Kasai, thirty-one-year-old Albert Kalonji, an agricultural assistant, wanted to retain more provincial authority than a genuine federation would permit. And in Léopoldville, capital of the Congo, Patrice Lumumba called for a unified country in a way that seemed to the other leaders to mean that he wanted to dominate the government.

The gravest fact in any total reckoning of the upheaval in the Congo is that the Belgians had prepared the Congolese for everything except self-government. They established comprehensive health and hospital services—but not hospital administrators. They prepared Congolese to be medical or dental assistants—but not doctors or dentists. They taught them to be government clerks—but not government officials. They taught them to construct buildings—but not to design them. They taught them to be good soldiers—but not to be officers. They gave them pensions and old-age security—but not the feeling that they were grownups capable of making decisions for themselves.

In education, the Belgians set up an impressive system of mass education surpassed by no other nation in Africa. For ninety-eight out of a hundred Congolese who went to school, however, the cut-off point came at the end of elementary school. There were 26,000 primary schools but only

300 secondary schools. At the top, it was not until 1956 that two universities were established by royal decree. Even here, however, white students accounted for a substantial part of the enrollment. Congolese students in both universities numbered less than 200.

In any event, at the time of independence in June, 1960, only seventeen men in the entire Congo were college graduates. Even among these, only two or three had any specialized training in government or public administration.

Opportunities for study in higher education abroad were virtually nonexistent. Thousands of promising young Africans from other countries had studied in Europe and the Americas. Not so the Congolese. Before 1959, perhaps not more than a dozen Congolese had been inside a Western university classroom. The Belgians discouraged foreign travel; they pursued a rigid policy of isolating the Congo not just from the West but from most of the rest of Africa.

Here, then, is one of the sharpest paradoxes in modern history. No colonial power did more for the Africans than the Belgians—in terms of housing, transportation, social welfare, basic education, and vocational training. In the end, however, no colonial power in Africa had to deal with a more violent or explosive situation.

The key to the paradox is that the Congolese got tired of being treated like children. No matter how devoted children may be to their parents, there comes a time when they want to be on their own. The Congolese were mindful of their economic advantages in comparison with most other Africans, but they were also mindful of their dependence on a generous outsider who was willing to give them everything except freedom. And in the end the freedom weighed more heavily than jobs, unemployment insurance, dispensaries, literacy, and a comfortable old age. Paternalism had worked beautifully—but only up to the point where people preferred the difficulties and dignity of adulthood to a congenial and perennial adolescence.

Even so, it is possible that the independence movement in the Congo might have been deferred for a decade or so had it not been for surrounding groundswells in Africa. Right across the Congo River, for example, fellow Africans were talking earnestly to their French masters about full independence. The French may have been less assiduous than the Belgians in taking care of the basic needs of their subjects, but one thing they did extremely well. They gave higher education to large numbers of Africans, unlocking the mysteries and complications associated with running a government. And Africans were being elected directly to the Chamber of Deputies in Paris, there to participate in the parliamentary process for all of France and not the colonies alone.

It is doubtful whether any single event preceding Congo independence made more of an impression on the Congolese than the visit in August,

1958, of General Charles de Gaulle to Brazzaville, capital of French Equatorial Africa, only a few hundred yards away from Léopoldville on the other side of the river. The French chief of state was characteristically forthright. He said that the question of independence for French Equatorial Africa was not for France to decide; as a matter of natural right it belonged to the African people themselves. France would be glad to work with the Africans before, during, and after independence according to the desire of the Africans themselves.

De Gaulle had spoken directly to the natural sense of dignity in people. As was to be expected, the people of French Equatorial Africa declared for freedom. Many people across the river had listened, too, and were coming to the same decision.

Among other external influences was the Pan-African Conference held in Ghana in December, 1958. Patrice Lumumba attended as head of the Congo National Movement Party. There he met the political giants of Africa, men like Nkrumah of Ghana, and Sekou Touré of Guinea. He had a sense of belonging to a continent-wide crusade. The Ghana Conference called for immediate independence of all Africa. Lumumba returned to Léopoldville fully ignited with the resolve to represent not only the Congo but the entire continent of Africa in the independence movement against Belgium.

"The Congolese people must stop sleeping," he declared. "The Congo is our country. It is our duty to make it greater and better."

These were strong and strange words for a people who had far less national consciousness than most of their fellow Africans, but they began to feel themselves caught up in a powerful undertow that meant more than liberation from the benevolent outsider; it meant personal emancipation and growth and a chance at adulthood. For it was not enough just to own a nation; they wanted to own themselves.

The Belgian government hardly knew what to make of all the stirrings and rumblings from the Congo. Only a few years earlier, in 1955, King Baudouin of Belgium had visited the Congo and was tumultuously received by his Congo subjects. True, there were indications that the continent-wide clamor for independence had some reverberations inside the Congo, but no one, including the Congolese themselves, believed that anything serious in the direction of freedom was likely to occur for many years. In fact, a few months after King Baudouin returned home, a Belgian professor, A. A. J. Van Bilsen, startled both Belgians and Congolese with a radical proposal of a thirty-year plan for an independent Congo.

Not thirty but three years later the serious trouble began. Sporadic demonstrations were taking place in the key cities. New parties were springing up all over; within the parties countless factions were asserting themselves. Almost any negative development, such as an increase in unemployment, or suppression of independence advocates, became the occasion for public protests or even rioting. In January, 1959, came the first mass outbreak of violence. Crowds swarmed through the streets of many cities shouting independence, attacking white people, looting and destroying European-owned shops.

The magnitude of the uprisings made a profound impression on the Belgians. They declared they had every intention of granting independence to the Congo and would work with the Congolese toward that end. However, no dates were mentioned. King Baudouin returned to the Congo in December, 1959, to put the full strength of the Crown behind the Belgian assurances. The acclaim that greeted him only four years earlier was now replaced by demonstrations and demands. One fact, however, seemed abundantly clear. The King had not lost his personal popularity. The demonstrations were not directed *at* him or *against* him but *to* him.

The Belgian government acted swiftly to convince the Congolese that Belgium was not standing in the way of independence. A round-table conference was scheduled for Brussels in January, 1960. To it were invited representatives of the various Congolese parties and factions. Belgian colonial administrators and government officials would meet with them on even footing and discuss the number one question—independence, how and when.

In all, some 150 delegates and officials sat at the Conference table, 96 of them Congolese. It was the most dramatic event in the short but intense history of the Congo independence movement. All the principal characters who were to make headlines in the coming months were there —Lumumba, Tshombe, Gizenga, Kasavubu, Kalonji, Nwamba, and Bolya, among others.

The contrast between the Belgians and the Congolese couldn't have been more dramatic. Many of the Belgians had been in government posts long before most of the Congo delegates were born. The average age of the Congolese was somewhere between thirty-four and thirty-five. The principal occupation represented among the Congolese was that of clerk. Only a handful of the Congo delegates had training beyond the secondary school. Some of them, such as Tshombe, had taken correspondence courses in accounting.

The Belgians asked the Congolese whether they could agree on a timetable for independence. Here the factionalism ended. The Congolese said they wanted freedom immediately; that is, within six months. They were astounded when the Belgians put up no argument but proceeded at once to the question of orderly transition. Some of the Congolese, no doubt, had expected that the Belgians would counter the demand for immediate independence with a proposal for an eight- or ten-year program for orderly takeover, with widespread and intensive training in self-government. On this proposal, the Congolese could have withdrawn their own demand for immediate freedom, after which a compromise might have been reached on the basis of a two- or three-year timetable.

If such were the calculations of some of the Congolese, they could experience no elation over the sudden and total concurrence of the Belgians. For the Congolese would have to organize and operate a major government for which they possessed neither immediate means nor qualifications. The starting date was July 1, 1960. The hundred-odd political parties lacked cohesion and clearly defined support; there were now so many of them that representative government was apt to degenerate into a free-for-all. Moreover, no central core existed which could keep the provinces from splitting off. Finally, the general rioting of January, 1959, had indicated the existence of explosive forces which the slightest weakness at the top might touch off again.

There was speculation in various capitals of Africa that the Belgians had readily agreed to immediate independence because they wanted to dramatize the inability of the Congolese to govern themselves, after which the Belgians would return, re-establishing and strengthening their hold on the basis of demonstrated need. A similar argument was that Belgium had no real interest in the Congo except for Katanga, where the government was a full partner in the operation of one of the world's most powerful and profitable mining companies, Union Minière. According to this thesis, Belgium was willing to cut loose the troublesome and expensive part of its colony as long as it could retain control, with the help of a few cooperative Congo leaders, over the incredibly rich mining province.

When such speculations came to the attention of the Belgians, they pointed out that no matter what they did they were bound to be accused of crass imperialism and bad faith. If they resisted the demand for immediate independence, they would be accused of typical colonial obstinacy and selfishness. If they offered to train Congolese for government functions, they would be accused of imposing their own way of doing things on people who said they would rather make their own mistakes than be efficient in the manner of the colonial power. Either way, they would be damned.

The truth of the matter, the Belgians said, was that they were fed up. They looked ahead and saw nothing but trouble, with the disorders of January, 1959, magnified many times, and with the probable result that they would be forced out of the Congo anyway—in rags and tatters. Now, while they still had ample reason for pride in their stewardship of the Congo, was the time to leave—especially since they were invited to do so.

In any event, the Belgians said, their hand was forced once General de Gaulle made what seemed to them to be grandiose pronouncements about self-government when he visited nearby Brazzaville. That was when the infection really took hold, they contended; after that, there was only one way to go—out.

In reply, Belgium's critics argued that a long-range program of preparation for Congo freedom should have been instituted many years earlier. They pointed out that Belgium did not have to wait for a round-table conference to establish the need for the orderly transfer of authority. Nor did General de Gaulle, they added, give birth to the independence movement in the Congo; all he did was to call attention to some universal aims in human society. The Congolese had overheard De Gaulle, experienced the shock of recognition, and moved more confidently in the direction it was inevitable they would take anyway.

Whatever the historical verdict on the Brussels round-table conference, the uncontested fact is that the Congolese leaders returned home bearing complete victory but not the means of making it work. True, the round table had reached agreement on some of the structural problems. The six provinces of the Congo were to continue as such but would be integrated into a single independent government, with a parliament in Léopoldville. The parliament would consist of two houses, a lower house for representatives directly elected by the people, and an upper house for senators chosen by the provincial assemblies. The parliament was charged with the responsibility for electing a national president who would appoint a premier, who in turn would appoint a cabinet. The Belgians would be phased out of their government posts and the Congolese completely installed by June 30, 1960. The provincial governments would exercise the main authority pending the formation of the central government.

So far so good. But this still left unanswered the functional questions: Whom would the people elect? Would the elected officials have the knowledge required to make government work? Who would operate the transportation services, the communications system, the hospitals, the large farms, the food-processing plants, the clinics, the social welfare agencies, the police department, the courts, the mails? Who would run the army? The Belgians had not trained a single Congolese officer.

Just as important: Could the multitude of parties be thinned out or consolidated so that the menace of factionalism could be averted and their programs made intelligible to the voters?

On the surface, it seemed logical enough to give the provincial governments primary authority during the transitional period. But this carried with it the danger that the provincial leaders would dig in and resist subordinating themselves later to a higher authority. Separatist feelings— or, rather, the absence of any highly developed national awareness— were enough of a problem already without fostering the conditions that would make them even stronger. If the aim was to build a unified Congo, one way not to do it was by fortifying the provincial psychology and habits.

In any case, even before the transitional period was over, the trouble started. Major tribal clashes, always a threat, flared up in various parts of the country; the provincial authorities struggled to bring them under control. Sporadic rioting against the white population added to the tension.

By May, 1960, only a month before independence became official, the nation was already on a downward spiral. There were some 110,000 Belgians in the Congo; suddenly, the exodus began. A general impression in the United States is that almost all the Belgians in the Congo were businessmen or plantation owners. Not so. Many of them were agronomists, machinists, engineers, electrical experts, sanitation specialists, doctors, veterinarians, aviation technicians, etc. When, alarmed by the rioting and an uncertain future, the Belgians pulled out of the country by the plane-load, the Congo began to run down. Agricultural machinery could not be kept in proper repair, with a dreadful reckoning to come in the food supply. Livestock could not be promptly treated for disease; infections spread. Roads were not repaired after the heavy equatorial rains, impeding the circulatory flow of the national economy. Schools tried to function without teachers. Shops stored their wares and closed down. The mails were unreliable.

Politically, the Congo was even more disorganized in the period just before independence than it was economically. All the later upheavals were foreshadowed in the inability of the Congo leaders to get together. Patrice Lumumba's party tallied enough votes in the general elections to make Lumumba the leading candidate for chief of state, but enough of the other parties pooled their strength to challenge his national leadership. Joseph Kasavubu, as head of the ABAKO (Federalist) party, pitted himself against Lumumba. In fact, with only one week to go before independence, Lumumba and Kasavubu each claimed to have a fully formed government ready to run the country. The newly formed Parliament broke the impasse. Kasavubu was elected president and Lumumba was appointed premier.

Five days later a free but sick Congo was born.

King Baudouin came to Léopoldville to take part in the official celebration. It lasted four days. Public elation, such as it was, seemed well under control, at least on the surface. Whether the Congolese were emotionally exhausted by the densely packed events leading to independence or whether they kept their joy to themselves, the ceremonies in the Congo seemed somewhat matter of fact.

On July 4 the fireworks began. In Equator province, workers went on strike because the pre-election promises of the government had not yet been met, though the government was less than a week old. A handful of people were killed when troops fired into a crowd.

The next day, tribal warfare broke out in Kasai province. Hundreds of homes were burned.

On July 6, chaos hit the armed forces. Belgian officers had remained at their posts, in keeping with the agreement with the new government. But all at once the army disintegrated. A large part of the 35,000-man force decided to fend for itself. The Belgians had failed to train Congolese to be officers, and thousands of soldiers became men on the loose with guns. Most of the Belgian officers fled for their lives. The Congolese government was unequal to the job of controlling its own army.

Now the disorders spread to the civilian population. The many thousands of whites still in the Congo—not only Belgian but American, English, French, German, Scandinavian, Italian, etc., many of them in the diplomatic service—tried desperately to evacuate. The combination of panic or near-panic among the whites and lawlessness among the Congolese produced a dangerously volatile situation. The atmosphere was one of terror as reports spread of looting, beatings, and rape in various cities.

At this point, units of the regular Belgian army went into action in an attempt to restore order. Paratroopers were dropped into the rioting areas. And now the Congolese government itself became panicky, fearing that the Belgians had come back to stay.

In the midst of all the pandemonium, Moise Tshombe announced the secession of Katanga. Furthermore, he said he welcomed the presence of Belgian troops and was asking Brussels for more. He also said he was asking Belgium to maintain its economic connections in Katanga. This was the first clear reference to the fact that the vast mining operations, in which the Belgian government owned a direct large interest, would continue to play a key and perhaps dominant role in Katanga.

This meant that the greatest single source of revenue for the central government would now be abruptly cut off. The Union Minière mines in Katanga accounted for more than fifty million dollars of government income. All this would now go to Katanga.

Confronted with civil war, secession, bankruptcy, tribal conflict, rioting, a mutinous army, attacks on whites, and the grim prospect of Belgium's return, the Congo government called on the United States for military help.

President Eisenhower said he was troubled by the Congo's difficulties but thought it inadvisable for any of the large powers to send troops.

Belgian paratroopers were able to restore a reasonable degree of order in many of the areas where the whites were in jeopardy, but the effect on the Congo government was far from calming. For with each additional Belgian soldier on Congo soil, there was a geometric increase in Premier Lumumba's anxiety. He feared he might never get them out again. Hence, his vigorous demands that the Belgian forces withdraw. The demands were ignored. The paratroopers continued to attempt to stop the looting and chase down the mutineers.

And now the Soviet Union came onto the stage, vigorously identifying itself with Lumumba's demand for full withdrawal by Belgium. There was more than a hint in the Soviet pronouncement that it intended to stay very close to the Congo situation.

Washington warned Moscow to stay out.

Other nations, large and small, now involved themselves in the debate. The ordeal of the Congo was no longer a purely African question. Like Spain in 1936, Korea in 1951, and Laos in 1960, Congo had all the raw materials for igniting multiple war.

The total situation of the Congo worsened by the hour. On July 12, Premier Lumumba formally and urgently appealed to the United Nations for military help against Belgian "aggression." He said nothing about the internal anarchy but it seemed clear he wanted to deprive Belgium of any justification for keeping troops in the Congo.

In New York, the Security Council debated the request within a few hours after it was received. It was argued that UN action in the Congo would represent an intrusion into internal affairs. The counter-argument was that affairs in the Congo now constituted a specific threat to world peace. Unless the UN acted boldly and promptly, it was said, it would be confronted with the need to risk countless thousands of lives in a Korea-type action. The request for military aid to Congo was voted by the UN on July 14, less than two days after the Congo request.

The Belgians assured the UN they would withdraw their forces if the United Nations could restore order.

Secretary Dag Hammarskjöld had to act swiftly to implement the resolution. He knew that Communist China had volunteered to put its troops at the disposal of Patrice Lumumba. He was also aware that Lumumba had been in communication with the Soviet Union on the matter of military assistance.

Hammarskjöld ordered a group of UN officials, then stationed in Jerusalem and the Gaza Strip to superintend the truce between Egypt and Israel, to Léopoldville. He sent urgent requests to the African nations for fully trained troops who would form a UN police force in the Congo. Meanwhile the UN's ace trouble shooter, the American Nobel laureate, Ralph J. Bunche, was already in Léopoldville in connection with the independence ceremonies. Bunche was assigned to the job of superintending the UN action. John McDiarmid, from the UN's staff, became Bunche's executive assistant.

The first troops for the UN army arrived on July 15. Within two days a total of almost 3,000 troops assembled on Congo soil—from Ghana, Guinea, Morocco, Sweden, Tunisia, and Mali—to be augmented later by crack units from Ethiopia, Ireland, and India. Most of them were flown in by mammoth Globemaster planes made available by the United States. President Eisenhower also authorized U.S. help in a massive air-lift operation to fly in food.

Day by day, the UN forces built up to an eventual total of 19,000 men.

The Belgian forces gradually withdrew, except from Katanga, where they were welcome.

The UN's first job was to stop the random violence wherever it existed —whether it took the form of tribal warfare, marauding armed soldiers who had mutinied, attacks on whites, or looting and destruction of property. It was a mammoth undertaking. The Congo covers an area almost as large as Western Europe. Each city had to be policed. Tribal uprisings could occur anywhere.

The UN did what it could to keep the entire Congo from going up in smoke. It was able to create enough law and order to make life and property reasonably secure, at least in the cities. But it could not dictate the national and provincial political stability which alone makes an ordered society possible. Nor could it prevent tribal violence and pillaging, resulting in death or homelessness for many thousands of Congolese. And coping with a mutinous army was like trying to meet the danger of fire after thousands of a nation's fire fighters have turned arsonists.

Yet the signal fact is that the general anarchy was brought to an end. And the danger that chaos in the Congo would result in big-power intervention and war was checked, although it has yet to be removed altogether.

The UN military operation, however, was just one side of a total Congo undertaking, though necessarily the larger one. The other side had to do with the total workings of a national society. Ralph Bunche quickly recognized that the business of establishing law and order called for more than policemen. The economy had to be restored. Goods had to be manufactured, shipped, or imported. Banks had to function. Schools and hospitals had to be reopened and staffed. Power installations had to be manned. Food had to be planted, and harvested. Roads had to be reopened or rebuilt; buses put back in running order; planes serviced; radio facilities made operable. Thousands of refugees had to be given shelter, food, medicine.

This quickly became a vital part of the UN mission in the Congo, although it never got into the headlines.

The UN mobilized experts from all over the world. It brought in industrial engineers, administrators, sanitation specialists, financial and trade experts, doctors, nurses, hospital administrators, mechanics, professors, teachers, farmers, builders, refugee specialists.

In general, the nonmilitary program was divided into four broad parts. The first was to meet the emergency situations, i.e., putting UN experts or technicians to work immediately in government departments as advisers, operating the hospitals, setting up famine relief facilities, caring for refugees, opening up lines of transportation and communication, etc.

The second was to set up an emergency training program under which Congolese could take over jobs in government.

The third was to lay the groundwork of a national system of education from elementary schools right through the university, with emphasis on the training of teachers, engineers, agricultural specialists, and doctors.

The fourth was to repair and develop the economy. This involved an almost infinite variety of projects—all the way from building drainage canals and roads to reconstructing pig-breeding stations and putting bulldozers back in working order. It meant meeting the perilous unemployment problem and reopening trade between the Congo and the rest of the world.

Obviously, the UN didn't do all these things as soon at it came into the Congo. But it had to draw up its plans right way and move into action without delay. For police action would be meaningless unless the basic problems of food, jobs, schools, hospitals, and a functioning economy could be met.

Meanwhile, however, the political situation in the Congo was unbelievably muddled and explosive in the early days following independence. Patrice Lumumba was making inflammatory and irresponsible speeches, some of them against the UN. He complained that the UN was not getting the Belgians out of the Congo fast enough and he threatened to call on the Soviet Union for help. He also wanted the UN to invade Katanga. At one point on July 20, the Congolese parliament was so appalled by his actions that it censured him for "Communist-leaning dictatorial demands and ultimatums."

Lumumba tried to deal with the problem of mutiny in the national army by buying the services of the soldiers. He kept upping the pay until the weekly offer exceeded the amount many Congolese earned in a full year.

Other contenders for power joined the bidding. Attempting to collect a personal army out of the large reservoir of soldiers-on-the-loose became standard operating procedure for would-be generals or political leaders. In some instances, the going pay exceeded the salary scale of the U.S. Army. This competition for soldiers was but another irrational element in a situation already peppered with Alice-in-Wonderland qualities.

Lumumba's flamboyant manner and his habit of personalizing the business of government added to the general disintegration. Since he made little distinction between the government and himself, some of the provincial leaders tended to regard him accordingly. Their dislike for Lumumba carried over to the central government.

The breakaway of Katanga was followed by the secession of part of the Kasai province. Albert Kalonji, with a small army he had hired on the open market, set himself up as king of South Kasai. Both in South Kasai and Katanga, hundreds of Belgians were returning to important government and military posts.

And now the large northeast province of Oriental became shaky. For a time no one really seemed to know whether it was in or out.

The infection spread, and the adjoining province of Kivu also decided to go its own way, at least to the extent of keeping all revenues that would ordinarily go to the central government at Léopoldville.

Thus, within a couple of months after independence, the fragmentation was well advanced, with four of the six Congo provinces in varying stages of separation. In at least two of the four, Belgians were again in prime positions of authority. The central government found itself with a sharply increased budget—to pay for the army and all the relief and reconstruction projects—but with only a fraction of the anticipated income from the provinces.

By the end of August, through personal arrangement between Lumumba and the Soviet government, 100 Russian trucks and ten Russian planes were placed at Lumumba's disposal for use in the civil war with South Kasai.

The rift between Premier Lumumba and President Kasavubu steadily widened. Kasavubu became increasingly apprehensive about Lumumba's opposition to the UN, his arrogation of authority beyond the constitution, his dealings with the Soviet Union, and the build-up of a personal political machine.

On September 5, Kasavubu declared that Lumumba had brought the Congo to a point of almost total dissolution and that he, Kasavubu, exercising the same authority under which he had appointed Lumumba to the premiership, was now dismissing him.

One hour later, Lumumba dismissed Kasavubu.

Thus the central government, involved in civil war struggles on four fronts, itself became a battleground between Kasavubu and Lumumba. Fighting crowds, upholding one man or the other, swarmed through the streets. Lumumba turned to the Soviet Union for help. Kasavubu turned to the United Nations. Belgium speeded up its arms shipments to Katanga. Soviet fighter planes tried to land in Léopoldville but were turned back by Kasavubu forces.

No one quite knew what government was in command or where. Two separate delegations from the Congo, each claiming to represent the government, arrived at the United Nations in New York. The United States stepped up its mammoth air lift of troops and food to UN authorities in the Congo.

A few days later, the thirty-one-year-old head of the national Congo army, General Joseph Mobutu, announced he was reorganizing the government, was putting both Lumumba and Kasavubu on the sidelines, was ordering all Soviet diplomats and personnel to get out of the country within twenty-four hours, and was forming a provisional "College of Commissioners" to run the country until things calmed down.

Lumumba promptly ordered Mobutu's arrest. Mobutu ordered Lumumba's arrest. When the smoke cleared, Mobutu was still the head of the army and Lumumba was in custody. Lumumba stayed that way until sometime in January, 1961, when he was sent to Katanga. He never came out alive.

Meanwhile, following the jailing of Lumumba in September, 1960, Antoine Gizenga announced that, as vice premier, he was now Lumumba's legitimate successor as chief of state. He made his claims, however, from his stronghold in Stanleyville, in the remote province of Oriental, and showed extreme reluctance to assume his office in Léopoldville. He seized the various assets of the national government then in Stanleyville. Like Lumumba, he seemed to feel that the only important sympathetic outside attention he could get was from the Soviet Union.

In Léopoldville, General Mobutu continued on the course he set for himself. He staffed his College of Commissioners with the best-educated young men he could find. He reorganized the army, made progress in the war against the secessionists, then announced that he was relinquishing his authority and restoring the government to its constitutional status. President Kasavubu resumed the post of president and appointed Joseph Ileo, a former department-store clerk, as premier. Ileo failed to command enough support in Parliament and in the country as a whole and was eventually replaced by Cyrille Adoula, a forty-one-year-old moderate.

Adoula, a former businessman and bank clerk, had somehow managed during all this time to steer an even course through all the ice floes and glaciers, not only coming out alive politically, but retaining the respect of almost all the key figures and factions involved in the Congo currents— Gizenga and Tshombe not excluded. Indeed, Tshombe, at the height of his opposition to the central government, found it possible to pay tribute to Adoula's fairness and integrity.

The early months of 1961 furnished the first hopes, however thin and tentative, that the Congo might make it as a nation, after all. The rebellion in Kasai had been put down; Kivu had been brought back into the government; Gizenga in Oriental had toned down considerably his once-strident claims as Lumumba's heir; many of the marauding soldiers had been reintegrated into a central army; and young Congolese trained by the UN in government courses were now being "graduated" into key administrative posts.

Equally important, the work of UN specialists and technicians in restoring the economy of the Congo was now beginning to bear fruit. The UN had put many old roads back into commission and was opening up new ones. Telecommunications were now functioning again. The airport was in full operation. Thousands of units of farm machinery had been repaired by the UN and were now in full use. Thanks to the UN the threat of widespread famine was fast receding, the schools were now on a regular schedule, manned by hundreds of school supervisors and teachers recruited by the UN from all over the world. Other schools—on the secondary and college level—were being planned and built.

The problem of outbreaks had not been completely solved. All at once, for no apparent reason, violence would flare up in one place or another. There would be isolated massacres of civilians or missionaries and tribal uprisings. But these were now decreasing both in severity and frequency.

All in all, there was a general air of optimism about the prospects of the Congo—not just in Léopoldville but at United Nations headquarters in New York. It seemed like a good time to turn all energies to the number one problem—national unity.

A reconciliation conference was held outside the Congo, on the island of Madagascar, in May, 1961. All the political leaders attended—Tshombe, Gizenga, and Kalonji included. It was agreed that the Congo would become a confederation with authority in all matters of common interest. It would issue currency, levy and collect taxes, maintain a central army, make foreign policy, etc. Further, it was agreed that an implementing conference would be held in June, inside the Congo, at Coquilhatville, Equator province.

The Coquilhatville meeting hit a snag when Tshombe retreated from the Madagascar agreement. In particular, he wanted a lot more autonomy for Katanga than a national government could permit. The matter of tax revenue from the Belgian-controlled Union Minière operations was another big question. Tshombe seemed unwilling to relinquish the $50 million annually paid him by the mining company. When Tshombe refused to take further part in the discussions, he was arrested at the order of Kasavubu, kept in a Coquilhatville prison for two weeks, then sent to Léopoldville, where he was confined under house arrest.

Toward the end of July, Tshombe said he had changed his mind and would abide by the Coquilhatville agreement. He signed a statement to that effect and was released; he returned to Katanga where he promptly denounced the agreement, declaring he had signed it under duress.

Once again the Congo fever began to rise. The United States became apprehensive about the increasing danger that all the gains of recent months would dissolve in the heat of new secessionist activity, led by Tshombe in the south and Gizenga in the north. For secession inevitably meant nationwide disintegration and this in turn meant that the Congo might be up for grabs in an international free-for-all. The Soviet Union had clearly indicated a prime interest in the Congo; in fact, the appearance of Mr. Khrushchev at the 1960 session of the UN General Assembly was a direct reflection of the importance attached by the Soviet Union to the emergence of the new independent African nations. And the Congo—literally, politically, geographically—was the heart of Africa.

One way or another, a divided and disintegrating Congo might either become a Soviet sphere of influence or repeat the tragic experience of Korea. The United States lent its full support, therefore, to the effort of the United Nations to pacify the Congo, reunite it, and strengthen it for the long ordeal of independence.

In this connection, it seems clear that the Soviet Union made a serious miscalculation in its assessment of U.S. policy in the Congo. The Soviet apparently believed that any showdown situation in Africa would find the United States siding with the imperialist powers. Indeed, at the core of Soviet propaganda activities in Africa was the attempt to make it appear that the United States had no real sympathy for the emerging nations. Soviet radio programs beamed at Africa made every effort to link secessionist Katanga with American policy. Everything was made to fit together snugly in the Soviet ideological analysis. Union Minière was one of the biggest capitalist enterprises in the world. It produced an important part of the world's total supply of copper, uranium, cobalt, and manganese. It did so by the sweat of African labor. It was owned in large part by one of the imperialist powers. It was the quintessence of everything the socially conscious African was against. It was inevitable, the Soviet ideologists seemed convinced, that the United States would go down the line with its European imperialist allies, thus dramatizing the role of the Soviet Union as the sole champion of the African peoples against enslavement and exploitation.

The analysis represented—and perhaps still represents—a mammoth Soviet miscalculation. For the United States has committed itself to an independent Africa in general and a united Congo in particular, making their own decisions about their own resources. Not that the U.S. decision was an easy one. The Congo posed one of the most complex dilemmas in American foreign policy since the end of World War II. If we went against our allies in Africa, there was a danger of weakening our position in Europe, where NATO had to serve as the main structural prop of whatever common defense could be established. But if we supported European interference in Africa, we would alienate not only Africa but a large part of Asia, clear the way for Soviet influence, and increase the chances of a senseless and tragic war. The decision was made to support an independent Congo.

British and French interests were involved in Union Minière. Along with the Belgians, they feared that if Katanga were reintegrated into the Congo, the central government might nationalize the mines. Even a separate Katanga, however, had its difficulties. Moishe Tshombe had undeniable leadership qualities; he was intelligent, resourceful, determined. He enjoyed the full confidence of the Lunda people in southern Katanga. But the Lundas were only one-third of the population of Katanga. The remaining two-thirds consisted mostly of Baluba tribesmen, traditional enemies of the Lundas. In any general election or test of self-determination in Katanga, victory for Tshombe was far from automatic..

It would be highly risky to include Baluba troops in any Katanga army. In building a fighting force, therefore, Tshombe had to hire foreign officers and advisors, some of them Belgian, some of them French officers and soldiers who had once served in Algeria. These mercenaries never numbered more than several hundred, but they were a fighting elite.

Meanwhile, some 3,000 United Nations troops were already in Katanga on the same basis as elsewhere—to prevent rioting and looting and to maintain order. Maintenance of law and order in Katanga, however, was far less a problem than in the other provinces, certainly as far as relations between whites and blacks were concerned. Tribal clashes between Balubas and Lundas were troublesome, to be sure, but even here UN troops and Katanga forces often worked side by side to keep tribal disorders or rioting in check.

With each passing month, the United Nations became increasingly concerned about the Katanga mercenaries, who, as the UN saw it, added to the risk of a full-scale war between the central government and the province. For Léopoldville had been badly stung by Tshombe's habit of agreeing in principle to the need for Congo unity, then going into reverse the moment he returned to Katanga.

Dag Hammarskjöld used the full weight of his office against any military showdown. The UN, however, did strengthen the Secretary General's hand with a resolution calling upon Tshombe to get rid of his mercenaries. Tshombe refused.

Then began a series of incidents between UN and Katanga troops. For their inception, the blame is at least evenly divided. The attacks on UN personnel in nearby Kivu may have made some UN troops jittery. On one occasion, UN forces reacted sharply to a Katanganese provocation. This was followed by a campaign of harassment against the UN forces. Tshombe did nothing to ease the tension when he inflamed the people against the UN, proclaiming that each citizen had the solemn duty to kill a UN soldier. The UN responded by strengthening its patrols. Several clashes took place.

Dag Hammarskjöld left New York for the Congo on September 9. He and his aides were killed when their plane crashed on September 17 just outside the Katanga border, five miles from Ndola, Rhodesia. The cause of the crash has yet to be fully ascertained.

The clashes between the UN and Tshombe subsided—at least for the time being. Then, in December, 1961, they broke out again, this time with increased severity. The fighting never reached the dimensions of a full military engagement—total casualties on both sides never exceeded several hundred—but the danger of wider involvement increased almost daily. More mercenaries and arms arrived in Katanga.

Tshombe said he would be willing to meet with Adoula to discuss the problem of peace in the Congo. He wanted assurances of personal safety, however, and appealed to President John F. Kennedy for his assistance in facilitating a safe round trip to Kitona, near Léopoldville, where the meeting would be held.

President Kennedy telephoned the U.S. Ambassador, Edmund A. Gullion, at Léopoldville. He instructed Gullion to escort Tshombe personally from Elisabethville to the conference table in Kitona and provide for his safe return. The *Columbine*, the four-engine plane used for national security purposes, was place at the Ambassador's disposal.

Both sides stopped shooting on December 19. The same day, Ambassador Gullion took off for Ndola, in Rhodesia, where he met Tshombe.

In talking to Tshombe, it quickly became apparent to the American Ambassador that the meeting with Adoula might not eventuate. Tshombe asked for all sorts of concessions and assurances that Gullion was in no position to give. President Tshombe threatened to withdraw. Ambassador Gullion stood firm. After several hours of deadlock, Tshombe finally agreed to take off for Kitona.

The Kitona meeting lasted more than two full days. The participants worked around the clock, taking only brief periods for snatches of sleep, and eating at the conference table. There were tense and difficult stretches. But Adoula and Tshombe got along well. Finally, eight points were agreed upon. In essence, they provided that Katanga would end its secession, get rid of its mercenaries, send its representatives and senators to Parliament in accordance with the Constitution, and proceed in other ways to play its full role in an integrated Congo. Tshombe insisted that any agreement was subject to full consideration and ratification by his Parliament and Cabinet.

Tshombe flew back safely to Elisabethville in the *Columbine*. Ambassador Gullion returned to Léopoldville and telephoned the President the good news about Kitona—and kept his fingers crossed. Then Gullion went to bed for the first time in four days.

Two days later, in Elisabethville, Tshombe saw reporters and virtually repudiated Kitona; he said he had been coerced by Ambassador Gullion.

The same day, Soviet Ambassador Valerian A. Zorin denounced the American role at Kitona for exactly the opposite reason. Ambassador Gullion, he charged, was actually serving Tshombe's interests.

These contradictory charges, from the extremes of left and right, were equally false and tended to be self-canceling.

Adoula served notice on Tshombe that he expected the latter to make good on the Kitona agreement. The central army went on the move against Tshombe.

Tshombe began to implement the agreements. By mid-January, the only major point outstanding concerned the mercenaries. Adoula made clear he would hold his ground.

Meanwhile, Adoula also moved against Gizenga. It seems likely that Tshombe had raised questions at Kitona about the separatist activities of Gizenga, as well as Gizenga's nominal post as vice premier of the national government. It seems equally likely that Adoula declared that Katanga would be asked to make no commitments that would not also apply to Oriental. Moreover, the central government had every intention of apprehending Gizenga as part of the reuniting of the Congo. The action against Gizenga was successfully completed by January 20.

What about Tshombe's future? One quickly learns in the Congo not to make predictions about anything that might happen a month later, or even on the morrow. Yet it is not inconceivable that the end of Katanga's secession, if it happens without major military action, might be accompanied by Tshombe's appointment to the Adoula cabinet, perhaps as finance minister.

The ordeal in the Congo is far from over. But the main elements of a federated, independent Congo at peace are visible at long last. If it should happen, the United States would achieve its most notable foreign policy success in at least ten years. And the United Nations, now in a crisis of confidence, would have an infusion of new hope created by the single most notable service in its sixteen-year history. No man in the world would have been more gratified by such an outcome than Mr. Hammarskjöld.

*—February 3, 1962*


# The Cosmos Is Still Friendly

All during the week, as reports spread on the anticipated solar eclipse and the rare alignment of the planets, mass anxiety mounted throughout the world. By Saturday evening, shock waves of morbid apprehension penetrated into the most obscure villages. In India, Hindu priests were surrounded by swirls of people fearing a collision of the planets. In Africa, pounding drums called attention to the ill omens. In Europe and the Americas, astrologers and crystal-ball gazers were besieged by terrified customers. In Chicago, one citizen offered a soothsayer half of everything he owned if he could contrive to keep the universe from blowing up over the weekend. And in Los Angeles, a man who feared the end of the world rushed to his bank to withdraw all his money.

By Monday afternoon, it was apparent that the doomsday forecasts had been exaggerated. The fever of apprehension subsided and people resumed their normal concerns.

What was most significant about the entire episode was that man's abode on earth was genuinely in danger but most people were looking in the wrong direction for the source of the trouble. The planets were not going berserk; it was man himself who was wandering precariously off course. And the eclipse of human intelligence, rather than the eclipse of the sun, was responsible for the long shadow obscuring man's future. A collision of nations was far more of a threat than any celestial accident. The universe showed no signs of withdrawing the conditions that made life possible; man himself, however, was showing every sign of rejecting this bounty.

Most curious of all was man's ability to detach himself from his own species in contemplating his destiny. He seldom even considered the totality of which he was a part. The concept of the human family had little claim on his imagination or his loyalties. The furthest his thinking could carry him was his status as a member of a national tribe. Thus virtually all his inventiveness and energy went into the effort to protect his tribe or to make it dominant over the others. He had reached the point where such tribal engagements could seriously lead to his own downfall, but this was not a governing fact. Men who were intelligent in most respects never got past the primitive point of national confrontation in their thinking. They locked themselves into the absolute conviction that peace could be sustained if the opposing ugly tribe could be expunged.

In the tribe called the Soviet Union, a delusion took hold that fantastic threats, some of them involving the detonation of city-sized fireballs, could gain respect for its point of view. And in the United States, where creative thinking directed to the human condition was the vital ingredient that went into its founding, weird misconceptions replaced the moral imagination. There was insufficient realization that the nation's security and freedom no longer could be maintained primarily through military means. All the working evidence demonstrated this fact. Year by year, the size and nature of the force swelled, and year by year the security diminished. A new primary approach was needed; in short, something far more powerful than giant explosives and chemical-and-disease bombs would have to be put to work in a massive way.

Such a new approach would have to begin with some philosophical convictions on America's role in history. If that role aimed solely at national greatness, then the greatness would never be achieved. But if Americans had a blazing awareness of their membership in human society, then they might fashion a larger role for themselves directed to a safe and orderly planet. The most important thing in the world was not national sovereignty. It was a condition that made it possible for people to grow, to be free, to utilize their resources imaginatively and sensibly.

This condition could not be achieved, however, as long as absolute national sovereignty remained the principal form of human organization.

And no progress could be made until enough people accepted the new imperative and made it the one great purpose to which they attached themselves. Motion in this direction could become a force in itself; potentially, it was the most powerful force in the world. And it had to begin with the belief that it was both necessary and possible.

There was no connection between the two, but at the time that large numbers of people were seized by fears of an interplanetary collision, scientists were meeting to explore ways of communicating with other planets. Eminent astronomers, physicists, chemists, and biologists came together to consider the serious possibility that means might be devised for exchanging messages with distant inhabitants of the universe. It was a mind-stretching notion, having its basis not in fantasy but in genuine scientific prospects.

Whether or not the interplanetary communications project ever materializes, an even more grandiose and demanding project awaits accomplishment. This is the need for human beings to communicate with one another, here and now. Perhaps the most advanced and wisest human minds might address themselves to this task, baffling though it is. For if this particular project is not achieved, no other may have any meaning.

The lack of respect for a common human destiny continues to be the main problem of the earth dwellers. To the extent that they fix their gaze and energies on this need, rather than on the dangers of cosmic collision and catastrophe, they will qualify themselves for survival.

—*February 17, 1962*

# Who Killed Benny Paret?

Sometime about 1935 or 1936 I had an interview with Mike Jacobs, the prize-fight promoter. I was a fledgling newspaper reporter at that time; my beat was education, but during the vacation season I found myself on varied assignments, all the way from ship news to sports reporting. In this way I found myself sitting opposite the most powerful figure in the boxing world.

There was nothing spectacular in Mr. Jacobs's manner or appearance; but when he spoke about prize fights, he was no longer a bland little man but a colossus who sounded the way Napoleon must have sounded when he reviewed a battle. You knew you were listening to Number One. His saying something made it true.

We discussed what to him was the only important element in successful promoting—how to please the crowd. So far as he was concerned, there was no mystery to it. You put killers in the ring and the people filled your arena. You hire boxing artists—men who are adroit at feinting, parrying, weaving, jabbing, and dancing, but who don't pack dynamite in their fists—and you wind up counting your empty seats. So you searched for the killers and sluggers and maulers—fellows who could hit with the force of a baseball bat.

I asked Mr. Jacobs if he was speaking literally when he said people came out to see the killer.

"They don't come out to see a tea party," he said evenly. "They come out to see the knockout. They come out to see a man hurt. If they think anything else, they're kidding themselves."

Recently a young man by the name of Benny Paret was killed in the ring. The killing was seen by millions; it was on television. In the twelfth round he was hit hard in the head several times, went down, was counted out, and never came out of the coma.

The Paret fight produced a flurry of investigations. Governor Rockefeller was shocked by what happened and appointed a committee to assess the responsibility. The New York State Boxing Commission decided to find out what was wrong. The District Attorney's office expressed its concern. One question that was solemnly studied in all three probes concerned the action of the referee. Did he act in time to stop the fight? Another question had to do with the role of the examining doctors who certified the physical fitness of the fighters before the bout. Still another question involved Mr. Paret's manager; did he rush his boy into the fight without adequate time to recuperate from the previous one?

In short, the investigators looked into every possible cause except the real one. Benny Paret was killed because the human fist delivers enough impact, when directed against the head, to produce a massive hemorrhage in the brain. The human brain is the most delicate and complex mechanism in all creation. It has a lacework of millions of highly fragile nerve connections. Nature attempts to protect this exquisitely intricate machinery by encasing it in a hard shell. Fortunately, the shell is thick enough to withstand a great deal of pounding. Nature, however, can protect man against everything except man himself. Not every blow to the head will kill a man—but there is always the risk of concussion and damage to the brain. A prize fighter may be able to survive even repeated brain concussions and go on fighting, but the damage to his brain may be permanent.

In any event, it is futile to investigate the referee's role and seek to determine whether he should have intervened to stop the fight earlier. This is not where the primary responsibility lies. The primary responsibility lies with the people who pay to see a man hurt. The referee who stops a fight too soon from the crowd's viewpoint can expect to be booed. The crowd wants the knockout; it wants to see a man stretched out on the canvas. This is the supreme moment in boxing. It is nonsense to talk about prize fighting as a test of boxing skills. No crowd was ever brought to its feet screaming and cheering at the sight of two men beautifully dodging and weaving out of each other's jabs. The time the crowd comes alive is when a man is hit hard over the heart or the head, when his mouthpiece flies out, when blood squirts out of his nose or eyes, when he wobbles under the attack and his pursuer continues to smash at him with poleax impact.

Don't blame it on the referee. Don't even blame it on the fight managers. Put the blame where it belongs—on the prevailing mores that regard prize fighting as a perfectly proper enterprise and vehicle of entertainment. No one doubts that many people enjoy prize fighting and will miss it if it should be thrown out. And that is precisely the point.

—*May 5, 1961*

# A Community of Hope and Responsibility

The other day a friend of mine, like countless thousands of others throughout the country, received a telephone call from his broker. The stock market was in a deep dive. The broker advised my friend to sell, while there was still something left to sell. And, like many others, my friend sold—not because he thought there was anything wrong or unsound about the companies in which he had invested, but because he had been hit by a chain reaction of fear. It didn't occur to him that he might be helping to produce the very crash he dreaded, or that he might be contributing to a state of panic that might crack the economy and do grave damage to the country.

When I spoke to my friend about this, asking whether he didn't feel any sense of responsibility beyond his own profit-and-loss position, he stared at me coldly and said: "Let someone else be responsible. I'm looking out for Number One."

I thought back to a conversation I had had with a Soviet economics professor in Moscow two years earlier. The Soviet professor said that Marxist scholars believed that capitalism would collapse ultimately—not solely because of inherent flaws in the structure of capitalism itself but because it wasn't really an ideology. He said that it inspired no sense of basic allegiance or willingness to sacrifice, the prime test of a strong ideology.

"Even your capitalists don't really believe in it," he said. "Whenever there is a real test of confidence, they turn and run. And the result is that the structure of capitalism will topple because it won't have enough support from the people themselves."

He went on to say that the difference between communism and capitalism as economic doctrines was that the first was built to cope with adversity while the second was prone to it.

I told the Soviet economist that I believed he was mistaken about the notion that all Americans reacted the same way and would crumple in any genuine showdown. And his greatest error was the assumption that America lacked an ideology.

As I say, this discussion with a Soviet economist came to mind when my friend told me the other day that he felt no special responsibility beyond his own financial condition. There was no connection in his own mind between what he did and the gloating that took place in *Pravda* and in Communist circles throughout the world over the gyrations on Wall Street. In fact, my friend prides himself on being militantly anti-Communist. He would yield second place in the decibel count to no one in his proclamation against communism. But his proclamations are meaningless alongside his actions. He doesn't comprehend that the best way of defending his society against totalitarianism is by doing all the things, small or large, that are required to make freedom work.

I think my friend would probably reply to this by saying that I am exaggerating his importance. After all, he might say, he is only one man. Why should I suppose that his one finger in the dyke could hold back the flood when everyone else was rushing for the dry highlands? More specifically, even if he hadn't told his broker to sell that Blue Monday, would it have made one whit of difference? Or would he have been left holding the bag—and an empty one at that?

In a sense, my friend represents the eternal and ultimate problem of a free society. It is the problem of the individual who thinks that one man cannot possibly make a difference in the destiny of that society.

It is the problem of the individual who doesn't really understand the nature of a free society or what is required to make it work.

It is the problem of the individual who has no comprehension of the multiplying power of single but sovereign units.

It is the problem of the individual who regards the act of pulling a single lever in a voting booth in numerical terms rather than historical terms.

It is the problem of the individual who has no real awareness of the millions of bricks that had to be put into place, one by one, over many centuries, in order for him to dwell in the penthouse of freedom. Nor does he see any special obligation to those who build the structure or those who will have to live in it after him, for better or worse.

It is the problem of the individual who recognizes no direct relationship between himself and the decisions made by government in his name. Therefore, he feels no special obligation to dig hard for the information necessary to an understanding of the issues leading to those decisions.

In short, freedom's main problem is the problem of the individual who takes himself lightly historically.

Having said this, I must admit that there are at least a few contributing factors. The individual is always responsible for the shape or direction a free society may take, but at the same time he is affected or conditioned by the general environment and by the general values he himself has helped to create.

My office is located in the largest city in the world. I look out from my window and see huge slabs of steel, concrete, and glass invading the Manhattan sky. A few of these new skyscrapers have distinction, grace, spirit, even elegance. They make for expansion of the mind. Most of the others, however, look alike. Their claim on the aesthetic imagination is quickly exhausted. Their sides contain row upon row of honeycombed slots, repeating themselves endlessly. It makes for a powerful spectacle, but it places at least some strain on the idea that an individual is a sovereign cause. An environment of compression, repetition, and massive routine does not quite furnish the ideal conditions for advancing a belief in the creative splendor and dignity of the individual.

When, suddenly, at the lunch hour or at five o'clock these monolithic hives disgorge their occupants, the notion of human individuality requires something approaching an act of faith. It would be a mistake to suppose that this has no effect on the human subconscious, which has pressed down upon it the evidence of individual inconsequentiality. Jefferson might have made at least a slight alteration here and there in his definition of human uniqueness if he had had to ride sixty floors in a crowded elevator four times a day. John Keats might have found it somewhat difficult to meditate on beauty or even to contemplate a Grecian urn after driving a car through midtown traffic or spending an hour in search of a parking place.

There is no point in extolling the concept of human individuality without recognizing the increasing difficulties such individuality is expected to sustain. The idea that a small box can light up from the inside and make it possible for the individual to witness events far away is surely one of the most magnificent ideas to come out of the inventive intelligence. Television still has this potential and someday, Mr. Minow willing, it may achieve it. At present, and for the most part, however, it has depressed individuality rather than expanded it. I make note of all the good things it has done, but its total effect has been to cheapen respect for life. The insistence of television on making people clobber one another constantly with fists or clubs, or making them fire bullets at each other—all this is having a debilitating effect on the preciousness and fragility of life, without which there can be no true respect for human individuality.

A casual attitude toward human hurt and pain is the beginning of the end of a free society. Long before a child learns how to read he learns how to turn on a television set. He is quickly introduced to a world of howling drunks, pampered idiots, wild-swinging and trigger-happy bullies, and gyp artists. He learns that sex is just another toy, to be discarded when a flashier one comes along. He learns that the way to express your disagreement with a man or your distaste for him is to clout him on the jaw or pour hot lead into his belly.

Education is not just what takes place in a building marked "school." Education is the sum total of all the experiences and impressions to which a young and plastic mind is exposed. The parent who insists on sending his child to the finest schools, but who sees no problem in allowing that child to spend at least an equal amount of time looking at TV gangster serials or Mickey Spillane, should not be surprised if the mind of his offspring gives back the meanness and the sordidness put into it.

A free society—at least this free society—has certain propositions that have gone into its making. These propositions aren't all political. One of the main propositions that had a certain vitality at the time this particular society was founded was that the individual man has a natural goodness inside him, that he is capable of responding to truth, that he is endowed with the capacity to recognize beauty and be enlarged by it.

These propositions, I submit, are now under attack—and not just by television. Whether with respect to motion pictures, or writing, or art today, I think we can find disturbing evidence that man is being cheapened—and cut down to a size much smaller than by natural rights he ought to be. The epic theme seems to be in retreat on a wide front. There seems to be a fascination with aberrations, a preoccupation with neuroticism, an obsession with aimlessness. The trend is to the harsh, the brassy, the abrasive. Nobility, sacrifice, idealism, beauty—these are too often dismissed as tall corn.

Not long ago a friend suggested that I see the film La Dolce Vita. It was, he said, quite remarkable and beautiful. I saw it. It was remarkable, all right; but I didn't see any beauty in it. The photography was striking, and I am even willing that the word beauty be used to describe some of the camera work. But I saw nothing beautiful about the people, or the lives they led, or their emotions, or their values, or what they did. The film was lacking in both sequence and consequence. The only point it had to make was that life was pointless. But what troubled me most of all was not the film itself but that our critical standards have themselves become so desensitized that the film could be called beautiful.

To offset this, fortunately, the other day I saw the Japanese film The Island. It had no frenzy. It had no bashings or thrashings or wailings. It didn't make heroes of degenerates. It was not afraid of honest emotion. All it did was to show real people trying to cope with real problems. It was concerned with fundamentals of human relationships and response. It dealt with the fact of human devotion, even sacrifice. And because of all this there was an essential beauty in it. According to some definitions, perhaps, the film will be regarded as corny or sentimental. If it is corn, then it is high time we relished the kernel.

Incidentally, I was interested in the reaction of a friend who also saw the Japanese film. When I asked him his opinion, he said: "I know you will probably think it stupid of me, but I rather liked it." He almost found it necessary to apologize for responding to the simple but beautiful appeal of the film. He was almost afraid to trust his natural responses. He had become so intimidated by the dry-eyed, hard-boiled approach to life that he felt sheepish about acknowledging the existence inside him of that which distinguished him most of all from the ape.

One more instance. Recently, outside an art gallery on 57th Street in New York, I overheard two women discussing an abstract painting in the window.The painting, to my eyes, lacked creative thrust. It seemed to follow along meekly behind the works of better-known abstract artists. One of the women said to the other: "It looks like an inferior work to me; but I hate to say it out loud. You know, one feels like an idiot these days if he doesn't lavish the greatest praise on anything that seems incomprehensible."

I see no reason why anyone should allow himself to be intimidated into a feeling of total nullity or grim acquiescence if he sees something he happens not to like. He has the best credentials in the world for reacting; he has his individual taste buds. They may not coincide with those of others; they may run counter to those of experts, but at least they are his own, and the more he uses them the keener they become. No critic of stature—whether in literature or art or music—expects people to blot out their senses whenever he speaks. The critic applies his special training and knowledge to the work before him. He defines his standards. He sees himself as part of the total process by which a culture advances toward excellence. He certainly doesn't resent disagreement. And he doesn't discourage or disparage individual reactions—not if he is worth listening to, that is.

What I have been trying to suggest is that a free society cannot long remain free if man is in full retreat from man. For such a society pays a high price if the individual loses faith in his own centrality or in his ability to respond to creative beauty or in the stark fact of his ultimate responsibility.

This is a great deal of weight for a free man to carry; but if it is political and cultural weightlessness we are seeking, we don't have to get into outer space to find it. We can find it right here on earth and it goes by the name of de-individualization.

There is no greater political or philosophical fallacy than the notion that freedom is not really an ideology. The ideology of freedom has the deepest foundation of all. It is fused with the nature of man. It exists in the molecular structure of man's own natural rights.

What is this ideology?

It is based on the proposition that government exists for the purpose of enhancing and protecting the natural and fundamental rights of individual human beings.

These rights do not have to be created or contrived. They exist. They are natural, essential, irrevocable. They come with the gift of life. The good society may recognize these rights but it cannot invent them. It cannot alter them; it cannot expunge them. Its obligation is to create the conditions under which they can grow and be secure.

Highest among these natural rights is the right of man to own himself. He cannot be owned by a nation, a group, or another man.

He owns the right to grow and to meet his potential.

He owns the right to appraise his abilities and to develop them and apply them, consistent with the rights of others.

He owns his thoughts and the right to nourish them and speak them, again consistent with the rights of others.

He owns the right to make mistakes, whether of thought or deed, without unreasonable punishment.

He owns the right to his hopes.

He owns the right to justice, whether his claim is against a person, an aggregation, or his own government.

He owns the right to contemplate human destiny and the mysteries of universal purpose, or the right to detach himself altogether from these pursuits.

He owns the right to hold grievances against his society and to make them known to other men in order to magnify his own voice.

He owns the right to make a better life for his young.

It is in these respects that a free society is not just a nation. It is an idea. It is a national sovereignty committed to the cause of human sovereignty. It seeks to create a proper environment for man's most enduring hopes. It is an instrument through which man may work for a fuller life—whether in terms of his physical needs or his creative and spiritual reach.

Our own free society has not yet fulfilled all these purposes. No one knows how near to or far from such fulfillment the American people may be. But the direction is clear. And the effort, however vast, will continue to be made. The great ideals and ordeals of human history go together.

The unfinished nature of our struggle should not separate or insulate us from an awareness of the needs and the rights of other peoples, nor does it sever this nation from the community of hope and responsibility in the world. The American people see a reflection of their own early history in those peoples who do not yet own their own nations. They see the cause of freedom from outside rule as a cause that connects all men. They accept that connection and are inspired by it.

The lands and cultures of man today are various, but they are all compressed into a single geographic abode. The question to be determined in our time is whether this abode can be preserved for man or whether it will become the arena of his last great combat. The means are now sufficient to punish nature itself, to put a torch to all of man's works, and to deprive him of the decencies that have given him distinction and pride.

In looking back at their own past, and in assessing their purposes and ideals, the American people also look to the duty that unites them to all mankind—to create an enduring peace under law for this generation and the generations to come; to make the world safe for its diversity; to advance the cause of independence wherever peoples are not free and to create a pattern of interdependence for the whole; to use the resources of nature and the intelligence of man in the common good; to serve man's capacity to be free, and to justify the fact of life.

This is the ideology. It is real and it is ours.

*—June 16, 1962*

## Short Strokes

A research organization has announced that the cash lost each year in the United States amounts to about $75 per capita. By "lost," the research people don't mean bad luck in business investments or bingo or poker or the horses. They use the word "lost" literally; that is, money that falls out of pockets or that is in wallets or purses which are misplaced, etc.

Completely unrelated but not irrelevant is another vital statistic. The total average income for most of the human occupants of this planet comes to about $69 per person. In short, the average American misplaces more money each year than almost anyone else earns.

There is something damnably itchy about these prickly statistics. You feel like scratching but don't quite know where to find the bite. It is like wearing unlined tweed next to the skin; the better the tweed, the more uncomfortable it gets. What do you do about unwanted distinctions? Does a man celebrate the discovery that he has the biggest garbage removal bill in town? Does he congratulate himself on the fact that the drip from his leaky faucet represents more water in one day than the average Asian family in a drought-stricken area will have to drink or use in a month?

Whatever one does or does not do about the jabbing statistics, one thing at least is clear. They don't lend themselves to adjustment. N philosophical formulation, be it ever so sophisticated, can possibly provide the accommodating ointment. The notion that we have to take the world as it is doesn't quite relieve the itch. What do we do? Perhaps we had better go on scratching—at least until we find the bite.

—*July 21, 1962*

# In Defense of the Genuine Conservative

A great political tradition is in danger today of acute contamination through unsavory association. The tradition is conservatism, both political and economic. The contaminating agents are a wide assortment of persons and groups who have appropriated the label for uses totally alien to the historical development it represents. It is a clear case of ideological grand larceny and something ought to be done about it.

The *term* conservative has a specific background and meaning. It stands for stability as opposed to innovation; for restraint as opposed to daring; for the preservation of inherited conditions as opposed to drastic reform. These ideas are not only compatible with a free society; they have an essential place in it, along with genuine liberalism. True conservatism is opposed to liberalism, but not destructive of it. The principal difference between conservatism and liberalism is represented not so much by disagreement over the nature of a free society or its goals as by disagreement over the approaches. Both conservatism and liberalism serve as the twin structural supports of constitutional government.

In any event, there has sprung up over the past few years a strange array of noisy haters and spoilers who have arrogantly appointed themselves the standard bearers of the conservative banner. In thought and action they resemble far more a pack of political desperadoes than the inheritors of Gladstonian ideas and manners. They claim to be conservatives, but exactly what is it that they would conserve? Would they conserve the Constitution of the United States? Only if some major surgery could be performed, especially on the first ten amendments. Would they conserve the one institution that has been specifically charged with the responsibility to preserve a constitutional form of government; namely, the Supreme Court? Only if they could expunge some Supreme Court justices and decisions they happen to detest. Would they conserve the ideals that animated the men who founded this nation—ideals that have to do with the basic nature of free man and his place in a free society? Only if these ideals could be twisted into their direct opposites.

They presume to speak in the name of Christianity, many of them, but they use it as though it were a blowtorch for consuming the

Christian spirit. In what they do and say they hold the Sermon on the Mount in contempt; if someone were to recite these gentle teachings, they would see red. Faith, hope, and charity are replaced by scorn, hate, and malice, and the chalice is filled to overflowing with bile.

There is a disheveled quality to their thinking, but some of them are not without intellectual pretensions. They claim affinity with such figures as Edmund Burke, Jeremy Bentham, Lord Acton, Alexander Hamilton, and, more recently, Senator Robert A. Taft. But names such as these are the synthetic props of respectability rather than any valid philosophical or historical underpinning. When they intone the name of Burke, do they agree with him that "it is better to be the citizen of a humble commonwealth in the Alps, without a prospect of influence beyond the narrow frontier, than a subject of a superb aristocracy . . ."? Or that "government is a contrivance of human wisdom to provide for human wants. Men have a right that these rights should be provided by this wisdom"?

Their particular animus is the word democracy. They believe that the United States is a republic and was never intended to be a democracy. But in this they are refuted by the one man in American history whom they claim as their progenitor, Alexander Hamilton. Hamilton did not hesitate to use the term "representative democracy." In fact, he described representative democracy "where the right of election is well secured and regulated, and the exercise of the legislative, executive, and judiciary authorities is vested in select persons, chosen *really and not nominally by the people*" [italics ours] as that government that would "most likely be happy, regular, and durable."

And how do they reconcile their contempt for the term democracy with the statement by that prime figure of nineteenth-century English conservatism, Lord Randolph Churchill, that he did not care if they called him a Tory so long as they also called him a democrat?

They claim Robert Taft as their patron saint, but they are lucky that he is not alive to tear himself loose from their unwanted affections. For Robert Taft was a genuine conservative. He may have had his foot closer to the political brakes of legislative progress than any man of his time, but at least he insisted on staying on the main road. He was not out to supplant democratic institutions, but to keep them free of overly centralized controls. Even here, however, he recognized that housing and education were national problems and had to be handled accordingly. There were few stronger voices on the issues of civil rights and racial equality. As it concerned the United Nations—an object of supreme contempt by those who now speak in his name—Senator Taft felt that what was needed was not weaker but stronger world organization. He believed in the need for world law and felt the United States should take leadership inside the United Nations in that direction. In fact, this was the central theme of his book on American foreign policy.

Genuine conservatism is now being libeled by know-nothings. There is no reason to doubt that the tradition will survive the ordeal, but it may be unpleasant while it lasts.

*—September 1, 1962*

# In Defense of the Genuine Liberal

The genuine liberal has had an even longer and more arduous problem with his label than has the conservative. In fact, one of the historical difficulties with liberalism is that the word has been seized and exploited by individuals, groups, and even political parties with diametrically opposed policies. In national politics, for example, we can't think of a single Presidential campaign in recent history when each side did not seek popular support by claiming to be the most liberal on key issues. Historically, the word has been invested with political magic.

In recent years, however, there has been an effort in some quarters to use the term liberal as a nasty word. Many of the same extremists who are trying to arrogate the conservative label to themselves have also been trying to make liberalism sound like an evil and alien doctrine with profound subversive implications. They equate liberalism with partiality toward the Soviet Union and with an emphasis on peace at the expense of freedom.

Paradoxically, the liberal is also under attack from the very forces he is accused of advancing. The affiliated, extreme Left has always regarded the liberal as the prime enemy. Marxist–Leninist strategy believes that the extreme Right wing has an important role to play in the sharp division of the country between extremes of Right and Left. In this analysis, a class struggle must be fought by the extremes.

Liberalism muddies the waters, according to the Marxist-Leninist thesis. It is most often associated with a strong middle class, and a strong middle class does not fit into a Marxist revolutionary pattern. Moreover, the liberal tries to convince people that necessary social and political change is possible without extreme measures. This is anathema to the Communist. He regards such talk as naïve and dangerous. It is dangerous because people will not be attracted to his banner if they can get what they need without violent upheaval. In dealing with liberalism, therefore, communism has pursued alternate strategies. It has tried to gain control of liberal causes, steering them into channels useful to its own purposes.

Failing this, it has attempted to wreck the liberal organizations associated with such causes.

In the 1930s, this rule-or-ruin strategy had a certain measure of success, especially in popular-front organizations. Since that time the genuine liberal has been increasingly aware both of the technique and its danger and has been developing the means for coping with it. The genuine liberal holds fast to his convictions about the need for constant improvement of his society, but he sees communism as a block and not as an approach toward that improvement. More particularly, he recognizes the American Communist party not as an independent political movement but as the extended foreign policy arm of the Soviet Union.

What does a genuine liberal believe? In the context of today's world he sees no contradiction between believing in freedom and believing in peace. For he believes neither in surrender nor suicide. He believes that the policies that are committed to the cause of a durable and enforceable peace also best serve the cause of freedom. Nuclear war may not destroy all life on earth, but it will certainly destroy the prime conditions for meaningful life. Peace without freedom is unthinkable; freedom without peace is impossible. Hence the genuine liberal never separates the two. He puts the making of enforceable peace at the top of the human agenda for our generation.

Ideologically, the genuine liberal is familiar with Marx and Engels, as he is with all the principal ideas about human organizations. But his ideological and historical kinship is not with Marx but with men such as Mill, Milton, Jefferson, Oliver Wendell Holmes, and William James. He believes in the perfectibility of man. He sets no limits to the possibilities of betterment of the human condition because he sets no limits to the potentialities of the human mind. He does not blind himself to the existence of evil, but he never loses faith in the essential goodness of man. He is concerned with those conditions and circumstances that can control the evil and provide the fullest outlet for the good. He sees a pluralistic free society as offering the best arena for meeting the problems, basic or contrived, that spew out of the fact of life itself.

In manner, the genuine liberal is disposed to accept the good faith of all those who disagree with him. He sees no weakness in admitting that he may be wrong. He is passionate but not punitive about his position. His purpose is not to lacerate an opponent but to locate the facts and put them to work. He is not a name-caller. If he disagrees with someone to the right of him, he doesn't shout "Fascist." If he disagrees with someone to the left of him, he doesn't shout "Communist." He has no conditioned reflexes about slogans or labels. Each situation has its own nature and its own requirements.

Genuine liberalism is under severe attack, but it is not in retreat. Since it holds to the idea that a human being is a sovereign cause and that the nation exists for the purpose of serving this cause, liberalism cannot expect this concept to be universally accepted or celebrated. Until this happens the pursuit will not be without pain—or excitement.

—*September 22, 1962*

# The Age of Desensitization

The greatest threat to the splendid variety of humans on earth is not represented by the pulverizing power of the bomb. An even greater threat is the numbness caused by the bomb. Our original sense of disbelieving horror has not been sustained; perhaps it could not be sustained. For we live in an age remarkable less for its destructiveness than for its desensitization. People have learned how to make their accommodations with the irrational. The missiles and the megatons have been metabolized inside the consciousness.

Adjustment is not an infallible value in the human catalogue. Adjustment can be anesthesia. It can be disaster. The end of man begins not with the existence of potential planetary devastation but with the absence of vital indignation.

It was only five years ago that the moral intelligence was able to ask pertinent questions. What were the implications, not alone of radioactive warfare, but of preparation for radioactive warfare? The experiments with the new explosives had the result of littering the sky with radioactive garbage, with seepage that infected the earth and found its way into human tissue. How was it that the nations setting off these explosives did not make a distinction between those measures that were essential to their own defense and those measures that inflicted widespread injury on other peoples with whom they had no quarrel? By what right or reasoning did nations arrogate to themselves the right to shoot up the natural environment which was the common property of all the planetary inhabitants?

The initial sense of horror over such outrages brought about their cessation. For more than three years there was forbearance. Then the Soviet Union let fly with new multi-megaton explosives, the infecting power of which was far beyond anything that had been tried previously. And once again the poisonous garbage pumped into the sky dropped down invisibly and indiscriminately on the society of humans, piercing their chain of life. There were protests, to be sure, but they were without volume or fury. And when the United States followed with its own test explosions, there was only a modest outcry. Each side could find its unholy justifications in the actions of the other. The Soviet Union self-righteously claimed that it knew the United States was going to test anyway. The United States said it had no choice but to resume because the Soviets had resumed. In any case, what was resumed was the race toward the finish line of civilization. The objective was security but the security decreased even as the speed of the runners increased.

Meanwhile, every malevolent idea about crippling man or producing mass suffering is given sanction the moment the word security is affixed to it. Thus, it is considered proper and essential to mass-produce odorless and invisible gases that can inflict heart attacks, or bombs that can disseminate germs to spread the very diseases that mankind over countless generations has been trying to eliminate. But nothing is more insidious in this apocalyptic inventory than the determination of each side to convince the other that it would not have the slightest hesitation to turn it all loose if it felt warranted in doing so.

If we could still think as humans we might be able to find a way out of the sickness, and in fact find a genuine basis for our safety and for the preservation of the freedom that is the highest prize life has to offer. But it is precisely because we have ceased to think and respond as humans, reacting on the level of tribal warriors, ignoring our membership in and obligation to the society of humans as a whole—it is precisely because of this that we have separated ourselves from the vision of what is required to achieve genuine security and fulfill the promise of a better world.

An age which is desensitized to evils and horrors is also desensitized to its glories and its opportunities. The essential task, then, is to regenerate the vital responses, to reopen access to the clarifying functions of conscience, to restore the capacity to dream about a better life. Despite all the billowing evidence to the contrary, man is still capable of good purposes and decent works. He can still recapture command of his existence and the forces that are shaping it. And this regeneration requires only an experience in self-recognition to become real. That is, when enough people can comprehend the reality of a human family, the beginnings of a genuine safety will emerge.

For the United States to discover its greatest power, it has only to regard itself as an instrument through which the ennoblement of man may be served. We can declare we will not fire into the body of mankind in the pursuit of our own security. We can say our purpose is to use human knowledge and energy in creating the finest life of which the human imagination is capable. We can make our voice the most resonant in the world behind the idea of world law—an idea that may yet create the conditions that alone can give reasonable assurance of peace and freedom.

*—October 27, 1962*

# The Noise Level Is Rising

As we left the office the other day we observed a young man on a delivery bicycle. He was navigating the vehicle with one hand on the steering gear. The other hand pressed a small transistor radio to his ear.

A few minutes later, at the corner of Madison Avenue, we paused briefly to observe some men at work putting in some underground cables. One of them was wearing a headband inside of which was a small radio set. On a small ledge was another radio, turned up full force. It had to be: It was competing with two pneumatic drills in full operation only a few yards away.

At the street crossing we waited while large trucks and buses thundered past. Then the traffic was halted in response to the hideous wailing siren and blast horn of a fire engine still several blocks away. When we arrived at the hotel for our meeting, someone's name was being paged over the amplifying system. Inside the elevator, a hidden loudspeaker told the passengers to face forward, announced the floors and the various services available at the hotel, and played screeching music between the blurbs.

The meeting we attended was in a fairly small room but a microphone and amplifier were used just the same. The volume was fully turned up. For more than two hours the human voice took on the ferocity and impact of cannonballs fired point-blank at the human ear.

When the lunch break came we went into the hotel restaurant. Nondescript music was being piped into the room. In order to be heard above the music and the conversation from the other tables, the diners raised their own voices. Many of those who were talking to one another were speaking simultaneously.

That evening we were taken to dinner at a fairly well-celebrated emporium. We were almost felled by the sounds as we were escorted to our table. Three trumpets were firing directly into a microphone; the drummer seemed beset by fear that his presence might go undetected and he pounded away like a man possessed. Under these circumstances, giving the order to the waiter called for a full mobilization of the human sound apparatus.

The next morning, shortly after sunup, the riveting began in a new skyscraper being built across the way from the hotel. One short block away, a tall building was being torn down to make way for a taller one, and the brutal noise of the large swinging iron ball crashing into brick walls came through over the riveting. When it subsided, briefly, we were able to hear a thundering jet overhead, its iron heart pounding into the sky as it gained altitude over New York.

Shortly after we arrived at the office, the air-raid signals went on, screaming, screeching, piercing, and stayed on for at least five agonizing, brain-addling moments. (By this time people are so confused about air alerts that they haven't the slightest idea of how to tell the difference between a test and the real thing, or what to do if it is real. And so they sit through the shrill howling noise, trying to concentrate on the matter at hand.)

The next day, we went out to International Airport for a flight to the West Coast. The roar of the jets warming up or on the runway was bad but not nearly so bad as the sickly sweet, tinny background music inside the plane.

Whether or not they realize it, the American people are waging unremitting war against themselves. The weapons are tranquillity-smashers and are fitted out with decibel warheads. They penetrate all known cranial barriers and invade the innermost core of an individual's privacy, impeding the processes of sequential thought, breaking down the sensibilities, and unhinging the capacity for serenity. The noise level is rising and the level of common sanity is falling.

Silence is not nothingness or the absence of sound. It is a prime condition for human serenity and the natural environment of contemplation. A life without regular periods of silence is a life without essential nourishment for both the spirit and the functioning intelligence. Silence offers the vital element of privacy, without which an individual becomes something less than himself, recognizable mainly by his own vapid mouthings and his twitchings.

People take on the characteristics of the things they value or desire. If they accept a high noise level they become noise-makers themselves. If they feel they cannot do without constant sound amplification, constant background music, constant bellowing and blustering, they create the conditions for their own diminution. More than anything else, they minimize thought. We can't escalate the decibels without shrinking the human mind.

We live at a time when thought alone represents the differences between safety and total madness. One of the prime requirements of such thought is privacy and a little silence, at least now and then. We will get them once we attach value to them.

*—December 8, 1962*

# Pope John and His Open Window

When the papal election ceremonies in the Conclave of Cardinals were completed the evening of October 28, 1958, well wishers in profusion pressed in upon Pope John XXIII. Indeed, the congratulatory urge felt by many of the members of the hierarchy was so strong that aides of the Pope tried to protect him by installing him in one of the offices of the Vatican Secretary of State and placing the Holy Seal across the door.

Breaking the seal is a profound sacrilege. But the enthusiasm of the pursuers, many of whom were cardinals and bishops, persisted and they swept the seal aside as though it never existed. Trying desperately to stem the tide, Dean of Cardinals Tisserant cried out to Monsignor Cardinale, then secretary of the Conclave: "Stop them! Do something! They will be excommunicated!"

Pope John smiled. "Very well," he said gently. "They will be excommunicated and my first act as Holy Father will be to grant them complete absolution."

Then everyone laughed and the tension was broken. The Pope quickly became engulfed by a human congratulatory tidal wave. It was a strenuous session for the seventy-seven-year-old pontiff, but he was equal to it. For the central and presiding fact about Pope John XXIII—indeed, the key to the many far-reaching changes that have come about under his Papacy—is that he likes people. The historic Ecumenical Council just recessed is a reflection of his desire to bring the Catholic Church into closer contact with the outside world, making it more responsive to needs of human beings everywhere, whether Catholics or not. He doesn't believe that God penalizes anyone for not being a Catholic. Religion is a matter of individual conscience. All religions are entitled to respect. Even non-believers who have had audiences with the Holy Father are told that he includes them in his prayers.

Pope John's genius for human relations and the importance he attaches to direct contacts with the outside world are highlighted by several specific incidents. Shortly after his election, he set out from the Vatican one morning on the first of a series of visits to Italian prisons. Asked by his aides to explain his purpose, he said simply: "It is somewhat more difficult for the prisoners to come to see me."

On another occasion, the Pope had left his car and was strolling back to his apartment in the Vatican when a distraught priest came up to him and begged his prayers for the paralyzed wife of a friend. The Pope said he could do better than that: he would go directly to the stricken woman at her home, which he did.

The third incident illuminates Pope John's central purposes. A Canadian dignitary asked him to explain the main objectives of his Papacy in general and the Ecumenical Council in particular. Pope John stood up, walked over to the window, opened it, and said, "What do we intend to do? We intend to let in a little fresh air."

Through that open window the winds of change have poured almost steadily for four years, culminating in the historic Ecumenical Council. What kind of change? First of all, change that meets the needs of a world that itself has seen more change in a half century than the world had known for the previous thousand years. Second, change that seeks to unite all Christendom and perhaps even to contribute to the spiritual unity of all mankind. Third, change that serves the cause of all people, and not that of Catholics alone.

Pope John has no intention to dictate change; his purpose is to set the stage for it. The Ecumenical Council, already one of the great events in the history of religion, was called for the purpose of having peoples of all Christendom consider what kinds of changes were required and how best to meet the problems involved.

Pope John's approach to the Ecumenical Council, in fact, reflects his own conviction that the Church is not the private possession of its hierarchy but a commmon responsibility shared by all its members. Accordingly, he makes an important distinction between dogma in theology and dogmatic attitudes. It is one thing to be strongly rooted in one's religious convictions; it is another thing to be rigid and authoritarian in one's attitude toward human problems and relationships with people of other faiths. A dogmatic attitude or approach toward the honest convictions of one's neighbors is itself a violation of the religious spirit. All men, whatever their belief, are important; God does not impose penalties or withhold blessings on people just because they are not Catholics. In this sense, all have access to the Deity.

In world affairs, Pope John does not believe his role is to denounce or assail but to utilize the full moral power of the Papacy in relieving tensions and in helping to create an atmosphere in which important and fundamental measures can be taken that can lead to a just peace under law. He believes the cause of human survival is too important for bluster or bombast. Moreover, in the event of a crisis, as in the case of Cuba, Pope John would like to speak from a position that will enable the Holy See to be as effective as possible in keeping that crisis from skidding into a nuclear disaster.

Underlying this concern is the conviction that the question of war and peace in today's world is no longer mainly a political or national issue. Nuclear war is primarily a spiritual and moral issue. Nuclear war smashes at the nature of man, and not just at man himself. That is, the effects of nuclear war are registered in the human germ plasm, deforming the basic units of heredity, cheapening and disfiguring life for generations to come.

Nuclear war is also directed against the vital balances of nature that make life possible. In this sense, modern war is not just a war by nation against nation, or a war by man against man, but a war against God.

A moral and spiritual issue is also involved in the punishment inflicted on nations and peoples outside the warring powers. Only two nations may be involved in a direct nuclear exchange but ten times as many people outside those two countries may be killed as are killed inside these nations. It is as though two occupants on the top floor of a large apartment house decided to wage war against each other by setting fire to the entire building. Anyone who ignores the moral issue involved in such a situation is a partner to the crime.

The action, therefore, of Pope John in issuing an anguished cry for humanity when the Cuban crisis was at its height was not solely the result of a sudden awareness of the implications of nuclear warfare. It was the result of a profound conviction that man's total spiritual and moral energies have to be mobilized in behalf of human safety and sanity.

"We entreat all statesmen not to remain deaf to the cry of mankind," Pope John declared. "Let them do everything in their power to save the peace. By so doing they will spare the world the horrors of a war that would have disastrous consequences such as no one can foresee."

It is only natural that Pope John's apprehension about world tensions should be a reflection of his interest in the conditions of human life. Freedom is the proper political environment for mankind; but freedom must not be stagnation or nothingness. It must be tied to the cause of social progress and a better life.

These are not the only questions to come before the Ecumenical Council. More than seventy subjects were introduced for consideration by the council. These have now been reduced to twenty; all are now being studied by special committees. In view of the reduction of the number of subjects, the work of the council is now scheduled for completion by Christmas, 1963.

Even before the Ecumenical Council was convened, Pope John made his position clear on various questions. He instituted specific reforms in the administration of the Holy See. He has combated bureaucratic tendencies in the Vatican. He has called for an avoidance of prayers and ceremonies offensive to non-Catholics. He has been especially severe in opposing false miracles and superstitions, such as weeping madonna statuettes and apparitions, etc. He has reinforced the policy against interference by the Vatican in the political affairs of nations. He has prohibited organized "crusades" against political enemies in the name of Christianity. Several Catholic organizations were forbidden to use the word "crusade" in their title. He has carried forward the realistic approach of his predecessors to social and economic problems; the complexity of modern industrial civilization requires advanced knowledge and flexibility. Similarly, colonialism in the modern world is an anachronism and must be replaced.

Pope John has set stern and sizable objectives for himself and the Church. Even for a Pope in perfect physical condition, this would be a severe assignment. Pope John is now eighty-one. Until a few months ago, he was in excellent health. Then he developed abdominal symptoms, with a severe hemorrhage. Despite the stern urgings of his doctor, the Pope insisted on addressing the Ecumenical Council and in participating at the canonization of three saints in St. Peter's Cathedral.

I watched the Pope as he fulfilled his papal duties during the canonization ceremonies. He did not allow his voice or his manner to betray the physical ordeal he was undergoing. His characteristic smile and warmth of manner did not fail him. But his pallor left no doubt about the weakness of his general condition.

Even after the Ecumenical Council recessed in early December, Pope John continued to perform his duties, holding audiences with pilgrims, reviewing the work of the council with his aides, and preparing his Christmas message. When I saw him again, he seemed somewhat stronger than a week earlier at the canonization ceremonies. His pallor had lessened. And the pastoral nature of his Papacy came through in the earthy anecdotes he related and the comments he made about world affairs. When concern was expressed over his insistence on maintaining such a punishing schedule, he looked up, smiled, and said he had decided to study a new language in order to make use of his spare time. As for any suffering caused by his illness, Pope John remarked that a lifetime of rich memories is a potent enemy of pain. He said he has so many satisfactions in his life to dwell upon that it was difficult to think about personal distress.

By remaining in constant good spirits, Pope John manages to get more latitude from his doctor than his illness would ordinarily permit. He knows that his work is important; before he dies he would like to see this earth become a far safer and nobler abode for man than it is now. This at least is his aspiration; if it is shared by enough men, the prospects of realizing it are reasonably strong.

—*January 19, 1963*

# A Declaration of Interdependence

ROME

A personal drama of historic proportions is being enacted in Rome, where Pope John XXIII is attempting to use his remaining energies and the resources available to him in an effort to halt the terrible drift toward a nuclear holocaust. He has not been well; but so long as he can think and act he is determined to awaken the world's peoples and their leaders to the peril of policies that have brought the human race to the present situation of terror.

Step by step in the past four years he has attempted to make his Papacy and the Roman Catholic Church in general completely relevant to the human situation. In this sense, he seems to believe that nothing could be less relevant than a church preoccupied solely with religious matters. Theology must not be narrowly defined. It must not be allowed to become a reflection of the irrelevancies that are so characteristic of the behavior of men and institutions in this modern world.

This was behind Pope John's moral intervention during the week of the Cuban crisis. And it was behind his decision from the start not to denounce or fulminate against hostile ideologies but to develop instead the constructive contacts and opportunities that would enable his voice to be heard where it would have to be heard if the present folly were to be arrested. Accordingly, he has welcomed the chance to discuss questions relating to the peace with representatives of all nations that are necessarily involved in the maintenance of peace.

It is ludicrous to say that Pope John, because he has refrained from denouncing communism and because he has met with a member of Mr. Khrushchev's family, has no understanding of the nature of communism or its aggressive intentions. The Pope has a most meticulous knowledge of the mainsprings and dynamics of communism. But he is equally knowledgeable about the circumstances that can lead to change in the world. And he has a profound respect for the power of ideas in a situation in which old ways of thought and actions no longer speak to people's needs or hopes.

Far from being remote or detached from the hard realities of the present world struggle, the Pope knows where these realities are pointing. Men must make distinctions between old realities that lead to a dead end, and new realities that can lead to a creative and safe existence for the human community. In this sense, his historic encyclical letter, "Peace on Earth," is in the nature of a declaration of interdependence for the human species. It holds up a bold new vision and dramatizes the higher reality of attainable new goals. It makes it clear that beyond the stress and clamor of nationalities there must be created a viable new form of world organization with authority to regulate the dealings among nations under justice and law. And he sees the United Nations as the organization which, properly strengthened, must become the framework for such a world community. This is genuine realism, for anything less is unworkable and dangerous.

In its analysis of the condition of man; in its assertion of freedom of conscience in religious and political matters; in its discussion of the dangers of a runaway nuclear arms race; in its comprehension of the nature of nuclear war; in its call for a strengthened United Nations under law and responsive to the needs of the world human community—in all these respects, the encyclical letter has historic proportions. It is at once eloquent and practical, diagnostic and therapeutic, historical and contemporary. Most important of all, it sets men's minds in a new direction, enabling them to break loose from notions of inevitability, defeatism, and despair.

This is not all. Pope John does not believe that religion should be completely theoretical. He places the human interest above the national interest. Nor can he justify a policy in which nations pump large quantities of radioactive poisons into the atmosphere, jeopardizing the health and violating the rights of peoples who are in no way involved in these disputes.

In short, Pope John believes in applied Christianity. He would like to see the pillars of the Church become the solid supports of a genuine structure for peace. He cannot separate the ethics of Christianity from the crisis involving the human family. And he believes that all other religions are similarly involved. That is why the encyclical is not addressed to Catholics alone but to all men of good will.

In sum, the moral and spiritual nature of the problem cannot be disguised or obscured by noisy and petty pronouncements having to do with national stance or posture.

Have the ideas in "Peace on Earth" penetrated through to Communist countries? This is the vital test of the Pope's conviction that persuasion is a far more effective instrument than denunciation. So far, the approach has been notably successful. The encyclical has been given prominent attention in the press and on radio and television inside the Soviet Union. It is of at least equal significance that Archbishop Slipyi, of the Greek Rite Catholic Church in the Ukraine, has been released from his long imprisonment and is now in residence in the Vatican.

In Mont Saint-Michel and Chartres, Henry Adams wrote that "Under any conceivable system the process of getting God and man under the same roof—of bringing two independent energies under the same control" has been an extraordinarily difficult and painful process. It is possible that Pope John has this kind of architecture in mind—not simply for adherents of any particular creed but for the generality of men.

It is usually presumptuous and always difficult to predict the historical significance of any event. Be that as it may, the central idea in "Peace on Earth"—the need for a human community under law—is the dominant imperative of twentieth-century man. This is the way to relevance. The individual who feels a terrible sense of detachment from living history can rid himself of his personal oppression. He can turn his thoughts to essential new goals. And energies follow thought.

—May 4, 1963

# Pope John XXIII

He leaned forward in his chair and smiled. "When I meet a person and talk to him privately, I try to put him at ease by reminding him that I am the same as he is. I have two eyes, a nose—a very large nose—mouth, two ears, and so forth. Even so, people sometimes remain rigid and incommunicative. You must feel completely relaxed. We will talk as man to man." And again he smiled.

I handed him a letter expressing the President's concern and good wishes for his health.

"I get many messages these days from people who pray that my illness is without great pain. Pain is no foe of mine. I have memories. Wonderful memories. There is much to think back upon. When I was young, I was an apostolic delegate in Bulgaria. I came to know and admire the Slavic peoples. I tried to study the Slavic languages, including the Russian. I never became really proficient but I did learn to read the language to some extent. I am sorry I never pursued these studies. Do you know the Russian language?"

"No."

"A pity. You really ought to learn it. You are much younger than I. It wouldn't take you very long. A very important language. The Russian people, a very wonderful people. We must not condemn them because we do not like their political system. They have a deep spiritual heritage. This they have not lost. We can talk to them. Right now, we have to talk to them. We must always try to speak to the good in people. Nothing can be lost by trying. Everything can be lost if men do not find some way to work together to save the peace. I am not afraid to talk to anyone about peace on earth. If Mr. Khrushchev were sitting right where you are sitting now, I don't think I would feel uneasy or awkward in talking to him. We both come from small villages. We both have peasant backgrounds. We would understand one another."

Again he smiled.

"Much depends now on keeping open and strengthening all possible lines of communications. During the terrible crisis over Cuba in October, the possibility of a nuclear holocaust became very real. I asked the statesmen to exercise the greatest restraint and to do all that had to be done to reduce the terrible tension. My appeal was given prominent attention inside the Soviet Union. I was glad that this was so. This is a good sign."

His voice betrayed his fatigue and general sense of depletion, but he spoke with eagerness. He knew his time was running short, but he was determined to use himself in the service of world peace. The Holy See might be useful in reducing tensions between East and West. Therefore it was logical to open up contacts. The Holy See was not attempting to arrogate to itself an unwelcome or unnatural role. But the grimly significant feature of the present world crisis was precisely that there were so many elements of danger and so few elements of control. Any person or agency in a position, near or far, to help strengthen the controls had a positive obligation to do so.

Did he know that his efforts were likely to be criticized or mis-construed? Certainly, but this was no warrant for lack of initiative or irresponsible inaction. The worst that could be said was that the Pope was taking Christianity literally. He couldn't imagine Jesus concurring in the notion that human security and freedom depended on the manu-facture and amassing of hydrogen bombs which, if used, would put a torch to the human nest. The fact that two or more nations, in the act of warring against one another, would in actuality also be at war with the human race—if this fact had no profound moral and spiritual sig-nificance, then what fact did?

This question, along with all the other central questions related to peace and the human future, formed the basis of his historic encyclical, "Peace on Earth," in April. A few weeks later, the progressive nature of his illness became critical. Even so, he followed events carefully. He looked for evidence that the nations were making progress in organizing their relationships and halting the arms race. He was heartened by the world-wide response to his plea for peace. His hopes were never higher than at the end. Some men will recognize that a claim has thus been laid on them in terms of their own efforts and obligations. The sustaining prospect is that there may be enough of them.

We live in an age which looks to physical motion for its spectacular achievements. A man encased in a metallic capsule spinning through outer space; the heart of an atom pried open and releasing vast stores of energy; streams of electrons flashing images of something happening thousands of miles away—these are the main articles of wonder in the modern world. But they do not have the impress on history of an eighty-one-year-old man dying of cancer, using the Papacy to make not just his own church but all churches fully relevant and fully useful in the cause of human unity and peace. Human advocacy harnessed to powerful ideas continues to be the prime power. The peace sought by Pope John need not be unattainable once belief in ideas is put ahead of belief in moving parts.

*—June 15, 1963*

*The explosion of the first atomic bomb over Hiroshima fixed the magazine's course for the ensuing years. It is doubtful, however, whether any aspect of the magazine's interest in atomic energy and its implications had sharper point or focus than the campaign to put an end to nuclear testing. The effective beginning of widespread public awareness dates perhaps from Dr. Schweitzer's world-wide appeal, "A Declaration of Conscience" of May 1967, and culminates in U.S. Senate ratification of the limited nuclear test-ban treaty, by a vote of 80 to 19, on September 24, 1963.*

## The Genie and the Dinosaur

There was a tone of unmistakable heartbreak and even tragedy in President Kennedy's reply, at his May 8 news conference, when he was asked about the prospects for a nuclear test ban. The situation at the moment, he said, was grim. There had been no progress in the talks at Geneva and time was running out. And when he looked beyond the failure of a test ban, it was like peering into a cosmic furnace. He foresaw the spread of nuclear weapons to various other nations. And then? Then, he said, the genie will be out of the bottle for fair, and the world may never be able to get him back in again.

What was most striking about the President's response, however, was the seeming air of personal helplessness with which he answered the question. He sounded more like a historian or an observer than a man engaged within an inch of his life in the deadliest game ever played on this planet. It was as though he were objectively interpreting events, rather than intimately and decisively controlling them.

The President's apparent mood of helplessness may be an accurate reflection of the position in which he finds himself. It is not only Mr. Khrushchev's refusal to go beyond three inspections that makes for Mr. Kennedy's feeling of near-paralysis on the question. At least as important is the situation inside the United States. Any test-ban treaty would have to go before the Senate for ratification—and the President is by no means certain the Senate would accept the seven inspections he has offered, let alone the three proposed by the Soviets. Even more serious, perhaps, is the absence of an informed and active public opinion on the issue. For only prodigious public pressure, combined with the full weight of Presidential advocacy, could produce the two-thirds vote required for ratification.

The President knows that the failure to achieve a test-ban treaty would jeopardize the military security of the United States and result eventually in a net gain for the Soviet Union. Paradoxically, however, the principal opposition to the President at home comes from those who are identified with the hard-line, anti-Soviet approach. It is difficult for this group to comprehend that old concepts of military security no longer hold in a nuclear age. The fact that war has now become an instrument of mutual suicide and possibly even global disaster has made no dent in the thinking of the hardliners. They cannot quite grasp the brand-new truth that American security no longer depends primarily on raw military power but on a workable way of ending the arms race, backed by a strong world organization. And they have yet to perceive that their past successes in blocking a test ban, when the United States could have had one, have redounded sharply to the advantage of the Soviet Union, which has used its tests to narrow the nuclear gap between itself and the United States.

The problem, therefore, is not solely how to keep the genie from escaping from the bottle. The problem is what to do about the dinosaur mentality in our midst. Survival with freedom today imposes the severest strain on the mechanism of human thinking yet to come before the species. The governments of this world will not be able to keep this generation from being incinerated in a nuclear furnace unless they perceive the differences between tradition and innovation, between habit and insight, between a mediocre acceptance of existence and a full awareness of the preciousness and possibilities of life.

If the President of the United States is weighed down by genies bursting out of bottles and dinosaurs already prancing on the lawn, the antidote will have to come not from court wizards but from an alert, rational, and responsible populace. If enough people can somehow mobilize enough energy to communicate their concern, then, at least, the terrible loneliness of the Presidency on this important issue may be eased. And a substantial combination may be put into the field where the important decisions will be fought out, as is proper in a pluralistic society.

Ultimately, the future of the nation rests where it began—in the ability of its citizens to stay on top of the big issues, retaining those men who serve them best and throwing out the others. Right now, no political penalty is attached to failure to achieve a test ban or to any of the major undertakings concerned with world peace. The reversal of this process could mark both an upturn in the national prospects and the beginning of hopefulness all around.

Jefferson's admonition on the relationship between government and people on critical matters has been quoted so many times that it has become something of a political chestnut. Even so, there is no better way of saying it:

"I know no safe depository of the ultimate powers of society but the people themselves and, if we think them not enlightened enough to exercise their control with a wholesome direction, the remedy is not to take it from them, but to inform their discretion by education."

*—May 25, 1963*

# Why Johnny Can't Write

One of the first questions in the final examination of a California high-school English class asked the student to write a 500-word essay describing a character in a play by Shakespeare. Another question asked him to reconstruct a vivid conversation from a recent novel he had read. There were at least four other questions involving skill in English composition. All this was to be done in two hours.

An examination in a Midwest college asked the student to write a short essay on the subject: "The status symbols today are those other than money can buy." The paper was to be completed in an hour.

These tests reveal little except the unfortunate role of schools in fostering and sanctioning bad writing habits. If Johnny can't write, one of the reasons may be a conditioning based on speed rather than respect for the creative process. Speed is neither a valid test of nor a proper preparation for competence in writing. It makes for murkiness, glibness, disorganization. It takes the beauty out of the language. It rules out respect for the reflective thought that should precede expression. It runs counter to the word-by-word and line-by-line reworking that enables a piece to be finely knit.

This is not to minimize the value of genuine facility. With years of practice a man may be able to put down words swiftly and expertly. But it is the same kind of swiftness that enables a cellist, after having invested years of effort, to negotiate an intricate passage from Haydn. Speed writing is for stenographers and court reporters, not for anyone who wants to use language with precision and distinction.

Thomas Mann was not ashamed to admit that he would often take a full day to write 500 words, and another day to edit them, out of respect for the most difficult art in the world. Flaubert would ponder a paragraph for hours. Did it say what he wanted it to say—not approximately but exactly? Did the words turn into one another with proper rhythm and grace? Were they artistically and securely fitted together? Were they briskly alive, or were they full of fuzz and ragged edges? Were they likely to make things happen inside the mind of the reader, igniting the imagination and touching off all sorts of new anticipations? These questions are relevant not only for the established novelist but for anyone who attaches value to words as a medium of expression and communication.

E. B. White, whose respect for the environment of good writing is exceeded by no other word artist of our time, would rather have his fingers cut off than to be guilty of handling words lightly. No sculptor chipping away at the granite block in order to produce a delicate curve or feature has labored more painstakingly than White in fashioning a short paragraph. Obviously, we can't expect our schools to make every Johnny into a White or a Flaubert or a Mann, but it is not unreasonable to expect more of them to provide the conditions that promote clear, careful, competent expression. Certainly the cumulative effort of the school experience should not have to be undone in later years.

Speed is not the only demon. Neatness is often valued above style. A composition paper full of corrections and crossed-out lines may be far more valuable to the teacher in appraising a student's awareness of the preciousness of the right word or phrase than an immaculately typed essay. Writing is one subject in which the student ought to be encouraged to ramble around and even be messy, if need be, in search of his answers. Nor is there anything particularly heinous about the use of a dictionary during an English examination or even a test in spelling. Not everyone can spell, even with the most conscientious study; but everyone can develop the habit of using a good dictionary effectively and consistently.

It would be a mistake to blame it all on the English teacher. Poor writing habits are developed in a wide range of courses. Homework assignments aren't always integrated. It is not unusual for a child to be given three overnight writing assignments, any one of which requires several full days' work to be done properly. Moreover, the teacher doesn't always have complete authority in the preparation of examinations, especially those of a year-end or state-wide nature. The root of the problem is that not much thought has been given to the requirements of good writing. The concept of expression as an intricate and highly demanding art has never fully been accepted.

The area in which a poor education shows up first is in self-expression, oral or written. It makes little difference how many university courses or degrees a man may own. If he cannot use words to move an idea from one point to another, his education is incomplete. Taking in a fact is only part of the educational process. The ability to pass it along with reasonable clarity and even distinction is another. The business of assembling the right words, putting them down in proper sequence, enabling each one to pull its full weight in the conveyance of meaning—these are the essentials. A school is where these essentials should feel at home.

—*June 8, 1963*


# The Default of the Educated Man

Not long ago I spoke on the subject of the United Nations at a teachers' convention in Portland, Oregon. A woman approached me after the talk. She said she disagreed completely on the suggestion that teachers give visible support to the UN. She wanted the UN to get out of the United States and the United States to get out of the UN.

"You probably think you did some good with this propaganda of yours about the UN," she said. "That's where you're wrong. What if you had an enthusiastic response? It doesn't mean a thing. You told the teachers it was important to write to people in government on important public issues. That's a laugh. How many letters do you think you will get out of this crowd? A dozen, maybe? It's less than nothing alongside what I've done and the people working with me have done."

I asked the lady what she and her friends had done.

"Last week alone, just by myself, I wrote five hundred letters against the United Nations. I wrote them to the President, Senators, Congressmen, businessmen who advertised in newspapers or magazines that supported the UN, to letters-to-the-editor departments. And more than thirty people in my group have been doing the same thing."

There is good reason to believe the lady was not exaggerating. For many months, the mails of public officials and periodicals have been flooded with angry letters on a wide variety of subjects, of which peace in general and the United Nations in particular seem to be prime targets. At times the mail against the UN has run as high as fifteen to one. Whether the Portland lady and her group are part of a nationwide systematic effort I have no way of knowing. But there can be no doubt that the mails have become a battering ram for extremist views.

Obviously, the President and the Congress are not allowing themselves to be stampeded by letters alone. Public opinion polls on the UN refute the mailbag. But the preponderance of negative mail is disturbing nonetheless. Even if four-fifths of it is discounted, that still leaves a substantial number. What troubles and mystifies the lawmakers most of all is the relative absence of pro-UN mail. It would appear that the lady from Portland was even righter than she knew. By and large, educated people can be counted upon not to write on important public questions.

The matter baffles me. One of the attributes of a truly educated man in a free society is his awareness of the way that society functions. Yet an astonishing illiteracy exists among otherwise intelligent, educated people about the workings of public opinion. Letter-writing to officials is part of the phenomenon of public opinion—not the only part and perhaps not even the most effective part—but it is a part nonetheless. Yet this fact somehow doesn't seem to make a dent in the thinking of many well-educated persons. And so they become part of a massive default—a default gleefully exploited by those who are using every trick in the democratic book, as is their right, to create the impression that their view is the dominant one.

"I don't see much point in writing letters to people in government," a professor of sociology told me. "The letters will not be read. They may be tabulated, perhaps; but they will not be read."

It seemed to me that the professor may have missed the point. Even if the letters are tabulated, this is a significant fact. What is wrong with tabulation? Elections couldn't be held without tabulation. Would a man be justified in declining to vote because he is given no opportunity to explain the reasons behind his preferences?

Another stereotyped objection by many intelligent persons to letter writing on political issues is that the President and Congressmen don't really attach importance to them. This is an assumption. I can bear witness to the fact that on the various occasions when I have had the opportunity to discuss foreign policy issues with the President—and this includes the three previous occupants of the White House—the President has referred to public sentiment as reflected in his mail. These references have been even more pointed in discussions with Senators. One of the favorite topics in conversations among Senators has to do with comparative evaluation of their correspondence.

Of course letters are important. They have never been more important. The President has the obligation to lead, but the people have the obligation to respond, one way or the other. It would be a mistake to expect the President to get too far out in front. Only as he becomes aware of the fact of attention and support can he feel strengthened in proceeding on a certain course. In particular, the President's talk at American University on June 10, in which he proposed a new context for our approach to the atomic age, calls for a profound response. That speech serves as something of a litmus-paper test of the credentials of any citizen who would like to feel useful on the key peace issues of our time. It is difficult to take such credentials seriously unless he has taken the trouble to write to the President about the talk. And, while he is at it, he might also write congratulatory letters to Senators Dodd and Humphrey, who introduced the resolution signed by thirty-two senators calling for a moratorium on nuclear testing.

—*June 29, 1963*

# Not So Fast

The ultimate test of education is represented by the ability to think. We are not talking about casual or random thought. We are talking about sequential thought, that is, the process by which one frame of ideas is attached to another in workable order so that they fit together without rattling or falling apart the moment they come in contact with a logical objection or query.

Sequential thought is the most difficult work in the entire range of human effort. Even when undertaken by a highly trained intelligence, it can be enormously fatiguing. When attempted by untrained minds, it can produce total exhaustion within a matter of minutes, sometimes seconds. For it requires an almost limitless number of mental operations. The route must be anticipated between the present location of an idea and where it is supposed to go. Memory must be raked for relevant material. Facts or notions must be sorted out, put in their proper places, then supplied with connective tissue. Then comes the problem of weighting and emphasis.

Sequential thought, like any other advanced form of human activity, is the result of systematic training. Just sitting in front of television screens watching baseball games for a dozen years or more doesn't automatically qualify a man to throw strikes with blazing speed. Either he has the educated muscles to pitch or he hasn't. The same is true of thought. A man who doesn't know how to use the muscles of his intelligence can hardly be expected to cope with a problem requiring concentration and the ability to think abstractly.

How, then, can a person be taught to think sequentially? It isn't necessary to devise special courses of study for this purpose. All that is necessary is for existing courses to foster those conditions that promote proper habits of thought. The problem lies not with the curriculum; it lies rather with the way education is generally organized.

Fragmentation is the enemy of sequential thought. Yet there is a large degree of fragmentation in the way a youngster is called upon to meet his educational obligations. He may have four or five different courses of study. In the space of a few hours he has to shift his focus of attention drastically several times, resulting often in a blurring of the significance of what he is being taught. Each class or course tends to be something of a universe in itself. This may provide welcome relief in some cases but it also violates many of the basic laws of concentration as they apply to intellectual absorption and retention. This is hardly reassuring at a time when the relationships among the various fields of learning have become of primary importance to education.

Homework assignments are only rarely correlated. On some nights a student may have three or four major assignments, making it virtually impossible to do them all adequately. We have never been able to understand why a homework paper in history, say, and an assignment in English composition cannot be combined. Far better to give a youngster a chance to put his history paper into decent English than to require him to go racing through separate assignments in both subjects. More basic still: why shouldn't the school attempt some measure of coordination in homework assignments, with each course having at least one night a week in which genuine concentration and sustained work would be expected and made possible?

H. L. F. Helmholtz, the noted German physicist who died seventy years ago, described three principal stages in effective thinking. In the first stage, a problem is carefully examined in all its aspects and all directions. In the second stage, ample time is allowed for a problem or an idea to get through to the subconscious in order that the mind may work on it and develop it even when not specifically focused on it. The third stage involves the conditions or circumstances under which an idea is brought to full term and makes its appearance. Helmholtz's analysis may not hold for all people—nothing is more individualistic than a man's thoughts—but at least he emphasizes the need for thought about thinking. Most of our confusion, James Harvey Robinson once wrote, comes from this failure to give thought to thought.

If we are to help Johnny to think—which is to say, if we are to help him become truly educated—it becomes necessary to respect the natural requirements of thought. Somewhere along the line in recent years a speed-up has taken place in large areas of education. Johnny is expected to read faster, study faster, write faster, and think faster. No doubt this is less the fault of educators than of the world itself. But the problems posed by an Age of Speed are not met by snap judgments, one-page memos on complex subjects, lightning-fast reading techniques, or rapid writing. We meet our problems only as we comprehend them and give them sustained and sequential thought. The quickest way to compound these problems is to put them in a pressure cooker.

*—July 6, 1963*

# Notes on a 1963 Visit with Khrushchev

*On April 12, 1963, SR's editor had a seven-hour meeting with Nikita Khrushchev. Because the editor's role at that meeting was not as journalist but as private emissary, no report of the visit was published at that time. The account was published in the November 7, 1964, issue of SR, following the ouster of Nikita Khrushchev as Prime Minister. It appears in this volume in the sequence of events.*

The asphalt road from Sochi to Gagra along the edge of the Black Sea curls, climbs, and dives through the rugged and verdant hills that drop down to the water. The automobiles proceed cautiously, not only because of the sudden turns but because this road is a paradise for bicycle clubs. Long skeins of cyclers, their backs bent low and their bodies seemingly fused into the frames, come shooting at you in endless swift files around the curves.

It was on this road, some sixty miles from the airport at Sochi, that Nikita Khrushchev had his country retreat. The house, large but not ostentatious, was set back from the road behind a low wall in a grove of silver-streaked pine trees. The place appeared to be lightly guarded. One man was posted at the gate and waved us in when he recognized the driver.

As soon as we turned into the estate, I discerned a heavy-set figure standing in the driveway in front of the house. It was Mr. Khrushchev, patiently waiting to welcome us. He was wearing a green-and-tan tweed cape and a large gray unblocked fedora. I said I regretted that our various connections en route from Moscow had made us a half-hour late. He replied that he would refer our apologies to the chef and suggested we proceed immediately to the luncheon table.

The dining room with its large glass doors looked out on the sea. Mr. Khrushchev did the seating, explaining that Mrs. Khrushchev was in Moscow. Lunch was actually a full Russian dinner, with a vast assortment of appetizers, fish, soup, pancakes, veal, wines, cheeses, and pudding. The Chairman steered the table conversation; he had an anecdote to fit every course.

When I found some excuse for not going all the way with the substantial pourings of vodka, the Chairman told of the time he was in the company of some Georgians, who, in keeping with tradition, were drinking out of a massive wine bowl. As the bowl was passed, each man was expected to hold his own in terms of the duration and depth of a single gulp. The Chairman said he knew he was traveling in fast company but decided to take the bowl and the plunge nevertheless. "Served me right," he said. "I was sick for a week."

During tea, he told the story of a frustrated tea drinker whose wife never gave him sugar for his tea. When away from home, he took out his resentment against his wife by thickening his tea with sugar to the point where he could hardly get it down. At home or away, therefore, the poor chap went through life without ever getting his tea just the way he liked it.

This is not to say that the luncheon was entirely without serious conversation. The Chairman asked whether we had observed all the flags on display along the roads and streets. This day, April 12, marked the anniversary of Yuri Gagarin's first flight into space.

"I was down here at the time and rushed up to Moscow to congratulate him," the Chairman said.

I said I understood from Eugenii Fedorov, one of the leading scientists of the Soviet Union, that ordinary people would eventually be able to go up into space; in fact, that this was the way many people would want to take their vacations.

"It will be an interesting development, but it won't happen next week. Still, things are being simplified very rapidly and we hope before long to announce that we have trained a female cosmonaut."

"It would be interesting to get a woman's reaction to a moon voyage," I observed.

"It would be interesting to get anyone's reaction to the moon," he replied. "Right now, however, it is difficult to predict when this will happen. My scientists tell me that they are ready right now, today, to put a man on the moon. But they can't assure me they can get him off and back home again. Of course, I told them it would have to be a round trip. I understand that the United States is very eager to be the first to do it. I say all the more power to you and good luck"—and he swept his arms in front of him in a polite gesture of stepping aside.

I asked the Chairman if he came to his Black Sea retreat in order to rest.

Not always, he replied. Sometimes he came here when he had important problems to think through or important speeches to write. He would walk through the pine grove or along the beach, and he would read and dictate. At such times, he would shut off the telephone and tell the people in Moscow not to bother him.

"There are some things that can be done right only if you take the time they require," he said. "A chicken has to sit quietly for a certain time if she expects to lay an egg. If I have something to hatch, I have to take the time to do it right. It is here that I thought through the problem of what to do about Stalin—whether to tell the people the truth about the man—especially about the tyrannical and irresponsible methods he used in personal dictatorship, or to perpetuate the myth of his greatness.

"Not that everything that happened in his regime was bad," the Chairman continued. "We made progress in a number of respects. But we were also held back in many ways because of the unbelievable irrationality and brutality of Stalin.

[Four months earlier at my meeting with him at his office in the Kremlin, he said that there was "an important difference between Lenin and Stalin; Lenin forgave his enemies, and Stalin killed his friends." He also said how astonished he was, after all this time, to meet reasonably intelligent people who still thought Stalin was sane.]

"It was not an easy decision to make, whether to tell the people the truth. Men had gone off to war and had died with his name on their lips. It would come as a profound emotional shock to them—and many others —to know what kind of man Stalin really was.

"I came down to this place and thought carefully about this problem and then decided to tell the Party Congress everything I knew. It was here that I also drew up the new economic program to increase production.

"It is very quiet here, as you can see," he said. "I have some visitors now and then; it's good to have a respite. Two weeks ago, some Somali government officials were here for some brief talks. You are not the first Americans to visit this place. A few months ago Secretary Udall was here. He made a fine impression on me. He said he had learned some things in observing our hydroelectric power developments. It is a big man who is willing to admit he can learn something from others.

"Also your John McCloy was here a few years ago. A very fine American and a gentleman. We went swimming together in the Black Sea. I think he enjoyed it. Then, your Walter Lippmann was here a couple of years ago. He went swimming too. Also, your Eric Johnston was here. Americans make lively conversation.

"Now, if you aren't too sleepy, we will walk around the grounds—if you would like to see the place."

I assured him we would, although I confess I got up somewhat heavily from the table.

Outside, we walked through the soft flooring of the grove of pine trees. The Chairman identified the trees as belonging to the rarest species of pine trees in the world. This was the only place, he said, where such trees had survived from their ancient beginnings. He was fond of these trees and had given many of them individual names but, like his grandchildren, there were so many of them that he was tempted to give them numbers instead.

The shaded walk soon led to a modern ranch-style structure on a hilltop. A glass wall fronted on the sea.

"This is my sport house," the Chairman explained. "First we will see the swimming pool."

We walked through a small indoor gymnasium and came upon the glass-enclosed pool. I judged it to be about thirty feet by seventy-five feet.

"The glass doors are electrically operated," Mr. Khrushchev said. "Here, I will show you."

He pressed a button and the giant doors began to retract.

Tongue in cheek, I told the Chairman that nowhere in the capitalist world had I seen a private swimming pool as magnificent as this.

The Chairman, with an equally straight face, consoled me, saying our society was still very young and that we would probably have one in due course.

When my daughters marveled at the swimming pool, the Chairman invited them to try it. They said they had not brought bathing suits.

"Don't let that worry you," the Chairman said. "Papa and I will look at the rest of the sport house and then we will have our serious talk on the terrace and you will be all alone. You will have the pool to yourselves and will be undisturbed."

The girls decided they would like to complete the tour of the house first. The Chairman escorted us into the small gymnasium, with its exercising equipment. When I asked what form of exercise he preferred, he pointed to the badminton racquets.

"I play badminton twice a day. Early morning and late afternoon. Then a swim and a rubdown."

I picked up one of the badminton racquets and bounced it against the flat of my hand.

"Do you happen to know anything about this little game?" he asked.

I confessed to a modest knowledge of the sport.

"Very well," he said, "we will have a go at it."

We picked up the racquets and started to play. The proprieties seemed to me to require that I hit the shuttlecock high and to his right side, just as I would if I were playing with one of my daughters.

After a minute or two of this kind of play, the Chairman shook his head.

"*Nyet!*" he said. "That's not the way to play. My gymnasium instructor says that to play this game right you've got to hit the bird hard and fast and only a few inches above the net, like this—" Wham! And the bird came straight at my head.

Now that the ground rules were explicit, I no longer felt bound by excessive restraint. We went at it. I was astounded at the speed of the Chairman's reflexes and his agility. He not only kept the bird in play but made it whistle as he rifled his shots.

When we stopped, I observed that he was not winded or flushed. In a few days he would be sixty-nine. I thought of some newspaper stories I had read in Rome only four or five days earlier to the effect that he had had a heart attack or a stroke and that he had gone to the Black Sea to recuperate. Under the present circumstances, these stories were less than convincing.

I asked the Chairman if he would permit me to take some photographs of him at his favorite sport. He assented readily and played badminton with my daughters while I operated the camera.

The tour of the sport house was resumed. Just outside the small gymnasium was the sun deck. Even on the coldest days, the Chairman said, he would come here to enjoy the sun. On these occasions he made ample

use of a giant bear coat. He held it up; it was a massive garment indeed.
"Maybe the girls would like to see my disappearing act," he said.

He climbed into the coat, grinned, and went into a going, going, gone routine, finally sinking into the coat until he was completely out of sight.

Suddenly, there came a few growls from inside the encased mass. My daughters were delightfully terrified. Then suddenly the top flap flew open and he reappeared with a loud "Boo!" It was obvious that he had developed certain skills as a grandfather.

The Chairman put the bear coat down and said the time had come for serious talk.

"The girls are free to do what they wish," he said. "Papa and I will get down to business."

The girls went back to the pool and the Chairman and I sat at a small table inside the glass-enclosed terrace. We had our interpreter, Oleg Bykov (my own choice), and a rapporteur, Boris Ivanov, both of whom had accompanied us from Moscow.

This was my second meeting with Mr. Khrushchev in four months. In December 1962, the trip to Moscow was concerned with religious matters. I was acting in behalf of church leaders who felt the time might be opportune for exploring the possibilities of enlarged religious freedoms inside the Soviet Union. In particular, the object of the mission was to obtain the release of Bishop Josef Slipyi, head of the Ukrainian Rites Catholic Church. Bishop Slipyi had been interned for seventeen years.

On that previous visit, we had three hours together in his office in the Kremlin. He was relaxed, optimistic, confident. But now, in April 1963, he seemed somewhat weighted down, even withdrawn. I couldn't be sure, but he seemed to be under considerable pressure.

Understandably so. Many things had happened to change the atmosphere since December. The Chinese had been exploiting the Russian missile withdrawal from Cuba, charging that Nikita Khrushchev was guilty of appeasing the imperialistic Americans. They claimed he had demonstrated his unfitness to lead the world revolutionary movement and that he had no real desire to overthrow or defeat the capitalist West, preferring to coexist with the very forces Marx and Lenin said must be violently overthrown. In return, Nikita Khrushchev had asserted that appeasement was in no way involved. He said the missiles had been installed in Cuba because of the possibility of an American invasion. Once the invasion threat was removed, there was no need to keep missiles there. At any rate, he had said that a nuclear holocaust over Cuba had been averted; this was the important thing. Anyone who knew anything about atomic weapons, he had declared, knew there was no alternative to peaceful coexistence. He had charged that the Chinese were absolutists who were attempting to use ideological dogma in places and situations where it didn't fit.

Even so, as the result of Cuba, it seemed clear that Nikita Khrushchev felt compelled to prove he was not an appeaser. He could try to do this either by being tough and militant, or by producing evidence that his coexistence policies were yielding results.

It was evident, just after Cuba, that he had decided in favor of the latter course. He was apparently confident he could conclude an early agreement with the United States banning nuclear tests, thus proving the practical wisdom of his policies. But the hoped-for agreement had become stalled over the question of inspection, and there was mounting uneasiness inside Mr. Khrushchev's own inner councils about the effect of this impasse on the situation inside the Communist world. The Chinese had pounced upon this failure, referring to it as yet another example of Khrushchev's ineptness. Some of Khrushchev's own advisers began to stress the need for unity inside the Communist world. They wanted to set reasonable limits to the differences between the two countries.

It was not at all surprising, therefore, that Mr. Khrushchev should seem preoccupied at Gagra. He had two critically important events coming up in rapid succession—the plenum of the Communist Party and the confrontation with the Chinese. Either one called for important leadership decisions and actions. The combination of both would put him to the severest test since coming to office. He had come to Gagra before when he had serious problems to think through; this time the totality of his policies was involved.

At that meeting—December 7, 1962—I had stated the case for the release of Bishop Slipyi. Bishop Slipyi had been imprisoned since 1947. I was authorized to say that Pope John was hopeful that the Bishop might spend his few remaining years—he was now in his seventies—at some distant seminary.

The Chairman had said at that December meeting that he would like to establish good relations with the Vatican and that he had a profound regard for Pope John, but he feared that the release of Bishop Slipyi would have exactly the opposite effect.

"In what way?" I had asked.

"The moment he is released, there will be big headlines saying the Bishop was tortured by the Reds," he had said. "This would not exactly help the cause of improved relations."

I had replied that it was my understanding that Pope John was not seeking the release of Bishop Slipyi for the purpose of propagandist exploitation. He was genuinely concerned about the health and well-being of the Bishop. As a matter of basic human justice, he hoped the Bishop would be freed.

The Chairman proceeded to expound on the case of Bishop Slipyi for almost twenty minutes. He traced the long history of rivalry between the

Ukrainian Rite Orthodox Church and the Russian Orthodox Church. He spoke about Bishop Slipyi's predecessor, Metropolitan Sheptytsky, who died, the Chairman said, under circumstances that suggested his departure from this earth may have been unnaturally accelerated, although he did not say by whom. In any event he said the Bishop had been imprisoned for good and sufficient reason.

My purpose was not to argue that point, I had said. But it was seventeen years since the arrest took place. Surely any further punishment could serve no useful purpose.

You may be right, he had said, adding that he would look into the matter and let me know.

At that December meeting, as I got up to leave, the Chairman reached into a drawer and took out two letters on which Christmas greetings to Pope John and President Kennedy had already been engraved. Then he signed the letters and asked me to deliver them on my return to Rome and the United States.

Several weeks later, after I had returned to New York from the December meeting in Moscow, I had received a telephone call from the Soviet Ambassador in Washington. Ambassador Dobrynin asked if I could come to Washington soon. He had some news to transmit to me.

Two days later, at the Soviet Embassy, the Ambassador said he had been asked to convey the greetings of Premier Khrushchev and also to say that the Premier was happy to arrange for the unconditional release of Bishop Slipyi. The Ambassador asked where and how and to whom the Bishop should be delivered.

I thanked the Ambassador for the good news and immediately communicated with Father Felix Morlion, President of Pro Deo University in Rome, who was then in the United States. Throughout all the arrangements leading up to the appointments in Moscow and the Vatican, Father Morlion had occupied a liaison role.

Father Morlion telephoned Rome immediately and conveyed the good news. Within a few hours Vatican officials drew up a plan for Bishop Slipyi's return to freedom. The plan, accepted immediately by the Soviet government, called for the Bishop to be flown to Vienna, where he would be met by the Pope's personal representative and flown to Rome.

The plan was successfully carried out within a week. Bishop Slipyi was brought to the Vatican where Pope John, despite his now advancing illness, greeted him and told of his joy at seeing him reunited with the Church. Following this meeting, the Bishop was escorted to a secret retreat some miles outside Rome. No reporters were permitted to see the Bishop. Indeed, it was only after the Bishop had arrived at his secret retreat that the news of his liberation was released.

The day following this announcement, I received a telephone call from Ambassador Dobrynin in Washington asking me if I had seen the afternoon newspapers. I said I had not. The Ambassador suggested that I do so. Then he read to me a news story under the following headline:

BISHOP TELLS OF RED TORTURE

He asked me if I would care to make any comment concerning what appeared to be a breach of good faith. I said I had no direct knowledge of what had happened but I was absolutely certain that there had been no breach of faith. I said I would telephone the Vatican directly and find out what I could.

Vatican officials were profoundly shocked when I told them of the news break in the U.S. Bishop Slipyi had spoken to no newsmen. They termed the story a pure concoction. They said they would set the record straight immediately. In particular, *Osservatore Romano* would carry a front-page statement quoting Pope John to the effect that the news stories about Bishop Slipyi were without authority and were repudiated by both Pope John and Bishop Slipyi.

What troubled Vatican officials most of all was that this incident might interfere with further attempts to bring about release of churchmen imprisoned in Communist countries.

I telephoned Ambassador Dobrynin and informed him that the news stories were completely unauthorized and that the next issue of *Osservatore Romano* would set the record straight on the authority of the Pope.

We began our terrace discussion, therefore, with matters that carried over from our talk of four months earlier.

I thanked the Chairman for his affirmative response to the request for Archbishop Slipyi's release.

Once again, I expressed the regrets of Vatican officials at what had appeared to be a breach of faith in some of the news coverage that followed the Archbishop's release and of the profound elation of Pope John at being reunited with Bishop Slipyi.

The Chairman said he understood, adding that some journalists didn't know what to do with good news.

He then inquired about the health of Pope John, saying he had often thought of, and been inspired by, Pope John's desire to contribute to world peace in whatever time remained to him.

This seemed like a propitious moment to transmit to the Chairman the advance copy, translated into Russian, of Pope John's encyclical, "*Pacem in Terris.*"

The Chairman said he was pleased to know about the encyclical. "Are there any parts of the encyclical," he asked, "that ought to be discussed now?"

This gave me the opportunity to call his attention to some of the key passages of "*Pacem in Terris*" dealing with the need to end the nuclear arms race and to regulate the affairs of nations in the human interest. The Chairman nodded frequently as I read from the sections. He again praised Pope John for his service to world peace and said he would study the entire encyclical.

I brought up the matter of Archbishop Beran, of Czechoslovakia, who had been interned for some years. Cardinal Augustus Bea, of the Vatican, had told me of his great concern for the Bishop's health.

The Chairman said he was unfamiliar with the case of Archbishop Beran, and that this was a matter that concerned the Czechoslovak government.

Recognizing this, I said that Cardinal Bea was hopeful that the Chairman might be willing to use his good offices to explore the matter with Czech government officials.

The Chairman said he would take the matter under advisement.

The discussion then turned to the matter of a nuclear-test ban. The Chairman had been quoted in news dispatches from Moscow as saying that the United States had not been acting in good faith on the matter of a nuclear-test ban, reneging on its own proposals for three inspections, and that there was reason to doubt whether the United States really wanted a test ban. If he had been correctly quoted, I said, his conclusions were inaccurate.

I had come to see him, I said, on no official mission; I was a private citizen. President Kennedy, knowing I was to see the Chairman, had asked me to try to clarify the Soviet misunderstanding of the American position on the test ban. If the Chairman construed the American position on inspections to mean that we actually did not want a treaty banning such testing, then that interpretation was in error.

The Chairman leaned forward in his chair. There was a perceptible tightening in his expression.

"If the United States really wanted a treaty, it could have had one," he said in measured tones. "If it wants one now it can have one. The United States said it wanted inspection. We don't believe inspections are really necessary. We think they are an excuse for espionage. Our scientists proved to me that new instrumentation makes it possible for you to detect any violations from outside our borders. But we wanted a treaty and the United States said we couldn't get one without inspections. So we agreed, only to have you change your position."

"There was a misunderstanding as to what our position really was," I said.

"A misunderstanding? How could there be a misunderstanding? Fedorov had a meeting with Wiesner in Washington last October. Wiesner told him that the United States was ready to proceed on the basis of a few annual inspections. Ambassador Dean told Kuznetsov the same thing. Kuznetsov is a very meticulous reporter. He always tells me exactly what happened. How can there be a misunderstanding?"

The President had asked me to say that he had a high regard for Ambassador Kuznetsov and did not doubt for a moment that the Ambassador reported the conversation with Mr. Dean as he understood it. He also had a high regard for Ambassador Dean, who, like Ambassador Kuznetsov, had a reputation as a meticulously correct reporter. Rather than carry on a fruitless debate over the precise nature of the Kuznetsov–Dean conversation, the President was disposed to regard the matter as an honest misunderstanding; he felt a fresh start should be made. It would be a tragedy of the first magnitude, he believed, if a misunderstanding were allowed to get in the way of an agreement that both countries critically needed in their own self-interest and that would represent the first great step toward controlling the nuclear threat.

The Chairman shook his head.

"It is not just one conversation. As I told you, there was the talk between Wiesner and Fedorov. Also, our scientists came back from Cambridge, where they met with American scientists who said the same thing. How could there be a misunderstanding?"

With due respect, I ventured to suggest that an honest misunderstanding, under the circumstances, was possible and plausible. An American representative might urge the Soviet representative to revert to the previous Soviet position, which accepted three inspections, as the basis of an agreement. In so doing, the American representative was suggesting what he considered to be the basis for negotiations that could lead to a prompt and fruitful resolution. The Soviet representative, however, might interpret the statement not as a basis for fruitful discussion but as the specific content of a treaty. The result was an honest misunderstanding.

In any event, I said, the President was acting in absolute good faith when he said that no misunderstanding, logical or otherwise, should obstruct so important an undertaking. I had firsthand evidence to offer on this point. A number of citizens' organizations had come together to develop public support for the President's position in favor of a nuclear-test ban. In discussing this matter with the President, I had shown him the texts and layouts for a series of full-page newspaper advertisements calling for a test ban. The President was deeply interested in these materials and had constructive suggestions to make. It seemed to me inconceivable that he would have encouraged this public campaign if he had publicly advocated a test ban only for propaganda purposes, as the Soviet press had charged.

I had brought one of the advertisements with me and I held it up so that the Chairman could see it. The headline read:

We Can Kill
The Russians
360 Times Over

The Russians Can
Kill Us Only
160 Times Over

We're Ahead,
Aren't We?

The Chairman stared hard at this advertisement while the text was translated for him. He lifted his hand.

"Your figures are all wrong," he said. "We're not that far behind. But, as the ad says, what difference does it make? Nuclear war is sheer madness. Now, back to our discussion. Your talk with the President has persuaded you of some things. Now let me tell you about the picture as we see it here. After Cuba, there was a real chance for both the Soviet Union and the United States to take measures together that would advance the peace by easing tensions. The one area on which I thought we were closest to agreement was nuclear testing. And so I went before the Council of Ministers and said to them:

" 'We can have an agreement with the United States to stop nuclear tests if we agree to three inspections. I know that three inspections are not necessary, and that the policing can be done adequately from outside our borders. But the American Congress has convinced itself that on-site inspection is necessary and the President cannot get a treaty through the Senate without it. Very well, then, let us accommodate the President.'

"The Council asked me if I was certain that we could have a treaty if we agreed to three inspections and I told them yes. Finally, I persuaded them."

When he said this, I thought of the earlier predictions by the Chinese Communists that if the Soviet Union accepted the American proposal of three inspections, the Americans would renege and ask for six, and if Khrushchev agreed to six, the Americans would renege and ask for twelve. And so on, indefinitely. The Chinese position was that the Americans were interested neither in a nuclear-test ban nor in coexistence in general. According to the Chinese, Khrushchev was naïve in pursuing a policy of peaceful coexistence when the people he wanted to coexist with had no desire to coexist with him. The Chinese had quoted Marx and Lenin to support their view that war was inherent in the nature of capitalist imperialism and that the world would have to sustain a violent ordeal before capitalism could be cleared away and the triumph of world socialism be assured.

Any failure of a nuclear-test ban, therefore, would have consequences far beyond the armaments crisis. It would have an effect on the struggle for power inside the Communist world, in the sense that the Chinese would exploit the test-ban failure as proof of the correctness of their total position.

Still another situation came to mind when the Chairman said it wasn't easy to get the Ministers to agree. This had to do with the U-2 episode several years ago. At that time, the Chairman had attempted to convince the council that the American President had nothing to do with the U-2 and that he could therefore proceed with plans to meet with him at the imminent summit conference. Then the President announced he had authorized the U-2 flight.

These, at least, were some of the speculations that came to mind when the Chairman spoke of the reluctance of the council to agree readily to his recommendation to accept inspection.

"People in the United States seem to think I am a dictator who can put into practice any policy I wish," the Chairman continued. "Not so. I've got to persuade before I can govern. Anyway, the Council of Ministers agreed to my urgent recommendation. Then I notified the United States I would accept three inspections. Back came the American rejection. They now wanted—not three inspections or even six. They wanted eight. And so once again I was made to look foolish. But I can tell you this: it won't happen again."

"The President had no intention of humiliating you or making you look foolish before your council," I said. "There is a genuine question in his mind concerning the adequacy of three inspections. Each year almost one hundred earth tremors or movements of varying magnitude occur within the vast land mass of the Soviet Union. Many of the seismograph markings caused by these movements are similar to the markings produced by underground nuclear explosions. Hence there is considerable feeling in the Senate that even eight inspections are minimal. In any event, the President would like to break the present impasse. He suggests that the negotiators at Geneva be instructed to proceed with the many questions apart from inspections that have yet to be worked out. These questions should represent no great difficulties but they have to be resolved nevertheless. The President would like to hold the question of inspections for last, and then he and you would work out this problem together."

"Not practical or possible," Mr. Khrushchev said, again shaking his head. "For various reasons I cannot go to Washington and I would assume that the President right now has good reasons for not coming to Moscow. Where does this leave us?"

"It leaves you with the rest of the world in which to find a place," I suggested. "Vienna served the purpose once before. And if not Vienna, then another place. But even if no place can be found, then there are other forms of communications."

"You don't seem to understand what the situation is here," he said.

"We cannot make another offer. I cannot go back to the council. It is now up to the United States. Frankly, we feel we were misled. If we change our position at all, it will not be in the direction of making it more generous. It will be less generous. When I go up to Moscow next week I expect to serve notice that we will not consider ourselves bound by three inspections. If you can go from three to eight, we can go from three to zero."

He leaned forward in his chair.

"Now there's something else you ought to know," he said. "My atomic scientists have been pressing me hard to allow them to carry on more nuclear tests. They believe that the security of our country requires that we develop new refinements in nuclear weapons. As you know, we have already successfully tested a 100-megaton bomb, but they want to follow this up with more variations. They say the United States has carried out 70 per cent more tests than the Soviet Union and that the world will understand. They want a green light to go ahead; I think I may decide to give it to them. It's time I put the security of my country first."

For a moment or two I said nothing.

"Well?" he asked.

"You are looking at a depressed man," I said. "I came here for the purpose of bearing witness to the President's good faith. You have apparently placed little weight on this. Your final response is that you are probably going to resume atmospheric tests. If you do, I cannot imagine that the United States will stand still and let its lead dwindle. So we will test again, and you will test, and we will test, and so on. This destroys any possibility that other nations can be persuaded not to test. The poisons in the air will multiply. None of this adds either to American or Russian security.

"There is something else that occurs to me at this point," I continued. "Last summer, President Kennedy was informed by a Soviet representative that missile bases were not being installed in Cuba. Perhaps it will be said that this was a misunderstanding. Under the circumstances, perhaps one misunderstanding can cancel out another."

Mr. Khrushchev looked at me severely.

"Very well," he said. "You want me to accept President Kennedy's good faith? All right, I accept President Kennedy's good faith. You want me to believe that the United States sincerely wants a treaty banning nuclear tests? All right, I believe the United States is sincere. You want me to set all misunderstandings aside and make a fresh start? All right, I agree to make a fresh start.

"Now," he said in unmistakably clipped tones, "let us forget everything that happened before. Forget all conversations involving Kuznetsov, Dean, Wiesner, Fedorov, and all the others. Now everyone will act in good faith and accept the good faith of everyone else. Very well. The Soviet Union now proposes to the United States a treaty to outlaw nuclear testing—underground, overground, in water, in space, every place. And we will give you something you don't really need. We will give you inspections inside our country to convince you we aren't really cheating. We make our offer; you accept it, and there's no more nuclear testing. Finished. If the President really wants a treaty, here it is."

"That's precisely the point," I said. "The President has come down a great deal from the original twenty inspections but he knows of no way he can come all the way down to three. The Senate would never accept it."

Mr. Khrushchev reached into the breast pocket of his blue suit and took out a "pull-out" watch—that is, a watch encased in a smooth metallic frame; when the two sides of this case are separated to show the time, the action also winds the springs. He toyed with the mechanism.

"We are repeating ourselves," he said. "Just so there is no mistake about it in your mind, let me say finally that I cannot and will not go back to the Council of Ministers and ask them to change our position in order to accommodate the United States again. Why am I always the one who must understand the difficulties of the other fellow? Maybe it's time for the other fellow to understand my position. But you can tell the President I accept his explanation of an honest misunderstanding and suggest that we get moving. I am willing to make a fresh start. Be sure to tell that to the President. But the next move is up to him."

The Chairman asked if there was anything else I wanted to discuss.

I said there was. In lecturing before various groups in the United States, and in talking about the problems involved in a just and durable peace, I would constantly be confronted by people who would ask: "How can you talk about peace with the Soviet Union in view of the fact that Mr. Khrushchev has already declared war on us? He keeps saying he will bury us."

And so I asked Mr. Khrushchev how he would answer these questions.

"What I meant was, not that I will bury you, but that history will bury you," he said somewhat testily. "Don't blame me if your capitalist system is doomed. I am not going to kill you. I have no intention of murdering 200 million Americans. In fact, I will not even take part in the burial. The workers in your society will bury the system and they will be the pallbearers. Don't ask me when it is going to happen. It may not happen tomorrow or the day after. But it will happen. This is as certain as the rising sun."

I asked Mr. Khrushchev if he would be willing to consider evidence to the contrary.

"Please," he said.

I pointed out that Marx's basic proposition—that the masses of people are impoverished under capitalism—was manifestly untrue in the United States. In fact, Marx's great failure was that he was unable to predict the profound changes that were to take place within the American economic structure. There was little resemblance between the capitalism Marx wrote about a century ago and the situation today. Instead of enslavement and impoverishment, the economic condition of the large masses of our people was vastly improved over what it was at the time of *Das Kapital.* We still had serious problems, of course. There was still a problem of waste—both with respect to our natural resources and our manpower; the nation was not yet making the most productive use of its Negro citizens. Even here, however, it would be a mistake to ignore important progress.

In any event, Marx had never fully anticipated the fluidity of a free society or the full significance of a considerable lack of acute class consciousness in the United States. Americans were productive and were improving their lot.

Mr. Khrushchev replied that if Marx were alive today he would not be dismayed by these developments but would say instead that all his predictions would come true. "I repeat," he said, "I have great admiration for the American people. Mark my word, when they become a socialist society, they will have the finest socialist society in the world. They are resourceful, energetic, intelligent, imaginative. What a wonderful thing this will be for them and for the world."

I told Mr. Khrushchev the United States would be glad to have his good wishes but I thought it important to point out that notions of historical inevitability or determinism did not really fit American history or the American character. Peaceful coexistence, as I understood it, meant that each state could hold to its institutions and there could still be peace.

"*Harrasho,*" he said. ("Just right.")

I knew I had prolonged our talk far beyond any reasonable limits. There was, however, one additional assignment I had been asked to carry out. Rex Stout, the mystery-story writer and president of the Authors' League, had empowered me to represent the league in seeking some solution to the copyright tangle with the Soviet Union. For the past ten years various attempts had been made to persuade the Soviet Union to respect American copyright. The main countering argument on the Soviet side was that the Russians read many times more of our books than we did of theirs and that we were therefore proposing an unfair balance of literary trade. Another problem had to do with retroactivity. Publication of American books without authorization in the Soviet Union had been going on for a long time; how far back in time would the Soviet liability go?

I told Mr. Khrushchev that the Authors' League authorized me to propose that any copyright agreement would be free of past liability. As of January 1, 1964, say, each country would honor copyright restrictions and seek permission for any literary works originating in the other country.

No retroactive payments would be required, although continued publication and distribution of books issued before January 1, 1964, would, of course, be covered by the new agreement.

Mr. Khrushchev shook his head.

"What kind of a deal is this?" he asked. "You get all the benefits, and what do we get? We publish maybe millions of copies of books by American authors. We read Hemingway, Faulkner, Mitchell Wilson, Jack London, Mark Twain, Sinclair Lewis, and many others. And how many of our writers do your people read? A few of the classical ones but hardly any of the contemporary ones. We are a nation of book readers. You are a nation of television watchers and comic-book buyers. How can you propose a deal when you are not in a position to offer anything?"

I told the Chairman that there was increasing interest among Americans in contemporary Soviet authors, but even if this were not the case, it was hardly relevant, one way or the other. American writers were entitled to payment for the use of their words. They also had the right to decide whether their books should be reprinted. If we could agree on this principle, then we could talk about the entirely separate matter of increasing the availability of Soviet books in the United States.

"You may think these are separate matters but we do not. I see no chance right now for a copyright agreement," he said. "But we would be glad to talk to you about developing something approaching parity in our literary exchange. Once that is done, we can consider the copyright problem. But, as I say, your country has a long way to go before you can equal ours in the matter of book reading. You know Tolstoy, Dostoevski, Gorki, and one or two others from the old Russia, but you know very little about our living writers—and we have some good ones. And even what you know of Tolstoy is badly corrupted. When I was in the United States several years ago I saw a version of *War and Peace* in comic-book form. It was made into a story of terror, wild sex, and brutality. How can you expect poor Tolstoy to rest in his grave with nonsense like that going on?"

I had no defense to offer for the offensive edition of Tolstoy and said so. But the context in which the Chairman made his remarks was incorrect. He said our people did not read books. An error. Last year, more than 300,000,000 books were sold in the United States. This did not include the comic books or the cheapies he had spoken about. Was he familiar with the large number of serious books now being published and sold in inexpensive paperback form? Again, this didn't excuse the cheap books, but at least the situation was somewhat different from the way he had understood it.

"You are to be congratulated," said the Chairman. "Now if only you can do something about your television, you will be making some real progress. Frankly, I could hardly believe my eyes when I was in the

United States, the kind of things you showed on television. If the sadism and violence you show are at all representative of the kind of life you have in America, God help you! All the killing and beatings and cheating and swearing and wife-stealing and immorality! A nation can't help being judged by the things it is interested in.

"But what is most surprising to me," he continued, "is that you apparently have no idea of the kind of harm this is doing to your children. They sit in front of the TV sets for hours at a time and take it all in. What kind of food is this for tender young minds? And you wonder why you have a juvenile-delinquency problem. Surely your capitalists, who put on these TV programs, must have some conscience and can be persuaded not to make money out of deforming children's minds. And if they can't, why can't your society do something about it? Capitalism isn't just an unjust economic system. It's a way of life that leads to a corruption of important values. Television is only one example."

Once again I asked the Chairman if he would be willing to consider some contrary evidence. And once again he said, "Please."

First, concerning television. I said he made it appear that there was almost no concern in the United States about this problem. Had it not been called to his attention that the chairman of the Federal Communications Commission had attacked irresponsible programming on television? Was he unaware of the various citizens' group that had been organized to combat harmful TV? Had he overlooked the numerous articles in the press on the subject? In any event, two important facts had to be stressed. The first was that the American people had freedom of choice. They were not confined to a government station; in many cities they had four or five or more channels. They also had freedom of choice over a wide range of programs dealing with serious music, good films, news reports, and public affairs. They could watch debates over government policy, in which the government itself would be seriously criticized. No penalties would be attached to such criticism. Moreover, some of our large capitalist companies would sponsor important music events and other similar high-quality programs.

Apart from all this, a major development in American television had probably escaped his attention. I referred to the fact that there were now some ninety educational television stations across the United States. These stations were free of what he called "trash." The fact that they were called "educational" TV stations did not mean that they were used just for instructional purposes. They provided general programs of genuine merit, combining public education with high-level entertainment. The national educational organization that supplied many of the programs for these stations was financed by a foundation that got its money through the sale of automobiles. Locally, the stations were supported on a community basis, and many capitalistic enterprises contributed to the upkeep of these local stations without commercial announcements or expectation of profit.

The Chairman said he hadn't intended to offend me or arouse me and was glad to learn about all these promising developments in the United States. And he was especially glad to know that so many people were eager to do something about the awful trash on television. He wished them all the luck in the world and said they would probably need it.

Apart from educational TV, there were other impressive indications, I said, of a healthy growth in the creative and cultural life of America. The fact that one child out of three was taking instrumental lessons in music; the fact that twice as many people attended concerts each year as attended baseball games; the fact that American colleges in their history—all these facts might indicate that the United States was not as backward or under-developed culturally as his earlier remarks would seem to indicate. The Americans were putting their freedom to good use.

The Chairman said he applauded these developments and could only say that if the American people had done this well despite their present system, just think of the kind of progress they would make when they turned socialist. And once again he looked at his pull-out watch.

It was late in the afternoon and the sunlight was waning. I was eager to put a final question to the Chairman. I asked him whether he was discouraged in his stated policy of peaceful relations with the United States and the West in general.

The Chairman said he wanted to believe that the terrible drift to war could be ended and that the two most powerful countries in the world could find some way to live in peace, but that the next move was up to the United States. He looked to President Kennedy, for whom he had high regard, to take the next step. Then he asked me to convey his greetings to the President and Mrs. Kennedy.

My daughters and their escort approached the terrace. We stood up to greet them. The girls had been swimming in the Chairman's pool (later, they told me that they had used Mr. Khrushchev's trunks—"they ballooned out like life preservers"). Then we all walked back to the main house. I thanked the Chairman for being so generous with his time. We got into the car and left.

—*November 7, 1964*


## The Test Ban and Beyond

It is important to identify two sets of questions that figure in the Senate consideration of the limited nuclear test-ban treaty. These questions are not now being openly discussed, but they are vital nonetheless, and the public is entitled to full disclosure and debate.

Neither set of questions is directly concerned with the merits of the test-ban treaty per se. They have nothing to do with radioactivity, or the spread of nuclear weapons to other countries, or the possibility of secret violations. They are strategic issues, fundamental in nature; unless they are fully resolved, it is doubtful that measures looking toward a less explosive world can be taken.

The first set of questions has to do with strategy in dealing with the Soviet Union. One group in government believes that the arms race should be pursued as an end in itself, forcing the Soviet Union to divert its resources and its energies away from its domestic economy. According to this argument, communism cannot survive the indefinite and unremitting pressure of unlimited arms production. Eventually, the people, in a state of acute deprivation, would turn on their masters. This viewpoint was advanced in government councils at one time by the late Secretary of State John Foster Dulles. President Eisenhower, however, disagreed with this position, believing it would be of definite advantage to the United States for the Soviet Union to improve its domestic economic capacity. He felt that a genuine advance in the living conditions of the Soviet people might be a healthy development, for an economic upgrading would not be an isolated phenomenon. Enhancing the importance of the individual in the economic sphere would mean that his importance in the political, cultural, and religious spheres would be enhanced as well. Under these circumstances, dogmatic Marxism would diminish and the basis for a non-belligerent relationship with Russia might ultimately be established.

This question was considered and debated at the highest levels during the Eisenhower administration; it persists today. President Kennedy has made his own position clear. He has given priority to the need to reduce and, if possible, to eliminate the mounting danger of a nuclear holocaust. For if this problem is not solved all other problems will be academic. Accordingly, he sees the limited ban on nuclear testing as a place to take hold in coping with the larger problem of establishing effective controls over war itself. On the narrower question of the effects of the arms race on the Soviet economy, there is reason to believe that the President sees far less danger from a government putting most of its resources into the well-being of its citizens than into the accumulation of shattering weapons of surprise attack. Moreover, the maximum threat to the United States is likely to come not from a nation that is making a reasonable degree of progress in attending to its own business but from a nation that is seeking to cover up its failures at home with adventures abroad.

The second set of subsurface questions has to do with the American economy. The debate here is between those who fear economic disaster if the nation goes in for serious cutbacks in military spending, and those who see the strongest opportunities in American history for a strengthened economy and for sustained well-being once the arms burden is lifted from the nation's back.

Those who take the former position are fearful that the test ban will lead to even more advanced measures in the field of arms control and reduction. They tend to see the continuation of the arms race as a useful end in itself. In their view, the American economy is now dependent on a high level of military spending; any shift downward from this level could be serious and even catastrophic. This position is often combined with the conviction that there must be no limitation on the raw fact of military power.

Opponents of this view see all sorts of exciting possibilities for the American economy under the circumstances of reduced military budgets. Men like Ralph Cordiner, chairman of the Board of General Electric, and Seymour Melman, professor of industrial engineering at Columbia University, have been pushing ahead with research on the essentials of conversion to non-military projects. They are optimistic about the ability of the American economy to make the transition; what they foresee is not just a situation in which military production can be absorbed, but a situation of substantial expansion.

There is no reason why these underlying issues should not be openly debated. The open discussion today may range over a wide variety of other issues, but the subsurface questions figure importantly in the thinking of the men who are called upon to ratify a test-ban treaty. This being the case, the public is entitled to a full view and a full debate.

And, as the debate proceeds, an interesting paradox may emerge. It is that some of the men who most loudly proclaim the virtues of the free-enterprise system may reveal the least faith in it when the chips are down. They inveigh against an increase in Federal powers, but ignore the powerful factor of government involvement when it comes to military projects. They denounce featherbedding and boondoggling but say little about the fact that a frighteningly large part of the American military program today is a vast boondoggle. The situation was bad when former President Hoover and his task force turned in their report some years ago; it is many times worse today under the circumstances of a 50-billion-dollar budget. The manufacture of weapons that are obsolete even before they are completed; determination of some budgets based on plant capacity rather than strict military usefulness; the accumulation over the years of weapons with a capacity to destroy the enemy many hundreds of times over—all these factors must now be taken into account. Extraneous surpluses, misused manpower, depletion of the national wealth—none of this adds to the national security. Secretary Robert McNamara has done everything humanly possible to check the waste; but he cannot control the political process which is central in the final determination of what is to be spent. And this is where the people come in.

If we combine the two sets of subsurface debates, what we find is that the opponents of a test ban pay higher tribute to the Soviet economy than they do to their own. They seem to feel that the Soviet economy has the ability to benefit from an easing or the end of the arms race, whereas our own economy cannot take up the slack. They say they are opposed to communism—indeed, their basic position is predicated upon it—but they tend to shrink from a full and free competition between the two systems in the non-military arena.

The ultimate question, therefore, has to do with one's basic faith and confidence in the ability of the United States to hold its own in the non-military showdown coming up in the world. Those who know most about this nation's history, its philosophy, and its institutions will find abundant nourishment for optimism. As usual, those who know the least will fear the most.

—*August 10, 1963*

## Just the Beginning

Reflections on the test-ban treaty:

The season of hope has begun. What kind of ultimate harvest is possible no one now knows. Moreover, it is too early to tell whether additional planting can be undertaken. But that is not important. What is important is that, after more than eighteen years of barrenness, the grounds of hope have been seeded with realism. It is not necessary to have extravagant expectations in order to warrant a genuine feeling of thanksgiving or even to justify modest celebration. There has been a break in a long stretch of unremitting failure and almost constant despair. There is also an opportunity to do more. Rejoicing over the achievement and the prospect is healthy and essential.

For a time during the debate, however, one wondered whether some of the treaty's supporters were forgetting what the treaty was all about. It was almost made to appear that the pact was a way of speeding up the arms race instead of slowing it down. Some of the supporters of the treaty, in their eagerness to assure one and all that there was nothing disadvantageous in the treaty, came close to making the treaty sound like a shrewd maneuver to guarantee American military supremacy, thus endorsing the argument of the Chinese Communists that the Russians were playing into American hands. In fact, some of the arguments for ratification made Nikita Khrushchev seem like a dunce for having agreed to the treaty in the first place—another pet proposition of the Chinese Communists.

The ban limiting nuclear testing has been so long in coming that we suppose we shouldn't cavil at any arguments, however misguided, in favor of passage. For the treaty is not an end in itself. It is part of—or should be —a large and delicate enterprise for making life less precarious for the humans who inhabit this planet. It is a portal to a more rational future. But the treaty can be substantially denuded of these possibilities if the driving force behind it is made to seem self-serving and grasping.

For a time during the debate many people seemed to forget that the precise purpose of the treaty was to compel the signers to give up something. The problem was caused in the first place by the desire of the major powers to hold on to everything, and, indeed, to grab for more. But the effect of almost unlimited grabbing in the past had been to leave almost everyone with an empty future. The accumulation of nuclear firepower had not achieved national security. It had intensified mutual insecurity, increased the yearning for more weapons, and exposed the human species to greater dangers. It was clear that, sometime soon, someone would have to give up something unless everyone was to lose everything. And this is what the treaty was designed to do.

It was therefore unfortunate that the debate should have stressed how much we could retain rather than how much the nations would have to relinquish in the cause of common safety and sanity. In this sense, the success of the test ban will be measured not so much by the number of nuclear explosives that were never detonated as by the large number of other sovereign manifestations that the nations must give up in the common cause of a workable peace.

If a few supporters seemed to miss the main point, the opponents of the treaty were at least equally astigmatic. Repeatedly, it was deplored that the United States would be barred under the treaty from testing bombs in the high-megaton range, or that we would be unable to proceed effectively with the development of an anti-missile missile. What was said was of course true, but what the opponents of the treaty seemed to overlook was that we weren't the only nation affected by the restrictions. A few years ago, the protesters were arguing that we had as much as we needed in the way of the big bombs but we needed more tests in order to sophisticate and refine our weapons, especially for tactical purposes. We tested and acquired the cuter and more adroit devices. Meanwhile, the Russians were testing, too. They were reaching for the big bombs. As a result of testing by both countries, the United States was in a less favorable position than it was before. The tests by both countries had left us with a net loss.

Dr. Edward Teller, who had said a few years earlier that we were well situated with our big bombs, now seemed to suggest that our big bombs were not big enough. He wanted more testing for this and other purposes.

Unfortunately, however, he could not assure the senators that another round of testing by both nations would not leave us with even less relative security than we had before the tests. Whatever his proficiency in the specialized field of bomb-making, Dr. Teller demonstrated no conspicuous competence in the area of history or political science. He said little about the previous experiences of nations with arms races. He avoided any detailed discussion of the extent to which American security depended less on the accumulation of force than upon the control of force. By and large, he gave the impression of a man determined to block the slightest limitation on military capability, lest it lead to more far-reaching measures. This, of course, was his right and he exercised it well; but it is a pity that the scientists who opposed Dr. Teller—men such as James R. Killian of M.I.T., former science adviser to President Eisenhower, George Kistiakowsky of Harvard, and Hans Bethe of Cornell were not given equal attention in the communications media.

The most original, though not necessarily the most convincing, argument against the treaty came from those who felt that it was healthy for the United States and the Soviet Union to have a nuclear arms competition. Any curbs in competition were unnatural and unfortunate, they said. Most progress in life, they declared, came from unfettered rivalry. It was a fascinating argument; it was like hearing an arsonist ask for approbation on the grounds that he could set bigger and better fires than any of his colleagues.

Another striking piece of testimony came from a former member of the Atomic Energy Commission. He said that industrial smoke and automobile gases represented an even more serious pollution danger than radioactivity from testing. Then he asserted that he accepted industrial contamination as an essential component of an industrial society. Similarly, he said he accepted radioactive contamination as an essential component of national security. It was a most impressive demonstration of risk-acceptance without the component of consultation with those for whom the risks were accepted.

We mustn't sound churlish. Perhaps the wonder of the debate was not that it should have produced such sizable and luminous irrelevancies but that, under the circumstances, it should have produced so few. On balance, the debate gave the nation a remarkable opportunity to consider some of the factors—vital and lethal—affecting its security and its future in general. And a central point was made often enough to register on those who followed the discussion. The point was that what was most important about the treaty lay beyond the treaty. If the treaty led to other things, no stronger argument could be made for it. It was this point, implict or explicit, that was actually at the heart of the debate.

In this respect, both supporters and opponents of the treaty are correct in saying that there is more to the treaty than is contained in its provisions. It is the first dent in the theory that superior force can provide safety. And it can unquestionably lead to even more substantial measures.

The debate, therefore, far from ending, has actually only begun. It will continue for a long time. It may be the most far-reaching controversy in our recent history. It could produce important new political alignments. It will be concerned primarily with the general question of peace and with the intentions of the people with whom the peace is being made; but the related questions will extend to the national economy and our total role in world affairs.

The debate is not to be shunned or deplored. It is a rich opportunity to think and choose. We need worry only in the absence of option.

*—September 21, 1963*

# New Realities

The challenge of communism in the world of 1963 is profoundly changed from what it was twenty-five years ago—or even ten years ago. At one time, communism could be regarded as a political and economic world ideology with headquarters in Moscow seeking to apply the theories of Marx on the widest possible scale. With the spread of communism, however, lines of separation have developed. In fact, the term communism today no longer is an adequate description for the various forces existing under that name in the world.

When we speak of communism today, therefore, what communism do we have in mind? Do we mean theoretical communism? Do we mean the national manifestations of communism? If the latter, do we mean the communism identified with the Soviet Union under Nikita Khrushchev? Or the communism identified with the Communist China of Mao Tse-tung? Or the communism identified with Tito's Yugoslavia? In each case, communism has a style of its own. In the Soviet Union, it is a corporate state in which dividends take the form of increased consumer goods and low prices for living essentials, and with incentives for increasing production—all under absolutist political control. In Communist China the more rigorous and literal ideas of communist ideology are being applied—often against the advice of the Soviet Union. In Yugoslavia, the economic system in some respects bears a closer relationship to some of the economic features of Sweden than it does to literal Marxism.

These varying expressions of Marxism may suggest a paradox: Karl Marx spoke in the name of universal historical forces. He recognized that history worked out differently in different places, but didn't allow sufficiently for variations in background, tradition, and cultures that would make for widely diverse approaches, whether in economics or politics.

Another apparent failure in Marx was the inability to foresee the variations in expressions of communism flowing out of the infinite variations of human personality. The differences among men are nowhere as deep as in their drives, ambitions, hopes, fears, outlooks, responses, and approaches. These variations, never fully reflected in the writings of Marx, Engels, and Lenin, have been a major factor in the different directions being taken by the various Communist nations in the world today. The personality of a Nikita Khrushchev gives a turn to Russian history substantially different from that of a Stalin. And the force of personality inside the Communist world may have a far greater impact on history than any theories of inevitable forces or historical determinism. History is still primarily what men make it.

The big question facing America in considering the challenge of communism, therefore, is whether our knowledge of it and our policies for dealing with it fit the present situation. If we are out of date in our understanding of the problem, it won't make any difference how large or sophisticated our nuclear arsenal may be. Our security depends not on bombs alone but on our ability to make an accurate diagnosis of problems and dangers.

The need for correct diagnosis is nowhere so acute as in the situation involving the Soviet Union and Communist China today. Obviously, it is not entirely within our power to determine the direction taken by the Soviet Union and China. But it is certainly within our ability to develop policies that deal with the reality of the present situation, strengthening those developments that are favorable to the United States and resisting those developments that are inimical to the United States.

What, therefore, are the issues between the Soviet Union and Communist China, and how do they affect the United States?

The first issue has to do with nuclear war.

Mao Tse-tung says he has no liking for nuclear war but quotes Lenin to the effect that war is inherent in the nature of a capitalist society. Moreover, the capitalist world is not to be trusted. It will not keep treaties or agreements, he says. It is intent only on expanding its imperial dominion to the entire world and in exploiting the working class everywhere, especially in Asia and Africa. He believes in a policy of toughness. He says that the only language the United States understands is the language of force. He says that the only chance of averting war is by creating a force so large and powerful that the capitalists and the militarists will not dare to attack. He is opposed to any limitation on the war-making capacity of communism, with respect to a ban on nuclear weapons or anything else. If war should come, he believes that from one-third to one-half of the human race will perish but that the socialist form of government will survive and that in from fifty to 100 years the human race will replenish itself. It is a high price to pay for peace, but not too high, he believes, in view of the destruction of capitalism and imperialism.

Mao finds it inexplicable and humiliating that Khrushchev, far from closing ranks with China against the hated Americans, without whose aid the enemy Chiang Kai-shek would have collapsed long ago, should be exchanging cordial toasts with the United States and negotiating treaties looking to peace and cooperation. He has scorn for the notion of neutralism or "uncommitted" nations. He believes that nations must take a stand one way or the other. His attack on India last year may very well have been a maneuver to sharpen the issue and to force the Soviet Union, which has been sending aid to India, to change its policy and make common cause with China against the enemies of socialism. He sees the world in blacks and whites; in fact, color to him is a prime exploitable fact.

Nikita Khrushchev says that whatever Marx and Lenin may have said at one time, they had no way of anticipating the nature of nuclear war. He doesn't believe that a policy of maximum risk is the best policy for averting nuclear war. He has firsthand evidence about the nature of thermonuclear explosives. He knows that a single bomb now contains more destructive power by far than all the bombs and explosives put together in all the wars in human history, including the second World War with its 1,000-plane raids and Hiroshima and Nagasaki.

Khrushchev knows that a single bomb can devastate 10,000 square miles. He knows that no system of defense, however intricate and ingenious, can protect a nation against all forms of nuclear attack. Some bombs are going to explode on target, whether from submarines or from missiles based on land. He knows that the Soviet Union, like the United States, will become a radioactive rubble pile as the result of another war. He didn't build the countless thousands of new housing projects throughout the Soviet Union just for the privilege of seeing them knocked down by nuclear bombs. He didn't construct the many hundreds of new mass-production plants and power installations just to see them leveled in another war.

He knows that suicide is not the ideal means by which to advance the cause of communism in the world. He therefore wants to shift the level of competition with the United States and the West to a nonmilitary level. He seeks victory through what he believes will be the eventual superior producing power of the Soviet Union, plus the predominant political and social influence of the Soviet Union, especially in Asia, Africa, and South America, and what he believes will be the ultimate collapse of the free enterprise system of the United States.

This is what he means by peaceful coexistence. It is not congenial coexistence, not quite. But it is at least a decision to reduce the risk of nuclear war. Hence, his desire for a ban on nuclear testing and a detente in general with the West. The spread of nuclear weapons to many countries, the speed-up in the arms race represented by unlimited experimentation—these are not consistent with the security of the Soviet Union, as Nikita Khrushchev sees it.

But differences on the question of nuclear war are not the only differences between the Soviet Union and Communist China. Some of the differences are historical. Russia may be a Communist society, but it hasn't detached itself altogether from its national history. The same is true of Communist China. The national experiences, ambitions, and fears of pre-Communist Russia play some part in its national policies today. The same is true of China.

The long history of both countries, especially during the eighteenth and nineteenth centuries, was not a harmonious one. China regarded Russia as part of the imperialist West—in many respects the most bitter part, for Russia was expanding into China. The territorial intrusions of the Western nations into China are not recognized by the present Communist regime. This most certainly includes the territory acquired by Russia in large areas contiguous to Siberia.

The Chinese today would like these territories back. The Russians have no disposition to accommodate them in this respect.

The result is a further intensification of the bitter feelings between the two countries.

There is also the matter of leadership of the Communist world. Mao Tse-tung would like Peking to be the headquarters of the world proletarian revolution. He would like to call the signals for world Communist strategy. Nikita Khrushchev would like to keep the headquarters right where it is.

It is no longer accurate, therefore, to speak of a Communist party, here or elsewhere. It is important to ask which Communist party, for there are rapidly developing throughout the world two fully formed Communist parties. The larger one is responsive to the leadership of the Soviet Union; the other is responsive to the leadership of Communist China. The first is inclined to be more sophisticated, more pragmatic in its approaches, more disposed to work for long-range results. The second is impatient, impulsive, arbitrary, revolutionary.

In the United States, the struggle for power between these two groups has already begun. The Chinese Communist division is doing all it can to re-establish the old Trotskyite revolutionary forces in the U.S. It would like to build up the raw materials here for national combustion. The old-line Communist party seems to regard the strategy of violence and imminent revolution as somewhat naïve.

The Chinese Communist division in the United States has discovered it can make rapid gains for its own purposes by combining with the anti-

Soviet forces in the United States without, of course, identifying itself. To the extent that the American people identify communism exclusively with the Soviet Union, the Chinese Communists can exploit anticommunism in dozens of ways for purposes congenial to itself.

The American people have the need, therefore, to update their knowledge of the problems and challenges represented by communism in its various forms and disguises. Not everything that represents itself as anti-Communist is the genuine article. Not all pronouncements labeled anti-Communist are genuinely anti-Communist in effect.

In the large, the United States today is called upon to make new assessments based on the profound changes in the nature of world communism.

The fact that Nikita Khruschev wants to win on the nonmilitary level should not mean that we should move toward a nuclear showdown.

Quite the contrary; we should welcome this nonmilitary competition as representing the only arena in which victory for freedom is possible. We need not be morose about the prospects. No nation in the world has more natural assets to put to work in a nonmilitary competition than the United States. The only pessimists are those who have little understanding of the nature of this society, of its history, of its ideas, and of its claim on the moral imagination.

*—October 5, 1963*

# The De-Regionalization of a Problem

The problem of race in the United States today is different in at least two major respects from what it was only a few years ago. First, the struggle of the American Negro for equality is no longer being fought primarily on the battlefield of civil liberties. The main field of combat today is the economic arena for jobs.

Second, the geographical center of the race problem is fast shifting from South to North. The traditional symbolic issues—and the resultant headlines—may continue to originate in the South, but the showdown forces and the combustibles are fast gathering in the North.

A strong inter-relationship exists between these major developments.

Until very recently, the eye-catching issues coincided with the central ones. The fight to admit an Autherine Lucy or a James Meredith to a state university in the South, or a few Negro children to a public school, or the difficulties attending desegration of buses or trains or railroad stations, or the sit-down strikes in restaurants—these news-making events were at the heart of the race problem in America. Even though the main spotlight may still be trained on these and similar issues today in places like Birmingham, the developments that have the deepest long-term significance are building up without corresponding visibility or attention. These developments go beyond the Bill of Rights in that they are concerned not just with how a man lives but what he does for a living. To be sure, this aspect of the race problem has always been a vital one but it has not been at the top of the agenda in the campaign against Jim Crow. All this, however, is now changing; a new and more complex phase of the struggle now opens.

The important bridge between political and economic equality is represented, at least theoretically, by education. Good jobs require special training. Trained and educated Negroes are now entering the economic arena in substantial numbers. As educational opportunities are expanded, these numbers will be multiplied. But American Negroes, highly trained or otherwise, as Joseph Lyford points out in this week's SR, are not finding jobs proportionate to their number or equal to their competence. With respect to both skilled and unskilled manpower, therefore, a problem of titanic dimensions is fast coming to a head. And the North will be even more of a testing ground than the South.

One reason for this, of course, is the redistribution of the Negro population. The greatest density now exists in Northern cities like New York, Chicago, and Detroit. And it is here that the war for jobs will produce its most explosive battles. Explosive, because the North has done so little thinking about the problem and is unprepared to deal with it on a showdown level, and because this is where the Negro will be able to make his stand with maximum effect. Whether or not the Negro is entitled to expect more in and of the North is not particularly relevant. What is relevant is that all the backed-up pressure from the social, political, and regional struggles will seek a substantial outlet in the North, much of it on the economic level.

As this happens, the total situation of the Negro in the North will be up for national scrutiny. It will no longer be possible for Northerners on their high-fare commuter trains to ride through Harlem without seeing it because their heads are buried in newspapers that tell of outrages in the South. The fact of massive squalor, such as the Harlem ghetto, will no longer be a secondary matter to Northerners who energetically deplore Southern race riots. Similarly, the helplessness of the Northern Negro in coping with a whole host of predators—in housing, employment, and commercial dealings—will no longer be a submerged issue for those Northerners who use a regional filter for their indignation.

The problem of the Negro has always been a national problem. But the focus and locus have been in the South. Now there is no longer any natural division between the centers of crisis and the centers of concern. The entire nation—horizontally, vertically, diagonally—is now involved. No longer need any individual feel oppressed by disconnection or distance from the problem. It lives where he lives. If he has business dealings, he is able to ascertain whether the firm has a policy against hiring Negroes. He is able to determine whether Negroes in his city or village have decent living conditions and whether their rent is within reasonable limits. He can look into hospital facilities available to the Negro. He can find out something about the practices of tradesmen who deal with them. Conscience need no longer operate at a distance.

The de-regionalization of the problem does more than offer potential relief for the frustration of concerned individuals. It deprives the entire nation of further excuses for further delay.

*—October 19, 1963*

# A Friendly Letter to Mr. Zorin

"How can one man [Frederick C. Barghoorn] create such a problem between our two great countries? . . . I do not understand how this single incident can color the whole range of Soviet-American relations."— Valerian A. Zorin, Deputy Minister of Foreign Affairs of the U.S.S.R., as quoted in press dispatches from Moscow.

Dear Mr. Zorin:

We understand that you raised these questions during a press conference at a time when American indignation over the arrest on espionage charges of Professor Barghoorn was reaching a powerful crescendo. The news stories said you expressed genuine bewilderment and concern and sought serious answers.

No more important or revealing questions than the ones you ask about the United States have come from the Soviet Union. In many ways those questions are even more vital to world peace than the emergency military questions for which the hot line between Washington and Moscow was devised. Questions involving military accident or miscalculation are fairly mechanical and are subject to reasonably prompt correction or clarification. Far more fundamental and difficult are questions involving miscalculation growing out of a nation's values or its philosophical underpinnings and the propositions attached to them. An emergency situation does not allow enough time for adequate discussion of deep philosophical conviction or intent. Hence, the peoples of the world and not just the peoples of our two countries have a genuine stake in the formulation of policy in the Soviet Union based on your correct understanding of why the United States moved powerfully and swiftly in the Barghoorn episode. This understanding will be relevant in any future assessment you make of those things that are certain to affect or bring about major American decisions.

First of all, we want to assure you that the implications of your question are quite right; the United States is prepared to turn itself inside out on behalf of a single man. It would be in serious trouble with its own citizens if it did not. Indeed, this is precisely what the United States was designed to do. It was designed to rescue the individual from the ages-old notion that he was comprehensively subordinate, and that his rights or suffering or longings or needs were of little consequence alongside the wishes or needs of the state. The design was not a superficial one. It took into account the available record of human experience. It involved an intricate structure of government, constituted in such a way that no government official could have an easy time immunizing himself from the consequences of his errors or putting himself beyond the reach of an individual who didn't like what was happening.

Most important of all, the design was based on the conviction that the only justification for a national government is to prevent bullies, including the state itself, from taking advantage of the individual because he is small and alone. According to this design, then, the individual is primary and the state is secondary. The individual in full possession of his rights becomes the central concern of the state. This means that the state must not merely come to the defense of a solitary individual who is under attack; the state must think through the total problem of what the individual requires in order to be himself, to function effectively, to grow, to think, and to exercise rights against the state itself. The individual must be able to shake his fist at the state, to denounce it, to take it into court and sue it and receive a verdict against it. If any one line of attack or defense he takes against the state should fail, he must have adequate recourse.

This, then, is the general idea. Many of our problems have come about not because the state has followed this design too closely but because it didn't follow it closely enough. The most important causes or movements in the United States today are those that are directed against government —local, regional, or national—for being less zealous than it should be in meeting its obligations to the individual.

We can understand why you expressed bewilderment. We appreciate— and we say this not with any intent to score points in a discussion but in an effort to state a recognizable and relevant fact—that you speak from the vantage point of a society that sees history as governed by inexorable and supremely impersonal historic forces. According to this view, there are basic laws that determine which way a society and the world itself are to be shaped. The fate of a single individual alongside these vast forces is not considered to be especially critical. The individal, to be sure, is not ignored, but his rights against the state are minimal rather than maximal. The term "destiny" is seldom applied to a single man; it belongs to the society as a whole. Cases in which one man is allowed to array himself against the state, which, for all its size and power, has no more standing in court than the man juxtaposed against it—cases such as these are unknown so far in your nation.

Against this background we can readily understand that you should be amazed and dismayed that an individual such as Professor Barghoorn could upset the flow of history. But this was to be expected and, under similar circumstances, would happen again. Indeed, surprise and bewilderment over the Barghoorn case would be warranted only if the United States and the American people did not fly into an uproar but contented themselves with a murmur of protest or nothing at all.

One of our poets and philosophers, Ralph Waldo Emerson, a contemporary of Marx, once wrote that the true test of civilization is represented not by its census or the size of its cities or the diversity of its crops but by the importance it attaches to the individual. For the kind of man a nation produces is the best indication of what that nation is all about.

Our purpose in writing you, we repeat, is not to deliver a sermon but to put before you some speculations bearing on the serious questions you pose. We want to assure you that this is not a one-way discussion and that our pages are available to you for response, riposte, or further questions.

*—November 30, 1963*

# The Legacy of John F. Kennedy

An American President is something special in the world precisely because American history has been something special. A nation founded on a decent respect for the opinions of mankind is bound to attract reciprocal sentiments. And when an American President gives life to the central purpose built into the design of that nation, the purpose being to advance the human cause on earth, it is natural that profound feelings of human oneness should be released. No matter that the purpose may have been dented or even battered through crisis or contention. Enough of it is left to produce a response, especially at a time of national tragedy.

The Japanese farmer and his family who walked eighteen miles through the night in order to stand silently in front of the American Embassy in Tokyo; the Warsaw bus driver who, upon being informed by a boarding passenger of the terrible news, halted his vehicle and wept openly; the students who carried memorial torches in Berlin; the long lines of grieving people who gathered outside official American stations or residences in London, Paris, Rome, Berlin, Moscow, Mexico City, Toronto, Athens, Istanbul, Beirut, Tel Aviv, Cairo, Teheran, New Delhi, Madras, Karachi, Léopoldville, Conakry, Tananarive, Hiroshima, and a hundred other cities; and the people everywhere who could only sit quietly with their sorrow—all this is more than a world expression of sympathy. It is a reminder of what this country is all about. It makes real the connections, seen and unseen, between the United States and the human community—connections that were basic in the thinking of the men who fashioned this nation.

John Fitzgerald Kennedy had immersed himself in history long before he made it. He had studied the American experience and written about it. When he moved to the White House he didn't superimpose himself upon American history; he fitted into it just as it fitted into him. He didn't have to wander through government archives looking for records of ideas and acts that had gone into the making of the American purpose. This knowledge was part of him and he put it to work.

At his command was immediate obliterative power, more power by far than had ever been collected in one place at one time. In the American arsenal were thousands of explosives, some of which contained more force than all the bombs and shells in all the previous wars in history put together. In toto, this destructive force represented the equivalent of 30,000 pounds of TNT for every human being on earth.

He regarded this power not as a source of true security, for, as he said, a nation's security could shrink even as its atomic might would expand. The power—not in our hands alone but in the hands of other nations—had to be brought under world control. It could not be unilaterally discarded—this would not create safety or sanity; it would have to be eliminated as part of a genuine world security system under law.

In this case, John F. Kennedy as President was confronted with issues involving human destiny. Woodrow Wilson used to say that his constituents included the next generation. The question before John Kennedy was whether there would be a next generation at all—here or elsewhere. This, for him, was not a melodramatic fact; he was not the melodramatic type. But it was a fact nevertheless and it never left him. He knew that his job was connected to the whole of the human future. No greater burden had to be sustained by any man in the history of the race.

John Kennedy came into office at a time when most of the world's peoples were shopping for a revolution. He knew he had to identify the United States with the desire for freedom of a billion people; he had to make this identification convincing to those who were then or had been under the domination or control of the nations with whom the United States had been closely linked for almost two centuries. He did everything he could to accelerate the historical process of national freedom. But he knew, too, that the issue went beyond independent statehood; it had to do with a conception of man himself. Did man own himself? Was government instituted to protect and cherish the concept of individual sovereignty, which is to say, a free man? Or was man a unit in a vast organism to which he was subordinate and secondary? In either case, man had to be fed, housed, educated, developed. These needs were insistent. Which ideology had most to say to him?

John Kennedy did not shrink from these questions. He knew that the future of the United States would rest not just on a superiority of nuclear fire power but on what we said to the majority of the world's peoples, and what we did after we said it. If we could make the idea of America relevant and vital; if we could use our wealth and resources responsibly and compassionately; if we could help develop the United Nations and its agencies in order to safeguard the human condition; if we could make it clear that the idea of freedom had to do not just with the way a nation ran its commercial enterprises but with the way a man grew and thought and raised a family, then we could face the ideological showdown with confidence. He had this confidence and did everything he could to transmit it—to his own countrymen as well as to other people.

He never minimized the extent of the ideological challenge. But he knew he could not meet it with obsolete information and concepts. He knew that the Communist world was itself in a condition of upheaval. He knew how important it was for the United States to make a correct assessment of these changes, for the wrong decisions could help create a conjunction of the two Communist forces. In this event, the center of gravity would be in Peking, with its fanatical hatred of the West in general and the United States in particular, and with a readiness to pursue policies that added greatly to the likelihood of nuclear war.

Wisdom begins with the ability to make valid distinctions. John Kennedy made distinctions not just between one part of an ideological camp and another but within each camp itself. He knew that the Soviet Union was in a process of profound historic transition. He made distinctions between its dominant character and thrust under Joseph Stalin and its dominant character and thrust under Nikita Khrushchev. The combination of the total irrationality and total power possessed by Stalin permitted no sensible dialogue under which reasonable and workable limits might be set to the struggle between the Soviet Union and the United States. Nikita Khrushchev was hard but at least he was rational. He could be expected to take advantage of every opening in order to advance his national interest but he was not deranged. He had no eagerness to see the Soviet Union incinerated in a nuclear war.

John Kennedy's policy, therefore, was to close off every possible opening through which the Soviet Union might advance its national or ideological interests to the detriment of other nations, and to keep open every channel through which sensible arrangements by the two countries might be made in their joint interest and in the human interest. One example of this policy was Cuba. Another was the nuclear test ban. Both seemed to point in starkly opposing directions, yet both were part of the same basic purpose; that is, a determination to resist encroachments and a determination to explore every opportunity to build a durable peace.

This policy was never better articulated by the President than in his June 10, 1963, American University commencement talk. With the possible exception of his September 20, 1961, talk before the General Assembly, the American University address was the most historic and important human document of his three years in office. The June 10 speech was an attempt to face new realities. It tried to cut through the insanity of mounting nuclear stock piles and mounting antagonisms. It tried to apply a human perspective to grave international problems. It tried to speak directly to the Russian people, not lecturing or scolding but giving full weight to their ordeals and difficulties and recognizing that common hopes can dissolve even the oldest enmities. The full text of this talk was published in the Soviet press.

The June 10 talk led in a straight line to what was perhaps the President's greatest triumph in the foreign policy area. This was the successful fight, in his words, to get the nuclear genie back into the bottle. He had to obtain Soviet adherence to a nuclear test-ban treaty and then he had to obtain Senate ratification, and he did both. He regarded this treaty not just as an end in itself but as a possible wedge into far more difficult and consequential problems between the two countries.

Questions of human dignity, world political upheaval, and ideological struggle were not the only burdens carried by the young President. Inside the United States another historic process was approaching its culmination. The American Negro was emancipated from slavery but not from humiliation. He received his liberation but not his rights. He was not so much freed as cast adrift. He was accorded no place of essential opportunity or dignity. And the same groundswell that a hundred years earlier had culminated in what another martyred President had called a fiery ordeal was beginning to make its tremors felt.

People today forget that Lincoln was condemned by many of his contemporaries because he didn't move faster, because he seemed to temporize, because he spent so much energy on persuasion. But Lincoln knew his main job was to hold the country together, appealing to reasoning people on both sides, and trying to effect a profound transition without insanity or national tragedy.

"We are not enemies but friends," Lincoln said in his first talk to the American people after becoming President. He spoke from an improvised platform on the steps of the unfinished new Capitol. "We must not be enemies. Though passion may have strained, it must not break our bonds of affection. The mystic chords of memory . . . will yet swell the chorus of the Union when again touched, as surely they will be, by the better angels of our nature."

The same men who have no hesitation today in acclaiming Lincoln for his leadership on the issue of human rights have no difficulty in denouncing John Kennedy for acting as Lincoln acted. John Kennedy tried to find an answer, not to force a solution. His job, no less than Lincoln's, was to keep even the bitter and basic issues from producing a national convulsion. He knew that fundamental questions of human rights could not and should not be deferred any longer. And he accepted the need to find every opening, develop every resource, command every initiative in that direction. But always in front of him, to paraphrase Madison, were the purifying but enfeebling limitations to the Presidential office in bringing about fundamental change.

John Kennedy did not find an answer to the dilemma, any more than any of his predecessors did. He could state the moral issue; he could use the full powers of the executive office and even of the National Guard to attempt to carry out the laws; but always he had to contend with the raw fact that the ultimate power was in the hands of the people themselves. The legislative process was only one reflection of this fact. The whole mechanism, often mysterious and always intricate, by which an idea gains acceptance and becomes living history, was another.

They accused him of half-hearted measures and lukewarm leadership on human rights issues in order to protect his political flank, but no President in the past eighty years incurred greater political regional liabilities. What was happening was that the American people were unwilling or unable to consider the real questions: Was there something in the way our government itself was constituted, with its separation of powers, its political machinery, its remaining unresolved lines of authority between the state and nation, that made it impossible for a President to give full effect to his ideas of fundamental justice among men? What is the role of public opinion and public action in producing the atmosphere and the impetus for change? At what point does vigorous leadership die for want of adequate consensus?

If the people looked to the President, the President looked no less to the people. He knew that on most big issues he would be helpless without them. Not that he expected public opinion to define every great question, carry it forward, move it triumphantly through the Congress, and deliver it to him for final signature. He saw his role and the role of public opinion as a process of creative interaction. He accepted the job of stating the case and giving it the proper degree of urgency. But the public also had the job to respond—one way or the other.

Often he would be urged by partisans of certain positions to go before the country on full television hookups in an attempt to mobilize public opinion. Last year, in the space of a single month, advocates of eight separate issues invoked the example of FDR's fireside chats as the best way to generate the necessary public support. He would generally respond by asking the person who made the suggestion to tell him or guess the number of fireside chats made by FDR during his thirteen years in the White House. The number given in reply would generally vary from one a month to one every other month, or a total for the entire Presidency running close to 100 fireside chats or more. Then he would supply the correct answer: eleven. The point he then made was that a President must be careful not to expend the full weight of his personal prestige on too many issues. He must husband his direct appeals to the people very carefully. There are dozens of important issues, but the President must decide which are the vital ones on which history turns. Again, the need for distinctions.

No Presidential working paper was consulted more frequently or pondered more carefully than the weekly mail tally. Allowances always had to be made, of course, for pressure tactics of organized groups. And he didn't permit himself to be thrown off stride by sudden flurries. But he was profoundly interested in the White House mail. When his mail showed no particular citizen support on the question of a nuclear test ban, he met with leaders of American public opinion, explained the issue as he saw it, invited questions, and then urged them to take part in public debate, whether they saw the issue his way or not.

Sometimes his mail would be misleading. More than a year ago he became seriously concerned because the White House mail, like the mail of the Congress, was running heavily against the United Nations. Indeed, on some days the anti-UN mail would be as high as fifteen to one. What made the matter especially serious was that the UN needed money to complete the pacification of the Congo and to maintain the emergency forces in Suez. He knew how difficult it was to persuade the Congress to authorize additional funds, whether through a bond issue or direct appropriation, if the negative mail was any indication of the condition of public opinion.

The President was overjoyed when he saw the results of private polls undertaken by several Congressmen and Senators who, concerned by the preponderance of anti-UN mail, went directly to the voters. These polls showed that the American people supported the UN, four to one, and favored its full development into an organization possessing the effective powers of world law. When these findings were confirmed by one of the major public opinion polls, the President made sure that every member of the Congress was appropriately informed. A major roadblock to passage of the UN bond issue was removed.

What had gone wrong? An analysis of a small portion of the mail showed that it was heavily patterned in content and was obviously part of an organized campaign by hate-UN groups.

The significance of this episode was not just that mail to government could be misleading but that extreme pressure groups were taking advantage of every opening in the catalogue of a free society to affect national decision. This was clearly their right and it was nothing new. But it was doubtful if ever before so many fanatics and near-fanatics had tried to put so much sand so skillfully into so many vital parts of the machinery of free government.

The period of danger and strain through which the country was passing was exploited in such a way as to undermine confidence in the men who had to make the big decisions. Suspicion of the UN was promoted and exploited. Issues of race and human rights became blood transfusions for bigots. Imputations of treason were laid to Presidents, members of the Supreme Court, and the Senate. The charges were ludicrous but this is not what was important. What was important was that enough fanatics believed these charges so that a streak of madness appeared in the national community. It was the kind of madness that could discolor an entire generation.

James Bryce, in his study of American institutions a half century ago, called attention to the relative ease with which the democratic process could be overloaded with pressure groups—to the point where the process would have difficulty in functioning. By the time John F. Kennedy came to the White House, the Presidency had become less a powerful pivotal station for affecting history than an arena for the most complicated balancing act in modern times. One set of pressures had to be weighed constantly against another. Movement in one direction was immediately met by resistance from another. Even the smallest legislative journey was a vast exercise of multiple force, pulling or pushing.

The original design for the Presidency had called for a proper number of check points on the executive power, but it never anticipated that ultimately the checks and pressures would multiply to the point where the President would spend most of his life running a gantlet.

"The laws," wrote De Tocqueville, "allow a President to be strong but circumstances keep him weak." Confronted with these circumstances, some Presidents sought to delegate authority to the greatest possible extent. John Kennedy had some buffers, to be sure, but he knew that he had to carry the main burden himself for putting through his program.

To sustain this kind of battering, a man must have love for his job or a superhuman disposition. John Kennedy had both. It is doubtful that any President ever paid more attention to his homework or tried harder to comprehend the full dimensions and all the implications of any decision he had to make. His press conferences were remarkable demonstrations of a man in full command of his office, prepared to answer questions covering literally hundreds of topics. Generally, he would begin by making sure he had understood the question thoroughly. He would state the arguments against his position, frequently better than they had been stated by an opponent. Then he would proceed to meet these arguments one by one, not by characterizing them but by providing relevant fact. He rarely left a sentence or an idea uncompleted. And always there was the effort to state a problem in reasonable terms in a way that might appeal to reasonable men.

The key to John Kennedy was that he was in the American rationalist tradition. Not every problem had an answer but every problem had its origins and component parts, each of which called for weighing and grading, and all of which were related to one another in a way that increased the probability of a workable answer. Even when he felt justified in making a summary judgment, he would feel more comfortable if someone he trusted went over the ground again.

John Kennedy would have no trouble in qualifying for inclusion in the kind of company Carl Becker wrote about some years ago in a striking book called *The Heavenly City of the Eighteenth Century Philosophers.* The men who founded the United States are among the principal characters in the book. They were men of reason and believed in the uses of history. What were some of the articles of their faith? A good government was distinguished from bad to the extent that it can develop a memory and put it to work. Tyranny and injustice were likely to recur if the conditions that favored tyranny and injustice recurred. Good men might retard or even combat the effects of the tyranny, but it was much more rational to avoid the cause. Even good men had a tendency to go bad under certain circumstances. Therefore, do everything possible to alter the negative circumstances and create the propitious ones.

The "heavenly city" of the American founding fathers was a condition of enlightenment in which human intelligence and rational thought could be addressed to the perfectibility of man and human society in general. This environment, like man himself, was highly delicate and had to be carefully nurtured. The result was an ingenious system under which the individual had greater protection against excesses or encroachments by officialdom than existed almost anywhere else on the face of the earth.

But the design was not without its inevitable flaws. The rationalist founding fathers did everything they could to protect the individual against government, but they had no way of protecting government against the irrational individual. One man with a gun could create chaos, could shatter the brain of the man whose decisions were critical to the life of that community, and could lay a burden of grief on the hearts of millions.

Confronted with this fact, some people now wonder whether the rational design ought not somehow be changed. Some may even say that the design is no longer workable. John Kennedy would be the first to remind them that not even the most totalitarian society can protect itself altogether against a man with a gun. Indeed, with his sense of history, he would be certain to point out that totalitarianism almost automatically fosters such violence, for that is often the only way to change it.

Is there, then, nothing we can do to halt and expunge the obscene and spreading violence? Is there no way to keep the face of the nation from being pock-marked and blistered by men putting their tempers to triggers? Is the shape of America to be determined by a barroom brawl?

There is something we can do.

We can re-examine the indifference to violence in everyday life. We can ask ourselves why we tolerate and encourage the glorification of violence in the things that amuse us and entertain us. We can ponder our fascination with brutality as exhibited hour after hour on television or on the covers of a thousand books and magazines. We can ask why our favorite gifts to children are toy murder weapons.

We can ask whether we are creating an atmosphere congenial to the spiraling violence until finally it reaches a point where living history is mauled and even our casualness toward it is pierced.

We can resensitize ourselves to the reality of human pain and the fragility of human life.

There is something else we can do at a time of emptiness and national deprivation.

We can be bigger than we are. We can rise above the saturating trivia, redefine our purposes, and bring to bear on problems that combination of reason, sensitivity, and vision that gives a civilization its forward movement. Our ideals are all right. W. Macneile Dixon once said, but they are unreal until they become articulate.

We can give not just added protection but added dignity to public office and reduce the sense of loneliness of public servants who are regarded as easy game for the predatory attacks of extremists.

The best defense against spreading madness is to carry on, to strengthen the belief in a rational society and in the natural sanity and goodness of man, to take all reasonable precautions but not to allow the precautions to distort or disfigure our lives. "The fact that reason too often fails," Alfred North Whitehead said, "does not give fair ground for the hysterical conclusion that it never works."

The sense of tragedy over the assassination of the President will not soon be dispelled, but in due time we may find warrant for some consolation in the fact of orderly succession, a miracle in itself, built into the structure of government. Even more basic is the fact that there is nothing to stop the American people from giving life to the ideas and purposes of the man whose memory they now cherish. The loss of John Kennedy becomes a total one only if our understanding of what he tried to do is emptied from our minds.

One of the unique characteristics of a free society is that it can assign immortality to a concept, an ideal, a set of working principles. If the impact of John Kennedy is confined to the circumstances of his death, then the tragedy is indeed a total one. But if there is accord with his purposes, then this may be a solvent for our grief. This, then, is the time for brave and reasonable men to come out of hiding.

John Kennedy believed in peace. He believed in freedom. He saw no conflict between the two. He believed in the creative potential of the individual man. He believed in the reality of hope. He relished laughter and the vigorous life of the mind. He loved life, and by life he did not mean segregated life; he meant all life. He believed in thought. He believed in reasonable exchange. He recognized obligations to people not yet born—to help provide them with a good earth and a decent world.

The ultimate tragedy of a man is represented not by death but by the things he tried to bring to life that are buried with him. The legacy of John Kennedy can be a large one—if that is the way the American people wish it to be.

—*December 7, 1963*

# Can Civilization Be Assassinated?

The instant reaction of most people to the assassination of the President was expressed in four words: "I can't believe it." This was not merely a sudden reflex response, like crying out in pain. It was a direct and accurate reflection of the inability of the human mind to deal with tragedy beyond a certain dimension. For man retains his sanity by assigning boundary lines to the range of improbables in life. He knows he may be confronted with accident, disaster, and death. But even this catalogue of horrors exists within a certain range of grim expectation. A tragedy may be stark, but as long as it is recognizable, the rational intelligence will try to cope with it.

But then the outermost limits of the improbables are violently punctured, and the mind turns blank. An embittered, unbalanced individual looks down a gun sight, squeezes a trigger, and the human intelligence staggers with the impact. When people say, therefore, that they still find it difficult to believe the President was murdered, what they are really saying is that it is virtually impossible to conceive that one sullen, warped mind could have produced such havoc all by itself.

Yet this is precisely the ultimate significance of the atomic age. Not just a President but all civilization is vulnerable to the weird turnings of a disturbed mind. It takes no more than a single individual to unhinge history. Consider the facts. Both the Soviet Union and the United States have placed in the hands of numerous individuals the power to start the chain reaction that could lead to the assassination of civilization. The Soviet Union operates submarines not far off the East and West coasts of the United States. These submarines are equipped with launching platforms for missiles with nuclear warheads. Every major city in the United States is within range. These missiles are subject to the decision of the submarine commanders. The United States, in addition to its Polaris fleet, maintains hundreds of jet planes in the air on a twenty-four-hour basis not far from the borders of the Soviet Union. These planes are fully loaded with hydrogen explosives. The greatest possible care has been taken to ensure that the commanders of these planes will not be given irresponsible orders; but the central fact is that the orders are transmitted to human beings who have to carry them out. The power, therefore, is subject to individual decision and motivation.

It is to be assumed that every one of the hundreds of men on both sides who have been given access to the final button has been carefully screened. But no system has been devised that can penetrate fully the mysteries of human personality and motivation. No psychologist or psychiatrist can probe deeply enough into those remote pockets of a man's mind where bitterness or venom may be stored. No psychologist or psychiatrist can predict unfailingly when a sudden impulse will seize a man's mind. No psychologist or psychiatrist can certify absolutely how each of a large number of individuals will react under an almost limitless range of circumstances.

A man doesn't have to be deranged or go berserk in order to commit an act of catastrophic irresponsibility. He can be impelled by the noblest motives of duty or righteousness. Several years ago a French air force pilot, disgusted by what he believed to be the inadequacy and incompetence of his government, decided to bomb an Algerian village. He was motivated by what he considered the highest impulses of patriotism— much the way an American general recently decided to substitute his understanding of what was happening in the world for the understanding of the President and the Secretary of State. These experiences were exceptional. It was only one French pilot out of many thousands and it was only one American general out of hundreds. But that is just the point. It takes only one man in our time to trigger the assassination of human society.

True, the most scrupulous safeguards have been established to guard against such a grisly event. Officials have painstakingly explained how extensive are the precautions and how small are the chances that these precautions might not work. But the danger, though small, is not nonexistent. The chances that a deranged assassin could penetrate the protective mechanism set up to safeguard the life of an American President were very small, but it happened. It was irrational. It was remote. It was most improbable. But it happened. In defense of the Secret Service, it is said that there was no way of X-raying the mind of every spectator in the line of march. Quite so. It is equally true that there is no way of X-raying the mind of every man in an atomic age who has the power to incinerate millions of human beings. The only possible defense is to take that power away from him. If the President's assassin had been unable to obtain the murder weapon, his bitterness would not have been lethal.

In any event, the key fact about the extensive precautions now taken against unintended nuclear war is that these safeguards are directed mainly to the danger of war through accident rather than to arbitrary decision by someone in a position to explode a bomb. The safeguards cannot possibly guard against the volatility, variability, and unpredictability of human personality.

It will be argued that only a few men possess the power to authorize a nuclear war. This is correct; but many men possess the power to detonate the bombs that could start a war without authorization. The proof of this fact resides in the very efforts taken by military officials to convince a possible enemy that no surprise attack, however vast, can destroy the certainty of retaliation. Even if the President, every one in line of Presidential succession, and the nation's top military commanders are all killed in the first wave of an attack, there will always be someone down the line to respond with nuclear force. This is what is meant by credibility. The enemy must believe there are literally hundreds of men in a position to punish him with devastating nuclear counterattack.

Few themes have challenged the thoughts of philosophers through the ages more than the idea of the fragility of human life. Even a drop of water, says Pascal, can suffice to destroy a man. But now, as the culmination of a century of science, man must also ponder the fragility of his civilization. Generally, a disaster had to be experienced before man developed the means to deal with it or prevent its recurrence. How does mankind protect itself against something that has never happened before? How does it protect itself against the supremely irrational, against something that lies far outside the range of the improbables? How can the same sense of biting reality that a man attaches to his next pay check be extended to questions concerning human destiny?

If human history is now drawing to a close, it is not because of any malevolence or incompetence deep within the species but because the human mind seems unable to convince itself that its own destiny is the issue.

—*December 21, 1963*

# Hail Automation, Hail Peace

Two fears are stalking America. One is the fear of automation. The other is the fear of peace. They are twin fears, born of foreboding over possible economic paralysis and loss of jobs. These fears are disfiguring the American future. They give opportunity the face of disaster.

There has hardly been a human society on this planet that has not dreamed of a realizable Utopia. In almost every case, these Utopias have had two things in common—peace and plenty. In such a favored state man would be freed of drudgery. He would be able to develop his most powerful and valuable resource—the human brain. He would regard education as the greatest of all adventures, for one exciting search would lead to another. In such a Utopia he would make a distinction between personal growth and impersonal accumulation. He would come to appreciate the difference between concepts and things. The absence of unremitting and exhausting physical labor would lead not to boredom but to all sorts of useful and satisfying activities. And peace would not be a land and time of nothingness but a period and place for bringing a nation's potential to full life.

All these hopes, misty and unattainable in the past, are now a tangible prospect. The present generation stands apart from all previous generations not just in the harm man can do to man but in man's practical ability to make of the planet a good earth, hunting down and banishing the so-far incurable diseases, nourishing the human body with vital foods grown on once-arid soil, collecting and utilizing energy from matter or from the sun or from the air itself, building schools by the thousands—not just for youngsters but for people of all ages who have come to comprehend that neither knowledge nor the human brain has any boundaries or limitations.

Confronted by this promise, many Americans seem to be reacting as though they had just been handed a sentence of doom. They are responding on the numerical rather than the historical level. They hear the word *automation* and immediately they spew out the number of jobs that would be lost in this or that industry. Or someone mentions *peace* and immediately they think of plants being shut down and salaries being shut off. And so they attach shrill sounds to their apprehensions, making it appear that an ominous blight is about to descend on America.

The time has come to identify and combat this frenzied nonsense. Automation and peace do not have to mean the end of the world. They can mean the beginning of a better one. It is the fear of automation and peace, and not peace and automation in themselves, that can produce disaster. For this kind of hysterical thinking can lead on the one hand to economic stagnation, and on the other to the perpetuation of an arms spiral that could end in war. What is really to be feared, therefore, is not the onset of innovation but the flight of ingenuity and the collapse of the moral imagination.

First consider peace, which is to say, a condition in which it may not be necessary to put upward of $50 billion into military spending. While the arms program accounts for more than half the government budget, it accounts for less than 10 per cent of the nation's total production. Does anyone seriously contend that this fraction cannot be made up? Are we to accept the proposition that America has no great remaining needs, that there are no cities that have to be rebuilt, no slums to be replaced, no new elementary and secondary schools to be erected, no colleges and universities that have to be expanded, no new cultural centers to be established and developed, no scientific and medical centers and research projects to be initiated? These are not sterile questions; they are full of life and promise. With confidence, imagination, and energy we can do more than replace the 10 per cent differential. We can multiply the present national output.

The effects of automation embrace virtually all aspects of the national economy. Some experts contend that within a decade or so automation could take over the tasks now performed by more than half the national work force. But this by itself need not produce widespread deprivation or destitution. Only a shrinkage in production or the blighting of our crops need bring about that condition. Automation will not reduce the production of the things people need. It can increase them.

The problem lies not with automation but with our conception of how the benefits of automation are to be realized. Instead of bemoaning automation we ought to be directing our attention to the shortage of imagination and intelligence that stands in the way of the fuller life that is now clearly attainable. It is not too soon to be studying and planning now to keep the greatest potential asset in the nation's history from disintegrating into a liability. It may well be that such study will indicate that a three- or even two-day work week for many millions of the American people is a practical and desirable development.

The fundamental problem will be represented by the ability of people to make productive use of their time. Here, then, is the ultimate test of a free society. What happens when people have maximum freedom? When peace and plenty are genuinely attainable, will this result in suffocating boredom or in a vast release of human creativity?

We make a mistake, therefore, if we look to economics for the answer. We must look to education, to our individual and national purposes, and to the preciousness we attach to human life and the possibilities inside it waiting to be released.

*—January 18, 1964*

# Educational Miracle

HONOLULU.

One of the major needs in the twentieth century has been for a world university in which the human condition and the human potential would form the radiating center of a curriculum. More particularly, the need has been for a school that could create the foundations on which a genuine meeting place between East and West might be built.

With very little fanfare, such an institution is now in the making. It is the East-West Center associated with the University of Hawaii in Honolulu. Launched less than four years ago, it has taken tangible and dramatic form in four major respects. First, it has a faculty and visiting scholars drawn from some thirty nations. Second, it has been able to attract more than 1,000 students from West and East, mostly the latter. Third, it has a highly developed course of study, most of it on the graduate level. And, fourth, it has a striking physical and architectural presence.

What is most remarkable about the enterprise is that it was quietly hatched in the form of a congressional legislative rider in 1960. It has since received $26,700,000 in government funds, constituting virtually its entire support. Based both on the results to date and on the potential, the Center may well represent the most imaginative and useful Federal initiative in higher education yet attempted. Indeed, the assumption of financial responsibility by the U.S. Congress for the Center is something on the order of a small miracle. The then Vice President, Lyndon B. Johnson, is generally credited with the strategy and the steering that made the miracle possible.

Broadly speaking, the East-West Center seeks not just to develop a dialogue between cultures but to create the working knowledge that can be diffused far beyond the campus and, in fact, even beyond the countries whose students and scholars are participants in the program. In this sense, the Center is both a headquarters for cultural interchange and a generating agency for new ideas and approaches to a world fumbling for ways to accommodate its diversity and pluralism.

But the Center is much more than a bridge for carrying philosophical traffic. It provides Asian students with the special training to become public health officers, specialists in food production, engineers (general, electrical, civil), biologists, chemists, physicists, meteorologists, curators of art museums, librarians, motion-picture producers, etc. And it takes from Asian scholars and gives to American students the ideas and techniques developed in other countries for comprehending and meeting problems concerned with man's relationship to himself, to other men, and to his total environment.

In general, the work of the Center is divided into three parts. One part is the scholarship program that brings in a large number of highly qualified students for two years of postgraduate study (580 students from twenty-eight countries are now taking part in this program). Second, an advanced institute provides senior specialists and scholars with research and laboratory facilities. In some cases, the specialists are in residence; in others, they participate in international seminars and conferences. Third is the program for technical training, in which the United Nations and the Agency for International Development are among the cooperating groups and beneficiaries.

Unfortunately but perhaps inevitably, the Center has not escaped serious difficulty. As a recipient of government funds, it has had to come up each year for congressional review in order to explain and justify its budget requests. The job of a congressional appropriations committee, quite properly, is to hold on to the people's money in every way it can. The going at such hearings can be pretty rough. Seasoned budgeteers from government agencies have developed the hide and the techniques for defending their requests without twitch or trauma. Educators are not too well conditioned for this kind of combat. Chancellor Alexander Spoehr managed to save the Center's budget from congressional cutting a few months ago but the ordeal was apparently more than he was prepared to endure or to repeat. His resignation followed shortly upon his return from Washington. Since that time, Thomas H. Hamilton, president of the University of Hawaii, has served as acting chancellor, with the help of John M. Allison, former Ambassador to Japan.

Before long, some way may have to be found to satisfy congressional concern that the people are getting their money's worth and to meet the Center's need to plan ahead with confidence. A university cannot exist on a year-to-year basis; the very nature of education requires long-term commitments. A school must anticipate its growth requirements or die. The clear need, therefore, is for an arrangement under which specific financing will be substantially assured several years in advance while providing for periodic and effective congressional review.

At some point soon, too, the leading American foundations may wish to consider taking over some or all of the underwriting. The sums involved may be steep but it is difficult to think of any major educational enterprise today that is yielding a greater return for the amount spent, or is serving a more essential purpose.

The East-West Center at Honolulu is not, of course, the only educational institution with a world point of view or with the potentiality for becoming a true world university. But it is in an excellent position—geographically, philosophically, educationally—to make powerful strides in that direction. It deserves to be encouraged, supported, enlarged.

—March 21, 1964

# Rice, Hope, and IRRI

LOS BAÑOS, PHILIPPINES.

Rice is a four-letter word spelling life to more than a billion earth dwellers. In many places, it is more than the principal food; it is often the only food. But there is a grim inversion. The crops are poorest where people need them the most.

Countries such as Australia, Italy, Spain, and the United States, with a relatively low per-capita consumption of rice, manage to grow from three to four times as much rice per hectare as India, Burma, Thailand, Laos, and the Philippines, where per-capita consumption of rice is the highest in the world. In fact, throughout the dense population belt of Southeast Asia the gap between available rice and empty bellies is growing wider all the time.

Another deadly paradox is that the food value of rice tends to be lowest where the need for nourishment is greatest. The rice of Cambodia and Laos, for example, has far less protein than the rice of Australia, where protein is abundantly available from other sources.

Any genuine improvement in the human condition on this planet, therefore, must be concerned with rice. If rice yields can be increased in the hot countries and if the protein content can be stepped up, the benefits would be among the most far-reaching in human history.

This is the background of what is literally one of the most exciting and revolutionary undertakings in the world. It goes by the name of the International Rice Research Institute, located in the hills of Los Baños in the Philippines, less than two hours by car from Manila. IRRI was organized four years ago this month as a joint project of the Ford and Rockefeller foundations in association with the Philippine government and the University of the Philippines. Director of the Institute is Robert F. Chandler, Jr., former president of the University of New Hampshire and now associate director of Agricultural Sciences for the Rockefeller Foundation.

Working with Dr. Chandler are agronomists, microbiologists, biochemists, plant physiologists, entomologists, virologists, plant breeders, geneticists, statisticians, agricultural economists, and agricultural engineers. They come from more than a dozen countries and constitute one of the most remarkable teams ever to be recruited for the purpose of prying into the secrets of rice.

The main goal of IRRI is to prod nature into breeding a new strain of rice that will withstand tropical hazards. Storms and high winds take a terrific toll of the tall, weak-strawed plants characteristic of rice in hot climates. Another defect of tropical rice is that it tends to produce heavy foliage at the expense of the grain. These two defects—lodging and shading—can be reduced by cutting down on the fertilizer, but this would lead to even greater liabilities.

It might be supposed that the simplest way of meeting these problems would be to import a strain of rice with short, stiff straw. Unfortunately, the taste characteristics of such rice are not congenial to the palates of tropical peoples. IRRI's assignment, therefore, is to give birth to a new breed of rice, one that is suitable to the growing conditions of hot countries and is also palatable. For good measure, IRRI would like its new breed to have maximum protein advantages.

The survival features of such a new breed of rice would enable farmers of countries such as India, Burma, and the Philippines to double and even quadruple their annual production. And augmented protein would mean better health for human beings.

In pursuit of these objectives, Dr. Chandler and his team have collected 10,000 different kinds of rice from all over the world. The desirable and undesirable characteristics of each strain are observed and recorded as the basis for crossing and recrossing. The IRRI has its own experimental rice fields in the valley just below its research laboratories. Each rice strain has its own clearly marked plot and furnishes the vital raw materials.

IRRI has not yet found the precise combination for producing its new breed, but it is well on the way. Dr. Chandler is making no public predictions, but he reflects the quiet confidence of IRRI that the main objective will be met within a decade. Already IRRI's scientists have accumulated abundant data on the variability of growth factors in rice. They have charted numberless correlations involving water and sunlight requirements, condition of soil, fertilizer, and insect repellents. Among the many significant findings is a way of fortifying rice systemically against pest invasion. Of high significance, too, is the training program of specialists from rice-growing areas throughout the world. The kind of knowledge they have helped to create at IRRI enables them to put programs for improving rice into local and regional operation. IRRI has also compiled the *International Bibliography of Rice Research*, which includes all significant literature about rice throughout the world.

It should be said that IRRI is not without critics. No one has taxed IRRI with inadequacy or incompetence. The objections are raised for exactly the opposite reasons—that it is apt to be all too successful in its program, resulting in an intensification of the world's number-one problem: overpopulation. Fortunately, neither the sponsoring foundations nor the Philippine government has been persuaded by these objections. The way to ease population pressure is not by indifference to hunger and disease. The mark of a civilized society is represented by the value it places on human life and its insistence that the human creature be provided with the conditions for maximum health of body and spirit.

There is a curious sense of self-Olympianism about those who deplore health programs for the peoples of heavily crowded countries on the grounds that this would only intensify the world's population pressure problems. If such critics or members of their families were ill, it is doubtful that they would spurn medical attention out of fear that their survival might contribute to the population surplus. Why is there any difference in principle between taking care of the health needs, say, of an art dealer in New York and a street vendor in New Delhi? Or fighting an epidemic in Connecticut and a famine in Korea? The moment a child is born anywhere in the world he has an equal claim on survival and on the compassionate response of the entire human community. Ideas about natural rights, so basic in the American historical experience, must stand on a universal base or they will fall apart completely.

It is a mistake to suppose that human misery, left unattended, results in population reduction. A low birth rate is the result not of poor conditions but of improved standards of living and widespread education. Problems of population pressure are met not by ignoring disease and hunger but by mounting an entirely different kind of offensive—one that educates people, whatever their condition, in the methods by which the size of their families can be limited. In the meantime, the job of the scientist, like that of the doctor, is to put all his knowledge to work in bettering the human situation.

By any yardstick, IRRI is already a success. But the achievement of its main goal could change the course of human history. For if rice means life, then IRRI spells hope. It is the kind of hope that justifies the dream that the inventive and scientific genius of man can be used primarily for his own good.

                                                                —*April 4, 1964*


# Douglas MacArthur

They demanded for him the highest honors but they saw to it that he was deprived of a decent burial. They said he was a man to be respected and venerated, but even before he was laid to rest they jumped up and down on his casket with microphones and amplifiers. They acclaimed him as a hero but they did their best to make him sound like a knave.

Who are "they"? "They" are the extremist supporters who never really understood him. They never understood him in life or death. They had a craving for someone who could be proud and powerful, a military hero who would symbolize both the national honor and glory. He symbolized all these things but he was not a militarist. He was not a lover of big bombs or a brandisher of hot swords. Yes, there was grandeur to the man. He could be hard, haughty, impatient. He could drive forward when he had an objective to reach, and he was disdainful of obstructions. And no one surpassed his genius for invoking patriotism, all of which misled the extremists into thinking they had found their man, with white horse to match. But he was not a tub-thumping jingoist who contrived to juxtapose the national cause against the human cause. He may have been autocratic in manner but he was democratic in purpose. His main job in life was done in soldier's uniform but this was not the way he wanted ultimately to be remembered.

"Could I have but a line a century hence crediting a contribution to the advance of peace," he once said, "I would gladly yield every honor which has been accorded me in war."

And again, he had expressed the hope that if a future historian should judge him worthy "of some slight reference," it would not be as a military commander but as a man determined to create a genuine basis for justice and peace.

But in the headlines and in the flaming newspaper stories after his death, what he had prayed would not happen did happen. They extolled him as a great military figure, which he was, but they gave very little notice to the things of which he was proudest and which may help to change history for the better. He was proud to be called the liberator of the Philippines but he was at least equally proud of his insistence that the civilian government of the Philippines come ahead of the military. He was proud to have received the articles of military surrender from the Japanese but he was even prouder that the central purpose of his occupation was to create civilian rule within the shortest possible time. And he was especially proud that Japan was the first nation in human history to renounce war and the means of war.

This renunciation was written into the new Japanese constitution that took shape under the occupation. Two other features of that constitution he believed were also of historic significance. One was the clause decreeing the end of feudalism and the social injustices inherent in it. The second was a bill of rights and the establishment of an independent judiciary.

He regarded the Japanese constitution not merely as an expression of ultimate aspiration but as a statement of working principles. He didn't come to Japan for the purpose of helping to lay down a superficial veneer but to participate in the making of a profound revolution in the democratization of a nation—and he never hesitated to use the word "democracy" even though the extremists at home who professed to worship him had the strongest contempt for the term. He sponsored a program of land reform under which millions of acres were turned over to the peasants who had worked the land for absentee owners. He fought against the usury that impoverished countless numbers of farmers and tradesmen. He helped to set free the largest politically and socially disfranchised group in Japan—women. He made it possible for Japanese laborers to be represented through organized collective bargaining.

All these were substantial achievements, and they were all interrelated; but it is possible that the clause in the Japanese constitution renouncing war was the achievement that meant the most to him personally.

He liked to recall the time that Prime Minister Shidahara came to him and agreed that the best way of serving and saving Japan was by abolishing war as an international instrument. "The world will laugh at us as impractical visionaries," the Prime Minister said, "but a hundred years from now we will be called prophets."

He spoke at a joint session of the Congress of the Republic of the Philippines three years ago in what was perhaps his last important public appearance. He said the great question of our time is whether war could be outlawed from the world. "If so, it would make the greatest advance in civilization since the Sermon on the Mount. It would lift at one stroke the darkest shadow which has engulfed mankind from the beginning."

He was never called a visionary, yet he felt most at home with visions of a better world.

"Many will say, with mockery and ridicule," he declared, "that the abolition of war can be only a dream—that it is but the vague imagining of a visionary. But we must go on or we will go under. And the great criticism that can be made is that the world lacks a plan that will enable us to go on."

His main rebuke of leaders in government was not so much that they interfered with the military but that they weren't sufficiently imaginative in creating the design for a world under law.

"Leaders must not be laggards," he said. "They have not even approached the basic problem, much less evolved a working formula to implement this public demand. They debate and turmoil over a hundred issues; they bring us to the verge of despair or raise our hopes to Utopian heights over the corollary misunderstandings that stem from the threat of war. . . . Never do they dare to state the bald truth, that the next great advance in the evolution of civilization cannot take place until war is abolished."

The term "common man" may sit awkwardly on the lips of many extremists, but he had no hesitation in using the expression or in investing it with uncommon significance. The common man, he said, understands that there is no greater issue before the world than the need to outlaw war. But his leaders are at least fifty years behind him.

"We are told we must go on indefinitely as at present," he said. "With what at the end? None say; there is no definite objective. They but pass along to those that follow the search for a final solution. And, at the end, the problem will be exactly the same as that which we face now.

"Must we live for generations under the killing punishment of accelerating preparedness without an announced final purpose or, as an alternative, suicidal war . . . ? Sooner or later the world, if it is to survive, must reach a decision. The only question is, when? When will some great figure in power have sufficient imagination and moral courage to translate this universal wish, which is rapidly becoming a universal necessity, into actuality?

"We are in a new era. The old methods and solutions no longer suffice. We must have new thoughts, new ideas, new concepts, just as did our venerated forefathers when they faced a new world. There must always be one to lead, and we should be that one. We should now proclaim our readiness to abolish war in concert with the great powers of the world. The result would be magical."

He carried these ideas into assemblies where they needed most to be heard. In January, 1955, at a banquet meeting of the Los Angeles County Council of the American Legion, he talked about the implications of atomic warfare. He began by saying that many of those present had been his comrades in arms. Then he asked: "How is it that the institution of war has become so integrated with man's life and civilization? How has it grown to be the most vital factor in our existence?"

He startled his listeners by telling them that as soldiers they could no longer regard war as a relevant way of safeguarding values or defending a nation. The reality of scientific annihilation, he said, had destroyed the possibility of war being used "as a medium of practical settlement of international differences. Science has clearly outmoded war as a feasible arbiter. War has become a Frankenstein to destroy both sides. No longer is it the weapon of adventure whereby a short cut to international power and wealth—a place in the sun—can be gained. If you lose, you are annihilated. If you win, you stand only to lose. No longer does it possess the chance of the winner of a duel. It contains rather the germs of double suicide."

This was what he believed, yet they are now trying to make it appear that he was prevented by politicians from using atomic bombs against China in the Korean War.

He had deplored the use of the atomic bomb against Japan and had no intention of using it in the Korean War. He believed that victory was possible in both cases without nuclear bombs, and he said so. Yet he has now been made to say the opposite in death.

His great mistake—one that his extremist supporters regarded as an act of patriotism—was to persist with his own ideas even after President Truman opposed them. A President of the United States is Commander in Chief of the Armed Forces. It is his right and responsibility to make ultimate decisions concerning America's politics and actions in the world. In 1951 the President could no longer countenance opposition in the field to his decisions on Korea.

It is possible to disagree severely with MacArthur over Korea, but it is unfair to allow even so substantial an event to blot out a view of the whole man. For if it is true that his extremist supporters have an incomplete view of Douglas MacArthur, the same is equally true of his critics. Both groups have reacted to the military posture, to the rakish tilt of the cap, to the mystique of the man. And both groups have failed to see beyond the clusters of medals. They have never taken the trouble to find out who he was philosophically; they have never gone into his library and observed the esteem he had for men such as Thomas Jefferson, John Stuart Mill, Abraham Lincoln.

Someday, a biographer will succeed in writing a full-length portrait of Douglas MacArthur. It will not be an easy undertaking. It will require an almost superhuman capacity for balance and perspective. But it is clearly in the national interest that it be written. And it is in the human interest that it be read.

*—May 2, 1964*

# Black Wind Rising

The civil rights movement in the United States is entering a new, explosive, and tragic phase. Leadership is passing into the hands of haters and racists. Responsible Negro leaders such as Roy Wilkins, Martin Luther King, Bayard Rustin, and James Farmer are finding it increasingly difficult to be heard above the battle cries of showdown-minded partisans. White leaders who for years have dedicated themselves to the struggle for human equality are not only losing rapport; they are becoming the particularized targets for condemnation and abuse by extremists.

In any great protracted social struggle there is always the danger of polarization. The gravitational pull is to the extremes. People who work steadily and conscientiously toward a central and far-reaching goal usually find that their main opposition comes not from the other side but from the hotheads in their own ranks. The reformers and the idealists are cut down not by the enemy but by their own fanatics and assassins. Militancy is no longer defined as resolute and responsible leadership but as direct action leading to violent showdown.

Inevitably, the extremes of black and white tend to mirror one another. Each talks about the other in racist terms. Each contends that the other understands only the language of force. Each has disdain for the moderate; in fact, the moderate often becomes the prime target.

This is not to say that there is no range of differences within the extremes themselves. Among the white extremists, there is a well-known spectrum of groups ranging from the night riders to the supporters of the new political party. The differences among the black extremists are not so well known. A struggle for power is now in progress between the super-extremists and the general extremists. Both factions agree that gradualism has served only to provide the whites with time to consolidate their position. They agree that the Supreme Court decision will not be implemented voluntarily and that the only rights the Negro can expect are those they carve out for themselves. They believe in the inevitability and necessity of a violent showdown. They are contemptuous of whites who are engaged in civil rights activity. They are scornful of old-line organizations such as the National Association for the Advancement of Colored People.

No greater mistake could be made than to think that the critical problem of extremism in the civil rights movement can be met simply and solely by rounding up and hauling in the leaders. The problem has its origins and its main explosive force in the condition of the Negro in America and not just in the irresponsible and dangerous activities of the men on top. Moreover, the main volcanic centers today are to be found not in the South but in the North. In the Negro ghettos of large cities such as New York, Chicago, and Detroit—this is where the incendiary materials are building up.

New York's Harlem has all the volatile makings of one of the worst race riots in history. If it comes, the villains will not just be the black hotheads and know-nothings who incited people to riot. The villains will include all the whites who have abused, shunned, cheated, hounded, and outraged the Negro beyond human endurance: the landlords who overcharge and whose tenements violate all the laws of housing safety; the housing inspectors who ignore the violations; the white merchants who shortweigh, shortchange, and pass off inferior merchandise; education officials who are clearly incapable of meeting the incredibly difficult challenge of operating a school system in Harlem; white employers who may deplore racial injustice but who have yet to institute decent employment practices in their own firms; union leaders who proclaim their interest in the workingman but who draw color lines as rigid as the most segregated community; in short, everyone who thinks the problem is at a distance.

Not much time is left. The white people of America are going to have to do something dramatic and they have to do it fast. The passage of the civil rights bill is the least, not the most, that is required. The main work has to be done not just by legislation but by enough individual Americans who accept a moral obligation and responsibility in their everyday attitudes and actions. The problem is broad enough so that no man need feel there is no part of it where he can take hold and become relevant.

Meanwhile, it might be a good idea for whites to listen more to, and strengthen the position of, men such as Wilkins, Rustin, King, and Farmer. They may seem like radicals to the uninitiated, but within the civil rights movement they represent the best hope against the racists and the inciters to violence. If they go, the last retaining walls of sanity go with them.

The time has come for the moderates among blacks and whites to close ranks against the pressure from their extremes. This calls for greater mutual respect and greater recognition of a common cause. A national tragedy is in the making. If it is to be averted, the eyes and consciences of the nation will have to be opened wide—and soon.

—*May 30, 1964*

# Garbage in the Air

Fifteen years ago or so, if you did a lot of flying either in commercial or private planes, you began to notice the change in the atmosphere over the world's large cities. A grayish murk was settling over the metropolitan centers, marking them off from the surrounding countryside. Year by year, since then, the murk has been intensifying. It is now more black than gray. And it is reaching out from the large cities like a brackish fog over large areas of countryside.

Hundreds of millions of people throughout the world have to consult their memories for a notion of what clear light really is—or clean air, for that matter. The sun comes through, but it is filtered light and not the real thing. Only rarely, after sustained rains and strong winds, is it possible for most city dwellers to know how blue a blue sky can be, or to experience the sensation of fresh air.

A decade ago the existence of an atmospheric pall over Los Angeles first pressed itself upon the national consciousness. There, a combination of wind currents, natural overcast or haze, industrial smoke, and the gases of combustion engines produced a hazardous and ugly concentration, causing eyes to smart and lungs to protest. "Smog" it was called, and it was supposed to be a geographical phenomenon. Since that time, however, city after city in the world has come under heavy atmospheric pollution. Wherever you fly in the world today—Madrid, London, Frankfurt, Bangkok, Tokyo, Manila—you can identify large cities from the air not by their towers but by a thick black veil. Not until you are fairly close can you begin to penetrate the curtain and discern a specific configuration. Your inevitable reaction is one of disbelief that human beings could exist in the center of such atmospheric contamination. And from the perspective afforded you by the cockpit of your plane you find it even more incomprehensible that people don't even seem aware of the steadily increasing assault on their environment.

Of all the cities, none seems to be under more of a filth fog than New York. Some of the sources of the pollution are clearly visible. Industrial plants between Newark and Jersey City throw up huge plumes of smoke that fan out and descend on New York. Even worse are the tall smoke-stacks of the power companies and New York City's own garbage in-cinerators inside Manhattan itself. Seen from the air, these chimneys in action look as though they were designed to protect the city against air attack by laying down a massive smoke screen. Meanwhile, heavy smoke from thousands of smaller chimneys—from hotels, apartment houses, and office buildings—pump hundreds of tons of soot into the Manhattan air. All this, of course, is in addition to the choking gaseous emanations from buses, cabs, and cars. The same city trucks that spray and clean the streets give off heavy emanations of foul exhaust. Gutters are clean but lungs are filling up. Statues from Egypt or Greece, transplanted to New York parks, show more effects of erosion in a few years than took place over centuries in their original homes. The stone sides of new buildings, after only a year or two of exposure to New York's soot and gases, become heavily streaked. This is the same grisly grime that now coats over the once-pink tissue of the human respiratory tract.

New York City has ordinances against chimney smoke, but enforce-ment has become a joke. Indeed, the city itself is among the worse offenders. It operates a large incinerator on the East River Drive, pump-ing garbage smoke over a large part of the metropolitan area. What makes the situation in New York paradoxical and ludicrous is that city officials wage a widespread educational campaign to persuade people not to litter the street with candy wrappers or cigarette boxes. The city itself adds to the poisonous garbage that litters the air.

The nation is alarmed, and properly so, about the steep rise in the incidence of cancer. A report issued by the U.S. Surgeon General has linked cigarette smoking to this increase. Is there no connection between malignancy and air contamination, much of it from smoke and fumes? Is it unreasonable to expect that the U.S. Surgeon General should also undertake a report on air pollution?

The problem of impure air is not an isolated one. It is related to the larger problem of environmental poisoning now so characteristic of con-temporary living. Brooks and streams are being contaminated by the widespread use of detergents, the chemical composition of which does not permit water to become purified through nature's replenishing chain. Our rivers are infected by poisons from insecticides, killing millions of fish. Even greater numbers of birds have been affected. Meanwhile, the nation itself is being despoiled at a fearsome rate. A million acres are taken out of cultivation each year for new superhighways. Another million acres are being claimed by expanding cities. Asphalt, cement, and black hydrocarbons now become the main features of the human environment.

Any verdict on man—modern man—is bound to show him as incredibly inventive but just as disdainful of the connection between cause and effect. He has devised ways of turning wheels faster and doing things more efficiently than they have ever been done before, but he has given only the most superficial attention to the cheapening of human life that sometimes results from the process. Most astounding of all is the importance he attaches to individual cleanliness even as he creates a total environment of poison and filth. Parents teach their children to clean their fingernails but are apparently unworried about the dangerous layers of dirt that get into their bodies. Vast enterprises are developed to kill off body odors and make the human being a sweet-smelling delight. But what about the horrendous odors and poisonous gases that emanate from the backs of buses, trucks, and cars? How is it that the passion for daily baths and deodorants has not been extended to the environment itself?

Even if environmental fouling were not a health hazard and were solely a matter of natural disfiguration, it would warrant a torrential outpouring of human anger. No man need apologize because his sense of beauty and wonder is assailed. A considerable portion of beauty is disappearing from the world. If the process is to be stopped, indignation in appropriate depth and quantity will have to be registered.

It is perhaps significant that the expedition to the moon, now in preparation, will sterilize and sanitize every object, however small, carried by our space ships. The purpose is to avoid contaminating the moon. This is a commendable purpose. Perhaps a bit of the same intensity of effort and expenditure might be directed to getting rid of some of the colossal contamination now burdening the earth.

—*June 6, 1964*

# Return of the Native

On the plane from Australia we met a young American couple and their ten-year-old son. They were en route to the United States after an absence of almost a year. It was a significant homecoming, for when they had left they didn't expect to return ever again. They were originally part of a distinct and unique group in human history. They were "nuclear migrants"—perhaps several thousand of them—products of the atomic age who had left the United States to find what they hoped would be a more reasonable and rational environment in which to live, work, and bring up their children. In particular, they were refugees from threats of nuclear war, nuclear testing, nuclear fallout, and what they felt was a desperately unhealthy national mood of tension and apprehension.

This particular family had lived in Orange County in southern California. Both husband and wife were teachers. They were aware of the ease with which one of the recurrent international crises could erupt into full-scale war; and they were profoundly concerned by the effects of the national insecurity on their son. And when the Cuban crisis occurred, with its portents of saturating horror, they decided they had had enough. They had read of highly educated Americans—scientists and doctors and professors among them—who felt that the time had come to make a new life elsewhere, not because they held their American citizenship lightly but because they felt that the United States had become caught up in a spiraling madness that was totally inconsistent with the nation's heritage of reason.

Many of the nuclear migrants had gone to Australia and New Zealand. One attraction was the relative absence of radioactive fallout in the Southern Hemisphere. Another was the English language and the existence of Anglo-Saxon institutions. Australia was favored because of the dynamic quality of a country still in the process of being settled. Newcomers to Australia were given every assistance in finding appropriate jobs and good homes.

My fellow plane passengers said they had decided to migrate to Sydney, on the southeast coast of Australia.

"We had heard that the weather was not unlike that of California," the man explained. "But what really attracted us was the psychological and political climate. People were not caught up in a mass-anxiety neurosis. You could read newspapers without being vibrated from one crisis to another.

"When we arrived in Australia, it was even better than we had hoped. Both my wife and I got jobs as teachers. We never knew how really free academic freedom could be until we taught in Sydney. There was very little special privilege. People weren't easily impressed by fancy manners or bank balances. And my boy stopped having nightmares about nuclear war."

Having just been in Australia, I could attest to all the attractions, both natural and sociological, of the country. But I was puzzled. What caused them to decide to return to the United States?

The man was silent for a moment.

"It wasn't an easy decision," he said. "At first we relished being able to have conversations with people without even mentioning the bomb. Then I found myself going to the library or the American Embassy to pick up airmail copies of *The New York Times*—just to avoid the feeling of being cut off altogether. And every now and then I would meet another American and we would hungrily ask each other about news from home.

"Finally, we got to resenting the absence of concern in talking to our neighbors or our professional colleagues. It's a sports-loving country. The weather is ideal. But that's precisely the point. The more we read and the more we thought, the more we realized that this was probably the finest place in the world for a vacation; but it was too much of a good thing— at least for us.

"In the end, we discovered what I suppose we should have known in the beginning. We discovered that what we missed the most were the very things we tried to get away from in the first place. What made the situation impossible for us ultimately was that we knew that Australia was exposed to as much danger as anyone else—except that no one seemed to be worried about it. And we became even more disturbed by the reluctance of the Australians to accept their involvement in the world than we were by the extremists back in the United States who had made life so unpleasant for us because they disagreed with us. We felt incredibly remote."

"You mean you are returning to Orange County?"

"Yes, Birchers and all. I don't know if I can get my old job back. I'll probably find something."

"What about the anxiety neurosis?"

"It'll be pretty tough to take but I might as well face it. I suppose I can stand anything except total separation and detachment. And it will be easier to take it this time knowing what the alternative is. Some other Americans there are making the same decision."

I had the feeling that my friend may have underestimated the Australians, who struck me as a remarkably well-balanced and well-informed people. Even so, with or without respect to the nuclear migrants, the evidence is clear that in the twentieth century man has no escape from man. On this planet, at least, the human confrontation will continue until such time as man defaults his way to the final encounter or comprehends the preciousness of life and creates the means for safeguarding it. The choice today is not between escape and disaster. It is, as it always was, between the satisfactions that blind and the responsibilities that awaken.

*—July 4, 1964*

# Nehru, Man and Symbol:
# A Fragmentary Appreciation

He was not one man but a procession of men. In him you witnessed a national hero, statesman, philosopher, historian, author, educator.

He was also a triumphant assortment of paradoxes. He was a supreme rationalist who presided over a nation with the most pervasive and complex religious make-up in the world.

He was an intellectual product of Western civilization who was accepted as symbolic leader by many hundreds of millions of Asians and Africans who feared the West.

He was an accomplished logician who lived on intimate terms with the imponderables and intangibles.

He was an avowed optimist who found it difficult to keep from brooding.

He had sensitivities so finely attuned that he could be jarred by the slightest vibrations, but he was able to make history-jolting decisions.

He believed the highest function of the state was to help develop the individuality of the individual, but no other nation in the world contained as many natural obstacles to the emergence of that individuality as the nation he governed for seventeen years.

With such a man, you cannot essay a full evaluation or appreciation. The best you can do is to pursue certain qualities and attributes.

*First, the courage of the man.*

August, 1947. With national independence and partition of the subcontinent between India and Pakistan, 450 million people became caught up in a vast convulsion. Hindus and Moslems, with a long history of tension between them, became part of a chain reaction of violence and horror. No one knows how many died. But 12 million people became homeless. Rumors of atrocities and actual atrocities interacted to produce a spiraling madness.

For a while, the situation was relatively calm in New Delhi, with its large Moslem population. Then, suddenly, the storm broke. Late one night a Hindu mob, inflamed by stories of Moslem terror to the northwest, swept into Connaught Circle, the main shopping area in New Delhi. The rioters smashed their way into Moslem stores, destroying and looting and ready to kill.

Even before the police arrived in force, Jawaharlal Nehru was on the scene. He plunged into the crowd in the darkness, trying to bring people to their senses. He spied a Moslem who had just been seized by Hindus. He interposed himself between the man and his attackers.

Suddenly a cry went up: "Jawaharlal is here! Jawaharlal is here! Don't hurt Jawaharlal!"

The cry spread through the crowd. It had a magical effect. People stood still and dropped their arms to their sides. Looted merchandise was dropped. The mob psychology disintegrated. By the time the police arrived people were dispersing. The riot was over.

The next day friends rushed to Nehru, admonishing him for exposing himself to a mob at the height of its frenzy.

"You could have been killed," one of them said. "Then what?"

"That's for you to determine," he replied quietly. "Many others could have been killed last night. Then what?"

The fact that Nehru had risked his life to save a single Moslem had a profound effect far beyond New Delhi. Many thousands of Moslems who had intended to flee to Pakistan now stayed in India, staking their lives on Nehru's ability to protect them and assure them justice. In years to come this confidence of India's Moslems in Nehru was to become a major factor in building a nation and holding it together.

Not many weeks after the communal rioting subsided, the Prime Minister and a foreign guest were driving in his private car about fifteen miles south of Delhi. The traffic piled up behind a caravan of camels in a village preponderantly populated by Moslems. Only recently this village had figured in mass violence.

The combination of the heat, the heavy, chalky dust from the dry dirt road, the temper of the camel drivers, and the screams of people in the stalled buses, trucks, wagons, and automobiles provided the combustible materials for a communal riot. Young Moslems from the village suddenly appeared with knives. They surrounded Nehru's car. One of them recognized the Prime Minister and shouted angry words at him.

Nehru stepped out of his car, walked up to the young man, spoke to him quietly. Suddenly a cheer went up for the Prime Minister. The Moslems surrounded him, expressing their devotion and loyalty. Then some of them began to weep in shame for their actions. Nehru spoke with them, answering their questions, telling them of his hopes.

On the drive back to New Delhi his guest expressed concern for the Prime Minister's personal safety. Mr. Nehru agreed the risk might be real, but he could not let it get in the way of things that had to be done.

### The human quality of the man.

January, 1951. Sunday. The clerk at the Imperial Hotel in New Delhi handed us a message. It was from Miss Sindhi at the Prime Minister's house. The P.M. was having some people over that afternoon and hoped we could come. Nothing special. Just relaxed talk.

Primed for a long bull session on philosophy and politics, we arrived at the P.M.'s house at about three o'clock. Mr. Nehru was at the door, greeting his guests. He seemed to be in excellent spirits. We were ushered to a large enclosed veranda. We looked around the room and recognized Dr. Sarvepalli Radhakrishnan, the eminent philosopher and vice-president of India; also, Shiva Rao, prominent author and long-time friend of the Prime Minister. Among the other guests to whom we were introduced were two cabinet ministers and a justice.

Mr. Nehru came into the room, his young grandson riding his shoulders, kicking Grandpa's ribs and demanding more speed.

"The gallop comes later," Mr. Nehru said, hoisting the boy over his head and placing him on the floor. He told the youngster he had a surprise for him. "In fact, I've got a surprise for everyone. This afternoon we shall all have a good time. I've arranged for entertainment."

The entertainer was a magician who went through a bewildering assortment of tricks. He caused long knives to turn into short knives, wine to turn into milk, and he made a chicken emerge from a paper cup. Then he demonstrated his accuracy with a bow and arrow, hitting a vertical thread at about twenty feet. Finally he invited a member of the company to step forward. Mr. Nehru, enjoying himself hugely, prodded the Finance Minister into joining the act.

As soon as the Finance Minister discovered he was to be a living prop in a latter-day version of a William Tell episode, he seemed to waver somewhat. Mr. Nehru gently chided him into going on with the act. The Finance Minister was directed to a chair directly above which, six inches from his head, a circular wreath was suspended by several thin threads.

The magician announced that with one arrow he would sever all the threads, causing the wreath to fall around the Finance Minister's distinguished shoulders. Almost as an afterthought he added that he would perform this feat while blindfolded.

Mr. Nehru spoke up.

"They tell me that good finance ministers are hard to find these days," he said. "I don't know whether I ought to allow him to go through with this. Oh well, I suppose it's too late to do anything now."

The magician clapped for silence, put on his blindfold, picked up his bow, tested its tautness, and inserted the arrow. Then he paused and, still blindfolded, paced off a few steps to his target, groping and stumbling on the way. Finally, he retraced his steps, assumed his battle station, and raised the bow and arrow.

"No, no," Mr. Nehru cried. "You're aiming at the wrong man! You're aiming at the justice. We can't afford to lose *him*. The man you want is about sixty degrees to the left."

Suddenly the magician let fly. The arrow pierced the strings and the garland fell neatly over the shoulders of the Finance Minister, who, suddenly released from his encounter with non-fiscal suspense, joined in the laughter.

After a while the group exchanged stories. The Prime Minister presided over the ice cream and punch bowl, the youngster at his side tugging at Grandpa's pants and asking when he could have a fast horseback ride.

The closest anyone got to serious talk was when Mr. Nehru told of a visit he had had the previous day from an old school chum who was now a wealthy industrialist.

According to the Prime Minister, the industrialist came up to him and complained that things had gone much too far. Taxes were crippling him and something had to be done about it. He said he had to pay a stiff tax on his private house in New Delhi. He also had to pay a tax on his hunting estate. As if this were not enough, he had to pay a tax on a house he kept in Bangalore. But worst of all was the tax he had to pay on his beach home in Juhu.

"Now I ask you, Jawaharlal, how do you expect me to keep up these houses with taxes like this?"

"Have you ever considered giving up a house or two?" Nehru asked.

"Now what kind of advice is this to give a lifelong friend?" the man asked.

The group laughed.

"What makes the story so ironic," Mr. Nehru said, "is that here I am, fighting back legislation to confiscate luxurious property, and this chap wants me to give him a tax refund. I suppose each man has to have his own dream world."

In this manner the afternoon passed. After the farewells, Dr. Radhakrishnan offered to drive us back to the hotel.

Inside the car, Dr. Radhakrishnan said we had just seen a side of Nehru that few people knew.

"There is something eternally young, even boyish, about the P.M.," he said. "People tend to think of him as a man lost in brooding, not even knowing how to laugh. Not so; he loves to laugh, as we have seen. It is very good for the nation that he can laugh. It helps to freshen his spirits. The important thing about Nehru is that he continues to think young. A man like this can never grow old. He will never look old, no matter how old he is. But he must take better care of himself. He works too hard."

*The man as author, poet, historian, philosopher, thinker.*

He liked to write, felt incomplete when he was unable to assemble his thoughts and commit them to paper. He regarded writing as the most demanding, the most exhausting, but also the most satisfying of the creative arts. Writing enabled him to discipline his mind, to think sequentially and creatively. Being able to give life to a concept through words; using language as a vehicle of persuasion or as a voyage of intellectual exploration and discovery—these meant much to him.

At times he could write like the most detached and aseptic historian. At other times he would write with extreme sensitivity and grace. In describing a natural setting, he could be all poet. In his writing, as in his life, he was many men.

For many years his writing, quite literally, kept him from losing his mind. This was during his various imprisonments as an agitator for Indian freedom. No one knows how many hundreds of thousands or millions of words he wrote while in jail. His autobiography came out of prison. He did a work on history, *The Discovery of India*. There were also, to be sure, the various pamphlets and tracts that made him the intellectual leader of the fight for freedom.

Of all his prison writings, however, perhaps none is more remarkable than the collection of letters to his daughter, Indira, later published under the title *Glimpses of World History*. The letters, running to almost 1,000 pages in the book, constituted something of a liberal university education, ranging as it did over the whole of the human historical record —European, Asian, African, American, Australian. It took in not just the development of national and continental civilization but the creative thrust and splendor of mankind. Nehru's own insights and his appreciation of the human potential are in evidence throughout. What makes the book unique in the history of literature is that his prison was totally bereft of historical materials. He wrote *Glimpses of World History*, with its thousands of facts and events and names, without reference books or notes of any kind. As a demonstration of human intellectual capacity, the book stands by itself.

It is doubtful whether any writer before or since has fused in one person more thoroughly the complex essence of East and West. He was a fascinating amalgam of cultures; his formal education was English but his traditions were Indian. His intellect was rooted in the Enlightenment but his spirit in the Vedas. Few men of our time have been so avowedly rationalist, yet there were the strongest spiritual connotations in his feelings about India and her people.

"I have been attached to the Ganges and Jumna rivers in Allahabad ever since my childhood," he wrote in his will. "And, as I have grown older, this attachment has also grown. I have watched their varying moods as the seasons changed, and have often thought of the history and myth and tradition and song and story that have become attached to them through the long ages and become part of their flowing waters. . . . The Ganges reminds me of the snow-covered peaks and the deep valleys of the Himalayas, which I have loved so much, and of the rich and vast plains below, where my life and work have been cast.

"Smiling and dancing in the morning sunlight, and dark and gloomy and full of mystery as evening shadows fall; a narrow, slow, and graceful stream in winter, and a vast, roaring thing during monsoon, broad-bosomed almost as the sea, and with something of the sea's power to destroy, the Ganges has been to me a symbol and a memory of the past of India, running into the present, and flowing on to the great ocean of the future."

Intellectually he could never quite comprehend, and sometimes he had difficulty in coping with, India's numberless castes. He disclaimed affiliation with or affinity for the religious aspect of Hinduism, yet he presided over a nation that sensed and responded to a profoundly spiritual quality in him. Gandhi was a godhead; he easily fitted into a theology. Not so Nehru, a supreme logician. Yet when Gandhi's mantle passed on, it passed to Nehru. No one questioned its appropriateness. There might be all the difference in the world between the thought, style, and outlook of the two men, but there was a seamless connection between the two in their devotion to the Indian people and in the response of the Indian people to them.

"I have received so much love and affection from the Indian people," Nehru wrote, "that nothing I can do can repay even a small fraction of it. Many have been admired, some have been revered, but the affection of all classes of the Indian people has come to me in such abundant measure that I have been overwhelmed by it."

*The leadership capacities and the charismatic quality of the man.*

April, 1955. The Asian-African Conference at Bandung. An event of profound importance for most of the world's peoples, symbolizing not just their freedom from outside rule but their full membership in the human race. Much of the drama flowed out of the juxtaposed presence of the two men who represented the two largest nations in the world—Jawaharlal Nehru of India and Chou En-lai of Communist China.

Both men knew that what was happening in their countries would have a great bearing on the way most of the newly independent nations would be developed.

Chou En-lai, speaking in English through an interpreter, was the first of the two to address the meeting. He identified China with the aspirations of Asia and Africa. He said that history was riding with China. This was said more in the form of an announcement than a claim. He invited the Bandung delegates to visit China and see the marked progress made under socialism. His manner was not bombastic or aggressive but matter-of-fact, austere.

When Nehru spoke some time later, the contrast between the two men couldn't have been more startling. It wasn't only that he spoke without a manuscript or without an interpreter. He had warmth, personal rapport. He became part of each individual, speaking to the best inside him. He was creating strength, awakening the individual's capacity and his hopes rather than attempting to convert a man to any large impersonal system.

He held up no glorious certainties of historical determinism, only the saturating uncertainties of the human situation. But this was in the nature of freedom, which guaranteed nothing except a chance to do better; and freedom was within their reach.

At Bandung the delegates may have been impressed by Chou En-lai, but they believed Nehru. And even when they did not agree with Nehru, they believed *in* him. This was the way it was with his own people. They might not have comprehended him at times, but they believed in him and knew that good would come out of such a man. Even though they were unable to connect themselves to his intellectuality, they never had trouble in understanding his integrity. And they knew that where he wanted to go was where India had to be.

At Bandung Chou En-lai was surrounded by bodyguards; Nehru by men who wanted to talk to him—men from new nations who suddenly were obligated to make history and needed the kind of confidence that a Nehru could impart to them. He was Olympian but he was never aloof.

The morning before the last session of the conference at Bandung, Nehru invited us to breakfast with him at his villa in the hills several miles outside the city. We sat on a veranda overlooking a flowering countryside. Nehru had already been down among the flowers, sniffing with satisfaction. His mood was deeply reflective. He spoke of the future of Asia with special reference to China and India. He said he had given the matter much thought. It was obvious, he said, that what happened inside India would have important effects outside India—not just in Asia but Africa. Here were two giant display cases for millions of people. The Indian display case, with all its complexities and difficulties, showed it was possible to have a progressive society without taking individuality away from the individual. The state should never subordinate the individual; rather the state itself had the obligation to be infinitely inventive in trying to serve him and ennoble him. India had 400 million people; most of them were poor. They needed jobs and food and medicine and schools and homes. It was precisely the kind of total need that the Chinese Communists said could never be met outside of a totally controlled society. They said what had to be done couldn't come fast enough or deep enough without the machinery available to a total Marxist state.

These were the questions most of the world's peoples had to decide, Nehru said. And he believed that India, despite all difficulties, was making progress and could do even better.

We asked what he considered to be the main strengths and weaknesses in the development of Communist China.

He said, characteristically, that it was not for him to dispense such judgments; this was a task more appropriately done by history. But he added, also quite characteristically, that he would suppose that any leader of a state might have a certain caution in applying rigidly and literally economic or ideological doctrines that were based on the world as it was a century ago.

Was this a reference to the ideas of Marx and Engels?

Yes, he replied. There was much that was valid and valuable in Marx. But the world had undergone profound changes since Marx published his theories, and the attempt to pursue these doctrines as though they were natural law was itself retrogressive, in a sense.

Moreover, he added, Marxism provided too narrow a creed for the problems it had to meet. It gave so much emphasis to economic factors that it underestimated the power of all the other concerns of man. Life consisted of much more than economic growth. He was not at all certain, he added, that the Marxist ideas were completely understood by all those who attempted to apply them.

Then his eyes twinkled and he sat back in his chair and told of an incident at the conference involving Chou En-lai to illustrate his point.

"We were assigned to a subcommittee whose job it was to prepare a draft for a short statement for the conference. It was a simple statement that was required, and we were able to agree readily on the general substance. I invited Chou En-lai to write the first draft. He declined, saying he preferred that I do it.

"I did—in English, of course, and then read it to him through his interpreter. He was appreciative but said there were several key words that tended to change the meaning from what he understood the statement was supposed to say.

"Again we discussed the purpose of the statement in general and the troublesome words in particular. We had no difficulty in agreeing on the intended sense of the draft. All that remained now was to translate a few English words into Chinese. The attempt to do this took several hours—and even then I was not completely satisfied that the translation was precise.

"Do you know what came to my mind when I left that meeting? I said to myself: 'Good Lord, just imagine what Karl Marx must be like in Chinese!'"

He laughed, then said: "I'm perfectly serious, you know."

There came to my mind a conversation with the P.M. in New Delhi some years earlier. Then, too, we were discussing what Stuart Chase called "the tyranny of words." In particular, words such as "inevitability," "free will," and "determinism."

Imprecise though these terms were bound to be, I had asked Nehru whether he accepted the idea of implacable historical forces beyond man's reach.

In matters such as these, he had replied, it was well to avoid absolute judgments.

Even so, I had said, it was perhaps fair to ask how he reacted philosophically to the eternal debate over free will vs. determinism.

"I would still try to avoid absolute judgments," he had replied. "Actually, I think it possible to reconcile the two. Do you play bridge?"

"Very little and very poorly," I had said.

"No matter," he resumed. "Determinism is like the cards that are dealt you. Free will is how you play them. The interaction between the two determines what you are as a person—or even a nation."

*The man as prophet and politician.*

Jawaharlal Nehru may have been able to reconcile free will and determinism, but he was never able to reconcile the conflict inside himself between prophet and politician.

As prophet, he had profound kinship with Mahatma Gandhi. Whenever you asked him about his innermost beliefs he was certain to say that the most important conviction of his life—one taught him by Gandhi—was that good ends never justified bad means. Violence, even in a good cause, defeats the good.

"We must not appease evil," he had said in our recorded conversation in 1951, "but we must also remember that evil is not surmounted by wrong methods that themselves produce more evil. I have felt more and more that the basic lesson Gandhi taught was right, that means should not be subordinated to ends.

"I know these ideas cannot easily be translated into life. A political leader cannot function like a prophet. He has to limit himself to people's understanding of him; otherwise, he cannot function at all."

"What happens when the moralist becomes politician and is faced with the need to get things done?" I asked.

"I am not a moralist or even a very good politician. I have dabbled in various things because they interest me. The politician has to compromise. That is what makes him a politician. But it may make a difference if he at least begins with certain convictions or principles. Anyway, I think Gandhi was right about ends and means and about violence. I hope to come as close as I can to making this a working philosophy."

Some years later, in a letter, he returned to this theme.

"A leader must not only feel what is right," he wrote, "but he has also to convince masses of people about it. Thus, he tends to compromise or else he would cease to be the leader. The only example I know in contemporary history of a leader who refused to compromise with what he thought was right is Gandhi—and Gandhi was assassinated in the end, as prophets often are."

Yet even Gandhi, faced with the terrible gravitational pull of events, could acquiesce in compromise, even if he was not an architect of it.

Shortly after independence armed raiders from the northwest moved into the Kashmir. Nehru didn't hesitate. He ordered military action. He didn't wait to consult Gandhi.

Once having acted, Nehru told Gandhi he had decided to use force in the Kashmir because this was the only course open to him. He was sorry if what he had done had brought pain to Gandhi.

Gandhi put his arm around Nehru's shoulders. He didn't have to say anything.

The battle between politician and prophet inside Nehru never left him. Long before he had the responsibility for governing a nation he defined goals in terms of necessity instead of workability or attainability; he could move toward an objective without having to develop a consensus in order to achieve it; he could advocate rather than legislate. Once in office he found himself plagued by some of the very tactics that had been so effective in gaining independence for India. Separatist movements sprang up throughout the country; this or that state would want its own language or cultural or political autonomy. The methods used to advance these objectives, naturally enough, were the same ones that had been used to such good effect against the British. In order to deal with these methods, it was necessary for Nehru to be tougher than his personal make-up would warrant.

We were in India in 1961 when the P.M. was having severe difficulties with Master Tara Singh, the Sikh separatist leader. In quest of his objectives, Singh went on a hunger strike. I asked Nehru how he felt being the target of this device, as contrasted to the time when he himself was an agitator identified with Gandhi, who made personal hunger and suffering into one of the most potent political weapons in history.

His face clouded over. I could tell it was painful for him to think about it.

"Frankly," he said, "I don't like it. I don't think this is the right way to go about persuading a government."

For the first time in the years since we had known him he seemed to stammer somewhat. Then he realized the irony of the situation. He smiled.

"I think I told you that a politician has to act in a certain way," he said. "What else is there to be done? I can't give in to the man and allow India to become a mass of splinters."

"Do you feel the hunger strike is—well, hitting below the belt?"

"In a sense, yes."

"How did you feel about it when Gandhi used it?"

"To tell the truth, I didn't feel quite right about it even then. If I analyze my feelings, I suppose I felt rather awkward about it. But you don't have to try very hard if you want to catch me in an inconsistency. This is the occupational disease of any philosopher who finds himself in the position of an operating leader."

It was at that 1961 meeting that I discerned for the first time the visible evidence in Nehru of physical deterioration. One side of his face seemed rigid, as though he had suffered a stroke. His posture was no longer as erect as it had once been. The fatigue came through in his voice. For more than a half century he had made India his life and work. Thinking he might be looking forward to a time when he might lay down his burden and return to his writing and thinking, I asked what he would do if it became possible for him to be freed of his government responsibilities.

"You mean, what would I do if I retired?"

"Yes."

I had thought his face would light up at the prospect. Just the opposite. He looked as though nothing would be more unwelcome.

"Well, I suppose there are some things I might do," he said without any particular enthusiasm in his voice. "I like to walk. I would probably walk quite a bit, in the mountains. I might want to read a bit. But I really haven't thought much about it."

More than ever we realized that Nehru loved his job and had no thought of leaving it; he loved everything about it, the contradictions, the inner struggles, the endless pressures and counter-pressures, the physical strain and the anguish and the multiple problems and complexities and the insolubles. Most of all, he loved the direct connection he had with the people of India and the destiny of his nation.

Before leaving him we had one more question to ask—even though we knew he was annoyed whenever it came up. But everyone was asking the question all through India, and indeed, throughout the world: After Nehru, who? In talking to newspaper editors and members of the government, I had encountered considerable feeling, some of it bitter, because Nehru had not selected a successor. One editor said he couldn't understand why Nehru couldn't anticipate the chaos and disintegration that would afflict India upon his death in the absence of a designated successor. A prominent member of the Congress party told me that the battle for his successor might go on for months. He said Nehru was neglecting his responsibility.

I put the question to the Prime Minister. But I approached the subject somewhat gingerly.

"People say that the greatest part of Gandhi's legacy to India was you," I said. "Now, who is your legacy to India?"

He didn't hesitate a moment.

"Four hundred million people who are capable of selecting a leader for themselves. I am not going to do it for them. It would be insolent of me to do it."

"But suppose they don't have that capacity?"

"They do. Anyway, it is rather depressing to me to believe that everything we have tried to do about preparing people to rule themselves has failed. I don't believe we have failed, at least not in that respect."

"They say—even some of your friends say—that if you fail to designate a successor, the attempt to choose one would tear the country to pieces. They say that all your good work could be undone if you don't train a man to take your place."

"I think we will do all right. I think the country will do quite all right."

At that time it is possible that he was the only man in India who held that view. Today the Indian people know how right he was. They have been able to select a successor, a good man and a wise man. They have been able to do so without upheaval or disintegration. And they have gained in strength because of it. They have vindicated Nehru's confidence in them. They have also justified his highest aspirations. Nehru's death, in a real sense, marks the coming of age of a free and mature India. His legacy is what he wished it to be.

*—June 20, 1964*


# Visit to Gettysburg

From the veranda of General Dwight D. Eisenhower's home you can look out over historic terrain. It is gentle, soothing countryside; the soft, early summer green deepens where it meets a distant stand of trees. Even in an age conditioned to harsh and jarring reconciliations, it is difficult for the mind to sustain the thought that these quiet fields were once the setting for one of the most violent encounters in history. The blood in the earth runs deep at Gettysburg but the eye sees only an enchanted land.

It was the serenity of Gettysburg that attracted General and Mrs. Eisenhower. But the political wars have shattered the stillness. For many weeks now, the battle for a Presidential nomination has rolled into the historic farmhouse. The invaders have the same objective: to capture the favor of a man who has no desire to direct or become enmeshed in partisan political warfare. He came to Gettysburg after forty years as soldier and eight years as President of the United States; he came in retirement and he had a clear idea of what he wanted to do and what he didn't want to do.

"The last thing in the world I wanted to do in my retirement was to try to run a political organization or give orders or pull strings," he said. "Trying to dictate who the man should be who would offer himself to the voters for the most important job in this country is completely out of keeping with what I want to do—or, indeed, what I believe *anyone* has the right to do."

As he spoke, we spied several of his unframed oil paintings on the floor propped up against the wall behind a chair. One of them was of a young boy, a fishing pole on his shoulder, walking down a quiet country road. The tallness of the trees on the sides of the road contrasted with the tininess of the child. Another of his paintings, also unframed, had as its theme a cluster of birch trees. Still another, this one framed and hung near the door leading from the veranda to the living room, was of a large barn, its age showing through the droop of its hanging doors, its flaking shingles, and its faded paint.

"I don't know anything about painting," he said. "Sometimes I work for hours without getting the right shading or texture. For example, the face of the farmer on that canvas against the wall. I just can't seem to get the shadows right on the side of his face. The more I try the worse it gets."

He smiled. "Sometimes I work on a portrait off and on for years without getting it right."

He didn't say so specifically but it seemed clear that he infinitely preferred to work on his paintings than to become enmeshed in political controversy on the basis of personalities.

He reminded us that he was not the standard-bearer for the party in the last election. Even so, people persisted in coming to him, asking him to pronounce judgments or make choices or dictate what ought to be done. He said he was not a king-maker. He didn't believe the party was a one-man affair. One-man rule of anything was obnoxious to him.

One could understand his distaste for political in-fighting. But it was natural, was it not, for the country in general and his party in particular to be interested in his views about the nomination?

It might be natural, but it created difficulties, he said. Some months ago a prominent newspaper reporter came to see him about the political campaign and asked him for his Presidential preference. The General said he wasn't going to sponsor any candidate. This was up to the party. Nor was he going to lobby. His main concern was that the best men make themselves available for the nomination. It was important that the party be in a position to choose from among a number of good men. The reporter then asked him if he thought Henry Cabot Lodge would make a good President. The General thought Ambassador Lodge had excellent qualities and that he would certainly be among the men who deserved consideration by the party.

The story and headline covering this interview made it appear that the General was backing Ambassador Lodge exclusively for the nomination. After he tried to correct the story, people thought he was repudiating Ambassador Lodge. Then he had to try to remedy that. He commented dourly that this was the way it seemed to go. A story created an erroneous impression or it had a misleading emphasis. You try to correct it and the emphasis is so strong in the other direction in the corrected version that that has to be corrected, too. After a while, you feel like giving up.

He gave another example. Recently he spoke to Governor Scranton as part of his effort to persuade as many good men as possible to make themselves available. He urged the Governor not to make things overly difficult for those who wanted to back him openly. In fact, the last thing he said to the Governor as he went out of the door was that he hoped the Governor would be flexible in his idea of what constituted a draft.

Then the story broke in the newspapers that General Eisenhower was now advocating the nomination of Governor Scranton. He tried once again to make it clear he was pushing no candidate in particular but hoped that the best men in the party would make themselves available. As happened before, this was headlined in some newspapers and news broadcasts as a repudiation of Governor Scranton. The thing became hopelessly confused.

We asked the General if he felt the newspapers had properly reported his meeting with Senator Barry Goldwater just before the latter voted negatively on the civil rights bill in the Senate. Didn't the fact that the Senator's announcement of his vote coincided with the account of his visit to Gettysburg create a misleading impression—as though there were some connection between the two events?

"A pertinent question," he replied. "The Senator called on me here to explain his position on the bill. He said he would vote against the bill as a matter of conscience. I said I respected any man who acted out of conscience. I also said my conscience put me in favor of the Civil Rights Bill and that, if I had been a member of Congress, I would have voted for it."

President Eisenhower then recounted the balance of the interview. The Senator said he felt that a few provisions in the bill went too far. General Eisenhower said that this might be possible, but, considering the extent of the deprivations suffered by Americans of darker skin for one hundred years, perhaps the country could afford a pendulum swing just a little bit to the other side. Finally, the General said he disagreed sharply with the Senator on his vote against cloture. Here, too, if he had been active in politics he would have put everything he had behind cloture.

Senator Goldwater told the General that the extended Senate debate had served the purpose of enabling the Senators to learn a great deal. President Eisenhower replied that this might have been true in the early days of discussion but that nothing new had been advanced in the extended days of the debate. In any event, he reiterated he would have opposed Senator Goldwater as strenuously as he could on that issue.

Some people in the Senator's staff gave the story of the meeting to the newspapers. The General was disturbed when he saw the account and the misleading impression it created.

While no one made the mistake of saying that the General endorsed the Senator's position, his own position had not been made clear. He telephoned the Senator and protested what he felt was a misrepresentation. Nothing had been said about the fact that he favored the civil rights legislation. Nothing had been said about cloture. The Senator told the General he was profoundly sorry that the story had been misreported and that he would call the newspapers immediately to set the matter straight.

We asked President Eisenhower if he was satisfied with the correction. He said he hadn't seen all the newspapers but he knew, on the basis of his own experience, that a correction never really caught up with the original. In any event, the matter was of serious concern to him, especially since it was about civil rights.

"A modern political party in a free society should move in only one direction—forward into the future," he said. "When I say I favor the middle of the road, I don't mean that I favor a position so weak it is meaningless. My definition of the political road is all of its usable surface. That is where the road is highest and where the traction is best and where you can bring the most people along with you, as contrasted with the ruts and ditches on the extreme sides."

He added he was concerned about the emphasis on political labels. He saw no hard and fast lines dividing genuine conservatism and genuine liberalism. It was being made to appear these days that there was an irreconcilable gap between the two. There shouldn't be any disagreement between conservatives and liberals on the need to make a better life for human beings. The difference, he said, should be over the means for doing it, not over the need to do it. Unfortunately, now and then the debate went beyond the means to the objectives. He was concerned about the growth of extremism in our political life and the failure to understand what the traditions were that must be conserved.

We asked the General how he reacted several months ago to attempts by various individuals and groups to persuade his brother Milton to become a candidate for the Presidential nomination.

"I'm going to forget the name Eisenhower and speak as objectively as I can," he said. "Milton is a remarkable man. I know few men who have the same genuine qualities of constructive leadership or the same intellectual capacity. Once he starts to speak you respond almost immediately with your confidence in him. Another most remarkable man is Robert Anderson. He not only has a grasp of the most abstruse subjects but he has the ability to transmit that understanding to others. Either one of these men would serve the American people with distinction. Unfortunately, neither is a candidate."

As we squared around in our seat, the leg of our chair brushed against his painting of the little boy walking down the country road. We picked it up again and looked at it. It had an unmistakable quality of openness and ungrudging friendliness.

"Ever since people heard I did some painting, I've received countless requests to donate my pictures," he said. "I haven't done so because I paint for my own pleasure. There's a hospital that's been after me to give them a painting. I'd like to do it, but the precedent would have the effect of making me stop my daubing—and it's fun."

It was late and we got up to leave. Outside, a large orange moon was sitting on the horizon, imparting a soft light to the fields of Gettysburg. Whatever the carrying power of the political battlecries, it was comforting to know that there were some moments, at least, when the stillness returned to Gettysburg and the longing for quietude was met.

*—July 11, 1964*


# Paul Brand and His Mission

Eighty-five miles from Madras, in the crowded southeast of India, history is being made at the missionary medical school and hospital at Vellore. Here battles are being fought and won against the blackest of all human diseases, leprosy. Already dramatic changes in the scientific understanding of leprosy have come about because of the pioneering work done at Vellore by Dr. Paul Brand and his associates. As a result of their brilliant accomplishments, and those of their fellow researchers at leprosy centers throughout the world, this dread disease can today—for the first time in history—be cured outright or brought under effective control by means of surgery and drug therapy.

Throughout history no scourge has been burdened with more superstition and dread than leprosy.

The very word "leper" came, in fact, to carry such connotations of horror and loathsomeness that it has been, as a matter of simple humanity, largely replaced by the more accurate term "leprosy patient or victim," just as the word leprosy has been replaced—to a limited extent—by the term "Hansen's disease." In fact, until recent centuries, to be a "leper" was to be a candidate for expulsion not just from a community but from human sympathy and grace. Fifteen hundred years before Christ "lepers" were cast out of Egypt and forced to live in the "City of Mud." Almost two thousand years later King Philip of France was to incinerate them, using Nero's excuse for persecuting the Christians: they had poisoned the wells of the people. For many centuries, throughout Europe, victims of leprosy were forbidden to enter cities. They were forced to wear gray gowns and to warn people of their approach with

wooden noisemakers. During the day food would be left for them outside the city gates, generally on a hillside; they were permitted to gather
in the food only at night. A healthy person who came into contact with
the afflicted, even though accidentally, was required by law to report this
fact, and would usually be banished.

Chinese records tell of a mandarin in an interior village during the
latter part of the eighteenth century who tricked "lepers" to their doom.
He invited all leprosy victims in the vicinity for a special feast, declaring
they would be permitted to enter the city gates. They came from miles
around. In the middle of the banquet the house was set on fire by order
of the mandarin. A few of those trapped inside managed to escape; as
they emerged from the building they were shot by sentries stationed there
for that purpose by the mandarin.

The name in literature and medicine most prominently associated with
the struggle against leprosy belongs, of course, to Father Damien, the
Belgian Catholic priest who contracted the disease on the island of Molo-
kai in Hawaii while in the service of leprosy victims. Father Damien's
life and work had the effect not just of dramatizing the predicament of
the afflicted but of improving their treatment and conditions of living in
general.

Today leprosy patients are no longer burned or shot, but popular
notions about their disease have changed very little from what they were
in the earliest times. Leprosy is still regarded as more of a curse than an
illness; most people would still react in blind horror and superstition if
informed that a "leper" was about to enter the room.

Even in medicine, where the scientific method is a basic law, knowledge of leprosy has lagged far behind the understanding of other diseases. Indeed, some of the same elements that have gone into the making
of popular fallacies about leprosy victims have not been altogether absent
from some medical discussions or opinions about the disease.

Leprosy—in the middle of the twentieth century—has 14 million sufferers
throughout the world. It cripples more people than all other diseases put
together. Fortunately, the creative work of men like Paul Brand has
opened up the brightest prospect of the almost total extinction of the
disease and its unhappy physical and psychological effects on mankind.

Paul Brand, whose work on leprosy may well give him a place among
history's most honored names in medicine, is a forty-nine-year-old English
orthopedic surgeon, recognized throughout world medical circles for
his work in restoring crippled or paralyzed hands to productive use. His
principal work now is as director of Orthopedic Surgery, Christian Medical College at Vellore.

Paul Brand went to Vellore as a young man in 1947. His wife, Margaret,
also a surgeon, joined him at Vellore a year later. Together they constitute
one of the most remarkable husband-and-wife medical teams in the world

today. Paul Brand has restored to thousands of leprosy patients the use of their hands and arms. Margaret Brand has saved thousands of patients from blindness, some of them leprosy victims, some not. Both of them teach at the medical college, undertake important research, and work at the hospital and in field clinics.

Paul Brand's main purpose in coming to the Christian Medical College and Hospital at Vellore in 1947 was to see whether he might be able to apply his highly developed skills in reconstructive surgery of hands to the special problems of leprosy sufferers. Commonly, the victims' fingers tend to "claw" or partially close up because of the paralysis of vital nerves controlling the muscles of the hand. Paul Brand wanted to try to reactivate the fingers by connecting them to healthy nerve impulses in the forearm. This would require, of course, reeducating the patient so that his brain could transmit orders to the lower forearm, instead of the hand, in order to activate the fingers.

He wasn't at Vellore very long, however, before he realized he couldn't confine himself to problems caused by the claw-like hands of the diseased. He would have to deal with the total problem of leprosy—what it was, how it took hold in the human body, how it might be combated. He immersed himself in research. The more he learned, the greater was his awareness that most of the attitudes toward leprosy he had carried with him to Vellore were outmoded to the point of being medieval. The fact that he had actually reflected the fairly primitive state of existing medical knowledge about the disease didn't ease his determination to pit the scientific method against the old mysteries.

He was to discover that the prevailing ideas about "leprous tissue" were mistaken. Wrong, too, was the notion that the shrinkage or apparent falling off of toes and fingers and the atrophy of the nose were direct products or manifestations of the disease.

As head of Vellore's research section, Paul Brand first needed to find out as much as he could about tissue from the affected parts of his patients. Medicine had long known that leprosy was produced by a bacillus somewhat similar to the organism that causes tuberculosis. This discovery had been made by Gerhard Henrik Hansen almost a century before; the term "Hansen's disease" had eventually become synonymous with leprosy. As in the case of tuberculosis, the *bacillus leprae* produce tubercles. The leprosy tubercles vary in size from a small pea to a large olive. They appear on the face, ears, and bodily extremities. It was commonly thought that the bacillus was also responsible in some way for the apparent disappearance and loss of fingers, toes, hands, and feet that is such a prominent and distressing feature of Hansen's disease. It had, of course, long been known that the disease often caused the bones of the extremities to be absorbed gradually into the body: a victim's fingers might retract and shrink till the fingernails rested against his knuckles. But Dr. Brand was puzzled by those relatively rare but dramatic cases, not explainable by the absorption principle, in which one or more of the extremities disappeared literally overnight. Were such disappearances due to some form of unprecedented, hyper-swift atrophy that struck only by night, overwhelming both bone and tissue?

Very little, Dr. Brand soon found, had been done in the field of leprous-tissue research: could it be that there was something in the flesh of finger stumps and toes that differentiated this tissue from healthy cells? Was the *bacillus leprae* an active agent in the atrophy? Dr. Brand put the pathologists to work. Through research they came up with the startling finding that in terms of the problem at hand, there was no significant difference between healthy tissue and the tissue of a patient's fingers or toes.

One point, however, was scientifically certain: The *bacillus leprae* killed nerve endings. This meant that the delicate sense of touch was missing or seriously injured. But the flesh itself, Dr. Brand ascertained, was in many cases indistinguishable from normal tissue.

As is often the case in medical research, some of Paul Brand's most important discoveries about leprosy came about not as the result of systematic pursuit but through accident. Soon after arriving in Vellore he became aware of the prodigious strength in hands of leprosy patients. Even a casual handshake with them was like putting one's fingers in a vise. Was this because something in the disease released manual strength not known to healthy people?

The answer came one day when Paul Brand was unable to turn a key in a large rusty lock. A leper victim of twelve observed Dr. Brand's difficulty and asked to help. Dr. Brand was astonished at the ease with which the youngster turned the key. He examined the boy's thumb and forefinger of the right hand. The key had cut the flesh to the bone. The boy had been completely unaware of what was happening to his finger while turning the key.

Dr. Brand had his answer at once. The desensitized nerve endings had made it possible for the child to keep turning the key long past the point where a healthy person would have found it painful to continue. Healthy people possess strength they never use precisely because resistant pressure causes pain. A leprosy patient's hands are not more powerful, he reasoned; they just lack the mechanism of pain that would let the patient know when to stop applying pressure. Because of this lack, serious damage could be done to flesh and bone.

Was it possible, Dr. Brand asked himself, that one reason his patients lost fingers and toes was not because of leprosy itself but because they were insensitive to injury? In short, could a person be unaware that, in the ordinary course of a day's activity, he might be subjecting his body to serious physical damage? Paul Brand analyzed all the things he himself did in the course of a day—turning faucets and doorknobs, operating levers, dislodging or pulling or pushing things, using utensils of all kinds. In most of these actions pressure was required. And the amount of pressure was determined both by the resistance of the object and the ability of the fingers and hands to tolerate stress. Lacking the sensitivity, a leprosy victim would, Dr. Brand reasoned, continue to exert pressure even though damage to his hands might be incurred in the process.

He observed the hospital's leprosy patients as they went about their daily tasks and was convinced he was correct. He began to educate them in stress tolerances; he designed special gloves to protect their hands; and he set up daily examinations so that injuries would not lead to ulceration and to disfigurement, as had previously occurred. Almost miraculously, the incidence of new injuries was sharply reduced. The patients became more productive. Paul Brand began to feel he was making basic progress.

Some mysteries, however, persisted. How to account for the occasional but nonetheless puzzling disappearance of fingers, in part or whole? Why was it that every so often parts of fingers would vanish from one day to the next? Were they knocked off? There was nothing to indicate that the bones of leprosy victims were any more brittle than the bones of healthy people. If one of them cut off a finger while using a saw, or if a finger were somehow broken off, it should be possible to produce the missing digit. But no one ever found a finger after it had been lost. Why?

Paul Brand thought about the problem. Then suddenly the answer flashed through his mind. It had to be rats. And it would happen at night while the victims were asleep. Since the hands of the sleepers were desensitized, they wouldn't know they were being attacked and so would put up no resistance.

Paul Brand set up observation posts at night in the huts and wards. It was just as he had thought. The rats climbed onto the beds of their prey, sniffed carefully, and, when they encountered no resistance, went to work on fingers and toes. The fingers hadn't been "dropping off": they were being eaten. This didn't mean that all "lost" fingers had disappeared in this way. They could under exceptional conditions be knocked off through accidents and then carried off by rats or other animals before they might be observed. But a major cause of the disappearance had now been identified.

Paul Brand and his staff went to work in mounting a double-pronged attack against the invaders. The program for rodent control was stepped up many times. Barriers were built around the legs of beds. The beds themselves were raised. The results were immediately apparent. There was a sharp drop in the disappearance of fingers and toes.

All this time Paul Brand kept up his main work—reconstructing hands, rerouting muscles, straightening out fingers. Where fingers were shortened or absent, the remaining digits had to be made fully operative. Thousands of leprosy victims were restored to manual productivity. One of the grim but familiar marks of many leprosy sufferers is the apparent decay of their noses. What caused the shrinkage? It was highly unlikely that the nose suffered from the kind of persistent injury that frequently affected the desensitized hands and feet. What about rats? This, too, seemed unlikely. Enough sensitivity existed in a patient's face, especially around the mouth, to argue strongly against the notion of rodent assault.

As Paul Brand pursued the riddle, he became convinced that neither injuries nor rats were involved. Finally, a brilliant British plastic surgeon, Sir Harold Gillies, came to Vellore and solved the riddle. The shrinkage was due, he hypothesized, to the effect of *bacillus leprae* on the delicate membranes inside the nose. These membranes would contract severely. This meant that the connecting cartilage would be yanked inward. What was happening, therefore, was not decay or loss of nasal structure through injury. The nose was being drawn into the head.

It was a startling theory, running counter to medical ideas that had persisted for centuries. But could it be proved out? The best way of proceeding, Dr. Gillies felt, was to perform surgery that would push the nose back, and make it stand out again from the face. He therefore reconstructed the nose from the inside. It was a revolutionary approach.

Unfortunately, the operation couldn't work in all cases. Where the leprosy was so far advanced that membrane shrinkage left little to work with, it was doubtful that the operation would be successful. But there was a good chance that, in those cases where the disease could be arrested and where the shrinkage was not extreme, noses could be pushed back into place.

Soon it was clear that the revolutionary theory worked well in practice, and following Dr. Gillies's lead Dr. Brand developed modifications of the technique which have proved highly successful. As a result, the nose-restorative operation developed at Vellore has been used for the benefit of large numbers of leprosy patients at hospitals throughout the world.

Next, blindness. Of all the afflictions of Hansen's disease perhaps none is more serious or characteristic than blindness. Here, too, it had been assumed for many centuries that loss of sight was a specific manifestation of advanced leprosy. At Vellore this assumption was severely questioned. Intensive study of the disease convinced Paul Brand and his fellow researchers that blindness was not a direct product of leprosy but a by-product. A serious Vitamin A deficiency, for example, could be a major contributing cause of cataracts, which, left unattended, would often destroy eyesight. Enriching the diets of patients with Vitamin A helped to prevent eye cataracts and consequent blindness. Where cataracts were already formed, it was possible to remove them by surgery, provided that the disease had been stabilized and made quiescent.

It was in this field that Dr. Margaret Brand became especially active and effective. On some days she would perform as many as a hundred cataract operations; many of them on arrested-leprosy cases, but most of them on ordinary patients in no way afflicted with the disease. This number would seem high to the point of absurdity to many European and American eye surgeons, for whom twelve such operations in a single day would be considered formidable. But the eye surgeons at Vellore have to contend with literally thousands of people waiting in line to be saved from blindness. They often work fourteen to sixteen hours a day, using techniques that facilitate rapid surgery.

Dr. Margaret Brand was part of a field medical-and-surgical team that would make regular rounds among villages far removed from the hospital. Surgical tents would be set up. Electricity would be supplied by power-takeoff devices from the jeep motors.

Cataracts, however, were not the whole story in blindness among leprosy patients. Many victims at Vellore didn't suffer from cataracts yet were losing their sight from eye ulcerations. Did the *bacillus leprae* produce the infection and the resultant ulcerations and blindness? Or, as in the case of fingers and toes, was the loss of function a by-product in which other causes had to be identified and eliminated?

The latter line of reasoning proved to be fruitful. Human eyes are constantly exposed to all sorts of irritations and dust and dirt in the air. The eyes deal with these invasions almost without a person being aware of the process. Thousands of times a day the eyelids close and open, washing the surface of the eye with soothing saline fluid released by the tear ducts.

Paul Brand and his colleagues believed this washing process didn't take place in leprosy sufferers because there was a loss of sensation on the eye surface caused by the atrophy of nerve endings. This hypothesis was easily and readily confirmed. They observed the eyes of their patients when subjected to ordinary irritations. There was, as they had suspected, no batting of the eyelids; therefore, there could be no washing process. The big problem, then, was to get the eyelids working again.

Why not educate these patients to make a conscious effort to bat their eyes? There being no impairment of their ability to close eyes at will, it ought to be possible to train them to be diligent in this respect. But the experiments quickly demonstrated the disadvantages of this approach. Unless the patient concentrated on the matter constantly, it wouldn't work. And if he did concentrate, he could think of almost nothing else. No; what was needed was a way of causing eyelid action that would clean the eyes automatically.

In the case of fingers or toes, it was possible to educate leprosy victims in stress tolerances and to give them protective gloves or shoes. How to keep dirt and foreign objects from getting into the eye? Eye goggles might be one answer but they were not airtight, were cumbersome, would fog up because of the high humidity, and were too easily lost. Something more basic would have to be found.

The answer, again, was found in reconstructive surgery. Paul Brand and his team devised a way of hooking up the muscles of the jaw to the eyelid. Every time the patient opened his mouth, the new facial muscles would pull the eyelids and cause them to close, thus washing the eyeball. In this way he could literally talk and eat his way out of oncoming blindness. Countless numbers of patients have their sight today because of this ingenious use of surgery in facilitating the use of nature's mechanism to get rid of dirt and dust in the eyes.

Gradually, as the result of research at Vellore and other leprosy centers throughout the world, the terrible black superstition about leprosy is receding. Contrary to popular impression, leprosy is not highly contagious. In fact, it is virtually impossible to transmit Hansen's disease to a healthy person. As with tuberculosis, of course, persons in weakened condition are vulnerable in varying degrees. The disease is not hereditary; again, however, as with other diseases, increased susceptibility can be passed along from parent to child.

Basically, leprosy is the product of filth, poverty, and malnutrition. It is not, as is generally supposed, a disease of the tropics and subtropics. It can exist wherever unsanitary conditions, hunger, or poorly balanced diet exist. It has occurred in countries as far north as Iceland. Scarcely a country in the world has been untouched by it. But the important thing is that it is eradicable, and its victims can be cured or appreciably helped and rehabilitated. And today it can once and for all be rescued from the general ignorance and associated superstitions assigned to it over the ages.

Medical researchers have given high recognition to Dr. Brand and his colleagues for their new insights into the nature of leprosy, but even greater accolades within the profession have come his way because of his work in rehabilitative surgery. He has been able to transform hands, long clawed and rigid because of nerve atrophy brought on by leprosy or other causes, into functioning mechanisms. Almost legendary in India is a case of a lawyer on whom he operated. For many years the lawyer had been at a disadvantage in court. His gestures, so essential a part of the dramatic courtroom manner, were actually a liability; judge and jury were distracted by his hideously deformed and "frozen" hand. Then one day the lawyer raised his hand to emphasize a point. The hand was supple, the fingers moved, the gesture was appropriate. Paul Brand had operated on the hand, hooking up muscle and nerve connections to the forearm, then educating the patient to retrain his command impulses.

Paul Brand and his staff have performed thousands of similar operations on patients at Vellore. But they have also gone far beyond surgery into what they consider an even more vital phase of the total treatment.

This is psychological rehabilitation. A man who, afflicted with leprosy, has been a beggar for twenty years is not considered to be fully treated at Vellore until he is mentally and physically prepared to be a useful and proud citizen in his society. At Vellore handicapped patients are given the kind of training that will enable them to be as self-supporting as possible. They gain a respect for the limitless potentialities and adaptabilities of the human organism. They learn that even as low as 10 per cent mobility can be made to yield a high return in terms of effective productivity. And, in the Emersonian sense, self-reliance creates self-respect.

It is not necessary, of course, to provide any precise assessment of the relative importance of the three main phases of Paul Brand's work— taking the black curse and superstition out of leprosy, reconstructive surgery, and personal and psychological rehabilitation. All are important; all are interrelated. But one aspect of his work may perhaps be more evocative and compelling than any of the others. He is a doctor who, if he could, would move heaven and earth just to return the gift of pain to people who do not have it. For pain is both the warning system and the protective mechanism that enable an individual to defend the integrity of his body. Its signals may not always be readily intelligible but at least they are there. And the individual can mobilize his response.

For the millions of Hansen's disease patients in the world today whose lack of pain places them in mortal jeopardy, Paul Brand and his colleagues are doing everything they can to provide substitute warning systems. Eventually, if their progress continues, they will master the phenomenon of pain and the ultimate good therein.

*—October 3, 1964*

# China and the Bomb

A situation long dreaded has now materialized. China is producing atomic weapons. A nation whose foreign policy is based on the inevitability of war now knows how to make the explosives that could devastate a planet. We are well into the age of world nuclear proliferation.

American newspaper coverage of China's atomic test has given prominent attention to Secretary Rusk's prediction that it will be some years before Communist China will become a major nuclear power. Unfortunately, press and public seem to have drawn more reassurance from this statement than Mr. Rusk may have intended. The danger is a critical one for the world even though it may not mature for a few years. The essential question is not whether it will take China five or fifteen years to develop the means of destroying any nation on earth. The question rather is what do we do *now* by way of meeting or reducing that danger? What ideas or plans do we have *today* that we can put to work before the point of maximum peril is reached? Assuming we could find some way of getting through to the Chinese people, what would we say to them? A breathing spell is not quite the same as a plan for purposeful survival. A policy based on deferred danger can be acquiescence in a perilous drift. In sum, there is precious little reassurance and even less nourishment in the probability that Chinese nuclear strength will not peak for a few years.

One policy, easy to advance and even easier to cling to, is a policy based on nuclear superiority. This policy is not good enough. We may have ten thousand times the atomic power of China ten years from now, but this in itself is no assurance of security. The critical factor may be represented not by the comparative size of American and Chinese stock piles but by the political and ideological leverage China possesses as the result of her nuclear capability. China's strategic exploitation of her nuclear muscle may be more significant in the long run than any specific atomic potency. Even in purely military terms, however, it is not necessary for China to equal or come remotely close to the size and might of American nuclear striking power in order to become a fearsome nuclear threat. It takes only a certain number of bombs to devastate a nation. The fact that we may have more than enough nuclear explosives to shatter every conceivable enemy several times over may be more impressive to us than it is to the Chinese, whose reckoning may be based on the number of bombs required to destroy their enemies just once rather than ten times over—or 500 times over. Overkill capacity, like a big paunch, may be comfortable to contemplate but may have limited practical application and it tends to get in the way. Instead of counting our bombs, we ought to be counting our ideas.

A second policy that will not work is the notion that we can achieve security by threatening overwhelming retaliation if the Chinese should make any misstep in our direction. It is naïve to suppose that a potential enemy would not already have taken this ultimatum into account. It is even more naïve to believe that the response of the potential enemy will not be to issue an even sterner atomic ultimatum of his own. Nor can we proceed on the assumption that all sides concerned can be counted upon to draw back if a crisis should bring them to a point of nuclear confrontation. It may be well to recall that one of the main items in the Chinese indictment of Nikita Khrushchev was that he backed down in Cuba. The Chinese contended that the Americans would never have dared to go to war over Cuba. Mr. Khrushchev, they said, was an appeaser. The Chinese were wrong about the United States, and it is possible we may be equally wrong about them if our policy is based on the assumption that they will draw back from the nuclear brink in any crisis involving what they think are their national or ideological interests.

A third policy that is not likely to work is that of stoical and fixed indifference to the existence of the Communist Chinese. If President Kennedy was right when he said that we must end the arms race before the arms race ends the human race, then we must face the fact that China is now part—and an ominous part—of the atomic arms race. There is no point in pursuing agreements on arms reduction or limitation with the Russians or anyone else if the Chinese are free to go their own way. It is possible that the Chinese leaders would resist any efforts looking toward comprehensive and workable world disarmament so long as they are committed to the idea that war is inherent in the nature of capitalism. But this fact, if it is a fact, does not mean that all possible pressure should not be brought to bear on the Chinese directly or that we should make no attempt to mobilize world public opinion as an integral part of any thrust toward world nuclear control. I don't see why we should be afraid to talk to the Chinese about workable disarmament or anything else. The prospects of such an exchange are less consequential than the gain that will accrue to us when we stop our shadow-boxing and deal with things as they are.

It would be a grave error, however, to suppose that all problems will be resolved if only the Americans agree to talk to the Chinese—assuming, of course, that the Chinese would be willing to talk to the Americans. A dialogue on matters of substance between these two major powers would represent an advance over the present situation; ultimately, however, enduring world peace requires a grand design—a design broad enough to accommodate diversity but strong enough to keep possibly obstructive or rambunctious elements of that diversity from tearing down the house. In short, peace calls for more than a détente or even live-and-let-live agreements between political enemies. It calls for a world organization capable of sustaining universal membership and strong enough to pierce the national sovereignty barrier in those matters of common danger and concern to the people who inhabit this earth. Man in his corporate identity comes before the nation. If this sounds revolutionary, place the blame on those who gave the idea its most powerful impetus—men such as Jefferson, Madison, Hamilton, Rousseau, Milton, John Stuart Mill.

The most effective policy that the United States can adopt toward the Chinese, therefore, is to make the cause of a strong United Nations the fundamental objective of our foreign policy. China's threat to world peace is reduced in direct proportion to the development of the United Nations —not just as an effective peace-keeping mechanism but as a repository of the hopes of people everywhere for a better world.

Are we expecting too much of the United Nations? We are if we think that the UN should tag along as a secondary factor in world affairs. But if we have a concept of the UN as a source of workable world law and justice, then our expectations are not excessive. Obviously, such a UN will not come into being overnight. But at least the acceptance of world law as the objective creates a positive momentum even as it establishes a new context for international affairs.

As it concerns China's relationship to the United Nations, it is possible that the debate over Chinese admission to the UN has missed the real point. The real question is not whether China should come into the UN but rather what kind of UN China should come into. World momentum for making the UN a universal body is growing. At some point, perhaps soon, there will be a decision for including China. That is why it is all the more important that no time be lost in equipping the UN with the kind of structure and authority adequate to universal membership. This clearly means a buildup of responsible and balanced authority in the UN.

It is not reasonable to suppose that China would constitute more of a threat inside such a strengthened UN than it would outside it. In any event, the UN is the proper forum for the pursuit of all vital issues concerning the peace—whether with respect to disarmament, peace-keeping machinery, aid programs, or resource development.

All these ventures take time. They require planning, special effort, moral imagination. If we have a respite of a few years, the time to start moving is now.

*—November 28, 1964*


# Winston Churchill and the Human Potential

What is it that is most significant about the response to Churchill's death? Is it the size and depth of the outpouring of acclaim and grief? This is not what is most significant. Several times during the twentieth century—most notably following the deaths of Franklin D. Roosevelt, Mahatma Gandhi, Pope John XXIII, John F. Kennedy, Jawarharlal Nehru—there have been world-wide demonstrations of loss deeply felt. What is most significant about the response to Churchill's death is the reflection in it of the changes he created in the people he reached. In speaking to the strength inside people, he caused that strength to come into being.

The human potential is the most magical but also most elusive fact of life. Men suffer less from hunger or dread than from living under their moral capacity. The atrophy of spirit that most men know and all men fear is tied not so much to deprivation or abuse as it is to their inability to make real the best that liest within them. Defeat begins more with a blur in the vision of what is humanly possible than with the appearance of ogres in the path or a hell beyond the next turning. Because of Winston

Churchill, millions of people discovered their ability to live more fully. They knew they faced total danger, but he helped them to find their capacity for total response. They also learned it was far less painful to pit the whole of themselves against a monstrous force than it was to sit on the sidelines half alive. And the beginning of the end of the Hitlerian nightmare came not when the Nazi military juggernaut was at last slowed down but when free men became unblocked inside, when they stopped equivocating about values, when they put aside relativistic notions of good and evil, and when they came to respect the rights of generations yet unborn. In the presence of greatness, they lost what they most needed losing, their cynicism and awkwardness. It was not rhetoric alone that enabled them to do this. It was the recognition the rhetoric gave them that history was what men made it.

Courage to him was more than a spirited charge into a hurricane of flying bullets. It was a wondrous human assortment—hearty laughter, warm feelings, and the enjoyment of living in general. The ability to feel fully alive was to be seen not solely in terms of a full adrenalin response to danger but in comprehending the creative possibilities that come with the gift of life. There was nothing freakish about versatility; what was unnatural, rather, was the man who permitted himself to develop in only a single direction. The highest privilege was the freedom to choose; the meanest affliction was to live without option. He gave options to a world quickly running out of time and space.

In all the acclaim accorded Winston Churchill, little has been said about his impact on the philosophy of his time. Yet one of his most profound contributions to his age was the evidence he offered that men are not at the mercy of historical determinism, that they do not need to worship their helplessness, as has happened occasionally under existentialism. Churchill stands in the great tradition of Franklin–Holmes–James in the proof he offers that the uniqueness of man is represented by his ability to reverse old forces and create new ones. Churchill claimed he did no more than to sound the roar. He did much more. He shattered the notion of a philosophical or political inevitability. In so doing he gave reality to freedom and nobility to reality.

All this was possible in Churchill not because of his courage alone, or because of his knowledge of the human potential and how to reach it, but because he could look beyond causes to their consequences. He had a highly developed sense for the anticipation of crisis. He was a superb politician but he had none of the average politician's fear of identifying an unpleasant fact or of calling for sacrifice. In an atomic age the only thing greater than the danger is the propensity for drift. The most cherished national possession is the lull.

The consequences will be averted not by any abstract belief that justice and the good, if left to themselves, automatically triumph in the end, but by the energies and actions of enough men who, like Churchill, believe in their capacity to do the impossible.

—*February 6, 1965*

# Vietnam and the American Conscience

Vietnam is profoundly complex, but it is not so complex as to defeat the American intelligence or disable the American conscience. Some facts and implications are clear, no matter how murky the general situation.

The first fact is that the United States today needs far greater support from the Vietnamese people in whose name it went into Vietnam in the first place and whom it is seeking to save today. The United States military forces have had to cope not just with secret agents from North Vietnam but with the growing opposition of the populace as a whole. In briefings of new U.S. military personnel, the point is stressed that most Vietnamese are either sympathizers with or secret members of the Vietcong. The retaliatory bombings by the United States of North Vietnam targets do not meet the problem represented by internal opposition within South Vietnam itself.

The second fact is that most of the military equipment used against American and South Vietnam military forces has come neither from Communist China nor North Vietnam but from the United States. It is ludicrous to talk about bombing supply lines from North Vietnam as a means of shutting off the flow. According to some estimates, up to 80 per cent of the military equipment used by the Vietcong originates in the U.S. In largest part, it is either captured by the Vietcong or turned over by supposedly loyal South Vietnamese. No one knows how much of the equipment finds its way to Communist China. A Chinese official interviewed in Peking several months ago said he was almost reluctant to see the Americans leave; they had contributed so heavily to the Chinese arsenal.

The third fact is that the legal justification invoked by the United States for its involvement in Vietnam has long since been nullified. Under the terms of the 1954 Geneva Agreement, all foreign forces and military equipment were to stay out of Indo-China. The United States came with military force into Indo-China, most notably in Laos, South Vietnam, and Thailand, declaring it had done so at the request of the governments involved, which was not a violation of the treaty. But nothing in the treaty gave the United States the right to finance revolutionary movements or to participate in undercover subversion. (In Laos in 1960 and 1961, the United States financed and equipped the effort of General

Phoumi Nosavan to overthrow the only elected government in the history of Laos. At the same time, the U.S. continued to pay the salaries of loyalist forces and to furnish their supplies. Thus the United States was in the astonishing position of underwriting both sides of a civil war. Eventually, the situation was restored to its pre-revolutionary status, but only after many thousands of civilians were killed or became homeless.)

In South Vietnam, the inability of the Diem government to maintain the support of its own people constituted a severe drag on the war effort. Eventually, the Diem government was overthrown and the Premier assassinated. Later, Frederick E. Nolting, Jr., former Ambassador to South Vietnam, said the United States had been directly involved in the anti-government plot. Whether Premier Diem was or was not authoritarian and backward is beside the point; the American people have never given their government a warrant to engage in subversion or murder. Since Diem, regimes in South Vietnam have come and gone; which of them has enjoyed genuine legitimacy it is difficult to say. In any case, what is the legal basis for our presence now? Our presence was requested by a government no longer in existence, and one that our own ex-Ambassador said we helped to overthrow.

The fourth fact is that our policy in Vietnam in particular and Asia in general has not been of a piece. Basically, an important objective of our foreign policy is to keep the Soviet Union and Communist China from coming together in a unified and massive ideological and military coalition. But our policy in Vietnam is producing exactly the effect we seek to avoid. Nothing that has happened since the original rupture between the two major Communist powers has done more to bring the Soviet Union and Communist China together again than recent American actions in Vietnam. The Communist Chinese have long argued that the Russian idea of coexistence was an anti-Marxist and antihistorical notion that could only be advanced by naïve sentimentalists. They claim war is inevitable because of the nature of capitalism. As evidence, they assert that the United States, despite its claim that it sought only to promote the internal stability of Indo-China, was actually pursuing a war against Asian peoples as an extension of the very imperialism Asians had fought so hard to expel. The Soviet Union, which is no less concerned than the United States about Chinese expansion throughout Asia, also has to be concerned about its standing in the world Communist community. It cannot allow itself to appear indifferent to military action involving a member of that community. Any expansion of the war by the United States into North Vietnam would force the Soviet Union to identify itself with North Vietnam and thus with China. In any event, in pursuit of one goal the United States appears to be losing a larger one. If the Communist Chinese had deliberately set a trap for the United States, they could not have more effectively achieved the result they sought.

The fifth fact is that American newsmen have had a more difficult time in getting unmanipulated news out of Vietnam than out of almost any crisis center in recent years. James Reston, associate editor of *The New York Times*, testifying before a Congressional investigating committee in 1963, said the news in Vietnam was being managed in a way inconsistent with the traditions 'of this society. In the past two years there has been some improvement in news policy on Vietnam but the American public has yet to be fully informed about the nature of the American involvement, the degree to which U.S. arms have been sustaining the attackers, the extent of the popular opposition, and the inability of the South Vietnam government to mount an effective response against the guerrillas.

The sixth fact is that President Johnson has genuinely tried to keep the military lid on in Vietnam, recognizing the ease with which the hostilities could mushroom into a general war; but he has been under extravagant pressure, much of it political, to translate American military power into a dramatic solution. The national frustration about Vietnam has far exceeded the national comprehension of the problem, for much of which the government has only itself to blame. In any event, there has been comparatively little counter-pressure in support of a policy of restraint and an eventual nonmilitary settlement—a failing that the American people have it within their means to change whenever they wish to do so.

The United States is concerned, and properly so, that the loss of South Vietnam would lead to grave consequences—territorial, political, psychological—throughout Asia and indeed most of the world. Already, the fact of developing atomic power in China has made a deep impression on many nations whose histories have pitted them against Western outsiders. American policy-makers fear that U.S. withdrawal from Vietnam or even a reluctance to press the war would weaken or destroy the image of the United States as a resolute, dependable, and successful foe of aggressive communism in the world. These are not illogical or nonhistorical fears, but it is equally logical and historical to raise questions about the damaged image of the United States that is emerging from the present actions in Vietnam. There has been an outpouring of anti-American sentiment not just in Asia but throughout the world—and it would be a mistake to charge it all to Communist manipulation or propaganda. Even among our friends in France, Great Britain, and West Germany there has been a sense of shock and outrage. If we thought we were building prestige by taking to the air and dropping bombs in Vietnam, we have built strangely indeed.

It is tragic that most of the debate over Vietnam has vibrated between total war and total withdrawal. It is made to appear that the only choice is between absolute victory and absolute defeat. There *is* an alternative—

if our main objective is to promote the stability and security of the area. And that alternative is to involve the United Nations, with all its limitations, to the fullest possible extent. Any general war growing out of the combustibles in Vietnam would bring catastrophe to most of the world's peoples. On the principle of no-extermination-without-representation, they have a right to ask that they be consulted now, while there may yet be time.

The situation in Vietnam is far more complicated than it was in Korea, but no one can say that no good can come out of a UN effort similar to the one existing in Korea. Korea has had numerous truce violations and difficulties, but because of the UN, Korea at least is not aflame today. Secretary General U Thant has provided an opening for such an effort by calling not just for restraint but for "shifting the quest for a solution away from the field of battle to the conference table." To the extent that the United Nations could be brought into this quest, the chances for a constructive outcome will be increased.

There are no easy answers to Vietnam. But some answers may be less volatile and more morally imaginative than others. Moreover, at some time soon the United States will have to recognize that a military policy without a full ideological and social program will not only fall short of its goal but may actually boomerang. In any case, the prospect for finding a workable answer to Vietnam will increase, not decrease, in direct proportion to the unblocking of an American conscience and the activation of an informed debate.

*—February 27, 1965*


## Double Jeopardy: UN and Vietnam

The United States pressed for a showdown in the recent session of the United Nations General Assembly against states that hadn't met their payments for the peace-keeping operations of the UN. The United States argued that it was not for individual nations to determine whether assessments were unreasonable and improper. They were obligated to support the UN whether they liked it or not. France and the Soviet Union didn't like it. Desperate attempts to find a formula for averting an ominous confrontation all failed. The General Assembly adjourned in the deepest gloom it has known since 1945.

It might be argued that the United States didn't take into account the fact that a showdown could be far less damaging to the Soviet Union in particular than to the United Nations in general. As against this was the need to gain acceptance for the principle of compulsory obligations in matters concerned with keeping the peace. In the sense that the development of a higher sovereignty for preserving the peace is the largest single challenge of the twentieth century, a defense can be made for the American position on assessments.

But the American argument for supporting the authority of the United Nations was negated only a few days later by the United States itself when it spurned the call by Secretary General U Thant for a conference looking toward an effective resolution of the war crisis in Vietnam. The principle we sought to uphold against the Soviet Union and France we set aside when our own interests were directly involved. Is it argued that the two cases are not similar? That the first case involved financial obligations and the second a situation in which the United States was already committed to a fixed course of action? The underlying principle in both cases has to do with the primacy of the UN in dealing with threats to world peace. The action in Suez and the Congo, which produced the financial crisis, was carried out in the interests of world peace. The action of the Secretary General in calling for a conference over Vietnam was advanced in the interests of world peace. It is difficult to assert that the UN enjoys supranational status in fixing dues for peace-keeping operations while downgrading the role of the UN in peace-keeping itself.

Perhaps it will be said that the UN had no effective way of acting in Vietnam since not all parties to the dispute were members of the UN. But the point at issue here is not whether the UN could or could not have been effective in mounting an armed action in Vietnam similar to its action in Korea or Suez or the Congo. What the UN tried to do was to initiate negotiations in a situation fast spiraling into a large-scale war. The United States declined U Thant's request with thanks. It was almost as though we were sending regrets for our inability to accept an invitation to a ball.

If France and the Soviet Union seemed cavalier in their attitude toward the United Nations, the attitude of the United States verged on condescension. One would suppose by this time that the United Nations does not exist for the purpose of making polite inquiries to concerned parties in questions of war and peace but for the hard and impersonal purpose of keeping this planet from atomic incineration.

Sooner or later the American people are going to have to make up their mind about what they want their government's position on the United Nations to be. So far, our position on the UN has been to give it full backing—up to the point where it impinges on the basic thrust of our foreign policy. Essentially, the UN has not been primary in our foreign policy. Primary elements include our nuclear stockpiles, our bases, NATO, SEATO, and our direct presence in various countries.

But if Vietnam has taught us anything, it is that the old policy of alliances, stockpiles, and bulging muscles is no longer the prime or workable instrument it was in the pre-atomic world of disconnected national units. NATO hasn't worked in Europe. SEATO hasn't worked in Indo-China. Raw force hasn't worked in Vietnam, either for France or the United States. But our response to the new facts of life is to put more of the unworkables to work instead of making a total commitment to the development of a collective mechanism for creating workable world law.

It is not solely geography that is interconnected in an atomic age. Actions are interconnected. We are pursuing a policy in Vietnam without regard to the effects on other elements bearing on our total security. The whole effort to keep the Soviet Union and Communist China from coming together in a vast military coalition; the need to keep the nations of Africa and Asia from veering toward Communist China; the need to keep a world organization competitive with the UN from being formed with Peking at the center; the need to create conditions that will make possible increasing control over the highly combustible nuclear arms race—all these are interconnected; all are affected adversely by the decision to spurn the good offices of the UN in Vietnam.

Equally important but largely disregarded is the connection between Saigon and Selma. Until President Johnson spoke before Congress last week, it was becoming increasingly difficult for Americans to explain to themselves or anyone else the contrast represented by the resolute policy of the United States in putting down disorders in Vietnam while observing zealous circumspection in Alabama. The President did honor to himself and the nation in recognizing the role of the U.S. in the Selmas of the South. He will do equal honor to the nation and the hopes for world peace in recognizing the role of the UN in the Vietnams of the world.

*—March 27, 1965*

# How to Lose the World

In the aftermath of the poison-gas episode in Vietnam, one fact at least may be worth pondering. The decision to use gas was made without the knowledge of either the President or the State Department. It is to President Johnson's credit that he did not feel obligated to close ranks and endorse an action that, whatever the military argument, was wicked, incompetent, and prejudicial to the vital interests of the United States. The action was news to him and he said so.

Inevitably and forcibly, hard questions flow out of these events. How much scope now exists for important decision-making outside the top councils of government? Was the decision to use gas in Vietnam a wild and isolated abuse of authority in the field? Or has a pattern slowly been emerging that is only now partially visible? It has just been revealed that undercover agents of the U.S. Government several years ago secretly adulterated a large shipment of sugar en route to the Soviet Union. President Kennedy learned of this sabotage and was able to intercept the cargo and undo the damage. Even more ominous is the charge made by Frederick E. Nolting, Jr., former U.S. Ambassador to Vietnam, that the United States was directly involved in the subversion and overthrow of the South Vietnam government in 1963 that resulted in the murder of President Ngo Dinh Diem. The fact that this charge has not been publicly examined or investigated is no less disturbing that the charge itself. If the charge is true, was it a field decision? Did the President know of it only after the event?

What about the degree of involvement by the United States in the attempt to overthrow the constitutionally elected Laotian government of Souvanna Phouma in 1960? This action precipitated a civil war, with the United States in the astounding position of underwriting both armies. What is the responsibility of American citizens for the deaths of thousands of human beings in Laos during that phase of the war? Had the President been consulted? Either way, when and how did it become the business of men acting for the United States to engage in sabotage and subversion?

Is it felt that the only way to cope with totalitarian and revolutionary world forces is to maintain undercover operations of our own, with power to unhinge governments or otherwise engage in secret mischief, or to turn over to the military substantial autonomy of decision in matters affecting the position of the United States in the world? If so, we badly misread history. It is impossible to find men wise enough to be entrusted with that kind of power. Such power engulfs men and makes decisions of its own.

What is most ironic is that the United States Government was itself designed by thinkers who knew that men and raw power don't go together. This to them was the most important lesson in history. The Philadelphia Constitutional Convention was an exercise in the control and distribution of power. More than any collective undertaking in history, that convention tried to create a structure of government in which even the best men would be kept separated from power that could be used capriciously or willfully and therefore dangerously. The best way to protect citizens against abuses of power by men in government was to circumscribe the power, define it, refine it, subordinate it to law and due process. This design was good enough to create a system of government that has been in continuous operation longer than any other in the world.

The notion that we can best cope with threats to our security or to world security by setting up vast cloak-and-dagger operations, or by creating authority outside the framework of the constitutional government, is itself a threat to the freedom of the American people. We cannot engage in subversion abroad without subverting the history and institutions of the United States.

There is something far more menacing to the United States than any lack of undercover power or restrictions on the policy-making powers of our agencies, military or otherwise. What is most menacing of all is the lack of respect for the moral principles that affect our station in the world. What the world's peoples think about the United States is in the end the most important factor affecting our world leadership capabilities and our security. Why should it have been necessary for Michael Stewart, British Foreign Secretary, to remind the United States that "a decent respect for the opinions of mankind" should have precluded the use of chemical weapons in Vietnam? How is it possible that government officials, if *The New York Times*'s report is correct, were "surprised" by the world outrage which followed the disclosure that the United States was using gas, however "routine" or "benevolent," as the official description had it? The kind of detachment from reality represented by this insensitivity is itself a clear and present danger. Has Communist propaganda against the United States done anything to hurt us as much as the harm we do to ourselves, as in the use of gas in Vietnam?

These things have not happened overnight. They have come into being piece by piece over a period of years. It is a denial of their own responsibility for the American people to expect that a President, upon coming into office, can deal with these problems by a single speech or stroke of the pen. The kind of power he is now called upon to tame requires all the help he can get. This means public opinion. This is the way America works, if we want it to work.

*—April 10, 1965*

# The No. 1 Crisis

A crisis even more dangerous than Vietnam or the Dominican Republic is threatening the peace of the world. It is the crisis of the United Nations. The UN lacks funds. It lacks means. But, most serious of all, it lacks centrality in the foreign policies of the major nations—the U.S. included.

In explaining American policy on Vietnam, for example, the President said the United States had gone into Vietnam with force to keep the peace because "there was no one else to do it." The United Nations was not even mentioned.

Twenty years ago, at San Francisco, the United Nations was founded for the express purpose of keeping world peace. It has been a turbulent twenty years, but if it hadn't been for the United Nations, the world might have slid into another great war—a war in which all the destructive genius of the human race would have been brought into play.

## The UN in Korea

In 1950, the United States called upon the United Nations to halt the Communist aggression against South Korea. The United Nations responded. The Communists were pushed back to the original boundaries. The truce in Korea today is an uneasy truce, but at least it is a truce. United Nations forces superintend the truce today, investigate border violations, put out the sparks.

## The UN in Suez

In 1956, world war threatened as the result of the British and French invasion of Suez. President Eisenhower recognized that British and French interests in the Suez Canal were in jeopardy, but he also recognized that nothing is more dangerous in a nuclear age than unilateral military action. He declared that the United States could not maintain a double standard; we could not condone action in our friends that we condemned in our foes. He said no principle was more vital to the safety of the human race today than the principle of world law, and he supported action by the United Nations in halting the war in Egypt and in maintaining UN police action to prevent a resumption.

Since 1949, the UN has supervised the truce between Israel and her Arab neighbors and has kept violent incidents from erupting into full-scale conflict.

## The UN in the Congo

In 1960, following the departure of the Belgians and the achievement of full independence by the Congo, bitter internal fighting developed. Many nations, including the United States, felt that the internal upheavals of the Congo could lead to major war. The United States called upon the United Nations to pacify the Congo and to take military action against dissident forces. The United Nations undertook what turned out to be the most difficult assignment in its history. But it succeeded in putting an end to the war in the Congo. Equally important, it helped train Congolese to run their own government, operate their own schools and hospitals, maintain communications, build roads, develop their own resources. Again, the ordeal of the Congo is far from over, but at least the spark has been checked.

*The UN and the U.S.*

Two highly combustible danger zones have flared into open conflict— Vietnam and the Dominican Republic. The United States has declared that both situations represent threats to the peace.

The United Nations, which was created to keep the peace, has had no role in either Vietnam or the Dominican Republic. The United States has opposed such a UN role—despite U.S. commitments to the UN as the one agency with peace-keeping responsibility.

True, in the case of Vietnam, a direct role by the United Nations similar to its role in Korea or the Congo might have been impossible because of the direct confrontation of the major powers in the area, one of which was Communist China, which does not belong to the UN.

But the United Nations might have been able, and might still be able, to play a *useful role in Vietnam by using its good offices to arrange a cease-fire and bring about negotiations.*

The United States not only spurned the good offices of the UN in Vietnam but one of its State Department officials publicly criticized the United Nations Secretary General, who was performing his clear duty— to use the United Nations to the fullest to prevent threats to the peace from developing into major war.

In the case of the Dominican Republic, the United States intervened with force when a group attempted to restore the constitutionally elected government that had previously been overthrown in a military coup. If a genuine threat to the peace was involved in the uprising, how does the U.S. justify ignoring the UN altogether, despite our clear obligations under the Charter not to act unilaterally? (Even on the basis of regional arrangements, how do we justify acting first and calling in the Organization of American States afterwards?) And if a general threat to the peace was not involved, how do we justify intervening in the internal affairs of another nation?

In either case, is it United States policy to apply the Monroe Doctrine against the United Nations? Are we saying to the world, in effect, that the United Nations must stay out of the Western Hemisphere? Do we say that the purposes, functions, and operations of the UN are not to be considered as applying to the Americas? If this is not our intention, how do we propose to reassure the world on this point? And if we interpret the section of the Charter referring to regional arrangements as authorization for military intervention, then what is there to prevent the entire world from being fenced off into regional military spheres, with large nations openly dominating vast areas, by military or other means? One of our main reasons for going into Southeast Asia in general and Vietnam in particular was to keep the entire area from being dominated by Communist China. Yet by upholding a regional unilateral role for ourselves in the Dominican Republic we define a role for Communist China in Asia and contradict the basis for our own presence there.

The impression grows that American foreign policy lacks a clear and unifying principle and contains more elements of improvisation than the security of the nation can afford or the safety of the world can sustain. And if it should be said that such a unifying principle does in fact exist and is represented by our determination to resist and throw back any advance by communism, the reply must be that this policy has not been singularly successful. The bombing of North Vietnam has actually had the effect of strengthening popular opposition to the United States; the attacks of the Vietcong have been stepped up; and Communists throughout the world have been given a propaganda weapon against us more potent than any they have employed so far. And, while the situation in the Dominican Republic is vastly better than it was a few weeks ago, the effect of our military intervention in the rest of Latin America, according to competent observers, has been to enlarge the role of Communist leaders as champions of national independence and as hate agents against the United States.

The struggle against world communism will be difficult and largely meaningless until we translate democracy into a clearly understood and dramatic ideology that ties individual liberty, national independence, and social justice together into a coherent and workable whole. And we will never have a truly unifying principle for our foreign policy until we define, pursue, and advance the principle of world law through the United Nations.

The twentieth anniversary ceremonies of the United Nations in San Francisco provide President Johnson with a magnificent opportunity not just to restore American hopes in the UN but to redefine our foreign policy with the United Nations as the major element. The full weight of this country should be put into a world-wide effort to save the UN and make it relevant and effective in those matters concerned with the common safety and betterment of the world's peoples.

*—June 19, 1965*

# Memories of A. E. S.

It was during the 1952 Presidential campaign and it happened in Springfield, Illinois. He had been nominated barely a week when a regiment of pressure-packed lobbyists zeroed in, brandishing their special-interest voting power. The freshly assembled team of Stevenson aides, many of them new to national politics, adroitly sheltered their chief without unduly antagonizing the wheeler-dealers. But there arrived on the scene one of the most powerful politicos in the Texas Democratic party. He sought Stevenson's support for private ownership of offshore oil rights.

Clearly, this was one case where a direct meeting with the candidate couldn't be averted. Texas was the key to the Southern vote. Stevenson met alone with the Texas politico. Meanwhile, the Governor's aides, glum and apprehensive, maintained a vigil in the adjoining office, every now and then sending in a note suggesting some special angle or idea for compromise.

After about two hours the Texas politico was the first to emerge. He stared straight ahead, walked directly to his car, and drove off. Stevenson came out, serene and grinning.

"It must have been pretty tough in there," someone said. "What did you work out?"

"Oh, it wasn't so tough," Stevenson said. "I didn't have to work out anything."

"What happened?"

"I just tried to make him see that a man doesn't try to be President just to give away the resources of the American people."

"Did you convince him?"

"I don't know. Anyway, I gave him something to think about."

This was what really counted with Stevenson. There was a measure of victory even in defeat if he could give people something to think about. The test of freedom to him was not the number of people who had unhampered movement but the number of people who had capacity for abstract thought.

Some months after his 1952 defeat in the national elections he was asked if he didn't think it was almost foolhardy for any Democrat to try to win against General Eisenhower, the nation's number-one military hero and a man of phenomenal popular appeal. He admitted that this was probably true, but he believed that a Presidential campaign offered too good an opportunity to talk to the American people to pass up. Win or lose, running for the White House provided the most magnificent access on earth to millions of human minds. And anyone who believed as deeply as he did in the educational process couldn't help feeling some measure of satisfaction in being able to talk sense day after day to large numbers of people about the complex issues that affected the safety and well-being not of Americans alone but of all the people who inhabited the earth in a time of peril.

He was more at home worrying about complexities than ministering to simplicities or driving forward with certainties. An idea wasn't worth much if you didn't have to brood over it or peel back the outer layers until you finally got to the center, where the intangibles resided and where the negatives and positives tended to look alike. He seldom read a book without making marginal notes, generally in the form of questions. A book to him was not just a reading experience but an opportunity for dialogue.

In his personal library was a substantial collection of Americana, most of it history and biography. And of all the books in the latter category, the subject of Abraham Lincoln easily accounted for most of the titles. And what interested him most in the life of Lincoln was the decision-making process. "Why would Lincoln do this?" was a question on one of the pages of a book dealing with Lincoln as Commander in Chief. This question pertained to some obscure decision by Lincoln. In a history book which seemed to question Lincoln's delay in issuing the Emancipation Proclamation, Stevenson wrote in the margin: "Have a heart; he was only trying to figure out the best way of holding the nation together."

Jefferson fascinated him, but the man in American history whom he scrutinized most intently and consistently was Lincoln. He felt there was a sense of tragedy about Lincoln long before that night in Ford's Theatre. The tragedy had something to do with the ordeal of finding the right answers at a time when any answer, right or wrong, meant that many good people were going to be hurt. He believed that Lincoln's face, with all its shadows and indentations, was its own best autobiography. "Sometimes it pains you just to look at the man," he wrote on a photograph of Lincoln in which the lines and shadows under the eyes looked like a furrowed field at dusk.

One of the many stories he would tell about Lincoln concerned the Senator who tried to persuade the President to give one of his political aides a postmaster's job. "I'm afraid not," said Lincoln. "I don't like his face." "Surely you can't be serious," the Senator said. "No man can be held accountable for his face." "That's where you're wrong," said Lincoln. "After forty, every man is responsible for his face."

Anyone who could tell Stevenson a story about Lincoln he hadn't heard before was his friend. Like Lincoln, he felt uncomfortable about facing an audience—or even a small company of friends—unless he could think of a story appropriate to the occasion.

Socrates declared that the unexamined life was not worth living; Stevenson believed that a life without laughter was not worth examining. His gift for producing laughter didn't depend on retailing processed humor; his native wit enlivened any meeting or situation, public or private, in which he had a part. Like Lincoln, too, he was an accomplished paradox spotter and could transform an opponent's arguments into a sanguinary battlefield on which his adversary's conflicting ideas would war with themselves.

He didn't dislike action but he resented the time it took away from creative brooding. Early in the 1952 campaign he asked us to visit him in Springfield. "Not far outside the city there's a hilltop," he said shortly after we arrived. "It's not more than a couple of hundred feet high, but you can look out over a great panorama of the American plains. You can see long vistas from mountaintops or skyscrapers, but you won't have a stronger feeling about America than you can get from this particular vantage point. When Lincoln was in Springfield he used to come to this hilltop alone, spend hours there, and let thoughts come to him because he was ready to receive them—something that didn't happen when people or problems were crowding in upon him and he was tyrannized by his schedule. After I became governor, I would go out to that hilltop by myself. Sometimes I would stay out there eight or ten hours at a time. It helped me. It helped me a great deal. But in the weeks ahead there's not going to be much of a chance to do any thinking at all; certainly not the kind of thinking that comes more or less naturally on that hilltop. I'm going to be on the road. The big danger is that I'll be giving out much more than I'll be taking in. That's not the kind of deficit that is going to do anybody any good.

"Anyway," he continued, "I want somebody on that hilltop or its equivalent who can be thinking and looking far ahead and who can prod me into doing the things that it would be easier not to do. Don't try to think of the things that are politically shrewd; I'm pretty well stocked in that department. Try to think of the next generation."

We accepted the assignment and took its terms literally. The things we thought about most were not the things that readily made for votes; instead, we thought about the architecture of peace, the need to bring nuclear weapons under control, the changing shape of Asia and Africa. Stevenson rejected neither the subjects nor the difficult risks they posed. When he accepted an idea he didn't just convey it or retail it. He stewed in it, worked over it, made it his own. He wanted to be prodded, as he had put it, but he couldn't be manipulated or stuffed.

Sometimes we wondered whether he ever regretted taking positions long before the nation really wanted to deal with them. In fact, we felt more than a little guilty for our own small part in getting him to do just what he had asked us to do—to put the tough ones in front of him and make him look at them. Not until years later—just last year, in fact—did we know how he really felt on this matter. He was the principal speaker at a public dinner at which we were to receive an award. With a characteristically light and witty touch he said he had come to join in tribute to a man whose ideas, particularly on nuclear testing, had cost him 3 million votes—according to the political analysts. Then, even more characteristically, his expression and voice turned reflective and serious, even somber, and he said he had no regrets. He was far ahead of his times on the issue of banning nuclear testing, but it is possible that the nation would not have been able to take that vital step when it did without his having prepared the way.

No decision he ever made in life required more soul searching and anguish than the decision to accept the appointment as head of the United States delegation to the United Nations. Many of his friends, in fact, were appalled when he didn't accept at once; he said he wanted ample time to think it over. His profound interest in the United Nations, his concern for world peace, the luster he would bring to the world assembly and the lift his presence would give his fellow delegates at a time when there was some question about the extent of the American commitment to the UN—all these reasons seemed to his supporters to call for prompt and enthusiastic acceptance.

"I just don't know," he told us. "I know everyone wants me to jump up and down with delight and say this is the thing I want to do more than anything else in the world, but I just don't know. I don't want to be a lawyer arguing a case whether he believes in it or not. I'm not just interested in explaining or defending a policy; I want to be involved in the making of that policy."

A man of his stature was in a position to help shape policy, we argued, just by being there. Certainly he was in a much stronger position to influence American policy from a summit inside the UN than from any station outside the UN or outside the United States government.

"I'm not absolutely certain of that," he said. "Once I take it, I can't walk away from it—even if I don't like a policy I have to defend. Something like this could tear you to pieces."

Of course it was difficult, we argued, but who was better equipped to surmount it? And who was there who could bring more to the UN than he? Besides, the fact that he had been offered the job was already public knowledge. If he turned it down now, the rejection could be interpreted not just by his supporters but by people everywhere as proof he didn't think the UN was important enough. And the job of making the UN important, as he himself had argued many times, came close to being the most important job in the world. "More Power to the UN," had been the title of one of his talks.

Even as we pressed the case for acceptance, we knew he knew he would take it. He would have to take it. But first he wanted to be able to think it through, to have a reasonably clear idea of where he was going and the kind of problems that were likely to come up. And he felt justified in seeking assurance that he would be consulted on major questions of U.S. foreign policy that were likely to come before the UN. He received the assurance and he took the job.

As he had feared, however, some major U.S. foreign-policy decisions by-passed the UN, and more than one consultation came after the fact.

He gave his job the best he had, even when the positions he had to defend seemed to him to be lacking in that quality of careful thought and arduous analysis that might anticipate the effects of certain actions.

A few months ago he went to lunch with a small group of magazine editors. "Suppose," one of them asked him, "you were able, just by waving a magic wand, to do the one job in the world you wanted most to do other than what you are now doing. What would it be?"

"Other than the Presidency, of course," he said with a smile, "I suppose I would have to say it would be the job of U.S. Secretary of State. Assuming you could really be involved in making policy and not just be an administrator, that job, with its infinite complexities and challenges, is the one I would have to choose. Apart from that I think I might like to be in your business, editing a newspaper or a magazine. You know, my father owned a small newspaper and I always felt that this was something I might like to return to at some time."

His last public speech was at the twentieth anniversary Commemorative Meeting of the United Nations at San Francisco. He seemed somewhat tired, even wan. He had never been a stranger to fatigue, but had always seemed to find new energy just in the act of getting up to speak. This time, however, the old bounce and verve were not readily apparent. But there was no failure of the moral imagination or lack of resonance in the ideas themselves.

"Man in his civil society has learned how to live under the law with the institutions of justice, and with a controlled strength that can protect rich and poor alike," he said. "And in this century, for the first time in human history, we are attempting similar safeguards, a similar framework of justice, a similar sense of law and impartial protection in the whole wide society of man.

"This is the profound, the fundamental, the audacious meaning of the United Nations. It is our shield against international folly in an age of ultimate weapons."

Such, at least, was the advice of a thoughtful man to an age whose greatest need is time for thought.

*—July 31, 1965*

# What Matters about Schweitzer

*Over the years, various editorials on the life and work of Albert Schweitzer have appeared in SR. When Dr. Schweitzer died in 1965, an appreciation published in the issue of September 25, 1965 drew on previous editorials directed to his life and work.*

The compound at the Schweitzer hospital in Lambaréné is a narrow rectangular affair grooved into the gritty hillside and flanked by the clinic and dispensary, both of them topped by deep red corrugated-tin roofing. On Saturday evening, September 4, the compound slowly began to fill up with people. Not on the busiest days of the hospital, when long lines of people waited to be treated, nor even at Christmas services or Easter Sunday, had the compound held so many people.

No call had been sent out. No one had said that this was the place to come to at just this time, but a loneliness was settling over Lambaréné. For the great doctor had been ill in his small room for more than a week and the word had gone out that his life was slowly receding. And everyone seemed to know somehow that the end was very near.

They came to the compound by torchlight. They came by canoe up or down the Ogoué River, or on foot from Lambaréné and the small villages, taking the road or the jungle paths. The sick ones got up from their slab beds in the wooden huts that served as wards. Patients came from the leper colony over the hill. And the doctors and nurses on the hospital staff left their quarters to join the Africans in the compound.

Some of the Africans began to sing hymns, in French, softly. More and more voices picked up the hymns and soon each person was joined to the other by the blending of human sound. Then, after the singing, individual Africans or members of the staff spoke as they felt. By what they said, the Africans proved that Albert Schweitzer was not so detached from them as some of his critics had contended. "We have heard that some Europeans say he has done us no good," one of them said. "How do they know? They have never come here to see us. The grand doctor, he came here and stayed for most of his life and gave us all he had to give, and that was a great deal."

An African patient stood up to say he understood that in Europe and America some people charged that the hospital was unclean and not very scientific. "But this is the hospital we come to when we are not well," he said. "There are other hospitals, but this one we know. We have known it for a long time. Our fathers came here when they were ill. It is for us."

Nurses and doctors joined in the witness. They told why they had left their own countries to work without pay in a jungle equatorial hospital. There was nothing self-serving about them as they spoke of their purpose. They had come to Lambaréné because they hoped their offer of help might be accepted. They also spoke of what it was that Schweitzer meant to them. And everyone knew without anyone's having to say it that the work of the hospital would go on. This was what the commitment to Albert Schweitzer was all about.

The meeting in the compound ended and the people began to disperse.

Then, at 11:30 P.M., the door to the doctor's quarters opened and Rhena Eckert came out and said that her father had just died.

Two weeks earlier Albert Schweitzer had called in his daughter and handed her a letter. In it, he was making known for the first time his wishes about how the hospital was to be run after his death. The letter said he wanted his daughter to be general head of the hospital and he named the doctors who were to be in charge of the medical services. Those who have been close to the hospital in the past few years can quickly recognize the good sense of the doctor's last request. Rhena joined her father at the hospital a few years ago after her own children became full grown. She quickly established herself as a competent, conscientious, knowledgeable associate of her father's.

So the Schweitzer hospital at Lambaréné will go on. But this will not resolve all the questions about Albert Schweitzer's life and work—questions that have been raised for half a century. The people who have raised the questions will no doubt continue to do so. They will contend that the hospital was the product of extraordinary publicity, and that the doctor was arbitrary and autocratic, especially toward the Africans. Or they will by-pass the hospital altogether and say it is a shame he squandered his talents in the jungle. They will say that his theology, however impressive it may have been a half century ago, lacks sophistication today. Or that his philosophy has borrowed too heavily from Hegel. Or that his reputation as Bach authority or organist or organ builder draws on the public's capacity for being impressed by extraordinary versatility.

But none of these questions is relevant or vital. For they all miss the main point about Schweitzer. The main point has nothing to do with the sanitation at Lambaréné or Schweitzer's alleged autocratic attitudes, whether toward blacks or whites. Nor has the real point anything to do with the level of sophistication of his theology or philosophy, or his rank as musician or organ technician. There are solid grounds for according him high honor and distinction in all these professions and undertakings; but again this is not really the central and overriding fact about Schweitzer.

The main point about Schweitzer is that he helped make it possible for twentieth-century man to unblock his moral vision. There is a tendency in a relativistic age for man to pursue all sides of a question as an end in itself finding relief and even refuge in the difficulty of defining good and evil. The result is a clogging of the moral sense, a certain feeling of self-consciousness or even discomfort when questions with ethical content are raised. Schweitzer furnished the nourishing evidence that nothing is more natural in life than a moral response, which exists independently of precise definition, its use leading not to exhaustion but to new energy.

The greatness of Schweitzer—indeed the essence of Schweitzer—was the man as symbol. More important than what he did for others was what others have done because of him and the power of his example. At least a half-dozen hospitals in impoverished, remote areas have been established because of him. Wherever the Schweitzer story was known, lives were changed. A manufacturer in the American Midwest read about Schweitzer, sold his farm-implement manufacturing company, and used the money to build a string of medical clinics in the Cameroons. A Japanese professor raised money in Schweitzer's name and started an orphanage. A young German medical-school graduate, with no means or resources save a fund of inspiration, went to South America and started a hospital. Tom Dooley and his hospital in Laos are now well on the way to becoming an American legend. A beautiful, talented young Dutch girl learned about Schweitzer and selected a medical career. Six years later she was chief surgeon at the Schweitzer hospital in Lambaréné. She left several years ago to found a hospital of her own, in southern France, carrying on in the Schweitzer tradition.

And there is also the story of Larimer and Gwen Mellon and the work they are doing in Schweitzer's name in Haiti.

At the age of thirty-seven Larimer Mellon was making a career out of being a rich man's son. Just bearing the Mellon name was something of a full-time job. When he read about Schweitzer, the effect was explosive; it blasted him out of one life and into a totally different one. He returned to college to complete his undergraduate education, sitting in classes alongside students half his age. Then he enrolled in medical school.

At forty-four he received his medical diploma. With his wife, Gwen, he decided to found a hospital dedicated to Schweitzer. They selected Haiti not solely because of the high disease rate and the illiteracy of the people but because it was part of North America—very close to the most prosperous nation in the world. Some seventy miles north of Port-au-Prince, in Haiti, Larimer and Gwen Mellon selected the site of what was to become the Albert Schweitzer Hospital of Haiti.

Then there is the case of a young American named Fergus Pope. Less than a decade ago he was traveling through Africa on a motorcycle safari. Out of curiosity he stopped at the Schweitzer hospital. That visit changed the entire course of his life. He returned to school, completed his undergraduate requirements, something he had not previously intended to do, worked his way through medical school in London, served his internship in a New Jersey hospital, and returned to Lambaréné less than a year ago as a fully accredited physician to make good his promise to himself. In the meantime he had married and become the father of three children. He brought his entire family with him to the Schweitzer hospital. Dr. Schweitzer was overjoyed at the presence of the children at the hospital. The entire staff, in fact, was caught up in the adventure of a young American family on the hospital grounds.

What was it about Schweitzer that caused Larimer and Gwen Mellon,

Ruth and Fergus Pope, and all the others, to set their lives on a new course? It was the enduring proof Schweitzer furnished that we need not torment ourselves about the nature of human purpose. The scholar, he once wrote, must not live for science alone, nor the businessman for his business, nor the artist for his art. If affirmation for life is genuine, it will "demand from all that they should sacrifice a portion of their own lives for others."

Thus, Schweitzer's main achievement was a simple one. He was willing to make the ultimate sacrifice for a moral principle. Like Gandhi, the power of his appeal was in renunciation. And because he was able to feel a supreme identification with other human beings he exerted a greater force than armed men on the march. It is unimportant whether we call Schweitzer a great religious figure or a great moral figure or a great philosopher. It suffices that his words and works are known and that he is loved and has influence because he enabled men to discover mercy in themselves. Early in his life he was accused of being an escapist. He was criticized for seeming to patronize the people he had chosen to serve. Yet the proof of his genuineness and his integrity is to be found in the response he awakened in people. He reached countless millions who never saw him but who were able to identify themselves with him because of the invisible and splendid fact of his own identification with them.

We live at a time when people seem afraid to be themselves, when they seem to prefer a hard, shiny exterior to the genuineness of deeply felt emotion. Sophistication is prized and sentiment is dreaded. It is made to appear that one of the worst blights on a reputation is to be called a do-gooder. The literature of the day is remarkably devoid of themes on the natural goodness of man, seeing no dramatic power in the most powerful fact of the human mixture. The values of the time lean to a phony toughness, casual violence, cheap emotion; yet we are shocked when youngsters confess to have tortured and killed because they enjoyed it and because they thought it was the thing to do.

It mattered not to Schweitzer or to history that he would be dismissed by some as a do-gooder or as a sentimental fool who frittered his life away on Africans who couldn't read or write. Schweitzer brought the kind of spirit to Africa that the dark man hardly knew existed in the white man. Before Schweitzer white skin meant beatings and gunpoint rule and the imposition of slavery on human flesh. If Schweitzer had done nothing else in his life than to accept the pain of these people as his own, he would have achieved eminence. And his place in history will rest on something more substantial than an argument over an unswept floor in a hospital ward in the heart of Africa. It will rest on the spotless nature of his vision and the clean sweep of his nobility.

The tragedy of life is not in the hurt to a man's name or even in the fact of death itself. The tragedy of life is in what dies inside a man while he lives—the death of genuine feeling, the death of inspired response, the death of the awareness that makes it possible to feel the pain or the glory of other men in oneself. Schweitzer's aim was not to dazzle an age but to awaken it, to make it comprehend that moral splendor is part of the gift of life, and that each man has unlimited strength to feel human oneness and to act upon it. He proved that although a man may have no jurisdiction over the fact of his existence, he can hold supreme command over the meaning of existence for him. Thus, no man need fear death; he need fear only that he may die without having known his greatest power—the power of his free will to give his life for others.

The individual in today's world feels cut off from the large forces or movements that determine his future. This leads to fatalism and default: Schweitzer demonstrated that one man can make a difference. He had no specific prescription or formula for the individual. All he hoped for was that the individual would be able to peel off the layers of hardened artificialities that separate him from his real self. Man's resources do not exist outside him. His responses must come from within. A thinking and feeling man is not a helpless man. The sense of paralysis proceeds not so much out of the mammoth size of the problem but out of the puniness of purpose.

It may be said that only a Schweitzer had the knowledge and personal power to answer satisfactorily the question: "What can one man do?" Certainly we can't all be Schweitzers. But what should concern us is not what it takes to be a Schweitzer but what it takes to be a man. Nature has not been equally lavish with her endowments, but each man has his own potential in terms of achievement and service. The awareness of that potential is the discovery of purpose; the fulfillment of that potential is the discovery of strength.

For Albert Schweitzer, the assertion of this potential was not directed to charity but to justice. Also, moral reparations. "We are burdened with a great debt. We are not free to confer benefits on these people, or not confer them, as we please. It is our duty. Anything we give them is not benevolence but atonement. That is the foundation from which all deliberations about 'works of mercy' must begin."

As for the right time to act? The time, inevitably, is now. It can only be now. "Truth has no special time of its own," he said. When circumstances seem least propitious, that is the correct time.

Much of the ache and the brooding unhappiness in modern man are the result of his difficulty in using himself fully. He performs compartmentalized tasks in a compartmentalized world. He is reined in—physically, socially, spiritually. Only rarely does he have a sense of fulfilling himself through total contact with a total challenge. He finds it difficult to make real connection even with those who are near him. But there are vast surges of conscience, natural purpose, and goodness inside him demanding air and release. And he has his own potential, the regions of which are far broader than he can ever guess at—a potential that keeps nagging at him to be fully used.

Albert Schweitzer was fully grown, fully developed, fully used. Did this make him happy? The question is irrelevant. He was less concerned with happiness than with purpose. What is it that has to be done? What is the best way of doing it? How does a man go about developing an inner awareness of important needs outside himself? How does he attach himself to those needs? Is he able to recognize the moral summons within him? To the extent that the individual is unconcerned about these questions, or lives apart from them, he is unfulfilled and only partly alive.

One night in 1957 at the hospital in Lambaréné, long after most of the oil lamps had been turned out, I walked down toward the river. It was a sticky night and I couldn't sleep. As I passed the compound near Dr. Schweitzer's quarters, I could hear the rapid piano movement of a Bach toccata. The doctor was playing on the upright piano next to his bedside.

I approached the doctor's bungalow and stood for perhaps five minutes outside the latticed window, through which I could see his silhouette in the dimly lit room. The piano had an organ footboard attachment so that he could keep his feet in playing condition. While he played the toccata his feet moved over the footboard with speed and certainty. His powerful hands were in total control of the piano as he met Bach's demands for complete definition of each note—each with its own weight and value, yet all of them laced intimately together to create an ordered whole.

I had a stronger sense of listening to a great console than if I had been in the world's largest cathedral. The yearning for an ordered beauty; the search for creative abandonment—yet an abandonment inside a disciplined artistry; the desire to re-create a meaningful past; the need for outpouring and release, catharsis—all these things inside Albert Schweitzer spoke in his playing. And when he was through, he sat with his hands resting lightly on the keys, his great head bent forward as though to catch any echoes.

He was now freed of the pressures and tensions of the hospital, with its forms to fill out in triplicate; freed of the mounds of unanswered mail; freed of the heat and the saturating moisture of the equator. Johann Sebastian Bach had made it possible for Albert Schweitzer to come to Lambaréné in the first place; it was Schweitzer's books on Bach that provided royalties to support the hospital in the early years. Now Bach was restoring him to a world of creative and ordered splendor.

The doctor knew in some way that I was standing outside, listening to him play, for when he finished the toccata he called out to me by name and asked me to come in. For one half-hour or so we chatted in the thin light of the oil lamp near the piano. He was speaking personally now—about his hopes mostly. First, he would like to see his hospital in complete running order. Second, he would like to be able to train others to run the hospital after he was gone. Third, he would like to have just a little time—to work quietly and finish his two books. One was his major theological work, *The Kingdom of God*. The other was his final volume *The Philosophy of Civilization.*

He did not wish these longings of his to give the impression he was unhappy in his work. Now and then something would happen that would give him a sense of fulfillment and deep reward. Only a few days earlier, for example, he had received a letter from a professorial colleague in France about an examination paper turned in by a nineteen-year-old boy. One of the questions on the examination was worded: "How would you define the best hope for the culture of Europe?" The boy had written: "It is not in any part of Europe. It is in a small African village and it belongs to a man in his eighties."

Dr. Schweitzer looked up from the letter. "At times like this, when the hospital has gone to sleep and everything is at peace, it makes me proud that a young man would think as he does, whether what he thinks is true or not. But in the morning, when the sun is up and the cries from the hospital are sounded, I do not think of such fancy ideas. I have all I can do to sit still while reality stares me in the face. And sometimes, if I am lucky, I can stare back."

*—September 25, 1965*

# Back to the Fundamentals

Question for today's class in contemporary civilization: What is it that man makes or grows or processes more of than anything else in the world?

Is it iron or steel or any other metal? No.

Is it brick or mortar or any other material for his shelters or edifices or monuments? No.

Is it grain or wheat or anything he needs to sustain life? No.

The product in greatest abundance made by man is explosive, obliterative force. It takes the form of fission and fusion bombs of varying sizes and potencies. They have been accumulating in man's storehouses and are primed for instant use. These explosives represent the destructive equivalent of 100,000,000,000,000 pounds of TNT. This comes to 28,000 pounds of explosive force for every human being now alive. All the foods and medicines and books and clothes in the world put together do not amount to 28,000 pounds per person, nor even a substantial fraction of it.

Question: Where is all this force located?

It is located at present in the United States, the Soviet Union, France, Britain, and China. Within a few years this power elite will be expanded to a dozen nations or more. At that time the holocaust-making potential may exceed the destructive equivalent of 50,000 pounds of TNT for every person on earth. Not all the men who will have access to this power will have profound convictions about the infinite value of the individual, or about the preciousness of life in general, or about the ease with which the membranes of civilization can be ripped wide apart. Some of the men who will be in a position to start the chain reaction will be fretful, puny, impulsive, irresponsible. They will differ from their historical predecessors solely in the absence of any limits to their malevolent capacities. The gap between human evil and human power will be closed.

Question: What would happen if all the nations possessing nuclear explosives should let them all fly?

In such a case, the earth's atmosphere would become drenched with radioactive charges, invading the human germ plasm, poisoning crops, soil, and streams, and unhinging the vital conditions of life itself. This would mean that the peoples of the warring nations would not have been at war solely against each other. They would have been at war against the whole of the human race and, indeed, against the life environment.

Question: Isn't there any way the belligerent nations could confine the effects of their radioactive exchange to their own territories, thus sparing hundreds of millions of people with whom they have no quarrel?

Nuclear warfare converts the entire globe into a single battlefield. At one time soldier was pitted against soldier. Slowly, over centuries, the circle broadened. By the time of World War II whole cities of the warring nations were under total attack from the air. In a nuclear war, only two nations may be directly involved, but their victims will be world wide. The worst suffering of all will be inflicted on generations yet unborn.

Question: Isn't the fact of overwhelming retaliation a sufficient deterrent to an aggressor nuclear nation?

It might actually be an incentive. Never before has a potential aggressor been in a position to use weapons that combine total power with total surprise. While the aggressor can never be certain he has hit all the vital targets, he knows he can hit enough of them to obtain a critical advantage.

Question: How can a nation that has been hit in a surprise nuclear attack be sure where the attack came from?

It can't.

Question: This being the case, shouldn't all other issues give way to this one? Why doesn't everyone drop everything he is doing and address himself to this problem?

That would seem to be the great unanswered question of the twentieth century.

Question: If the men at the head of the nations are not to be expected to take the initiative in bringing nuclear weapons under control and in creating the machinery of world law that alone can provide for a common security, where is one to look?

In the mirror. The ultimate responsibility for good or evil rests with the individual. The things that animate him and disturb him are transferable to the group and to government. Public opinion is the accumulation and expression of individual concerns. So long as the individual allows himself to be preoccupied by personal or national irrelevancies, he will make no contribution to his personal or the national survival. The educator who prides himself on the advanced learning he imparts to students is actually a purveyor of gross illiteracy if he transmits no awareness of the danger of world anarchy or the means by which it can be eliminated. The scientist who stands tall in his profession is actually a pygmy if he takes no responsibility for what he makes. The titan of industry who presides over efficient and high production is no more than a transient spectator to the demolition of his industry if he fails to comprehend the implications of a world without law.

The biggest lesson of all to be learned about contemporary civilization is that nothing anyone is doing today makes any sense unless it is connected to the making of a genuine peace.

*—November 6, 1965*

# Just Right

The man opposite me in the lounge compartment of the airplane was discussing the war in Vietnam. It was important, he said, to keep the fighting from running the serious risk of a direct clash with Communist China. He identified himself as a stockbroker and said that anything approaching an atomic war would crack the market. Business knows no nation could survive nuclear war, he said. At the same time, he was concerned about the possibility that the fighting in Vietnam might come to a sudden end. That, too, would have a negative effect on the market—not so severe, of course, as a nuclear war, but severe enough to cause a reduction and curtailment of war orders, with a resultant sharp sell-off.

The present level of fighting, he thought, was just right—not steep enough to risk nuclear war but deep enough to maintain the present level of government defense spending and feed the present industrial boom.

Several days later the afternoon newspapers ran headlines about peace feelers from North Vietnam that were conveyed through India. The final editions carried related stories saying that stock prices at first tumbled in response to the peace scare but then rallied near the closing as later news disclosed that the "feelers" were not of recent date and had already been discounted. Thus reassured, investors returned to the buying side.

My fellow airplane-traveler was not unique. The nation may have accustomed itself to a just-right war. Vietnam has been metabolized into the national economy. Consciously, very few Americans would vote against ending the war in Vietnam on the grounds that continuation of the war was good for the economy at home. But on the subconscious level, where values first take shape and decisions begin, we may have adjusted too easily to the fact that the Vietnam war has become an important prop of the current prosperity. The reality of such an adjustment hasn't offended us or gnawed at us.

Some people, thus confronted, would doubtless say that we have to take things as we find them. They would say that the Vietnam war is bound to require a higher level of defense spending than otherwise, serving as a stimulus to the entire economy; they might add that it is unreasonable to expect anyone to shun the indirect benefits of that combination of circumstances. Quite so; but the issue here is not whether individuals should renounce their portion of war prosperity. The issue is whether the American people may lack a burning compulsion to put an end to war—not just the Vietnam war but war in general—because they have been able to make the adjustment, an adjustment that involves relatively little pain and that indeed is linked in their view to a booming economy.

There is no point in talking about the need to avoid military humiliation or defeat in Vietnam. The idea of a just-right war is itself a national disaster. How does anyone determine a just-right way for a soldier or a civilian to die from the sudden eruption of TNT or fire? How many casualties are just right when announced in the morning newspapers alongside stories about officials deploring rising prices?

Our eyes are fixed on the wrong things. We are looking at the prosperity indices instead of the coffins returning from the war front. We are listening to the stock ticker instead of the heartbeats of frightened people cowering in their crude underground pits against the mounting sounds of oncoming war.

There was a time, only a few weeks ago, when a thin thread of hope was being delicately woven out of the wild infinity of loose ends in Vietnam. The United States had suspended its aerial bombing; the Christmas cease-fire led to a Buddhist-holiday cease-fire of slightly longer duration. The severity of the ground fighting had diminished somewhat. There was talk of reciprocal de-escalation. The expeditions to foreign places of Vice President Humphrey, Ambassador Goldberg, and Ambassador Harriman gave dramatic world focus to the President's desire to find a way of ending the fighting in Vietnam.

But then, abruptly, the thread snapped. The bombing was resumed. On both sides the ground fighting took a sharp climb. Thousands more soldiers were pressed into battle. Civilian casualties began to mount again.

No one knows what course the war will take. One thing, however, is certain. A just-right war cannot be kept in bounds. The American people will find no answers to Vietnam unless they start asking the right questions. And questions are the result not just of curiosity but of values and basic approaches to life. When, therefore, the American people get both Vietnam and their historic values into focus, a vital mood will be created in which constructive possibilities will come to life. We will not drift into such a mood. It can only come into being through awareness and conviction.

*—March 5, 1966*

# What Is Owing to the Vietnamese?

The life expectancy of the average Vietnamese is about thirty years. This means that most of the people in Vietnam today have known nothing but war in their lifetimes. They were caught in the wild crossfire between the French and the Japanese during World War II. Then, with the defeat of Japan in the larger war, Nationalist Chinese troops occupied the northern half of Indo-China and British troops the southern half. Meanwhile, a Vietnam guerrilla army under Ho Chi Minh seized Hanoi and proclaimed a war to free the country of all outsiders.

For a time, in 1945, it appeared that Ho Chi Minh would be able to obtain American support, since the United States had proposed international trusteeship for the area once the war against the Japanese had been won. When American aid failed to materialize, Ho Chi Minh entered into a halfway-house-to-freedom agreement with the French under which Vietnam would become an independent republic inside the French Union.

Within a year the Vietnamese were convinced that the French never intended to give them even token independence. Large-scale fighting between the Vietminh and the French spewed out of a series of episodes and lasted until the middle of 1954. By that time French casualties were said to have exceeded 170,000. Vietnamese casualties, including civilians, were four times as high. The war created a French government crisis; Prime

Minister Pierre Mendes-France arranged for a cease fire and negotiations at Geneva in 1954.

Out of Geneva came a series of agreements, one of which was that all foreign military activities would cease in Indo-China. Another provision was that the political future of North Vietnam and South Vietnam was to be resolved by free elections. South Vietnam decided not to go through with the elections. The Viet Cong, aided by North Vietnam, launched a guerrilla campaign of terror and assassination against the South.

The United States, which had not participated in Geneva, established a military and political presence in South Vietnam, Laos, and Thailand. When the South Vietnam government was beset by internal difficulties, the United States turned against the government it said it·was trying to save from the Communists and became a silent partner in its overthrow, according to the later testimony of the American ambassador who was there at the time. In 1965, when military disaster seemed imminent, the United States took a direct role, sending its own troops in large numbers into battle and bombing targets in both North and South Vietnam from the air.

The main concern of the United States in going into Vietnam is the threat of Communist Chinese expansion into Southeast Asia. It was feared that if Laos or Vietnam toppled, the rest of Indo-China would be under critical immediate Chinese pressure with Burma, India, and Pakistan not far down the timetable. Thus the struggle in Vietnam must be seen against the larger background of the world struggle for a balance of power.

The purpose of this brief historical recital is not to make an argument but to ask a question. What is it that the Vietnamese people have done to warrant such unremitting punishment—punishment beyond reason or imagination—over a quarter century? Their lands have been crossed and crisscrossed by war since before most Vietnamese were born. Their crops have been trampled or burned by soldiers from a half-dozen mighty nations. Their little huts have had to be built and rebuilt. And now at night there is the terror of the Communist Viet Cong, and during the day there are the pitched battles and the bombing. And if their village is near a road on which military trucks travel or is on the line of march, there is the double jeopardy of having their villages chewed up by the ground fighting or blasted down by dynamite raining out of the sky.

A generation ago they built thin tunnels under their villages to protect them against the Japanese and French. They still take to their tunnels today. This makes a problem for the Americans, who often have no way of knowing whether Viet Cong or innocent families are in the tunnels. We call to them to come out but they are badly frightened and do not always respond. Sometimes we use grenades or other blast-and-fire devices. When the dead bodies are hauled out we sometimes discover we have killed people whom we wish we hadn't. The difficulty from the start, in fact, has been that it is often virtually impossible to distinguish between innocent villagers and the Viet Cong we are trying to hunt down. And so there have been lives lost through error. How do we go about rectifying such errors? Is it enough to charge it to the nature of war?

Our officials in the area have complained that the villagers seem to lack conviction and will favor whatever side happens to occupy their area at a given time. Why should conviction come easy after a quarter century of random war in which many of the underlying issues have to do with the clash of interests of foreign nations? The wonder is not that the Vietnamese seem to bend with the wind but that they can bend at all.

There is a question about Vietnam more important than any of the questions now being asked. How does the rest of the world make it up to the Vietnamese whose constant and unwanted companion has been violence and terror and whose only crime has been their geography? The question applies not just to Americans or French or British or Japanese or Communist Chinese or Nationalist Chinese but to the full category of humans who have the obligation to make better sense of their world.

Whatever one's stand may be on American policy in Vietnam today, all can agree to a single proposition: The Vietnamese have a moral claim on history. How do we go about making it right with them? How do we help give them a horizon? How do we demonstrate that life is a gift and that there are wondrous things to be felt and warm hopes to come true?

If we did nothing else in our lives than to achieve this purpose, we would not be out of balance, focus, or grace.

—March 26, 1966

# The Delegation of the Survival Instinct

Survival depends on the instinct for survival. Basic dangers must be sensed in order to be identified. One of the principal problems of modern man, however, is that he has delegated his survival instincts to the state and has therefore become increasingly incapable of comprehending fundamental threats to the species of which he is a part. He has no difficulty in discerning threats to the nation—the nation sees to it that he is fully alerted and mobilized—but he has hardly any response to the fact of overriding danger to the human species.

Primitive man had at least one important advantage over modern man. His response mechanism to surrounding dangers was superbly developed and in excellent working order. He may not have been capable of writing lyric poetry or of calculating a price-earnings ratio, but one thing he most certainly could do: He could sense and define a danger before it became full blown. He didn't waste any time between the initial awareness of the threat and the defense.

Civilization was an interruption of this uncomplicated interaction between man and his environment. The more dependent man became upon group organization and upon social and collective techniques, the more de-individualized his instinct for survival became. The development of adroit and intricate tools and methods for collectivizing the response to danger blurred the individual's sensitivity to fundamental hazards. The group became the custodian of man's survival instincts. In so doing, it desensitized man, at least to the extent that his basic allegiances and obligations were directed to the nation rather than to humanity.

Wisdom, however, is not mobilized at the same rate as is power. The absolutely sovereign state has been far more adept at developing its consciousness of self than its awareness of the human species and its needs. It has put muscle ahead of conscience. Paradoxically, the nation can survive only as it becomes integrated into a larger and more interdependent whole, one that bears some relationship to the totality of the human situation. But the energy and the momentum that are necessary to bring this about can only come from the people themselves, and it is precisely this kind of energy that is wanting because of the weakening of the instinct for survival.

The great failure of education—not just in the United States but throughout most of the world—is that it has made man group conscious rather than species conscious. It has celebrated man's institutions but not man himself. It has attached value to the things man does but not to what man is. Man's power is heralded but the preciousness of life is unsung.

The fragility of life is the dominant fact of life but this is not the central fact of education. Human pride is circumscribed. Pride is readily summoned out of national achievement but it does not readily extend to the human family as a whole. There are national anthems but no anthems for humanity.

The essential question, therefore, is whether modern man comprehends that the fundamental threat today transcends anything now being starkly called to his attention, whether through headlines or discourse with his neighbors. This threat is represented by the fact that man is at war against his environment without knowing it. The weapons he has devised to protect the nation are actually environment smashers, engines of mass suicide rather than useful devices of what was once known as war. Meanwhile, in a thousand other ways man is altering and cheapening the basic conditions on which life depends—covering the earth with asphalt and cement, making the sky an open sewer for his poisons and wastes, infecting his reservoirs and streams. Nothing is more precarious than the delicate balances of environment on which life depends. Nothing is so little respected or understood.

If the instinct for human survival is atrophying but not yet dead, where will regeneration come from? It cannot come from the group, however exalted the purpose of the group may be. The hope has to reside where it has always been—with the individual. The challenge here is supremely personal. It does not lend itself to easy superimposition or force feeding. What the group can do—and it makes little difference whether the group is formally or informally defined—is to arrest its own impatience with the individual long enough to sustain his search for the regenerating truths. This is the only way the group is likely to get the truth.

*—April 9, 1966*

# The Trouble beyond Vietnam

If there is a deep malaise in the American soul over Vietnam, it is not because the American people have difficulty in understanding that aggression, whether by Communists or anyone else, must be turned back. Nor is it because they lack the staying power to see it through.

The deep malaise is the result of a steady accumulation of jabbing, wrenching events in Vietnam itself. The repeated, underlined purpose of the United States in going into Vietnam is to make it possible for people to have a government of their own choosing. Yet repeated, underlined events in Vietnam indicate that the government we are attempting to uphold may not be the government the people would choose to keep. The uprisings a few weeks ago were calmed only when a promise of free elections was made by the South Vietnam government. But now that political matters seem in hand, the head of the South Vietnam government says there may be no elections after all. What happens, then, to the argument that the problem in Vietnam is external, rather than internal, and that the end of Vietcong terror will see the return of stability and security in South Vietnam?

These are not the only things about Vietnam difficult to understand. It also is difficult to understand the insensitivity and maladroitness of some American officials who sought to reassure the American people after the newspapers published stories about a shortage of bombs in Vietnam. Never before in history, one U.S. official proclaimed, has one nation rained as many bombs on another nation as the United States has rained on North Vietnam. Why should this be reassuring? Why should it make Americans feel better about Vietnam? Why should it be satisfying to know that the most powerful country in the world can exert so much force at

604 The Editorial Page, 1940–1966

will? Why not also say that never before in history has any one nation been able to inflict as much damage on another without being in the line of fire itself? Why should the rest of the world be impressed with unprecedented bombing when so many memories are fresh with the personal knowledge of what air bombings do to human beings?

Why should it be comforting to read that the wrong targets have been hit or that villagers have been killed? There was a lull in the bombing at the beginning of the year. After thirty-eight days the bombing was resumed because it was said Hanoi gave no indication of wanting to come to the negotiating table. It is now 120 days since the bombing was resumed. The evidence is at least three times greater that the resumption hasn't had the intended effect either. Why, then, is the bombing continued?

Shortly after the denial that any bomb shortage existed, it was ascertained that the United States had re-purchased from West Germany at $21 per bomb a supply of bombs that we had sold West Germany earlier at $1.70 per bomb, and that had been produced originally at a cost of $330 per bomb. Stories like these are not effectively dispelled just by reminding ourselves that we have to stop Vietcong terror in Vietnam.

Another example of inexcusable maladroitness is represented by the American official who told newsmen that the United States could engage in provocative action against China without fear of retaliation. This kind of inflammatory, idiotic arrogance should have no place in the foreign policy of the United States—not in a world made volatile by atomic power attached to the fuses of human psyches. If the Chinese are half as irresponsible as we say they are, such cockiness could act as a time bomb in the Chinese mind, ticking away like an apocalyptic clock.

The feeling grows that a grim inversion of our foreign policy may be taking place. Day-to-day decisions seem to be shaping long-range policy instead of being shaped by them. Not just the enemy but we ourselves are being hurt by the inability to admit we may have made some mistakes. Every word of criticism has to be laboriously refuted, whether or not the facts support the refutation. It is not particularly edifying to learn that the government frequently employs the device of "cover" stories as a way of explaining otherwise embarrassing actions or decisions.

A nation is known not just by its songs but by its concerns. It is disquieting to learn that some government officials seem more concerned about the fact that other nations may not respect our strength than they are about the fact that other nations may not respect our wisdom. There is an almost neurotic compulsion to refute the notion that we may be overly reluctant to use force, but there is no corresponding compulsion to dispel the idea that we may not be sufficiently aware of the limitations of force.

Little wonder there is a growing sense of disquiet in the American soul. It involves the relationship of Americans to their own history and its meaning for them. It involves their understanding of the national purpose. It involves, finally, their sense of connection with their government. There seems to be a feeling that the country is being steadily separated from the moral base on which so many of its traditions have rested.

What is most striking of all about U.S. foreign policy, of course, is that it is not beyond effective change. A definition of basic aims, not just in Vietnam but in the world; an unambiguous declaration that the support and strengthening of the United Nations is a major objective; respect not just for the ends but the means; recognition that we don't cope with our adversaries by imitating them but by holding to standards that give us the vital leadership that in the end represents our best hope for genuine security—these are the essentials that might re-energize the nation.

*—May 21, 1966*

# The Four Centers of U.S. Foreign Policy

Long before he came to the White House, Woodrow Wilson said that the foreign policy of the United States could never be fully comprehended unless one examined it from the vantage point of the Presidency. He didn't mean by this that the public's understanding of a foreign event or crisis was necessarily inferior to or different from the President's. What he meant was that a President's decision often had to surmount and resolve an incredible array of converging and diverging pressures and counter-pressures.

If the process of decision-making was complicated a half-century or more ago, consider how it has become compounded since. The President's post today is not just a station for the contemplation of world affairs. It is a battleground, a zone of sustained conflict for all the elements and groups that are involved in the decision-making process. Officially, these groups include the pertinent Cabinet members, Congressional committees and Congress as a whole, representatives of relevant government departments or agencies, the President's own aides, and the National Security Council, consisting of many of the same people who see the President individually. On the unofficial level, the pressures involve the full range of the press and public opinion.

Essentially, the problem is represented by the fact that there are now four centers of foreign policy inside the American government, all of them potent, all of them posts of action and advocacy that have to be heard and reconciled.

First of all, of course, is the State Department, with its world-wide establishment for carrying out American foreign policy and for gathering information and assessing all the political, historical, and diplomatic factors involved in problems coming up for decision.

Second, there is the policy-analysis and policy-making function of the Department of Defense. The Secretary of Defense is not solely a coordinator of military affairs and operations. He presides over a substantial organization concerned with collecting and scrutinizing voluminous data —political, historical, diplomatic, as well as military—and is involved in the multiplicity of foreign situations with which the United States must deal.

Third, a full and separate organization concerned with matters that affect foreign policy is the Central Intelligence Agency. Like the State Department, it has its representatives all over the world. It not only gathers information but carries out major undertakings in the foreign field. It also seeks to bring into single focus the full range of views of other government agencies in its preparation of "national estimates" covering a wide variety of situations. Recently, *The New York Times* called attention to the activities of the C.I.A. in mounting policies and programs, some of them at odds with State Department positions, some of them actually subversive of other governments.

Fourth, the U.S. Mission to the United Nations carries with it a wide range of duties and responsibilities that pertain to America's foreign policy. It necessarily operates from a somewhat different perspective from that of the State Department or the Department of Defense. The American Ambassador to the UN, ideally at least, succeeds in direct proportion to his ability to support the United Nations in its effort to substitute objective yardsticks for the traditional unilateral actions of nations. World public opinion is a major factor in the UN equation.

Theoretically, the National Security Council is supposed to coordinate and bring into focus the particularized views or approaches of the different centers of foreign policy inside the government. But it is not expected to eliminate the complications resulting from the separate thrusts or pressures applied directly to the President.

The result is that the President has to deal with at least four major foreign policy units, each of them possessing full-blown staffs engaged in comprehensive appraisal, recommendation, and, often, action. By now, most Americans have been made aware of the problem of overlapping military authority, facilities, and operations, with the U.S. Army, the U.S. Navy, and the U.S. Air Force each containing most of the elements of a full and separate military establishment. The attempt to consolidate all these agencies into a Department of Defense has come a long way, even though total unification has yet to be achieved. What Americans in general do not realize is that even more serious proliferation now exists in the field of foreign policy. And the penalty for overlapping in the foreign policy area is even more severe than in the military. For the United States cannot afford to be fragmented in its dealings with the rest of the world. It cannot afford conflicting spheres of foreign-policy formulation. It cannot afford to limit the ability of the President to create clear lines of consistency in carrying out clearly defined purposes.

The American people are in serious error if they suppose that the President has only to invoke his Constitutional powers in order to remove or reduce internal pressures and counter-pressures in the making of foreign policy. He cannot abolish, nor can he readily curtail, agencies created by Congress. When he comes into office, he is confronted by numberless ongoing programs. Everything is in process, and the process has a momentum not easily reversed or even slowed. Early in his Presidency, John F. Kennedy was told of an advanced plan for staging a U.S.-backed revolution in Cuba. The plan turned out to be a colossal miscalculation and blunder, and President Kennedy took the responsibility. But what is significant here is not just that the President made the mistake, as he later acknowledged, of going along with the scheme, but that a duly constituted part of the United States Government had the authority and the means to attempt to export a revolution.

(Incidentally, the branch of the C.I.A. concerned with the preparation of "estimates" is believed to have supplied negative advice on the Cuba undertaking, but the operational branch of the C.I.A. proceeded just the same.)

President Dwight D. Eisenhower, after the death of Secretary of State John Foster Dulles, undertook a series of initiatives for turning back the growing danger of nuclear war. He felt that the new leadership in the Soviet Union should be given every opportunity to demonstrate that it didn't hold to Stalin's views about the inevitability of war. Moreover, the President felt that growing differences between the Soviet Union and Communist China made it necessary for the United States to strengthen the position of those Soviet leaders who favored improved relations with the West, as against the violent anti-Western stand of the Chinese.

Various joint efforts and parleys were initiated. But these measures had to be aborted when both Premier Nikita Khrushchev and President Eisenhower were confronted with the fact that an American spying plane had been downed deep inside Soviet territory. Premier Khrushchev told his Council of Ministers he was certain the plane operated without authorization or knowledge of the President and that the imminent Big Four Conference in Paris could therefore proceed. The President, however, was persuaded that he would expose himself to serious criticism and even ridicule if he said he knew nothing about the flight. The upshot of the entire episode was that the President's hopes for an effective détente were negated by a lack of coordination within the government.

Still another example of misapplied authority occurred in Laos in 1960, when the popularly elected government of Souvanna Phouma was overthrown in a military coup, which in turn brought on a civil war. This writer does not know which agency of the U.S. Government facilitated the coup, directly or indirectly, but he does know that there was a strong difference of opinion inside the U.S. Government on the matter, and that for several months after the coup the United States was in the incredible position of paying the salaries of the armed forces both of the government and the insurgents.

Eventually, the government was restored to Souvanna, with the backing of the United States. But the episode resulted in further strengthening the Communist forces in Northern Laos, with a degree of public support that might not have been possible otherwise.

Yet another contretemps took place in 1961 at a time when the State Department was doing everything it could to strengthen U.S. relations with Burma and, in fact, with all nations in South and Southeast Asia that were under pressure from Communist China. The C.I.A. dropped guns and ammunition into a corner of Burma where a small contingent from the Chinese Nationalist Army had been hiding out since the end of the Chinese Civil War. The incident soon became public knowledge. Inevitably, the disclosure produced a strong reaction in Burma. The revelation that the United States not only had violated the sovereignty of Burma but had exposed that country to possible reprisals from China brought on demonstrations by the Burmese against the American Embassy in Rangoon. The State Department's attempt to create good-will with Burma was not furthered, to say the least.

The C.I.A., of course, is by no means the only U.S. agency involved in actions running counter to our public declarations about self-determination as a cardinal principle of American foreign policy. Consider the case of the overthrow in 1963 of President Ngo Dinh Diem and his government in Vietnam. There is reason to believe that the C.I.A. was strongly opposed to the coup. But the State Department went along with the enterprise, at least tacitly, thus involving the United States in the overthrow of a government we said we had gone into Vietnam to protect against overthrow by others.

The inadequacy of the Diem government is not the only issue here. One issue is whether the United States should become involved in the subversion of other governments. Another issue concerns the line of authority under which such decisions and actions take place. To what extent does authority exist for undertaking "minor probes" or "projects," which in the aggregate represent major actions and policies, thus confronting the President with events in motion? In any event, one serious effect of the Diem overthrow and assassination was that it jeopardized the historical and moral position of the United States. Another effect was that it made the United States responsible for the performance of successor governments in Vietnam.

U.S. policy in Vietnam today does not belong exclusively to President Johnson any more than it belonged exclusively to President Kennedy. The basic decisions that were to affect the course of American policy for years to come were made in 1954 at the time the French withdrew from Indochina. Prime Minister Mendès-France, of France, later revealed that one of the major obstacles in the Geneva negotiations concerned the role the United States would play in the future of the area.

The key article of the Geneva treaty called for all foreign forces and military influence to be withdrawn from the nations of Indochina. M. Mendès-France said he was asked during the negotiations whether he could provide assurance that the departure of France would not be the signal for the arrival of the United States, in which case the terms of the treaty would be meaningless. The Prime Minister said he replied that he had no reason to believe that the United States had any such intention. A treaty was signed calling for evacuation of foreign forces and for free elections. The French left and the United States began to move in.

The 1956 elections provided for by the Geneva accords were called off by the South Vietnamese government. It is important to point out, however, that the prospects for free elections in the North were less than substantial. In any case, the Vietcong, backed by North Vietnam, began its unremitting campaign of terror and assassination in the South. The process of violence and disintegration that set in has continued almost without interruption from that moment to this.

It is not clear what was behind the American decision to run counter to a treaty that had just been signed. For the effect was exactly the opposite from the one intended. The effect was to make Ho Chi Minh, whom the United States had earlier supported in the war against the Japanese, partially or largely dependent on Communist China, despite the long history of Vietnamese resentment toward and fear of its great northern neighbor.

It seems reasonable to ask whether the same sources whose later advice worked out so poorly in the case of Cuba had drafted the plan and the recommendations for the original involvement in Vietnam. In any case, President Johnson inherited a situation in which the practical range of decision was severely circumscribed by the stark effects of previous decisions and actions.

And in Vietnam today, one of President Johnson's biggest difficulties is represented not just by those who are clamoring for an all-out military effort, even at the risk of a major war, or by those who are demanding that the United States abruptly withdraw from Vietnam altogether, but by the cross-currents inside the U.S. government itself. The President is pushing for negotiations with North Vietnam and all concerned parties, including Communist China. Yet any indication that such negotiations may in fact be possible seems to touch off prodigious pressure by American military and diplomatic representatives in South Vietnam to forestall any such event. Their argument is that the South Vietnamese government is opposed to negotiations and that we cannot afford to run counter to a government already beset with critical difficulties. The bombing, therefore, becomes as much a device to bolster the morale of Saigon as it is a means of interdicting the supplies from Hanoi.

The United States is locked in. We cannot use our full force in Vietnam because to do so would represent an irresponsible invitation to the Chinese to take part in an unspeakable holocaust. To pull out altogether would represent an irresistible invitation to the Chinese to move in. And the only alternative, a negotiated peace, becomes increasingly difficult not just because of what happens in Hanoi but because those who represent the President in Saigon seem to be doing everything they can to block the policy of negotiation that he has declared offers the best chance for ending the war.

None of these matters can be viewed as isolated phenomena. They all reflect the fact that the conduct of U.S. foreign policy has become enormously complicated not just by events but by the existence of different hubs of foreign policy inside the same government. It is unfair and unreasonable to expect any President, however bold and confident, to conduct the nation's foreign policy on the basis of dealing with entrenched departments which operate inside different contexts.

The aim of U.S. foreign policy must be to try to shape events, and not just to be shaped by them. However, day-to-day actions, even on a fairly low level, in the aggregate have often become high-level policy, whether the President agreed with it or not. The danger is that a separation is taking place between American policy and American purposes. The level of action is being detached from the level of intent.

Some years ago, a commission under former President Herbert Hoover made important recommendations for the reorganization of the Armed Forces. It is equally important now that a high-level commission be appointed to study the process by which American foreign policy is made and implemented, and to scrutinize the operations of all government agencies that have an effect on that policy. The study now being undertaken by Senator Henry M. Jackson of Washington gives promise of high usefulness in this direction, and it ought to be broadened.

Such a study ought to consider possible correlations between the often unworkable foreign policies of national sovereignties and the present condition of world anarchy among the nations. For the absence of law among nations not only leads to crises among them but actually tends to create disorganization within the nations themselves. The effects of anarchy are both external and internal.

What is needed is not just greater streamlining and coordination in American foreign policy, but the existence of a unifying principle. World law is that principle, endorsed by history in general and the American Constitution-makers in particular.

*—July 2, 1966*


# The Computer and the Poet

The essential problem of man in a computerized age remains the same as it has always been. That problem is not solely how to be more productive, more comfortable, more content, but how to be more sensitive, more sensible, more proportionate, more alive. The computer makes possible a phenomenal leap in human proficiency; it demolishes the fences around the practical and even the theoretical intelligence. But the question persists and indeed grows whether the computer will make it easier or harder for human beings to know who they really are, to identify their real problems, to respond more fully to beauty, to place adequate value on life, and to make their world safer than it now is.

Electronic brains can reduce the profusion of dead ends involved in vital research. But they can't eliminate the foolishness and decay that come from the unexamined life. Nor do they connect a man to the things he has to be connected to—the reality of pain in others; the possibilities of creative growth in himself; the memory of the race; and the rights of the next generation.

The reason these matters are important in a computerized age is that there may be a tendency to mistake data for wisdom, just as there has always been a tendency to confuse logic with values, and intelligence with insight. Unobstructed access to facts can produce unlimited good only if it is matched by the desire and ability to find out what they mean and where they would lead.

Facts are terrible things if left sprawling and unattended. They are too easily regarded as evaluated certainties rather than as the rawest of raw materials crying to be processed into the texture of logic. It requires a very unusual mind, Whitehead said, to undertake the analysis of a fact. The computer can provide a correct number, but it may be an irrelevant number until judgment is pronounced.

To the extent, then, that man fails to make the distinction between the intermediate operations of electronic intelligence and the ultimate responsibilities of human decision and conscience, the computer could prove a digression. It could obscure man's awareness of the need to come to terms with himself. It could foster the illusion that he is asking fundamental questions when actually he is asking only functional ones. It could be regarded as a substitute for intelligence instead of an extension of it. It could promote undue confidence in concrete answers. "If we begin with certainties," Bacon said, "we shall end in doubts; but if we begin with doubts, and we are patient with them, we shall end in certainties."

The biggest single need in computer technology is not for improved circuitry, or enlarged capacity, or prolonged memory, or miniaturized containers, but for better questions and better use of the answers. Without taking anything away from the technicians, we think it might be fruitful to effect some sort of junction between the computer technologist and the poet. A genuine purpose may be served by turning loose the wonders of the creative imagination on the kinds of problems being put to electronic tubes and transistors. The company of poets may enable the men who tend the machines to see a larger panorama of possibilities than technology alone may inspire.

A poet, said Aristotle, has the advantage of expressing the universal; the specialist expresses only the particular. The poet, moreover, can remind us that man's greatest energy comes not from his dynamos but from his dreams. The notion of where a man ought to be instead of where he is; the liberation from cramped prospects; the intimations of immortality through art—all these proceed naturally out of dreams. But the quality of a man's dreams can only be a reflection of his subconscious. What he puts into his subconscious, therefore, is quite literally the most important nourishment in the world.

Nothing really happens to a man except as it is registered in the subconscious. This is where event and feeling become memory and where the proof of life is stored. The poet—and we use the term to include all those who have respect for and speak to the human spirit—can help to supply the subconscious with material to enhance its sensitivity, thus safeguarding it. The poet, too, can help to keep man from making himself over in the image of his electronic marvels. For the danger is not so much that man will be controlled by the computer as that he may imitate it.

The poet reminds men of their uniqueness. It is not necessary to possess the ultimate definition of this uniqueness. Even to speculate on it is a gain.

*—July 23, 1966*

# Report from Geneva

GENEVA, SWITZERLAND.
A sense of shock and revulsion seizes the world when a young man, laden with gun and ammunition, mounts a college tower and proceeds to slaughter people at random. There seems to be little concern, however,

about a rapidly developing world situation in which the sky itself could become an atomic gun-mount with the entire human race vulnerable and exposed to nuclear holocaust. What gives the matter special point is that the world has not yet found an adequate way of safeguarding human society against irrational decisions and actions on the level where nation confronts nation.

Here at Geneva, representatives of a special United Nations committee have been meeting for the purpose of finding some way of keeping modern weaponry under control. The delegates recognize that the continued development and spread of nuclear explosives and missiles can create a situation, not too far distant, when "civilization" will be forced to move underground in order to cope with the ceaseless threat of a sudden hurricane of nuclear fire.

Two specific areas were marked out for possible agreement by the Geneva Conference. One involved a halt to the further spread of nuclear weapons. The second involved an extension of the present ban on nuclear testing to all environments, whether in the air, sea, outer space, or underground.

At the start of the current session last January, there seemed to be reasonable grounds for believing that effective agreement was possible in both areas. Of all nations, the United States and the Soviet Union had most to lose by the proliferation of nuclear weapons. Both countries had spent enormous sums on their nuclear arsenals in pursuit of a commanding world position. If, therefore, a dozen or more countries were to build or acquire nuclear weapons, the practical effect would be to reduce heavily, and perhaps ultimately to wipe out, the military superiority of the major nuclear powers. To be sure, these major powers would continue to possess superior stockpiles, but the significance of such superiority would be measured more in terms of prestige than military might, since a relatively small number of nuclear weapons could destroy any nation, large or small. Hence it seemed inconceivable that the United States and the Soviet Union would lose any time in reaching agreement on the best way to slam the door on the spread of nuclear weapons. And if these two nations could agree, it was not considered likely that other nations would stand in the way of general agreement.

Similarly, a comprehensive test-ban agreement was regarded by the UN delegates as being in the best interests of both the U.S. and the U.S.S.R. Underground testing is prodigiously expensive. The refinements in the size and type of nuclear weapons produced would not be enough to offset the cost or the grim consequences of a world nuclear arms race.

But the expected agreements on non-proliferation and on a comprehensive test ban have not materialized at Geneva. The two nations that stood to gain most by agreement have been unable to agree.

On the non-proliferation issue, the United States took the position that atomic weapons could not be excluded from the arsenals of its military alliances. The Soviet Union took the position that the United States was proposing a treaty containing a loophole that would give West Germany access to nuclear weapons.

Thus the problem at Geneva was not just the need to work out the precise details of a treaty but to deal with the reality of Germany. In private discussions with other delegates, the Russians expressed their bewilderment at the attitude of the Americans. They found it inconceivable that the United States should permit West Germany to rearm at all, let alone be part of a nuclear force and perhaps even have access to the atomic trigger. Twenty million dead Russians in one war—quite apart from the toll of previous wars—represented enough reasons to oppose any treaty which would make an exception for the one nation which, the Russians insisted, could not be trusted with access to overwhelming force.

The Americans have replied by saying, first, that their draft proposal would not have the effect of giving West Germany command of any nuclear switchboard, and that, second, it is a serious error to assume that what has happened before will necessarily happen again; Germany today is not the Germany of the Thirties.

The Russian rejoinder is that the United States itself has publicly assured its NATO allies that they are full military partners. If the United States is to be taken at its word, say the Russians, NATO becomes the loophole through which West Germany becomes a nuclear power. And if the United States contends there is no danger of a revival of German militarism, they add, it is ignoring the evidence of a neo-Nazism observed by the German press itself.

In any case, the Russians say they are not prepared to sign a nuclear non-proliferation treaty that implicitly or explicitly excludes West Germany. Finally, the Russians profess to be mystified by the fact that their own proposed draft for a non-proliferation treaty has been virtually ignored by the United States. They would like their draft to have detailed study and consideration. They would like some indication by the Americans that the Russian draft even exists. Morever, the Russians believe it is now their turn to furnish a document that will be regarded by the Americans as a basic draft, since it was the American draft that was accepted by the Russians as the basis for the test-ban treaty.

The despair at Geneva produced by this state of affairs was relieved, at least temporarily, when Secretary of Defense Robert McNamara some weeks ago proposed a consultation procedure inside NATO on the use of nuclear weapons.

Behind the scenes, influential Russians have indicated that this formula might be satisfactory to their government. They have been waiting for the United States to incorporate the McNamara formula in its official proposals. The fact that the United States has not done so has been interpreted, not just by the Russians but by other delegates here, as evidence of a difference of opinion within the ranks of the U.S. policy-makers.

Americans in key positions have attempted to offset this impression by getting word through to the Russians that the United States might be prepared to revise its draft to reflect the McNamara view if the Russians would provide some specific indication that they would respond affirmatively to such a proposal.

Through the same intermediaries, informal word has come back to the Americans that the Soviet delegation feels such an approach is too iffy. The Russians contend they cannot reasonably be expected to provide advance response to a proposal that is not official and that in fact has not been fully formed.

The American reply is that the United States is understandably reluctant to introduce drastic new proposals unless it knows there is some point to the exercise.

Again, the Russians say the Americans have not hesitated to introduce any number of other new ideas and approaches, such as a plan for scientific detection of violations to go along with the new U.S. proposal for a cutoff in the production of fissionable materials for weapon purposes. Since the Americans did not think it important to find out in advance what the Russian reaction would be in this case, the Russians see no reason to follow a different procedure with respect to the McNamara proposal.

The Russians privately add that the failure of the U.S. Government to follow up Secretary McNamara's consultation formula may actually reflect a new American decision to accept all the perils of a world-wide dissemination of nuclear weapons rather than to face up to the awkward and difficult political situation involved in standing up to the Germans. As confirmation, the Russians point to a recent article by John W. Finney, in The New York Times, saying that Washington, once eager to have non-proliferation, has cooled off considerably.

In short, the Soviet assessment of the present American position is that the United States attaches greater importance to the need to avoid disturbing its relationship with Bonn than to the need to check the spread of nuclear weapons.

When this interpretation is called to the attention of the Americans, the response is that the Russian estimate is wide of the mark. True, the United States intends to maintain good relations with Bonn, but it has no intention of putting nuclear weapons in German hands or of barring Germany from responsible participation in NATO. As for The New York Times article, the Americans say the Russians persistently make the mistake of measuring U.S. newspaper "background" articles by their own controlled-press yardstick. But the Americans privately admit that the absence of any counter-statement or denial at the time of publication did serious harm—not just among the Russians but among members of other delegations.

If the Russians really want to find out whether the United States is serious about wanting a non-proliferation treaty, say the Americans, then let them accept the U.S. proposal. True, such a treaty would not satisfy the Russians about Germany, but at least it would have the effect of setting up some barriers against the infinitely precarious spread of atomic force. Moreover, such a treaty could create a positive momentum and might lead before long to a better answer on Germany than now seems attainable.

The Russians concede there is apparent logic in the argument that even an imperfect non-proliferation treaty is better than none, but they contend it is even more logical to suppose that an exception made for West Germany now will harden rather than soften with the passage of time. And the Russians can conceive of no greater danger to them—or to the rest of the world—than a resurgence of German militarism with access, direct or indirect, to atomic force. Besides, the ability of West Germany to create situations that can force the hand of the United States is something the Russians believe has not been taken sufficiently into account.

And so the argument goes, round and round like a giant waterwheel, requiring only the slightest impetus to keep it turning and always coming back to the same point.

What do the other delegates think—the delegates from the other sixteen nations who have been meeting in Geneva? How do they assess the American and Soviet positions?

The dominant feeling in the closing sessions of the Geneva Conference is one of sadness at another great opportunity missed. This feeling is somewhat tempered, however, by the recollection that the test-ban negotiations leading ultimately to a successful treaty seemed at times even more inconclusive and futile than the current multilateral negotiations over non-proliferation. Yet once President Kennedy and Premier Khrushchev, in direct exchange, were able to establish the fact of a common serious intent to do away with atmospheric tests, and were able to agree on the *broad* outlines of a treaty, all the intricate spadework and detailed discussions that had gone into the previous UN disarmament negotiations suddenly became highly essential and useful. Similarly, many of the delegates at Geneva feel that the key to any non-proliferation treaty, or an enlargement of the present test-ban, is in the hands of President Johnson and Premier Kosygin. The delegates feel they have gone as far as they can go in the basic groundwork and in attending to the point-by-point details. They do not believe their work has been entirely wasted or is without significance—once there is a summit understanding between the U.S. and the U.S.S.R.

Some of the delegates attach high value to proposals made by the United States in the closing days of the conference. In particular, they believe that the U.S. offer of a plant-by-plant shutdown of nuclear manufacturing installations should be kept alive. They are also impressed by the U.S. description of a new detection system for monitoring a cutoff in the production of fissionable materials for weapons purposes.

At the same time, some of the same delegates say that these U.S. proposals, impressive though they are, would have shown to even greater advantage if they had not been put forward during the non-proliferation debate. They feel the U.S. might have waited until the outlines of a non-proliferation treaty were completed.

In procedural terms, this would appear to make good sense. Certainly the United States should have done everything possible to avoid any impression that its new proposals were in any sense diversionary or obfuscating, however meritorious they may have been in themselves.

Questions of procedure and sequence aside, however, one fact that emerged above all other facts at Geneva is that nothing concerned with peace can be kept separate from anything else concerned with peace. In the long run, attempts to halt the spread of nuclear weapons cannot be divorced from the problems arising out of continued possession and manufacture of nuclear weapons by nations that already have them. The smaller nations with a potential nuclear capacity see little justice or sense in a situation that deprives them of the right to initiate manufacture but does nothing to deprive the nuclear nations of the right to continue manufacturing and stockpiling. Also, the non-nuclear nations object to a situation in which they would be barred from any future nuclear development while the nuclear nations would be left free to make new kinds of nuclear weapons.

Non-proliferation, therefore, is tied to a comprehensive test-ban, just as a comprehensive test-ban is tied to other potent forms of warfare using chemical and biological weapons. And all are related to the total problem of disarmament; just as disarmament is related to the circumstances that make disarmament possible.

Germany is only one case in point. Communist China is another. India over the years has disavowed any intention of joining the nuclear club. The development of nuclear capacity by China, plus the eruption of fighting along the Chinese-Indian border, plus the present activity by China in helping Pakistan in nuclear development—all this has given India some sober second thoughts about nuclear abstention.

Japan, too, confronted by the stern fact of geography with respect to Communist China, feels some compulsion to develop its own nuclear muscle.

Egypt and Israel are also potentially capable of making nuclear explosives. Any move by one in this direction will produce a heightened response by the other. Sweden could make the bomb if it wanted to and has already served notice on the large nations that their failure to arrive at atomic control measures among themselves could well result in a reversal of Sweden's traditional reluctance to get into advanced arsenals. At least six other nations could make nuclear weapons within a decade.

In a very real sense, the world nightmare dreaded for so many years has already come to pass. The United States, Great Britain, France, the Soviet Union, and Communist China, representing the five most powerful nations in the world, all have nuclear weapons. Only a fraction of the atomic explosives already stockpiled could destroy not just all life on earth but the conditions that make life possible.

In retrospect, the most serious failing in history is chargeable to those who were in a position in 1945, at the end of the Second World War, to pursue world controls over the development and spread of nuclear force. In the United States, the emphasis was on the pursuit rather than the control of atomic force. The Soviet Union was committed to an all-out effort to offset the U.S. nuclear advantage. Indeed, the Soviet Union exploded a hydrogen bomb before the United States did.

But ruminations over the growing materialization of a nightmare are without point. The only point is to find out what can be done now. Another disarmament conference would serve only to vibrate from the small to the large; from the particular to the general; from the military to the political; from partial to comprehensive; from the immediates to the ultimates; from the individual nation to the alliance; from the alliance to the world.

Therefore, other initiatives are essential. The first step is not a cosmic one. It calls for the President of the United States and the Premier of the Soviet Union to enter into direct communication on the non-proliferation issue. If the President agrees with Secretary McNamara's consultation-rather-than-possession formula for solving the German question, it is reasonable to believe the two countries can come to general agreement. If they do so reasonably soon, other nations are likely to withdraw their own demands or objections. The standby details of a treaty worked out at Geneva can be brought forward by way of expediting agreement on the minor issues.

The second step is for the United States to seek high-level agreement on a comprehensive test-ban. Underground explosions have too small a yield for the cost involved. The Soviet insists that existing scientific instrumentation, operated at great distances, rules out the need for on-site inspection. The United States wants physical verification. A possible compromise may be found in the recommendations of the recent Toronto Conference, held under the combined auspices of the American Assembly of Columbia University, the Canadian Institute of International Affairs, the Institute for Strategic Studies, and the Carnegie Endowment for International Peace. Experts from various countries, including the United States and the Soviet Union, participated in the unofficial Conference. They were able to agree on the feasibility of a remote detection system plus a procedure of "challenge-and-response" as a way of ending the present inspection deadlock. This recommendation, and indeed the full report of the Toronto Conference, warrant serious official consideration as the basis for effective agreement.

But even agreements on non-proliferation and test-ban enlargement, important and consequential though they may be, are only part of a far wider need. That need is to create a new context for a workable peace. The present context is one in which the foreign policies of individual nations have right of way over the ability of the United Nations to deal with the tensions or conflicts produced by those same national policies. Therefore the United Nations must be brought to full strength—in procedures, powers, membership. For the world requires a better mechanism than it now has for preventing conflict or for dealing with it whenever and wherever it arises.

The UN will never be a cure-all. But at least it should be able to act with a reasonable degree of effectiveness in behalf of the common interests of the world's peoples, a function that no single nation is equipped either to define or discharge by itself.

For the United States to realize its greatest power and security, it has only to become an eloquent and persistent advocate for such a United Nations. This is the kind of advocacy that carries with it the full resonance of American history and the prospect of a wider response than most men now dare hope.

—September 3, 1966

# U Thant

Representatives of many sovereigns have called on him and sought to persuade him to continue to serve. Heads of the world's religions have tried devoutly to move him. Philosophers and poets and artists of the earth have sent messages.

He is one of a small handful of men who occupy a new station in human history. Their job is to prevent nations from coming into violent collision. It is an extraordinarily difficult undertaking, for no creature on earth possesses greater stubbornness and falser notions of what constitutes reason and justice than the absolute sovereign state.

U Thant has said he would like to retire from his post. But many of the same nations that have made it impossible for him to do his job well are now imploring him to continue. A grotesque double standard, in fact, exists in the attitude of some of the nations that constitute the UN. The moment representatives of these nations walk through the doors of the UN, they abruptly reverse the principle which alone makes it possible for their own national governments to function. What is absolutely indispensable in the operation of their governments are adequate authority and the assured means of support. They know the alternative is anarchy. Yet they themselves represent the prime elements of anarchy on the world level. They reject totally the concept of compulsory taxation in the world community, though they would not countenance a situation in their own communities in which individual citizens remained the judges of whether or not they should pay and how much. Nor would they permit their citizens to set aside the peace-keeping functions of their governments, yet they constantly block effective peace-keeping machinery on the world level.

It is unreasonable to expect any man of purpose, intelligence, and understanding to accept a responsibility without the means of discharging it. When U Thant says that the United Nations cannot carry out its basic purposes without authority or revenue, he is not dictating the conditions for his own continuation as Secretary General. He is calling attention to the basic principles of survival for the organization itself. Whether he or another man occupies the office, the principles remain the same. And if the principles are not respected, neither he nor anyone else will be able to save the UN. The issue as he sees it, therefore, is not how long he remains, but how soon the United Nations can be made to take its underlying problems seriously.

Only recently, he has traveled to the capitals of certain nations and talked to the heads of governments in an attempt to win their adherence to a policy of adequate moral and financial support for the peace-keeping functions of the UN. He has been unsuccessful. Some of these same nations are now imploring him to stay in office.

He feels profoundly the impotence of the UN in the Vietnam war. Even more deeply is he dismayed by the gap between the proclaimed willingness of nations to negotiate and their refusal to do so when confronted by opportunities to engage in exploratory talks for which he himself helped to set the stage.

He is not embittered. Despite all reversals and difficulties, he retains a rock-like belief in the future of the United Nations. He knows there is nothing else on which the future of the human community can be built— nothing else that gives greater promise of protecting human beings from the holocaust-producing weapons now in the hands of an increasing number of national sovereignties. He is a man of limitless good faith and good will. He has incredible qualities of patience and personal serenity. He comes from the East but he is equally at home in the West.

He has extraordinary intellectual and spiritual endowments but they are not infinite. He has known—increasingly often in recent years—the terrors of fatigue. His formal working day begins early in the morning and continues to nine at night. Even then, the telephone and the work pursue him at home. Saturdays are full working days. On Sundays, the locale but not the intensity of the work changes. He is a man who loves the life of the mind but in the past nine years he has found the time to read fewer than a dozen books. On two or three occasions during those nine years, Adlai Stevenson almost bodily lifted him out of his office to take him to a movie or to the theater.

Not all of the problems of his job are the historic ones. He is expected to endure an incalculable amount of pettiness. Not long ago, he was asked by a delegate for an appointment, and he promptly fixed a date. On the day of the appointment, he was virtually anchored to the chamber of the Security Council. He sent a message to the delegate, suggesting that they meet in a room adjacent to the Security Council chamber. Later, the delegate complained bitterly that it was only because he represented a small nation that the Secretary General did not see him in his office.

Apart from all problems, puny or prodigious, there is the yearning to return home. Family life in Burma is close-knit. He would like to spend time with his mother. She is eighty-three.

The most powerful arguments for him to remain at his post have come not from officialdom but from everyday people all over the world. The letters have arrived by the hundreds from people who understand his ordeal, yet who beg him to stay on. He now knows he has a constituency of common folk; they have made him a custodian of their hopes. If he finally decides to stay, it will be not just because a way has been found to enable him to perform more fully and effectively the duties of his office, but because of the manifest public support that might enable the UN to become what it has to be.

—*October 1, 1966*

# The Second Front in Vietnam

Let us take a simple statement and pursue some of its implications. The statement, generally presented as a bedrock cause for U.S. involvement in Vietnam, takes this form:

"Adolf Hitler could have been stopped in the Thirties if the free nations had acted promptly and decisively. It was when aggressive Nazism discovered that the free nations were more concerned with their comforts than their convictions that Nazism made its greatest gains. If the United

States had had the wisdom and courage to stand up to Hitler early enough, the lives of millions of people could have been saved.

"The world today is undergoing another test of nerve. Communist China —expansionist, aggressive, restless—seeks to take over all Asia. The initial target is Indochina; in particular, Vietnam, Laos, Thailand, and Cambodia. If China should succeed in gaining direct or indirect control over any one of these nations, it will not stop until all four have come under its dominion. After that, unremitting pressure will be directed against Indonesia, Burma, Nepal, India, Pakistan, the Philippines, Japan, Australia, and New Zealand. The time to stop Communist China is now and the place is Vietnam."

This particular analysis and prescription have been expounded many times but never more emphatically than by Thanat Khoman, Foreign Minister of Thailand, during his recent visit to the United States, when he spoke in vigorous support of American policy in Vietnam. He declared that the United States, in defending the nations of Southeast Asia, was properly acting in its own self-interest. If it failed to act now, it would set the stage for larger conflict later.

We don't happen to agree with this particular historical analogy. There are significant differences between the situation as it existed thirty years ago and the situation today. But our purpose here is not to argue that point. Our purpose, rather, is to examine some of the implications of a policy based on the validity of the analogy. What it means is that the Vietnam war is incidental to a larger problem and purpose. But the price the Vietnamese people have had to pay for their geography is far from incidental. Whether as victims or wards, the Vietnamese have been caught up in one of history's bloodiest meat-grinders. The arrival of the Vietcong has meant assassination, intimidation, raw terror. In the attempt to liberate them from the Vietcong, the Americans have rained bombs down on the Vietnamese, defoliated their crops, burned their villages. It is not easy to distinguish Vietcong from noncombatants. According to estimates four Vietnamese have died for every member of the Vietcong who has been killed.

It makes little difference whether you are among those who give the strongest support to present U.S. policy in Vietnam or among those who are its severest critics. Both groups can recognize that we have a special obligation to the Vietnamese. Their present condition calls for a program of care and mercy—a program not less imaginative or far-reaching than the prosecution of the war itself.

Winston S. Churchill, grandson of the British war leader, recently visited hospitals in Vietnam. He reported that medical treatment is indescribably wretched. Countless thousands of civilians wounded by war are without adequate medical attention.

Representatives of the American Friends Service Committee report that thousands of Vietnamese children urgently require sustained medical care. Many of them are suffering from serious burns. Many of them need homes.

American surgeons, sent on missions supported by private funds, report that there is a virtually endless procession of people who have been maimed and who require plastic or reconstructive surgery.

CARE reports thousands of people who are hungry and on the move.

Is this something that Americans should take in their stride? Do we make the necessary adjustment just by saying that all wars are horrible? Or do we say that nothing in our history lays more of a moral claim on Americans? The test of the United States in Vietnam will be represented not by our ability to exterminate the Vietcong but by our determination to save lives where we can, to make mercy just as central as military operations, and to put the individual human being first.

It is estimated that it costs the United States about $100,000 to kill one member of the Vietcong. How much is it worth to us to keep people alive? Why should instant dollars be available for bombs but only pennies wrapped in red tape for medical care and rehabilitation? Why should the American people be satisfied with the explanation that the hospitals seen by Mr. Churchill are under the jurisdiction of the South Vietnam government and that it would be interference to try to set things straight? In military matters, we have no difficulty in running the war the way we think it should be run. Why should we be any less forthright where human values are at stake?

At least a dozen private agencies are working in the area of social care and medical relief in Vietnam. Readers of *Saturday Review*, through their contributions to the Cam Ne Fund, have sent plastic surgeons to Vietnam. All these efforts have to be expanded. But these efforts cannot be regarded as a substitute for the massive program that only the United States Government itself can mount and carry out. Would the United States be content to run the war in Vietnam largely through the efforts of volunteer agencies? Why should its approach to the suffering resulting from the war be any less dynamic or far-reaching?

The Congress of the United States ought to insist that any appropriations for the war in Vietnam be made on the principle of moral balance. Every dollar authorized for military spending should be matched by a dollar for relief, hospitals, medical care, restoration, reconstruction, and rehabilitation. There is a second front we can open up in Vietnam. We ought to be flying sick, maimed, and homeless children by the planeload from Vietnam to the United States. If hospital facilities are inadequate, and if homes cannot be found in Vietnam, we can find them here. We should also be constructing emergency medical facilities for the population at large with a spirit that makes it clear this is the most important thing on our minds.

Despite what has been said recently in some quarters, life is not cheap in Asia—or anywhere else. The conditions of life may be wretched and difficult to endure, but there could be no greater indictment than for Americans to take the position that the life of any individual, however illiterate and miserable he may be, is cheaper than the life of any American, however eminent or prosperous. The fact that we should have to remind ourselves of these things, with years like 1776 and 1787 in our history, is profoundly disturbing in itself.

*—October 29, 1966*

# Is It Possible to Be an Optimist?

Is it possible to be an optimist in a world which has turned most of its organized brain power and energy into the systematic means for debasing life or mutilating it or scorching it or obliterating it? What basis is there for hope when the human future is increasingly in the hands of men who do not comprehend the meaning of the new power and who are, some of them, puny and fretful and prone to act out of frustration or false pride or mistaken notions of grandeur?

Is it possible to believe in the ability of the human species to eliminate the mass injustice that leads to mass violence—or the mass violence that feeds back into mass injustice? Can anyone have confidence in the capacity of human intelligence to sustain the natural environment on which humans are absolutely dependent—at a time when the progressive despoliation and poisoning of air, land, and water are fast outrunning efforts to protect the environment?

Questions like these are producing a profound upheaval within the body of contemporary Western social philosophy. For the essence of modern social thought is its belief in the idea of human progress. With a few exceptions such as Spengler, the leading thinkers of the past few centuries have generally accepted Aquinas's idea that man "advances gradually from the imperfect to the perfect." Pascal underscored this notion when he said that man is a creature capable not only of undergoing experiences but of comprehending them, and that the unending accumulation of experiences is therefore bound to be reflected in his own learning, understanding, and growth. Bacon, Descartes, Kant, and Hegel, each in his own way, have attempted to break free from the Aristotelian concept of fixed limitations on human potentiality, or the Lucretian idea of cataclysmic disaster, or the prophetic notion of doom.

No group of thinkers has had more to say about the potentialities of human beings, especially under conditions of freedom, than Americans such as Franklin, Jefferson, Emerson, William James, Holmes, Pierce, and Dewey. Each has added depth and strength to the idea that human-kind is capable of almost infinite development. Indeed, emerging from the ideas of the American social philosophers is a definition of human uniqueness: the ability to do that which has never been done before.

Today, however, the bedrock of modern social philosophy has been badly shaken by a long series of somber developments pointing toward the ultimate decimation of the human species. The habit of violence is no less significant than the technology of violence. There has been a grow-ing desensitization to human hurt.

Albert Schweitzer perhaps reflected the dilemma of many of his col-leagues when he said that any optimism he might have for the human future rested less on his knowledge of history or on his analytical faculties than on a pervasive wish that everything would come out all right. Yet there is no real contradiction between the two. The capacity to hope is not the natural enemy of the analytical intelligence. It is a source of energy for creating new options. It helps to create new uses for logic. It sets people in motion and thus gives rise to new swirls, new contexts, new combinations. It gives reality a new face.

History is an accumulation of causes and effects, but it is far from being a procession of inevitables. Time and again, supposedly inexorable forces have been reversed by human acts proceeding out of positive human decisions. To say that man is locked into error and delusion runs counter to human experience. This is not to underestimate his propensity for error. But neither should we underestimate man's ability through an act of will to create a wide and exciting range of new possibilities. The only ultimate prison he need fear is his inertia and indecision.

Pessimism has one thing in common with optimism. It is not only a mood but a movement. The main characteristic of pessimism is that it tends to set the stage for its own omens. It is self-fulfilling. It shuns prospects in the act of denying them. It narrows the field of vision, obscur-ing the relationship between the necessary and the possible.

The prime fallacy of pessimism is that no one really knows enough to be a pessimist. It is unhistorical to rule out the conversion of impondera-bles under pressure from powerful ideas into positive forces. And the reason there is no inconsistency between the exercise of reason and the optimistic outlook is that the search for new approaches or answers often has to be built on new grounds—and optimism is the range-finder for locating such grounds. Optimism is also a way of paying our respects to the mysterious process of change in human affairs and to the marvelous suddenness with which new prospects are revealed when urgently sought. The achievement of a limited ban on the testing of nuclear weapons was one example. Extending that ban to all levels of testing and to all nations can be another. Creating a basis for a reasonably decent and war-free existence on this planet can be yet another.

It *is* possible to be an optimist in today's world—without having to strain or synthesize. It is necessary only to attach oneself confidently to a plan for accomplishing an essential purpose—and then to help bring that plan to life with advocacy and work. The only thing more dangerous than nuclear force in today's world is failure to perceive the lines of connection between the individual and the ideas and forces that shape his world.

*—November 5, 1966*


# A Man for All Seasons

*On January 13, 1967, Grenville Clark, distinguished American, world citizen, and architect of the concept of world peace through world law, died in Dublin, New Hampshire, after a long illness. His life provided proof of the proposition that the highest justification and reward of a free society is the free individual who can help shape the policies of the government and the form of that society. The editorial which follows appeared in* SR *two months before his death:*

Grenville Clark, who makes you think of a company of Americans like Madison, Jefferson, and John Adams, has just turned eighty-four. He has never held public office and is not popularly known, but it is doubtful if any living American is more deserving of the Nobel Peace Prize. If the United Nations ever achieves the maturity of a workable government with adequate, responsible powers, the role of Grenville Clark in making it possible will have been a key one.

I first met him in 1945, shortly after the end of the Second World War. He had joined with the late Owen J. Roberts, associate justice of the Supreme Court and the late Robert P. Bass, former governor of New Hampshire, in inviting forty-eight Americans to a conference in Dublin, New Hampshire, where he lived, for the purpose of considering the revolutionary new situation in the world represented by the development of nuclear weapons. I learned that he was widely respected by his peers as a lawyer with a keen interest in world affairs, and that he had been consulted by four Presidents on matters of foreign policy and national defense.

Clark made the opening presentation at the Dublin Conference. He attempted to look ahead twenty years or more. He said he thought it unreasonable to assume that the wartime alliance between the United States and the Soviet Union could hold up under the pressure of events. He forecast a struggle for the balance of power under conditions of uncertainty and insecurity for both countries. He saw the emergence of a world atomic armaments race. Despite published assurances to the contrary by

U.S. Government spokesmen, he anticipated the development within a few years of nuclear weapons by the Soviet Union, and by other countries within a generation. He said it would be difficult to keep the atomic armaments race from leading to a world holocaust unless strong measures were taken to create a world authority with law-enacting and law-enforcing powers.

He believed the moment in history had come for creating the instruments of workable law. He spoke of the need for a world government which would have "limited but adequate" powers. It should be "limited" in the sense that it would not interfere with internal functioning of the nations. It should be "adequate" in the sense that it would be able to deal with the historic causes of war and would seek to insure justice in the relations among nations. In short, he proposed world law as the only alternative to the existing world anarchy.

Listening to Grenville Clark that day at Dublin, New Hampshire, was an unforgettable experience. He was then, as he is today, a magnificent example of the man of reason joined to the man of good will. He summoned historical experience, always giving proper weight to his analogies, always making the essential qualifications. The political philosophy reflected in his talk placed him in the tradition of John Stuart Mill, the Physiocrats, the leaders of the Philadelphia Constitutional Convention, and jurists like Oliver Wendell Holmes. When he spoke about the need for world law, he was not just trying to prevent world war; he was speaking to a condition necessary for human progress.

As the result of Clark's leadership, the Dublin Conference produced a document that commanded national attention and served as the effective beginning for the world law movement in the United States and elsewhere. Clark was its main architect and champion; he was also its primary source of energy and inspiration. Since then he has put everything aside in order to work for the ideas contained in the Dublin Declaration. He is one of the few men in the world, in fact, who has given full time to the most important need on earth. With Professor Louis B. Sohn of Harvard University, he wrote the book, *World Peace Through World Law*, which addressed itself to the multiplicity of problems involved in the transformation of the United Nations into a source of enforceable world law. The book recognizes that a world legislative body must be "weighted" in representation. For the present one-nation, one-vote system of representation makes the enactment of world legislation cumbersome and potentially inequitable. The book presents carefully developed ideas that indicate the practicality as well as feasibility of weighted representation. In 1959, the American Bar Association awarded him its Gold Medal, referring to *World Peace Through World Law* as a "major contribution to world literature" on the subject of peace.

Clark has tackled the bugaboo of absolute sovereignty in a way that has disarmed even the most pronounced adherents of unfettered national determination. At the Dartmouth Conference between prominent Americans and Russians in 1960, the meeting was virtually at a point of tension-saturation. The Americans were steadfast in their advocacy of a plan for disarmament with full inspection and control. The Russians reacted sharply to what some of them described as a plan for violating the sovereignty and security of their country. The tone of the meeting became somewhat harsh and strident. Grenville Clark, who until that moment had been silent, asked to speak.

He began by saying he accepted fully the genuineness of the desire of the Russians present to reduce and eliminate the danger of war. He spoke of the enormous number of casualties suffered by the Russian people in the Second World War. He referred to the siege of Leningrad and the heroism of its people. He spoke of the contribution made by the Russian people to victory in the war. He spoke movingly and with great dignity. Then he spoke of the need to avert even greater wars in an age of nuclear weapons. He defined the basic principles that had to go into the making of a workable peace. He described the opportunity before leaders of public opinion in getting acceptance for these principles. He called on both Americans and Russians to see the problem of disarmament in a larger and more historic setting than weapons alone. When he sat down, both sides gave him sustained applause. And from that moment, Grenville Clark's name was magic with all the Russians who had heard him and many who hadn't. He had demonstrated not just the power of logic but the prodigious force that is represented by an understanding of the next man's experience and problems. Even more, he had proved that even the most hardened positions tend to dissolve in the presence of honest good will and friendliness.

In 1964, despite advancing age, Grenville Clark took off on a world tour to advance the cause of world peace through world law. And wherever he went, whatever the local political and ideological situation, he made converts and friends, for the two were synonymous. To know him is to believe him.

In November 1965, he received the "Publius Award" of the United World Federalists, an organization that seeks wide acceptance for many of the ideas he helped to define and enlarge. Many of his friends in law and government, whether or not they were world federalists, came to honor him that night. He had earned their love and trust. He has a view of a better world and he has done his best to make it real.

*—November 26, 1966*

# Christmas in Vietnam

From Vietnam come news dispatches about truce periods over the Christmas and New Year's holidays. According to the Hanoi radio, the Vietcong has offered a forty-eight-hour cease-fire for Christmas and a similar cease-fire for New Year's. The news reports say that this initiative produced a flurry of consultations between South Vietnamese and U.S. officials who, apparently, had been taken by surprise. They were in the process themselves of considering a holiday truce offer when the Vietcong announcement beat them to the punch.

The news report reminded readers that U.S. and South Vietnamese officials were disadvantaged last year when the Vietcong was the first to offer a twelve-hour Christmas truce, but that the United States topped the Vietcong with a proposal for extending the truce to thirty hours.

"What authorities are weighing now," the news report said, "is the propaganda advantage of a longer truce period against the military disadvantages of giving the Communists more time to organize and concentrate their forces undisturbed. Officials also are considering how long a cease-fire should be observed at Tet, the Buddhist New Year, which falls next February 9. The Communists made no mention of that holiday period in their announcement."

If the news account is accurate, the American people can ponder the moral poverty implicit in the attitude of the officials involved. The governing principle, apparently, is not what can be done to save lives at a time when a religious holiday provides an opportunity to do so. The governing principle is whether a propaganda advantage exists and, if so, whether it can be an offset to military factors.

It is difficult to comprehend why this particular holiday-truce initiative should have remained in the hands of the Vietcong after the experience last year. It is even more difficult to comprehend why we should be put in the position of backing into a cease-fire because there is no other choice. If there is so little moral imagination in this case, what reasonable expectations are there for a wider approach to the possibilities for bringing the fighting to an end altogether? Things do not happen in isolation. If a Christmas cease-fire is regarded as a necessary evil, this says something about the prospect for mounting strong initiatives to set a stage for ending the war through negotiated settlement. The President has said that military victory is impossible. He has also made it clear that the United States believes that only a political settlement can end the war and bring peace to Vietnam. If that is the case, then a Christmas cease-fire provides an opportunity to get into the kind of reciprocal de-escalation that Ambassador Arthur J. Goldberg has said represents our present intention and objective.

The protracted pause in the military activity last Christmas, far from being a liability, should be regarded as a promising precedent. This time, the United States should announce that it is willing to maintain a cease-fire indefinitely, that it will not be the first to resume the fighting, and that it is prepared to use the cease-fire as a basis for negotiations with all those involved in the fighting.

The indications are substantial that the South Vietnam government will be opposed to such a move. The South Vietnam government has little interest in a negotiated settlement, as it has taken pains repeatedly to emphasize. But this doesn't mean that the United States is obligated to have its foreign policy made in Saigon. If there is any chance to end the fighting or reduce it, we ought to grasp it with both hands.

A Christmas cease-fire, by its very nature, is a grim paradox. What it says, in effect, is that men can come to their moral senses only on special occasions. Death is deferred for a few hours; men can look up at a sky without the squint that comes from fear of raining dynamite; homes and huts can stand without jeopardy; children can come out of the tunnels in which they have spent so much of their lives. Then the period of religious significance designated by the calendar comes to a close and the world resumes its normal abnormalities. Men take up their guns and the air is filled with talk of the impossibility and inadvisability of premature settlement. It becomes too easy to make the adjustment again to the ongoing violence of the war, too difficult to say that the way to stop the violence is to stop it. Pope Paul's plan for an indefinite continuation of the cease-fire may sound to some like an unrealistic call for a prolongation of the spirit of Christmas. But all other realities have been exhausted. There is left only the reality of human decency and common sense.

—*December 10, 1966*

# There's Something in the Air

### 1. *In the U.S.A.*

The main point made repeatedly at conferences on air pollution during the past two years has been that little could be done unless the public became aroused. That objective has now been achieved. During the past year, air pollution as a major problem has exploded into the national consciousness. The issue has been brought home to the American people by books, magazines, newspapers, television, and radio. The result is that the public is now ready for the drastic measures that only a few months ago would have seemed beyond popular support. In fact, it is possible that the American people are actually ahead of government in their readiness to move swiftly and decisively.

Another major change in the air pollution situation is that the problem no longer affects seriously only a few American cities and population centers. If the concern has become a national one, so has the problem. The airshed over the United States is steadily filling up with poisons. Only a few years ago, the sky over the nation was clear except for the pall over the cities. Today, however, the pall extends hundreds of miles in every direction. It is not unusual for the eastern half of the United States, all the way from Maine to Florida and extending west from Boston to Des Moines in the upper half of the country and from Miami and Atlanta in the Southeast to New Orleans and even Dallas in the lower half, to be covered by a pollution blanket. Arizona, traditionally regarded as the state with the driest and cleanest air, now has to cope with heavy smoke drifts from its mining and smelter operations. The Thanksgiving weekend air pollution episode affected not just New York City but the entire East Coast. Such dangerous inversions can be expected to recur with increasing frequency and severity—not because of new meteorological phenomena but because of the steady buildup in airborne poisons.

Each year for the past decade in the United States, several million acres have been taken out of cultivation for our spreading cities and for the construction of superhighways. This represents double jeopardy. First, it impairs nature's restorative cycle by which air is purified. Soil, vegetation, trees are part of the vital balance of nature. Second, what was formerly open space becomes filled up with pollution-causing agents—people, furnaces, incinerators, manufacturing, automobiles, buses, trucks.

The poisons in the air are no longer transient. They are fast becoming cumulative. The air pollution buildup is developing at a faster rate than nature's ability to neutralize it, or man's attempts to combat it. The gap between the intensification of the problem and the response to it becomes wider all the time.

All this sets the stage for the key question: What would happen if the rate of population growth, industrial growth, automobile growth, and highway growth of the past two decades were to remain constant or increase during the next two decades, assuming the same pace of national attack on the problem?

*The conclusion is inescapable that most of the large cities in the United States could be regarded as uninhabitable within a decade.*

This does not necessarily mean that the air pollution over the nation's large cities will reach and remain fixed at a lethal level. What it does mean is that enough serious episodes will have occurred within a decade so that the large cities will be considered unsafe as permanent places for habitation or business. This is why a vast acceleration of anti-pollution planning activity, both local and national, is now critically needed. The federal government must play a major part in such a stepped-up program. It would be a mistake, however, to assume that the cities and states should no longer have responsibility for attacking the prime sources of pollution.

The reason for a prodigious expansion in federal aid is clear. No municipality has the resources for carrying out all the measures essential to cope with the increasing sources of pollution. Any comprehensive program for the largest cities requires an expenditure of hundreds of millions of dollars, both public and private, if critical episodes are to be averted.

There is nothing more important that the United States Government could do to help safeguard the nation's air than to mount a "Manhattan District" program behind the development of the fuel cell as a source of energy.

Gas turbine engines, propane gas, liquefied petroleum, natural gas, electric motors—all these promise relief from air pollution. They should receive strong research-and-development support from the federal government. However, a major breakthrough in replacing the combustion engine may have to await the development of a fuel cell.

The United States Government mounted a $2 billion project for harnessing nuclear power. It did so because it believed that atomic energy was essential to national survival. The same is no less true of the fuel cell. The combustion engine has revolutionized the way of life not just in the United States but throughout the world. But it has produced large clouds of carbon monoxide, lead, oxides of nitrogen, and pyrobenzine, and literally has become the greatest nonpolitical enemy of the human species on earth. It carries the smell of death inside it.

No one knows how much the development of the fuel cell would cost, any more than anyone in 1940 knew how much it would finally cost to liberate atomic energy. But the need is great enough to warrant the effort. The abandonment of major American cities would be incalculably more costly.

This does not mean that everything else should be deferred until a fuel cell is developed. Mention has already been made of the need for a federal crash program to speed up the availability of efficient gas-turbine engines, or engines powered by propane gas or natural gas or liquefied petroleum gas. (Chicago is already operating propane-gas buses.) The federal government should also promote research in chemicals that can be added to gasoline, diesel fuels, and heating fuel oils to reduce excess smoke and noxious fumes. Such chemical additives already exist; they are far from being finished products, but at least they are good enough to indicate that a substantial increase in research and development is clearly justified.

The federal government should also be involved in the regulation of large smokestacks, beyond a specified capacity. Such capacity is of interstate significance. While all smoke emitters, however small, contribute to the over-all density and drift, the large stacks are specific and clearly identifiable offenders over a large area, and ought to come under federal statutes, in addition to local and state regulations.

The federal government should require air-pollution control equipment, and clearly defined performance characteristics, for all such stacks. The costs of installing such equipment should be fully tax deductible by industry within a reasonably short period.

The federal government should promote research in the improvement and sharp cost reduction of electrostatic precipitators and scrubbers. Especially is it important to promote research in the development of sulfur recovery from smokestack gases.

Again, this is not to say that the local units of government should be relieved of the central responsibility for controlling or eliminating airborne garbage and poisons. An effective nationwide program involves combined operations, with separate though related activities going forward on the national, regional, state, and city levels. But more and more, the national government will have to get into the business of setting minimum safety standards and establishing *enforcement* procedures in those cases where large air masses of poisonous drift exist.

The fight against air pollution has won its first and most important objective. The public consciousness has been pierced. Those in authority no longer need fear inadequate public support for hard measures. All the parts are now in place for a prodigious step-up in planning and implementation. Delay or inadequacy can be chargeable neither to public opinion nor technology but to government.

Air pollution is but one aspect of the whole environment. It is impossible, for example, to separate the causes and effects of impure air and impure water. Poisonous chemicals in air affect streams and reservoirs. Contamination of both air and water affects crops, livestock, and wildlife. Waste disposal through burning can create air pollution; through dumping it can create water pollution. Dumping also creates sanitation hazards.

As these and similar conditions are studied, it seems clear that *whole systems* are needed. The attack on air pollution must be part of a comprehensive program to protect the total environment. What is needed on a national scale is a plan for interrelating and coordinating problems of air pollution control, water pollution control, solid-waste disposal, noise abatement, congestion, and protection of both natural and man-made facilities that give pleasure and well-being to its citizens.

## 2. In the World

It is not now too early to begin thinking and planning on the highest levels for a world attack on the problem of contamination. Week after week, reports are published on the increasing concern of city officials in Europe, South America, Asia, and Africa about the fast-developing hazards of environmental poisoning. Tad Szulc writes from Madrid about a blanket of dust and smoke so thick that it is sometimes difficult to see from one side of a thoroughfare to the other. From Paris, Stephen Coulter reports that 180,000 tons of toxic matter are now being pumped into the air of Paris and the suburbs every year. The number of vehicles coming onto the streets is constantly increasing—carbon monoxide gas pollution from cars and trucks has tripled since the early 1920s.

London, according to correspondent Colin Chapman, no longer has to cope with soot pollution fumes caused by coal burning. City ordinances now forbid burning of soft coal. But the danger to Londoners now is from carbon monoxide and sulfur dioxide.

Rome's problem, according to Alan McElwain, may not be as serious as that of New York, but it is severe enough to warrant serious counter-attack. There are now about 500,000 automobile registrations in Rome and new cars have been coming onto the roads at an average of 100,000 a year.

Tokyo, writes Robert Trumbull, is one of the worst. Oxygen tanks have been installed at ten of Tokyo's busiest intersections for the use of traffic policemen who must stand for hours in a miasma of automobile exhaust fumes. Early in 1966 an air sampling revealed the presence of sulfuric acid in the atmosphere in a proportion of .5 milligrams to the cubic meter—.1 milligram above the point generally accepted as being a serious danger to public health.

And so it goes. Berlin, Frankfurt, Amsterdam, Warsaw, Moscow, Kiev, Karachi, Calcutta, Bombay, Singapore, Jakarta, Hong Kong, Bangkok, Cairo, Tel Aviv, Johannesburg, Buenos Aires, Caracas—all these and others are now apprehensive about the blackening canopy overhead. Meanwhile, scientists examining the ice near the Arctic polar cap report detectable traces of lead.

The United Nations has not been able to fulfill the major hopes of the Preamble to its Charter because the large nations have consistently failed to provide the authority required for these purposes. But surely the protection of the world's air supply is an issue that transcends ideology and national interests. There is no reason why the United Nations cannot now begin to plan for a coordinated world attack on the environmental poisoning of the planet earth. Indeed, its activity in this area may produce a general strengthening of the organization, all of whose members have to breathe.

—*January 28, 1967*

# The Ordeal of the Short Distance

An astronaut with a taste for irony can look down on the earthball and ponder the melancholy fact that it will take him longer to travel a few blocks in the average city than to circle the entire world. For the city has become a stage for the humiliation of modern man engaged in the act of short-distance travel. Man has fixed his gaze on the distant places, but he has given absurdly little attention to his everyday need for circulating in the immediate vicinity. His genius in science and invention has gone into the large leaps; what happens on wheels and on foot is a disgrace to the race. Man's new access to the universe gives him cosmic grandeur but a trip to the other side of town gives him the willies. The symbol of the age is not the spaceship but the bottleneck.

In today's world, life in a metropolitan center is a morose demonstration of the failure of otherwise intelligent men to manage their environment. Consider, for example, just one aspect of New York City's short-distance crisis. There are three superhighways running from inside the city to the outlying main arteries. All three superhighways are relatively new but they were obsolete even before the concrete was laid. They provide for only three lanes of traffic in each direction, instead of the minimum of five or six that are clearly required. There are few turnoffs for disabled cars. These highways now have to be rebuilt at prodigious cost.

Are we to believe that the men who planned these major arteries didn't know the car population was rising? If so, they are plainly in the wrong business and should be barred from further interference with the movement of vehicles. It is possible, of course, that the designers were chained to inadequate budgets. In that case, they should have refused out of professional pride to proceed with ventures that were patently doomed. It is quite possible that the congestion on these three "expressways" has been responsible for more cases of twitching, hypertension, adrenal exhaustion, and elevated blood pressure in New York than business and marital difficulties combined. New York City may have a surfeit of brainpower, but there is no evidence that any of it has gone into its highway planning.

The automobile, conceived as a device for swift and convenient locomotion, is rapidly becoming a thing of fits and starts, an isolation chamber for sealing people off from continuous movement. The automobile horn is now less a device for alerting people to danger than it is an outlet for the boiling desperation of traffic-snarled and snarling drivers who don't know what else to do. This, of course, creates and compounds other problems: Noise pollution and air pollution come out of the same bottleneck.

Can nothing be done about the size of automobiles? Whatever the advantages of the large car on open highways, the moment it gets onto a city street it becomes an unholy instrument of congestion and air poisoning. Space in the heart of any large city is limited and valuable. Buildings are taxed according to the amount of land they occupy. Because of this, the emphasis is on vertical construction. An automobile, for no functional reason, is a horizontal phenomenon. It takes up space in defiance of all the logic that pertains to the operation of a large community. Moreover, the passion of designers to make cars look like frankfurters has resulted in front seats that require an unnatural sitting position and rear seats that make human legs an encumbrance. A long protrusion jutting far out over the rear wheels represents an ultimate tribute to baggage but makes parking the exercise of the devil. The net effect of this squeezed-out design is to reduce by one-third to one-half the number of cars that can pass a heavily trafficked point within a given time.

It is too easy to blame the automobile manufacturers. Less than a decade ago, Detroit put a major thrust behind smaller and lighter cars. It soon developed that when a man went into a salesroom to buy a compact car, he wanted the biggest one he could get. Competitive escalation in the size of compacts reached the point where some automobile owners could boast that their compacts were larger than some full-size cars. An automobile, like government, tends to reflect the level of public taste.

The penalty for oversized and overpowered cars is not confined to slowdowns in traffic. Quite literally, people have to pay through the nose for extra horsepower. The combustion engine has converted city streets into public gas chambers. The motors in automobiles, of course, are far less malevolent than diesel engines in trucks and buses, but there are more of them and they are generally in need of repair.

It is while en route to an airport that the automobile has its most poignant confrontation with the jet age. Few roads leading out of the average large city are as clogged as the approaches to the airports. No amount of detailed explanation can convince a man who has just missed his plane that there are good reasons why it should take him longer to drive six miles than to fly 600.

Airports are not built. They are rebuilt—sometimes three and four times within a decade. Again, are we to believe that the airport planners were carefully insulated from the facts showing that increasing numbers of Americans were taking to the air? Chicago's O'Hare Field was built against the background of the continual failures of nearby Midway, where three successive reconstructions were outmoded before they were completed. Yet O'Hare, despite the hundreds of millions spent in the original construction and in various enlargements, is still ten years behind its needs. Landing strips are inadequate. Ramps for arriving planes are insufficient. It is not at all unusual to be incarcerated in a plane for an additional half hour or more because of piled-up air traffic or lack of unloading gates. Even worse, perhaps, is the agony of getting from ticket counter to boarding area. Marathon runners can take this distance in stride; the average passenger must concentrate not just on getting to the gate in time, but on the cardiac implications of the chase.

John F. Kennedy International Airport in New York is another dramatic example of the inexplicable shortsightedness of men in an industry that is supposed to be synonymous with vision and progress. JFK Airport is now forced to handle three times as much traffic as it was designed to receive only a few years ago. The runways are not long enough and there are not enough of them. The ground approaches for automobiles are farcically outmoded; it is not unusual for passengers to miss planes because they were landlocked inside the airport grounds.

The most successful design of any individual air terminal building in the United States belongs to TWA at JFK Airport in New York. It is more than a structure; it is a magnificent example of applied sculpture. But the interior design is a lamentable anachronism. The space for boarding passengers can accommodate perhaps only half the required traffic.

The short-distance ordeal is not ended when the passenger boards the plane—not even when the plane starts to move. There is still the trip to the runway. At major airports in Chicago, New York, and Washington, sometimes as many as twenty planes are herded together with jet engines running, waiting for runway clearance. The cabin air-intake system sucks in the exhaust from the planes ahead. Jet exhaust is highly concentrated, highly toxic. The four engines of one plane at full takeoff thrust produce each second a spew equal to that of 5,000 automobiles of average horsepower accelerating at full power from a standing start. Medical authorities report varying degrees of brain damage from excessive exposure to jet-exhaust gases. Airplane spew can be reduced by having the control tower direct startups, and by careful positioning of planes waiting for takeoff. Also, more research is needed to find chemical additives for fuel that can reduce the amount of poison in exhaust.

Jet planes have brought the large cities closer together but many cities of small and intermediate size have poorer interconnections than they did fifty years ago. Passenger railroad facilities have been sharply reduced and, in some cases, eliminated altogether. The jet travel time from Chicago to New York is ninety minutes, and from Los Angeles to Chicago it is little more than three hours, but if you are more than a hundred miles away from places like Concord, New Hampshire; Castine, Maine; Hutchinson, Kansas; Elmira, New York; Ripon, Wisconsin; Big City, Michigan;

or hundreds of other cities of 100,000 population or less in any state, you will find the Jet Age has passed them by, and that they have even less train service than they did a half-century ago—if indeed, they have any train service at all.

One of the most distasteful short-distance ordeals in the world, of course, as international travelers can attest, is represented by the stretch from one end of a U.S. Customs inspector's counter to the other. In terms of courtesy and helpfulness, the U.S. Customs inspector deserves high marks. But he is forced to administer procedures that are incredibly crude. No other major nation, including the Soviet Union, subjects arrival passengers to as much red tape as does the United States. At the end of the vacation season, the inspection-and-customs room at JFK Airport in New York looks like a combination of a dollar sale at Macy's and the world's largest taffy pull. Why should the United States be one of the very few nations in the world that still require their inspectors to go rooting through luggage? What is it that the United States has to fear from its own citizens that other nations do not fear from theirs?

This brief account of short-distance ordeals doesn't begin to exhaust the list of senseless exasperating experiences in getting from one place to another. A few others:

Contending with staggered traffic-light systems that are calibrated to the volume of city traffic that would ordinarily be found on city streets at 3 A.M., but that are preposterous for midday traffic.

Missing a poorly marked turnoff on an automobile expressway, the result being that you have to drive ten miles before you get back on the right road.

Being almost blinded by the neon glare of a virtually continuous run of gasoline stations on an ordinary highway, and then almost losing your sight looking for a gasoline pump on a superhighway where stations may be more than twenty miles apart.

Being trapped inside a taxicab that is piled up in traffic and that is stuck alongside the billowing rear-end of a city bus.

Any experience on a subway train or surface transportation vehicle during peak hours.

Finding yourself stuck at a highway toll station behind a driver who has nothing less than a $50 bill and is trying to find out how to get to Nogales, Arizona.

Short-distance travel ordeals are not inherent in the fact of modern civilization. They have come about and have been intensified because human brainpower hasn't been trained on them in sufficient degree. There is no reason why human society need be condemned to a mass frustration neurosis caused by bottlenecks. City planning can be as exciting and challenging as programming computers or seeking cures for so-far incurable diseases. If the country attaches enough importance to the matter, it is possible that some of its best minds may turn to it. We'll all go out of *our* minds if they don't.

*—February 11, 1967*

# Morale and Morality in Vietnam

The photographs accompanying the lead article in this issue by David McLanahan by no means exhaust the pictorial horrors of the war in Vietnam. It would be possible to publish equally dramatic photographs of American soldiers whose legs had just been amputated after being spiked by poisonous bamboo shoots planted by the Vietcong. It would also be possible to publish gruesome photographs of Vietnamese teachers and village leaders who had been beheaded by the Vietcong because they refused to cooperate.

It should not be necessary to write this preamble to an editorial on nonmilitary casualties in Vietnam caused by our bombing policy or by the difficulty in distinguishing between innocent villagers and Vietcong. But there is an unfortunate tendency in some quarters to assume that anyone who talks about wounded civilians is either oblivious of Vietcong terrorism or doesn't know that war is hell.

The response of Americans to the problem of civilian casualties cannot be confined to their indignation over Vietcong actions or to the fact that people are going to be hurt in war. The essential question Americans must ask is whether human beings, Americans or Vietnamese, may be dying because of mistakes in policy, serious miscalculations, or missed opportunities to end the war honorably. The question has to do with human values and not just with military policy.

Secretary of the Air Force Harold Brown, at a recent press conference, referred to the inevitable "risk factor" for civilians in any military operation. It is difficult to regard the Secretary's statement as a complete or satisfactory explanation for the death of thousands of Vietnamese, most of them in South Vietnam, who have been killed by the bombing from the air, or by the widespread burning and leveling of villages. No one knows how many Vietnamese have failed to come out of their dugouts when summoned because they were paralyzed by fear and were thereupon incinerated inside the tunnels.

There is much in the news about wrong targets being bombed from the air, not just in Vietnam but in Laos and Cambodia, and even about American soldiers being hit by their own bombers, but little is said about civilian casualties resulting from the difficulty of making accurate identification of Vietcong. Increasingly, the tendency in dealing with the Vietcong is to saturate the general target area. Few chances are taken with suspects. This is not simply a matter of holding suspected Vietcong for interrogation, but of pouring lead and fire into a village which is believed or known to contain Vietcong. Members of the Vietcong did not come to these villages by invitation. The Vietnamese in these villages desperately wish only to be left alone—by everyone. The United States has announced it is in South Vietnam to protect the people against the Vietcong. How do we protect them, how do we liberate them, when we set fire to their huts or destroy their villages in the attempt to get at the Vietcong? Does a policeman fulfill his duty if he machineguns a crowd in the attempt to get at a murderer?

An American aviator, writing in the November issue of *Flying* magazine, says he looked down on his assigned target and reported by radio to his base that there must have been some error in his instructions, for he saw nothing below but a village with women and children moving about. He was ordered to hit the village just the same. He dropped the bombs but later admitted he was careful to see that they landed in an open field.

In drawing up targets for bombing and ground attack, our military forces lean heavily on briefings supplied by South Vietnamese intelligence officers, some of whom have proved to be overzealous or incompetent. Long lists of targets to keep our aviators busy have not been wanting, but no one can certify to the accuracy of the designated targets or can assure our aviators that they may not on occasion be unwitting participants in random slaughter.

Administration officials have acknowledged that the bombing has not produced the expected military results. Why, then, are the bombings continued? One of the main reasons openly given is that the bombings help to bolster the morale of the South Vietnamese government. This admission amounts to an indictment that history will not take lightly. It is an indictment of those who can be buoyed up by news that bombs and fire have been rained down on people in their homes and not just on military supply lines and installations. The incredible irony, of course, is that many of the villagers who are hit are citizens of South Vietnam, not North Vietnam. It is even more an indictment of ourselves, for we *know* the bombings are having a limited military effect at best.

Another highly relevant factor in any consideration of civilian casualties has to do with the possible prolongation of the war because of missed opportunities to negotiate. The Washington *Post* has substantiated stories appearing in various world capitals to the effect that exploratory talks which might have led to negotiations were under way in December of last year but were aborted by the bombings of Hanoi. Also, Secretary General U Thant of the United Nations has been quoted as saying that a genuine opportunity for negotiations *did* exist in 1964 and 1965, but that he was told by Adlai Stevenson, U.S. Ambassador to the U.N., that our government feared the negotiations would have an adverse effect on the morale of the South Vietnamese government, possibly causing its collapse.

What, then, is our main purpose in Vietnam? Is it to maintain a government of our own creation in South Vietnam, or is it to bring about an honorable settlement that can end the war under conditions that would provide for the stability and safety of the area? How many American soldiers and Vietnamese have been killed or wounded because of missed or spurned opportunities to get into valid negotiations? If it is true that possible openings for such negotiations have in fact existed, despite official assurances to the contrary, then it is not the morale of the South Vietnamese government but the moral position of our own government that is in jeopardy.

There is no doubt that Hanoi has been watching American public opinion carefully. There is no doubt that President Johnson is right when he says that North Vietnam will have little incentive to sit down at a peace table if it holds to the mistaken idea that American public opinion will force a withdrawal from Vietnam. But it is equally true that the Administration itself, because of a declared policy that is sometimes at variance with its own actions, because of air bombings that produce an unnecessarily high rate of civilian casualties, and because it apparently underestimates the instinct of a free society to find its way to the hard facts, is bringing about the very situation it fears. The American people cannot be expected to ignore or overlook questions that go to the roots of their own history. If the government requires public support as an essential ingredient for mounting a successful policy in Vietnam or anywhere else, it has the obligation to mount policies that are worthy of support.

The major issue in Vietnam before the American people has long since ceased to be whether we ought to stay in Vietnam or get out. Most Americans recognize that abrupt unilateral withdrawal could set the stage for wholesale chaos and slaughter in South Vietnam. They similarly recognize that total war in Vietnam could become the torch for world war. The major issue is how best to bring the war to an end with a minimum expenditure of human life, creating not just a situation of safety and stability but a situation in which the scientific and compassionate intelligence of the United States can be put to its fullest use in restoring Vietnam and in rehabilitating people who for thirty years have known nothing but war and daily peril. These are the declared aims of the American government. Any compromise or distortion of these aims is chargeable not just to the American government but to its people. This is in the nature of a free society.

*—March 25, 1967*

# Vietnam and the Fourth Group

Until recent weeks, American public opinion on the war in Vietnam has tended to form into three groups. One group has advocated the direct use of military force to whatever extent might be necessary to crush North Vietnam, regardless of the risk of wider war. A second group has favored complete military and political withdrawal, regardless of the risk of chaos and widespread slaughter. The third group, according to most of the indications, has been the dominant one. It has supported a course, outlined by the President, that seeks to avoid either total escalation or total pullout, putting our main emphasis on ending the war through negotiations. Beyond negotiations, this third group sees a chance for the Vietnamese, under the auspices perhaps of the United Nations, to have a test of self-determination, and an opportunity for the United States to help rehabilitate all of Vietnam, North and South.

In recent weeks, however, a fourth group in American public opinion has been taking shape. It is drawing much of its strength from the third group. This fourth group consists of those who formerly supported the President's declared policy for an honorable peace through negotiations but regard the bombing as inconsistent with that objective. It is also becoming apprehensive and aroused over the growing evidence that the President's policy is being negated or contradicted within the Government itself.

The evidence of contradiction is accumulating. It is now known that as long ago as August 1964, U.N. Secretary General U Thant conveyed a message about possible negotiations to the U.S. State Department. The message made known Hanoi's willingness to participate in talks with the United States. The suggested place for the meeting was Rangoon, Burma. President Johnson had previously emphasized the desire of the United States to avoid a punitive settlement; he had urged Hanoi to come to the peace table as the only possible means of ending the war and sparing the people of Vietnam. U Thant had supported the President's plea in a private communication to the government in Hanoi. The reply from Hanoi was encouraging. But after relaying the message to Washington, U Thant was unable to get any response out of the State Department for more than four months. Finally, U Thant learned that the State Department, despite public statements to the contrary, was opposed to negotiations at the time because it feared that peace measures might produce another collapse of the government in South Vietnam. Later, it was reliably learned that the State Department had failed to inform the President of the opportunity for negotiations presented by U Thant.

Several weeks after the failure to get talks started in Rangoon, the

President announced he was authorizing air bombing in Vietnam. One of the reasons publicly given was that Hanoi had shown no positive response to the effort to end the war through negotiations aimed at a just peace.

A second item of evidence now coming to light has to do with quiet exploratory talks with North Vietnam that had been painstakingly arranged and that were about to take place in Warsaw, Poland, as recently as December, 1966. On the eve of the exploratory talks, the United States bombed the city of Hanoi, despite its earlier assurances it had no intention of attacking civilian targets. That was the end of the talks. The U.S. State Department denied that the bombing had occurred and stood by the denial until the testimony of eyewitnesses, Americans among them, became irrefutable. President Johnson sought to reactivate the Warsaw negotiations by assuring Hanoi that he was banning bombing operations within a specified distance of the city; but it was too late. The basis for negotiations or even for a direct exchange of views at that time had been destroyed.

A third fact concerns the repeated statements by Dean Rusk, Secretary of State, to the effect that the United States would stop the bombing if it had any indication that North Vietnam was prepared to respond with de-escalation moves of its own. The Secretary's position, on the face of it, was reasonable enough. It takes two sides to scale down a war. It now develops, however, that a message saying Hanoi was willing to enter into reciprocal de-escalation was conveyed to the U.S. State Department early in January 1967. The message said that Hanoi was prepared to offer a permanent cease-fire if the United States would stop the bombing. Despite this fact, the Secretary continued to say he had received no sign of Hanoi's willingness to cut back on the war.

Such facts are known not just to a few. They are being discussed with consternation in Congressional quarters, in capitals throughout the world, in the United Nations, in the Vatican, and wherever foreign correspondents are gathered. These facts represent a liability in America's relationship to the rest of the world. They reflect the historical position of the United States.

This is the background against which a new public opinion is emerging in the United States. This public opinion has had no difficulty in supporting the declared policy of the United States in Vietnam. But it is now discovering that the declared policy may not be the real policy. It is discovering that the government itself is not of a piece on vital questions in foreign affairs and that sectors of the government can move in direct contradiction to the President. The President has succeeded in persuading most of the American people against an irresponsible enlargement of the war or an irresponsible and precipitate withdrawal, but he appears to be less persuasive inside his own house. It is difficult to arrive at any other conclusion on the basis of this record.

Whatever the vagaries of American public opinion, there are finite limits to its capacity to be manipulated. A free society has a way of developing an instinct for reality. It also places a proper value on its good name before the rest of the world. American public opinion may be many things but it is not cynical. It is also the major element in any effective conduct of government policy, at home or abroad. It demands respect, not as an indulgence, but as the firmest of all its natural rights.

*—April 1, 1967*

*One of the shortest and most dramatic wars in history began on June 5, 1967, and ended on June 11, 1967. The war began after Arab armies mobilized on the borders of Israel and President Gamal Abdel Nasser, of the United Arab Republic, announced he was barring ships bound for Israel from passage through the Strait of Tiran at the entrance to the Gulf of Aqaba. The turning point of the war came when the Israeli air force caught the planes of the United Arab Republic on the ground the first day of the war. Israeli soldiers scored decisive victories in the fighting in the Sinai peninsula and in the Gaza strip. The war ended when belligerents observed the order of the United Nations for a cease-fire.*

*The issues raised by the war, however, extended to the life of the U.N. itself. To what extent could the basic principles underlying the U.N. transcend the differences of its members? To what extent were the major powers willing to accept a course of action decided by the world body as a whole, even though that action might run counter to their own interests? In short, would the crisis in the Middle East create a pattern for peace-making or would it lead to a magnification of the world power struggle?*

# What Have We Learned?

What has been learned? What have we learned from one of the most instructive weeks in human history? If we have learned well, it is possible that the human race stands a fair chance of securing to itself the blessings of reason and fulfillment on earth to a greater degree than has been possible so far. If we have learned poorly, then it may be only a short time before the onset of new eruptions from which there can be neither recovery nor appeal.

The first lesson proceeds out of this question: Suppose General Nasser had had nuclear bombs at his disposal? Would he have withheld the use of such weapons if they could have prevented defeat? Even if we assume he would have been willing to forgo the enormous advantage of a lightning atomic blow as part of a surprise attack on Israel, would he have persisted with such restraint at the point of military disaster and humiliation?

Similarly, suppose the Arab armies had overrun Israel? If all that stood between Israel and the annihilation of her dream of a free and independent existence was her use of nuclear explosives, is it likely that those explosives would be kept in their sheaths?

These questions are hypothetical only in point of time. It may be no more than three to five years before Egypt and Israel—and at least a half dozen other small nations—come into possession of nuclear weapons. When that happens, the possibility that regional nuclear war can be kept from mushrooming into world nuclear war will shrink almost to the vanishing point.

The continuing spread of nuclear weapons means that the future of the human race may well depend on a decision by a General Nasser to see his country die rather than to use nuclear weapons and thus run the risk of world destruction. Such restraint presupposes a quality of spiritual strength and moral splendor—not an invariable characteristic of military men at the heads of governments—or any men, for that matter, in positions of national power. Would Adolf Hitler have hesitated to use atomic bombs—if they had been available—regardless of the incalculable price to humanity?

A lesson to be learned by recent events, therefore, is that the world is confronted by the grimmest of all deadlines in preventing the spread of nuclear weapons and in bringing existing stockpiles under effective control. Until such control is an accomplished fact, humanity will exist in a condition of almost total peril. How will the control be achieved? There is no real steam behind present official efforts to bring about nonproliferation. The reason for this is that the men who are at the head of the nuclear nations are not eager to give up anything, and many of the smaller nations do not wish to be prevented from becoming as powerful as anyone else. The fate of nonproliferation and control of nuclear weapons, therefore, is in the hands of men whose surrounding circumstances incline them to possession and spread rather than to reduction and control.

Nuclear nonproliferation can be achieved, therefore, only if enough people set up an irresistible demand for it. The political penalties for indifference to such a demand must be sufficiently stern to be respected.

A second great lesson of recent events concerns the United Nations. It is now clear that the peacekeeping function cannot be separated from the peacemaking function. The United Nations was able to stop the fighting in the Middle East in 1956 but it was unable to create the conditions that could keep the war from recurring. It couldn't prevent the Arab armies from massing on Israel's frontiers. Hence the U.N. was on shaky ground in demanding that Israel withdraw without effective guarantees that the peace of the entire area would be assured.

Whether it welcomes the fact or not, therefore, the United Nations is confronted by the need to create the conditions of peace and not just to cope with problems created by the outbreak of war. But the U.N. Charter never envisioned the need to deal with basic causes of war. It is this tragic fallacy—the fallacy that there can be a separation between the pursuit of peace and the control of war—that could become the obituary of the U.N.

From the very inception of the U.N., the world's statesmen have insisted that the U.N. could never be more than a realistic reflection of the attitudes and tempers and ideological diversities of its members. Why should this be so? Why shouldn't the whole of the U.N. be greater than the sum of its parts? The need in the world is not for a magnifying mirror for the unilateral and erratic behavior of individual national powers but for a control mechanism that can compel responsible and noncombustible behavior in the world arena. Certainly the United Nations must be a corporate body, with authority adequate to its functions in the field of world law. Just as there is a deadline for preventing the spread of nuclear weapons, so there is a deadline for revamping and upgrading the philosophical and physical being of the U.N. Voices of the past will insist it is impossible to give the United Nations enforceable authority in matters concerned with world law, for they have become so hypnotized by ideological differences and by tradition that they have no sense of vital change or the forward thrust that comes from advocacy.

Fundamentally, a lesson to be learned from recent events is that any attempt to make peace or keep peace, or any attempt to invoke law, must rest on abstract, objective concepts of justice, self-evident to a world consensus if not to some of those directly affected. The Israelis cannot be expected to relinquish the gain of their astounding victory unless they receive workable assurances that the traditionally belligerent policy of the Arab nations toward Israel will be replaced by a policy of peace and recognition. This, too, requires a U.N. that is able to establish and maintain the conditions of peace, quite apart from its ability to mount emergency deliberations after the peace has been shattered.

The U.N. Security Council attempted to deal with the Arab-Israeli confrontation in a vacuum. The debate centered almost entirely on accusations of aggression. Did the aggression consist of the surprise attack by the Israelis, as the Arab and the Soviet representatives contended? Or did it consist of Arab belligerence and the closing of the Gulf of Aqaba, as the Israelis contended? To attempt to resolve such a debate on the level of accusation and fulmination is a denial of all juridical experience.

What machinery is provided by the United Nations to underwrite the safety of individual nations? What body or agency of the United Nations is empowered to enforce world law in the name of world justice? How has world law been defined? How is it to be interpreted?

The United Nations has been severely criticized in recent days by people who somehow expected it to have all these powers. Their condemnation should not be directed against the U.N. but against the statesmen who consistently and insistently blocked all efforts to strengthen the U.N. and to give it precisely the kind of authority it needed so badly in the Middle East crisis. The wonder is not that the United Nations was not fully effective in that crisis but that, considering the stark limitations placed on its authority, it functioned as well as it did.

Similarly, U.N. Secretary General U Thant has been castigated because he withdrew the U.N. Peacekeeping Forces from the Middle East as soon as serious trouble loomed. People were bewildered because this was precisely the time when additional U.N. forces should have been sent to the area. What they failed to take into account was that Egypt had the right to request the removal of the forces. The anomaly inhered not in the action by the Secretary General but in the fact that he had no choice but to act as he did under the terms of the Charter.

There is much to be learned from recent events, and not much time to learn it. The sum total of all these lessons is the need for a concerted effort to revamp the United Nations in order to enable it to deal with root causes of war. The ability of enough men to understand these lessons will weigh more heavily in their future than virtually anything else they may have learned in the totality of their education. In an age where specialized knowledge is both pursued and prized, nothing is more paradoxical or costly than the improvisation and amateurishness that have gone into the most important work in the world—the making of peace.

If people want a safer and more rational way of conducting human affairs than now exists on this planet, they cannot wait for sovereignty-minded statesmen to take the initiative. The statesmen will become relevant in these matters only as there is an unmistakable demand that they do so.

—*June 24, 1967*

# Epilogue:

# The Age
# Of Acceleration

There was no problem, Hegel liked to think, that was not penetrable by thought. This is encouraging enough, but Hegel lived at a time when the problem of scrutinizing living history was not yet battered and confounded by acceleration. The trouble with trying to penetrate the vitals of the past quarter century is that 1940 was more than a hundred years ago. Into a few decades have been compressed more change, more thrust, more tossing about of men's souls and gizzards than had been spaced out over most of the human chronicle until then. The metabolism of history has gone berserk.

What is most significant, therefore, about the past twenty-five years is not the extent of change but the pace of change. A man's legs are forty times longer than they were a generation ago, measured by his increased speed and mobility. He has developed more potent energy during the past twenty-five years than during the previous twenty-five hundred years. And the rate of acceleration continues to increase, a specific reflection of the fact that the number of scientists now alive is larger than all the scientists in all the ages of man put together before 1920.

The acceleration has done more than to impair the faculty of human observation and comprehension. It has created a tendency toward disorientation. It has unhinged the sense of vital balance that enables a man to locate himself in time and place. In the centrifuge of the twentieth century man is whirling away from the center of his own being. The farther out he spins, the more blurred his view of himself, of what he might be, and of his relationship to the nameless faces in the crowd. The separation is not just between body and place; it is between mind and reason.

The connection between the acceleration and man's anxiety has been widely observed and documented. The same is true of computerization and its tendency to wash the color out of human personality. Less fully identified and scrutinized is the fact that ultimately the acceleration produces irreverence. Men in increasing motion cover ground but have none to stand on. Values take on a free-floating quality. The disconnection makes for distortion and an unfamiliarity that breeds contempt. It is not just a matter of rejecting values; it is a matter of being disconnected from the things that give rise to values. Obviously, not all irreverence is bad.

The irreverence that challenges, that peels back the layers of sham, that releases bitterness or anger against attempts to cheapen life—this in itself is an assertion of values. But the main vein of irreverence in our time is quite different. It is nihilistic, brutal, anti-human. Basically, it is directed against life itself.

The symptoms are fundamental. They are not just a street mob goading a man on a ledge to take the plunge. Nor a crowd in a subway passively observing one man carving up another. Nor people paying for the privilege of seeing people get hurt. Nor rapacious comedians mistaking verbal brutality for wit. Irreverence in the twentieth century has a more pervasive accent. It involves the basic mood of large numbers of people and the kind of culture they are prepared to support. It is visible in the abrasiveness of human relations that many people either prefer or seem to take for granted.

These things haven't occurred because of some historical quirk. They are the product of specific gravity and direct cause. They reflect and are part of a dominant theme. The theme is the volcanic eruption of the scientific intelligence, throwing hot lava over the whole of man's estate, most especially over the national structures. A nation meant many things to an individual, but most of all it meant protection—protection against other tribes, protection against disorder from within. This protection, from without or within, required force. Then, suddenly, out of the acceleration came a new kind of force that changed everything about the state except its awareness that a fundamental change had come about. Man became deprived of his protection. The power was total, obliterative, suicidal. The feasibility of war became obsolete but the habit of war and the situations that produced war remained unchanged.

The nations possessing nuclear weapons knew that any general use of atomic force could shatter the natural environment that made life possible. Yet each dreaded having the other think it lacked the nerve to go through with the apocalypse if it had to. And so each made unambiguous proclamations about its readiness to use all the power at its disposal in behalf of its vital interests. But the use of the power would expunge these vital interests, along with everything else. Thus the central need was to find some way of creating security which, when employed, would not be destructive of that security.

The ultimate effect, therefore, of the acceleration has been to make life tentative. Life that is tentative has a tendency to become cheap. What does it mean to live in an age when the defensive level of human beings has been reduced to that of insects against a blowtorch? The most enshrined phrase in the lexicon of philosophers is the dignity of man, yet dignity does not depend only on political charters or declarations. Dignity also means solidity; it means a moral contract accepting life as infinitely precious. How much reverence for life is possible when everyone knows that the flick of a finger can incinerate a billion human beings and that a nod can release tons of disease germs? A painful world man can train himself to endure, but a world that on the whim of a madman can become a crematorium or a disease chamber—this is the giant thief that steals a man's dignity and his reverence for life.

Man and his society are in a constant condition of interaction. At a time when nations can vaporize civilization, the individual takes on the temper of the total organism of which he is a part. He doesn't have to react on the level of conscious decision; he can reflect an environment that no longer fully comprehends the fragility and uniqueness of human life.

Any attack on the problem must begin not so much with a definition of acceleration as with a definition of man. If the theory of human perfectibility is rejected, then it may be only a matter of time before he becomes ground up in the wheels he has sent spinning so furiously. But if human uniqueness is defined as the capacity to conceive that which has never been conceived before, then acceleration can be relieved of its terrors. Man's difficulty has never been in doing things; it has been in choosing what to do. The ultimate test is not of skills but of purposes and desires. Man has already transformed nature; are we to say he is unable to transform himself? Is it reasonable to believe that a species that has demonstrated a capacity to lift itself off its planet is unable to raise its sights in devising a rational future? If awareness of the consequences of the present drift leads to a desire to avert them, the Age of Acceleration can lead to an Age of Balance.

Thomas Jefferson looked forward to a time when all barbarism would disappear from the earth. If he were alive today he would take note of the persistence and extension of barbarism but, as a believer in human perfectibility, he would warn against the conclusion that men are essentially barbarous. With Franklin, Emerson, William James, and Holmes, he would resist theories of historical inevitability. He would not be intimidated by the momentum of events into believing that a great reversal could not be brought about. He would also probably try to remind us that no idea figured more largely in the making of American society than that history was what men wanted it to be, and that civilization is what happens when men have intelligent desires.

There is hope, then, in a plastic definition of man. This goes beyond the recognition of a divine itch or the sudden notion that there is an extra minute before midnight. Hope today—and it may be the only hope —resides in the world-wide emergence of the articulate and communicating citizen. What he wants and what he does mean more and more to the governments of which he is a part. The American experiment has succeeded in a way that Madison and Hamilton never dared dream it would. Its essential claim—that nothing is more important than man—has been echoed in every continent. The individual man has come into his own. Thinking, feeling, musing, complaining, fending, creating, building, evading, desiring, he has become more important to the operators of his governments than ever before. The question, therefore, is not whether man is capable of prolonging and ennobling his stay on earth. The question is whether he recognizes his prime power—and also his duty—for accomplishing that purpose.

What will cause Everyman, who lives everywhere, who is preoccupied with different things and who lives under different systems, suddenly to find both unison and resonance in calling for safety and sense on earth? Next, what is it he is expected to say? Finally, who will do the effective listening?

On the first question: Despite national boundaries and belligerently different ideological systems, the main confrontation in today's world cuts across national boundaries and ideological lines. The ultimate divisions take place within the societies, not between them. On one side are those who comprehend or sense the meaning of the acceleration, who perceive that new connections among men have to be created regardless of their diversity, and who move almost instinctively toward building those universal institutions that can serve the city of man. On the other side are those who think in terms of separatism, the perpetuation of group egos, the manning of tribal battle stations, and the lures of compartmentalization.

It is out of this transcendent confrontation that Everyman will make his voice and weight felt. He needs to be encouraged to believe that what he feels and wants to say can be part of a universal thrust. And it is here that writers, especially novelists, poets, and playwrights, have their finest opportunity. If we have learned nothing else, it is that the ideas of the poets and artists penetrate where everything else has failed. The question, therefore, is not so much whether Everyman is capable of response, whatever his station, as whether he has something and someone to respond to.

On the second question: It would be exhilarating, to say the least, if a shout were to go up all over the world for a human society under law. This is not likely to happen in the next twenty-four hours. All that is necessary to happen is the direct expression of raw concern. There is primitive, colossal energy in the simply stated but insistent call by enough people for a situation of reasonable safety on earth, for an end to anarchy in the dealings among states, and for easier access by members of the human family to one another.

On the third question: Even the most insulated and arbitrary government or system has to be concerned today about the turnings of the popular mind. Some systems may be less attuned than others but at some point all must pay attention.

The same acceleration that has produced disarray and irreverence can give man confidence in achieving big goals within the short time it is necessary to achieve them. It can give him confidence, too, in the reach of his intelligence for finding answers of almost infinite complexity. Progress lies not in a rejection of acceleration but in a proper respect for the possibilities of mind.

". . . We ought not to die before
we have explained ourselves to
each other."

*—Thomas Jefferson*
*to John Adams*

# Index

# Index

Academy of Social Sciences, 291
Ace, Goodman, 40
*Act of Love, An,* 217–218
Acton, John, 462
Adair, J. Carlton, 426
Adams, Henry, 474
Adams, John, 6, 626
Adoula, Cyrille, 445, 449–450
Advertising, 43
    *Saturday Review,* 18, 25, 27, 47–48,
       65, 71, 75
Aeschylus, 181
Afghanistan, 226
Africa, 225–226, 551, 578
Agency for International Develop-
    ment, 531
Agopard, 182
Agriculture, 308–313, 314, 405
Ahmed, 212–214
Air pollution, 274–275, 315, 378–379,
    507, 540–542, 624, 630–635,
    636, 637
Airports, 636–637
Alexander the Great, 129
Alexandria, 182–183
Alexandrov, Igor, 303–305, 308–309
"All Quiet on the Western Front," 82
Allen, Hervey, 217
Ali, Mohammed, 216, 226
Allison, John M., 531
Alpert, Hollis, 40
Amerada, 23
American Assembly, 618
American Bar Association, 627
*American Commonwealth,* 104
American Communist Party, 295–296,
    300, 464

American Dental Association, 57
American Friends Service Committee,
    326, 622–623
American Institute of Mining and
    Metallurgical Engineers, 23
American Unitarian Association, 194
Americans, foreign view of, 169–172
Amherst College, 43
Amoros, Sandy, 339
Amory, Cleveland, 24, 39–40, 44
Anderson, Marian, 409
Anderson, Robert, 559
Andover, N.H., 411–417, 418
Annenberg School of Communica-
    tions, 40
*Anthony Adverse,* 217
Antibiotics, 56
Ants, 121
Apathy, public, 264–266
Aqaba, Gulf of, 255, 263, 644, 646
Aquinas, Thomas, 624
Arabs, 229, 231, 255–264, 581, 644–
    646
Architecture, 371–373, 378–380
Aristophanes, 175, 181
Aristotle, 136, 160, 173, 612, 624
Armour, Robert, 40
Arnold, H.H., 190
Art, 39, 70, 458
Arts, 179–184
Asia, 225–226, 433, 550–551, 575,
    578, 608
Astor, John Jacob, 158
Athens, 85–86, 134, 161
*Atlantic,* 151
Atomic Bomb Casualty Commission,
    329, 347, 350–351